The Selected Works
of
Eugene V. Debs

THE SELECTED WORKS OF EUGENE V. DEBS

This groundbreaking project by Haymarket Books will republish more than 1,000 of the articles, speeches, press statements, interviews, and open letters of labor leader and socialist activist Eugene Victor Debs. More than 1.5 million words will be reproduced in six thick volumes—the vast majority of which seeing print for the first time since the date of their first publication.

Eugene Victor Debs (1855–1926) was a trade union official, magazine editor, political opinion writer, and public orator widely regarded as one of the most important figures in the history of American socialism. Five times a candidate for president of the United States and twice imprisoned for his role as a strike leader and antiwar agitator, Debs remains today an esteemed and iconic figure of twentieth-century political history.

The Selected Works
of
Eugene V. Debs

Volume II:
The Rise and Fall of
the American Railway Union,
1892–1896

edited by
Tim Davenport
and David Walters

Haymarket Books
Chicago, Illinois

Published in 2020 by
Haymarket Books
P.O. Box 180165
Chicago, IL 60618
773-583-7884
www.haymarketbooks.org
info@haymarketbooks.org

ISBNs: 978-1-60846-770-9 (hardcover)
978-1-60846-765-5 (paperback)

Trade distribution:
In the US, Consortium Book Sales and Distribution, www.cbsd.com
In Canada, Publishers Group Canada, www.pgcbooks.ca
In the UK, Turnaround Publisher Services, www.turnaround-uk.com
All other countries, Ingram Publisher Services International,
IPS_Intlsales@ingramcontent.com

This book was published with the generous support of Lannan Foundation and
Wallace Action Fund.

Cover and text design by Eric Kerl.

Printed in Canada by union labor.

Library of Congress Cataloging-in-Publication data is available.

10 9 8 7 6 5 4 3 2 1

Contents

————

1895

Appendix

Introduction

Although mythologized in popular culture as the "Gay Nineties," replete with barbershop quartets, handlebar mustaches, and penny-farthing bicycles, there was little joyous or whimsical about the final decade of the nineteenth century for most Americans. This was a time of relentless economic crisis and popular disaffection, of mass unemployment and exploitative working conditions—ushered in by an economic crisis remembered as the Panic of 1893. America's gross national product would drop by more than 7.5 percent in about 18 months.[1] Joblessness hit a nadir in the last days of 1893, with nearly 3 million people out of work, an unemployment rate of between 15 and 20 percent.[2] With money tight and jobs scarce, take-home pay of factory workers would tumble by more than 13 percent, with the average worker receiving just $376 in the year the economy cratered.[3] A modest rebound in 1895 was quickly swamped by another economic trough. The percentage of unemployed workers in the United States would not fall below double-digit levels until 1899.[4]

These "Grim Nineties" were, in short, a time of troubles—an era in which employers maintained profitability through imposition of unilateral wage cuts as capitalist enterprise contracted around them, leaving workers to struggle for preservation of their jobs and lives. The sordid underbelly of America's concentrated economy, dominated by massive price-fixing trusts, was starkly exposed. A relative handful maintained a life of wealth and leisure. The great majority scrapped and suffered. In response, dynamic new political protest movements and labor organizations began to emerge as the nineteenth century sputtered to a close.

This historical era is documented in this second of six volumes that constitute *The Selected Works of Eugene V. Debs*. It is an interval marked at one end by the collapse of Debs's effort to bring about federation of the existing brotherhoods of railroad workers through a centralized directorate known as the Supreme Council of United Orders of Railroad Employees, and at the other by his reassessment of political beliefs in the wake of the disheartening defeat of the People's Party and its fusion with William Jennings Bryan and the Democrats in the general election of 1896. These were the years in which Gene Debs, vigorous and in the prime of life, first emerged as a national public figure, the head of a new labor organization, the American Railway Union (ARU)—though the union would be short-lived, mortally wounded soon after birth when a sympathy strike against Pullman's Palace Car Company was crushed by the allied forces of the state, military and judicial.

☙

Debs's mid-1890s articles and speeches tell the story of three strikes—one in which he was an interested observer and commentator, and two in which he was a direct participant. The first of these, with which this volume begins, was the seminal Homestead Strike of 1892. Homestead was a strike over steel, the durable and rust-resistant alloy of iron and carbon that played a pivotal part in the post–Civil War boom of the transportation industry. The recipe for steel was not complex: iron ore and hardeners were heated by burning coke, a form of concentrated carbon rendered from coal through a protracted baking process. With its ready access to an almost unlimited supply of locally made coke as well as direct rail access to the high-quality ore of Michigan, by the 1880s western Pennsylvania had emerged as the center of steel manufacture in America. Within this region no town was more important than Homestead, a company town of about 12,000 people located on the bank of the Monongahela River seven miles outside of Pittsburgh—home of the massive and modern flagship of the Carnegie Steel Corporation, the Homestead Works.[5]

Andrew Carnegie[6] was a technological innovator, aggressively adopting new production techniques and investing in new facilities that allowed the production of more finished metal in less time. On July 1, 1892, the fifty-six-year-old "titan of industry" launched a new consolidated enterprise, the Carnegie Steel Company—employer of 13,000 workers, and the largest steelmaker in the world. At that time Carnegie's Homestead enterprise occupied 110 acres and included 16 open-hearth furnaces and two modern Bessemer converters, capable of producing nearly 800,000 tons of steel ingots per year. The works also included finishing mills that turned out armor plate and structural steel beams for bridges and buildings. Carnegie would personally extract tens of millions of dollars during his final years in the steel business before departing the industry in 1900.[7]

Regarded by the public—although not necessarily by those who worked for him—as a humane albeit frugal employer, owing to his well-publicized philanthropy, no such popular illusions were harbored about Carnegie Steel's managing partner, Henry Clay Frick, the "Coke King of Western Pennsylvania." Hailing from a bourgeois family, Frick had entered the business in the

Connellsville region, located about 50 miles south of Pittsburgh, becoming a partner at the age of 21 with two others in a coke business utilizing 50 ovens. A new railroad in the vicinity promised to make Frick's venture extremely lucrative. He saw the brass ring and grabbed, dumping his two early partners and merging with another local operator. The company formed by this new alliance, H. C. Frick & Co., would by the end of the 1880s count among its holdings more than 10,000 coke ovens, operated by 11,000 employees, as well as mineral rights to over 35,000 acres of prime coal land.[8] Carnegie respected Frick for both his efficiency and his anti-union ruthlessness.

Before he joined forces with Frick in 1889, Carnegie and his steel works had, grudgingly and after a protracted fight, been heavily unionized by the fledgling Amalgamated Association of Iron and Steel Workers (AAISW). New managing partner Frick had no compunction against launching a labor war to break the union, however. With Carnegie away on an extended 1892 sojourn to Great Britain, Frick made preparations for a lockout of the Homestead Works to smash the union once and for all. He presented a greatly reduced wage schedule to the AAISW in May, a new scale to be accepted by June 24, 1892. Knowing full well the union would never accede to his unilateral demands, Frick spent the month of June securing the perimeter of the Homestead Works with a tall wooden fence topped with barbed wire. In addition, Frick secretly contracted with the infamous Pinkerton Detective Agency[9] for 300 armed guards in anticipation of "trouble" for a July 6 restart of the Homestead Works on a non-union basis.[10] Two armored barges were constructed for the transport of these armed Pinkerton toughs, and plans were made for their secret insertion inside the fortified Homestead Works in the dead of night via river landing.

Frick's Pinkerton plans leaked to the union, and following collapse of his bad-faith negotiations, the anticipated trouble became a reality. Locked-out union members and their supporters lining the banks engaged in a protracted gun battle at the river's edge with the armed Pinkertons in the wee hours of July 6, with casualties on both sides. The Pinkertons were trapped in their fortified barge, with the strikers raining down gunfire. The stalemate was finally broken at 6 p.m., when the Pinkertons surrendered to strike leaders, having been promised safe passage to the railway station. This earnest guarantee was overruled by the mob, however, and a number of the disarmed Pinkertons were badly beaten as they walked a lengthy gauntlet of strikers.[11] National Guard intervention to break the strike soon followed, with the subsequent prosecution of strike leaders for treason and the failed assassination attempt of H.

C. Frick by the anarchist Alexander Berkman[12] garnering national headlines. Debs detailed these events in the pages of the *Locomotive Firemen's Magazine,* a monthly publication that he would continue to edit through October 1894.

☙

During 1892, initial discussions began that would culminate in the formation of the American Railway Union (ARU), an industrial union that was to include all railroad workers, from the best-paid conductor or engineer to the simplest maintenance worker. Periodic informal meetings of the railway brotherhood magazine editors in Chicago brought together strong federationists like Debs, Brotherhood of Railroad Conductors founder George W. Howard,[13] and Louis W. Rogers,[14] editor of the Brotherhood of Railroad Trainmen's monthly prior to the launch of his own publication, *Age of Labor.* Also central to the effort were fellow labor magazine editors John A. Hall of *Switchmen's Journal*[15] and Sylvester Keliher of *Railway Carmen's Journal.*[16] Debs continued to focus his own efforts on the Supreme Council until its termination in June 1892,[17] with discussions by the editors for a new federative structure resumed that fall and continuing into 1893. Keliher's carmen were the most committed to the idea of federation of all the railway brotherhoods, with its annual convention instructing its top two officers to pursue the matter further.[18] As discussions continued, a conceptual leap was made from the renewal of a federation of existing railway brotherhoods to the establishment of a new industrial union encompassing all railway workers.

According to the testimony of American Federation of Labor president Samuel Gompers, the ARU was not in the first instance the brainchild of Debs. Rather it was the man who would become the organization's vice president, George W. Howard, who first gave voice to the idea. Gompers recalled Howard boasting to him early in 1893 after a Kansas City speech, "I have a plan to organize the railway workmen of America into one union. All they need pay is one dollar a year, and in less than three years we will smash the brotherhoods." Gompers indicates that Howard predicted the future success of said enterprise would depend upon his ability to bring the acclaimed orator Debs into the project. Howard had asked for the American Federation of Labor's blessing for this effort to supplant the existing railway brotherhoods, which were not themselves affiliated with the AF of L, but this appeal had been rejected in no uncertain terms as deleterious to the cause of organized labor.[19] Certainly one must consider the source—by the time he recounted the tale in 1905, Gompers and Debs were bitter political foes and Gompers had an incentive to minimize Debs as a mere pawn in a duplicitous union-wrecking enterprise—but circumstantial evidence does indeed lend support to Gompers's ascription of the core idea of an industrial union called the ARU to Howard rather than Debs.[20]

A formal session, announced to the press, was held in Chicago at the Leland Hotel on February 8 and 9, 1893, chaired by Howard and attended by 21 representatives of various railway brotherhoods. These included both the thirty-seven-year-old Gene Debs and his beloved younger brother, Theodore.[21] The assembled delegates agreed upon the name American Railway Union for a new federative organization of craft unions, with Howard promising to the press that a mass public meeting of railroad employees would be held in Chicago in the near future.[22] A three-member committee on Constitution and Declaration of Purposes consisting of Howard, Debs, and Keliher was named to draft a manifesto and organizational law for the new industrial union.[23] Those assembled also issued a call for a permanent organizing conference, which was to be held in Chicago from April 11–17, 1893. The ARU was to "be formed of all classes of railway employees working on trains, tracks, in shops, offices, anywhere," according to Debs.

George W. Howard would once again serve as chairman at that conference's opening session.[24] At the close of the conference Debs, Howard, and Keliher were elected as officers of the new order, joined on the nine-member board of directors by *Age of Labor* editor Louis W. Rogers; W. S. Missemer, head of the Brotherhood of Railway Carmen; W. H. Sebring of the Order of Railway Conductors; James A. Clarke of Chicago, a former top official of the Order of Railroad Telegraphers; Henry Walton of Philadelphia, a member of the Brotherhood of Locomotive Engineers; and Debs's successor as secretary-treasurer of the Brotherhood of Locomotive Firemen, Frank W. Arnold.[25]

With officers elected and a constitution and manifesto already adopted, a call was issued for a public meeting to be held the evening of Tuesday, June 20, 1893, at which "the new doctrine of labor equality and protection for the weakest will be expounded and the good points of the new movement discussed." Those who attended this session at Uhlich's Hall in Chicago were addressed by an array of ARU officers, including the group's four top leaders—Debs, Howard, Rogers, and Keliher. This gathering was not delegated, but was rather a mass meeting open to any and all railway employees, including "every track-walker, engine-wiper, and section man, as well as engineers, conductors, and dispatchers."[26] This so-called "first bow on the public platform"[27] has frequently been misidentified as the date of birth of the ARU. Rather than a starting point, June 20 marked a denouement in an ongoing process of formation—a date after which there could be no further denial that a new industrial union had emerged from the ashes of the old federation of established brotherhoods. Two of the ARU's elected directors with deep ties to the old brotherhoods made a hasty exit at this juncture, with Frank Arnold of the Firemen and W. S. Missemer of the Carmen gone by June 21. Sylvester Keliher, editor and secretary-treasurer of the Carmen, chose a different course, breaking with Missemer and the old brotherhood and casting his lot with the ARU. He submitted a formal resignation to the Brotherhood of Railway Carmen at once, to take effect August 15.[28]

Regardless of whence the idea originally sprung, the ARU was instantly connected with the personage of its greatest public champion, the charismatic orator Gene Debs. It would consequently be him who the officials of the old brotherhoods blamed for the attrition of their memberships and depletion of their finances during the difficult years of the mid-1890s. Despite claims that the ARU sought to organize the unorganized in the railroad industry—those 85 percent of railroad workers not part of any established railway brotherhood—the old orders were racked by membership attrition, which they attributed to new competiton, the ARU. Particularly hard hit was Keliher's Brotherhood of Railway Carmen, a craft union of railroad car inspectors and repairmen, which lost not only Keliher, their outstanding figure, but Grand Chief Carman Missemer as well, the latter declining to run for reelection.

Adding insult to injury, Keliher's departure was allegedly accompanied by a circular letter from his desk sent to all lodges of the order offering them fresh charters as lodges of the ARU in exchange for their charters with the old organization.[29] As the Brotherhood of Railway Carmen was a young order with little institutional loyalty, having been established only in October 1888, Keliher's proposition proved attractive, and membership plummeted, with the brotherhood rapidly shedding 112 of its 150 lodges. Slashing cuts to the salaries of union officials followed. ARU vice president Howard attempted to win final surrender late in 1893, visiting Keliher's replacement, BRC founder Frank Ronemus, to ask, "What can you expect to accomplish with the handful of members you have left? We have practically all the former members of your brotherhood in the ARU and within the next six months we will have the last of them." According to Ronemus's testimony, a position as assistant secretary-treasurer of the ARU was offered as an additional inducement for him to terminate the old order. Ronemus declined. With its coffers depleted, the organization's official organ was suspended in June 1894 as Ronemus and his associates battled through lean times. It would not be until 1899 that the Brotherhood of Railway Carmen had recovered sufficiently to relaunch its monthly magazine.[30]

While the troubled situation of the carmen epitomized the ARU's effect upon the membership and finances of the old railway craft brotherhoods, a similar dynamic was seen in every department. In 1899 the *Cyclopedia of Fraternities* tallied a loss during 1894 and 1895 of 8,000 members by the Brotherhood of Locomotive Engineers, 4,000 members by the Brotherhood of Locomotive Firemen, and a similar number by the Brotherhood of Railroad Trainmen.[31] Substantial losses were experienced by the Order of Railway Conductors, while the Order of Railroad Telegraphers and the Switchmen's Mutual Aid Association were almost completely annihilated.[32] For all protestations that the new ARU bore no ill will toward the existing railway brotherhoods, the practical effect of its launch upon the membership and finances of these groups, amplified by the contracting incomes of workers during the ongoing depression, proved devastating. A bitter enmity developed between the old orders and the new industrial union. When the acid test came at the time of the Pullman boycott of 1894, there would be few willing allies among the railway crafts to rally their members to the ARU banner. Divided allegiances among railroad workers, in 1894 as in the past, would aid strikebreaking by management and help speed the Pullman boycott to its unsuccessful conclusion.

☙

But the Pullman defeat was in the future. The new ARU began its life with a widely publicized victory, the second great strike that this book details. The Great Northern Railway was an arterial line running from St. Paul, Minnesota, across that state, through North Dakota, Montana, Idaho, and Washington, to the coast of the Pacific Ocean. The road was the subject of a major work stoppage beginning April 13, 1894, triggered by company efforts to impose the latest in a series of wage cuts. Strikers temporarily disabled the line before leaving, decoupling cars from engines and thereby making a fast restart difficult. Picket lines were formed in an effort to deter the hiring of strikebreakers. The ARU fanned the flames of discontent, issuing a circular letter to its members on April 16 illustrating the Great Northern's failure to pay wages commensurate with those of other transcontinental lines.[33] With its system gridlocked, the company immediately pursued relief from the courts, citing its role as a primary carrier of mail to the Pacific Northwest in its application for a US Circuit Court injunction in St. Paul on April 16. Alleging more than $200,000 in damages, the complaint sought to bar strikers from disabling engines or cars or interfering with their operation. The company's request was rapidly granted by Judge Walter H. Sanborn.[34]

Hearing of the strike by ARU members, Debs hurried from Terre Haute to

St. Paul, arriving on Wednesday, April 18, to take command of the work stoppage.[35] Workers remained united against the Great Northern's wage reductions; the company was anxious to bring the fight to a hasty conclusion by any means necessary. On April 28, Great Northern president James J. Hill sent a telegram to Washington asking President Grover Cleveland to intervene with federal troops to protect the sanctity of the mail, hoping to end the strike through the introduction of armed force.[36] This plea was rejected, however, moving Hill to take another tack, convening a meeting of the St. Paul Chamber of Commerce and challenging Debs to present the ARU's position in an effort to pressure the strikers to accept the new wage scale. The Chamber of Commerce proposed binding arbitration as a solution, with the decision to be rendered by a committee dominated by regional businessmen. Convinced of the righteousness of his cause, Debs quickly accepted the proposal and induced Hill to match his commitment. To Debs's delight a decision was rendered in favor of the striking workers by Charles A. Pillsbury and other prominent shippers on the arbitration committee, who sought the speediest possible restoration of the transportation network upon which they depended. The strike was ended after just 18 days, with Hill agreeing to return wages to their August 1893 level, putting $146,000 a month into the pockets of Great Northern workers.[37]

The whirlwind Great Northern victory catapulted Debs to a place on the national stage, with news of the victory by the eloquent young labor leader burning up the wires of the Associated Press. Debs returned from the Twin Cities to Terre Haute to a massive celebratory throng that crowded the city's railway terminal to honor the returning hero. He was proudly marched behind a brass band to the Terre Haute House Park to deliver a rousing victory speech to his home folk.[38] It was a great day for Debs. The Great Northern victory and his triumphant Terre Haute homecoming would mark a personal high-water mark of Debs's career as a labor organizer. Moreover, the triumph helped to deepen his commitment to the blossoming ARU, an organization that gained thousands of new members in its aftermath.[39] Industrial unionism seemed clearly to be the right path.

ς⁊

George Mortimer Pullman, namesake and president of Pullman's Palace Car Company and the company town for which it was created, was not a person born to great wealth. His father was a carpenter from upstate New York who invented a specialized machine for moving buildings from one place to another, a patented process that provided a steady if unspectacular income to support his large family. George attended school for just four years before leaving to work as a shop assistant for an uncle in his general store. After several years of childhood labor, George left the world of retail to apprentice as a cabinetmaker.[40] He would eventually follow his father into the house-moving trade, taking over as sole proprietor of the family business following his father's death in 1853. The next year he obtained a contract from the state of New York to move about 20 warehouses and other buildings from the banks of the Erie Canal as part of a state-financed project to widen the waterway. This and other contracts provided a small nest egg that allowed Pullman to set up shop in the emerging town of Chicago, which at the time had a massive need for building movers in conjunction with a project to raise the elevation of the business district to make way for a new sewage system.[41] This government work would be the initial source of the Pullman fortune.

The growth of railroads in the years immediately following the Civil War provided a lucrative field for speculative investment for young capitalists of the day. Sitting in the geographically strategic transportation hub of Chicago, George Pullman witnessed with his own eyes the steady westward expansion of the nation's railways over the vast expanses of the Great Plains and Mountain West. Multiday train travel would require adequate facilities for overnight accommodation, Pullman observed—why not provide a means for such overnight travel in comfort? Together with a business partner, Benjamin C. Field, Pullman developed the concept of the luxury sleeper car, a well-ventilated behemoth with a complex suspension system that rode smoothly over rough rails and featured polished walnut accoutrements and comfortable mattresses featuring (novelty of novelties!) fresh linen.[42] Pullman sleepers were costly to construct, bearing a price tag of $18,000 in an era when simple sleeper cars could be produced for $4,000, but demand was intense and a lucrative manufacturing business was spawned. This manufactory "went public" in 1867 with the launch of Pullman's Palace Car Company, a corporation capitalized through the sale of $100,000 worth of stock in dividend-paying $100 shares.[43] The firm would soon expand from the construction of sleeper and dining cars to their operation for the various railroads under license, providing a key channel of corporate profit for Pullman and a lucrative enterprise for the railways alike.

Between 1880 and 1893, a company town called Pullman, located a few miles outside of Chicago, would be established as a manufacturing and service center for the growing palace car fleet. Pullman was envisioned as a model company town, an idyllic enclave in which millions of dollars of corporate funds had been invested to build well-constructed, thoroughly habitable homes, parks, public buildings, and a modern urban infrastructure, all with a view to housing an orderly, productive, malleable proletariat. No charity was involved in the proposition—the Pullman Company remained the sole property owner within city limits and used its monopolistic position to charge rents and utility fees well in excess of prevailing rates in nearby Chicago. The company even structured rental fees for the Greenstone Church building to ensure a 6 percent rate of return on its capital investment in the facility.[44] The town rapidly grew in population to more than 12,000, as the Pullman enterprise expanded in tandem with America's growing railway system.

The rapid growth of the Pullman Company was short-circuited by the deep national depression of 1893, with many of the company's repair and manufacturing shops falling idle in the economic contraction. With orders diminished and travel reduced by the economic crisis, wages were slashed and layoffs enacted. Fatally, however, no comparable adjustment was made in rental and utility fees charged in the company-owned town. Many workers fell into debt to their erstwhile employer and landlord, with little hope of extrication. A mood of anger and despair prevailed. A substantial percentage of the Pullman workforce, approximately one-third, had joined the American Railway Union following the union's victory in the Great Northern strike, made eligible for union membership by the 20 miles of track running through the company's car works. These unionized workers spearheaded a protest against wage cuts, layoffs, and the company's refusal to lower rent, gas, and water bills on par with the lower wage rates unilaterally enacted by the company. Adding to worker antagonism was the company's failure to cut commensurately the salaries of officials and foremen, and to halt or reduce the payment of cash dividends to stockholders.[45]

Negotiations between a workers' grievance committee and company officials began around the first of May and reached an impasse on May 9, when President Pullman appeared at a scheduled meeting to refuse demands for either restoration of wages to previous levels or reduction of rents in accord with lowered wage levels. This session not only failed to reach an amicable understanding, but it further inflamed the tense situation when several members of the strike committee were abruptly terminated from employment after the meeting.[46] Arbitration to settle the matter was vociferously rejected by the company; a strike was set in motion.

In the early-morning hours of May 11, 1894, representatives of the various Pullman shops gathered at Turner Hall in the neighboring town of Kensington to discuss further action. Following heated debate, a vote was taken and, by a margin of 42–4, delegates approved an immediate strike. The following morning, workers reported for duty as scheduled, but when summoned by their leaders, they downed tools and left the premises, with between 80 and 90 percent of the company's workers heeding the call for a stoppage. While initiation of the strike was technically an action of the Pullman workers themselves rather than an official action of the ARU, the union's heavy representation among the most militant Pullman workers had the effect of drawing ARU officials into the conflict.[47]

Strikers, generally wearing a white ribbon tied through a buttonhole as a badge of solidarity, held a series of public meetings at Turner Hall in Kensington, headquarters of Pullman strike leaders, with ARU officials addressing some of these gatherings. The workers were realistic about their chances of victory doing battle against a wealthy and powerful corporation during a period of massive unemployment, with strike leader Thomas Heathcoate declaring,

> We do not expect the company to concede our demands. We do not know what the outcome will be, and in fact we do not care much. We do know we are working for less wages than will maintain ourselves and families in the necessaries of life, and on that proposition we absolutely refuse to work any longer.[48]

Strikers placed their hope for victory in the possible intercession of the American Railway Union and expansion of the strike beyond the narrow confines of the Pullman shops.[49] This assistance appeared to be forthcoming when ARU president Gene Debs addressed the assembly on May 14 to assure strikers that he held a deep distaste for the "paternalism of Pullman" and that in standing up for their rights, he was with the idle workers "heart and soul."[50] Behind the scenes, Debs and the ARU were themselves realistic about the strike's prospects for success, as well as potential negative repercussions for the union if it were to be drawn into the conflict prematurely. An informal meeting of ARU officers held in Chicago on June 1 determined not to expand the strike against the Pullman Company until every opportunity for settlement had been exhausted.

The desire of Debs and the American Railway Union leadership to contain and manage the Pullman strike was undercut by an external event—the previously scheduled opening of the First Quadrennial Convention of the ARU at Uhlich's Hall in Chicago on June 12, 1894. Two days prior to the event, 75 delegates had streamed into the city from points around the West, with about 206 delegates in attendance for the initial gavel.[51] General Master Workman James R. Sovereign[52] of the Knights of Labor addressed the gathering on June 14, and an alliance between the two industrial unions was agreed upon, bolstering the confidence of delegates of the union's power. The next day the matter of the Pullman strike was brought before the convention for the first time, with striking employees of the company making impassioned pleas before the assembled delegates. The decision was made by the convention to appoint a 12-member committee consisting of six ARU delegates and six Pullman employees to conduct further negotiations with company officials in an effort to force binding arbitration, under threat of an expanded strike. George Pullman refused to meet with the committee, however, arrogantly declaring that there was "nothing to arbitrate." Momentum began to build for a general stoppage of all Pullman traffic under ARU auspices.

After a Sunday recess, the ARU convention was diverted by other matters for several days, including a bitter two-day debate on the race question, with the convention ultimately voting against advice by Debs and prohibiting black workers from membership in a narrow 112–100 roll call vote.[53] It would not be until June 21 that the Pullman matter again occupied the delegates, who heard a report from their Pullman committee before voting unanimously to call a general halt to the handling of all Pullman cars until the company would reverse their previous position and agree to arbitration. No such retreat would be forthcoming.

On June 25, 1894, Debs, Howard, and other members of the ARU board of directors filled the Empire Theater in Chicago to rally the troops for a selective work stoppage, in which union members would refuse to link or move Pullman cars. Such a boycott of sleeper cars was intended to slash the company's revenue from operations, thereby forcing the corporation into good faith negotiations. Unfortunately for the ARU, the battle would not be so simple. The operation of Pullman sleepers by the Pullman company under franchise was legally mandated by contracts signed by numerous railroads, including most member companies represented in the Chicago-based General Managers' Association (GMA). Having witnessed the potential power of the ARU in its recent Great Northern victory, these railroads were by now united and determined to strangle the troublesome new industrial union in its crib; smashing a Pullman sympathy strike was seen as an ideal opportunity.[54] The GMA held an emergency meeting on June 25 at the Rookery Building in Chicago, unanimously issuing a declaration that the "unjustifiable and unwarranted" sympathy strike by the ARU would not be tolerated, with the united action of member railroads promised to defeat the strike. Regular meetings of the GMA ensued, with a consensus reached on June 26 providing that any railroad employee refusing to handle Pullman cars should be immediately discharged.[55] Battle lines were set.

The boycott went into effect on June 26, with the switchmen—historically the most militant of the railroad crafts—playing the decisive role in refusing to handle Pullman cars. A spate of terminations for refusal to inspect, switch, or haul Pullman cars followed, unsurprisingly provoking a reaction.[56] By June 28 as many as 40,000 railway workers were off the job, impacting all of the primary Chicago-based lines. This more than doubled the following day, with nearly 100,000 men on strike and at least 20 railroads substantially impacted or halted altogether.[57] The Pullman strike was strongest in the Midwest, the West, and the Southwest but weak in the populous Northeast as well as in the Deep South, where the ARU had comparatively few lodges organized.[58] The boycott was peaceable during its initial days, with no violence or destruction of property. Nevertheless, public reaction was sharply negative, with the capitalist press decrying the strike as the "Debs Rebellion" and depicting the ARU president as an economic dictator in the making.

The affected Chicago-based railroad lines that had organized since 1886 as the General Managers' Association provided a nexus for united action against the Pullman boycott. The 24 railroads and terminals participating in the GMA refused to parley with Debs and the ARU, instead publicly expressing their intention of fighting the boycott by all means available and making use of their press connections to win the battle of public opinion.[59] The organization coordinated the hiring of strikebreakers (primarily from among unemployed workers in the East), devised plans to ensure Pullman cars were attached to trains carrying mail, and agitated for government action against the ongoing strike. Efforts to halt the strike through the courts began immediately, led by the Santa Fe Railroad, then under federal bankruptcy receivership, which successfully obtained an injunction from US circuit court judge Henry C. Caldwell on June 27 prohibiting strikers from interfering with the property or operation of the line within his Southwestern judicial circuit. Two days later, circuit court judge William A. Woods extended this order to cover the Illinois division of the same line. These early localized injunctions were supplanted by blanket injunctions obtained by US district attorneys that declared such interference illegal on all lines within a given jurisdiction. The first of these was issued in Chicago on July 2 by judges Woods and Peter S. Grosscup, with potential obstruction of the mail and interstate trade providing the rationale for such action.[60]

At the federal level, the railroads had a staunch supporter of their interests in the corridors of power in attorney general Richard Olney.[61] Olney, the Ivy League-educated son of a Massachusetts textile manufacturer and banker, had more than two decades of experience as a corporate lawyer and member of boards of directors of several prominent railroads before he was tapped as the nation's chief law enforcement officer by President Grover Cleveland in 1893. As a staunch defender of the unfettered rights of private capital in general and railroads in particular, Olney was an eager point man in Washington, DC, for the railroad companies subjected to the Pullman boycott, and he emerged as chief strategist within the Cleveland administration for defeat of the ARU strike, which Olney saw as a lawless attack on the prerogatives of capital.[62] Olney was ready from the onset to use any means necessary to quell the escalating strike. Even before a boisterous throng of thousands began spontaneously overrunning the railroad yards to shut down traffic at Blue Island, south of Chicago, on July 1 and 2, Olney had busied himself convincing President Cleveland of the necessity of federal military intervention elsewhere, gaining an order on July 1 to send troops to Los Angeles and Trinidad, Colorado.[63] When Cleveland issued orders on July 3 to General Nelson A. Miles[64] to transport regular army soldiers to Chicago to suppress the growing disorder there, he was only revisiting a tactic already used in other locales. Cleveland was adamant in his quest to restore interstate transportation, declaring that even if "it takes every dollar in the Treasury and every soldier in the United States Army to deliver a postal card in Chicago, that postal card shall be delivered."[65] Uniformed troops with rifles and bayonets arrived in Chicago the following day, setting up camp along the lakefront and at other strategic points.

The presence of troops to halt a work stoppage in Chicago proved inflammatory, in a very literal sense. On July 5 rioting erupted in the Chicago stockyards, with waylaid boxcars looted and burned. The day after would see a further descent into chaos and destruction when, on the worst day of rioting, as many as 700 railroad cars would be destroyed, along with other railroad property. Several thousand rioters on the Grand Truck line at 49th and Loomis in Chicago assaulted a company of state militia guarding a wrecking train that was clearing the line, with the guardsmen firing into the crowd. An advance with fixed bayonets was made and several people were seriously wounded, while a rain of rocks, bricks, and bottles was unleashed by the mob. Four were killed and 20 wounded in the battle, including several women.[66] Not a single wagon of meat or livestock would be moved to or from the stockyards from July 4 to 10, leaving cars full of perishable food to rot in the sun.[67] Consumers felt the impact immediately as far away as New York City, where peaches formerly selling for $1 a box now demanded $3.60, and the price of poultry and meat likewise shot up rapidly.[68]

A July 7 letter from Debs to President Cleveland fell upon deaf ears.[69] Additional federal troops were dispatched to Chicago, and on July 8 President Cleveland issued a proclamation against public lawlessness. All individuals participating in public demonstrations or obstructing railroad traffic were to disperse and return to their homes by noon the following day, or face being treated as public enemies by the government and its military forces.[70] With industry and transportation tottering, and wanton looting and rioting offending public sensibilities, positive public sentiment for the ARU's boycott quickly evaporated. Railway employees also wavered in their resolve. A July 7 "monster mass meeting" of shop workers of the Missouri and Missouri, Kansas & Texas railroads in Sedalia, Missouri—home to an estimated 1,000 railroaders—ended with a tepid resolution registering their opposition to the Pullman strike, while dutifully sending "heartfelt sympathy" and vague promises of "pecuniary aid" to those out of work.[71] With federal troops in place amid warnings by the president to cease and desist or face the wrath of military authority, the Pullman boycott was effectively defeated. Only the final details of the union's surrender and the contour of the inevitable legal repercussions against Debs and other leading ARU officials remained to be determined.

❧

On July 10, 1894, Cook County district attorney Thomas Milchrist convened a special grand jury, to which was presented subpoenaed copies of ARU telegrams as evidence of a criminal conspiracy to interfere with movement of the US mail. No other evidence was presented. The grand jury deliberated only a few hours before returning indictments on ARU president Debs, vice president Howard, secretary Keliher, and *Railway Times* editor Rogers. All four were arrested that same day before being released on a joint bail of $10,000. While the grand jury was doing its work, deputy marshals and postal inspectors raided the offices of the ARU in Chicago, seizing the union's books and documents, including unopened personal mail. This document trove would provide copious raw material for a future legal proceeding, and on July 17 Debs and other ARU officers were arrested for contempt of court, alleged to have violated an injunction of July 2. It would be this contempt charge, not the ultimately unproven conspiracy indictment, that would send Debs and his compatriots to jail.[72]

With public sentiment enraged by one-sided coverage in the press and solidarity of strikers beginning to weaken, by July 12 Debs and the ARU were ready to sue for peace. An emergency session of labor leaders, including prominently President Samuel Gompers of the American Federation of Labor, was convened in Chicago, to which Debs presented a document for delivery to the General Managers' Association declaring a willingness to immediately end the work stoppage if the railroads would hire back strikers without prejudice.[73] This effort to save face and place was met with stony silence by company officials. Facing inevitable defeat, the union quickly folded its hand, calling off the Pullman sympathy strike at 9:30 a.m. on July 13, unilaterally and with no guarantees. The Pullman Company would remain shuttered until August 2, when the repair department reopened, but defeat of the original Pullman strike was readily apparent from the moment of the ARU's inevitable surrender in its sympathy action. Company employment rolls included 2,337 workers by August 23, of whom about three-quarters were former Pullman workers and the remainder newly hired employees.[74]

Things were worse for the railwaymen. In the aftermath of the strike, the railroad companies exacted brutal revenge, blacklisting strike leaders and ARU activists and chasing them from the industry. The example of one blacklisted engineer, Ben Carroll of Covington, Ohio, is illustrative. Fired from his job on the Southern Railway, Carroll found himself unable in the aftermath of the 1894 strike to find another position on any line, owing to his inclusion on the blacklist. His wife and four children were found by local authorities in January 1896 occupying an unheated home, with scant clothing and not having eaten in two days. The family was relegated to the emergency care of local authorities.[75]

Debs was quick to recognize the paralyzing effect of the managers' blacklist in deterring otherwise sympathetic railway workers from further participation in the ARU. Henceforth the ARU would attempt to beat the blacklist by becoming an underground organization, Debs and his associates determined, complete with secret meetings and a concealed membership list.[76] The move of the ARU to an underground status was formally announced to the membership through a circular dated December 27, 1894.[77] While Debs optimistically predicted in an August 1895 interview with the union-friendly *Chicago Chronicle* that "seven-eighths" of the nation's 880,000 railway workers were with the union, in actual fact relatively few were willing to risk permanent loss of employment to attend meetings of an ineffectual secret society. ARU membership rolls plummeted, as did the union's financial resources. By 1897 the union had atrophied into a small core of committed activists, an impotent force in the field of labor-management relations and collective bargaining.

☙

Debs is widely remembered for his two stints in jail, and for the grace, dignity, and unbroken defiance with which he bore unjust punishment. On November 16, 1894, Debs and eight other ARU directors were arraigned as part of a group of alleged conspirators in Chicago before federal judge Peter S. Grosscup. The case was held over until December 4, at which time a defense motion to quash would be heard, with a trial to be held on the conspiracy charge after the first of the year. In the meantime, Judge William A. Woods ruled on a citation for contempt of court, in which Debs and other ARU officers were charged with having violated a July 2 injunction effectively prohibiting participation in strike activities. Woods delivered a 60-page ruling running to 27,000 words on December 14, declaring the officers guilty of contempt and sentencing Debs to six months in county jail as most culpable, while handing down three-month terms to ARU officers Howard, Keliher, and Rogers, as well as directors William E. Burns,[78] Martin J. Elliott,[79] James Hogan,[80] and Roy M. Goodwin.[81] Ten days were allowed for appeal and a decision was made by the legal defense team to apply directly to the United State Supreme Court on a writ of habeas corpus since constitutional issues were involved, with a further stay granted until January 8 to allow time for this process. While this appeal was presented, Debs continued to speak on behalf of the ARU, visiting several cities in Wisconsin and Minnesota to state his case in the court of public opinion.[82]

January 8 arrived, and Debs and his fellow ARU officers were incarcerated. At the request of their legal defense team, the place of incarceration was moved from the overcrowded and bleak Cook County Jail to the comparatively idyllic conditions of the McHenry County Jail in Woodstock, Illinois, located about 50 miles northwest of Chicago. There the ARU prisoners were received by a sympathetic county sheriff, who invited the passive and intellectual prisoners to share meals at the family table in his home adjacent to the jail. Reading, writing, and the discipline of military drill were part of the daily routine, with every courtesy extended the prisoners—who were visited by journalists including the renowned Nellie Bly, who documented the comparatively easy conditions of their confinement for readers of the *New York World*.[83]

With a major trial for conspiracy under the Sherman Antitrust Act of 1890 slated to begin against them before the end of January, and their appeal still in the hands of the Supreme Court, new bail was granted to the jailed ARU leaders after just 17 days had been served. The first two weeks of incarceration had proved eventful, however, as a split took place among the defendants, with Vice President Howard quitting the ARU. Howard immediately moved on to his next organizing project, envisioned as a national labor organization open to all workers, emulating ARU-style low membership dues, to be known as the American Industrial Union (AIU). Debs and the other ARU leaders refused to abandon their industrial railway union to follow Howard into his new endeavor, though. Howard would spend the next year attempting to breathe life into what would ultimately be recognized as a stillborn organization.[84]

Jurors in the ARU conspiracy trial were sworn in in Chicago on January 26, with the government presenting its case over the following week. The first week of February came to a close with Debs on the stand, reading several manifestos in which he called for lawful behavior on the part of strikers and condemning potential acts of sabotage or violence. On February 8, in the middle of cross-examination of Debs, the trial was suddenly postponed owing to the illness of juror John C. Coe, stricken by pneumonia. Coe was visited in person by Judge Grosscup, who deemed him unlikely to be able to continue the trial for more than two weeks.[85] Because no alternate juror was available, proceedings were tentatively postponed until May 1, although with the tide of both public sentiment and testimony in the courtroom seemingly tilting against the prosecution, there would be no resumption. The charges would ultimately be dropped.

With the trial postponed, Debs made use of his time out on bail to conduct a western tour, visiting North Dakota and Montana en route to the San Francisco Bay Area.[86] At the end of the first week of June the Supreme Court finally issued its unanimous ruling rejecting the ARU attorneys' writ of habeas corpus, and Debs immediately began his journey back to Chicago for re-incarceration, although no certified copy of the Supreme Court's ruling returning the defendants to jail would be received until June 10. In the interim, former vice president Howard requested that his confinement take place apart from the others, so he was brought to the Will County Jail in Joliet to serve the remaining time on his three-month sentence. The other ARU directors were told to report to the office of the federal marshal on June 11 for their return in one group to Woodstock. The appointed hour for surrender, 4 p.m., came and went; Debs failed to appear. An arrest warrant was issued that evening, but Debs was not located. The matter was resolved at 11 a.m. the next day when Debs checked in to the marshal's office for transportation—quite obviously hungover from a night of alcoholic excess. Debs explained his unexcused absence with an implausible claim that he had suffered incapacitating illness brought on by eating "bad cucumbers" while having dinner with a friend—a laughably weak explanation that would be ridiculed for many months by wags in the conservative press.

In jail, the "Cooperative Colony of Liberty Jail" resumed its daily regimen of reading, writing, and military drill. The ARU political prisoners were visited periodically by family members, friendly journalists interested in a good interview,[87] and sundry radical worthies. Among the latter were Chicago Socialist Labor Party stalwart Tommy Morgan,[88] who visited Debs on September 4, accompanied by former Haymarket prisoner Oscar Neebe and touring Scottish socialist Keir Hardie.[89] As part of this visit, Debs, Hardie, and Morgan would jointly sign a letter of intent to establish an "International Bureau of Correspondence and Agitation" that would "bring into active and harmonious relation all organizations and persons favorable to the establishment of the Industrial Commonwealth founded upon collective ownership of the means of production and distribution."[90] While it would not be until the last days of 1896 that Debs would come out by publicly self-identifying as a socialist, this document lends support to the idea that Debs's acceptance of the socialist idea predated his time in Woodstock Jail.[91]

With its leadership figuratively decapitated, the ARU's coffers continued to attenuate, as tens of thousands of dollars were committed to payment of legal fees while membership and dues revenue contracted.[92] By August, when the three-month sentences of Debs's jailed ARU associates were slated to end, finances were so poor that Debs was forced to send his brother scrambling to borrow $775 from a financial angel to cover advance costs for the five to return to the road as union organizers. While acknowledging that "just now we have to strain to a point," Gene predicted that by the first of the year "we will have more money than we have use for" as "we are dead sure of coming right for the whole world is bound to come our way."[93] This assessment proved fanciful. During its last two years of existence, the ARU would be unable to pay its president his salary of $75 a month.[94] Loans from supporters would tide over the ARU and its ongoing legal and organizing expenses, but Debs would ultimately spend years of his life repaying these tens of thousands of dollars of accumulated union debt.

❧

Gene Debs would remain in jail at Woodstock until November 22, 1895, serving the full six months of his sentence for contempt of court to the day. The potentially more serious trial for conspiracy was never completed. Juror Coe's illness was used by a failing prosecution to avoid a precedent-setting loss in the courtroom, Debs later claimed. Debs's final days at Woodstock were spent drafting a major address about the ramifications of his legal experience in the aftermath of the Pullman affair. This speech, entitled "Liberty," was delivered to an enthusiastic crowd of thousands that packed the Chicago National Guard artillery armory and marked another personal highlight for Debs as a nationally acclaimed union leader. The defiant statement he made at Battery D on the necessity of united political action by the working class to achieve its own liberation would be frequently reprinted throughout Debs's life.[95] In his epic two-hour address, Debs equated the ongoing battle of the labor movement for economic justice with the battle of colonial heroes to win freedom from autocratic British rule in the Revolutionary War of 1775 to 1783. Liberty was "a birthright" that had been "wrested from the weak by the strong," in Debs's view, and thus the object of a supreme fight that would end with construction of a new world:

> There is nothing in our government it cannot remove or amend. It can make and unmake Presidents and Congresses and courts. It can abolish unjust laws and consign to eternal odium and oblivion unjust judges, strip from them their robes and gowns, and send them forth unclean as lepers to bear the burden of merited obloquy as Cain with the mark of a murderer. It can sweep away trusts, syndicates, corporations, monopolies, and every other abnormal development of the money power designed to abridge the liberties of workingmen and enslave them by the degradation incident to poverty and enforced idleness, as cyclones scatter the leaves of the forest. The ballot can do all this and more. It can give our civilization its crowning glory—the Cooperative Commonwealth.

Despite his rhetorical bravado, on the ground things were grim for the ARU. Debs put up a brave front, holding on to hope that the mortally wounded union would still yet recover to assume mass membership and influence. Debs began his first post-Woodstock year with a meticulously planned three-month organizing tour that would take him through the Midwest and the South. With the fall election approaching, Debs called on his listeners to act as a solid bloc in electing loyal candidates, declaring before a packed house in Milwaukee that "boycotts and strikes had proved ineffective and reactionary, and the only way for labor to get its just dues in this country was for the workingmen to swarm the ballot box with a unity of purpose and sweep everything before them."[96] With the reins of political power in working-class hands, fundamental reform would follow for organized workers, Debs argued. This notion of a dual-winged working-class movement combining independent party politics with the separate and parallel activity of mass industrial unions anticipated the ideology of the Socialist Party of America.[97]

Debs was greeted enthusiastically during his 1896 organizing tour, with organized workers from every trade and middle-class sympathizers filling the large music halls and auditoriums into which he was booked. Debs would generally precede or follow these mass oratorical spectacles by a day with closed presentations at smaller ARU organizing events. With the blacklist of ARU members restricting open agitation and enrollment, Debs and his fellows nevertheless sought to rebuild his shattered union as an underground organization, only gradually coming to the realization that constructing a mass organization through secret membership and surreptitious tactics was impossible. Moreover, railroad managers and company spies were not Debs's sole obstacle in reconstructing the ARU. From its creation, the ARU remained in essence a dual industrial union from the perspective of the old brotherhoods. This common threat pushed the old organizations to join hands in an anti-ARU alliance, an informal agreement consecrated on January 21, 1896, in Princeton, Indiana, at a session attended by D. L. Everett, a top official of the Brotherhood of Locomotive Engineers, grand master Frank Sargent of the Brotherhood of Locomotive Firemen, grand chief conductor E. E. Clark of the Order of Railway Conductors, and grand master Patrick Morrissey of the Brotherhood of Railroad Trainmen.[98] Unwilling or unable to join in federation against the bosses only a few years earlier, these four powerful brotherhoods now expeditiously united to defend their fiefs from the existential threat of industrial unionism. Taking advantage of his published tour dates, the four great railway brotherhoods began to coordinate organizing efforts by their own officials, holding meetings several nights in advance of Debs in an attempt to warn away railroad men from the silver-tongued Hoosier's siren song.[99]

ↂ

As trade-union organizing faltered, the political path began to burn bright. The vessel for unified working-class political action, from Debs's perspective, was the People's Party—the so-called "Populists"—a fledgling political organization endorsed by the ARU's "First Quadrennial Convention" in 1894. While Debs saw independent working-class politics through the People's Party as the means to break the impasse represented by the two "old parties" with their respective anti-labor perspectives, there were those in the People's Party who saw their own answer to a shortage of charismatic national leadership in the person of Debs—a widely known, earnest, and eloquent labor leader of a new type, a man whose public reputation had quickly regenerated owing to the unfair judicial persecution he had suffered. The moment to step forward as a political leader was never more ripe, but Debs would not budge, refusing the efforts of People's Party activists to draft him as the party's presidential nominee in 1896. The party instead sought victory through expedient fusion with the Democratic Party behind a tolerably reformist candidate, William Jennings Bryan, who promised monetary reform that would help common people.

Although he had earlier proclaimed himself to be a supporter of former Colorado governor Davis Hanson Waite,[100] a politician of impeccable populist bona fides, after the decision was made to co-nominate Bryan, Debs dutifully took to the road in support of the Democratic-Populist fusion ticket, making a series of campaign speeches to labor crowds in the fall of 1896.[101] The defeat of Bryan at the polls left the People's Party looking opportunistic, unprincipled, and weak, marking the beginning of the end for the organization as an effective force in American politics. The decks were thus cleared for a new role for Eugene V. Debs as 1897 dawned: socialist political leader.

General Series Notes

The Selected Works of Eugene V. Debs will present his most important writings in six chronological volumes. Each book will include a brief introduction touching upon the major activities of Debs's life during the period of coverage and pointing toward key elements of his evolving thought. Archaic spelling, idiosyncratic punctuation, misspelled names, misquoted sources, and typographical errors appearing in the original published versions have not been treated as sacrosanct, but rather have been silently corrected and standardized for consistency and readability. A few words from defective source documents that had to be guessed from context are provided within square brackets, as are substantive clarifications provided by the editors. The inclusion of full articles rather than excerpts has been given high priority, although a few items have been shortened for reasons of space or clarity. These editorial alterations have been marked by ellipses (. . .) for very short deletions and asterisks (* * *) for longer content removals.

Titles of articles and speeches as they appeared in the press varied greatly from publication to publication. Those appearing in *Locomotive Firemen's Magazine* were written by Debs himself and have been generally retained without change unless the same title was used multiple times, as Debs was wont to do, e.g., "Federation," "The Knights of Labor," "The Supreme Council," etc. A few Debs-generated titles that are particularly non-descriptive of actual content have been editorially revised. The titles of articles and speeches appearing in publications edited by others have been either kept or rewritten for clarity as deemed most appropriate; those appearing previously in reprints of Debs's works have been retained to avoid confusion in almost every instance. In every case of a title change, the original title as published is provided at the end of each piece, along with other publication information.

Material has been chosen with a view to illustrating the evolution of Debs's thinking. Mundane contemporary affairs have been accorded low priority; matters touching on the events of the broader labor movement and society at large have been given closest attention. No material has been omitted or deleted for ideological reasons. We emphasize that Gene Debs was neither a saint nor a savant, but rather an evolving human being that was a product of his times, exhibiting at various times crassly individualistic aspirations; ethnic, racial, and gender biases; and ideological inconsistencies. We have attempted to chronicle these foibles and flaws rather than hide them through tendentious selection of content.

Debs never wrote a full-length book in his lifetime, nor did he attempt to compile his memoirs.[102] All of his literary output was of an oratorical or journalistic nature, with the great majority of this material published as newspaper or magazine articles or speeches reproduced in pamphlet form. The editors attempted to review at least cursorily each of the approximately 420 Debs articles, speeches, and statements from the time period encapsulated by this volume. Some 162 items were chosen for inclusion, together with five related items in an appendix. Of these, just four have appeared in previous collections of Debs's speeches and articles.

Scholars should note that internal circular letters and the "daily strike bulletin" of the ARU were not successfully located and are not included in this volume. It is hoped that many of these rare printed documents will eventually resurface from the archival mists. Many hundreds of telegrams ostensibly signed by Debs were dispatched during the 1894 Pullman strike, some of which have been preserved. However, as part of his testimony to the special federal committee investigating the cause of the strike, Debs indicated that many or most of these were not actually written by him, but rather were the product of other officials and functionaries of the ARU and sent over his signature for reasons of economy and to aid in the projection of central authority. As a result of their undetermined and varied authorship, only two of these telegrams unquestionably written by Debs have been included here.

While the editors have received no financial support from any individual or institution in the preparation of this volume, they have nevertheless benefited immensely from the activity of others in the world of Debs scholarship, including those whose work is listed in the footnotes below. The editors wish to thank additionally Gene Dillman and Vince Kueter for graphics of rare ephemera, as well as Cinda May and Kendra McCrea of Cunningham Memorial Library, Indiana State University, and Ben Kite of the Eugene V. Debs Foundation for their courtesy and assistance. Martin Goodman of the Riazanov Digital Library Project has aided in the acquisition of certain rare publications from East Coast libraries. Historians Paul Buhle, John Holmes, and Micki Morahn were very helpful in answering queries. Similarly, the importance of our friends in the community of radical booksellers to the cause of independent scholarship, especially John Durham and Alexander Akin of Bolerium Books in San Francisco and Lorne Bair of Winchester, Virginia, is not to be underestimated. We also thank Nisha Bolsey and Amelia Ayrelan

Iuvino, who skillfully handled the project for Haymarket Books, Eric Kerl who designed the cover and text, as well as the entire Haymarket editorial board for their unflinching support of this expanding project.

The outstanding contribution to Debs scholarship was made by historian J. Robert Constantine and former Tamiment Library archivist Gail Malmgreen, with their twenty-one-reel microfilm collection and printed guide, *The Papers of Eugene V. Debs, 1834–1945.* The editors note their debt to this pioneering effort to chronicle and collect the speeches, articles, and correspondence of Gene Debs—it is impossible to imagine the successful completion of this project without such a thorough and expert plowing of the field having previously been made. This material has already been harvested by Mr. Constantine for his outstanding three-volume collection, *Letters of Eugene V. Debs,* published by University of Illinois Press in 1990. The editors hope that these volumes edited by Mr. Constantine will occupy every shelf next to the volumes of *The Selected Works of Eugene V. Debs,* and that the two series will be viewed as integral parts of the same project.

It is a matter of regret that Bob Constantine, the dean of Debs studies, died in 2017 at the age of 93, before the editors were able to communicate news of this project to him. It is to his memory that this series is dedicated.

Notes

1. According to US Chamber of Commerce figures, the years 1893 and 1894 saw consecutive GNP declines of 4.8 percent and 2.8 percent, respectively, which were only offset by a recovery in 1895. From: John W. Kendrick, *Productivity Trends in the United States*, 293; cited in Charles Hoffmann, *The Depression of the Nineties: An Economic History* (Westport, CT: Greenwood Press, 1970), xxviii.

2. Hoffman, *Depression of the Nineties*, 97, 103.

3. Albert Rees, *Real Wages in Manufacturing, 1890–1914*, 33; cited in Hoffman, *Depression of the Nineties*, L.

4. Paul H. Douglas, *The Problem of Unemployment* (New York: Macmillan, 1931), 2, 26; cited in Hoffman, *Depression of the Nineties*, 107.

5. Note the parallel between Homestead, Pennsylvania (located just outside of Pittsburgh) and Pullman, Illinois (located just outside of Chicago). Due to high urban property values, new company manufacturing towns were frequently established on the peripheries of urban population centers.

6. Andrew Carnegie (1835–1919), a so-called "titan of industry" of the late nineteenth and early twentieth century, is remembered both for his anti-labor role in the Homestead Strike and for his philanthropic "Carnegie Libraries." Ironically, Carnegie—a mid-level railroad company administrative employee in the 1850s—established his fortune through early investment in a firm that manufactured railway sleeping cars, T. T. Woodruff & Co. Carnegie would see his gamble on the profitable fledgling company rewarded handsomely, providing the initial capital for his entry into the lucrative field of steel manufacturing.

7. Paul Krause, *The Battle for Homestead, 1880–1892: Politics, Culture, and Steel* (Pittsburgh, PA: University of Pittsburgh Press, 1992), 286.

8. Arthur G. Burgoyne, *Homestead: A Complete History of the Struggle of July, 1892, Between the Carnegie Steel Company and the Amalgamated Association of Iron and Steel Workers* [1893]. (New York: Augustus M. Kelley, 1971), 9.

9. The Pinkerton Detective Agency, first established in 1850, became deeply involved in counterintelligence against the labor movement and provision of armed security to strikebreakers in the aftermath of the great strike of 1877. Allan J. Pinkerton (1819–1884) helped build the national reputation with a series of melodramatically titled volumes glorifying his firm's work, such as *The Molly Maguires and the Detectives* (1877) and *Strikers, Communists, Tramps, and Detectives* (1878).

10. David P. Demarest, ed., *"The River Ran Red": Homestead 1892* (Pittsburgh, PA: University of Pittsburgh Press, 1992), 24.

11. Demarest, *"The River Ran Red,"* 72.

12. Alexander Berkman (1870-1936) was a Lithuanian-born Jew who emigrated to the United States in 1888 and became romantically involved with anarchist Emma Goldman in 1891. A committed anarchist, Berkman unsuccessfully attempted to assassinate coal and steel maganate Henry Clay Frick with a pistol and a dagger on July 23, 1892. He would serve 14 years in prison for the crime, resuming his literary and political activity upon his release. Berkman died in France in June 1936

following injuries sustained from a self-inflicted gunshot wound.

13. George W. Howard (1848–19XX) was a career railroader who worked a variety of jobs running the gamut from brakeman to general superintendent in the Western United States. In 1888 he launched a new pro-strike dual union, the Brotherhood of Railway Conductors, an organization that he headed until its dissolution by merger with the older and larger Order of Railway Conductors in 1892. Credited by Samuel Gompers with first having the idea of the American Railway Union, Howard was elected vice president of the organization at the time of its formation in 1893, and he toured exhaustively, speaking on the union's behalf. In 1895, shortly after being jailed with Debs and other ARU leaders for contempt, Howard broke with the ARU and established a new organization, the American Industrial Union.

14. Louis W. Rogers (1859–1953) was a native of Iowa who taught school there before becoming a brakeman. He was employed on the Chicago, Burlington & Quincy at the time of its 1888 strike, during which he became a union activist. Rogers was fired from his position after the strike and moved into journalism, while continuing to maintain a membership in the Brotherhood of Railroad Brakemen. Formerly the editor of *The Patriot* in St. Joseph, Missouri, Rogers was chosen as editor of *Railroad Trainmen's Journal* in September 1891. He was active in the American Railway Union from its inception and served as editor of its official organ, *The Railway Times,* which launched in January 1894. (See: *The Railway Times,* September 2, 1895, 2.)

15. John Anthony Hall (1854–1892) went to work in the transportation industry in 1872 as a railway telegrapher, followed by stints as a station agent, brakeman, switchman, and yardmaster. After being fired as one of 11 yardmasters to lose their jobs joining the switchmen in the 1889 Burlington Strike, Hall wrote a sympathetic account of the conflict for the general public, *The Great Strike on the "Q"* (1889), before returning to work as a switchman on the Santa Fe. Hall was co-opted as a functionary of the Switchmen's Mutual Aid Association shortly thereafter, first as general organizer, then as editor of the brotherhood magazine when that post fell open. As a member of the SMAA Grand Lodge, Hall attended virtually every session of the Supreme Council of United Orders of Railway Employees during that institution's brief existence. In June 1892, after addressing a convention of the Brotherhood of Railroad Carmen along with Debs and L. W. Rogers, Hall slipped while trying to catch a moving train and was crushed to death beneath a wheel. After the accident, Debs published a long biographical eulogy of Hall and indicated the two were close cothinkers. See Debs, "John A. Hall," *Locomotive Firemen's Magazine,* vol. 16, no. 8 (August 1892), 734–737.

16. Sylvester Keliher (1863–19XX) was a founder of the Carmen's Mutual Aid Association in Minneapolis in 1888. This organization merged with the Brotherhood of Railway Carmen of America in 1890, at which time he was elected secretary-treasurer of the united organization and editor of the organization's monthly magazine, a role which put him in touch with Gene Debs, George Howard, and other leading spirits of railway federation. Together with Debs and Howard, Keliher worked on the committee to draft a constitution for the new ARU in February and

March 1893, attending every important organizing meeting and gaining election as secretary-treasurer. A political actionist and a socialist, Keliher would later be elected national secretary by the Social Democracy of America in June 1897.

17. Nick Salvatore, *Eugene V. Debs: Citizen and Socialist* (Urbana, IL: University of Illinois Press, 1982), 115.

18. Sylvester Keliher, "To the Brotherhood," *Railway Carmen's Journal,* vol. 13, whole no. 28 (July 1893), 387.

19. Samuel Gompers, "Editorial," *The American Federationist,* vol. 12, no. 7 (July 1905), 438–439.

20. Gompers repeated a similar tale in his posthumously published autobiography, changing the date of Howard's words to 1891 and adding the detail that at that time Howard came to Gompers's hotel to offer him the presidency of the forthcoming industrial union of railway workers. According to this second version of the story, it was only after being rebuffed by Gompers that Howard indicated he would therefore ask Gene Debs to assume the ARU presidency instead. See Gompers, *Seventy Years of Life and Labor: An Autobiography* (New York: E. P. Dutton, 1925), vol. 1, 404–405. "Gompers probably rewrote history here," Debs biographer Nick Salvatore has subsequently opined—a sentiment the editors of this volume share. See Salvatore, *Eugene V. Debs,* 368, n3. Nevertheless, Howard's documented chairmanship at several key foundational meetings and his presence on the three-member Committee on Constitution with Debs provides powerful circumstantial evidence to support Gompers's basic recollection that Howard, not Debs, was the originator of the ARU idea.

21. "Railroad Men Unite," *Chicago Tribune,* vol. 52, no. 40 (February 9, 1893), 1.

22. "New Federation," *Indianapolis Journal,* February 10, 1893, 4.

23. For the listing of committee members, see "Constitution of the Railway Union: It Is Submitted and Discussed in Detail in Secret Session," *Chicago Tribune,* vol. 52, no. 103 (April 13, 1893), 2.

24. "All Railway Men: National Federation Will Embrace Every Branch," *Chicago Tribune,* vol. 52, no. 102 (April 12, 1893), 9.

25. Sylvester Keliher, "Dawn of a New Era," *Railway Carmen's Journal,* vol. 3, whole no. 26 (May 1893), 259.

26. L. W. Rogers, "Federation Outdone: The American Railway Union Opens Its Campaign," *The Age of Labor,* vol. 2, no. 14 (May 20, 1893), 2.

27. The words are those of L. W. Rogers.

28. Keliher, "To the Brotherhood," 388. It was, incidentally, this same date of August 15, according to the testimony of vice president George Howard, that the ARU actually began organizing itself on a local basis. See United States Strike Commission, *Report on the Chicago Strike of June–July 1894* . . . (Washington, DC: US Government Printing Office, 1895), 12.

29. No copy of the document has been located to verify the accuracy of the BRC's allegation.

30. Frank L. Ronemus, "Origin, Progress, and Attainments of the Brotherhood Railway Carmen of America," in *International Official Souvenir: Tenth Biennial Convention*

Commencing Week September 9, 1907 . . . (Chicago: Grand Lodge Brotherhood Railway Carmen of America, 1907), 21, 27–29.

31. Formerly the Brotherhood of Railroad Brakemen.
32. Albert C. Stevens, ed., *Cyclopedia of Fraternities* (New York: Hamilton Printing and Publishing Co., 1899), 279. Cited in Ronemus, "Origin, Progress, and Attainments of the Brotherhood Railway Carmen of America," 23.
33. Stephen Marion Reynolds, "Life of Eugene V. Debs," in *Debs: His Life, Writings, and Speeches* (Girard, KS: Appeal to Reason, 1908), 7–8. No surviving copy of this circular letter is currently known to exist.
34. "Injunction Issued," *St. Paul Dispatch*, April 18, 1894, page unspecified. Copy in *The Papers of Eugene V. Debs, 1834–1945*, microfilm edition, reel 9.
35. Salvatore, *Eugene V. Debs,* 120.
36. Salvatore, *Eugene V. Debs*, 121.
37. Bernard J. Brommel, *Eugene V. Debs: Spokesman for Labor and Socialism* (Chicago: Charles H. Kerr Publishing Company, 1978), 33.
38. Debs, "The St. Paul Victory: Speech in Terre Haute," this volume.
39. Debs biographer Nick Salvatore indicates that the ARU gained about 2,000 new members every day immediately following the Great Northern strike, with total membership reaching the 150,000 mark—dwarfing the cumulative total of 90,000 of all the other railway brotherhoods. (See: Salvatore, *Eugene V. Debs,* 125.) ARU membership figures should be regarded with suspicion, however, as the union boasted that its membership approached 100,000 not long after its formation, when its actual membership roll was obviously a small fraction of that. Despite the strong likelihood of inflated membership claims, positive publicity around the Great Northern victory no doubt spurred an impressive growth in ARU membership.
40. Liston Edgington Leyendecker, *Palace Car Prince: A Biography of George Mortimer Pullman* (Niwot, CO: University Press of Colorado, 1992), 15–17.
41. Leyendecker, *Palace Car Prince,* 24–26.
42. Leyendecker, *Palace Car Prince,* 74–75.
43. Leyendecker, *Palace Car Prince,* 79–84.
44. Stanley Buder, *Pullman: An Experiment in Industrial Order and Community Planning, 1880–1930* (New York: Oxford University Press, 1967), 67.
45. David Ray Papke, *The Pullman Case: The Clash of Labor and Capital in Industrial America* (Lawrence, KS: University Press of Kansas, 1919), 17–18.
46. Papke, *The Pullman Case,* 18.
47. Papke, *The Pullman Case,* 18–19.
48. *Chicago Times,* May 13, 1894, 1. Quoted in Almont Lindsey, *The Pullman Strike: The Story of a Unique Experiment and of a Great Labor Upheaval* (Chicago: University of Chicago Press, 1942), 126.
49. Lindsey, *The Pullman Strike,* 126.
50. Debs, "First Speech to Striking Pullman Workers," this volume, 239–40.
51. Although the ARU and later historians have recited a figure of 400 delegates, a simple count of attendees generates a much lower figure. See: *The Railway Times,* June 15,

1894, 6.

52. James Richard Sovereign (1854–1928) grew up in the Midwest, gaining employment as a cattle driver and bridge-and-tunnel construction worker. He joined the Knights of Labor (K of L) in 1881 and went to work on a K of L newspaper in Dubuque, Iowa, *The Industrial Leader,* three years later. He was elected head of the Iowa K of L organization and in November 1893 was elevated to the top post in the national organization when a faction of more aggressive Midwestern populists and Eastern socialists forced out cautious general master workman Terence Powderly. Within the Populist movement, Sovereign was an advocate of fusion with the Democratic Party. His tenure as general master workman of the Knights came to a close in November 1897. In later years, he was a newspaper publisher in rural Washington state.

53. Debs, "The Race Line and the ARU," this volume, 264.

54. Lindsey, *The Pullman Strike,* 131–132.

55. Lindsey, *The Pullman Strike,* 136–137.

56. Lindsey, *The Pullman Strike,* 134. Lindsey incidentally estimates the number of strikers on June 28 at 18,000.

57. Papke, *The Pullman Case,* 26.

58. Papke, *The Pullman Case.*

59. Papke, *The Pullman Case,* 27.

60. Lindsey, *The Pullman Strike,* 160–161.

61. Richard Olney (1835–1917) was born to a well-to-do family in Massachusetts. A graduate of Harvard Law School, Olney was a leading railroad attorney during the 1880s, serving as general counsel for the Chicago, Milwaukee & St. Paul Railroad as well as a director of a number of other lines, including the Chicago, Burlington & Quincy and the New York Central. Named attorney general by President Grover Cleveland in March 1893, Olney was an advocate of judicial intervention to suppress labor disputes on the railways, helping to spur Cleveland to send in federal troops to shut down the ARU's 1894 Pullman boycott.

62. Lindsey, *The Pullman Strike,* 148–149.

63. Lindsey, *The Pullman Strike,* 163, 247–250.

64. General Nelson Appleton Miles (1839–1925), a Massachusetts-born Medal of Honor winner during the Civil War, was commander of the US Army's Department of the East from 1894 to 1895. He was subsequently named commanding general of the US Army, a post that he held until its abolition in 1903.

65. Papke, *The Pullman Case,* 29–30.

66. Lindsey, *The Pullman Strike,* 208–209.

67. Lindsey, *The Pullman Strike,* 210.

68. Lindsey, *The Pullman Strike,* 261.

69. Eugene V. Debs and J. R. Sovereign, "Open Letter to President Grover Cleveland," this volume, 284–86.

70. Lindsey, *The Pullman Strike,* 211–212.

71. "Sympathy for Pullman Strikers," *Chicago Tribune,* July 8, 1894, 4.

72. Virgil J. Vogel, "Introduction" in William H. Carwardine, *The Pullman Strike* [1894]

(Chicago: Charles H. Kerr & Co., 1973), xxix.

73. Eugene V. Debs, et al., "Proposal to the General Managers' Association from the Board of Directors of the ARU," this volume, 292–93.

74. Vogel, "Introduction," xxxii.

75. "Pathetic Case of a Man Who Went Out on the Debs Strike," *St. Louis Post-Dispatch*, vol. 47, no. 155 (January 12, 1896), 7.

76. Debs, "Term Half Over: Interview with the *Chicago Chronicle* at Woodstock Jail," this volume, 467–69.

77. Existence of this ARU circular was briefly mentioned in wire reports datelined December 31, 1894, although no surviving copy of the document is known.

78. William E. Burns (1856–19XX) was born in Baltimore County, Maryland. He began working for the railroads in 1874 as a fireman on the Pennsylvania Railroad. Initially a member of the Firemen's International Union until its merger with the B of LF, Burns spent 15 years as a fireman and engineer for the Illinois Central Railroad, beginning in 1879 and gaining promotion in 1882. A delegate to 12 consecutive conventions of the B of LF, he was elected vice grand master in 1891. Burns was a leading delegate on the floor at the June 1894 ARU convention and was elected to the Board of Directors by that body. In June 1897 Burns was elected general organizer of the Social Democracy of America.

79. Martin J. Elliott (1860–1903) began working in the Pennsylvania coal mines at the age of nine. In 1880 he moved west, working as a hard metal miner in Colorado, where he remained until 1885. He briefly went into business but failed and returned to Pennsylvania and to work in the mines. He became a railway switchman in 1888, later working as a brakeman in Wyoming and Montana. He quit the railroad to become a functionary of the ARU in June 1894. He was a state legislator and a socialist activist in Butte, Montana, during his final years. He died in Utah in 1903 following kidney surgery.

80. James Hogan (1867–19XX) was the youngest of the ARU's officers. He first worked as a brakeman at Pennsylvania in 1885, joining the Brotherhood of Railroad Brakemen two years later. He worked for major railroads in Missouri and Utah, gaining promotion to conductor in September 1890. Hogan attended an initial public meeting of the ARU on June 20, 1893, going to work for the union as an organizer in October of that year. Following his release from Woodstock, Hogan was the chief Western organizer for the ARU. In June 1897 he was elected vice president of the Social Democracy of America.

81. Roy M. Goodwin (1863–19XX) was born and raised in Iowa. He left home at age 18 to become a switchman in Minnesota, soon gaining promotion to the supervisory role of yardmaster. He worked for the Great Northern Railway as a yardmaster after that, remaining until the April 1894 strike on that line, when he resigned to join the ARU as an organizer. Goodwin continued as an organizer for the ARU at least through 1896.

82. See, for example, Debs, "Accused of Every Crime But Selling Out: Speech in St. Paul, Minnesota," this volume, 390–94.

83. See Nellie Bly, "Interview with Eugene V. Debs at Woodstock Jail," this volume, 623–35.

84. Although maintaining a small presence and generating some interest in Chicago and isolated locations in New York state, traces of the AIU vanished by early 1896.

85. "Debs Trial Put Off," *Chicago Inter Ocean,* vol. 23, no. 325 (February 12, 1895), 10.

86. For an example of these public speeches, see Debs, "The ARU's Fight is For All Humanity: Speech at Fargo Opera House," this volume, 404–26.

87. See, for example, "Debs's Busy Life in Jail: Interview with the *Chicago Chronicle*," this volume, 635–40.

88. Thomas J. "Tommy" Morgan (1847–1912) was the son of a nailmaker from Birmingham, England, who had been active in the Chartist movement. Morgan was one of the leading English-speaking international socialists in America during the last three decades of the nineteenth century, having been a member of the Social Democratic Workingmen's Party of North America—one of the organizations which unified to become the Socialist Labor Party—from 1876. Morgan was active in a citywide labor federation in the city of Chicago and the Knights of Labor. A staunch political activist, when the Socialist Labor Party moved to anarchism in the mid-1880s, Morgan formed a new organization, the United Labor Party, which succeeded in electing seven of its members to the Illinois legislature in November 1886. Morgan was also a founder of the International Association of Machinists (IAM), of which he was general secretary in 1894 and 1895. Morgan quit the SLP to join the Social Democratic Party in 1900 and was a founding member of the Socialist Party of America in August 1901.

89. James Keir Hardie (1856–1915), a former Scottish coal union organizer, was a founder of the Independent Labour Party in Great Britain in 1893, one of the key constituent groups of the British Labour Party. Hardie was a pacifist and a committed opponent of World War I.

90. "Agreement: EVD, Thomas J. Morgan, J. Keir Hardie, and Frank Smith [September 4, 1895]," in J. Robert Constantine, ed., *Letters of Eugene V. Debs, Volume 1, 1874–1912,* (Urbana, IL: University of Illinois Press: 1990), 102. Frank Smith was Keir Hardie's personal secretary and a fourth signatory to the notice of intent.

91. Debs would later pen an article assigning primary credit to Victor L. Berger for converting him to socialism with a visit and a timely gift of a copy of *Das Kapital* while incarcerated at Woodstock. (See Debs, "How I Became a Socialist," this volume, 640–44.) Anecdotal evidence about the prisoners' reading habits and their charming decision to establish themselves as a "cooperative colony" at Woodstock Jail lends support to the alternative thesis that Debs and his associates were already de facto utopian socialists at the time of their initial incarceration, and implies that Debs's political identity emerged organically, independently of the fortuitous appearance of Marxist missionaries bearing gifts.

92. Actual paid membership of the ARU (and by extension the union's revenue stream through remissions of $1 annual dues payments) appears to have been greatly inflated by ARU officials. According to the printer of *The Railway Times,* a broadsheet

newspaper with a comparatively modest production cost, press runs during June and July 1894, the peak of the union's size and influence, ranged from 2,000 to 5,000 copies. (See testimony of Henry O. Shepard in *United States of America vs. Eugene V. Debs, et al.: Proceedings on Information for Attachment for Contempt* (Chicago: Circuit Court of the United States, Northern District of Illinois, n.d. [1894]), 47.

93. EVD. to Theodore Debs, August 16, 1895, in Constantine, *Letters of Eugene V. Debs: Volume 1,* 99.

94. Reynolds, "Life of Eugene V. Debs," 7.

95. Debs, "Liberty: Speech Delivered on Release from Woodstock Jail at Battery D, Chicago," this volume, 511–24.

96. Summation of Debs's thesis by an unnamed journalist in attendance, published in the *Stevens Point [WI] Daily Journal,* vol. 1, no. 65 (January 9, 1896), 2.

97. This orientation also, it should be parenthetically noted, moved Debs into direct opposition to the union-first, politics-second perspective of Samuel Gompers and the constituent craft unions composing the American Federation of Labor. A bitter personal battle between Debs and Gompers would rage for the rest of their lives.

98. For a brief account of this meeting of the four brotherhoods, see, for example, "Done to Head Off Debs: Monster Meeting of Brotherhood Railroad Men at Princeton, Ind.," *Louisville Courier-Journal,* vol. 86, whole no. 9,884 (January 22, 1896), 5.

99. See, for example, Brotherhood of Locomotive Firemen functionary J. J. Hannahan's itinerary in "The Visit of Debs," *Atlanta Constitution,* vol. 28 (February 10, 1896), 2.

100. Debs mentioned his presidential preference in a January 19, 1896 interview with the *Cleveland Leader,* reprinted as "A New Leader of Labor" in *Appeal to Reason,* February 1, 1896, 2.

101. See, for example, "An Uprising of the People: Speech for William Jennings Bryan at Duluth" and "Patriotism Versus Plutocracy: Speech for William Jennings Bryan in Cleveland," this volume, 598–02, 603–7.

102. Debs's friend and biographer David Karsner—brother-in-law of future Trotskyist leader James P. Cannon—helped cobble together a series of ten articles that had been published in the *Washington Times* in the summer of 1922 as a slim posthumous volume under Debs's byline, *Walls and Bars* (Chicago: Socialist Party, 1927).

Eugene V. Debs from a carte de visite housed in the Special Collections Department of Cunningham Library at Indiana State University. Debs had rapidly thinning blonde hair and piercing blue eyes. He was a gifted public orator who spoke with an earnestness that listeners found compelling. The image is undated but would appear to be from the second half of the 1880s—shortly before his tenure as president of the American Railway Union. (Courtesy Debs Collection, ISU.)

Debs gave up his paid position as secretary-treasurer of the Brotherhood of Locomotive Firemen in the fall of 1892 to pursue "other business interests." One of these enterprises was a publishing house specializing in books for railway workers, later moving to publication of socialist literature. Debs would continue to publish books for about ten years.

Debs remained the editor of the B of LF's official organ, *Locomotive Firemen's Magazine,* through September 1894. The amount of coverage of the American Railway Union in its pages during 1893 and 1894 is comparatively minimal, a conscious effort by Debs to steer clear of the controversial topic.

In the spring of 1894, several "armies" of unemployed workers, numbering in the hundreds, converged on Washington, DC, to present a "petition in boots" for increased public infrastructure spending. It was hoped that the march would build to an enormous crescendo. Instead, the leaders Jacob S. Coxey (shown riding) and Carl Browne (on horse, looking backward) were arrested for walking on the grass before they could speak.

Top officials of the ARU (left to right, from top)

1. **Eugene V. Debs (1855–1926), President, ARU**
This image was apparently an official portrait that was sold to members of the ARU.

2. **Louis W. Rogers (1859–1953), Managing Editor, *Railway Times***
Previously publisher of The Age of Labor, *Rogers was later prominent in the theosophy movement.*

3. **George W. Howard (1848–19XX), Vice President, ARU**
Likely the originator of the ARU idea, Howard broke with Debs and his compatriots early in 1895 and tried to establish a new organization encompassing all workers, the American Industrial Union.

4. **Sylvester Keliher (1863–19XX), General Secretary, ARU**
The youngest of the four top leaders of the ARU, Keliher would follow Debs into the socialist movement, gaining election as secretary of the Social Democracy of America.

Uhlich's Hall in Chicago was both the site of the First Quadrennial Convention of the American Railway Union in June 1894 as well as strike headquarters for the union during its ill-fated Pullman boycott. Later known as the Schweitzer-Turner Hall, the building was also home for the founding of the American Labor Union and for conventions of the IWW.

A sense of the bustling activity at ARU headquarters is reflected in this contemporary painting, with ARU secretary Sylvester Keliher seated at his desk next to a stenographer as he listens to incoming reports, while other ARU officials work. Hundreds of telegrams were sent from ARU headquarters in Chicago to coordinate strike activities, which were particularly effective in stopping traffic in the western states.

This drawing from the *Illustrated American,* a news weekly, shows workers exiting through the main entrance at the Pullman works. (Issue of July 14, 1894.)

Armed deputies attempt to move an engine through strikers at Blue Island, south of Chicago, on July 2. Switchmen played a particularly important role in the strike, refusing to link Pullman cars and sometimes rendering switches inoperable. (*Harper's,* July 14, 1894.)

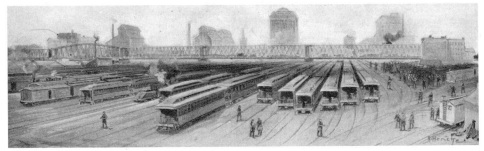

On July 3 the ARU strike appeared to be on the verge of success, with railway traffic effectively paralyzed across the West. This painting shows the complete blockade on the Chicago & Northwestern, near Halsted Street in Chicago. (*Harper's,* July 14, 1894.)

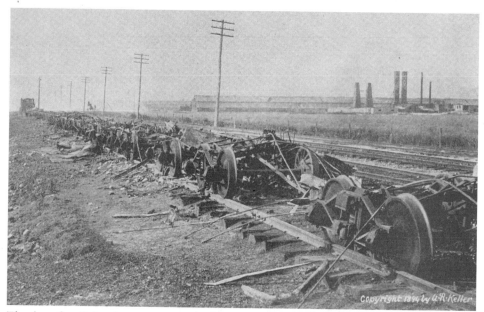

The day after federal troops entered Chicago on July 4, rioting erupted in the city, with hundreds of boxcars and coal cars burned over the next three days. These skeletons remained in the aftermath on the Panhandle Railroad at 39th Street.

National Guardsmen fire into the crowd at Loomis and 49th Street during July 7 rioting. The crane is part of a railroad wrecking car, used to clear derailments. (*Harper's;* art by G. W. Porter).

The July rioting in Chicago was followed by a wave of vilification of the ARU and the organized labor movement in the bourgeois press that tilted public opinion decisively against the strikers. This lurid centerfold from *Life* magazine depicts "The Downtrodden Workingman" as an ill-kempt, destructive, gun-wielding goliath. The caption warns, "While other men are losing money in these hard times, he strikes for higher wages—and with tender solicitude for the property and rights of others."

(Issue of July 19, 1894; art by F. T. Richards.)

KING DEBS.

This frequently reprinted *Harper's Weekly* cover drawing depicts "King Debs" wearing his American Railway Union crown, petulantly blocking the "highway of trade" and obstructing the movement of mail, perishable food, and passengers. The Pullman strike was highly personalized, with Debs depicted as a public enemy by strike opponents.

(Issue of July 14, 1894; art by W. A. Rogers.)

THE VANGUARD OF ANARCHY.

Harper's followed up its "King Debs" issue with a second Debs cover depicting prominent leaders of the Populist movement as a troupe of bloodthirsty anarchist clowns transporting their king. Illinois governor John Altgeld leads the parade, accompanied by US senator William A. Peffer and Governors Davis H. Waite of Colorado, Henry H. Markham of California, and Sylvester Pennoyer of Oregon.

(Issue of July 21, 1894; art by W. A. Rogers.)

Chicago jeweler S. N. Clarkson & Co. crafted gold buttons and charms with ARU logos. The signal torch at left was the motif used on the official seal of the ARU Grand Lodge. The shaking hands over a signal torch at right anticipates the two logos of the Socialist Party of America.

THEY ALL LAND THERE AT LAST!

"They All Land There at Last!"—This color lithograph from *Puck* magazine shows the goddess of Justice in a "Law and Order" tiara disposing of labor leaders Debs, Terence Powderly, Martin Irons, Jacob Coxey, and Hugh O'Donnell, as well as Governor John Altgeld of Illinois, in a human garbage dump. (From *Puck;* art by Louis Dalrymple.)

The ARU collected $1 annual dues on a fiscal year basis, with the dues year running from May 1 to April 30. The last year of operation was 1896–1897.

In June 1897 Debs and the remaining members of the now moribund ARU dissolved in order to join with a socialist colonization group called the Brotherhood of the Cooperative Commonwealth. These two groups together established a new utopian socialist organization, the Social Democracy of America.

(Image courtesy Vince Kueter.)

This posed photograph of seven of the eight jailed ARU leaders is said to have been taken at Woodstock Jail in front of a false backdrop. Shown standing are George W. Howard, Martin J. Elliott, Sylvester Keliher; seated are William E. Burns, James Hogan, Roy M. Goodwin, and Eugene V. Debs. Missing is Louis W. Rogers.

Andrew Carnegie
(1835–1919)
Carnegie Steel Co.

Henry Clay Frick
(1849–1919)
Carnegie Steel Co.

Hugh O'Donnell
(1869–19??)
Homestead strike leader

Alexander Berkman
(1870–1936)
Attempted assassin

James J. Hill
(1838–1916)
Great Northern Railway

George M. Pullman
(1831–1897)
Pullman's Palace Car Co.

James R. Sovereign
(1854–1928)
Knights of Labor

Samuel Gompers
(1850–1924)
American Fed. of Labor

Jacob S. Coxey, Sr.
(1854–1951)
"Coxey's Army" Leader

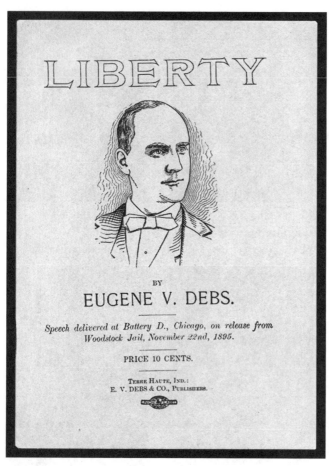

LIBERTY

BY
EUGENE V. DEBS.

Speech delivered at Battery D., Chicago, on release from Woodstock Jail, November 22nd, 1895.

PRICE 10 CENTS.

TERRE HAUTE, IND.:
E. V. DEBS & CO., PUBLISHERS.

Debs's "Liberty" speech, made to a mass meeting of several thousand people at the Chicago National Guard artillery armory following his release from Woodstock Jail, was the first Debs speech to be widely reprinted as a piece of propaganda literature of the American socialist movement. Although it might appear at a glance to be a first edition, this version of the pamphlet with a pictorial cover was actually an early reprint by the Debs Publishing Company, circa 1897.

At left, a Chicago newspaper sketch of Debs delivering his seminal address at Battery D. No photos are known of Debs speaking as head of the ARU, nor were any recordings of his voice ever made.

At right, a white and blue commemorative ribbon worn by attendees of the "Liberty" speech.
(Courtesy Gene Dillman, Old Politicals Auctions.)

Chicago's Greeting
TENDERED

Eugene V. Debs

UPON HIS
RELEASE FROM WOODSTOCK
JAIL

Friday, November 22, 1895

1892

The Battle of Homestead[†]
August 1892

It cannot be expected that the *Magazine* will give anything approximating a full account of the Homestead horror. Such a report would require every page of this number. Nevertheless, we deem it prudent to introduce so much of the record as will supply the reader with the main facts and serve for future reference.

As we write, July 14, 1892, Homestead is in charge of a military force and is under martial law. The report is that "all is quiet."

We go back to the closing days of June for a beginning, and find that while the steelworks were in peaceful operation, the fiend, Frick,[1] was preparing for murder; he was fortifying the Carnegie steel works. His idea was to transform them into a fort. He built a strong fence, unusually high, and surmounted it with barbed wire. He had within the enclosure large dynamos for producing strong currents of electricity, with which the wires surmounting the fence could be instantaneously charged, so that if a man touched the wires he would fall dead as quickly as a felon at Sing Sing.

In addition, he had prepared the most effective machinery for scalding men to death with hot water or killing them with jets of cold water thrown with tremendous force by his engines. Nor was this all. There were loopholes in the fence through which his mercenaries could shoot down workingmen without danger to themselves.

And it now appears, by his own statements to a congressional committee, that the hiring of the Pinkerton thugs to man his works began in June, before the lockout. Hence it is seen that the fiend, Frick, had determined not to enter into any compromise about wages that would satisfy the workingmen, but had deliberately planned to kill them when the hour arrived to perpetrate murder.

On July 1 the lockout occurred, and immediately Frick prepared for scabs to take the place of the locked-out men. The men, however, concluded that they would take charge of the Carnegie steel works at Homestead, and see to it that scabs did not take their places.

This having been done as a preliminary step, the fiend, Frick, called upon the sheriff of Allegheny County to put him in possession of his works, as follows:

[†] Published in *Locomotive Firemen's Magazine* [Terre Haute, IN], vol. 16, no. 8 (August 1892), 737–739.

Dear Sir:—

You will please take notice that at and in the vicinity of our works in Mifflin township, near Homestead, Allegheny County, Pa., and upon the highways leading thereto from all directions, bodies of men have collected who assume to and do prevent access to our employees to and from our property, and that from threats openly made we have reasonable cause to apprehend that an attempt will be made to collect a mob and destroy or damage our property aforesaid and to prevent us from its use and enjoyment. This property consists of mills, buildings, workshops, machinery, and other personal property. We therefore call upon you, as Sheriff of Allegheny County, Pa., to protect our property from violence, damage, and destruction, and to protect us in its free use and enjoyment.

Carnegie Steel Company, Lim.
H. C. Frick, Chairman
Carnegie, Phipps & Co., Lim.
H. C. Frick, Chairman

This was done early in July, and the sheriff, Mr. McCleary, addressing a chairman of the strikers' committee, said:

Mr. Chairman and gentlemen of the Advisory Committee:—
The Carnegie Steel Company has called upon me in my official capacity as Sheriff of Allegheny County to protect the property and buildings of the company, located here. I thought it would be a wise move to come here this morning and personally look over the ground.

To this the committee responded as follows:

The Advisory Committee is not only ready but anxious to assist you in preserving peace and protecting property hereabouts. In proof of which we now offer you any number of men, from 100 to 500, to act as your deputies. They will serve without pay and will perform their duty as sworn officers of the law, even though it cost them their lives. Furthermore, the committee will give bond of either $5,000 or $10,000 for each man, no matter how many, that they will do their duty.

The sheriff made frequent attempts to respond to the demands of Frick, but the men summoned to act as deputies for the purpose of ousting the strikers generally begged to be excused, but some were sworn in and the following proclamation was issued:

Proclamation—To Whom It May Concern

Whereas it has come to my knowledge that certain persons have congregated and assembled at and near the works of the Carnegie Steel Company, Limited, in Mifflin township, Allegheny County, Pa., and upon the roads and highways leading to the same, and that such persons have interfered with workmen employed in said works obtaining access to the same, and that certain persons have made threats of injury to employees going to and from said works, and have threatened that if the owners of said works attempt to run the same the property will be injured and destroyed.

Now, I, William H. McCleary, High Sheriff of said county, do hereby notify and warn all persons that all acts enumerated are unlawful, and that all persons engaged in the same in any way are liable to arrest and punishment.

And I further command all persons to abstain from assembling or congregating as aforesaid, and from interfering with the workmen, business, or the operation of said works, and in all respects preserve the peace, and to retire to their respective homes, or places of residence, as the rights of the workmen to work, and the right of the owners to operate their works will be fully protected, and in case of failure to observe these instructions all persons offending will be dealt with according to law.

William H. McCleary,
High Sheriff of Allegheny County,
Office of Sheriff of Allegheny County, July 5, 1892

It will be understood that the sheriff's efforts were all made prior to the 6th of July, the day of battle.

It may be well to say just here that the population of Allegheny County, Pa., is probably near 1 million. Still the sheriff could not summon a sufficient number of men to dislodge the strikers. Why? Simply because the great mass of the people of Pittsburgh and Allegheny County are in sympathy with the locked-out workingmen, and hold the fiend, Frick, in utter detestation as the sworn, inveterate, and relentless foe of organized labor.

This brings us down to the morning of July 6, forever memorable in the history of labor, as much so as the 20th of April, the day on which the minutemen of Lexington and Concord fired the shot "heard 'round the world."

The Pinkerton thugs had been concentrated at Pittsburgh. There were 300 of them, all armed with Winchester rifles, one of the most deadly weapons known to modern warfare. To convey them to Homestead, two model barges were provided, floating forts, ironclad, constructed to shield the murderers and to resist attack. These barges were towed up the Monongahela River under cover of darkness. Every movement of Frick was secret and skulking, the purpose being to land the murderers undiscovered and place them in the works. Once there, electricity, scalding water, and bullets would overawe the workingmen, or, should they resist, cooling boards[2] and coffins would be in active demand.

On came the flotilla. A landing was made and the battle began. The *Pittsburgh Dispatch* of July 7 furnishes the incident as follows. It seems that the workingmen had been apprised of the approach of the Pinkerton flotilla, though the *Little Bill*, the towboat, was not yet in sight. Says the *Dispatch:*

> Soon the grey streaks of dawn appeared in the sky. No boat had yet hove in sight, though thousands of eyes were straining to catch the first glimpse of her. Suddenly a cheer from the lower end of the town announced that the headlights of the approaching steamer had been sighted. Those at the mill could not see her, but the word was passed along to them so quickly that they were aware of her approach.
>
> A few moments later the red lights of the boat were discovered through the fog by the men at the mill. Another cheer went up, followed by a grand rush for the water's edge. The boat came up rapidly, the *Little Bill* between the two great clumsy-looking barges, and passing up to a point directly opposite the center of the mill yard ran the barges close up to the shore.
>
> A moment later and 40 or 50 men stepped out from a door in the end of the largest barge to the small deck on the bow. Each man carried a Winchester repeater, and on every face there was a look of determination. In the doorway behind those on the deck there could be seen many more faces and the glistening barrels of many more rifles.
>
> A gangplank was thrown out and the men on the boat started toward it, then glancing at the multitude of determined men on the shore, they hesitated.
>
> "Don't step off that boat!" was the cry from 50 men on the shore, but a commanding voice from the boat said, "Forward." Just as the first man was about to step on the gangplank the first shot was fired. No one seemed to know from whence it came, but someone yelled that it had come from a porthole in the side of the boat and volley from a score of millworkers' guns followed.
>
> Then followed a momentary silence, as the invaders quietly ranged in line, broken by a volley from 40 rifles. Most of them must have fired

into the air, as, with the solid mass of humanity only a few feet away from them, they could not have missed had they fired point-blank. But many of them fired into the crowd and several men fell.

A wild scramble of 3,800 or 4,000 men and women followed. Up the steep bank, 40 feet high, and down the riverbank toward the village they scrambled in a wild frenzy of terror. Men fell and were trampled under foot by those who came after.

All this time the invaders were keeping up a rattling fire, which was briskly returned by a couple of hundred of the millworkers, some of whom had stood their ground while others had retreated to the mill yard at the top of the bank and were screened behind piles of metal and steel piled along the front.

The first man to drop was Martin Murray, shot through the side. A moment later Joseph Sodak stooped to pick up Murray, when a bullet struck him on the upper lip just below the nose, dropping him dead beside Murray. In the meantime, Henry Streigle, who had retreated to the top of the hill and was firing at the men on the boat, fell over with a bullet through his neck. He died in a few moments. On the boat the man who seemed to be leading the armed party was shot and fell on the deck. After he had been carried inside and the men on the boat had all retreated into the covered barges, firing ceased on both sides.

Then came a conference between the leaders on the shore and a stout, middle-aged man on the boat who seemed to be a leader. Said the millworker who had stepped down to the water's edge:

"On behalf of 5,000 men I beg of you to leave here at once. I don't know who you are or from whence you came, but I do know that you have no business here, and if you stay there will be more bloodshed. We, the workers in these mills, are peaceably inclined. We have not damaged any property, and we do not intend to. If you will send a committee with us we will take them through the works, carefully explain to them all the details of this trouble, and promise them a safe return to your boats. But, in the name of God and humanity, don't attempt to land. Don't attempt to enter these works by force."

The leader on the boat, resting his rifle across his left arm, stepped to the front and, speaking so that those men on the bank above him could hear, said:

"Men, we are Pinkerton detectives. We were sent here to take possession of this property and to guard it for the company. We don't wish to shed any blood, but we are determined to go up there and will do so. If you men don't withdraw we will mow every man of you down and enter in spite of you. You had better disperse, for land we will."

A deathly silence followed this speech. Then the leader of the mill-workers spoke again. Every man within the sound of his voice listened with breathless attention.

"I have no more to say," said he, "what you do here is at the risk of many lives. Before you enter those mills you will trample over the dead bodies of 3,000 honest workingmen."

It will be observed that after the workingmen had been killed by the murderous Pinkertons, the Homestead men sought for peace, and that their overtures were disdainfully thrust aside and the defiant threat made that they, the Pinkertons, would "mow every man of you down, and enter (the mills) in spite of you." Then the battle raged with increased fury until in the afternoon the Pinkertons surrendered, gave up their guns and ammunition, and were ready to leave Homestead.

Thus ended the bloodiest battle ever fought between workingmen and the hirelings of capitalists in this or any other continent, and when the battle was over, victory perched upon the standard of labor. The thugs were vanquished. Their prestige was utterly wrecked.

It should be remembered that the workingmen of Homestead were not armed as were the murderous invaders. Their guns were not Winchester rifles. They were not aware until it was too late of the banquet of blood their friend Frick had prepared for them, but such arms and means as they had were splendidly utilized. We could fill pages with incidents of splendid heroism on the part of the workingmen and of their wives and mothers.

After the battle, quiet reigned at Homestead, the locked-out workingmen were in possession of the town and of the Carnegie steel works.

Frick besought the sheriff to place him in charge of his works. The sheriff protested his inability to respond, and then the governor of Pennsylvania was asked to send troops—the State Guard—and he finally responded and 8,000 armed men marched upon Homestead, took possession, declared martial law, and with rifles and Gatling guns, and all the pomp and circumstance of glorious dress parades, was inaugurated.

The Pinkerton thug business, the bloody battle, the murder of innocent men, aroused the nation's representatives in Congress assembled, and an investigation was ordered, and is going forward as we write.

What the result will be no one knows. Possibly the states will enact laws by which Pinkerton thuggery will be abolished, and in many ways benefits may result from the bloody battle at Homestead.

Public Opinion†

August 1892

———————

The public is the people, not a faction or a fraction, but the general body of a state or community; and opinion is conviction, belief, settled judgment; hence public opinion is public conviction, belief, and judgment of all the people.

The assumption is that public opinion is always right, and if it could be shown that at any time the people were a unit in conviction, belief, and judgment upon any proposition whatever, the conclusion would necessarily follow that the proposition thus endorsed by public opinion was right. But public opinion, being the judgment of fallible men, does not create an infallible standard for men who choose to investigate subjects which bear upon the welfare of individuals or communities.

A moment's reflection discloses the fact that public opinion is often a mere craze, the result of some hue and cry, that it is manufactured for the occasion by demagogues and knaves for a purpose, and that in its operations it often inflicts the most serious calamities. Like a stream swollen by cloudbursts, it sweeps along, resistless for a time in its course, without the power to remedy the wrongs it inflicts.

Public opinion often, however, settles down in the advocacy and approval of the most flagrant errors; indeed it is seen, not infrequently, supporting stupendous outrages upon human rights, discarding justice, and clamoring for the supremacy of iniquities which blotch civilization and intensify men's distrust of this accredited factor in human affairs.

Notwithstanding such facts, society is so constituted that public opinion, not necessarily the opinion of the entire body of the people, but of a majority of the people in a state or community, must be respected. It is a force of great and unquestioned power and, right or wrong, upon any given proposition, makes itself felt.

We have said that public opinion is often a mere craze, brought about by a hue and cry for or against individuals or organizations, laws and institutions. Men engage in agitation, in the press and pulpit, on the rostrum, at all times, in all places, and by every means in their power, to create public opinion or change public opinion, and this work and warfare goes forward

———————

†   Published in *Locomotive Firemen's Magazine,* vol. 16, no. 8 (August 1892), 686–687.

ceaselessly. This agitation, right or wrong, is inherent in free speech, untrammeled discussion, and it has been said that errors, even though they be embodied in laws, cannot long exist when there is free speech and a free press to combat them. As a general proposition, we think such conclusions are supported by the facts, but it must be said that some errors are so antiquated and have had the endorsement of public opinion so long that to uproot them approximates the impossible. They appall the great body of men. Only heroic souls attack them, only men who dare martyrdom by challenging vastly superior forces, are the *avant-couriers* of reforms. Such is history, and history is forever repeating itself.

Take, for instance, public opinion in the United States touching chattel slavery, a crime of unspeakable enormity. Sixty years ago, aye, a far less number of years in the past, and public opinion endorsed the stupendous iniquity. The church of God and His Son favored it. Federal and state legislatures enacted laws to perpetuate it. The press lent its power to sustain it. The great body of the people was a unit in its support. But a few intrepid men and women assailed the infernal wickedness, a sin that had come down to the nation from past generations. The assault upon the institution, from small beginnings, grew steadily in force. Men dared and died; still the grand work went forward. It culminated in the bloodiest war of all the centuries, but when the last bugle blast calling men to arms was blown, when the war drum was hushed to silence, the battle flags were furled, and 5 million slaves stood forth emancipated and free, behold, public opinion had changed, and now there is not one of our 65 million people to approve of conditions that existed as late as 1860.

In the days of chattel slavery the Negro slaves worked for their masters, for which they received food, clothes, and shelter; their surplus earnings went to enrich their masters. The slaves owned no land, no houses, nor any other description of property. They toiled, multiplied, and died, and public opinion approved. But as we have said, public opinion changed, and the slave went free, and now thousands of them own land and houses and are educated, and they are striding on to still better conditions, and public opinion favors the new departure.

What do we hear nowadays on every hand? This: the cry of white slavery; not chattel slavery, not of the slave block and pen, but of white men's huts, far worse than the old-time slave quarters. We hear of squalor and degradation to which the average plantation slave was a total stranger. We hear of great industries being carried forward by men and women whose compensation decrees their degradation, as certainly as if Jehovah had thundered it from his eternal throne. There is no disputing the facts, nor are they disputed, and with reference to them, what can be said of public opinion? This: there are valiant men and women who are discussing the situation as they have opportunities, and are creating public opinion. Those who are engaged in robbing wage-toilers of just compensation, and are forcing upon them conditions against which human nature revolts, feel moderately secure in their strongholds. They have wealth; the same was true of the slaveholder. They have pulpit, press, and legislatures to approve their course; the same was true of the slave owner. But the wage toilers are agitating. They have a press, occasionally a pulpit, and of themselves they have an army of evangelists who, in lodges and shops, are creating public opinion. The work is going grandly forward and emancipation day is drawing nigh.

There need be no misgivings about results. The fact that traitors, apostates, sneaks, and scabs are found here and there, identified with the armies of labor, is the old, old story, but they cannot impede the triumphant march. The plutocrats, whose purpose is to enslave white men, reduce them to helots, is to be defeated, defeated by the patience, intelligence, and patriotism of organized labor and a wise public opinion true to conviction, belief, and judgment, or it is to be defeated as was the purpose of the South to perpetuate chattel slavery. This nation cannot exist with 6,000 millionaires and 60 million slaves, white or black, and public opinion will, in due time, shape itself to the mighty issue.

The Pinkertons at Homestead[†]

August 1892

From time to time for years past the *Firemen's Magazine* has devoted such space as was required to the discussion of Pinkertonism as one of the phases of our plutocratic Christian civilization. In this regard the *Magazine* has not failed in doing its duty to the great brotherhood it represents.

We have sought to draw a line between *capitalist* and *capital*. We have at all times endeavored to demonstrate that workingmen have no *grievance* against capital, nor yet against honest, fair-minded capitalists; that only the heartless, soulless, inhuman capitalists, the robber gang of capitalists, the venal villains who wield the power of capital to rob and degrade workingmen are those who excite the loathing and enmity of wageworkers.

The four thousand employees of Carnegie & Co. at Homestead, Pennsylvania, have been engaged for years in pouring capital into the laps of capital, content if they could build for themselves humble homes, obtain the necessities of life, rear their children as become American citizens, and save a few dollars for a "rainy day," for sickness and old age, and secure for themselves a decent burial.

By virtue of their brain and brawn, their skill and muscle, their fidelity to duty, Homestead grew in importance. It obtained a worldwide fame. The chief proprietor, Andrew Carnegie, a Scotchman by birth, an aristocrat by inclination, and a Christian with Christ omitted, waxed fat in wealth while the men toiled on. The works spread out, area expanded, buildings and machinery increased, night and day the forges blazed and roared, the anvils rang, wheels revolved, and still Carnegie grew in opulence. Taking his place among the millionaires of the world, he visits his native land,[3] and sensation follows sensation as he dazzles lords and ladies, dukes and dudes, by the display of his wealth in highland and lowland.

All the while, four thousand or more of the hardy sons of toil keep the machinery at Homestead in operation. The Monongahela [River] is not more ceaseless in its flow than are Carnegie's workingmen in their devotion to his interests. Suddenly Carnegie, to use a phrase, "gets religion," and begins to blubber about the duty of rich men to the poor. He out-Phariseed all the Pharisees

---

†   Published in *Locomotive Firemen's Magazine,* vol. 16, no. 8 (August 1892), 726–728.

who made broad their phylacteries and made long prayers on the corners of the streets in Jerusalem that they might be seen of men, while they were "devouring widows' houses"[4] and binding burdens upon the backs of men grievous to be borne,[5] for Carnegie, bent on show and parade, seeking applause, ambitions of notoriety, concluded to bestow a portion of his plunder to build libraries bearing his name to perpetuate his fame.

This Andrew Carnegie, in 1889, began to preach his "Gospel of Wealth," the purpose of which was to demonstrate that wealth creates "rigid castes,"[6] not unlike those that exist in India among the followers of Buddha, the Carnegies being the priests and the workingmen the pariahs, and this Buddhism of wealth being established, Carnegie, the author of the "gospel," lays back on his couch of down and silk and writes, this condition "is best for the race because it insures the survival of the fittest."[7]

Andrew Carnegie, who for a quarter of a century has coined the sweat and blood and the life of thousands into wealth until his fortune exceeds many times a million, proclaims "that upon the sacredness of property civilization itself depends."[8] This Carnegie, a combination of flint and steel, plutocrat and pirate, Scotch terrier and English bulldog, rioting in religious rascality, attempts to show that he is animated "by Christ's spirit,"[9] and remembering that when Christ wanted "tribute money" to satisfy Caesar, He told Peter to "go to the sea and cast a hook, catch a fish and in its mouth the required funds would be found,"[10] Carnegie and his Phipps[11] and Frick, wanting cash wherewith to pay tribute to Mammon, have cast hooks into the sea of labor and, securing from five thousand to ten thousand bites a day, have hauled in that number of workingmen and taken from their mouths such sums as their greed demanded wherewith to enlarge their fortunes and enable them, with autocratic pomp and parade, to take the place of Jumbos in the procession.[12]

Under the influence of his "Gospel of Wealth," Carnegie, having prospered prodigiously, having millions at his command, concluded the time had arrived for him to array himself in purple and parade before the people of Great Britain. He was ambitious of applause. He wanted to sit in an open carriage drawn by a half dozen spanking high-steppers and hear the roar of the groundlings as the procession moved along the streets. In the United States Carnegie was not held in much higher esteem than "Robert Kidd as he sailed."[13] Indeed, the freebooter never robbed as many men as Andrew Carnegie, though their methods were somewhat different. Kidd never wrote a "Gospel of Wealth." He never played the role of hypocrite. When he struck a rich prize on the high seas, captured the valuables, killed the crew, and sunk the ship, he did not go ashore and bestow his booty to build a church or found a library, but like Carnegie he was influenced by a "Gospel of Wealth," which was to get all he could and live luxuriously while he lived and then, like the rich man spoken of in the New Testament, go to "hell."

Kidd had heartless lieutenants, cold-blooded villains, but it is to be doubted if he had one equal to H. C. Frick, into whose hands Carnegie, when he left home for his triumphal march through Scotland, committed all power over the Homestead workingmen. The fellow Frick proposed to reduce the wages of these men from 15 to 40 percent, an average of 27.5 percent, and this reduction, whatever it may amount to, is sheer robbery, unadulterated villainy. It is an exhibition of the methods by which Christless capitalists rob labor, and this is done while the brazen pirates prate of religion and the "Spirit of Christ," who plunder labor that they may build churches, endow universities, and found libraries. Is it required to say that hell is full of such blatherskites?

But direct and immediate robbery on the part of these plutocratic Pharisees is not the only purpose they have in view, nor perhaps the chief purpose. They have in view the abolition, the annihilation of labor organizations. This purpose, on the part of the fellow Frick, is now openly avowed. It was the Order of Amalgamated Iron Workers[14] that antagonized the reduction of wages from 15 to 40 percent. The men would not submit to robbery. They comprehended the intent of Carnegie's "Gospel of Wealth." They knew it to be a gospel of piracy rather than of peace. They saw Frick's operations to transform the Homestead steel works into a fort. They saw the murderous devices perfected to kill by electricity and scalding water. Carnegie's gospel was finding expression in numerous plans for wholesale murder. But the workingmen were not intimidated. They saw the shadows of coming events, but their courage did not desert them. They themselves had built the steel works. From their toil had flowed a ceaseless stream of wealth into the coffers of Carnegie and his associates. Around these works they had built their cottages and had hoped to live in them the remainder of their days. They made no unusual demand for wages. It was the same old "scale." There was no good reason for its change. Still they were willing to concede something to the greedy capitalists. They were willing to make some concession in the interest of peace. Having done this they resolved to stand by their rights and to resist oppression and degradation.

What is the plea of Frick? By virtue of the capital these workingmen had created, Carnegie had been able to introduce new machinery, whereby it was claimed the men could make better wages, and it was resolved that the men should not be the beneficiaries of improved machinery; only Carnegie & Co.

should pocket the proceeds. Such was the teaching of the "Gospel of Wealth." The pariahs were to remain pariahs forever.

The day of the lockout came, July 1, 1892. The steel works at Homestead were as silent as a cemetery. The workingmen were remanded to idleness. Their offense was that they wanted fair wages—the old scale—and that they were members of a powerful labor organization, created to resist degradation, to maintain fair prices.

Between July 1 and the morning of July 6 unrest was universal; excitement increased with every pulse beat. The workingmen had charge of Homestead. Frick was in exile, but he was not quiet. He wanted possession of the steel works. His purpose was to introduce scabs to man Fort Frick, to get his dynamos to work and send streams of electricity along his barbed wire, to touch which was death. He wanted to have seas of hot water to be sent on its scalding, death-dealing mission if a discharged workman approached the steel works. He wanted the muzzle of a Winchester rifle at every porthole in the fence, and behind it a thug to send a quieting bullet through the head or the heart of any man who deemed it prudent to resist oppression.

What was the scheme? To introduce Pinkerton thugs armed with Winchester rifles, a motley gang of vagabonds mustered from the slums of the great cities, pimps and parasites, outcasts, abandoned wretches of every grade, a class of characterless cutthroats who murder for hire, creatures in the form of humans but as heartless as stones. Frick's reliance was upon an army of Christless whelps to carry into effect Carnegie's "Gospel of Wealth."

Oh, men, who wear the badge of labor! Now is the time for you in fancy, at least, to go to Homestead. You need to take in the picture of the little town on the banks of the Monongahela. You peer through the morning mists and behold the Frick flotilla approaching, bearing to the landing 300 armed Pinkertons, each thug with a Winchester and all necessary ammunition to murder Homestead workingmen. The plot of Frick was hellish from its inception. There is nothing to parallel it in conflicts labor has had since Noah built his ark. No man with a heart in him can contemplate Frick's scheme without a shudder.

The alarm had been sounded. The Homestead workingmen were on the alert. They were the "minutemen," such as resisted the British troops at Concord and Lexington in 1775. The crisis had come. Nearer and nearer approached Frick's thugs. Four thousand workingmen are on guard. Now for Carnegie's "Gospel of Wealth." In quick succession rifle reports ring out from the "model barges," and workingmen bite the dust. Homestead is now something more than the seat of the Carnegie steel works. It is a battlefield, and from Thermopylae to Waterloo, from Concord to Yorktown, from Bull Run to Appomattox there is not one which to workingmen is so fraught with serious significance.

Amidst fire and smoke, blood and dying groans, the workingmen stood their ground with Spartan courage. It was shot for shot, and the battle continued until Frick's thugs surrendered and left the workingmen of Homestead masters of the field. A number of the thugs were killed, others were wounded, and the remainder, demoralized, were glad to surrender and return to the slums from which they were hired by Frick.

Rid of the gang of mercenary murderers, the workingmen proceeded to bury their dead comrades, the gallant men who preferred death to degradation, and who are as deserving of monuments as was ever a soldier who died in defense of country, flag, or home. Of these there were ten who were killed outright on the morning of the battle.[15]

The fiend Frick, of coke region infamy, is the man directly responsible for the Homestead tragedies, and the blood of the murdered men are blotches upon his soul which the fires of hell will only make more distinct, and still this monster simply represents a class of Christless capitalists who are now engaged in degrading workingmen for the purpose of filching from them a portion of their earnings that they may roll in the luxuries which their wealth purchases.

Carnegie wires from his triumphal march through Scotland that he has no word of advice to give, and constitutes Frick the Nero of Homestead, consenting thereby to the employment of Pinkertons to murder his old and trusted employees.

It would be easy to reproduce here the arguments pro and con, showing the underlying causes which led to the murder of workingmen at Homestead. But we do not care to introduce them here, except insofar as the fact is brought out that the country has a class of capitalists who conduct vast industrial enterprises and who, not content with honest dividends upon honest investments, are ceaselessly seeking to rob labor of its legitimate rewards, and the better to accomplish their nefarious designs are determined to break up, if possible, labor organizations, the one barrier that keeps them from accomplishing their purpose.

The Homestead slaughter of workingmen must serve to remind the armies of labor of what is in store for them if the Carnegies, the Phipps, and the Fricks can, by the aid of Pinkertons, come out victorious.

It occurs to us that the Homestead tragedies will serve to bind labor organizations in closer union. If not, then the blood of workingmen as it calls from the ground, exhorting the living to emulate the courage of the men who fell at Homestead, might as well call upon a herd of "dumb, driven cattle."[16]

Ralph Waldo Emerson wrote of the first shot at Concord and Lexington on the 20th of April, 1775, as "The Shot Heard Round the World." The first shot of the Pinkertons at Homestead has been heard around the world, and its reverberations ought to continue until the statutes of all the states make the employment of Pinkerton thugs murder in the first degree.

It required Lexington, Concord, and Bunker Hill to arouse the colonies to resistance, and the battle of Homestead should serve to arouse every working-man in America to a sense of the dangers which surround them.

H. C. Frick†

August 1892

Carnegie's man, Frick, is *sui generis*.[17] In the theory or science of evolution, the student would be perplexed to determine from what he had been evolved. To intimate that God made him would be such an unmitigated insult to high heaven as would throw angels and archangels into spasms, and yet Frick resembles a human being.

H. C. Frick, the man responsible for the Homestead murders, may have been evolved from a cobra. He is evidently 99 parts venom. There is a crawling, venomous thing called a centipede, with a hundred feet, each foot a fang emitting poison wherever it crawls, but we will not wrong cobra or centipede by attributing to either of these frightful abominations the propagation of such a monster as H. C. Frick.

It was said by some classic ancient that every man has a tiger in him, but Frick seems to be the embodiment of such reptiles as men everywhere abhor.

For a number of years the civilized world has been excited over the butcheries of "Jack the Ripper," the monster who murdered and mutilated unfortunate women at Whitechapel, London; but Jack the Ripper was, or is, a gentleman of refined feelings compared with H. C. Frick, the detestable wretch, the horned toad, evolved by Carnegie's "Gospel of Wealth." We take it back, we would not offend the sensibilities of horned toads nor dungeon toads by

---

† Published in *Locomotive Firemen's Magazine*, vol. 16, no. 8 (August 1892), 731–732.

instituting any comparison between them and H. C. Frick, the manager of the Carnegie steel works at Homestead, Pennsylvania.

H. C. Frick is a monster, not in physical development, not in weight or stature, but in incarnate fiendishness; and here, again, we may be doing the devil rank injustice, since for cool, premeditated, deliberate infernalism, we know of nothing the devil has ever done, or has been credited with doing, equal to Frick's schemes to murder and maim workingmen at Homestead.

We would like to have our readers contemplate this convert to Carnegie's "Gospel of Wealth," laying his plans to kill workingmen.

Look at Frick. He is well groomed; everything betokens wealth. He looks well fed. He has the strut and swing of an autocrat. Under him are thousands of workingmen. Day and night they toil. Frick regards them simply as cattle or chattels.

The fact that these men exhibit independence, self-respect, and ambition to live like men rather than like dogs enrages Frick. His bosom is full of implacable hates; they burn like fire. He had transformed the coke regions into a hell and had reigned there, chief devil; had seen blood flow at his command; had seen men, women, and children starving in their dens. He liked it. His beastly, venomous nature gloried in such scenes of gloom and suffering, agony and death. He thirsted for more blood, more death. He longed to inaugurate hell upon earth, and concluded to transform Homestead into a miniature Golgotha.[18]

To catch the idea it is only required to contemplate Frick as he premeditates the most speedy methods to kill the workingmen of Homestead, if they came within range of his murderous appliances.

One scheme was to kill by electricity. To do this, he surrounds his works with a strong fence surmounted with barbed wire. This done, he arranges to charge the wires with electricity. He proposes to kill by lightning. To touch his wires is death. In the state of New York the authorities ascertained that electricity was just the thing to kill murderers, and Frick believed it would be just as effective in killing workingmen. He chuckled with fiendish glee as he saw the scheme advance to perfection.

But, said Frick, in spite of lightning some workingman may escape death, in which event I must have other means of murder, and he bethought him of the efficacy of hot water; at once appliances were provided for scalding men to death, a scheme more devilish than lightning, because there is more torture in it. In addition, the barricade fence was pierced with portholes for the convenience of such murderers as he might hire and arm to kill workingmen.

H. C. Frick was now ready to give the world an exhibition of the power of

Carnegie's "Gospel of Wealth." One thing only was wanting: men as murderous as himself to do his bidding and kill workingmen for a stipulated price per day or week. In the Pinkerton thugs he found the men he wanted, who would agree to commit murder for $15 a week.

Three hundred of these murderers were hired and armed and transported to Homestead. They were ready to commit murder and they did commit murder. The program was not fully carried out. These things did not obtain possession of the dynamos nor of the engines to murder by scalding workingmen to death. They did not get inside of "Fort Frick," where, from behind defenses, they could shoot down workingmen. What murder the hired thugs did perpetrate was done by shooting from their floating forts, another device provided by the forethought of Frick.

We are anxious that our readers should have, as near as possible, some rational conception of the miscreant monster H. C. Frick, an unnatural production, a prodigy of depravity who, controlling capital, has had his greed so abnormally developed as to render him the most brutal specimen of viciousness to be found on the continent. Soulless and heartless, his hatred of workingmen exceeds that of any other man living, and has no parallel among all the dead who have lived to earn eternal detestation.

We do not doubt that there will be men sufficiently degenerate to apologize for Frick. We do not doubt that there are men who are unhappy because Frick's plans to murder workingmen at Homestead, in part, miscarried; men who had hoped for a Pinkerton victory, though every home in Homestead held a corpse. But everywhere, throughout all this broad land, there are millions of voices lauding and magnifying the courage of the Homestead workingmen who gained a victory over the murderous gang of thugs, and in so doing this has made the name of H. C. Frick, who planned and schemed for their own destruction, the synonym of all that is detestable and infamous among men.

The Switchmen's Strike[†]

September 1892

On August 13, 1892, the switchmen in the local yards of the Erie and Lehigh Valley railroads, to the number of 350, went out on a strike with the sanction of Grand Master Sweeney of the Switchmen's Mutual Aid Association.

The immediate cause of the strike was for an advance in wages, aggravated beyond endurance by the fact that the officials of the roads not only declined to grant the advance, but autocratically refused to confer with committees of switchmen or recognize the association.

The switchmen demanded that their pay should be "$65 per month for night switchmen and $70 per month for night conductors, $60 per month for day switchmen and $65 for day conductors, 26 days of ten hours each to constitute a month's work. They also demanded that all time over ten hours be paid for at the same rate per hour of 25 cents for night switchmen and 27 cents for night conductors, and 23 cents for day switchmen and 25 cents for day conductors per hour. It is claimed that the roads against which the strike was ordered were only paying 21 and 22½, and 19 and 21 cents for night and day, respectively."

The demand of the switchmen was simply for the same wages paid by other roads for performing the same work, and was eminently just, and should have been granted by the officials.

The Switchmen's Mutual Aid Association is an organization that has never made an unjust demand for wages. The duties of switchmen are not only of the most perilous character known to the train service of railroads, but, as circumstances have shown, in importance to the service are equal to those performed by any other class of trainmen. And to adjust wages upon a basis of simple justice has been the honorable and praiseworthy purpose of the order, and it has been from the first a matter of profound amazement that railroad officials have uniformly disregarded the importance of the services of switchmen and kept their wages at the lowest point they could.

In the case under consideration, railroad officials precipitated the strike by a gross insult to organized labor, and it is this autocratic, overbearing, and

---

†   Published in *Locomotive Firemen's Magazine,* vol. 16, no. 9 (September 1892), 832–833.

relentless hostility to organized labor which all labor organizations are now called upon to contemplate with a seriousness never before exacted.

The crisis has come. It was supreme folly to brush it aside—to pooh-pooh at it. The fate of one organization is to be the fate of all, provided organizations, single-handed, propose to fight organized capital aided and abetted by the military machine, and the horde of scabs which infest the country like swarms of locusts.

The present is no time to hug delusions. Organized labor demands a living; organized capital proposes degradation. If the Almighty were to write the issue in letters of fire in the heavens above us, they could not be more vividly outlined and presented.

The present is no time for hairsplitting. If workingmen do not now take sides in favor of organized labor, they are scabs at heart, regardless of their flaunting banners and loud professions.

We do not hesitate to say that our sympathies are with the switchmen, with them in their dignified attitude to resent the autocratic humiliations which the policy of organized capital toward organized labor proposes to inflict. This is the crucial test. To be less than this is to join the enemy. To be less than this is to applaud scabism. To be less than this is to glorify Pinkertonism and the military machine which protects scabs, sheds blood, drapes the homes of honest men in mourning, and fills the land with funeral dirges.

We do not discuss here and now acts of violence—burning, etc. We are not in sympathy with such proceedings. We go back to the beginning: Railroad officials, by acts of injustice, by acts of unpardonable insolence, by acts intended to humiliate and exasperate, are responsible for the strike in progress as we write, and for all the outrages inflicted. Switchmen deprecate these acts, and organized capital, having aroused the mob element by acts of injustice, finds it convenient to charge all the wrongs to organized labor, when in fact the guilt is directly chargeable to the heartless officials who deem such outrages cheap, provided they can use them to crush organized labor.

From the day the strike was inaugurated, August 13, to the day we write, August 20, it has spread until it involves a vast network of railroads, including the Vanderbilt lines and that infamous concern known as the Reading, and is still spreading.

As we write, the military machine is in full operation. Troops with shotguns are protecting scabs. The star-spangled banner symbolizes the triumph of capital and scabs and the suppression of honest labor. The reeking slums are sending forth their moral and physical deformities to take the places of men who dared demand honest wages, who dared organize for the protection of American homes.

It is not required that we should enter into lengthy details of the progress of the strike. We have not the space, nor yet the inclination. We prefer to say to the readers of the *Magazine* that one by one, acting single-handed and alone, their fate is sealed. They can live a little while by sufferance. With hats in their hands or under their arms, they will be permitted to exist. Capital, the military, and scabs in alliance, they will dictate terms. As in prisons, they may be honored as "trusties," but the moment they demand, by virtue of independence and the rights of American citizenship, that their wages shall be such as to make their homes something better than dens, they will be in trouble, and single-handed, they will go down as certainly as lead thrown overboard finds the bottom of the sea.

The outlook is full of peril or of promise to organized labor; of peril if the organizations, seeing one in danger, decline assistance; promise if all, with one accord, make an "injury to one the concern of all." In the one case disaster and degradation is inevitable; in the other, victory could be secured in an hour.

It is not required to say we devoutly wish for the triumph of the switchmen. They deserve victory. Alone they are passing through the Red Sea, and the hosts of Pharaoh are upon them. We would like to see the pillar of fire that is to guide and guard them,[19] and we would like to hear the shout, "The switchmen have triumphed gloriously, and their enemies have been taught that organized labor has a mission in the world that will never be abandoned."

The Homestead Horrors[†]

September 1892

Reflecting men are asking themselves, whither are we drifting? Are the Homestead horrors the dark shadows portending coming events? Are the free institutions of the republic and the liberties of the people in danger?

From the center to the circumference of the land there is unrest. It is asserted in Congress, in the dignified and conservative Senate that there are mighty forces in operation ominous of conflicts, the results of which cannot be contemplated with any degree of composure.

It will doubtless occur to many that the supreme demand of the times is to find the causes for the effects which we daily witness and which daily assume more alarming proportions.

Transactions at Homestead serve to bring into prominence other incidents which, though less serious, are of the same tenor and are the results of similar causes, and grouping these malignant symptoms, the conclusion is that peaceful remedies must speedily be found if Homestead horrors are to be avoided.

The employment of Pinkertons by capitalists to aid them in overcoming their employees, who, having been mercilessly plundered, resolve upon resistance, has been fruitful of universal discontent.

It has been well known from the first that the creatures called "Pinkertons" are, in a large majority of cases, made up of characterless vagabonds, ready and willing, for small compensation, to murder men unhesitatingly if ordered to do so.

These outcasts, organized and armed, have been for years hired by piratical capitalists, when circumstances demanded their assistance to overcome employees who had struck because wages were insufficient to purchase subsistence, or who resisted humiliation and degradation imposed by some vulgar beast permitted to act as boss. The term "Pinkerton" long ago became the synonym of all that is odious, hateful, and abominable in human affairs. They were known to be callous-hearted villains, characterless dwellers of slums, criminals by instinct, and dangerous anywhere, but when armed and equipped by piratical plutocrats, as in the Homestead horror, they become a thousand-fold more dangerous to life and liberty and to the peace of communities.

---

† Published in *Locomotive Firemen's Magazine*, vol. 16, no. 9 (September 1892), 771–774.

These mercenary thugs, operated in defiance of all law, and those who employed them, whatever the difference in wealth and position, were of the same genus; therefore, H. C. Frick, who employed 300 of these murderers to do bloody work at Homestead, in all regards stands forth as despicable a wretch as the vilest of the gang.

These thugs caused the Homestead horror, for which one man, H. C. Frick, is responsible; all the bloodshed at Homestead, on the morning of July 6 [1892], stains his soul. A man of wealth and surrounded by all the luxury wealth can purchase was still a monster of such insatiable greed that rather than yield to demands for wages under which the Carnegie mills were making fabulous fortunes for their owners, he deliberately prepared for the scenes which resulted from his villainous plans.

The demand now is to suppress Pinkertonism by law. Laws are made by representatives of the people in legislatures and in Congress.

Workingmen, if united, can, in a majority of cases, elect men pledged to the suppression of Pinkertons.

If true to their interests, two years will not elapse until the Pinkerton disgrace of the country and of the age will be effectually suppressed.

The supreme hour for workingmen to act has come. If the question of crushing out Pinkertonism does not unite workingmen to vote *only* for men *pledged* to annihilate Pinkertonism, destroy it root and branch, then the question arises, what question is likely to demand, with greater emphasis, the united vote of workingmen?

It will not fail of notice that organized capital has already placed John McLuckie[20] and Hugh O'Donnell[21] under bonds of $10,000 each to stand trial for murder in the second degree, the charge growing out of the killing of a number of Pinkerton thugs when they were murdering Homestead workingmen.

Now, then, H. C. Frick admits that he hired 300 Pinkertons, equipped them with deadly rifles, mustered them upon barges, and shipped them to Homestead.

Did he order them to murder the Homestead workingmen? That has not been shown, but they did perpetrate murder and committed the awful crime with rifles which Frick purchased. Does that render him liable to arrest upon a charge of murder in the second degree? Why not? If McLuckie and O'Donnell were liable to such a charge because they were identified with the Homestead strikers, why is not Frick also liable, by being identified with the Pinkerton murderers?

For a few days there was talk of having Frick arrested. Those who studied the matter closely were forced to the conclusion that in a moment when organized labor should have had courage, enough and to spare, it, from some cause, became weak and timid, and trembled in the presence of the power of organized capital.

Frick's own testimony, showing him to have been in collusion with the Pinkerton murderers, was far more explicit than any testimony brought against McLuckie and O'Donnell. In any event, if it was shown that McLuckie and O'Donnell were implicated in the proceedings resulting in the death of Pinkertons, proof still more positive was at hand showing that Frick was more directly involved in the plot by which a number of workingmen were killed.

It is barely possible that the attempt upon the life of Frick by Alexander Berkman, the Russian refugee, Jew, and anarchist, served to postpone legal proceedings against Frick, but if the wretch pulls through it is to be hoped that as soon as he is able to walk about the necessary papers will be served upon him, as it will be interesting to know to what extent wealth obscures murder in Pennsylvania.

The history of the Homestead horrors discloses the fact that the sheriff of Allegheny County, in which Pittsburgh and Homestead are situated, could not, after numerous trials, summon a sufficient number of men to take charge of the Carnegie mills. In this fact is a lesson of wonderful significance, demonstrating as it does that public sentiment was hostile to Frick and all of his murderous schemes. The people, except to a beggarly extent, would not obey the sheriff's summons. They did not want to be the tools of Frick to be used against honest workingmen. They could not be made to act as guards of mills transformed into forts for the purpose of killing workingmen. They knew the man, Frick, to be a tyrant who had used his power to impoverish and degrade workingmen, and what is true of Pittsburgh is also true of every city in the land, and a vast majority of the American people.

The Homestead horrors disclosed a purpose on the part of plutocratic employers to disrupt labor organizations, and those who are students of labor problems see, in the stand taken by the Carnegie concern, the coming conflict between organized capital and organized labor, or, more properly speaking, between an alliance of capitalists and labor organizations. Everywhere throughout the country the capitalistic alliance is in course of perfection. It is not demonstrative in its preparation. Its movements are stealthy and therefore all the more dangerous.

This is seen in the Frick program to overthrow the amalgamated order of ironworkers. First, he fortified his mills, made elaborate preparations to kill workingmen if found necessary, by electricity and hot water. Then, quietly, he hired and armed mercenary murderers. These things accomplished, Frick was prepared to measure arms with a powerful labor organization.

The amalgamated order was scarce less confident. It had a large fund, reported at $250,000. The conflict came. The Pinkerton thugs were defeated. That is the *one* plume in the cap of the amalgamated order, and has been said, ought to lead to the enactment of laws in every state for the suppression of the armed thugs. But in all else, insofar as the Homestead mills are concerned, Frick has won. The amalgamated order is overwhelmingly defeated, and there is rejoicing in the camps of the capitalistic alliance. It is a notable victory for the alliance.

Organized labor may, we think, contemplate the situation with profit.

How did it happen? What forces came to the relief of the Carnegie concern to enable it to defeat the Homestead employees?

In the first place the laws of Pennsylvania were on the side of Frick—more properly speaking, on the side of the capitalistic alliance. The sheriff being unable to find men to oust workingmen and guard the mills and shoot down employees, the governor of the state was appealed to. For a few days the governor thought the civil authorities had the power to respond to the request of Frick, but after repeated demands the entire military force of Pennsylvania, eight thousand men with muskets and batteries, was ordered out under the command of an aristocrat who had no more sympathy with workingmen than if they were prairie dogs, and with all the pomp and circumstance of war, the standing army of Pennsylvania,[22] with guns, banners, and music, concentrated at Homestead, and the old employees of the Carnegie mills, whose only offense was that they resisted degradation, were at once subjected to all the annoyances, oppressions, humiliations, and degradations which a military machine had the power to inflict. The scenes enacted by this standing army were the same as distinguish the military machine in the meanest despotisms that curse the world. So disgraceful were they, so well calculated to create universal abhorrence, that the governor had to interpose and reduce the army, General Snowden and all his shoulder-strapped lickspittles, to mere deputy sheriffs; but this was not done until the whole country regarded Pennsylvania as the coworker with Frick in perpetrating the most damnable outrages that ever disgraced the country.

It is seen that the powers the laws of Pennsylvania confer are all for the purpose of subjugating workingmen. This Frick fully understood, but the amalgamated order seems to have been entirely oblivious of the fact.

Again, Frick knew that the country was full of scabs, men who would gladly take the places of the locked out employees, provided they could once again obtain admission to the mills. And here again, the standing army of Pennsylvania was utilized to afford the scab element protection and thus enable Frick to reduce wages to any level his degenerate soul might designate. Viewing the whole affair, it is seen that Frick has won a series of notable victories, and that the amalgamated order has suffered disastrous defeats and will not again be recognized by the Carnegie concern, the forces arrayed against the amalgamated order being capital, the military machine, and scabs.

The amalgamated order having a large membership and a large fund, having been able to dictate terms in numerous instances, concluded it was able to "go it alone." This confidence was the natural outgrowth of success and was natural, but the result of the Homestead conflict clearly indicates that the leaders of the amalgamated order were wanting in that astuteness which provides for extraordinary occasions such as Frick inaugurated.

The amalgamated order had small comprehension of the powers of endurance which capital possesses. It had a large fund, but it does not seem to have calculated how rapidly a fund disappears when it is applied to the support of five thousand people. In fact, aside from its power to stop the operation of an industrial enterprise, it does not seem to have had any views at all as to the final outcome of a conflict with the Carnegie concern.

It is not the only order of workingmen in the United States that has made the mistake of fighting organized capital or the capitalistic alliance, single-handed or alone, nor is the Homestead defeat of labor the first on record in which a labor organization overestimated its strength, nor is it the last if labor organizations continue to disregard the power and importance of federation.

It is worthy of notice that labor organizations throughout the country are passing resolutions of sympathy with the Homestead workingmen and denouncing Frick, Carnegie, and all other wage robbers. This is well if it leads to that general uprising in the ranks of labor which sets men to thinking how labor may unify for the triumph of labor against the capitalistic alliance. If it does not do this, if labor organizations form aristocratic notions, jealousies, or from any other cause prefer isolation, then the Homestead horrors will result in no benefits whatever to labor. One by one, labor organizations will disappear or be shorn of their power whenever the capitalistic alliance deems it prudent to crush them out of existence or leave them as mere skeletons, to rattle around for the "moral, social, and intellectual improvement of their members."

It is reported that men in some of the Carnegie mills struck out of "sympathy" for the Homestead workingmen. "Sympathy" is not the word; the better term is "*principle.*" Frick concluded not to recognize the amalgamated order.

Here is something upon which labor organizations can unite, a vital principle, and upon which they must unite if labor organizations hope to withstand future attacks; otherwise, defeat is inevitable.

H. C. Frick and Alexander Berkman[†]

September 1892

Let it be understood in the first place that we abhor the crime of assassination—and regard a man guilty of the crime as a wretch whose depravity defies exaggeration.

Just here we inquire in what consists the difference between H. C. Frick and Alexander Berkman, the would-be assassin? As a matter of course we refer to their moral *makeup*.

It is easy to say that Frick is rich in money, while Berkman is poor; that Frick lives in a palace and fares sumptuously, while Berkman is a moneyless tramp; that Frick is a native-born American, a country where it was once declared "all men are born equal"—while Berkman was born under the rule of the most Christless despotism that now disgraces the earth.

Frick has arrived at a position in which piratically secured millions enable him to associate with cultured men and women, while Berkman, being an exile and poor, has been, by the decrees of fate, required to accept associates quite different. These differences could be indefinitely extended.

Frick is an employer of men, thousands of them, and to a certain extent controls their destiny. He can determine their wages, make their home dark or bright, as he may choose, give them wages by which they may have plenty of food, good dwellings, and proper raiment, or he can so reduce their wages as to prevent them from having such things, make life one long continued struggle against hunger, poverty, squalor, and degradation—while Berkman possesses no such power.

Why proceed further with differences?

[†] Published as "H. C. Frick and Alexander Bergman" in *Locomotive Firemen's Magazine,* vol. 16, no. 9 (September 1892), 779–780. Original has "Bergman" for "Berkman" throughout.

In what regards are H. C. Frick and Alexander Berkman similarly constituted? In what respects do the two monsters resemble each other?

To arrive at a just and rational conclusion, we must consider their acts and the motives which prompted them.

H. C. Frick, desiring to gain possession of the Carnegie mills at Homestead, employed a band of 300 Pinkerton assassins. He armed them with the most deadly weapon known to our advanced Christian civilization, the Winchester rifle. Each thug had one of these guns and was provided with a large supply of ball cartridges. Thus armed and equipped, he ordered them to Homestead. Arrived, these thugs proceeded to murder a number of innocent men in the interest of Frick.

It is well to have Frick in this matter painted to life—to see him in all of his surroundings of wealth and power plotting the Pinkerton raid upon Homestead. There is in every movement fiendish depravity, cruelty, and inhumanity that defies characterization. It was savagery and displays the ferocity of his nature, and distinguishes him above all others as a pitiless, bloodthirsty monster.

Such are the human brutes whose acts create assassins in all lands—men who brood over the wrongs inflicted by men in position to exert their power to promote evil in the world and who make the helpless their victims.

They are moral deformities, moral lepers, whose souls are unclean.

Alexander Berkman, the Russian Jew, born where the poor are forever oppressed and forever in the grasp of despotism, thought he saw in Frick a target that he should shoot at—and in doing this he thought he could be of some service to his fellow men. He saw the blood of innocent men on the soul of Frick and concluded to kill him. Had he accomplished his purpose, his own miserable life would have paid the penalty.

In the foregoing we have Frick, the man responsible for the Homestead murders of workingmen, and Berkman, the imported assassin, side by side, and it is possible someone can draw the line and show where there is a preponderance of depravity. If it is found on the side of the outcast Berkman, it will be in order to give the reasons for such a conclusion. But judged by their acts and motives, Berkman stands a fair chance of coming out on top.

Magazine Editor's Biennial Report and Resignation to the Sixteenth Convention of the B of LF†
[excerpt]
September 12, 1892

———

To the Officers and Members of the Grand Lodge
of the Brotherhood of Locomotive Firemen:

Sirs and Brothers: —

I have the honor to submit, herewith, my report of the publication of the
Locomotive Firemen's Magazine for the two fiscal years ending July 31, 1892, as
required in section 24, page 11 of the Constitution.[23]

*   *   *

The Policy of the Magazine Reviewed

I deem it prudent, in discussing *Magazine* affairs, to review its policy during
the past two years. Such a review is due the order and is equally just and becoming to myself—and all the more appropriate because such references as are
made to the policy of the *Magazine* are in the nature of a valedictory.

From the first, under my management, the *Magazine* has had a policy based
upon the well-defined purposes of the Brotherhood of Locomotive Firemen. At
the start, a few noble souls, some of whom still survive the wear and tear of toil,
believed there was a necessity for the organization and a place for it, that there
was an inviting field spread out before it which ought to be occupied and cultivated in the United States and Canada, in fact, for the firemen of the continent.

I do not suppose that in those now faraway days, the men who founded
the order grasped the full measure of the mission of the Brotherhood. Like "the
men who rounded Peter's dome," they builded better than they knew.[24] They
put in operation forces which since that day have encircled a continent, and
which, applied to problems of labor, have wrought results of a character which
this convention cannot contemplate without feelings of honest pride. I confess

———

†   Published as "Report of Editor and Manager of the *Magazine*" in *Journal of Proceed-*
    ings of the Third Biennial Convention (Sixteenth Convention) of the Brotherhood of Lo-
    comotive Firemen, Held in Cincinnati, Ohio, September 12, 13, 14, 15, 16, 17, 19, 20,
    and 21, 1892. (Terre Haute, IN: Moore and Langen, 1892), 279–293.

to a reverence of these brave men akin to awe. They were the men who first lighted the lodge fires of the order, flung out the first signal lights, and with that faith which is "the substance of things hoped for, the evidence of things not seen," pointed the way to the highland of victory and prosperity which the brotherhood now enjoys. They had faith in education, in its conquering power over debasing ignorance, and therefore founded the *Locomotive Firemen's Magazine,* the organ of the order which for twelve years has been, by the partiality and confidence of the brotherhood, committed to my hands. I need not, nor shall I, in this report, attempt a recapitulation of the more commanding features of the *Magazine* since I assumed control of its pages—nor is it required, since all the facts are on record and are as unchangeable as the laws of the Medes and Persians. They speak for me. They are my witnesses. I could not if I would, and I would not if I could, silence their utterances. They will speak to the brotherhood long after my retirement, and all through coming years they will speak to me and I shall be glad at all times to give them audience.

What has been the policy of the *Magazine?* Stated tersely, it has been first to promote the welfare of the Brotherhood of Locomotive Firemen. In no spirit of bravado, here and now, I challenge the records of its pages. It would be the sheerest folly to assume that no mistakes have been made, that infallibility has distinguished discussion. I make no such declarations, but this may be said: that like a ship in mid-ocean when neither sun nor stars appeared to enable the navigators to determine latitude and longitude, the purpose was to reach the destined port. The *Magazine* has often been surrounded with embarrassments, when adverse tides and winds prevailed which only increased my solicitude for the good of the order, and so far as the *Magazine* is concerned the flag of the Brotherhood has never been lowered, has never been trailed in the dust, has never been dishonored, but, unfurled, it has floated defiantly, never as the symbol of discord and war, but rather as the ensign of independence, manhood, and equal rights.

Need I remind this convention of a time when the great Brotherhood of Locomotive Engineers, guided by false lights, subjected this Brotherhood to exasperating humiliations which no diplomacy coupled with humiliating pleadings could remove? Need I refer to the duplicity and double-dealing to which this Brotherhood was subjected in the vain effort to have degrading laws of the B of LE so changed and modified as to remove stigma from the Brotherhood of Locomotive Firemen? Or need I refer to the policy of the *Magazine* which, after all prudent means had failed, created a sentiment which in spite of the hostility of the grand chief helped to place the two great brotherhoods in harmonious relations upon a basis of equal rights? The pages of the *Magazine* are luminous with the facts in the notable contest, in which the sense of right in the great Brotherhood of Locomotive Engineers overcame the petty prejudices and Jesuitical policy of its grand chief and created harmonious relations made conspicuous by the fact that at this biennial convention, for the first time in its history, the B of LE sends to this convention a committee to confer with the representatives of the Brotherhood of Locomotive Firemen.

The policy of the *Magazine* has been to permit no attacks from any quarter upon the Brotherhood of Locomotive Firemen without at once assuming not only the defensive, but the aggressive, demonstrating to all the ability of the brotherhood to maintain its independence and to carry forward its enterprises without regard to opposing forces.

Fealty to Labor Organizations

The policy of the *Magazine* has been to sympathize with all labor organizations and, as opportunities offered, to give them aid and comfort. In this policy there have been no exceptions. Comprehending, in some measure, the importance of labor organizations, and knowing the sentiments of the rank and file of the Brotherhood of Locomotive Firemen, it has been the policy of the *Magazine* to give expression to that sentiment on all proper occasions. Having a lofty scorn for an aristocracy in labor, it has been the policy of the *Magazine* to excoriate those infirm creatures who, because they hold office and are decorated with titles, put on more style than the nobility of Europe and assume that the simple incident of wages is quite sufficient to create an aristocracy in labor circles, and that a $4-a-day man may of right contemplate with contempt a man who receives $1 a day. The policy of the *Magazine* has been to expose such arrant nonsense and to denounce it with deserved severity. As an incident of this policy, I may refer to the position taken by the *Magazine* on the Homestead strike of the members of the Amalgamated Association of Iron and Steel Workers.

The articles which appeared in the *Magazine* upon that strike were so eagerly sought after that the general officers of the Association wrote for copies of the *Magazine,* and the articles were read in the lodges of the Association, eliciting rounds of applause. I refer to this incident because the Homestead strike assumed national importance, to a degree that the two houses of Congress at once created investigating committees whose duty it was to analyze the facts and report, preliminary to congressional action. What that may be is still undetermined, but it is certain if workingmen are true to themselves, the deliberations of Congress will be in the nature of the emancipation of labor from the degrading conditions which now crush it to the earth.

I do not propose, in this, my final report, to invite attention to every incident in which the policy of the *Magazine* is made conspicuous, but I do myself simple justice by referring to the case of the Knights of Labor, in which certain villainous concerns at Rochester, NY, perpetrated an outrage which the *Magazine* helped to expose, and earned the approval of all organizations of workingmen.

In conducting the *Magazine,* I have assumed that the Brotherhood of Locomotive Firemen is an organization of workingmen. I have fired an engine. I have not forgotten what the term "fireman" means. I know what it is to break and shovel coal into a firebox. I shall never forget my years of toil in front of the firebox. Good luck to the boys who are still working for promotion![25] And it is because firemen are workingmen that I have sought to make the *Magazine* the exponent of their views upon labor subjects. Laboring men have a fellow feeling for laboring men—and the policy of the *Magazine,* under my control, has been to keep to the front the conquering fact that the Brotherhood of Locomotive Firemen is not an organization of aristocrats, but of workingmen who sympathize with their fellow toilers in all departments of labor.

To give the largest power possible to organized labor, the Brotherhood of Locomotive Firemen favored federation and the *Magazine,* in full accord with the sentiment, did all in its power to bring about the alliance, and success crowned its efforts. At one time four organizations were in line under the banner of federation. The outlook was cheering—notable victories were secured—all that was expected of federation had been accomplished; clouds were disappearing. At this supreme juncture there came a reaction. Like a clap of thunder from a clear sky, one of the orders in the alliance, by the action of its grand officials, blasted every hope and by conspiracy inaugurated disaster. The officials of the B of RT entered into a conspiracy with the officials of the Northwestern railroad system to slaughter every switchman in its employment who was a member of the Switchmen's Mutual Aid Association, an organization at the time a member of the supreme council of the federated orders.[26]

I am aware of all the duplicity and prevarication of the officials of the B of RT to exculpate themselves from their acts of treason, but the "damned spots" will not out, nor will the ghosts of the murdered switchmen down. It is shown by their own testimony, a part of the record of the order, taken in their own convention behind locked doors, secret and sacred, that the grievance committee, with the authority and by direction of the grand (?) officers of the order, entered into a conspiracy with the officials of the Northwestern railroad system to discharge all the switchmen in its service. In this infamous conspiracy it was stipulated that members of the B of RT should be sent east, as the agents of the order and the railroad, to employ men to take the places of the switchmen. The men were employed, they did take the places of brotherhood switchmen, and the Northwestern Railroad Company paid the expenses incurred by the B of RT men to secure the services of these scabs.

This incident of conspiracy, treason, duplicity, and infamy resulted in the overthrow of federation, disrupted the Supreme Council, which gave up the ghost and forever disappeared on June 20, 1892. It was a child of promise and gave splendid indications of usefulness, but it fell a victim of conspiracy and was stabbed to death by traitors.

* * *

Sectarian Wrangles

The Brotherhood of Locomotive Firemen knows no sect. Its doors are open to all manly men and they may worship according to the dictates of their consciences, with none to molest them nor make them afraid. The brotherhood is not a nursery for bigots or fanatics. It cultivates no superstition. It advocates no sectarian creed or dogma, and it has been the policy of the *Magazine* to voice such sentiments of toleration as would prevent the introduction of the blighting effects of sectarianism. Notwithstanding this, sectarian prejudices in certain localities have crept into our lodges and threatened their disruption. In this connection, I suggest that this convention may with eminent propriety indicate, by resolution or otherwise, its abhorrence of bigotry and proclaim that the order will not tolerate men in its lodges who promote sectarian animosities.

Union Label

The policy of the *Magazine,* as has been said, has been to promote the welfare of all organized labor. It has taken the broadest possible view of such subjects, because they are intimately interwoven with the welfare of the B of LF. Union labor is seeking to protect itself from scabism by the introduction of union labels upon goods, such as hats, clothes, boots and shoes, cigars, etc. The idea is for buyers to inquire, when making purchases, for the union label, and, unless it is shown, to withhold their patronage. The propriety of this movement is seen at a glance, and it enables all persons interested in the welfare of organized labor to aid its triumph. I shall hope that this convention, by resolution, will place itself upon record as uncompromisingly in favor of the use and observance of the union label.

The policy of the *Magazine* has been to advocate every proposition made by labor organizations to secure the enactment of laws calculated to mitigate any of the wrongs to which labor has been subjected, hence it has been in harmony with all legislative committees which have sought to bring to the attention of legislatures measures in any way calculated to remedy existing evils. While legislative committees are of unquestioned importance, and have accomplished much good, the one grand essential is to have certain bills prepared, calculated to benefit labor, and then interrogate candidates. If they pledge themselves to support the measures, vote for them; if they decline to give assurance of support, vote against them regardless of the party tag they wear.

It is to me, as it should be to every member of the order, a source of pride and satisfaction to have the testimonials of the foremost men in the movement of the popularity of the *Magazine,* and it is simply echoing the universal verdict to say that it occupies a commanding position in the field of economic discussion. The *Magazine* today is more widely and more extensively copied than any labor publication on the continent. Its articles are to be found in almost every issue of the scores of labor periodicals devoted to almost every industry known to our civilization. Lawyers, doctors, divines, statesmen, statisticians, economists, and students of social science are numbered among its readers. In a letter under date of September 1 received by me from the labor editor of the *Boston Globe* by one of the great metropolitan papers of the country, the *Magazine* is alluded to in the following language:

> During the seven years that I have been labor editor of the *Boston Globe,* I have seen many labor publications and am deprived by the hard experience of severe knocks of the luxury of being able to "enthuse" easily. I cannot forbear, however, taking the time in the bustle and hurly-burly of getting up copy for Labor Day, to say to you that you ought to feel proud of the magazine you are producing, and the members of your brotherhood should also experience a glow of satisfaction that they have one among their number who is capable of such a production. It is beautiful in appearance and typographical makeup, it is chock full of meat, and it strikes good solid blows, every one a hundred pounds to the square inch, in the cause of labor's final emancipation. If the last number is a sample of the way you get up every number you must feel perfectly satisfied when you look it over fresh from the bindery. I know it has been no small factor in making the B of LF the strong, compact, and fearless organization it is today.
>
> —Cyrus F. Willard, *Boston Globe*

The pathways we have traveled together for nine years have led through many pleasant places—by flowery fields and dewy meads, by winding streams and sparkling fountains. We have marched together where the landscapes were of enrapturing beauty—by cottage homes and palatial residences. We have bivouacked with comrades, have been cheered by their fraternal greetings, and have shared their generous hospitalities. But this is not all. We have tramped with our comrades over arid deserts and through dark defiles. We have clambered up mountain roads and walked beside yawning chasms. Nor does this tell the story. We have stood shoulder to shoulder with them in many a conflict, when the enemy, well equipped, was defiant and fierce, when many faltered, when some fled and others turned traitors.

The brotherhood has seen its magazine on the warpath only when an enemy was to be hunted down, when lurking foes were to be driven from ambush and exposed, when the right was assailed, when justice and truth demanded that their professed votaries should come to the rescue. On such occasions the *Magazine* has responded with alacrity. For these things the Brotherhood of Locomotive Firemen has not yet demanded an apology, nor will it until the Carnegies, the Fricks, the McLeods,[27] the Depews, and all enemies of organized labor achieve a victory for corporate greed and corporate autocracy.

In surrendering to this convention the offices I have held in the great Brotherhood of Locomotive Firemen, I confess to varied emotions. The twelve years I have held office, necessitating the most intimate, confidential, and responsible relations, have created ties which cannot be sundered without regrets. Here and now I dismiss all but pleasant memories, and wherever I am and whatever fortune betides me, I shall hope for the continued prosperity of this my beloved order which has had so many years of my early manhood, and shall never be more happy than in knowing that its career develops constantly increasing power and usefulness.

Respectfully submitted,
Eugene V. Debs,
Editor and Manager

"My Retirement Is Certain":
Speech to the Sixteenth Convention of the B of LF, Cincinnati, Ohio[†]

September 19, 1892

My retirement from the Grand Lodge is certain. I have been in office twelve years, and find the work very exacting. While I don't expect to disconnect myself with organized labor, to continue in my present position would materially interfere with my plans for the future. A life purpose of mine has been the federation of railroad employees. To unify them into one great body is my object, but I don't believe it can be done on the present lines. Now the men are organized in classes for distinct departments. Class enrollment fosters class prejudices and class selfishness, and instead of affiliating with each other, there is a tendency to hold aloof from each other. Class organization is well enough, but they should be united when the time comes for federation. With the present differences in organization and differences among the grand officers, federation is impracticable and impossible.

It has been my life's desire to unify railroad employees and to eliminate the aristocracy in labor, which unfortunately exists, and organize them so all will be on an equality. To this I am going to turn my attention. I have yet no plans formulated, but they will come later, after a needed rest.

These are my reasons for declining a reelection. To the firemen I have given my best years, and naturally they will always be first in my thoughts and always will have my best wishes for success in the future.

---

†   Published in *Cincinnati Enquirer,* September 20, 1892. Copy in the *Papers of Eugene V. Debs* microfilm collection, reel 9, notebook 1, 46.

The End of the Switchmen's Strike[†]

October 1892

On the morning of August 25 [1892] the wires flashed the tidings that the switchmen's strike at Buffalo had been declared "off"—and that the "515" switchmen "called out" could seek work, and if possible secure the positions they had abandoned.

The strike had a duration of about two weeks, from start to finish. It is a mistake to say that it resulted from the fact that the switchmen demanded an advance of wages—not only is it a mistake to say that, but it is false and vicious.

There is not even a remote probability that a strike would have occurred in arranging a schedule of wages. There would have been pros and cons, but out of it all would have come a peaceful settlement, but for one thing, and that was that the railroad officials, in a spirit of autocratic meanness, refused to recognize the order of switchmen and treat with its officials. Under such conditions a strike was inevitable. There is not an organization of railroad employees that would not have struck under such circumstances. It was an unavoidable outcome of the matter. And here it should be said that the railroad officials were absolutely responsible for the strike. Their hostility to organized labor provoked and brought about the strike. Had they conferred with Grand Master [Frank] Sweeney, the chief executive officer of the Switchmen's Mutual Aid Association, there is not a remote probability that a strike would have occurred.

These railroad officials reasoned logically. Evidently they said, "no other organization will come to the rescue of the switchmen; acting alone we can *whip* them." How well they reasoned the sequel shows. Other organizations gave the switchmen oceans of sympathy, carloads of taffy, but not so much as an ounce of substantial aid. In that regard the switchmen were left to paddle their own canoe through the rapids, the Hell Gate of the strike, alone and unaided.

Let it be distinctly understood that the *Magazine* does not excuse the destruction of property by strikers. It has no word of condonement for such crimes. They not only do no good, but they are fruitful of incalculable wrongs to organized labor. In saying this we do but speak the sentiments of the great

---

†   Published as "The Switchmen's Strike" in *Locomotive Firemen's Magazine,* vol. 16, no. 10 (October 1892), 869–871.

body of switchmen, members of the Switchmen's Mutual Aid Association. They are not anarchists, but men who stand as high in the ranks of organized labor as do the men of any other organization. They are hardworking, honorable, self-respecting men whose duties are perilous, and who, as a general proposition, are never justly paid. That in the organization are turbulent men, who are not guided by honorable methods to secure justice, need not be denied, but in this regard the order of switchmen constitutes no exception. Such men are in all organizations, as the records fully demonstrate, and the order ought not to be—and in the estimation of honest men will not be—held responsible for the acts of those who, at Buffalo, disregarded law and order. We dismiss such incidents for the consideration of more important questions.

The Buffalo strike becomes notable because of the small number of men, say "515," who were engaged in it. The number was so small as to create national surprise, when considering the force required to stay its progress and conquer the little band of strikers. The civil authorities of Buffalo and of Erie County immediately became utterly demoralized—cowards to the backbone—provided they had any spinal column. Their chicken hearts suddenly went down into their boots, and they yelled frantically for troops, and from Brooklyn to Lake Erie the "Empire State" resounded with drumbeats and the tramp of soldiers. Writers of flapdoodle exhausted their descriptive powers of the pomp and circumstance of glorious war, as multiplied thousands of soldiers with guns and batteries moved on to the seat of war to conquer "515" switchmen, who had dared to demand an advance in wages, and who were loathe to see degenerate scabs from all the slums of cities take their places. Then the American eagle screamed in response to the military brass band and the beating of the war drums. Generals located their "headquarters" and their "hindquarters," and the game of war was played with the "joker." Pickets were "thrown out," bayonets were "fixed," guns loaded, officers drew their lusty blades, and the campaign was inaugurated.

The enemy, "515" strikers, spread out over about as many square miles, were mighty thin. Some mounted trestles and grinned as the troops marched and countermarched, while occasionally some fool switchman threw a rock or a coupling pin to break the monotony of the campaign and enable reporters and Associated Press agents to write their hair-breadth escapes of platoons and magnify the battles in which generals and colonels participated, and won the gratitude of railroad officials and their scabs, and possibly will apply for pensions.

While such things were going on, the great majority of the "515" switchmen were quietly minding their own business, firing neither coupling pins nor rocks at the grand army of the "Empire State," leaving perhaps 50 switchmen to dare the army to win such renown as they could by capturing, killing, or wounding them. Were it our mission to write burlesques of the military, Pennsylvania and New York at Homestead and Buffalo would supply raw material sufficient to last a lifetime. But with all the ludicrous and disgusting features of the military pomp and parade, the army at Buffalo was there to kill if an opportunity offered, and if real estate in boneyards was not in demand at advanced figures, the fact is not to be set down to the credit of the military machine.

Away from the military, Grand Master Sweeney was trying to solve the strike problem. He saw defeat close at hand, if he was required to continue the struggle alone, and he therefore appealed, like a drowning man, to "sister (?) organizations." He wanted to meet all the "grand officers," having an idea that somehow the "grand officers" could save him—turn the tide of battle and place the switchmen "on top." Some of the "grand officers" responded. They came at his call like homing doves, each with the message under his wing that they "had no grievance and couldn't fight." Their souls were profoundly stirred with sympathy, compassion, condolence, tenderness, and fellow-feeling, but no kick—no strike—no declaration of war; with them all was serene, and while their bowels of compassion were greatly perturbed, there was nothing in their craw indicating help to the switchmen.

This conclusion fully aroused Grand Master Sweeney to the seriousness of the situation. There was no help for him; the last hope had fled, gone glimmering like a schoolboy's tale. Hope had whispered in his willing ears, and the story she told inspired his faith that a wrong had been done in the switchmen's order, which all would realize was equally an indignity offered every other order of railroad employees. He believed it, but like Dead Sea fruit, when it touched his lips, turned to ashes.

Grand Master Sweeney, like Lee at Appomattox, deemed it unwise to sacrifice more men, yielded to the inevitable, and declared the strike off. The action was dictated by wisdom and prudence of the highest order. To have continued the strike would have been madness; to have sacrificed another man would have been in the nature of an unpardonable blunder.

Of all the incidents of the strike the brutal beating inflicted upon Grand Master Sweeney defines fitting characterization, and to couple Mr. Sweeney's name with dishonorable transactions in any matter connected with the strike we regard as the acme of perfidy on the part of those who make the intimation. The switchmen were defeated, and here, we ask, which one of the orders of railroad employees under similar circumstances would have won a victory? Not one. The switchmen made a gallant fight—all honor to them. Their honor was not wrecked. The order is intact. We wish it in the future a career of prosperity.

We have not forgotten the CB&Q struggle.[28] Defeat crushed the engineers and firemen on that system, but not elsewhere, and the switchmen will survive the Buffalo battle. There are other battles in store for railroad employees. It requires neither a prophet nor the son of a prophet to foretell their coming, and when they do come we hope that having outgrown the indifference which marked their policy when Sweeney pleaded for help, they will unify and win victories, in spite of corporations, scabs, and the military.

Homestead and Treason[†]

November 1892

October 1, 1892, the news was wired over the country that a number of the members of the advisory committee of the Homestead strikers had been arrested for treason against the great state of Pennsylvania. Those arrested, says the dispatch, were Chairman Thomas J. Crawford, William Bair, George Royland, John Direken, and T. W. Brown. "The informations," says the dispatch, "were made by County Detective Belzhoover before Chief Justice [Edward H.] Paxon, of the Supreme Court of Pennsylvania." The petition "charges Hugh O'Donnell, Thomas J. Crawford, John McLuckie, and thirty others, all members of the strikers' advisory committee, with treason. It states that the defendants, who are inhabitants and residents of the commonwealth of Pennsylvania, did ordain, prepare, and levy war against the commonwealth of Pennsylvania to the end that the constitution, laws, and authority were defied, resisted, and subverted; and that the said defendants on July 1 [1892], with hundreds of others, armed and arrayed in warlike manner—that is to say with guns, revolvers, cannons, swords, knives, and clubs—did unlawfully, maliciously, and traitorously assemble in the borough of Homestead and then and there, with force and arms, did falsely and traitorously and in hostile and

†   Published in *Locomotive Firemen's Magazine,* vol. 16, no. 11 (November 1892), 972–973.

warlike manner array themselves in insurrection and rebellion against the commonwealth of Pennsylvania, contrary to the duties of allegiance and fidelity of the said defendants."

The foregoing is an unexpected and a novel proceeding—and it will be well if the workingmen of the United States give it, as clergymen would say, "prayerful attention." Carnegie, Frick & Co. have their backs up, and their blood is hot. They have sought by every method at their command to get back into their mills the locked-out workingmen of Homestead. They have failed. In their place is a number of unskilled, conscienceless scabs, vagabond creatures, and the mills have made a show of work, but it is understood they are making no money, the business is going to the everlasting bowwows, and hence the anger of the millionaire proprietors, and hence also the trumped-up charge of treason.

It is well under the circumstances to understand, as fully as necessary, in what the crime of treason consists. The highest authority upon the subject, so far as the United States is concerned, is its Constitution. The language of the Constitution is as follows:

"Treason against the United States shall consist only in levying war against them, or in adhering to their enemies, giving them aid and comfort."

We do not know what language is used in the constitution of Pennsylvania to define treason against that state, but presume, as in the constitutions of other states, the language is similar to that used in the Constitution of the United States, that is, "levying war against the state, or adhering to its enemies."

The reader will not fail to observe that the charge of treason as made against the Homestead strikers is simply that of "assault and battery with intent to kill," and the question arises, who did the Homestead strikers assault, with "swords, guns, knives, and clubs?" The state of Pennsylvania? Not at all; only a gang of hired mercenary thugs, armed to the teeth for the purpose of committing murder, and instructed to commit murder by the Carnegie concern—hence if anyone committed treason it was Frick and his pals—and not the strikers, who defended their homes against an invading band of cutthroats.

However, this phase of the affair does not particularly concern us at this writing; on the contrary, our purpose is to point out the desperate methods organized capital has adopted to intimidate and crush workingmen and compel them to submit to the "plan of degradation" now clearly defined by millionaire employers. Again, referring to the Constitution of the United States, we have the following:

"A well organized militia being necessary to the security of a free state, the right of the people to keep and bear arms shall not be infringed."[29]

Hence it will be observed that the Homestead strikers had a constitutional right to have swords, guns, knives, clubs, and revolvers, and they had a constitutional right to use them to beat down the murderous gang of Pinkertons who invaded their homes for the purpose of killing them and who did kill them.

It will be noticed that Carnegie & Co. have on their side the supreme judge of Pennsylvania—that is to say, that high official, so far as is known at this writing, favors the Frick theory of treason, and it is therefore not surprising that the Homestead strikers, say five thousand workingmen who defended their homes against an invading gang of thugs, are somewhat depressed. In this connection, the dispatch says:

> The borough is yet quivering from the shock of last night's bombshell. Business is practically suspended and anxious groups stand at every corner discussing this latest coup. "What does it mean?" That is the query on every tongue. The thought of the states of Pennsylvania interfering in the struggle is frightening to the sturdy workers. They would accept with derision riot, murder, or conspiracy suits brought by the Carnegie Steel Company, but to be arrested by the state, and on a charge of treason— that is different; it is unknown danger and therefore ominous. What the result will be no one here attempts to predict but what the effect is is visible on every face—desperation. Men soberly propose to their fellows that they secure a band and flags and, marching to Pittsburgh, apply en masse for admission to jail, to save further uneasiness and to end at once all suspense. Incident with this fear in the minds of the Homesteaders is another passion which may yet dominate: It is anger.

The question here arises, if the Homestead strikers are becoming "desperate" and "angry," what will be the condition of millions of workingmen throughout the United States as they contemplate the spectacle of their fellow toilers persecuted, throttled, manacled, imprisoned, and degraded because they dared to resist a horde of armed mercenaries, hired and equipped to murder them? Are all workingmen to become desperate and angry and continue in this frame of mind and peacefully continue to carry forward the industries of the country while listening to the clank of the iron shackles of their fellow toilers as, in felon's stripes, they march to and from their tasks behind prison bars? Is it not possible that Carnegie et al. are carrying their devilish methods of intimidation too far for a peaceful solution of the labor problem?

This latest movement by the infamous Frick, if workingmen can be aroused, means trouble. They behold capital, scabs, the military, and the courts in alliance to subject them to conditions which arouse desperation and anger, and things which provoke trouble are beginning to move at a rapid pace.

The Homestead strikers need money to feed and clothe them during the inclement season. Let the flow of money be quick, full, and continuous. The Homestead strikers need cash to enable them to employ the most eminent legal ability on the continent to defend them against the charge of *treason*. Who, of the millions of workingmen of America, will decline to contribute their mite? Money talks. If it is supplied as the workingmen of America can supply it, the trial of the Homestead workingmen on the charge of treason may be made the most notable event for labor that has occurred since skill and muscle built the seven or the 700 wonders of the world. If there is a Demosthenes, a Cicero, a Burke, or a Webster living, let his talents be secured, let his voice be heard in the trial of the Homestead workingmen on the charge of treason.

The nations are coming to America to celebrate the 400th anniversary of the discovery of America. Is the spectacle in reservation for them of seeing Carnegie and Frick driving their workingmen to dungeons? It looks that way. Organized capital is now stabbing organized labor. In certain localities men may contemplate results, and if resistance to wrong is to be adjudged treason by the courts, the army will do whatever remains to be done to accomplish the purpose of organized capital.

The End of the Homestead Strike[†]

November 21, 1892

As we write, November 21, the wires flash the news that the Homestead strike has authoritatively been declared off, and all the men are left to do the best they can, which to many of them means a long march through a wilderness of sore trials.

It now occurs that the officials of the Amalgamated Association long since admitted that the strike was lost, but from various causes were prevented from doing what common sense dictated and which finally has been done.

[†]   Published as "Homestead" in *Locomotive Firemen's Magazine,* vol. 16, no. 12 (December 1892), 1105–1106.

The statement is made that the strike has cost the Homestead workingmen at least $2 million in wages. In addition to this, it has cost them, or most of them, all their savings—how much will never be known. Besides, it has cost a vast sum that has been contributed to aid the strikers to maintain their independent attitude in the hope of winning a victory; the sum total approximating doubtless $4 million.

The fight was for a principle, for a right, an eternal right, and no friend of labor will cry over the defeat. The statement is made that the Carnegie concern has lost more than the employees, but that does not count. The concern had the cash in bank, and the bottom of the flour barrel was never reached.

Though the strike is declared off, Homestead, like Marathon,[30] is historic. It is a Mecca, and to it labor pilgrims may go and find inspiration for courage in future contests which are to come. At Homestead the banners of the Pinkertons went down for the first time in the history of that infernal crew. The battle at Homestead, though lost to the men immediately engaged, opened the eyes of millions of men, unstopped their ears, aroused them from their lethargy, and gave them to understand that the plutocratic class had determined to enslave them, and in the light of such facts a victory for labor was won.

The announcement is made that a large number of the Homestead strikers are in destitute circumstances, and it has also been announced that December 13 was to be Homestead Day for the purpose of contributing means to aid the strikers. Let December 13 be Homestead Day. Let the contributions be made to aid the destitute families of Homestead, whom Frick & Co. deny the privilege of going to work, so that during the inclement season they may be made comfortable. The demand is imperative; let it be heeded by the workingmen of America.

Notes

1. Henry Clay Frick (1849–1914) was, to use an anachronistic title that lends clarity, the chief executive officer of the Carnegie Steel Company from its formation through a merger in 1892. Frick was himself a magnate in the production of coke, a key component of the steelmaking process, and was involved in a miners' strike that lead to the April 1891 Morewood Massacre, in which nine striking miners where shot and killed by National Guard troops. In July 1892 Frick survived an assassination attempt by anarchist Alexander Berkman, an attack that only built public sympathy for Frick's militantly anti-union position.

2. Perforated wooden boards for the temporary storage of dead bodies, packed with ice to slow the decomposition process.

3. Carnegie was on an extended visit to his native Scotland during the Homestead strike.

4. Allusion to Matthew 23:14.

5. Allusion to Matthew 23:4.

6. Reference to a widely read 1889 article in which Carnegie wrote: "We assemble thousands of operatives in the factory, in the mine, and in the counting-house, of whom the employer can know little or nothing, and to whom the employer is little better than a myth. All intercourse between them is at an end. Rigid castes are formed, and, as usual, mutual ignorance breeds mutual distrust." Carnegie, "Wealth," *North American Review,* vol. 148, no. 391 (June 1889), 654.

7. From Carnegie, "Wealth," 655.

8. From Carnegie, "Wealth," 656.

9. Carnegie, "Wealth," 661.

10. Allusion to Matthew 17:27.

11. Henry Phipps, Jr. (1839–1930) was a cofounder and the second largest shareholder of Carnegie Steel Co. Like Carnegie, Phipps was not an active manager of the company at the time of the Homestead strike.

12. Jumbo was a captive African elephant brought to America from the London Zoo as a feature attraction by P. T. Barnum in 1882. The elephant died in a Canadian rail yard accident in 1885.

13. Apparently a reference to a popular children's song of the late 1830s that included the line "His name was Robert Kidd, as he sailed." William Kidd (1654–1701), was an executed Scottish pirate who, legend had it, used the alias "Robert Kidd" while on the water engaging in larceny.

14. Actually, the Amalgamated Association of Iron and Steel Workers (AAISW).

15. The final toll of the July 6, 1892 "battle of the barges" included seven strikers and three Pinkertons killed. More than 100 strike leaders and active participants later faced an array of charges, including murder, conspiracy, and treason.

16. Allusion to "A Psalm of Life" (1838), by Henry Wadsworth Longfellow (1807–1882), the fifth stanza of which reads: "In the world's broad field of battle / In the bivouac of Life, / Be not like dumb, driven cattle! / Be a hero in the strife!"

17. That is, one of a kind.

18. Golgotha was an execution site immediately outside of the walls of Jerusalem where, according to the Bible, Jesus and two thieves were crucified.

19. Allusion to Exodus 13:21–22.

20. John McLuckie, a former steelworker of radical pro-strike views, was the mayor of Homestead, Pennsylvania.

21. Hugh O'Donnell, a young, skilled steelworker active in the Amalgamated Association of Iron and Steel Workers (AAISW), emerged as the leader of the Carnegie millworkers in the Homestead strike. The prosecution of O'Donnell and McLuckie was an attempt to decapitate the leadership of the Homestead strikers.

22. Actually, the Pennsylvania National Guard.

23. Debs's biennial report included extensive lodge-by-lodge subscription figures for *Locomotive Firemen's Magazine*, with paid totals of 6,847 for 1890, 7,456 for 1891, and 5,434 for the first seven months of 1892. These figures were dwarfed by the number of B of LF members, said by Debs to be 26,000—a ratio of just one subscriber per five members of the order. (See: Debs Report, 283.) The actual circulation of *Firemen's Magazine* was far greater, however, with monthly print runs for the first seven months of 1892 ranging from 33,000 to 35,000. (Report, 285.)

24. Allusion to "The Problem" (1847), by Ralph Waldo Emerson (1803–1882).

25. Locomotive firemen worked under the supervision of the better paid and more esteemed locomotive engineers and uniformly aspired to promotion to this superior position.

26. The Brotherhood of Railroad Trainmen (B of RT), formerly the Brotherhood of Railroad Brakemen, engaged in a bitter jurisdictional struggle with the Switchmen's Mutual Aid Association on the Northwestern railroad system in the spring of 1891— a dispute which ultimately led to the expulsion of the B of RT and the disintegration of Debs's Supreme Council of the United Orders of Railway Employees project. For more on this conflict see Eugene V. Debs Selected Works: Volume 1, pp. 549–58; 617–34; and passim.

27. Archibald Angus McLeod (1844–1902) was president of the Reading Railroad from 1890 until 1893.

28. Reference to the bitter 1888 strike of the Chicago, Burlington & Quincy Railroad. See numerous articles on the same in *The Selected Works of Eugene V. Debs: Volume 1*.

29. Second Amendment to the United States Constitution.

30. The Battle of Marathon took place in 490 BC, during the first Persian invasion of Greece. The battle was won by the unified citizens of Athens and Plataea, who successfully drove the Persians from the Greek mainland.

1893

Evolution[†]

January 1893

In writing of evolution there is no purpose to investigate or criticize Darwinism relating to "man's place in nature." We take man's place in nature as it stands today regardless of his creation. His remote ancestors may have been apes or tadpoles, or he may have been created as the Bible proclaims. In any case there has been, going forward in processes of evolution, a steady unfolding of mental powers, whatever may be said of man's early physical endowments. It is quite possible that in the processes of evolution, man has lost in physical strength and gained in mental vigor. Indeed, investigation, we think, would lead to such a conclusion. This mental energy, it is noticed, exhibits greater development in some men than is found in others and, as a result, the men of the largest brain or mind power manage to rule those of inferior intellectual grasp. To state a general proposition, the evolution of intellectual power is consequent upon education, which is the great unfolding force. Hence it follows that those who command the largest educational advantages control those of inferior opportunities. To equalize these opportunities is the great purpose of the American free school system, to secure to all mind evolution, the unfolding of its powers, so that the humblest citizen may become a thinker and be prepared to maintain his independence in all conflicts that may arise between contending classes.

If a man is qualified so much as to read correctly, he, to a certain and to a very large extent, becomes responsible for the progress he makes in mental evolution. Being able to read, he can, if he will, avail himself of the advantages which books confer upon those who read. In that case the processes of evolution go forward with an ever-accelerating rapidity. As he reads, his mind expands, unfolds, grasps, and solves, and instead of being ruled by others he becomes a force and a factor in government, and in all affairs pertaining to his welfare.

In commerce, in finance, in industries, and in labor the processes of evolution are challenging the attention of men of thought. Intelligent workingmen are profoundly interested in these wonderful exhibitions. They behold new forces in operation and are studying with intense concern to ascertain in what regard they contribute to their well-being. In the evolution of business affairs, they behold the concentration of wealth and the power which wealth confers in the hands of

---

†   Published in *Locomotive Firemen's Magazine*, vol. 17, no. 1 (January 1893), 6–9.

the few. They behold the machine everywhere taking the place of men. Unable to counteract such processes of evolution, even if they were desirous of doing so, they inquire with ever-increasing solicitude, what must the end be? What, if anything, is evolution contributing to the welfare of those who toil?

If the concentration of wealth in the hands of the few, if trusts, syndicates, corporations, and monopolies are the results of evolution on the one hand, it may be affirmed that labor organizations are also the fruits of evolution, and it is just here that comes into view the theory of survival. In evolution as it relates to animals and plants, the strongest survive, the weak go to the wall—disappear—sometimes styled "the survival of the fittest," but always the strongest. It must be granted that when large mind forces are in alliance with wealth, immense strength is developed, and as against ignorance and poverty, the latter must succumb, except incidentally and spasmodically, as in the early days of the French Revolution.

But when the eye surveys the field of organized labor, the fact comes into view that evolution has already accomplished wonders for those who toil. The labor mind as a whole has unfolded to an extent productive of amazement. Grasping every problem that relates to its welfare, it is accomplishing results along the line of its active forces, that bear the stamp of practical wisdom, and in the discussion of the fittest, or the strongest, labor is developing staying qualities which are creating anxiety in the ranks of those who have believed themselves to be the favorites of evolution. They have claimed that their education and their wealth conferred upon them not only the power to rule, but the right to rule, while labor, on the other hand, points to the fact that its mind forces challenge scrutiny; that its skill is more to the world than money. And then, when labor calls the roll of its membership and the men step forth to be counted, the army, the standing army of labor, appalls those who surmise that labor is simply a machine to be operated for their benefit.

We unhesitatingly declare that such are some of the advantages that have come to labor by virtue of evolution, and quite as unhesitatingly do we aver that up to this day labor fails to comprehend, scarcely in any measure whatever, what emancipating blessings evolution has conferred upon it. It not only does not put forth its hand to grasp and utilize its inheritance of power, but, wedded to jealousies and selfishness, it courts defeat and prefers degeneracy to independence.

If this debasement were universal, we should say that evolution, going forward during all the centuries, had accomplished nothing whatever for labor—and if we wanted an illustration of the fact, we would point to the condition of labor on the Reading Railroad, where men yield up their independence and, like so many peons or helots, wear the badge of servitude placed upon them by Mc-Leod—men who dare not light a lodge fire and proclaim their emancipation from a slavish condition. For such men, neither evolution nor revolution could lift them in a thousand centuries one inch above the dead line of their degradation.

But, fortunately, such soul inferiority is not universal, nor yet a distinguishing feature in labor affairs of the period. Evolution has not simply unfolded the intellectual powers of the plutocratic class. It has laid its redeeming hand upon millions who toil and now, by rights divine, they are organizing—a movement preceded by thought and carried forward by thought, to be crushed out only when Gabriel or some other commissioned herald proclaims that the pendulum of time has made its last vibration.[1]

But there is a demand for still further evolution in the world of labor. While the armies of labor are divided, and are under the leadership of men who from any base ambition hold their positions to promote selfish ends and aims, plutocrats and their wealth will rule. With such men, evolution has no significance beyond the boundary line of their own mercenary meanness. But they cannot resist the silent, ceaseless operation of evolution. They will die not too soon for labor's emancipation from the thralldom of prejudices they promote. The labor world, if evolution proceeds—and go forward it must, for such is the law—will unify upon all questions where rights are involved. Labor organizations, separate as waves but one as the sea, will mass their tremendous power for self-preservation. It is the law—the trend, and we shall hope to see its sublime exhibitions of power. We should like to see it come as comes the dawn, with pencilings of light and rising orb, advancing in a cloudless sky to noontide glory. We should like to see it come as comes the vernal season, with its sunshine and shower, buds and flowers and fruits, while all the feathered songsters make the woodlands vocal with their melodies—but come it must, either gently or with exhibitions of wrath and terror. Labor is the subject of evolution and its forward strides arouse the nation. Too great to be intimidated, too resourceful to take a backward step, its future is destined to be the climax in the process of evolution, since man started on his upward march toward the elysian fields of independence.

The Labor View of the Election[†]

January 1893

The *Locomotive Firemen's Magazine* is not a politically partisan publication, only to the extent that when a citizen who is an enemy of labor aspires to office, the *Magazine* would have that aspirant defeated, regardless of party platform, banner, or shibboleth.

The country has passed through a presidential election in which labor was as conspicuously identified as any other interest that was or could have been named, and the question arises, wherefore this interest and solicitude?

In this discussion the *Magazine* discards all reference to the personnel of tickets, except insofar as such allusions refer to the welfare of organized labor.

Whitelaw Reid,[2] all of the years that he had been in a position to employ men, was distinguished as an inveterate enemy of organized labor. As an owner and publisher of a great newspaper, he had evinced a hostility to organized labor so relentless as to become a public scandal. This the *Magazine* deemed it its duty to expose in the light of established and notorious facts. Let this suffice.

The Democratic Party succeeds the Republican Party in the national government and in a number of states hitherto Republican in politics. In this sweeping change, are there any comforting lessons to labor? If so, what are the lessons?

The discussions of the campaign were largely economic. Such questions are abstruse and easily mystified. Hence labor has sought industriously for a few fundamental facts and principles to which it was easy to refer and which were impregnable to the attacks of sophistry, calculated to mislead the mind and culminating in erroneous conclusions. Manifestly, the pivotal question of the campaign was that of the tariff, and we doubt if, within the entire realm of economic questions, there is one upon which there is such a wide and honest disagreement; and yet, in this, as in every other question of national importance, there is a principle involved which, found and embraced, emancipates the mind from the thralldoms of error.

Admitting that the principle of protection is right, the next question is, should it be so warped and distorted as to protect a favored few to the neglect of the many? If a tariff does that, then justice is discarded and wrong triumphs. In a nutshell, should Carnegie and Frick be protected, whereby millions accrue

---

†   Published in *Locomotive Firemen's Magazine,* vol. 17, no. 1 (January 1893), 9–11.

to them, while their workingmen have their wages reduced and are made to realize that, though employed in carrying forward a tariff-protected industry, the same tariff affords them no protection, but even makes their condition worse? Nor is this all. Labor has asked the question, why should certain industries be protected, while others are left to succeed if they can without such protection? Various reasons were assigned for this admitted injustice, but it is evident that labor was not satisfied with the arguments adduced; such protection was not, in the first place, fair play. It did not afford all industries the same advantages. It taxed one to support another, and was therefore in direct conflict with the genius of American institutions.

Again, it was held during the campaign, if a high protective tariff protected certain industries against the importation of what is termed "foreign pauper labor products," it furnished labor no protection against the importation of "foreign pauper laborers;" they came by thousands and by tens of thousands, and offered their services for "pauper wages," and as a result, while the hue and cry in favor of protective tariff was loudest, organized labor, as in the case of Homestead, found it impossible to maintain wages, and thousands of workingmen are suffering because they had the independence to resist not only a reduction in wages, but the murderous policy of a protected industry to introduce scabs and thus compel unprotected labor to submit to conditions fruitful of poverty and degradation. In all of this, insofar as labor was concerned, strictly speaking, there was no partisanism. It was an economic question, and as a high protective tariff, as we have shown in the case of Homestead, did not protect organized labor, it was pronounced a failure, and the edict has gone forth for the modification of existing tariff laws.

There were other economic questions involved in which labor has a vital interest, as for instance the free coinage of silver. Here again comes into view a question in which labor has a right to be heard. First, because mining silver is a great American industry and gives employment to thousands of workingmen. Second, because free coinage affords a market for the product of the mines, and third, because silver coin is honest money, and no man ever failed whose silver dollars were equal to his debts.

Again, free coinage is in direct opposition to the policy of plutocratic millionaires, styled "goldbugs," whose policy has been and now is, by virtue of the single gold standard, to control the financial affairs of the nation and control values. Labor takes no stock in such a policy, and on a direct vote would overwhelmingly declare for the free coinage of silver, and the fact that when silver certificates are issued there is a silver dollar behind every certificate emphasizes the fact that whether a man has the coin or the certificate, he has honest dollars.

We could extend illustrations showing that in the political campaign just closed, labor was everywhere an issue, and that all political parties sought to give it prominence. It remains to be seen what the victorious party will do in legislatures and in Congress to redeem the pledges made to labor. Much is required to modify present laws, and to enact others which shall give to labor a standing in the courts of the country equal, in all respects, to that occupied by those who command money, and who, hitherto, when they have wanted a court went out and bought it. As the fruits of the election are gathered into law making bodies, the *Magazine* will endeavor to outline special requirements.

The Death of Jay Gould[†]

February 1893

At 9:15 a.m., Tuesday, December 2, AD 1892, Jay Gould died at his home in the city of New York, in the fifty-seventh year of his age, surrounded by his family.[3] According to well-authenticated statements, his death was as tranquil as when an infant goes to sleep upon its mother's breast. For some time previous to his death, he had been unconscious; suddenly his mind regained its throne, when he recognized each one of his family, called them around his couch, whispered to them his farewells, then, relapsing into a comatose condition, passed away.

In all of this there is nothing spectacular. Jay Gould died unobtrusively. The richest man in the world, he died like a man whose income is a dollar a day. Jay Gould abhorred pageantry. He never made a display of the pelts of the bulls and bears he had slaughtered. He hung no scalps upon his belt, nor decorated his wigwam with such trophies of his prowess. He was preeminently a modest man. He had no "dying words" for the public ear. His tastes were all simple. He was neither gourmand nor bacchanal. He did not drink stimulants, smoke cigars, nor chew tobacco. He was absolutely free from bad habits, and in such regard at least, he stood a towering example to all young men, even theological students. In stature and weight he was below the average. His head, "the dome

†   Published in *Locomotive Firemen's Magazine*, vol. 17, no. 2 (February 1893), 103–108.

of thought and palace of the brain," was superb. His eye, black and piercing, was a distinguishing feature, and once seen was never forgotten. His courage, daring, willpower, audacity, self-control, were known and read of all men. In tactics and strategy on fields where his battles were fought, he had no peer. He was in almost everything *sui generis*, to the world around him a sphinx, a riddle no one could solve. He was his own preceptor. He was a student of men—a mind reader. He discerned at once if the man he wanted as a tool was for sale, sized him up intuitively, and knew what he was worth, paid cash, and placed his collar on him. His estimate of judges, juries, and legislators was equally infallible. Of the laws that concerned him he was familiar with every technicality and saw at a glance the holes through which he could take a railroad train with entire safety.

The remarkable times in which Jay Gould lived and wrought produced no more remarkable man than Jay Gould. During a quarter of a century there was not a man on any continent, from prince to peasant, who occupied so large a space in the public mind as Jay Gould. Not even the Rothschilds, one or all of them together, were as conspicuous in the financial world, in the sense of being talked about. If he talked, the wires flashed his words over the land and under the sea. If he was silent, the fact was, if possible, of still greater consequence. Hence the sobriquet "Wizard," and it is not to be questioned that there were those who believed him to be master of the black art, because his methods were different from those of other men. As a consequence, he became an object of alarm to thousands of Wall Street speculators and gamblers, who breathed easy only when assured that Jay Gould was not in the market.

It is widely asserted that Jay Gould was a railroad wrecker, but those who make the charge are careful not to name the roads he wrecked. They doubtless refer to the Erie, but upon examination it is found that in his Erie deal he was fighting old Commodore Vanderbilt, and out-generaled him, that is all. True, old man Drew[4] got squeezed in that remarkable deal, but it was because at a critical time he deserted Gould and played into the hands of Vanderbilt, and when he found himself in a hole he pleaded with Gould to rescue him, but owing to Drew's treason he was left to pay the penalty of his treachery. In this there was nothing peculiar. Men do the same thing three hundred days of every year, but Gould had the fortune always of being selected for maledictions.

The times in which Jay Gould's lot was cast were corrupt. Wall Street was and is a den of robbers—a place which, when men enter it, they leave conscience behind. It is an arena where bulls and bears engage for the mastery. It is war to the hilt. There is neither compassion nor quarter. Ordinarily the longest purse, the largest bank account wins, but not always. Strategy, tactics, prescience, accurate knowledge of conditions and dash have won many a Wall Street victory.

It is said that Jay Gould engineered matters to bring about "Black Friday." Admit it—how was it done? And why was it done? A number of speculators were trying to down Jay Gould and his confrères. It was a battle on a gigantic scale in speculation possibly without parallel. Gold was locked up amounting to many millions; as a result, prices of stocks went down; men were wrecked. At a certain time the locked-up money was released, then prices went up. Those who understood the scheme made money; those who did not lost. Jay Gould, being the superior general, won. It is the same old story, repeated every day, not upon so large a scale, perhaps, but with the same purpose in view. Why then this ceaseless denunciation of Jay Gould? Why not arraign the entire brood of men who make money by similar processes? Indeed, if it is gambler rob gambler, who cares which one wins? But it is said that Jay Gould robbed women and orphans. Here again no specifications are made. It is one of those sweeping charges which no one seeks to prove because there is no specific proof. Nor does the public desire proof. It prefers to curse Jay Gould without proof. The captivating form of the charge is that Jay Gould was never more delighted than when "shearing lambs"—that being cold, cruel, and heartless, he delighted in seeing innocence suffer. Such a charge, we apprehend, is totally fallacious. It is true that Jay Gould was a speculator—to use a current and eminently just phrase, he was a gambler in stocks. He put up his money and took his chances. Let it be understood that this form of gambling has the sanction of law, that those who engage in it are often men of culture, pillars in society and in the church. Jay Gould was neither better nor worse than the rank and file of such gamblers, the only difference being that in tact, vigilance, the knowledge of men and conditions, he was superior to all the Wall Street gamblers of his time. He was not always successful, but he had the rare ability to learn important lessons from experience, a quality that all men do not possess.

It is well known that there are multiplied thousands of persons in the United States who, having accumulated a little money, conclude to go into Wall Street and gamble in stocks. These are the "lambs" we hear so much talk about. Of those who win, nothing is heard, but those who lose bleat so loudly that all creation hears, and quick as a flash all creation credits their misfortunes to Jay Gould, when it is doubtless true that in all his life he never knew one of these innocent creatures who tried to better their condition by taking a fly in stocks in Wall Street. Jay Gould's enterprises were on a magnificent scale. When a bull he tackled bears, and when a bear he skinned bulls—but he was never found shearing small fry. He did not fish for minnows; he did not hunt squirrels. His hooks were baited for whale and his gun loaded for b'ar. If Jay Gould wanted to buy certain stocks, he sought by such means as he could command to reduce the price; if he wanted to sell, his tactics were changed and he sought to advance prices. That he accomplished his purposes more frequently than other men accounts for many millions of his vast fortune, but not for all of his accumulations.

Jay Gould is credited with watering stocks.[5] The charge is doubtless true, and at the time of his death a large percentage of his fortune was doubtless pure water. Of all the schemes ever devised for swindling the public, stock watering is probably the most nefarious—but mind you, it is according to law, or there is no law against such public robbery. In this, as in other schemes for moneymaking, Jay Gould was like the rest of the pirates who engage in that sort of business. And it so happens that there is not sufficient public virtue to arrest and crush the outrage. It should be understood that in all cases where crime flourishes under the protection of law, or because there is an absence of law, the public is a partner in the crime and, as investigation would demonstrate, is responsible for much of the present debauchery. The point we make, therefore, is that it is unjust to single out one man for the purpose of denouncing him, when he is only one of many engaged in these disreputable practices; and when it is considered that the laws of the country are silent in such matters, the anathemas of press and pulpit directed against millionaire gamblers might prudently give place to ceaseless bombardment of lawmakers, who for considerations permit wrongs to multiply and go unpunished. In a word, while the state, speaking through its legislature, and the nation, speaking through its Congress, permit nefarious practices to go unpunished, the verdict must be that the state and nation are in league with brazen rascality and equally responsible for existing debauchery.

It is charged, and is doubtless true, that Jay Gould would not hesitate to buy anything on the market that could be turned to account in carrying out his schemes, and that he found judges and legislators for sale, ready to barter opinions and votes for boodle, is not to be denied. But Jay Gould was not alone in this business—only one of many who practiced the demoralizing policy. The public clothed moral deformities with power, and Gould purchased them as he would any other commodity; and yet the public vented its denunciations upon Gould, and continued to place such traitors to truth and justice in places of trust and responsibility—another case in which Gould's morality and business methods were in accord with the standards which the public erected for the measurement of men—hence the appropriateness of William H. Vanderbilt's expression, "The public be damned!" He had a sovereign contempt for the public, because the public, whatever its convictions, lacked the courage required to enact laws with adequate penalties to suppress the machinations of millionaires, when they put in operation machinery to rob their victims, and as Jay Gould was a prince among these fortune makers, it has been popular to visit upon his devoted head a double portion of cheap curses.

But men in the employment of the railroads of the country will ask, after all, what has been Jay Gould's treatment of men employed on his railroads? How has he treated workingmen in his employment when he has been in a position to make his word the law? It is said that at his death he owned or controlled 10,000 miles of railroads and had in his employment 100,000 men. What are these men saying now that Jay Gould is dead? How does Jay Gould compare with McLeod, Corbin, the Vanderbilts, Depew, and other railroad magnates? Has Jay Gould issued orders that his employees shall not belong to labor organizations? Has he employed Pinkerton thugs to murder workingmen? Has he ordered men to shave off their whiskers and button up their coats? Has he sought to inaugurate a policy of robbery and degradation? Try Jay Gould by these standards, and no railroad king in the land expands to grander proportions. Already, lodges of workingmen on lines of railroad controlled by Jay Gould are bearing public testimony of his generous treatment—and one word from such men is more than a thousand columns of newspaper detraction or the vapid utterances of pulpits—and the fact that he placed his interests in a man like S. H. H. Clark[6] is proof conclusive that he was animated by a sincere desire to promote fair dealing with employees on all of his great lines of railroad.

Those who denounce Jay Gould bear testimony that he loved his home, his wife and children; that he was in all things a model husband and father; that he was absolutely uncontaminated in habits and never used his wealth to promote social debaucheries. He did not belong to New York's aristocracy. He was not one of the "400." In this Jay Gould was better, immeasurably better, than the times in which he lived.

He loved money for the power it conferred to make money. He is said to have been charitable, but made no display of his gifts. His life was one continuous battle with speculators—bulls and bears—gamblers. In dealing with them he proved himself to be the superior of them all. They would have sacrificed him had they been able to have accomplished his ruin. They were heartless, but not conquerors. Jay Gould's dispatch to those who were in his confidence, after a battle, was like Caesar's *"Veni, vidi, vici,"*[7] or like Perry's "We have met the enemy and they are ours."[8]

A New Start:
Statement to the Press[†]

February 9, 1893

We have made a start.[9] We antagonize no one. We will organize closely for protection. We have asked for legislative reforms in the various states in matters affecting the interests of railway employees. They have been refused and laughed or bought out of the legislatures. By a compact union, we can make our voice heard in state capitals. Look at the number of men killed annually while on duty in our business whose lives could be saved if we could secure even humane legislation on our behalf.

We will strip our union of the secrecy which has so greatly retarded many labor unions. We will invite the press to hear us talk of our grievances and proposed reforms. Our cause is just. We have nothing to fear from an open discussion of our condition. We propose to conduct the union on simple business principles, keep expenses down, charge small dues, have no beneficiary features, and live simply for mutual protection and the bettering of the condition of all our members.

Strikes as labor weapons are obsolete. We have advanced to a higher scale. With the Australian ballot system[10] and a good, clean, compact organization, we have reason to hope for magnificent results from the American Railway Union.

---

†   Published as "Call It the American Railway Union" in *Chicago Daily Tribune*, vol. 52, no. 41 (February 10, 1893), 3.

Industrial Peace[†]

March 1893

The *Boston Labor Leader* of December 24, 1892 publishes a number of contributions on "industrial peace." Among the contributors is Mr. Edward Atkinson, the inventor of the Aladdin oven, a writer of operas, a robust hater of labor organizations, and probably the most ardent and uncompromising friend of scabs on the continent.

Mr. Atkinson is eminently spectacular. His self-importance could not be improved if he were a peacock or a turkey gobbler, but the real fun of the thing is the way he starts off. "Industrial peace" acts like a plummet in deepsea soundings—brings up things that set scientists to guessing. Mr. Atkinson evidently believes he has discovered the key that lets him into the secrets of what constitutes "industrial peace," and as the Yankees say, he is "tickled," as delighted as the small boy with a tin whistle or a kite, and is as satisfied with himself as were his ancestors when they hung a witch or whipped a Quaker.

One of the peculiarities of Mr. Atkinson is to introduce his discoveries in science and philosophy with Baconian profundities of dictum which he intends shall overwhelm his hearers. When he discovered that a workingman could get a square meal on three cents (provided he cooked his radishes in his Aladdin oven), his utterances were characterized by explosions of knowledge of dynamite detonation, and the same was true when he told the factory hands of Rhode Island they were capitalists and employed the millionaire proprietors of the mills.

In discussing "industrial peace" Mr. Atkinson is equally deep, as for instance he says, "Industrial peace is to be found in personal liberty," and "Personal liberty is maintained when men and women work for whom they please, at such prices as they please and as many hours as they please;" that is to say there should be no labor organization to dictate terms, all should be as free and independent as scabs. If a union man receives $2 a day it is entirely legitimate and in consonance with "industrial peace" for a scab to offer to do the work at $1 a day, and for organized labor to kick is to create industrial war, which the state ought not to tolerate. Mr. Atkinson's idea is to organize a great union of scabs to strike down organized labor, which Mr. George E. McNeill, in the *Labor Leader*, characterizes as follows:

[†]   Published in *Locomotive Firemen's Magazine*, vol. 17, no. 3 (March 1893), 186–188.

The project to form a trades union of men who will not unite upon the question of their wages and hours of labor, but will unite in a grand go-as-you-please scramble for place, reminds me of the military company that voted to parade in time of peace and to disband in time of war.

In this Christmas time our imagination is greatly awakened and the spirit of good will quickened, but I confess that in the wildest flight of dreams well told, none can compare with the dream of a union of non-unionists. Toady workers can combine as toadies, tramps may operate in groups, scabs will appear in numbers where the virus of competition manifests itself on the putrid surface of an enterprise thieves do combine to steal, but a union of non-unionists can only find its parallel in Dante's Inferno.

*   *   *

Liberty is not effeminate, not a toady, not even an Atkinsonian statistician. Liberty is not blind to wrong. Liberty is a spirit, a sentiment, a fact. It finds its best expression in the collective will of men organized for mutual welfare.

Mr. Atkinson evidently believes that industrial peace is industrial degradation, that peace means submission, and that organization means war, in all of which Mr. Atkinson is absolutely correct.

Mr. Atkinson knows several young men who are anxious to engage in the work of unionizing scabs for the purpose of securing industrial peace. If these young men can manage to buy a square meal for three cents, and can unionize scabs on that sort of a dietary platform, it may be that the time is not distant when American workingmen will be able to eat garbage with a relish and beat the Dagos and Huns at their own game.[11]

Industrial peace will come with industrial victory. It will be brought about by industrial valor. It will not come by disbanding labor organizations nor in declaring that the strike, as a weapon, is to be wielded no more. Mr. Atkinson may be able to impress upon New England scabs the glory of that sort of "personal liberty" enjoyed by those base-born creatures who are willing to live on a square meal costing three cents, and to obtain the three cents agree to work for the special benefit of those who reduce them to slaves. But we surmise that even with a Dago constituency, he will find his plans something less than a dazzling success.

Standing Armies[†]

March 1893

Some time since, Edward Everett Hale,[12] writing of "social problems" in the
Cosmopolitan, had a chapter on republics in which he said:

> Quite fundamental in the republican idea is the abolition of large stand-
> ing armies. The true republican expects that every man shall be a soldier
> and do his duty in repelling foreign invasion. It almost follows that in a
> true republic there are no wars of conquest. The republic of France, at this
> moment, is taxing itself beyond all measure simply to maintain an army
> which shall approach the strength of the army of Germany or that of
> Russia. If you asked the tsar of Russia, or the emperor William, in public,
> why Russia or Germany maintain such large armies, the answer would be
> an appeal to national pride and a declaration that it is necessary to main-
> tain such forces in order to preserve the independence of the respective
> empires. But if you could get the tsar of Russia or the emperor William
> into a confessional, and if he should tell you the absolute truth, certain
> that it would not be proclaimed anywhere else, he would say, "I should
> not remain on my throne a month if I did not have an army."

Manifestly, Mr. Hale states the republican idea correctly. He states the
American idea correctly. It was the intention of the founders of the American
republic never to have a large regular or standing army. They knew that such
an army would be a perpetual menace to the liberties of the people; hence
Congress alone has power to raise and support armies. But here comes in a
provision that Congress cannot appropriate money to support armies for a longer period than two years; hence if the appropriation is not made, the armies
become practically disbanded.

The purpose of the fathers of the republic is seen at a glance. They did not
intend that the liberties of the people should be crushed by a standing army or
a "regular" army, and therefore the power to raise and support armies was left
with Congress, the people's representatives. But to make it doubly sure that a
standing army—always and everywhere a menace to liberty—if raised, should
not exist longer than two years, Congress itself is forbidden to appropriate
money for its existence for a period longer than two years. Every two years the

---

†   Published in *Locomotive Firemen's Magazine,* vol. 17, no. 3 (March 1893), 192–194.

people choose their representatives in Congress, and thus hold the power in their own hands.

Let us see what has been the practice of the republic from the first, in the matter of raising and supporting standing armies:

Date		Strength of Army
1789	1 Regiment Infantry, 1 Battery Artillery	840
1792	Indian Border wars	5,120
1794	Peace establishment	3,629
1801	Peace establishment	5,144
1807	Peace establishment	3,278
1810	Peace establishment	7,154
1812	War with Great Britain	11,881
1815	War with Great Britain	9,413
1817-1821	Peace establishment	9,980
1822-1832	Peace establishment	6,184
1833-1837	Peace establishment	7,198
1838-1842	Florida War	12,530
1843-1846	Peace establishment	8,613
1847	Mexican War	17,812
1848	Mexican War	30,890
1849-1855	Peace establishment	10,320
1856-1861	Peace establishment	12,931
1862	Civil War	39,273
1863-1866	Civil War	43,332
1867	Peace establishment	54,641
1868-1869	Peace establishment	52,922
1870	Peace establishment	37,313
1871	Peace establishment	35,353
1872-1874	Peace establishment	32,264
1875-1885	Peace establishment	27,489
1892		Practically the same as 1885

The question arises, what service is this standing army of 27,489 men and officers performing for the country? Some of them are watching Indians, keeping them on their reservations, where a gang of thieves, paid to deal justly by the savages, are robbing and starving them to death—facts proven and denounced in the United States Senate. A portion of our army is housed up in forts scattered over the country, where the officers, in gaudy attire, attend balls and give gorgeous receptions, assume to be the aristocracy, for which the people are taxed from $30 million to $50 million a year, and in addition to this the government military mill annually grinds out a set of officers who are enabled by their salaries, to make angels turn up their noses in silent scorn of their worse-than-turkey-gobbler struttings.

But within a few months past, this "regular army" has been put to a use never dreamed of by the fathers of the American republic. It has been degraded by the president of the United States, who is commander-in-chief, to stand guard at the Couer d'Alene mines in Idaho while a Christless gang of capitalists imported scabs, black, white, and tan, to displace honest laborers, a work which the standing armies of Europe have performed for a thousand years and will continue to perform as long as workingmen permit it to be done.

There may be in some autocrat-cursed country an exhibition of military power more imposing, more impressive and degrading than was seen at Homestead, Buffalo, in the mountains of Tennessee and Idaho, but we have not read of it; and if in the king-cursed countries some things in the same line have occurred, we may thrust them aside and contemplate what the military machines are now doing in the great American republic, not to drive back foreign invaders, not to keep half-starved savages on their reservations, but to enable capitalists to crush organized labor, where gleaming bayonets, flashing swords, and big and little guns, loaded with shot and shell, command organized workingmen to stand aside while degenerate scabs willingly respond to the command of their masters to accept wages which transform American homes into dens and lairs, fit only for wild beasts, bats, and vermin.

From this time forward, if workingmen so will it, they will find themselves the victims of state standing armies, as much so as the subjects of the tsar of Russia or Emperor William of Germany, who, as Mr. Hale remarks, could not remain on their thrones a month were it not for their standing armies.

And just here a remarkable feature of the subject comes into view. These standing armies of states are largely made up, rank and file, of workingmen, men from every department of the industries of the country who, at a moment's warning, may be called upon to stand guard while scabs, as at Homestead and Buffalo, step in and accept such wages as employers see proper to pay, and thus become the architects of their own degradation.

Carnegie Returns†

April 1893

During the closing days of January 1893, Mr. Andrew Carnegie, after an extended sojourn abroad, found himself again on American soil.

During his absence the Homestead horror, under the management of H. C. Frick, occurred. Andrew Carnegie, having posed before the American public, and as much of the world outside as he could reach, as a sublimated millionaire, making money only for the purpose of conferring benefits upon the poor, would, it was believed, if appealed to, arrest and change the murderous and damnable policy of Frick in the management of the Carnegie mills at Homestead. He was appealed to by his old, tried, and faithful employees to interpose in their behalf and see that simple justice was done them.

At the time these appeals were made, Carnegie was in his castle in Scotland, wallowing and rioting in the wealth which his Homestead employees had made it possible for him to secure. In his castle halls there was music, and dancing, and feasting. Carnegie was surrounded by British and Scotch nabobs whom he was entertaining in princely splendor, and when from out of his mills, once the center of peace, prosperity, and contentment, but transformed into a hell by Frick, there came to him appeals for help, it was a supreme opportunity for Carnegie; one word from him, the principal owner of the property, would have sufficed. Frick, the bloodthirsty monster, would have cowered and slunk into quietude, like a wild beast under the lash of its keeper. But Carnegie did not respond; silent as a brass dog, he saw the electric batteries erected around his mills and the scalding water machinery completed to kill workingmen because they demanded fair wages. He saw Pinkerton murderers, hired from the slums of cities and armed with deadly weapons to murder at the word of command, flocking to Homestead; or if he did not see these murderous schemes progressing, he knew of them, but said not a word; he made no sign, or if he did take notice of them, it was to approve of Frick's plans and urge him forward in his satanic work, and as a righteous result, the ineffable infamy earned by Frick attaches, without a modifying circumstance, to Carnegie, and will remain upon his name, indelible stains, forever. Like the mark upon Cain, he will carry them to his grave.

---

†   Published as "Carnegie" in *Locomotive Firemen's Magazine*, vol. 17, no. 4 (April 1893), 273–276.

When Carnegie arrived in Washington city, report had it that during his stay "startling developments" would occur upon his arrival at Pittsburgh. It was reported that

> Carnegie was not at all pleased with the unpleasant prominence into which he was brought by the late Homestead riots. The fact that he has made millions of dollars out of his "protected" industries argued rather badly for him when an attempt was made to reduce the wages of his men. Moreover, it is said that some of the indicted men are old employees of the company, between whom and Mr. Carnegie the most cordial relations exist. It is believed, therefore, that Mr. Carnegie will use what influence he possesses to have the indictments quashed and the sentences of those men who may be convicted made as light as possible. Those who saw the Pittsburgh millionaire yesterday say that he has aged considerably in the last year, and that his appearance indicates the severe strain to which he has been subjected since the riots began.

This turns out to be the sheerest poppycock. His works have doubtless lost money by Frick's policy of robbery and murder, and have gained an infamous notoriety. These facts doubtless have caused the Scotchman unrest. He loves to make money, give a few thousands, now and then, just to advertise his purity and philanthropy and brace up his "Gospel of Wealth." He likes to strut and pose as an Abou Ben Adhem, one who loves his fellow man,[13] but his unqualified endorsement of Frick makes all of his pretension in that line just so much despicable duplicity. After a column of the most disgusting bosh about not hoarding money, and the assertion "I shall never accumulate money," he says:

> And now one word about Mr. Frick, whom I recommended to the Carnegie Steel Company (Limited) as its chairman, and my successor, four years ago.
>
> I am not mistaken in the man, as the future will show. Of his ability, fairness, and pluck, no one has now the slightest question. His four years' management stamps him as one of the foremost managers in the world. I would not exchange him for any manager I know. People generally are still to learn of those virtues which his partners and friends know well. If his health be spared, I predict that no man who ever lived in Pittsburgh and managed business there will be better liked or admired by his employees than my friend and partner Henry Clay Frick. I do not believe any man will be more valuable for the city. His are the qualities that wear. He never disappoints. What he promises he more than fulfills. Good workmen or able men who wish to do what is fair and right will learn to

appreciate Mr. Frick. Neither inefficient officials nor bad, unreasonable, violent workmen does he like, and these will not thrive with him.

The public will want to hear no more from Andrew Carnegie. He is hand-in-glove, heart and soul, body and brains, money and muscle, including electricity, hot water, and Pinkerton thugs, in alliance with Frick. What Frick has done is unequivocally endorsed, and he does not hesitate to outrage public opinion by beslobbering the monster with his fulsome eulogies. Had Carnegie concluded to bestow flatulent commendation upon any successful buccaneer, land pirate, or train wrecker, they would have been received by the American public as quite as appropriate as his florid endorsement of H. C. Frick, who is accounted as the most detestable villain, whose money gives him power to rob and degrade workingmen.

The American public did feel a lively interest in the utterances of Carnegie relative to the Homestead horrors. He had for years posed before the public as a mortal of seraphic mold, a millionaire hog with improved snout, with grunt and greed eliminated, a man who by some miraculous power had had all the devils cut out of him and, with eyes turned heavenward, panted like a wind-broken horse for opportunities to do good, and now where do we find him? Sitting on Frick's knees with his arms around his neck, besliming him as an anaconda does a calf preparatory to swallowing him neck and heels—Carnegie and Frick wedded and welded together by the cohesive power of plunder.

After this the American public will not care a pinch of snuff what becomes of Andrew Carnegie. He is rich and can rest in luxuries purchased by his ill-gotten money, and like the rich man we read about, he may be heard from eventually bemoaning his thirst and willing to part with his vast wealth, including his castle in the Highlands, for "a drop of cold water," which Frick would doubtless give him if he were not baking in a coke oven close at hand and himself quite as thirsty as Carnegie.

Coming Events†

April 1893

The dogma "history repeats itself" is of universal acceptation. Is it true? The answer is yes, and no—each correct from different points of view. We omit all records of physical phenomena. In such matters history daily repeats itself. The tides ebb and flow, comets come and go, as do the seasons. Earthquakes and cyclones, as of old, leave their reservations and go on the warpath to perpetrate their devastations. In recording such things history repeats itself. But in regard to matters relating to men and nations, as in bygone centuries, history does not repeat itself, and will never again repeat itself—that is to say, in all cases there will be such modifications as to destroy the parallels. Anything approximating a careful analysis of the subject must lead to the conclusion that coming events in human affairs are to be totally unlike the events which history has recorded of the past in that line.

We are not unmindful that in writing of the future the idea suggests infinity and therefore reaches beyond all mental grasp, and that no man knoweth what the future has in store for the world. Nevertheless we know what history has recorded, and we know what is now transpiring, and however exhaustive the search we find no instance in which history is repeating itself. Events as they occur are unlike former events, and it may be observed that when approximations are noticed there are such modifications as to create wide dissimilarity.

No one supposes that history will repeat itself in recording such events as relate to the Jews, to the rise and fall of the Assyrian, Persian, Egyptian, and Roman empires, and to others that could be named. Conditions have changed to an extent that makes the repetition of such records impossible. We are aware of the claim that human nature is "the same yesterday, today, and forever." Insofar as the attributes of human nature are concerned, the statement is doubtless true, and we would not change them if we could. We would not have man a machine—an automaton—but it is nevertheless true that human nature is susceptible of vast improvement, ranging upward from the degeneracy of the Hottentot to the full-orbed intellect of a Sir Isaac Newton, and it is this fact of mind development that is changing the character of events, and therefore, as a matter of course, making it impossible for history to repeat itself. Hence

---

†   Published in *Locomotive Firemen's Magazine,* vol. 17, no. 4 (April 1893), 276–278.

however schooled men may be in "mystical lore," and however capable of interpreting the "shadows of coming events," the event itself will, if it comes, be unlike events of the past.

We do not doubt that the law of cause and effect is irrevocable, nor do we doubt that the law exists in human affairs as certainly as in nature. Idleness is the prolific parent of vice; ignorance breeds superstition, etc., to the end of the chapter; but in the steady advancement of human nature, antagonistic forces have been put in operation which modify effects, change results, and hence history chronicles events essentially different from those which occurred in the past, when such antagonistic forces were not in operation.

Take for instance the dogma of a "divine right to rule," unchallenged for centuries. We now behold an opposing force in the field—call it truth, if you please. It is quite as much an attribute of human nature as error, and is everywhere wrecking error. It bombards thrones, autocracy, plutocracy, and aristocracy, and champions democracy, or the rights of the people. It is the eternal foe of ignorance and the hope of the world. It brings into flaming prominence the poetic prophecy of Bryant:

> Truth, crush'd to earth, shall rise again;
>   The eternal years of God are hers;
> But Error, wounded, writhes in pain,
>   And dies among his worshippers.[14]

This development of all the attributes of human nature is to change coming events. Nothing is more certain in human affairs, and within the entire realm of investigation there is nothing more cheering to the world of labor.

We do not doubt that the era has dawned when the capitalistic class will put forth its mightiest efforts to change the trend of labor affairs; all the signs point in that direction. But labor, observant of forces and factors, proposes that history shall record events quite different from those which have occurred in the past, when autocrats marshaled their hosts for the fray and labor paid all the penalties of defeat.

It is a campaign of education, pure and simple, and the supreme question is, what shall be the character of coming events? Labor can, if it will, require history to chronicle events such as the world has not known since "the morning stars sang together and the sons of God shouted for joy."[15]

Congress, Pinkertons, and Organized Labor†

April 1893

The Senate of the United States appointed a select committee to investigate and report to the Senate the facts in relation to the employment, for private purposes, of armed bodies of men or detectives in connection with differences between employers and employees.

This select committee has made its report, which shows that the committee examined 14 different witnesses on the thug side of the question, including the Pinkertons themselves, and with regard to the Homestead infamy, the part played by the thugs, H. C. Frick, the murderous monster and pimp of Carnegie, and Bob Pinkerton were examined, and eight other witnesses. The committee, in examining questions directly bearing upon labor and labor strikes, called in 17 witnesses. Four witnesses were examined upon questions relating to the power of the courts to interfere to prevent labor strikes, and 15 witnesses were examined upon the subject of arbitration and other matters of inquiry proper for the committee to pursue.

The investigation led to the admission on the part of the Pinkerton brothers, who hire, organize, arm, and equip the thugs, and then supply Carnegie, Frick, and others of their ilk, with as many murderers as they demand to kill workingmen, that the presence of these thugs served to unduly inflame the passions of the men who strike against oppression and degradation. There are, it was ascertained, in the ranks of the thugs, trained spies who, assuming to be mechanics, enter the ranks of the strikers and, obtaining information, report to employers and thereby enable them to spot and discharge certain men who dare protest against outrages, and thus make it possible for scabs to obtain the places of honest workingmen.

Having obtained such information from the two brother Pinkertons, whose names stand for as much infamy as fell to the lot of Judas Iscariot or Benedict Arnold, or any other villains our corrupt civilization has spread upon society, the committee reached the conclusion that if corporations would discontinue the employment of Pinkerton thugs on occasions of threatened or existing strikes, their interests would be better subserved.

The committee also reached the conclusion that the employment of the Pinkerton thugs at Homestead was "unnecessary." Prior to the introduction

---

†   Published in *Locomotive Firemen's Magazine*, vol. 17, no. 4 (April 1893), 259–262.

of the thugs by Frick, the committee found that "not the slightest damage was done nor attempted to be done to property on the part of the strikers." Hence it may be inferred that the passions of the strikers were inflamed by the introduction of a gang of armed thugs, ready and willing to murder the strikers at the word of command, and that they did not murder hundreds of them in the interest of Carnegie and Frick is a mystery, unless it is explained by the heroic determination on the part of the strikers to sell their lives as dearly as possible; a resolution that brought the thugs to terms, and sent them, for the first and only time, defeated and crushed, without having accomplished their murderous mission.

The committee, in its deliberations, reached the following conclusions:

1. Rights of employers and workmen are equal.
2. Employers have an undoubted right, provided they fulfill their agreements, to employ and dismiss men at pleasure.
3. Workmen can legally organize for mutual protection and improvement.
4. When dissatisfied with wages or hours, they should attempt to arbitrate.
5. Failing in this, they have a right to discontinue work, either singly or in a body.
6. Having discontinued, they have no right, legal or moral, by force or intimidation, to keep others from taking their places, or to attempt to occupy, injure, or destroy the property of their employers.
7. In all controversies, arbitration having failed, reliance should be placed upon the power and adequacy of the law.
8. Whether assumedly legal or not, the employment of armed bodies of men for private purposes, either by employers or employees, should not be resorted to, and such use is an assumption of the state's authority by private citizens.
9. States have undoubted authority to legislate against the employment of armed bodies of men for private purposes; but the power of Congress to so legislate is not clear, although it would seem that Congress ought not to be powerless to prevent the movement of such bodies from one state to another.

In the foregoing conclusions, nos. 1, 2, 3, 4, and 5 are those which will attract the most attention. The equality stated in no. 1, as matters stand, is totally misleading—the rights of employers and employees, only in a restricted sense, are equal—and this is seen in conclusion no. 2, in which it is glaringly shown that the employee has no rights whatever; the right to hire and the right to discharge an employee is placed absolutely in the hands of the employer; the employee is not consulted at all. He may be discharged for any cause which the whim or malignity of the employer may suggest, and according to this Senate committee, he has no redress; his work, his means of living, are taken from him, and he is forthwith remanded to the ranks of the idle, and he may go to the devil for aught the employer knows or cares; hence we ask what becomes of conclusion no. 1?

Does someone say that conclusion no. 3, which asserts that "workmen can legally organize for mutual protection and improvement," provide any remedy against conclusion no. 2? We answer, none whatever, because, conceding the absolute right of the employer to discharge an employee, any protest on the part of organized labor to remedy the outrage would be interfering with a conceded right of the employer.

To illustrate, A has a legal right to join a labor organization, but for the exercise of this legal right, B, the employer, according to conclusion no. 2, may discharge A "at pleasure," and thus it is seen that while the equality of "employers and employees" is asserted, the equality is a sham and deception, having no practical existence, so far as the conclusions of the committee are concerned.

To establish conditions in some measure approaching equality has been the earnest effort of organized labor. As for instance, A, an employee, is discharged. Just here organized labor comes in and asks of the employer, Why? and insists that A shall not be discharged without a hearing, something in the form of a trial, that he shall not be set adrift to gratify the spleen of some parasite and made to suffer penalties innocently. If the committee had suggested something of this sort, something to check the meanness or venom of underlings, it would have been far more creditable than the one-sided conclusions the committee reported. The other conclusions are a series of old chestnuts, which it were a waste of time and paper to discuss. There is just one way out of the woods for organized labor to pursue, and that is to go forward pleading the cause of union, federation, united, and compact organization and action, to create a bond of union so strong that unity will be secured when there is a conflict between right and wrong, truth and error, and to force the fight into legislative halls and to never cease the struggle until there shall be, in fact, in reality, truth in the declaration that the "rights of employers and employees are equal."

The Hawaiian Islands†

April 1893

During the year of 1778, Captain James Cook, a celebrated English navigator, discovered the Hawaiian or Sandwich Islands. There are eight islands in the group, having an area of about 6,000 square miles. These islands are situated between 18 and 22 degrees north latitude and are about 2,000 miles southwest from San Francisco.

Their products are tropical and semi-tropical, such as coffee, sugar, tobacco, arrowroot, cocoa, zano,[16] wheat, sandalwood, and taro. Cattle and sheep are numerous.

When Captain Cook discovered the islands 115 years ago, their inhabitants were savages and cannibals, and numbered, it is estimated, about 800,000.

Captain Cook having become involved in a dispute with the natives, they murdered him on St. Valentine's Day, 1779, and probably cooked him.

Some years after the discovery of the islands, the missionary spirit, particularly of the United States, centered largely in the interest of the heathen Hawaiians, and it was found that they, with exceptional readiness, received instruction, and when about 50 years had elapsed the Hawaiians had been converted to Christianity. Here and there an old timer had an idol hidden away, and a few retained a relish for human steaks and choice roasting pieces, but as a general thing they had abandoned their savage customs and adopted civilized ways.

But as is seen by the rapid decrease of native population, civilization did not agree with them, since in less than one hundred years of civilizing methods, the nation has decreased from 800,000 to about 35,000, and the remaining remnant, as the auctioneers say, are "going," and in another 50 years will be gone.

According to the census of 1890, the population of the Hawaiian group "consisted of 34,436 natives, 6,186 half-castes, 7,495 born in Hawaii of foreign parents, 15,301 Chinese, 12,360 Japanese, 8,602 Portuguese, 1,928 Americans, 1,344 British, 1,034 Germans, 227 Norwegians, 70 French, 588 Polynesians, and 419 other foreigners, in all, 89,990 souls." The proposition now is to

---

†   Published as "The Hawaiian, or Sandwich Islands" in *Locomotive Firemen's Magazine*, vol. 17, no. 4 (April 1893), pp. 271–273.

annex these islands to the United States, to make them one of the territories of the American Republic and eventually constitute them a state of the union.

Speaking of the products of the islands, it is proper to remark that leprosy commands special attention, so much so that one island is entirely given up to its transplantation from other islands, where it is permitted to develop and go to seed, and the crop is annually increasing.

Of the 89,990 souls on the Hawaiian Islands, not more than 2,675 would make desirable citizens, leaving 86,315 souls that ought never to be annexed to the United States under any circumstances. The Chinese, Japanese, and Polynesians are simply so many slaves who do the work of the islands, and the annexation would therefore not only afford no outlet to American labor, but would serve to degrade labor, as it is everywhere degraded in all tropical and semi-tropical lands, and it might therefore be prudent for organized labor to be heard upon the subject of annexation.

It is believed by some people who profess to be students of cause and effect, and of coming events, that in due time, and at no distant day, all of North America will be under the jurisdiction of the "star-spangled banner," sometimes called "Old Glory," and it may be, in addition, that Cuba will be included; but this thing of going 2,000 miles to sea to secure 6,000 square miles of volcanic islands is not thought to be "manifest destiny," but up to the present "manifest destiny" is a puzzle no one is able to solve; hence there is no telling what will occur, should Uncle Sam find himself the victim of a well-developed case of annexing fever. But this thing of annexing about 30,000 Chinese, Japanese, and Polynesians to get 6,000 square miles of lava beds and the largest volcano in the world ought not to be done with a hop, skip, and jump for the gratification of a few millionaires who alone will be the beneficiaries.

Law, Lawmakers, and Politics[†]

April 1893

The government of the United States is based upon constitutions called organic law, the foundation for all statute law. Every state in the union also has a constitution which must conform to the provisions of the Constitution of the United States. The constitution-making power is lodged in the people. It is this fact that proclaims and establishes the sovereignty of the people.

If there is anything wrong in the constitution of the republic or in the constitution of a state, it is the high prerogative of the people to abolish the wrong. A constitution may be amended by the people or abolished by the people. The people constitute a sovereign, all-pervading power. The theory is that in making and amending constitutions, a majority rules; but constitutions, in their provisions protecting all the people alike, guard the rights of minorities from encroachments by majorities, since majorities, like autocrats, if not restrained, become arrogant and oppressive.

Notwithstanding such guards and limitations, majorities often transcend such defenses and securities, which brings into action another shield against congressional and legislative arrogance known as the "veto power," a power lodged with the chief executive of the republic and of the states, which forbids the enactment of a law designed to work wrong to the people. In such cases, the veto is generally effective, since it requires a two-thirds vote of both houses, either of Congress or a legislature, to enact the law, though in some cases only a majority is required to set aside the veto, and in some of the states the constitution does not give the chief executive the veto power, holding that the will of the majority ought of right to be supreme.

There is also provided in all constitutions another safeguard against the operation of laws which strike down the rights of the people. This power is lodged in what is called the Supreme Court, where, under certain forms of procedure, an unconstitutional law may be abrogated, and multiplied instances of such decisions of supreme courts are annually recorded. Nevertheless, after the most critical disquisitions upon constitutions, it is found that the latitude given lawmakers has extraordinary sweep, and, as a result, under the operation of such powers, laws are enacted which strike down, under the decisions of the

---

†   Published in *Locomotive Firemen's Magazine,* vol. 17, no. 4 (April 1893), 264–267.

courts, the most sacred rights of citizens.

It would seem practicable to frame laws in such simple and easily understood language that "a wayfaring man, though a fool" might comprehend their meaning, but it so happens that laws touching great interests are so framed that only lawyers are able to solve their mysteries, and to the average man they might as well be written in Coptic as in English. In such laws, when the fee warrants the hunt, a provision, a technicality, a word easily tortured to mean anything or nothing, as may best suit the interests of the rich and powerful client, is found which often befogs judge and jury, so that brazen rascality goes unscathed while innocence, left to contend against such laws, receives the stamp of infamy. The records are burdened with such cases, the laws being so constructed that as a net, the whales go through unharmed while minnows are caught, or upon the principle of the man in search of game, and having doubts in a certain case whether he saw a deer or a calf, fired so as to miss it if it were a calf, and kill it if it were a deer.

All men are interested in the laws of the republic, state and national, because they are the subjects of law; their lives are, in a large measure, regulated by law—law touches their interests at a thousand points—therefore since politics is the science of government and government being based upon laws, every citizen, and none more than workingmen, has a profound interest in politics, an interest from which only cowardice or debased ignorance could by any possibility absolve them. It is here that the sovereignty of the people comes prominently into view. It is here that the ballot becomes the bulwark, the palladium of men's rights, their liberty, and their independence. It is not a partisan question, only insofar as men discover that one party favors just laws and their honest administration more than another party.

Such reflections are in line with the efforts of labor just now to secure the enactment by Congress and by legislatures of certain laws designed to place workingmen's interests on a level with the interests of capitalists; hence there are in every state labor legislative committees presenting bills and asking the representatives of the people to enact them into laws. These committees ignore parties and work to enthrone principles. They present to lawmakers conditions of long standing, in which they demonstrate by facts that flagrant wrongs exist; as, for instance, they show that in the operation of railroads, thousands are killed and maimed annually because of imperfect machinery, and they ask that this slaughter may be reduced to the lowest point practicable, by a law compelling the introduction of life-saving appliances. It is a case in which the dead appeal to the lawmakers; it is a case in which thousands of men present maimed hands and arms and legs, and demand redress. It is a case in which widows and orphans appeal to the lawmakers to rescue the wives and children of others from the same wretched fate.

Again, organized workingmen and all workingmen who have ideas superior to those of scabs and convicts demand the enactment of laws which shall put an end to penalties inflicted by employers upon their choice as freemen to join a labor organization. To join such an organization is a constitutional right, nor is there anywhere in this broad land a statute which prohibits such an exercise of inherent right. This being true, workingmen demand that employers shall not have the power, directly or indirectly, by contract written or oral, to inflict any penalty whatever for the exercise of such a right.

We would suppose that upon such a proposition the workingmen of America would be a unit, and that in every state they would bring their power to bear to induce legislators to enact a law emancipating them from such slavish bondage, that upon such questions they would mass their sovereignty and sweep away the last vestige of the power of employers to degrade and oppress them.

It would be an easy task to catalog laws which oppress labor, and to suggest other laws which would relieve labor of antiquated wrongs so flagrant that it creates astonishment that they have not long ago been abolished, as for instance the infamous co-employee abomination which strikes down the claim of A for damages because of the incompetency or negligence of B, a co-employee—a wrong that exists independent of statute and is based entirely upon the decisions of courts, running back into the twilight of English jurisprudence, when workingmen were mere cattle and their employers were masters. Still the infamy exists, and employers, who are the beneficiaries of the wrong, have hitherto been able to crush, in most of the states, all remedial legislation.

It is to be hoped that upon such things labor may be induced to unify, and taking the aggressive in politics, bring about the reform required.

Self-Made Men[†]

April 1893

The term "self-made men" is seemingly paradoxical—since men who rise from obscurity to eminence in any of the walks of life must have been assisted by agencies quite independent of themselves—and yet men are properly styled self-made who, without parents or friends to discover those inherent qualities of mind which achieve success, hew out their pathways to distinction self-directed.

It has been truly said that American institutions are preeminently favorable for the development of the mind forces of the masses of the people, that to use a phrase somewhat slangish, those who start out in life under unfavorable conditions may get "on top" if they have the required amount of "sand," that is to say courage, pertinacity, diligence, and that superiority of soul which patiently endures privation, that clear vision which sees victory from afar, and that tenacity of purpose which defies obstacles, and steadily marches toward the goal of success. In such regards, there is no country on the face of the earth that offers equal opportunities to those which distinguish the United States of America—nor, indeed, approximates them. Such facts, whatever may be said of them by those born rich, are of the greatest possible significance to that vast majority who were born poor.

The subject, self-made men, at once presents temptations for discursive writing. It brings into view the declaration of a self-evident truth that men in the United States of America, whatever may be said of other lands, are created equal, that is to say, birth establishes no prerogative for one class that is not equally the right of all other classes, among which, and all of which, are the rights to "life, liberty and the pursuit of happiness." It may be true, and from certain indications there are reasons for believing the statement, that opportunities for aspiring youth to overcome the disadvantages which poverty creates are not as numerous now as in the earlier days of the republic, and that, as a result, self-made men are less frequently heard of in public affairs. We doubt if such conclusions are well founded. On the contrary, we think, if the facts could be ascertained, the conclusion would be that self-made men are rapidly multiplying, though it may be true that there are fewer of the type in positions

---

†   Published in *Locomotive Firemen's Magazine*, vol. 17, no. 4 (April 1893), 267–271.

to attract the public gaze—the reason being that self-made men are making themselves along lines of endeavor other than political distinction.

It has been justly said that the largest share of the mind forces of the country is no longer attracted by the glare and glamour of political preferment. Indeed, it is asserted that the most brilliant intellects are not found in what is called the "learned professions." If this is true of men whose youth was favored with opportunities for education and powerful friends, wealth and its influences, it is reasonable that youths less favorably situated, as they unaided solve problems and advance, will also in a great majority of cases seek their welfare by identifying themselves with the great industrial enterprises of the period, and this is really what is happening.

It is true that our legislatures and congresses, courts and bare, are overrun with *half*-made men. The people, strange to say, tolerate these *misfits* for a time and then discard them, and as a result, there are judges without bench or ermine, lawyers without clients, legislators without a constituency. If we proceed with the investigation of dead failures, we find clergymen without pulpits and doctors without patients—and these exhibitions of failures are fruitful of determinations on the part of many a brainy youth who has his fortune to make, by virtue of pluck and perseverance not to accept elegant pauperism and decayed dignity as examples, but to make himself useful by mastering some trade, and with such equipment, await events, ready and qualified at all times for promotion, and here it should be said that the term "self-made" invariably implies success.

We read from time to time of railroad men who have advanced from indigence and obscurity to positions of responsibility, and it is noteworthy that in every instance they are self-made men, students from the start—students of men, of things, of books, of everything pertaining to their chosen calling—indomitable and indefatigable, they were always engaged in the *self-making* business. Such men—and it is a misfortune that their biographies are not printed—are splendid examples to all youths who must make themselves, must rise by their own willpower, or remain forever at the bottom of the ladder.

The biographical history of the United States abounds with the names of illustrious men who struggled up from conditions of extreme poverty, a poverty which triumphantly demonstrates the possibility of success when there is willpower and an unyielding purpose to advance, regardless of obstacles.

It is doubtless true that the most illustrious self-made man the United States has produced was Abraham Lincoln. The advancement of this youth from squalor and illiteracy to the summit of fame, to brighten as the centuries go by, reads like fiction—and yet every incident in the life of the great citizen from youth bears irrefutable testimony that where there is a will, there is a way to "sound all the depths and shoals of honor" and win victories all along the line. Poor, friendless, illiterate, required to toil as a mere farmhand or a flatboatman, he read, thought, toiled, and advanced—in everything a self-made man.

Henry Wilson[17] of Massachusetts was another splendid type of a self-made man—in some regards, perhaps, more pronounced than Abraham Lincoln. The son of a farm laborer in bleak New Hampshire from childhood till he was of age; one year at school was the limit of opportunities in that direction. Apprenticed to a farmer at ten years of age, he remained until he was twenty-one, but though his school days were few, he managed to read a thousand books during the period of his bondage. Quitting the farm, he learned the shoemaker's trade, and by frugality saved enough from his wages to enable him to add to his limited learning, and thus aided in overcoming the disadvantages of poverty, he steadily advanced to political positions till he reached the vice presidential office of his country. Henry Wilson, the "Natick cobbler," the poor boy and self-made man, represented the state of Massachusetts in the United States Senate and placed his name beside those of the most distinguished sons of that old commonwealth, and at no period of his career was Massachusetts required to blush for his words or acts.

If the Adamses, Websters, Everetts, and Choates had borne high and advanced the banner of the old Bay state in the arena of learning and statesmanship, Henry Wilson, the self-made man, never lowered it the fraction of an inch.

Andrew Johnson, the North Carolina youth, was, if possible, poorer than Henry Wilson—and in his boyhood and early manhood was more unfavorably situated for advancement. Scarcely knowing his alphabet when of age, simply a tailor, with an aged mother to support, he cut and stitched and pressed and studied, and in a state surrounded by an aristocracy of wealth and refinement, he became governor of Tennessee, a United States senator, and president of the United States.

We could fill the pages of the *Magazine* for a twelve-month with the achievements of self-made men who, in every department of human endeavor, have won success and renown, but the instances briefly referred to must suffice. If these awaken no aspirations on the part of the readers of the *Magazine* who find themselves in positions not dissimilar to Lincoln, Webster, and Johnson, then it were folly to extend the list.

We desire, however, to deduce from such incidents practical lessons for locomotive firemen of our brotherhood. They enter the service of railroads, hoping at least to become engineers. Thousands of them succeed—some reach higher positions. There are thousands of firemen who will never become engineers, simply because they do not desire promotion. They are ignorant and prefer to remain so. They complain of their hard fate but are everlastingly attributing their failures to the wrong cause. They are not students of anything. Ask them to undergo an examination and to write out the answers to questions, and they will decline because they cannot *spell.* They will expend dollars for beer and whisky, but never ten cents to purchase a dictionary or a grammar. Ask them to solve a simple problem in arithmetic, and their ignorance will compel them to decline the task. This illiteracy, stupidity, lack of ambition forever keeps them at the bottom. They see others advance, and instead of emulating their example, they prefer pool to school, and choose to hammer coal and shovel it into a firebox rather than employ their leisure in learning what they must know if they expect to rise.

What is the remedy? We know of but one. There is but one—and that is to resolve upon a change of habits—renounce follies and vices, obtain elementary books, and study. All self-made men have done this in the past, and men who are *making* themselves are doing it now, and will continue to do it as long as the world stands.

A Workingman's Congress[†]

April 1893

The *Magazine* propounds the question: Would a workingman's congress be a move in the right direction? If not, why not? What can be said in favor of such a movement? Is the time ripe for it? What could it do if convened?

Just now, what would be a move in the right direction for workingmen to make? We refer to organized workingmen, for they are the workingmen who think, who want to accomplish something for their own benefit and for the toilers who shall inherit their tasks.

We do not now discuss the federation of organizations, but rather the unification of the mind forces of organization; deliberation, rather than federation.

True, all organizations have their annual or biennial conventions for deliberation and for the enactment of laws for their government, and it occurs in these conventions that those whose expressions are made public are taking ever broader views of labor problems, and it would be difficult to chronicle a fact more creditable to the heads and hearts of men who have advanced to the responsible position of leaders.

It is worthy of remark that in all the labor organizations of the country are to be found men of broad and liberal views, students of industrial affairs, profoundly interested in the welfare of workingmen, but forever confined to their particular organization, they are handicapped; they never advance to their full measure; in a sense, fenced in. They discuss measures which relate to their particular organization when, in fact, labor questions in their legitimate scope touch the wageworkers of the nation, and in a labor congress there would be opportunities to bring into commanding and merited prominence labor questions in which all are vitally interested.

We are profoundly impressed with the idea that the country cannot know the wealth of mind forces which labor possesses until a labor congress is convened, and we are quite as much persuaded that such a congress would prove a revelation to those who regard labor organizations with a species of contempt and lofty disdain, as composed of men who are small intellectually and whose minds are chiefly occupied in accomplishing small things, men chiefly desirous of promoting organized jealousies, of feathering their own nests, to be wiped

---

†   Published in *Locomotive Firemen's Magazine*, vol. 17, no. 4 (April 1893), 262–264.

out of existence whenever organized capital deems it prudent to squelch them.

We do not state the position of affairs too narrowly. It is only required to read the monopolistic press to verify our declarations. In it you will find no complimentary declarations relating to organized labor, and the question arises, is organized labor doing those things which ought to be done and which can be done to change the estimate which a subsidized press ceaselessly puts forth?

We are not opposed to what organized labor is doing. On the contrary, we have only words of commendation for what we see and hear. Labor Day gives opportunities for parades, for many and valuable recreations, splendid addresses, etc., but we advocate something different, better, higher, more important. We should like to see a stately parade of labor's mind forces, free from badges, gewgaws, brass bands, and all things spectacular; a labor congress of labor's intellectual men debating questions which, day by day, are becoming the vital questions of the times in which we live; questions that are up for debate in the parliaments of the world, and in which labor, more than any other interest, is concerned. Such a congress, composed of labor's representative men, would arouse continental interest. The press would not and could not ignore it. The plutocratic class would stand amazed in its presence. It would be a proclamation that workingmen know their rights and are not ready to be enslaved. What says the labor press of the country? The labor congress proposition is up for debate. May we hope to have the views of others?

ARU Permanently Organized: Statement to the Press[†]

April 11, 1893

The union will be formed of all classes of railway employees working on trains, tracks, in shops, offices, anywhere.[18] They will be organized by the branch of work they do. There will be a central body composed of one delegate from each of those branches, and then there will be a president, secretary, and treasurer. That's the plan. There will be no benevolent features. It is formed for mutual protection and the promotion of the interests of the working railroad men. Its home will be in Chicago.

We will open permanent headquarters here as soon as we adjourn and send out from here our organizers over all railway lines.

We will hold a mass meeting at an early day in Chicago to talk to railway-men and the public and state our purposes.

This fall we will hold a grand convention in Chicago, which will form the basis from which will date hereafter our quadrennial conventions, for we are building to endure.

---

†   Published as "All Railway Men: National Federation Will Embrace Every Branch," in *Chicago Tribune*, vol. 52, no. 102 (April 12, 1893), 9.

Labor Deliberation[†]

May 1893

At Muskegon, Michigan, the state federation of labor recently held a meeting and deliberated upon certain propositions relating to labor, law, military affairs, and politics. "A short day for women and children" was proposed and adopted. It would have been better to have proposed that there be no workday at all for children, long or short. Children should have no labor tasks. Their bodies and their minds should not be dwarfed and stunted by toil. Children all over the country are made physical, moral, and mental deformities by excess in work, and the land everywhere is being filled with the degenerate progeny of women who were overworked in childhood. When parents become so debased and brutified as to drive their children to work during their tender years, their children should be removed from their custody. They are disqualified from rearing children.

A proposition was debated to appoint a union workingman as the commissioner of labor for the state. A move in the right direction and eminently consistent with the prevailing policy in such matters, since, if there is to be appointed a commissioner of banking, a banker or an acknowledged financier would be sought for, and so on through the list.

A resolution was passed "favoring the approval by the people of all legislation, before it becomes operative." In this resolution is found all the earmarks of the impracticable in lawmaking; a vagary of such proportions that even a cursory examination of it makes it ridiculous.

Suppose for instance a member of the legislature offers a bill, making it a felony to discharge a workingman because he belonged to a labor organization? And suppose the bill passes and becomes a law? What reason is there for submitting such legislation to the people for their endorsement? Suppose a legislature passes a bill appropriating money, say $100,000, to defray the expenses of the session. To submit the question to the people would cost, say, $200,000. But suppose all the acts of a legislature, as contemplated by the resolution, should be submitted to the people, say 150 acts or laws. What would be the outcome of such a proceeding? The mere mention of such contingencies illustrates the folly of all such schemes, and labor, when in council, should sit down upon them. They are the rankest vagaries—impracticable and practically impossible.

---

†   Published in *Locomotive Firemen's Magazine,* vol. 17, no. 5 (May 1893), 355–357.

The military question was brought forward by a resolution declaring it to be "contrary to the best interests of unionism for men to belong to the state troops." There were those in the convention who held that it was well "to have union men in the militia because in a pinch they would shoot over the strikers' heads rather than at them," and "during the debate on state troops one delegate created a sensation by stating that in one company of militia, the Flint blues, stationed at Flint, he knew of union men who were going to withdraw because they would not go out to fire on striking unionists." It is not surprising that labor conventions and assemblies are taking special interest in the militia business, the military machine, since it is becoming well understood that the states have no use under heaven for an army, except to respond to the requests of the Carnegies and Fricks and other robbers of labor.

Whether union workingmen should volunteer in such armies or keep out of them is a question of two sides. But it should be borne in mind that a soldier on duty is not permitted to exercise any discretion at all. Military power is absolute and is summed up in the motto "Obey orders." If this is not done, the next move is a speedy trial for treason and such penalties as the court may determine. If a union workingman soldier is ordered to shoot down a brother workingman and should be detected in firing over his head rather than at his heart, he would very speedily find out his mistake. Hence we are inclined to the opinion, if a workingman does not want to kill or wound a workingman for striking when oppressed, robbed, and otherwise outraged, he will act wisely by keeping out of the state's standing army.

A very excellent resolution was adopted favoring "the taxing of church property." There never was a rational reason why church property should escape taxation. In hundreds of instances, the church building, after going through the mummery of dedication, an auction is held and the pews are sold out to those who have the money to purchase, and those who have not are permitted to take the paupers' bench and go to heaven as freight. Whatever may be regarded as prudent for such church buildings as have their doors thrown wide open for all without charge, there should be agreement upon the proposition of taxing those buildings which sell their seats for cost, as do theaters and other buildings erected for amusement and profit.

After all, it occurs to our mind that the overmastering demand in these days is to so unify and solidify labor organizations as to realize that when one of them is attacked by capitalist rogues, all are attacked. For until this is done the triumphs of labor will be few and far between, and defeats will be far more numerous than milestones on a turnpike.

The Plan of the ARU:
Statement to the Press in New York City[†]

May 20, 1893

I am perfectly frank to say that I am opposed to the present labor organizations of the country—not to their purpose, but to their methods. My objections to the present labor organizations are many. They have tended not only to perpetuate the caste feeling that existed, but have created new castes, the lines of division between which have become stronger and more cruel than the lines that existed before labor organizations were an assured fact in America. There are in the United States from 800,000 to 1 million railroad employees. Not more than 150,000 are members of organizations. The reasons are many. The present organizations are altogether too expensive. Their machinery is cumbersome. It costs approximately $1.5 million to pay the expenses of the present railroad orders in the United States.

The various labor organizations war against each other. The leaders are jealous of each other. More strikes have failed from this cause than all others. In fact, the number of strikes that have resulted in victory on the part of railroad men would be found, if the records were to be carefully examined, to be surprisingly small. The locomotive engineers, for instance, never won a strike worth mentioning. There is altogether too much one-man power in the present organizations.

I think conditions can be vastly improved, and that not only the workingman but the railroad companies and the general public will be greatly benefited by the change. Our new organization is entitled the American Railway Union. Into it we propose to gather all branches of railroad employees. We do not intend to do away with road labor, and it is not our purpose to antagonize present organizations, but we do propose to make this new organization such a one as will successfully invite membership on the part of almost every employee of the railroads of America. Its expenses will be reduced to the minimum. We shall effect this by doing away with nine-tenths of the cumbersome machinery

---

†   Wire service report, datelined New York City. Published as "One Great Order" in *St. Paul Globe*, vol. 15, no. 142 (May 22, 1893), 1. Merged with the slightly expanded content published as "Railroad Interests" in the *Buffalo Enquirer*, May 23, 1893, 3, and "Boycott on Strikes" in the *Chicago Tribune*, May 21, 1893, 13.

that is now required for the conduct of labor organizations. There will be no initiation fee at all. The organization will not be a "secret, oath-bound society." An upright, truthful man will be bound by his simple word. There will be as few officers as possible, and no one man will hold the welfare of thousands of hardworking men in his hands.

We shall reduce expenses by consolidation in the matter of halls and meeting places. There is no reason why in any city where there are a number of railroad organizations each should have a hall of its own. We shall aim to have a meeting place in each city where all organizations may meet. In a big city like New York or Chicago we can better afford to own a building in which there may be two or three or more halls if necessary, so that as many organizations as need be may meet at the same time. Those, of course, need not take up the entire building, and if they do not we can rent the unoccupied part at such terms as will give us something of an income.

We shall establish a daily newspaper in the interests of railroad employees, and also a monthly magazine. Our daily newspaper will be published in Chicago. The capital is ready in plenty, and the plans are about completed. It will not be a large newspaper, but it will be large enough to contain not only the news of the labor world, and the railroad world in particular, but all the essential telegraphic news of the day as well. We shall furnish this paper at the cost of publication, our object in publishing it not being profit in any sense, except to the men who support it, and we believe they will profit by the possession of such a newspaper. We shall not run especially to editorials, but shall make news our chief feature, though of course we shall discuss questions of general interest. The magazine will be run on the same lines, as far as price is concerned, as the daily, but it will necessarily not be so much a medium for the distribution of news. The newspaper will sell for one cent, and the magazine will be put out at the lowest possible figure.

Another feature of the educational department will be the monthly meetings, which will, to a large extent, if not altogether, take the place of the ordinary weekly lodge meetings. To these meetings all members of the order in the town where they are held will be invited, and they will be addressed by the heads of the districts on such subjects as are of vital interest to the workingmen. We believe that these means will stimulate the thought of the railroad men greatly, and the one thing that is necessary above all others to the success of the labor movement is intelligent thought on the part of its members. Workingmen, especially those whose employment is purely physical and continuous, are not deep thinkers, and it would be wonderful if they were.

A meeting for the perfection of the American Railway Union's organization will be held in Chicago on June 20 [1893], and the plans, so far as they have been decided upon, may be roughly outlined as follows: The entire country will be divided into districts, of which there will be 12. From Chicago 12 organizers, one from each district, will be sent out, and they will go from center to center, organizing first district headquarters or capitals, and, after this is done, headquarters for subdivisions. The boundaries of the divisions have not yet been fixed. The subdivisions will be subordinate, of course, to the district capitals, and each subordinate organization will be entitled to delegates in proportion to its membership, say, one to every 200. There will be no yearly state conventions, nor grand conventions—these cost from $35,000 to $60,000 each—but there will be a quadrennial convention of the entire order, and 60 days before the holding of a quadrennial convention, the lodges or unions will meet at the district capitals and choose delegates to the quadrennial convention. Each district will be entitled to delegates in proportion to its membership. It is proposed that the quadrennial convention shall do its work in a day, or at most two days, and that its business shall be mainly the electing of a board of directors of, say, 20 or 30 practical railroad men.

To this board of directors will be entrusted the business of the order. It is expected that the district chiefs will make most of the addresses spoken of in the educational scheme, and if they have served as chiefs in the various parts of the country they will thereby become much better qualified to make these addresses valuable to the men.

We propose to make this an organization of rugged workingmen. We shall study economy. We shall include every branch of railroad employment from the lowest to the highest, and without doing away with special organizations we shall strive to bring all under one common fold. The first quadrennial convention of the American Railway Union will be held next fall.

"A Great Thing and Bound to Win":
Statement to the Indiana Press[†19]

May 25, 1893

The new order [the ARU] proposes to begin right where the other orders have left off. We must concede that they have been the source of great good. That no man can deny. Compare the condition of the railway employee today with what it was twenty or even ten years ago. There has been a vast improvement. But labor organizations must keep abreast with the times. The conditions that governed ten or twenty years ago have changed, and so must organized labor change in order to meet the new conditions which confront it. There is today a general feeling of unrest. The several organizations as they exist today do not meet the demands made upon them. They have outlived their usefulness for the simple reason that they can no longer accomplish what they were organized to accomplish. The men at the head of the new order are men of vast experience in these matters. When I was in New York a few days ago I laid my whole plan before men in whose judgment [I trusted]. I said it was a great thing and one that is bound to win. It is not the work of a day or a month, but was only evolved after thorough consideration and after every detail was weighed.

If there is ever another strike after this order is thoroughly established, I will miss my guess. Great bodies of men are bound to be conservative. It has been my experience that out of a large body, the majority is always right, or at least nearly always. A great body would never endorse the petty, ill-advised strikes that are continually occurring all over the country. It is our purpose to thoroughly organize every branch of railroad labor under the same laws—the same rules to govern all alike—and yet it will be under a perfect class system. The locals of the order will include engineers, firemen, switchmen, brakemen, conductors, shopmen, trackmen, and in fact every branch of labor employed by railroad corporations. Each class will discuss matters pertaining to its own branch of the work. For instance, the firemen will meet tonight, the brakemen tomorrow night, and so on. There would be little of interest to shopmen that would concern engineers and roadmen, and yet all will be governed by the same laws. Once every month the director who is the leader and organizer of

---

†   Published as "The New Railway Federation" in the *Logansport Pharos-Tribune* (Indiana), vol. 18, no. 123 (May 26, 1893), 5.

a district will be present to lecture to the whole body in mass meeting assembled, and it will be arranged so that the organizers will change places so that a different speaker will address the meeting every month. Our plan is to organize the men as the railroad companies organize them—the engineer, firemen, brakemen, conductor, switchmen, shopmen, and so on, each and every one at his post, each performing his duty, and all working in one harmonious whole.

I believe it is possible to so organize and conduct this vast organization that it will command the respect of the railroad companies. It will tend to eliminate the petty jealousy that exists now and will relieve the officials of the many annoyances with which they now have to contend. It can be conducted so as to command the respect of the public. The average businessman is now opposed to organized labor and is inclined to sneer or speak lightly of it, and there is some justice in what they say. The moment you can assure a businessman or the public that the great commerce of the country is not going to be interfered with because of some petty grievance in which they are not interested and that their interests and rights will be protected and looked after as much by the employees of a railroad corporation as by the company itself, you make them your friends. The chief source of friction and the great reason why men are not able to make satisfactory arrangements with their employers or, in other words, to sell their labor at the best price, is due to the fact that different labor organizations are in constant war with one another. They talk about the tyranny of capital, but there is no warfare that compares with that which is waged by different labor organizations against one another, and until that is put a stop to, it is absurd to talk about a rational and businesslike settlement of these railroad problems.

Strikers have done more harm to wage earners than anything that employers have ever imposed on them. Then the methods of the various orders are technical, and greatly involved, and my estimate is that it costs $15 million yearly to maintain these railway organizations. There are a great many officers who receive large salaries, and all of these expenses have to come from the railway workingmen. Then there are also expenses which it is impossible to analyze. They are called emergency expenses, and when a strike is ordered there are assessments levied upon the men to support those who have gone out upon a strike. The cost of conventions, meetings, hall rent, and salaries make up in the aggregate an enormous sum. And yet the railway employees get little benefit from these organizations. All these things we hope to eliminate and to provide greater benefits to wage earners at less cost. It is not our purpose to antagonize existing orders, but to harmonize labor interests.

The new organization must stand on its merits, and it will stand. We do not ask the endorsement of anybody. If our principles are right, the organization will not need the endorsement of anybody, and if they are wrong, nobody's endorsement would make it stand. The American Railway Union will start with 12,000 members. One order—the Railway Carmen—voted at its last convention in St. Louis to leave it to the discretion of its grand officers to merge that order into the new one, and this they have decided to do. On June 20 [1893], we will start by organizing Chicago, and then after that we will organize according to applications.

I have received thousands of letters, and out of these only one man raised objections to our plans. He is a New Jersey man, and he differed with me in his opinion of the plan of organization, claiming that there were certain things about it which would not work. Of course, he had a right to his opinion the same as every other man, and his views were stated in such good faith and so good-naturedly that I can only thank him for them. In this town [Terre Haute], one man objected to the organization on the ground it would antagonize the interests of the firemen. When he had succeeded in sending the news broadcast that I would be expelled from the order in advance of even charges being preferred against me, much less a decision being reached, he objected when I demanded that I be set aright before the public through the same medium he had employed to injure me. But the charges were withdrawn, and I do not care to discuss the matter further.

Labor and Legislation[†]

June 1893

Thoughtful workingmen are considering in what regards, and to what extent, labor can be benefited by legislation. But before we come to the consideration of legislative action, other matters preliminary to such questions demand attention.

In the first place, as workingmen we are to consider in what measures laws are required to secure for labor simple justice, because justice to labor works no wrong to society, but, on the contrary, promotes the general welfare, while injustice to labor is in every instance productive of general injury—necessarily so, since labor is the great force and factor in promoting the public welfare. Any injustice to labor

†   Published in *Locomotive Firemen's Magazine*, vol. 17, no. 6 (June 1893), 427–430.

is wide spreading and far reaching. Labor, contented and prosperous, measures the progress and prosperity of communities everywhere; while labor, discontented and impoverished, marks decay and retrogression in all branches of business.

Labor, having investigated conditions and arrived at conclusions relating to such laws as are required to correct prevailing wrongs, should be able to unify its forces for the purpose of securing the election of men of first-class capabilities to champion its measures in legislative bodies. If at this juncture there is division and faction, failure is inevitable, regardless of the justice of the measures proposed, the wrongs complained of, or the rights which labor ought to secure.

The fact ought to be recognized, and have weight, that comparatively few men are successful legislators. There are men in the ranks of organized labor in all regards capable of being lawmakers, but they are few in number and far between in location. This is not the result of mental incapacity, but is owing to the fact that workingmen have had, as a general proposition, neither the time nor the opportunities for study and mental discipline required to equip them for preparing bills embodying their demands, in matter and language required in statutes which must be constitutional in their provisions, and so constructed as to challenge the acumen of lawyers when appealed to, for the purpose of affording labor the relief it demands. Hence we infer that in selecting men to represent labor in legislative bodies, two prime questions should be considered: First, are the men the ardent, uncompromising friends of labor? Second, are they fully equipped by native ability, education, and experience to legislate— that is to say, to frame measures legal in form, free from ambiguity, and which if enacted into laws will accomplish the purpose for which they were enacted?

We are confident labor is making serious mistakes in this matter of legislation, by electing men who, however well-meaning and honest, are sadly lacking in equipment as lawmakers. They are always at the mercy of others. They propose measures they do not construct and are therefore incapable of analyzing them. They do not comprehend the intricacies of phraseology nor discover lurking technicalities. Wanting in legislative sagacity, amendments and provisos are injected, and when the bill becomes a law it is shorn of usefulness and labor pays all the penalties, or the bill finds its way into the custody of an unfriendly committee and by various subterfuges is placed where it cannot be reached, because its friends were incapable of applying such forces as experience and capability could wield to overcome opposition.

Viewing matters from such standpoints, what would seem to be the essential requirement? Manifestly, for labor to concentrate its votes upon the friends of labor whose qualifications for legislators are admitted, regardless of any connection with labor organizations. They need not necessarily be lawyers, but most certainly if they are lawyers so much the better, as lawyers are best equipped for framing laws; they, more readily than others, discover defects in bills; they are the best judges of phraseology, and know when a bill meets the demands of labor. Besides, there are to be found everywhere lawyers who are in profound sympathy with labor and who know the wrongs to which it is subjected, and are the best judges of legal remedies. Ordinarily, lawyers are equipped for presenting to deliberative bodies the strong points of a measure, and are trained to detect and expose the strategic movements of opponents, and as legislators, shape all laws. Hence as the advocates of labor measures, they become of great value.

In these times no labor bill that touches in any way the assumed prerogatives of employers and corporations can be introduced into legislative bodies without arousing fierce hostility. Money has its henchmen in these bodies, and throngs of them, as lobbyists, men who are selected as representatives because for a consideration they will "sell out." They are known to have their price, like certain witnesses who swear for their clients, shaping their statements without reference to truth but in a way to escape the penalties of perjury. To expose these debauched creatures or to render their schemes powerless has become one of the supreme duties of legislators who are governed by principle—not always nor indeed at any time an easy task—and labor in a special sense needs such men to champion its measures, and the lack of their assistance accounts to some extent for the slow progress labor legislation is making in the country.

Labor deems it prudent to have what it calls "legislative boards," to see that certain measures are introduced and to watch their progress. These boards constitute lobbies, and by their operations often do more harm than good, and serve directly to create opposition lobbies made up of shrewd and unscrupulous men whose operations cannot be as severely criticized as they deserve because labor, having a lobby, is required to remain silent. As a result, in the battle of lobbies labor generally suffers defeat.

In such cases labor is in the habit of saying, by acts if not by words, and often by declarations, that the enemies of labor, or those who oppose labor measures in legislation, will be watched and defeated when again they are proposed for legislative positions. To say the least of it, such intimations of reserved penalties are not wise; reticence as to what labor will do or not do would be preferable, since in scarcely any given case can anyone foretell what labor would do. It seldom unifies—far more frequently splits and factionizes. Labor boards for legislative purposes could be prudently reduced in number with a prospect of more favorable results. Insofar as the future welfare of labor depends upon the enactment of wise laws, we feel satisfied labor must, in several essential points, change its program; men must be found, first and foremost, who are capable; nothing in such positions condones ignorance and inexperience, however honest the representative of labor may be. The time has come when the champions of labor in legislative bodies must be not only earnest and honest, but so admittedly intelligent, so sound in legal lore and strategy, that whether in committee or on the floor they will be found the equals in all regards of the enemies of labor. To be watchful in these regards means future victory for workingmen. To neglect them is to insure defeat.

Russianizing the United States[†]
July 1893

A treaty has recently been negotiated between the United States and Russia, and simply awaits the proclamation of the president to become the law in all matters agreed upon by the contracting parties. Treaties, it is known, are compacts concocted in secret. In the United States, where it is published to the world that the government is of the people and by and for the people, the people are not permitted to know anything more of the agreements contained in a treaty, until it becomes the law, than if they were Russian exiles working in a Siberian mine. Fortunately, however, according to the adage that "murder will out," the people of the United States have managed to learn so much of the treaty as to create the belief that it places the United States in a position of unqualified shame and humiliation before the whole civilized world.

It so happens that Russia is a despotism, the most cruel, brutal, inhuman, murderous, abominable, and infamous upon the face of the earth, and the emperor "of all the Russias," is the one bloodthirsty monster who is responsible for all the banishments, murders, and tortures inflicted upon Russians because they dare hope for a change of government, because they ask for liberty, because they demand redress for wrongs, and no sooner is a whisper heard of discontent than imprisonment, torture, death, or exile follows. As a result, certain brave Russians plot the death of the autocrat, or they seek to inaugurate rebellion, they plot to

---

†   Published in *Locomotive Firemen's Magazine*, vol. 17, no. 7 (July 1893), 535–536.

overthrow the government, in doing which they have the unqualified and enthusiastic approval of ninety-nine hundredths of the people of the United States.

Thousands of these Russian patriots are caught; some are murdered, others
tortured, others imprisoned, while a ceaseless tide of others flow toward Siberia
to linger out their miserable lives in mines. Some of these patriots escape to the
United States and publish to the world the truth regarding Russian despotism.
The autocrat of Russia very much desires to put his paws on these patriots now
under the jurisdiction of "Old Glory," and, surpassing all belief, the United
States Senate votes that he may do so, and thus make the government of the
United States *particeps criminis*[20] to every horror Russia inflicts from murder
to exile in crushing out the spirit of liberty among her people. As we write,
the treaty is in the hands of President Grover Cleveland: If he does not hold
it for modification, so that Russian refugees who have sought asylum here are
safe from autocratic atrocities, then Russian detectives will invade our shores
and drag away any one whom it may be the tsar's pleasure to murder, torture,
imprison, or exile. In this connection, says the *Chicago Herald:*

> We shall not become bloodhounds for any European despotism. We are
> not going to help despots, no matter who they are or what their past in
> regard to us, to track fugitives from the knout, the galley chain, the mine,
> or the penal colony across our free prairies or into the seclusion of the free
> cities of this Republic. The fundamental blunder in the text of the treaty
> is that it does not discriminate between political and other offenses. Until
> that discrimination shall be made, and until the power of testing each case
> arising under it is vested in our own courts, giving refugees right of coun-
> sel, the treaty with Russia, no matter how satisfactory otherwise, will not
> be acceptable to the American people. We did not destroy fugitive slave
> laws on our own soil only to revive their principles for the accommodation
> of old world slavers or tyrants. In proposing such a clause as this to us,
> Russian diplomacy has audaciously asked the United States for a political
> accommodation that would be scornfully denied to her diplomats by En-
> gland, as England has denied it for generations to all powers; an accommo-
> dation she has no right to expect except from the petty, half-savage, tribal,
> or satrapic communities her bayonets pin down or her gold corrupts in
> Eastern Europe and Asia. No political partnership with despots!

It is to be hoped that the *Herald* is right, but it all rests with President
Cleveland; if he does not crush the infamous treaty, then the United States
from ocean to ocean becomes a hunting ground for such creatures as the autocrat of Russia may designate to entrap the victims of his wrath.

Should the treaty go into effect, and a Russian official be seen dragging some victim of Russian hate away to the infernal regions under the control of the tsar, it would not be surprising if it were found an exceedingly difficult task. Let it once be understood that the Senate of the United States, aided by the president, has placed such power in the hands of the Russian autocrats, and by common consent they would become objects of ineffable scorn and ignominy.

Chicago Anarchists Pardoned[†]

August 1893

On the night of May 4, 1886, there was a meeting held in Haymarket Square, Chicago. The attendance was estimated at about one thousand persons, who were denounced as anarchists.

Americans being in favor of law, order, and a stable government, anarchists, who oppose such conditions, are necessarily unpopular in the United States. The meeting in Haymarket Square, it seems, was called to publicly discuss numerous outrages perpetrated upon workingmen in Chicago by the police and Pinkerton thugs.

Governor Altgeld,[21] in his masterly message, extending pardon to three anarchists, makes the following statement showing the underlying causes of the Haymarket meeting:

> Again it is shown that the bomb was in all probability thrown by someone seeking personal revenge; that a course had been pursued by the authorities which would naturally cause this; that for a number of years prior to the Haymarket affair there had been labor troubles, and in several cases a number of laboring people guilty of no offense had been shot down in cold blood by Pinkerton men and none of the murderers were brought to justice. The evidence taken at coroners' inquests shows that in at least two cases men were fired on and killed when they were running away and there was consequently no occasion to shoot, yet no-

---

†   Published as "The Chicago Anarchists" in *Locomotive Firemen's Magazine,* vol. 17, no. 8 (August 1893), 645–648.

body was punished; that in Chicago there had been a number of strikes in which some of the police not only took sides against the men, but without any authority of law invaded and broke up peaceable meetings, and in scores of cases brutally clubbed people who were guilty of no offense whatever.

In this, the governor arraigns the government of Chicago and states facts which would make anarchists of Quakers. People shot down in cold blood, who were guilty of no offense, by Pinkerton thugs, and never brought to justice, and a brutal police clubbing people who were guilty of no offense whatever, and never punished for their infamous outrages, would, anywhere under heaven, create anarchists. It should be borne in mind that it is the governor of Illinois who arraigns Chicago for the perpetration of murders as black as that caused by the Haymarket bomb, for he says the Pinkertons, employed by Chicago, had in cold blood shot down a number of laboring people, guilty of no offense, and that none of the murderers were brought to justice. What more natural than that such murders should create excitement and result in fiery denunciation?

But we write for the purpose of getting before our readers the views of Governor Altgeld, as expressed in his message pardoning three of the convicted anarchists—Michael Schwab,[22] Samuel Fielden,[23] and Oscar Neebe.[24] Besides the three anarchists named, there were five others indicted for murder, viz: Albert R. Parsons,[25] Louis Lingg,[26] George Engel,[27] Adolph Fischer,[28] and August Spies.[29] Louis Lingg committed suicide, while Parsons, Fischer, Engel, and Spies were hanged.

Governor Altgeld makes the declaration that the convicted anarchists not only did not have a fair trial, but on the contrary, the purpose of the trial was to convict regardless of proof, and that conviction was obtained by methods the most scandalous and infamous that ever blackened the records of Anglo-Saxon jurisprudence. A miscreant by the name of Henry L. Rice was made special bailiff to summon men to act as jurors, who, it is shown, had openly and repeatedly expressed opinions relating to the guilt of the accused, and boasted that the indicted men would hang as certain as death, and Governor Altgeld shows that the trial judge outraged justice and fair dealing by using his position to secure conviction.[30]

No one attempts any defense of the man who threw the murderous bomb, but the man who threw the bomb could not be discovered. All efforts to find him utterly failed. He was the one and the only one guilty of murder, and in this connection Governor Altgeld says:

The prosecution could not discover who had thrown the bomb and could not bring the really guilty man to justice, and, as some of the men indicted were not at the Haymarket meeting and had nothing to do with it, the prosecution was forced to proceed on the theory that the men indicted were guilty of murder because it was claimed they had at various times in the past uttered and printed incendiary and seditious language, practically advising the killing of policemen, of Pinkerton men and others acting in that capacity, and they were, therefore, responsible for the murder of Mathias Degan. The public was greatly excited, and after a prolonged trial, all of the defendants were found guilty; Oscar Neebe was sentenced to 15 years' imprisonment and all of the other defendants were sentenced to be hanged.

It will be observed that the men tried and convicted, five of whom were sentenced to be hanged, two imprisoned for life, and one for 15 years, were not tried for committing the crime of murder, but for "uttering and printing seditious language, practically advising the killing of policemen and Pinkertons and others acting in that capacity."

Governor Altgeld, in issuing his pardon, sets forth the fact that petitions for executive clemency and letters have poured in upon him, setting forth the reasons why the governor should act. These petitions assert as follows:

1. That the jury which tried the case was a packed jury selected to convict.
2. That according to the law as laid down by the Supreme Court both prior to and again since the trial of this case, the jurors, according to their own answers, were not competent jurors, and the trial, therefore, was not a legal trial.
3. That the defendants were not proven to be guilty of the crime charged in the indictment.
4. That as to the defendant, Neebe, the state's attorney had declared at the close of the evidence that there was no case against him, and yet he has been kept in prison all these years.
5. That the trial judge was either so prejudiced against the defendants, or else so determined to win the applause of a certain class in the community, that he could not and did not grant a fair trial.

In commenting upon the foregoing, the governor leaves nothing in the dark, but shows most conclusively that the jury was packed and selected to convict—that the trial was throughout illegal, and that while the dead had passed beyond the reach of the clemency which justice and mercy demands, the survivors could be and ought to be pardoned. The governor fortifies his act of clemency by reciting, in detail, the questions propounded to men selected by Rice for jurors and their answers, and in reading them now, after passion has subsided and reason has resumed its sway, the infamy of the proceedings to convict in defiance of law, justice, and all things decent sends a thrill of horror through every fiber of the hearts of honest men. Judge Lynch, at the head of a mob, was never more cruel. It was an exhibition of civilized savagery without a parallel in all of the centuries.

It is of special importance for those who would have any clear conception of the farce trial, or a trial to convict, to know how Rice and the trial judge proceeded to secure a jury to convict. We give the official records of a case or two which illustrates the infamy of the proceedings:

H. N. Smith, hardware merchant, stated among other things that he was prejudiced and had quite a decided opinion as to the guilt or innocence of the defendants, that he had expressed his opinion and still entertained it, and candidly stated he was afraid he would listen a little more attentively to the testimony which concurred with his opinion than the testimony on the other side; that some of the policemen injured were personal friends of his. He was asked these questions:

Q. That is, you would be willing to have your opinion strengthened and hate very much to have it dissolved?

A. I would.

Q. Under these circumstances do you think that you could render a fair and impartial verdict?

A. I don't think I could.

Q. You think you would be prejudiced?

A. I think I would be, because my feelings are very bitter.

Q. Would your prejudice in any way influence you in coming at an opinion, in arriving at a verdict?

A. I think it would.

H. D. Bogardus, flour merchant, stated that he had read and talked about the Haymarket trouble; had formed and expressed an opinion; still held it as to the guilt or innocence of the defendants; that he was prejudiced; that this prejudice would certainly influence his verdict, if selected as a juror. *I don't believe that I could give them a fair trial upon the proof, for it would require very strong proof to overcome my prejudice. I hardly think that you could bring proof enough to change my opinion.*

The foregoing is in keeping with others who, though challenged for having formed an opinion and being prejudiced against the defendants, but were nevertheless forced upon the jury to try men impartially, whose life and liberty trembled in the balance. Every allegation set forth by the petitioners Governor Altgeld held to be absolutely true. First, the jury was packed to convict. Second, the law was ruthlessly bludgeoned out of court. Third, the defendants were not proven guilty. Fourth, Neebe was absolutely innocent, and fifth, the judge showed himself to be a monster. The trial was a crime and the execution of the men judicial murder.

What of it all? The trial was a monstrous perversion of justice—a disgrace to our civilization, a murderous stab at free speech, and if such infamous court proceedings could be made the rule in the United States the difference between Russia and America would not be perceptible. The three men rescued from prison is something in the line of redeeming the country from this odium of the trial, and Governor Altgeld deserves a monument for the moral courage he has displayed in breaking the fetters forged by a judicial crime, and thereby setting three unfortunate men, who were not legally convicted, free.

The Organization of Workingmen:
Speech to the Chicago World's Fair Labor Congress[†]

August 30, 1893

I appreciate the compliment of the Labor Congress in assigning me a place in its deliberations.[31]

Standing upon this platform, this mound of vision, surveying my surroundings and contemplating this labor congress as one of the auxiliaries of the World's Columbian Exposition, I realize in some measure the gigantic strides of progress the nations are making toward fraternity and federation.

It requires, I confess, a more far-reaching vision than I can boast to penetrate the future and determine the date when battle flags will be furled, when the drumbeats of war shall be hushed to silence and the parliament of the world shall assemble to deliberate under the sublimating influences of "peace" and "goodwill toward men." But if there is anything in the signs of the times calculated to inspire hope, the "medicine of the miserable,"[32] then it must be conceded that a labor congress as an appendage of the World's Columbian Fair is a token of cheering significance, a blazing signal in the wilderness of doubt and apprehension, a lighthouse on the stormy coast where labor has often been wrecked when seeking a harbor of security and repose.

I accept with diffidence the theme assigned me for discussion, "the organization of workingmen." I know the subject is trite, that it has been on the lips of ten thousand men for a century or more. I know from readings and from observation how toilsome has been the march of labor during all the centuries since Pharaoh's slaves built the pyramids, hewed out the Sphinx, and reared the obelisks, since other slaves built the seven wonders of the world, aye, the multiplied wonders along the track the nations have traveled.

In all of the ages past, the workingman has been doomed to toil and to silence. Born to toil and drudgery, uncomplainingly he bowed his head and back in token of submission, crawled in the dust at the behest of superiors, and accepted his cruel fate as taught by the gods and church, and, steeped in ignorance and superstition, had a vague idea that when his bitter task was ended,

---

†   Published as "The Organization of Workingmen" in *Locomotive Firemen's Magazine*, vol. 17, no. 10 (October 1893), 875–879. Reprinted as a pamphlet (Terre Haute, IN: 1893).

somewhere a better life was in store for him.

Nor is labor yet redeemed from the blighting curses of the past, nor has it moved anywhere in all of the shining zones that belt the earth a fraction of an inch toward improved conditions except by the lifting and emancipating power of organization.

In making this declaration I unhesitatingly challenge the world. If it is asserted that here and there, now and then, laws have been enacted for the amelioration of workingmen, the irrefutable truth stands forth that such laws have their origin in the councils of organized labor and were forced upon the statute books by the conquering energy of organized workingmen.

In saying this, I pronounce no undue eulogy upon the organization of workingmen. I am not required to proclaim that labor organizations are immaculate. I know they are human, and I frankly concede their errors. I know of the long captivity of workingmen, of the Red Seas they have passed, of their wanderings in the wilderness with burning thirst and consuming hunger in search of a promised land. Organized for victory, they have experienced defeat. Their enemies, entrenched in wealth and commanded by generals of consummate abilities, have often been able to demoralize the forces of organized labor and subject the defeated to penalties of harrowing severity. But labor's battles have not all been lost, nor are labor's hosts disbanded or discouraged. On the contrary, organized workingmen were never more confident of success, never more hopeful of the future of labor than now, and for this trust and expectation there are many and cogent reasons.

In the first place, experience has taught organizations of workingmen the supreme value of education, of mental development and intellectual grasp. The great brain of labor has lain comparatively dormant, except as exercised along the line of the chosen field of work. Learning in its best sense has not been in alliance with labor organizations. It has been thought sufficient for workingmen to be skilled in their trades to hew and saw to lines marked out by others and to be content with the ABC of knowledge, a species of slavery and degradation which forever held their noses to the grindstone of dependence and kept their feet tramping the same treadmill journeys in which there was neither development nor advancement. The men who thought controlled those who toiled. As in the academies where Plato and Aristotle taught, workingmen have been excluded from the benefits and blessings to be derived from science and philosophy which related to their emancipation from conditions imposed by centuries of ignorance and oppression. But the spirit of organization touched them, united them in one vast body, sent the red currents of life coursing through their veins, and they stood up and stood forth in a mighty army panoplied for war, proclaiming to the nations of the earth that while the stars shine above them and mind holds sway in the councils of men, labor shall not be enslaved—at least not in the United States of America, while our flag, christened "Old Glory," has a star or a stripe upon its ample folds.

In this emancipation being wrought out by organized workingmen, if one cares to listen, may be heard welling up from every organization of labor the demand for more and a higher education. This mind march of labor is phenomenal. Students multiply by the thousands, lodges are becoming schoolrooms, books are in demand, and a labor literature, daily increasing in power, is among the cheering signs of the times.

This mustering of the mind forces of labor has a majestic significance which ought to challenge the admiration of patriots and philanthropists of every school. If there are those who aver that this work is moving slowly, I do not hesitate to admit the affirmation and express my approval of the staid but sturdy character of the march. I am not an advocate of the spectacular. The present is the formative, the educational, the consolidating period of the organization of workingmen, and the work is proceeding in a way betokening ever-increasing force and strength, and this "Labor Congress" in this "White City" of the world,[33] the local center of the thought of all the nations, may be cited in support of the declaration.

The time is coming, fortunately, when we are hearing less of the old paternal pharisaism, "What can we do for labor?" It is the old, old query repeated along all the centuries, heard whenever a master wielded a whip above the bowed forms of slaves. It is the language of the slave-catcher, the slave-pen, the slave-block, and the slave plantation. We hear it yet occasionally, along lines of transportation, in mines and shops, but our ears are regaled by another and a more manly query, an interrogatory permeated with the spirit of liberty and independence, which is "What can labor do for itself?" The answer is not difficult. Labor can organize, it can unify, it can consolidate its forces. This done, it can demand and command. Such are the possible and the practical things labor can do, is doing, and will continue to do, until constitutions and courts and laws, based upon principles of eternal justice, make no distinction in dealing with the people.

Such grand achievements I do not doubt can be accomplished and be vastly expedited by the organization of workingmen. I am unable to discover anything in the program chimerical. It is not a fantasy, a dream, or a creation of the fancy. It is, on the contrary, an expression of faith in human attainments, when the mind, no longer fettered by ignorance nor deformed by bigotry, expands to its full-orbed power to bless the world.

I would not have it understood that I underestimate the power of the forces in league to circumvent the high aspirations of labor or to defeat the purposes of the organization of workingmen. I appreciate the herculean task that comforts labor, and how long and tedious and dreary will be the march before the hosts of labor will be able to celebrate their full emancipation. But were the obstacles in the way a thousand times more formidable than they appear, I would still have faith in the triumph of eternal justice, though it were but as "a grain of mustard seed" that labor would be able to remove them all and advance,[34] since the converse of the proposition would be that "right is to be forever on the scaffold" and the "wrong forever on the throne,"[35] in which event the duration of the earth has already been ample and its destruction by any of the processes from time to time suggested ought to meet with a hearty welcome.

It ought to be understood and it is conceded by men of thought, by statesmen who can lay any just claim to the appellation, that the supreme welfare of the social fabric depends upon the prosperity, happiness, and contentment of workingmen, and since the absence of this great fortune means the opposite, viz: adversity, poverty, and want, it requires no seer to foretell social calamities—crime and its attendant woes. Workingmen's organizations, having in view the maintenance of fair wages, are doing more for the well-being of society than all other agencies combined. I am not unmindful of what is said of the church and the school, nor am I here to wage warfare against either of them, nor against any other human agency for the mitigation of social ills, but dogmas and creeds, the refinements of religion nor the learning of the schools, never did demand or maintain fair wages for workingmen, and the fact that wages have been unjust accounts for a vast percent of the ignorance, squalor, degradation, and crime that now confront our much-vaunted civilization. The shylock policy of reducing wages has been and continues to be the prolific parent of innumerable ills, and against this policy the organizations of workingmen proclaim unyielding hostility.

If such dangers, resulting from persistent injustice to labor, threaten the social fabric, what may be said of the perils that environ our political system consequent upon a policy which seeks to reduce men who wield the ballot to pauperism? Do I cry "wolf" when there is no wolf? We hear on all sides cries of alarm caused by illiteracy. Men declare that ignorance is the one great peril of our institutions and that the school, and only the school, guarantees security. It is well. Organizations of workingmen are in active alliance with the school.

Their motto is "education," but in addition they demand just wages and fair conditions for work, because wages reduced to the point which barely suffices to keep soul and body together blocks the pathways to mental culture, and until the elevating power of honest wages is recognized and established, the state will continue to deplore the demoralizing results of illiteracy.

Wages are one of the supreme requirements of labor in social and political affairs. I am not here as a money worshipper. I know that dollars are called "tokens," and are said to be mediums of exchange, the yardsticks and balances of trade by which we weigh and measure the prosperity, happiness, and contentment of workingmen. If wages approximate labor's honest share in the wealth it creates, the homes of workingmen are bright and joyous, and as wages are reduced below that standard, there is gloom and squalor, and organizations of workingmen animated by the noble ambition to secure and maintain fair wages which, while providing a suitable living for their wives and children, enables them to meet every required obligation of the state.

Again, it should be said that when labor is honestly paid, communities and states feel at once the vivifying influence: Consumption keeps pace with production, trade and commerce proceed on lines of security and wide prosperity, and rewards are equitably distributed. To secure these blessings is the paramount purpose of organizations of workingmen.

Standing amid the marvelous displays of work and skill concentrated in this world-renowned White City from the four corners of the earth, I am prompted to deal in eulogistic words of work, but the majesty of the theme dissuades me. Had I the imagination, the genius, and the eloquence of an Ingersoll, I would make this labor congress an epoch immortal in the annals of labor. I would put tongues in workingmen's organizations whose words should echo around the world when this great Columbus Fair takes its place in the traditions of the centuries.[36] Here students may learn how inert and dead is the thing we call capital until it was touched by the vitalizing power of labor—labor of brain and hand. Here the federal government might have poured to exhaustion its accumulation of gold and silver—here the states of this mighty republic might have concentrated their wealth, and here, Chicago, the wonderful interoceanic city of the continent, might have drained her coffers until the Alpine pile of money amazed the nations of the earth, but Jackson Park[37] would have remained a barren land but for the play of the elements. But, touched by the hand of labor, behold the transformation! The weird fictions of Aladdin become facts for the contemplation of the world. Palaces, the description of which defies all languages, spring up as if by enchantment, and a fairy realm is created by the magic power and genius of labor. And here are concentrated, as never before in the history of all the ages, the products of skilled workers of every clime under the starry heavens, and as the millions come from the north and the south, from the east and west, from continents and islands, the exclamation is made, "Verily, the genius and skill of man is the marvel of the world."

These visiting wonderers may search in vain for something that kings, aristocrats, plutocrats, the rich and titled snobs of the earth have made. As well search for roses amidst the eternal snows of the Arctic zone. No! All things in the White City combine to eulogize labor, and workingmen's organizations, whatever the future has in store for them, may congratulate themselves that they are animated by the sublime purpose of redeeming their members from the thralldoms which centuries of cruelty and oppression have imposed upon them.

The Money Question[†]
September 1893

The money question is one upon which the most eminent doctors of finance disagree. Those who want a single standard, that of gold, and those who demand a double standard, that of gold and silver, in discussing the money question, exhibit all along the line such antipodal differences of opinion that any expectation of agreement is utterly futile. Hence men who care to familiarize themselves with the arguments and assertions of the disputants will have to exercise great fortitude and patience, and then take sides as their judgment may dictate. In this connection it should be said that the money question is not usually discussed dispassionately—either in private or in legislative bodies, and, to make matters still worse, sectionalism is introduced and epithets are unsparingly applied.

At this writing, while the panic is on, and banks are breaking, and large industries are going to the wall, we are simply interested in ascertaining what the effect will be, or is likely to be on labor interests. Many very prominent citizens, men who are supposed to understand financial affairs, have repeatedly

---

†   Published in *Locomotive Firemen's Magazine,* vol. 17, no. 9 (September 1893), 733–737.

declared that there existed no real legitimate cause for the panic, but such declarations amount to little or nothing when one sees the panic rushing along with the force of a cyclone. Under such circumstances, men realize there must be a cause for the panic, and whether legitimate or bastard, they want to know what it is. Here again, all is disagreement and confusion, and since a real cause must be found before a remedy can be applied, the squabble over the cause may not only protract the panic, but indefinitely augment its seriousness.

A great many people believe that the demonetization of the silver dollar, called the "dollar of the daddies," in 1873, was the starting point of the financial misfortunes of the country—because then silver dollars had their money quality knocked out of them, and the single or gold standard, it is charged, was established in the interest of "goldbugs" and "Wall Street sharks," and it is further charged that England took a hand in the demonetization of silver by sending to the United States large sums of money with which to debauch members of Congress, and placed the cash where it would do the "most good." Be this as it may, one thing is certain, there has since been a perpetual war over monometallism and bimetallism—the free coinage and the limited coinage of silver—together with its absolute equality with gold in its use upon some parity of value, but the advocates of silver have never scored a complete victory, and at this writing, the outlook for silver is anything but encouraging to its friends. It is not required that the *Magazine* should assume an attitude of antagonism to either gold or silver. So far as the Brotherhood of Locomotive Firemen is concerned, the coins of both metals are eminently popular, and we shall be glad to know that a parity between the metals can be established that may be indefinitely prolonged, and the business of the country established upon secure monetary foundations.

Those who contend that the "demonetization of silver" in 1873 is the initial cause of the present panic, notwithstanding the wrong was perpetrated twenty years ago, are met by investigators and writers in the interest of the "gold standard" who tell them that from the foundation of the government the gold standard has practically prevailed, and this assertion is fortified by the fact that from 1792, when the original Coinage Act was passed, to 1873, when the dollar was demonetized, only 8 million silver dollars had been coined, while, within the same period, 81 years, the American mints had coined $900 million of gold, which seemingly establishes the assertion that the gold standard had prevailed during the entire period.

In 1878, five years after the demonetization of silver dollars, the coinage of silver under an act of Congress began in earnest, and from that time to December 1892, 361,508,508 silver dollars had been coined of *full* legal tender quality—that is to say, the silver dollars have absolutely all the value of gold coins except the payment of interest upon the national bonds, which, as expressed in the bonds, must be paid in gold. Here it is seen that the 361,508,508 silver dollars have the same value in the United States as is conferred upon gold. But such statements, however concise, instead of elucidating the causes which have led to the present panic, serve to embarrass the investigation. Hence another chapter relating to silver must be introduced, which may be properly styled the notorious Sherman Law. This law put a stop to the coinage of silver dollars, but did not interfere with the full legal tender quality of the dollars already coined. The Sherman Law provided for the purchase of 4.5 million ounces of silver bullion every month, or 54 million ounces annually, and directed that this bullion should be paid for in treasury notes, to "be redeemable on demand in coin at the treasury of the United States," and the Secretary of the Treasury is directed to "redeem such notes in gold or silver coin, at his discretion." It is now claimed that the Sherman Law is the real cause of the panic. Why? It is easy to ask questions, and sometimes difficult to answer them, but in answering why the Sherman Law is the cause of the panic, or the initial cause, some space is required.

In the first place, the United States treasurer is required to keep on hand $100 million in gold coin, to redeem on demand its obligations payable in coin. This $100 million reserve fund is regarded sufficiently limited to maintain specie payment, hence any reduction of the reserve below the $100 million limit places specie payment, and therefore the credit of the government, in peril.

As has been stated, under the Sherman Law the government is required to purchase 54 million ounces of silver bullion annually, and pay for the silver in treasury notes redeemable on demand in coin, gold, or silver, at the discretion of the treasurer—but really the treasurer has little if any discretion in the matter, because of the proviso in the law as follows: "It being the established policy of the United States to maintain the two metals on a parity with each other upon the present legal ratio, or such ratio as may be prescribed by law." Now then, suppose A sells the government 1 million ounces of silver bullion, and receives payment in treasury notes redeemable in coin. Having received the notes, he presents them for payment and demands gold; should the treasurer refuse to pay gold and offer silver, that moment the "parity," the equality of the two metals would cease, and gold would be at a premium, hence, therefore, if A demanded gold, the treasurer would be bound to redeem the notes in that commodity, because it is "the established policy of the United States to maintain the two metals on a parity."

Under the operation of the Sherman Law, treasury notes amounting to about $200 million have been issued in payment for silver bullion; and

European nations wanting gold, their agents get possession of the treasury notes, present them at the treasury, and demand gold. These transactions have continued until the government reserve of $100 million in gold was seriously reduced. Notes of alarm were sounded. Gold continued to go to Europe on almost every ship. The reserve decreased, the press was full of warnings, and the panic started. Distrust took the place of confidence; confusion prevailed. Men who had money in banks became suspicious, runs followed, banks failed, industrial enterprises closed down. Men who had money locked it up, and thus as we write, the panic is sweeping along and wrecks mark its pathway, and boiled down we find a general agreement of opinion that the Sherman Law is responsible for the starting of the panic, and this opinion is confirmed by the fact that President Cleveland has called an extra session of Congress to repeal the Sherman Law and put an end to the purchase of silver bullion, which will put an end to the issuing of treasury notes, and put an end to the further depletion of the gold reserve for the maintenance of specie payments.

This, it is thought by some, will at once restore confidence and establish normal conditions, while others are as confident that the salvation of business depends upon the free coinage of silver the same as gold; that there must be no discrimination, since, so long as silver is required to play second to gold at the mints, the discrimination will be fatal to conditions of the largest prosperity.

There are others who scout the idea that it is possible to place the United States on a plane of the largest business activity and security of expansion without a larger volume of currency, and aside from the issue of paper money, they claim that the free coinage of silver alone can solve the vexatious problem. The advocates of free coinage, which means throwing the mints open to the coinage of all the silver offered, the same as gold, as was the condition prior to 1873, will secure the double standard, gold and silver, at a ratio of 16 to 1 or some other rational ratio, and indefinitely increase the volume of specie currency. These advocates of free coinage point to France, the most prosperous of European countries, with an area of 203,000 square miles and a population of 40 million, which maintains in circulation $700 million of silver or $17.95 per capita, and including gold, silver, and paper, $40.56 per capita, while the United States, with an area of over 3 million square miles and a population of 65 million, maintains a circulation in silver of only $8.85 per capita, and including gold, silver, and paper, only $25.15 per capita, or $15.41 per capita less than France.

Indeed, when statistics, showing the portion of the currency of the United States held out of circulation which is said to be in circulation, the amount of currency actually in circulation is far below $25.15 per capita, and it is just here that a large body of men attribute the present panic to causes other than the vicious forces embodied in the Sherman Law. Hence they say that the legislation all along the line from 1873 to the present, having been in the interest of gold and of flagrant injustice to silver, accounts largely for the present panic and widespread business demoralization.

Admitting, simply for the sake of argument, that silver is at the bottom of the present business demoralization growing out of legislation, in which the "goldbugs" have triumphed over the "silver fanatics," how stands labor? We hear much said about paying labor in "honest dollars." So much, indeed, as to leave the impression that the gold and silver factions have been animated all the time by a desire to do the fair thing by labor. But the inquiry is: What is the result? (1) Throughout the silver mining regions of the country the silver mines are forced to close down and thousands of men are out of employment, without a remote prospect of a day's work. Want stares them in the face, and funds are being subscribed and appeals made to the railroads to scatter these idle men abroad over the country. (2) Banks that hold the small accumulations of workingmen are closing their doors against depositors, and men and women shed tears as they see the doors close upon them and their little hoard. (3) Other industrial enterprises are either failing or temporarily closing their establishments and setting thousands of employees adrift, and these conditions have been brought about, admittedly, by vicious legislation. And to make matters worse, while all agree that legislation to down silver and exalt gold is the cause of the panic, the probabilities are that remedial legislation is by no means assured. Meanwhile, labor suffers—and only labor suffers. The bankers will continue to fare sumptuously; the owners of silver mines and closed factories will not be seriously inconvenienced; the real victims of vicious legislation will be workingmen and their families. While this suffering continues, Congress will convene, and the wrangle will begin again over silver. The country will again be deluged with historical *chestnuts* relating to silver, from the days of Abraham to the present. We shall have windy dissertations on monometallism, bimetallism, single standard, double standard, free coinage international conferences, Latin unions, the rupee, ad infinitum and ad nauseam, and while labor suffers and starves and the panic proceeds, the debates will go forward.

If there are those who anticipate legislation that will immediately restore confidence, let them dismiss the hallucination. Panics, like wars, are destructive. Confidence, once destroyed, recovers slowly, and once started, like earthquakes, they subside only when their force is exhausted. Our advice to workingmen is, be rigidly economical—save the dimes, hoard your earnings with miserly care. Let it be understood that the gold and the silver factions are at war. And while the war proceeds, confidence will seek retirement and take its surplus cash with it into its hiding places. Already, the wires report that from one state alone orders for $12 million for merchandise have been canceled. This canceling is likely to be many times multiplied, which means less work for railroads, less wages, and reduction of employees. Hence we say to railroad employees, let the severest economy prevail.

We do not belong to the ranks of calamity howlers. We do not care to paint the outlook either blue or black, but a man is colorblind who declares it to be rosy. Panics, as we have said, run their course, and this of 1893 is not likely to be an exception, and since, as it is claimed, it is owing to vicious financial legislation, the remedy would seem to be wise legislation, or legislation diametrically opposed to that which has produced the panic; and should such legislation be had, with the promptness the emergency requires, a full year would elapse before normal conditions could be established. Meanwhile, let the motto of workingmen be: Save every possible cent of wages while wages can be had.

The Pulpit and Socialism[†]

September 1893

Rev. Myron W. Reed is a very distinguished clergyman of the Presbyterian persuasion.[38] He is one of those divines who "finds tongues in trees, books in running brooks, sermons in stones."[39]

And good in many things the average theologian fails to discover.

One of the distinguishing characteristics of Mr. Reed's sermons is that he sees more in a text than the average orthodox preacher. In a recent sermon, he had for his text "And I Saw a New Heaven and a New Earth"[40]—and proceeded to show that if socialists do not yet see what was unfolded to the enraptured vision of Saint John, they are working industriously in that direction. Mr. Reed thinks there is even now a pressing necessity for a new heaven and a new earth

[†]   Published in *Locomotive Firemen's Magazine,* vol. 17, no. 9 (September 1893), 740–743.

in the United States. He says, "There ought to be a new earth, and what ought to be will be. No one will assert that this is the ideal social system—this one that we are living under. Isaiah would not be satisfied with it, nor Plato. We are not satisfied with it. It is a makeshift."

Mr. Reed points out that in New York City, "more than 800,000 people exist on a square mile." Does Mr. Reed think that with a "new earth," people would be less gregarious and more disposed to scatter? If so, then there should be a new set of people to inhabit the new earth: Otherwise, we should see a reproduction of great cities, tenement houses, squalor, and degradation such as the world now complains of, and which might be remedied in a year if people would go to the country, where there is only one to twenty persons to the square mile. Mr. Reed remarks that "prophets and poets," as did Saint John, "have seen" this "new heaven and new earth," that "Plato looked away and saw Atlantis;" the same may be said of Lord Bacon, he too saw Atlantis, the dream of the ancients, and located it in the middle of the Atlantic Ocean, and he refers to Sir Thomas More who, in his utopia, saw the new earth, an imaginary coast or island, also in mid-ocean, like Atlantis, where everything was very much like heaven, as fancy paints it.

Manifestly, things are not just right in this world, and insofar as the United States is concerned, the question arises, who's to blame? Mr. Reed points out that during one recent year, 23,000 evictions took place in the city of New York, and thousands of evictions take place in great cities every year, and yet the people continue to crowd to the great cities; they go from the country to the cities; they prefer the tenement houses with their filth and poisoned air to the delights of country life, and if we had a new earth, upon which the Creator would build a four-room cottage on every ten acres, the people, at least half of them, would go to the cities.

A New York paper, of recent date, names localities near New York where female help, as cooks, and for laundry work, housekeepers, etc., are in active demand but cannot be obtained because the girls want society, amusements, etc., and therefore remain where there are 800,000 people to the square mile and evictions mount up into the thousands annually.

Mr. Reed remarks:

> What a summer we had. War up in Idaho and Wyoming and down in Tennessee, and at Buffalo and Homestead. These little wars cost millions. Nothing was settled by them. Lockouts and strikes will continue. It is no wonder that we hear prophets and poets saying: "I see a new heaven and a new earth." They are very much needed.

Why do such things occur in the United States? Ah, because the people who have the ballot permit them. Who is going to create the new earth? God? Is this one a failure? Everyone says the earth, as it is, is "very beautiful," and God said, after He had completed it, that it was "good." The trouble has been with man. He is a failure—particularly in the United States of America—and yet, if we accept statistics, he has done fairly well. What is required to improve the condition of man in the United States of America? Here a man, if he is not a criminal nor insane, is a citizen—a sovereign citizen. He has the ballot—a wonderful weapon. He can make and unmake constitutions and laws. If there is anything wrong, he can right it. If an officer is incapable, or a rascal, the ballot can turn him out. If the laws hedge up our present opportunities, the laws can be repealed. What more is wanted? Here we have *free* speech, *free* books and newspapers. For five cents a man can purchase a newspaper every day that will take all his leisure to read it through, and with free libraries he can become familiar with the mind treasures of the world. What more does a man want? The free school is here, multiplied thousands of them, which, like springs of pure water, are inviting all to drink, slake thirst for knowledge, and go on their way rejoicing. What better earth does Mr. Reed or any other socialist want? What other "divinity" is demanded to "shape the ends" of the country, or of the government, or of individuals? Before socialism in its present form was heard of, the United States struck all the fetters from mind and soul, and men stood redeemed and disenthralled, free, absolutely free to work out their own destiny upon what was a new earth, not the vagary of Plato or Sir Thomas More or any other dreamer.

Mr. Reed says, "Poverty and ignorance get together and crime is born," but he does not say what the result is when wealth and education get together. He does not define the terms "poverty" and "ignorance." A man receiving $1 a day is poor compared with men whose incomes reach $1,000 a day, or $100 a day, or $60, $20, or $10 a day. A man may be said to be ignorant who can simply read and write, compared with a graduate of Harvard or Yale, or Dr. Briggs's theological seminary. People representing that description of "poverty and ignorance" are to be found by the thousands in the United States—men who are poor and ignorant, as compared with rich and educated. This sort of "poverty and ignorance" get together. It is found in all the workshops in all the factories and mines in the land, but *crime* is *not* therefore *born*. From the days of Plato, Saint John the divine, the prophets, and the poets, crime was born when the rich and the educated got together, and what was true in the faraway days, when this earth was new, has been true all along the centuries and is true now. The poor and uneducated have been the toilers, the builders, have constituted the army of progress and are now the hope of the world. In the ranks of the rich and the educated are those who rob the poor, as did the Pharisees, who "devoured widows' houses."[41] Christ gave them a "new heaven and a new earth," but not the kind they wanted. A few concluded to form a community and have all things in common. It was the socialistic idea, but they mistook the meaning of Christianity and exhibited profound ignorance of human nature. Ananias concluded to join the community, went in with a lie on his lips, and was carried out dead. And his wife followed suit, and the first society was wrecked, and all subsequent schemes of the sort have proven failures.[42]

We return to the proposition that in the United States of America we have the "new earth and the new heaven." Not the dream of Plato and Sir Thomas More, nor the thing which John saw while on the Isle of Patmos,[43] but a country extending from ocean to ocean, a country of boundless resources, capable of supporting a thousand millions of people, and this country is the new earth and the new heaven of workingmen, if they can be made to understand the fact. They can improve and embellish it until all of its square miles shall resemble the poet's wildest fancies of fairyland. Already this is a government of the people, by the people, and for the people. The workingmen are in the majority, and therefore this is their country and their government, their new earth and new heaven. They can have such constitutions and such laws as they desire, and such presidents, Congress, legislatures, and officers as they wish. They can maintain their individuality, be free and independent, and have just the kind of a new earth and a new heaven they may deem best for their happiness.

Mr. Reed, in his sermon advocating socialism, says, "I am as ready to buy meat of the United States as to buy it of Mr. Armour." Evidently it is the socialistic idea to have the United States turn butcher and supply the people with meat, turn grocer and retail soap and soda, turn gardener and furnish vegetables, organize a dairy and peddle butter and milk, and so on to the end of the chapter, and this would be a realization of Plato's dream and the vision of Saint John; Atlantis and Utopia, castles of moonshine which prophets and poets have built as their imaginations have dictated.

Workingmen are in the majority, and if they will unify upon common-sense lines and use the ballot to enthrone justice, the new earth and the new heaven will come—and come to stay. Wages will be just—homes will be beautiful and vocal with songs of contentment. The government will not reduce the man to a thing as in Sparta, under Lycurgus. Man will still be man, and not a part of the rolling stock of the government. Courts will inspire confidence, and judges will not be clothed in robes smirched in the filth of apostasy. Already we are reaching out for the new earth and the new heaven—not an Atlantis nor a utopia, a land of butterflies and buttercups, rainbows and moonshine, but a country in which fact supersedes fiction, and honest wages, reasonable hours of work, just laws, and high-minded judges hold sway.

Business Depression and Legislation[†]
October 1893

According to *Bradstreet's,* from January 1 to August 1, 1893, moneyed institutions of various descriptions to the number of 428 suspended, and during the same period, of the entire number, only 58 resumed business.

During the months of January, February, March, and April there were no premonitions the average businessman could discover of the impending storm, and during the four months named, only 26 moneyed institutions suspended. During the month of May the cyclone struck 54 institutions; in June the wrecks numbered 118, and in July the number swelled to 231, and the panic swept along, creating almost unparalleled depression in all departments of business.

Bradstreet's, of August 12, surveying the whole field of finance and industries, informs the country that up to August 1 the suspended banks had assets amounting to $105 million, and liabilities amounting to $102 million, and that of the 428 suspended institutions only 58 had resumed business. In commenting upon the industrial situation, the paper gives returns of 800 establishments of more or less prominence which have suspended operations since June 1, throwing out of employment 463,000 employees, and adds: "When it is realized that this report, complete as it may be, is quite incomplete so far as the country at large is concerned, . . . it becomes plain to casual observers that there are in all probability no fewer than 800,000 or 900,000 idle employees of manufacturing, commercial, and other enterprises at this time who were nearly, if not all, actively employed three or four months ago." Since the tables of *Bradstreet's* were compiled, the work of depression has gone steadily forward,

†   Published in *Locomotive Firemen's Magazine,* vol. 17, no. 10 (October 1893), 819–823.

banks have continued to suspend, and industrial enterprises have suspended operations, and the army of idle men has received enormous accessions.

Under such circumstances men are inquiring and investigating to ascertain the cause of the depression, of the panic, that is producing widespread alarm, extending from ocean to ocean, and from the British possessions to the Gulf of Mexico. At this supreme juncture the president calls Congress in special session, and in his message says:

> To the Congress of the United States:—
>
> The existence of an alarming and extraordinary business situation, involving the welfare and prosperity of all our people, has constrained me to call together in extra session the people's representatives in Congress, to the end that through a wise and patriotic exercise of their legislative duty present evils may be mitigated and dangers threatening the future may be averted. Our unfortunate financial plight is not the result of untoward events nor of conditions related to our natural resources; nor is it traceable to any of the afflictions which frequently check national growth and prosperity. With plenteous crops, with abundant promise of remunerative production and manufacture, with unusual invitation to safe investment and with satisfactory assurance to business enterprise, suddenly financial distrust and fear have sprung up on every side; numerous moneyed institutions have suspended because abundant assets were not immediately available to meet the demands of frightened depositors; surviving corporations and individuals are content to keep in hand the money they are usually anxious to loan, and those engaged in legitimate business are surprised to find the securities they offer for loans, though heretofore satisfactory, are no longer accepted; values supposed to be fixed are fast becoming conjectural, and loss and failure have invaded every branch of business. I believe these things are principally chargeable to Congressional legislation touching the purchase and coinage of silver by the general government.

In reading the foregoing it is seen that the president attributes the business depression, the panic, the wreckage of banks, the closing of factories and mines, the entire bad business to "congressional legislation." The arraignment of Congress by the president is of tremendous import. The indictment embodies the charge, by inference, at least, of incapacity, of inability to comprehend cause and effect, and blindly pursue a policy that fills the land with calamities and which portends still other trials and struggles, that the bravest of men cannot contemplate without experiencing thrills of horror.

Manifestly, if, as the president asserts, the misfortune the country is now experiencing is the result of vicious legislation by Congress, what hope is there that Congress is either capable or willing to apply the needed remedy? Indeed the question arises, is it within the power of Congress, however willing and capable, to apply any remedy that will restore the status quo of business until the panic, like the plague, cholera, yellow fever, or smallpox, has run its course and prostrated everything not abnormally prepared for resistance?

In this connection it is prudent to inquire, who can resist the force of the panic? We answer, the rich. They can not only stand the storm but grow richer in proportion to its violence. They are the wreckers on the storm-beaten coasts when the crafts go down or are driven upon the reefs and rocks. Thousands of the rich, we do not doubt, will suffer, but the term, in their case, has a limited meaning. There will be less luxury, but no decrease in the comforts of life. The real sufferers are the daily wage-men—men without work and without pay; men around whose homes the gloom increases to the point of despair. These are the real victims of congressional legislation, and of all vicious legislation. The charge is made upon the high authority of the president of the United States—not by agitators, not by anarchists, not by the depraved. Mr. Cleveland points out what the panic is doing in the way of disasters, and says, "I believe these things are principally chargeable to congressional legislation." What things? As *Bradstreet's* says, forcing into idleness 800,000 or 900,000 workingmen, employees of various enterprises. *Bradstreet's* admits that its report does not include the sum total of the idle. On July 31, Mayor Harrison[44] of Chicago said, "There are 200,000 idle men in Chicago," and he utters the terrible warning that, unless something is done by the government to brighten conditions, there will be deeds of violence that will shake the country like an earthquake. Everywhere the newspapers are trying to lie conservative. They speak hesitatingly, they are afraid to tell the truth, the naked, hideous truth. The *Philadelphia Times,* a conservative paper, reports the canvassing of 57 trades and callings in the city of New York having a membership of 99,950, and shows of those 36,177 are idle. There are probably in the city of New York more than one hundred organizations representing wage earners. We know of a city with a population of 125,000 that has 83 organizations, hence the *Times's* statement must be regarded as giving a low estimate. And it is notable that while the *Times* refers to conditions in New York, it is silent regarding the effects of the panic in Philadelphia, immediately under its nose and within reach of its reportorial force. The fact is, the country is left to conjecture regarding the direful outlook.

In a general way the *Times* discusses the panic and tells the truth. It refers to the "financial revulsion," saying it was "declared to be entirely a rich man's panic; that only speculators and gamblers were embarrassed by it," and proceeds to say,

> Whatever may be the causes which produce financial disturbances, and however the rich may suffer, the one class that cannot escape the bitterest dregs of the cup of misfortune is the working class. All ills of commerce, finance, and trade end in the homes of the poor, and they must bear the chief burden of business disturbance. The rich can live on greatly reduced resources; they can stop their mills or mines and be content with profits already accumulated, but the poor, who earn their bread from day to day as they consume it, when forced into idleness must face starvation.
>
> It is true that the present panic is a money panic; entirely a money panic in its origin, but it has permeated into every channel of commerce, industry, and trade, and today it affects every mill, mine, field, and forest where industry has its home. The scarcity of money, no matter from what cause, has halted improvements, has reduced consumption, and the inexorable law of supply and demand enforces a reduction of supply. To attain that, labor must be dismissed from employment, and the laborer left without means to support himself and his family.
>
> All panics of every kind and from any and every cause end in fearful cost to labor, and it is lamentable to see how many of our industrial people are misled as to the remedy. Of all classes and conditions in this country they most need stable and just laws; they most of all need honest money, and yet from nearly every industrial organization of the country we hear expressions of sympathy for those who are battling for cheap and dishonest money, the countless evils of which must in the end fall upon labor. Business that employs industry is disturbed today because our national money and our national credit have been impaired by insane concessions to cheap money advocates, and labor is today paying the fearful price of that folly.

It is true, deplorably true, that labor and only labor suffers by the panic—all else can wait until the storm has spent its force. The rich can close down their shells like a tortoise, pull in their heads, and sleep. The notable thing about the *Times*'s article is its closing paragraph, in which, like all champions of the plutocratic class, it seeks to throw the responsibility of the panic upon labor, intimating that it suffers because of its advocacy of a dishonest currency. When did labor control or influence the legislation of Congress, which Mr. Cleveland avers is responsible for the panic? Vicious damphoolism[45] never went further than to intimate such a charge. Labor never had a voice in the financial legislation of Congress. Labor never voted for a dishonest dollar of any description. Labor accepts the government's currency and has had an abiding faith in its honesty. It has made no war upon standard coins or redeemable paper. Whether in one party or another, labor has been loyal to honest money, has had implicit confidence in the fiat of the nation, and is not responsible for congressional legislation, which Mr. Cleveland says is "chargeable" with the present panic.

No sane man will challenge the propriety of greater activity in the ranks of labor to influence congressional legislation in the future. The *Times* demonstrates the absolute necessity for labor to take action, since it must bear all the ills.

Congress is now in session. Will it give relief to labor, which is now paying the "fearful cost" to which the panic has subjected it? As labor is not represented in Congress, and since it is subjected to a fearful strain, it has begun holding public meetings. In Chicago, on August 15, three thousand idle men deliberated upon their condition and passed a series of resolutions. Speeches were made. A report outlines proceedings as follows:

> Thomas I. Kidd, general secretary of the Woodworkers' International Union of America, was greeted with cheers. A part of his remarks were:
> "Send representative wage earners to Washington instead of lawyers and millionaires. Let the masses and not the classes be represented. If you would do that, there would not be 200,000 idle men in Chicago, our poorhouses and prisons would not be crowded, and women would not be selling their purity for morsels of bread. Look at the auditorium (and he moved his hand toward the structure); wageworkers cut and set the stone to build it, but they are the last ones welcomed there. Why? Because you shout for Cleveland and Harrison. Mrs. Vanderbilt gave $150,000 for a collar for her poodle dog, when ten thousand children were starving to death in New York."
> P. J. Grimes of the Hardwood Finishers' Union spoke briefly, saying: "Thousands in this crowd want work. It cannot be had. It is not their fault they are idle. The capitalistic press says it is. This is untrue. Many here know not where their next meal will come from. It is only summer now. What will winter produce? They will die like slaves. An empty stomach has no conscience. Our people sit on a volcano. Let them beware of the explosion."
> The following resolutions were adopted:
> "Resolved, That we demand of the present Congress to fix a true standard of values based upon the product of labor, and that the government issue the circulating medium to the people.

"Resolved, That the government employ the idle men on the roadways and on the public improvements of all kinds where the convicts are now employed, and that public work be done by the people and not by contract.

"Resolved, That the hours of toll be reduced to that point that all may be employed, so that machinery will be a boon to the toiling millions rather than a curse.

"Resolved, lastly, That the unemployed be warned through the press that Chicago has thousands of men willing to work, but unable to find it."

The meeting is significant—others will follow. It is not required to so much as suggest how the fire will spread or the character of the scenes to be enacted. Whatever may transpire inimical to peace and order as the result of the panic, let it always be remembered that President Cleveland says it is *chargeable to congressional legislation.*

Labor and Capital and the Distribution of Property[†]
November 1893

The question of capital and labor is not only being debated in congresses and legislatures, in lodge rooms and in the assemblies of labor representatives, but Mr. Justice Henry B. Brown[46] of the United States Supreme Court deems it entirely prudent to give the subject his attention, which he did in an address before the American Bar Association at its annual meeting in Milwaukee, August 31. We have only a synopsis of the distinguished gentleman's views, but enough of what he said to force the conclusion that he leans up to capital and capitalists like one who knows and appreciates the difference between a workingman and a millionaire.

The address of Mr. Justice Brown is spoken of as being "lengthy but interesting throughout." In the course of his remarks it is reported that the "distinguished jurist, by way of introduction, reviewed the history of strikes between capital and labor from the days of the great strike of the Israelites, the conflicts

---

†   Published in *Locomotive Firemen's Magazine,* vol. 17, no. 11 (November 1893), 879–883.

between the Roman patricians and plebeians, the feudal lords and the merchants of the Middle Ages, down to the struggles of the present day."

The ermined orator did not, so far as reported, give any particulars relating to the "great strikes of the Israelites." It is possible that he referred to the straw-strike, at a time when the Israelites were making brick for Pharaoh. This was not exactly a strike, but the brickmakers did appoint a grievance committee to go to Pharaoh and tell the general manager of Egypt their troubles.[47] Really, we feel much obliged to Mr. Justice Brown for his allusion to this strike, though it was not, properly speaking, a strike between "labor and capital, but rather between labor and the government. At the time of the straw-strike there were in Egypt 600,000 adult male Israelites. How many of them were directly engaged in making brick we have no means of knowing, but it was, evidently, a leading industry. The straw required in making the brick was to mix with the clay to improve its adhesive qualities, and was deemed in those days essential.

It is interesting to state how this straw-strike of the Israelites originated. It appears that God had appointed Moses the leader of the Israelites, for the purpose of getting them out of Egypt, by the way of the "wilderness" into the "promised land," or Canaan. Moses, therefore, asked permission of Pharaoh to let the Israelites go a three days' journey into the wilderness to worship. This three days' vacation asked for the Israelites, in the name of the Israelites' God, seemed preposterous; besides, Pharaoh neither knew nor cared for the God of the Israelites, and he not only flatly refused the request, but ordered that, as previous to this request, he had supplied the brickmakers with straw, thereafter they should hunt straw for themselves, but in no case was their task to be lightened; they were ordered to make as many bricks as when the straw was furnished, and their taskmasters were ordered to beat them in every case where the tale (count) fell below the required number.

It was this infamous order that resulted in the officers of the children of Israel organizing a grievance committee to lay their troubles directly before Pharaoh. But the effort to have the iniquitous order modified in any regard did not succeed. Pharaoh was obdurate and insolent, drove the grievance committee from his presence, remanded the brickmakers to their tasks, taunting them with the remark, "Ye are idle, ye are idle, therefore ye say let us go and do sacrifice to the Lord. Go ye, therefore, now, and work; for there shall no straw be given you, yet shall ye deliver the tale (count) of bricks." At this supreme juncture the grievance committee met Moses, the leader, and said to him, "The Lord look upon you, and judge, because ye have made our saviour to be abhorred in the eyes of Pharaoh and in the eyes of his servants to put a sword in their hands to slay us." Times did look blue to the brickmakers, as also to Moses, who immediately laid the matter before the Lord, and said to the Lord, "Wherefore hast thou so evil entreated this people? Why is it that thou hast sent me? For since I came to Pharaoh to speak in thy name he hath done evil to this people, neither hast thou delivered them." It was plain talk on the part of Moses. Pharaoh had been enraged, he had imposed heavy burdens upon the Israelites, and things had been made worse, generally. But the Lord assured Moses that he was not done with Pharaoh, but that he would, in the end, make the strike such a success that it would never be forgotten. Certainly, we are obliged to Mr. Justice Brown for his reference to the "great strike of the Israelites." The Lord set the example of doing Pharaoh and all Egypt immense honor, because of his infamous dealings with the brickmakers. In the first place, as a punishment, the waters of Egypt were turned to blood; (2) he filled the land with frogs; (3) he filled the land with lice; (4) swarms of flies filled all Egypt; (5) all the cattle, horses, asses, camels, and oxen were stricken with murrain; (6) every man and beast was afflicted with boils; (7) a storm of hail, thunder, and fire was sent so that everything was destroyed except the wheat and the rye; (8) locusts came next and devoured everything; (9) then came darkness that could be felt, lasting three days; (10) then came the final plague, when the firstborn in all the land of Egypt, from the firstborn of Pharaoh unto the firstborn of the lowliest in all the land, was slain.[48] This done, Pharaoh was willing to give the Israelites a vacation, to let them leave his country, but in a moment of madness he called out his army to slaughter the Israelites, but was caught in the Red Sea, when horses, chariots, and soldiers all went down to death.

What of it all? Not much, perhaps. Pharaoh treated workingmen unjustly; he would not listen to a grievance committee; his greed obscured all sense of right and justice, and ultimately he paid dearly for his exercise of power over defenseless men. God did not stop to consult public opinion, nor the courts of Egypt. He did not consider the rights of property. He saw the inhumanity of Pharaoh, his tyranny, his purpose to degrade workingmen, to increase their tasks and then beat them for their non-performance. These things aroused the vengeance of Jehovah, and then came the plagues of blood, frogs, lice, flies, murrain, boils, hail and fire, locusts, darkness, the death of the firstborn, and then the Red Sea disaster. After all these things, the children of Israel marched for forty years and finally entered the promised land.

For this wonderful display of divine power and vengeance there seems to have been one cause, and only one cause—the bad treatment of workingmen— and we are told that God is the same yesterday, today, and forever. We do not know that Mr. Justice Brown spoke either lengthily or learnedly upon the "great strike of the Israelites." We conclude he did not, because he jumped from the "great strike of the Israelites" to the strike of the brassworkers in Breslau as early as 1539, and to the strike of the tailors in Baltimore in 1795, concluding from his brief historical sketch that "it is apparent (1) that strikes, so far from being peculiar to modern industrial enterprise, as seems to be generally supposed, are as old as *civilization itself;* (2) that they prevail most *extensively* in the most enlightened and wealthy communities, and so far from being an *indication of extreme poverty,* are equally as frequent in times of general prosperity; (3) that the wit of man has as yet devised no scheme whereby they may be prevented or even alleviated." In saying this, Mr. Justice Brown writes himself down a superficial thinker. It was never claimed that strikes were an indication of "extreme poverty." What is the signification of "extreme poverty?" It is squalor, degradation, hunger, and nakedness. There may be instances on record where such people struck to better their condition, but, as a general proposition, it is not true. Men strike to prevent "extreme poverty," to prevent squalor and degradation. They strike, as did the Israelites, against inhuman treatment, tasks that kill soul and body. They strike against a reduction of wages and for an advance in wages; they strike for reasonable hours for a day's work and against hours that leave no time for physical recuperation and mental improvement; they strike for that which dignifies citizenship and secures liberty and independence; they strike that their homes may not be huts and dunghills, and their children outcasts from the day of their birth—facts which Mr. Justice Brown never discovered, and would not have appreciated had they been forced upon his attention.

It is not true, as Mr. Justice Brown declares, "that the wit of man has as yet devised no scheme whereby [strikes] may be prevented or even alleviated." Strikes have been prevented in a vast number of instances and as often alleviated when they have occurred, and beyond the vicious influences prevailing in high judicial circles, hopes are born and nursed into vigorous vitality that a reign of justice in the world is of possible attainment—and it is widely accepted as a probability that men who now are compelled to strike against oppression will, armed with the ballot, strike against an aristocratic judiciary and place men upon the bench whose public utterances are not framed to obscure their baseness.

It is not at all surprising that Mr. Justice Brown, in support of his plutocratic theories, should refer to the utterances of some "enthusiasts" who picture an "ideal state of society where neither poverty nor riches prevail," but workingmen who strike do not indulge in vagaries. On the contrary, they do believe a reign of justice is within the limits of "human character as at present constituted." The distinguished judge doubts if there was neither poverty nor riches in the world that such a condition "would conduce as much to the general happiness as the inequality which excites emulation and stimulates energy." He can conceive of nothing to "excite emulation and stimulate energy" except money—riches, and he doubtless had his own ambitions in view when he made the statement. He said, "Rich men are essential even to the well-being of the poor." "It is they," said the judge, "who in a thousand ways develop the resources of our country and afford employment to a countless army of workingmen. One has but to consider for a moment the immediate consequences of the abolition of large private fortunes to appreciate the danger which lurks in any radical disturbance of the present social system." In the foregoing, there is nothing new. It is the rehash of the same old idea, that workingmen are dependent upon the rich—that they live, move, and have their existence by the permission of the rich. It is the idea of the slave driver. Its purpose is to degrade workingmen until they are ready and willing to accept the domination of assumed superiors and obey their orders without complaint. This done, degradation has reached its lowest depths. This done, the slave accepts his bacon and corn bread, his dress to distinguish him as a helot, and then things go on swimmingly for the plutocratic masters. Mr. Justice Brown is of the opinion that for workingmen a sort of a millennial era has dawned. He said:

> While, in this country at least, private fortunes are larger than they have ever been before, the condition of the laboring class has improved in equal ratio. There was never a time when the working classes were so well paid, or when their wages could buy for them so many of the comforts of life as now. Not only are the workingman's wages higher, but his hours of labor are shorter. He is better housed, better clad, better fed, better taught, reads better and cheaper papers, sends his children to better schools, and enjoys more opportunities for recreation and for seeing the world than ever before. He not only practically dictates his own hours of labor, but in large manufacturing centers he is provided with model lodging houses for his family, with libraries, parks, clubs, and lectures for his entertainment and instruction, with cheap excursion trains for his amusement on Sundays and holidays; and not only absolutely but relatively to the rich is vastly better off than he was fifty years ago.

Thus spoke Mr. Justice Brown to the American Bar, August 31, 1893, at a time when multiplied thousands of workingmen were out of employment, not knowing where they could secure a meal of victuals. But supposing no clouds overspread the skies of labor and the picture painted by the judge was literally true, then it is seen that during the past 50 years great improvements have been made in the condition of workingmen. The question arises, who brought about this improvement? Not men of Mr. Justice Brown's type. Not rich men, but workingmen by combination, by strikes, by sacrifice, and as labor's emancipation has not yet come, and as the rich are still oppressing, and as the courts are still corrupt, labor has before it herculean tasks to perform. Hitherto the combinations of labor have been on a small scale and imperfect. Once unified, once redeemed from the fetters of envy and jealousy, once marshaled under one banner, and they will go forth from bondage under a God-ordained leader, such as was Moses in the great straw-strike of the Israelites.

The Teaching of Christ[†]

November 1893

Cardinal Gibbon,[49] in an address delivered at Chicago at a recent date, among other things said:

> The Savior of mankind never conferred a greater temporal boon on mankind than by ennobling and sanctifying manual labor, and by rescuing it from the stigma of degradation which had been branded upon it. Before Christ appeared among men, manual and even mechanical work was regarded as servile and degrading to the freemen of pagan borne, and was consequently relegated to slaves. Christ is ushered into the world not amid pomp and splendor of imperial majesty, but amid the environments of an humble child of toil. He is the reputed son of an artisan, and his early manhood is spent in a mechanic's shop. "Is not this the carpenter, the son of Mary?" The primeval curse attached to labor is obliterated by the toilsome life of Jesus Christ. Ever since he pursued his trade as a carpenter, he has lightened the mechanic's tools, and has shed a halo around the workshop. If the profession of a general, a jurist, and a statesman is adorned by the example of a Washington, a Taney, and a Burke, how much more is the character of a workman ennobled by the example of Christ. What de Tocqueville said 60 years ago of the United States is true

---

†   Published in *Locomotive Firemen's Magazine,* vol. 17, no. 11 (November 1893), 904–905.

today—that with us every honest labor is laudable, thanks to the example and teaching of Christ.

It is always a little difficult to discuss Christianity in connection with what Cardinal Gibbon calls "manual labor." Certainly Christ was referred to as "the carpenter's son," and as "the carpenter," and because he was a carpenter, and the son of a carpenter, the Jews, in his "own country," treated him scornfully, to an extent that "he could there do no mighty works,"[50] and from that day to the present, the church, though in some countries clothed with imperial sway, has done no "mighty works" for manual laborers. All along the line, the church has ceaselessly pointed to Christ as "the son of a carpenter" and "the carpenter," but to what extent such references have benefited carpenters, or the sons of carpenters, or manual laborers of any class, it would be difficult to find out. Cardinal Gibbon says, "Christ is ushered into the world not amid pomp and splendor of imperial majesty but amid the environments of an humble child of toil." Has the church emulated the humility of Christ? Is the church free from pomp and splendor? Cardinal Gibbon says, "Ever since he pursued his trade as a carpenter, he has lightened the mechanic's tools." When, where, in what Christian land has the mechanic's tools been lightened (by which is meant, we presume, that his toil has been lightened) by any act of the church? By any decree of the church? The church, like "men of words and not of deeds, is like a garden full of weeds."[51] We give the church credit for every generous word it has spoken.

We are glad to believe the acts and precepts of Christ were designed, as the cardinal says, to benefit manual labor, to elevate and dignify labor, but it so happens that in Christian lands labor has been required to fight its battles alone and singlehanded. True, in the United States, labor has advanced a little, that is to say, organized labor has shown a determination to move up to a higher plane, but as a general proposition it has moved by virtue of the force of organization. We doubt if, by searching all the records in all the archives of Christendom, there will be found so much as the "scratch of a pen" showing that the church ever formulated or fulminated a decree informing men that the degradation of labor was a crime and in violation of the precepts of Christ. Something may have been done in the way of emancipating slaves, redeeming them from chattel bondage, but even in this the church has been divided. But we are discussing manual labor aside from chattel slavery and we recall nothing indicating, even remotely, the obligations of the church to do more than to exhort to patience, to bear afflictions, and vague promises of something better when the tools of toil fell from the grasp of the toiler, and death removed his burdens.

Even as we write, we have before us the self-laudations of a divine, in which he tells how many addresses he has delivered before college students, how anxious he has been to have his church in vital alliance with higher education, and how literary and Shakespearean clubs have been profited by his labors, but in all this stilted self-commendation, there is not one word showing that he cared more for workingmen than he did for working cattle.

We do not hesitate to believe there is an awakening in the church betokening a livelier interest in "manual labor." We hail it as a cheering sign of the times, but once let organized labor put its trust in anything else than organization and its doom will be recorded then and there.

Every blow organized labor strikes for the emancipation of labor has the endorsement of Christ. It is, reverently speaking, in alliance with Christ to oppose pomp and splendor, always and everywhere designed to degrade labor and fasten upon the world the abominations of paganism utterly regardless of the name it wears.

Progress of the Union: Statement to the Press†

December 1893

The sentiment in favor of the new order is widespread, growing so rapidly we cannot attend to the work of organization as promptly as we would like. Since I have been away from home it has been a constant jumping from one city to another, organizing lodges, two nights seldom finding us in the same city. The West is by no means yet organized, but sufficient work has been done to assure an exceedingly rapid growth. The success with which the American Railway Union has thus far met is very gratifying, and many months will not pass by before the country west of the Mississippi will be thoroughly organized.

For some two or three years I have foreseen that nothing short of a federation, in which all branches of the service were consolidated, could eventually

† Published in the *Terre Haute Express,* unspecified date, December 1893. Reprinted in the *Railway Times* (Chicago), vol. 1, no. 1 (January 1, 1894), 1.

expect to retain a firm footing, that which would insure it a continuous existence. Conditions in the railway world have changed wonderfully within the past few years, change to such a magnitude that organized railway labor must necessarily change to be in a present to meet this change.

At the present time the big railroads of the country number only about 20, that is, of course, the big systems and other roads controlled by them. Organized railway labor in its present condition has shown that it is unable to cope successfully with such large organizations.

Mr. Debs referred to the number of men annually being dropped from the various lodges of the old orders for non-payment of dues.

There is no such thing as suspension or expulsion for this cause in the new union. When men are suspended or expelled for non-payment of dues, when possibly they cannot pay, it engenders an ill-feeling, and when strikes are declared these men quite naturally are the ones to take the places of the strikers. Such conditions will not exist in the American Railway Union, for no member can be expelled on account of not paying dues.

One branch of the railway service never before organized and one which Mr. Debs believes will add great strength to the new order is the clerks. Here a rather laughable incident was referred to.

It was while I was out West that an employee of the auditing department asked to have the auditing clerks of the system organized. A number of the clerks said that the company had informed them that in case an organization was attempted, they would be discharged. There is a good deal of difference between a clerk and a switchman, but a party of these switchmen simply walked in and said to the clerks to organize and that should the ax fall, the headsman would be invited to come on to the switchyards and finish off the job.

The Columbian Fair[†]

December 1893

In writing of the great American Exposition, held in Jackson Park, Chicago, at once the mind relaxes its grasp upon the magnificence of the Exhibition, its cost, its national and international importance, and its historical significance, and while the heart beats like a muffled drum, enters the house of mourning, where, cold in the embrace of death, lies Carter Harrison, slain by an insane wretch. During all the months from May to the closing days of October, Carter Harrison, as a citizen and as the chief executive officer of the great metropolis of the West, had in a thousand ways given éclat to the Columbian Fair. On all occasions, his great intellect, his wide information, his profound knowledge of men and affairs had given to the great undertaking of the United States and of the nations of the earth embellishments which only great and cultured mind forces are capable of bestowing. In the midst of royalty and titled aristocracy, the Democratic mayor of Chicago, the untitled American sovereign, the exponent of Republican simplicity towered aloft, the peer of the highest and the superior of all snobdom, regardless of titles and self-assumption of superiority.

To murder such a man at any time is a national calamity; to strike him down at the time when the crime was perpetrated defies, we care not how gifted the pen, adequate characterization. We shall not attempt it. The president of the United States touched the button that set the machinery in motion on the day the fair opened, and the booming of cannon was heard around the world. Flags were unfurled to the winds, and the grand celebration of the four hundredth anniversary of the discovery of a new world began. Six months sped by, the day approached for closing the great celebration in a manner worthy of the event—when the finger of a crazy assassin touched the trigger of a death-dealing weapon, and in 20 minutes the soul of Carter Harrison had taken its eternal flight—and gloom, like a pall, fell upon a great city and upon a great nation, and the fair passed into history blotched with blood. As we write there is not a capital in all Christendom, nor scarcely in pagan lands, where the untoward event is not commented upon with sorrow.

†   Published in *Locomotive Firemen's Magazine,* vol. 17, no. 12 (December 1893), 994–996.

It is folly to discuss theories relating to cranks. Insanity is often methodical, and to such an extent that experts find it difficult to trace the dividing line between reason and madness. Insanity in its mildest forms is dangerous, and the time has come to beware of cranks, creatures who brood over fancied as well as real ills—bigots who imagine themselves the ambassadors of heaven and who stand ready, if not restrained, to light the fires of hell upon earth, and satiate their cannibal thirst with a brother's blood. Carter Harrison owes his premature and awful death to the murderous insanity of a crank who had become melancholy over a fancied wrong.

In writing of the great Columbian Fair, it scarcely suffices to say that from first to last, as an enterprise, it was a splendid success. Ordinarily, such a statement might be accepted as referring to finances. We speak of the fair in a far broader sense. It was a success financially. From first to last, the paid admissions amounted to 21,468,910, as follows: May, 1,050,037; June, 2,676,113; July, 2,760,263; August, 3,616,493; September, 4,658,907; October, 6,799,107; and the total revenues, from all sources, aggregate about $10.5 million.

Such figures illustrate the financial side of the fair. But when we attempt to estimate its educational influences upon the American mind, figures, whether numerals or the figures of rhetoric, become almost expressionless. To say that the Columbian Fair was grand, wonderful, unique, conveys to the mind no adequate conception of the enterprise. It stands out as the latest of the wonders of the world. We make no attempt to accomplish the impossible. To have seen it was to have made the voyage around the world—the acquaintance of the nations of the earth, in their own climes and environments, "from Greenland's icy mountains to India's coral strands," from the homes of the Eskimo to the homes of the Dahomeyans[52]—Christian, pagan, and savage—all were grouped in Jackson Park. Costumes, houses, huts, and customs, with products of field, farm, mine, factory, and studio, requiring days and weeks to enable the mind to grasp the alpha of the fair, the task of reaching its omega being of such a herculean character that not one visitor in a thousand accomplished it.

The fair, after all, was the sublimest testimony the world has ever heard or seen, in all the centuries, of the civilizing, elevating, liberalizing force of labor. Everywhere, from the turnstiles through which the millions passed to review the wonders of the fair—over all, above all, surrounding all, the imagination, without an effort, could see written, as vivid as electric light, the announcement that the Columbian Fair is monumental of the achievements of labor.

We make no objection to the claim capitalists may set up that behind it all was money. We are quite willing to admit the alliance between money and labor in the accomplishments of great undertakings, but this must be said, because it is true that the greater credit is due to labor, because it is the creator of the capital with which, where justice holds the scales, it is in ceaseless harmony.

Referring again to the close of the fair, October 30, 1893, we repeat that but for the tragic death of Mayor Harrison,[53] the Columbian Fair would have passed into history as the grandest achievement the nations of the earth have known since Pharaoh built the pyramids.

European Military, Money, and Misery[†]
December 1893

Nations are no longer isolated. Electricity and steam have made them near neighbors. The concern of one is becoming more and more the concern of all. Thoughtful men in the United States cannot contemplate the steadily increasing armies of Europe with composure. Our attention is called to a recent article in the *New York Herald,* in which it is stated that at the date of the Crimean War, 1854, the aggregate strength of the armies of the great powers of Europe did not exceed 3 million, in round numbers, while today, after the lapse of 39 years, it is more than 20 million, an increase of 700 percent.

The people of the United States, at least a great majority of them, treat with indifference figures relating to European military affairs, growing out of the fact, perhaps, that they regard with quite as much indifference the military affairs of their own country. Here we have what is called a regular army of about 25,000 men, costing annually, say, $30 million, an establishment so small that it seldom occupies the attention of the average citizen. We notice, because the facts are forced upon our attention daily, that Europe is annually sending vast armies of immigrants to our shores, and workingmen complain

†   Published in *Locomotive Firemen's Magazine*, vol. 17, no. 12 (December 1893), 993–994.

because the influence of these arrivals is to reduce wages, but we do not stop to consider why such vast numbers come to us. We have tabulated figures relating to wages and production, with an occasional statement showing the deep degradation of the subjects of monarchies, but too seldom do we seek to know the real cause of the sad condition from which these wretched people would escape.

It is stated that in 1869 the fighting force of Europe was 7 million soldiers; the number in 1892 was 12.5 million, but as everybody anticipates war, laws have been enacted which, as soon as they take effect, the armies of Europe will show the sum total of 22,448,000 soldiers armed and equipped for war, costing annually $1,009,000,000, as follows:

Germany	5,000,000
France	4,350,000
Russia	4,000,000
Italy	2,236,000
Austria-Hungary	1,900,000
Turkey	1,150,000
Spain	800,000
England	602,000
Sweden and Norway	338,000
Switzerland	489,000
Romania	280,000
Belgium	258,000
Bulgaria	200,000
Holland	185,000
Greece	180,000
Serbia	180,000
Portugal	154,000
Denmark	91,000
Montenegro	55,000
Total	**33,443,000**

The population of Europe, in round numbers, is 300 million; if the United States should determine to have a standing army based upon population equal to that of Germany, it would number 6.5 million soldiers, and this military establishment would cost annually, at the wages now paid for soldiers, not less than $650 million, to say nothing of equipment.

Taking such a view of the subject, it is at once seen why it is that Europeans fly from their country to find homes in the United States, free from military despotism, and where their scanty earnings are not taken by the authorities to maintain in peace the pomp and circumstance of war.

Notes

1. Gabriel is one of three named angels in the Bible, appearing in Luke 1 and Daniel 8.
2. Whitelaw Reid (1837–1912) was the successor to Horace Greeley as chief of the *New York Tribune,* one of America's leading Republican dailies.
3. Railway financier Jay Gould (1836–1892) died of tuberculosis.
4. Daniel Drew (1797–1879) was an American steamship and railway financier. In 1857 he was made a member of the board of directors of the Erie Railroad. He became embroiled in a three-way battle with Jay Gould and Cornelius Vanderbilt for control of the line. In the long-running financial feud Drew would lose $1.5 million as a result of stock manipulation practiced by Gould and his associate James Fisk.
5. Stock watering refers to the issuance of corporate stock in excess of the value of the assets to support it, usually as part of a scheme to defraud investors.
6. S. H. H. Clark (1837–1900) was a high-ranking executive for two of Gould's properties, the Union Pacific and the Missouri Pacific railroads.
7. *I came, I saw, I conquered.* Words attributed to Julius Caesar (100 BC–44 BC) in addressing the Roman Senate about a recent military victory in 47 BC.
8. Terse announcement by Commander Oliver Hazard Perry (1785–1819) of victory over the British fleet at the Battle of Lake Erie in September 1813: "We have met the enemy and they are ours. Two ships, two brigs, one schooner, and one sloop."
9. At 10 a.m. on February 9, 1893, 24 men met at the Leland Hotel in Chicago to lay the foundation for a new organization called the American Railway Union. George W. Howard chaired the brief session, which concluded its business at 2 p.m. The decision was made to secure office space for headquarters in Chicago and to effect a permanent organization at another meeting in the near future. A committee on constitution and principles was appointed, which included Debs, L. W. Rogers, and Sylvester Keliher. The afternoon was spent meeting the steady stream of railway workers who made their way to the hotel to learn more about the provisional organization. Debs took the time to make this statement to the press.
10. The Australian ballot system refers to the secret voting by individuals in privacy by marking standard government-printed ballots. Secret voting was first adopted in Australia only in 1856 and made standard in the United States in the second half of the 1880s.
11. Debs's propensity to use ethnic epithets is discussed in the introduction of Volume 1.
12. Edward Everett Hale (1822–1909) was a prominent Unitarian minister and author.
13. Allusion to the poem "Abou Ben Adhem" by James Henry Leigh Hunt (1784–1859), a short work in which the eponymous subject's earnest profession to an angel of love for fellow man is rated the supreme value by God in spite of his lack of orthodox piety.
14. Stanza from "The Battle-field" (1841), by William Cullen Bryant (1794–1878).
15. Allusion to Job 38:7.
16. Perhaps a typographical error, as no agricultural product called "zano" can be identified in the contemporary literature.
17. Henry Wilson, born Jeremiah Jones Colbath (1812–1875), was the running mate of Ulysses S. Grant during his successful campaign for reelection. Wilson was vice

president of the United States from 1873 until his death in office in 1875.

18. From April 11 to 13, 1893, a second meeting of the provisional American Railway Union was held at the Hotel Greene in Chicago, with George W. Howard as the chair. The meeting heard a report of the three-member committee on constitution and declaration of principles, with the election of officers to follow on the second day. Debs was directly quoted here by the *Chicago Tribune* following the first day's session.

19. A short introduction to this piece hints that this Debs interview was not first published in this Logansport, Indiana, morning daily. The interview was probably granted to one of the Terre Haute newspapers the previous day and subsequently reprinted. The original has not been located.

20. Partner in crime.

21. John Altgeld (1847–1902) was a progressive Democrat who served as governor of Illinois from 1893 to 1897. Altgeld distinguished himself by opposing armed federal intervention during the 1894 Pullman strike as well as for his politically controversial pardon of the surviving radicals imprisoned in the aftermath of the 1886 Haymarket bombing. His political career was effectively short-circuited by these principled albeit unpopular decisions. Long in frail health, Altgeld died of a cerebral hemorrhage in the city of Joliet at the age of 54 while delivering a political speech.

22. Michael Schwab (1853–1898) was a German-American bookbinder and labor activist who was coeditor of the revolutionary socialist *Arbeiter-Zeitung* at the time of the 1886 Haymarket affair. He wrote to Illinois governor Richard Oglesby for lenience, who commuted his sentence to life imprisonment, from which he was pardoned by new governor John Altgeld on June 26, 1893.

23. Samuel Fielden (1847–1922) was an English-born Methodist minister and labor activist who spoke at the May 3, 1886 Haymarket public meeting that was bombed. Sentenced to hang for his part in "inciting" the so-called riot, Fielden wrote the governor for clemency and had his sentence commuted to life imprisonment, from which he was pardoned after six years by Governor John Altgeld.

24. Oscar Neebe (1850–1916) was born in New York City to German immigrant parents. He was office manager of the *Arbeiter-Zeitung* at the time of the Haymarket affair, to which he was connected only through personal associations. Sentenced to 15 years in prison, Neebe was pardoned in 1893 by Governor John Altgeld.

25. Albert R. Parsons (1848–1887) was one of the leading American-born revolutionary socialists of the late nineteenth century. A newspaper editor and labor activist who turned away from electoral politics in 1880, Parsons launched an English-language anarchist weekly, *The Alarm*, in 1884. He was also regarded as the most effective English-speaking radical orator in Chicago. Parsons spoke at the Haymarket Square rally which was bombed in May 1886, and sentenced to death for allegedly inspiring the bomber. Parsons was hanged on November 11, 1887.

26. Louis Lingg (1864–1887) was a German-born carpenter and radical political activist who emigrated in 1885 to avoid military conscription. Although not present at the 1886 Haymarket Square bombing, prosecutors presented evidence implicating him

in the making of the bomb. Sentenced to hang, Lingg committed suicide in his cell with a smuggled blasting cap the day before his scheduled execution.

27. George Engel (1836–1887) was a German-born shopkeeper and radical political activist. While he did not attend the May 1886 Haymarket Square rally that was bombed, Engel was charged by a state witness with conspiracy and sentenced to hang. Engel wrote a letter to Governor Richard Oglesby refusing to plead for clemency and he was hanged with Parsons, Fischer, and Spies on November 11, 1887.

28. Adolph Fischer (1858–1887) was a German-born printer who worked as a compositor at the Chicago *Arbeiter-Zeitung*. An anarchist by the mid-1880s, Fischer was active in the Lehr und Wehr Verein, a radical militia. Fischer was implicated in the 1886 Haymarket affair for having printed bilingual leaflets that urged workingmen to "arm yourselves and appear in full force." He was sentenced to death at trial and hanged on November 11, 1887.

29. August Spies (1855–1887) was a German-born journalist and radical labor activist who was the editor of the *Arbeiter-Zeitung* in Chicago from 1884. Spies was the German-language counterpart of fellow Haymarket martyr Albert Parsons, and was regarded as an extremely influential writer and public speaker. He addressed the assembly at the ill-fated May 1886 Haymarket Square rally and was later charged with conspiracy in connection with the bomb thrown at the event. Spies was hanged with Parsons, Engel, and Fischer on November 11, 1887.

30. Joseph E. Gary (1821–1906) presided over the 1886 trial of eight Chicago anarchists who were charged with inspiring a May 4, 1886 bombing and gunfight in which 11 people were killed.

31. The Labor Congress was held under the auspices of the World's Congress Auxiliary of the Chicago Columbian Exposition, which held a series of scholarly meetings in conjunction with the fair. The Labor Congress was held August 28 to September 4, 1893 at the newly constructed Art Institute of Chicago.

32. Allusion to a line from *Measure for Measure* (c. 1604), by William Shakespeare (1564–1616): "The miserable have no other medicine but only hope."

33. The main exhibition buildings of the 1893 Columbian Exposition shared a common neoclassical architectural theme and were faced with white-painted plaster, garnering the nickname "The White City." Most of these buildings burned to the ground in a January 1894 fire.

34. Allusion to Matthew 17:20.

35. Adaptation of a line from "The Present Crisis" (1845), by James Russell Lowell (1819–1891): "Truth forever on the scaffold, wrong forever on the throne."

36. The World's Columbian Exposition was conceived as a celebration of the 400th anniversary of the arrival of Christopher Columbus (c. 1451–1506) in the Americas.

37. Jackson Park, today a 500-acre park on Chicago's South Side, was the site of the Columbian Exposition.

38. Myron Winslow Reed (1836–1899) was the preeminent Christian socialist of the American West during the 1880s and 1890s. He is the subject of a biography

by James Denton, *Rocky Mountain Radical: Myron W. Reed, Christian Socialist* (University of New Mexico Press, 1997).

39. From *As You Like It* (1599), by William Shakespeare (1564–1616).

40. This quote by Reed and further references below by Debs trace back to 2 Peter 3:13: "Nevertheless we, according to his promise, look for new heavens and a new earth, wherein dwelleth righteousness."

41. Allusion to Matthew 23:14.

42. Allusion to Acts 5:1–11, in which Ananias and Sapphira sold a possession but failed to provide the full proceeds to Peter and were promptly stricken dead for daring to "lie to the Holy Ghost."

43. Allusion to Revelation 1.

44. Carter Harrison, Sr. (1825–1893), a former two-term member of Congress, was mayor of Chicago from 1879 to 1887, a period including the Haymarket bombing of 1886. Elected to a non-consecutive fifth term in 1893, Harrison was assassinated that same year by a disgruntled seeker of political patronage. Harrison's son, Carter Harrison, Jr. (1860–1953), would himself be elected five times as mayor of Chicago.

45. Damn fool-ism.

46. Henry Billings Brown (1836–1913) was appointed an associate justice of the Supreme Court in 1890 by President Benjamin Harrison. He is best remembered by history as the author of the majority decision in the 1896 case of *Plessy v. Ferguson,* which institutionalized racial segregation in America for more than half a century.

47. Allusion to Exodus 5.

48. Reference to Exodus 8–10.

49. James Gibbon (1834–1921) was made the youngest bishop in America by the Roman Catholic church in 1868 and the archbishop of Baltimore in 1877. In 1886 he was named a cardinal by Pope Leo XIII.

50. Reference to Mark 6:1–5.

51. Couplet from an archaic nursery rhyme, inspiration for which is sometimes attributed to Elizabethan author John Fletcher (1579–1625).

52. The kingdom of Dahomey was located within the boundaries of today's Benin, between Togo and Nigeria on the Atlantic coast.

53. Harrison was murdered on October 28, 1893, just two days before the close of the fair.

1894

Value of the Ballot[†]

January 1894

The *Alliance Independent,* speaking of the ballot, says:

> A man's ballot is the scepter of his individual sovereignty. By using it wisely, intelligently, he maintains his manhood and guards at all points against the insidious encroachments of tyranny. The ballot is the proud, invincible weapon of American citizenship, the invaluable possession of the common people—and is itself a recognition of man as man, that one man, no matter who his parents were, has as much right to a place and natural means to live as all other men, and that he should be equally benefited by the laws of society, each having one vote and one only. The ballot placed in every hand has cost millions and millions of lives, and comes down to us, out of the struggle of the ages, as our chief inheritance. It is the gift of earth's countless heroes, and bears to us their free, undying spirit.
>
> The ballot has with us displaced the sword we hope forever, and in the light of advancing truth shall peacefully settle the great questions which still divide men, questions of equity and individual rights. War, all the aggressive wars of history, have been engaged in for conquest, for wealth and power over labor. Today business is war, having the same object and compassing the same end.
>
> Getting as much as one can, while giving the least that one must is the barbarous rule of business, and it does not bring into battle with each other those having equal wisdom and power. The far-sighted, the cunning, the law favored and entrenched demand net-profit tribute and unequal exchanges from the others, from the masses whom they have made dependent by first robbing them of their birthrights to land, which is the necessary basis of liberty. The monster monopolies are veritable kingdoms grown up in the republic, aggressive despotisms, far advanced in their encroachments on liberty's basis, and reaching out after the whole earth. We are all for the time being in subjection to monopoly power, and must unite at the ballot box to cut its absorbing tentacles and get loose from its grasp.

The foregoing is a happy and forceful presentation of the value of the ballot, but in further considering the subject, a number of questions are forced

---

†   Published in *Locomotive Firemen's Magazine,* vol. 18, no. 1 (January 1894), 47–49.

upon the attention of the American people. (1) While the ballot is the symbol of citizenship and sovereignty, is it not being used to destroy both? (2) Is there not a purpose rapidly developing to restrict the ballot within narrower limits?

In replying to such interrogatories, however severely condensed, considerable space must be taken, for however easy it may be to formulate questions, it is not always, nor generally, an easy task to answer them, and questions which relate to citizenship, sovereignty, liberty, and independence should not be lightly dealt with.

The true American idea is manhood suffrage, that is to say, a native-born American, 21 years of age, who is not an idiot, nor insane, and who has not committed crime, is entitled to the ballot, and in most of the states of the union, under the laws, has this suffrage right conferred upon him. But there are states that have enacted laws which do not recognize manhood as alone sufficient to entitle a man to suffrage. There are a number of states that disfranchise paupers, men no longer able to provide for themselves, and who, therefore, become a public charge. There are many grades of the misfortune called poverty, and the pauper is supposed to have reached the lowest—and is therefore disfranchised, and takes his place with the insane, the idiotic, and convicted criminals, who are also disfranchised. Now, if the pauper could get a chance to earn so much as 50 cents a day, he could, with the aid of Edward Atkinson's Aladdin oven,[1] live on 9 cents a day, and put 41 cents in *bank;* and if then, like Jay Gould, he could get a patent mousetrap, or like old Commodore Vanderbilt, get a scow and a long pole, or like old John Jacob Astor,[2] get possession of a mink skin, he might rise, in course of time, to the serene and lovely altitude of a millionaire, but in the absence of such opportunities, he must be a pauper, and in several states pay the penalty of disfranchisement. The law, as a penalty for extreme poverty, disrobes its victims of citizenship, of sovereignty, and reduces him to the level of the insane, idiots, and criminals.

It is not required by the law that the pauper should be declared guilty of any crime, or that he should be crazy or a fool. If he holds out his trembling hands and asks for bread, for clothes and shelter, that answers the demand, and then the law reduces him to an outcast; the penalty, insofar as voting is concerned, is the same as is visited upon the most depraved wretch in a penitentiary.

It does not matter in what bank wreck, engineered by bunko desperadoes, his savings may have been wrested from him; it does not matter in what corporation mill, between the upper and the nether stones, he was reduced to pauper pulp; it does not matter that he may have been remanded to idleness because he belonged to a labor organization, and sought to live as becomes an

American citizen; it does not matter that he may have worked and obeyed the laws of his country until, bending beneath the weight of accumulating years, he asks for bread; it does not matter that when the bugle called to arms, he said "farewell" to home and kindred, and sprang to the front and followed "Old Glory" into the storms of battle; the moment he asks the great public for help, something to keep his protesting soul within his famished body, he is disfranchised. The pauper may be possessed of every virtue, he may have been animated by noble aspirations, may have been charitable and magnanimous, but misfortune overtook him and great states, because he has no money, rob him of the ballot and decree him an outcast.

In the states where this rape of manhood has been perpetrated, the idea prevails that money, not manhood, is entitled to the ballot, and it is eminently pertinent to inquire if the crime could have been committed had working-men—men, regarded as poor, as compared with the rich, had by their ballots protested against the iniquity?

Again, there are states which disfranchise men because it is assumed they are non-taxpayers—that is to say, their names do not appear on the list of taxpayers. They are not paupers—they support themselves by their work, as also those dependent upon them for support. And these men, like idiots, the insane, and convicted criminals, are disfranchised. Here, again, the plutocratic class magnify money and seek to degrade the poor, upon the vicious assumption that a man can live in a rented house, buy food and clothing, and yet pay no taxes, when it is known and admitted that every rent payer is a taxpayer, that every consumer is a taxpayer. In short, every person, no matter how poor, who is not a pauper is a taxpayer. Notwithstanding such uncontradicted facts, men are disfranchised because their names do not appear on tax lists as taxpayers, and here, again, the question arises, have workingmen, in the states where these poor men have been struck down by the plutocratic class and the ballot, to prevent the degrading crime, protested? Have they not stood idly by and seen the ballot, the "scepter of individual sovereignty," taken from the hands of their fellow toilers without an effort to prevent the crime?

In response to the question "Is not the ballot being used to destroy the citizenship and the sovereignty of the individual?" what we have said is a direct reply. There is no citizenship without the ballot, and only the citizen is sovereign, hence when a man is disfranchised, citizenship and sovereignty go down together—hence, also, the ballot is used to enact laws disfranchising the poor, thereby placing all power in the hands of the rich. Such is the trend of affairs, and if workingmen do not see it they are blind.

Is there not a purpose to restrict the ballot within narrower limits? Every time a man is disfranchised, except for idiocy, insanity, and crime, a flagrant departure from the true American idea is committed. On all occasions and on every hand is heard the cry that illiteracy is the one great danger that menaces the government, but of late comes another alarm; it is that wealth, consolidated wealth, is destined to overthrow our institutions. The rich are not illiterate. They can read and write and cipher, and it is the rich who are eternally repeating the *folly* that the illiterate, those who can neither read nor write, are to bring about the ruin of the government—and by their clamor, they are able, here and there, to disfranchise not only the illiterate, but men whose names are not on the tax list. In all of this is seen a purpose to do away with manhood suffrage, to deny poor men their rights, to create a governing class made up of rich men, as if the hope of the country was based upon money rather than labor.

A Grand Beginning:
Speech at the Formation of the ARU Lodge at Terre Haute[†]

January 10, 1894

There is no desire or intention on my part to say anything of the old organizations to belittle or injure them.[3] All have been organized for a purpose, which has been the benefiting of their members. This they have tried hard to do. But from the time they were first organized there has been no material change in their manner of seeking to benefit their members.

The conditions of the railway service have materially changed in the past ten years. No further back than ten years ago there were hundreds of small railroads from 100 to 300 miles in length, which were operated independently of any corporation or system of roads. With a few exceptions, no such state of affairs now exists. The big lines are branching out, absorbing the smaller lines until they are now in a position to successfully cope with the united strength of the

---

[†]   Published in the *Terre Haute Express*, January 11, 1894, unspecified page. Reprinted as "Started Grandly" in the *Railway Times*, vol. 1, no. 2 (January 15, 1894), 1.

six federated railroad orders. The brotherhoods remain the same as when first organized, having taken no steps to meet the onslaughts a united capital can wage. If I may refer to the past history of the orders now organized in the railway service, when engaged in strikes, I can recall nothing but a succession of defeats.

The strike on the Ann Arbor was a failure; the strike on the CB&Q was a failure; the Lehigh Valley strike[4] was a failure; in fact, every strike which has been declared by the grand chiefs of the old brotherhoods has been a failure. And why? Simply because there has been a lack of unity—a feeling of enmity and jealousy, a desire to build up one organization at the expense of another. This hatred and jealousy has existed in the brotherhoods for years. The opinion has prevailed that the man who makes $5 a day has nothing in common with the man making $1.10 a day; there has been a kind of aristocracy, the $5 man holding himself aloof from the $1 man. There is a contention between the switchmen and the trainmen, and so long as the present system of organization exists there always will be. History of strikes has shown that trainmen have taken the positions of switchmen at critical moments in time of trouble. There is that lack of confidence and unity which can exist only when all branches of the service are united under one banner, each striving to uphold and help along the other.

It requires a good deal of money to maintain membership in the old organizations; their laws require members to take out insurance, and other minor expenses foot up quite a small sum. These fees must be paid, and any member failing to do so is summarily expelled from the order. There are times when these sums cannot be had by the member, and no matter how industriously he may seek work in an effort to secure the necessary amount, the failure to do so brings the dreaded result. This state of affairs happens not only occasionally, but may just such happen daily. The result can plainly be seen. With the stigma of being a scab upon him, he is exiled from his former associates and brothers, jeered at and the epithet of "scab" constantly flung at him. There are thousands upon thousands of these men in the country, and the united strength of organized railroad employees embraces but 20 percent of the service.

A strike is declared. The organized men quit work, but the road officials have no trouble in filling their places. They know where to [look to find men to] fill the strikers' places. They have but to look around them to find the man who was jeered at, called a scab—an ex-brotherhood man. He is seeking revenge and gets it.

I might refer to dozens of strikes, all of which have been failures. On the Lehigh Valley alone, where five organizations went out at once, they were whipped, and today out of the 1,800 men who went out but 600 again secured places at its termination. The CB&Q had to spend $10 million to defeat organized labor, but they did it. And why were the men defeated? Simply because there was a lack of harmony, no thorough organization.

The railroads have constantly prepared and fortified themselves to fight organized labor. At Chicago an association of managers was organized, the purpose of which, as published, is to assist each other in combating organized labor, to listen to no protests of their employees. They are bound, should one of the roads in their organization get into trouble, to help them out of it. With such an existing state of affairs, how can railway labor, organized into different branches, all of which are more or less antagonistic to each other, expect to successfully cope with them? The situation requires that a closer union be effected, less jealousy, no antagonism, an organization where stands the $5 a day man and the $1 man both on equal footing, one not striving to be aristocratic over the other, but with friendship existing so that the poorly paid member may say to his more fortunate brother: "Your cause is my cause, your grievance mine; what is beneficial to you is likewise beneficial to me." When this is brought about, when the $5 man can look upon the $1 man as a brother who has interests in common with his own, then will strikes cease—or if one is declared, it will win, and win quick.

There is hardly one in this audience but remembers the E&TH strike.[5] Captain [G. J.] Grammar ordered a 10 percent reduction in wages. The engineers were willing to accept it, but the trainmen, switchmen, trackmen, in fact every branch of the service, said, "No," and when it was known that the protest came from both organized and unorganized [workers] the president of the E&TH the next day sent out notices that no reduction would be made. Aristocracy in this case was banished from the ranks of labor, where it did not belong. The engineers were possibly able to stand a 10 percent cut, but the man earning but $1.10 was not, and by making the cause of one the cause of all the road officials wisely withdrew the order.

Within five years, I firmly believe, at least within ten years, there will be just two railroad corporations east of the Mississippi River. These two systems will be those of the Vanderbilts and the Pennsylvania Company. I would say a few words to those of you that are employed on the Vandalia line. It is only a matter of a short time, I believe, when it will pass entirely to the Pennsylvania. Before the recent change you had every assurance you would always receive a fair and impartial hearing on all subjects and otherwise be fairly dealt with. Both Mr. [William Riley] McKeen,[6] the president, and also its general manager, I think, are two of the "whitest" and "squarest" men in the railroad business today. You will e'er long, however, be in the employ of the great Pennsylvania Company with its insurance attachment, which, whether you desire it or not, you must take out. You who have heretofore had your interests looked after will be called upon to help yourself, and you should be prepared.

For years organized and unorganized labor has been blinded. It has allowed others to think and act for it. The American Railway Union will endeavor to bring its members to a fuller realization of this fact, and will impress upon their minds the importance of studying and thinking for themselves. The union is founded on broad lines. It proposes to, so far as possible, bring about a kind of reform in legislative matters—not as Republicans or Democrats, but as a united body of railroad employees, comprising every branch—as will insure them the same justice as that accorded the corporation.

Corporations have [in the past] and are today scanning the field of railway labor. They know just when to attack. They know the weak spots. The courts are becoming a great feature in settling and preventing strikes. Numerous plans have been practiced by railroad corporations to gain in a contest with organized labor. In many instances they provoke the strike purposely to gain their ends. The Northern Pacific has introduced the latest scheme. Before ordering a reduction which would be sure to end in a strike, the corporation very cunningly places the road in the hands of receivers who act subject to the order of the court. The reduction was then ordered, and at the same time the road asked for an order restraining the men from striking, restraining the engineers from refusing to handle their cars. Is there any justice in a court that restrains men from quitting? Should the same men ask the court to restrain the corporation from discharging a man or from cutting their wages, they would be laughed at.

The Union Pacific has been pretty thoroughly organized, and the American Railway Union is in a flourishing condition. Nearly every other western road has made deep cuts in wages, but on the Union Pacific none has been asked. And why? Simply because there was an organization on the system that was a perfect one, and it was not antagonized.

There Should Be No Aristocracy in Labor's Ranks: Speech in Fort Wayne, Indiana† [excerpt]

January 23, 1894

In the creation of a new organization of railway employees, certain reasons prompting the movement are demanded and should be set forth with becoming candor. The number of men now in the service of the railroads in America has been estimated at 1 million, and of this number less than 150,000 are members of the various railroad brotherhoods, leaving 850,000 who are not enrolled in the ranks of organized labor. It is not my purpose to detract from the present railway organizations, as they have done [a great deal] for their members. The old plan of organization is not now practical. The railway corporations are consolidating as is shown by the 92 roads that passed out of existence, they being gobbled up by the larger corporations, and now practically only 20 organizations represent the business—and when vital issues are at stake, but one exists. The general managers have formed an organization so that strikes will not cripple any road, they helping each other in time of disputes with men and equipment. The corporations are getting closer and closer together, while the employees are getting further and further apart.

By this means many organizations have lost strikes, because they have not been united thoroughly. As a rule I am opposed to strikes and believe them the height of folly, but strikes are the only weapon that the laboring man has. The surest way to win a strike is to be prepared, and that we have not been prepared is shown by the many failures. Whenever a railway company permits its employees to strike, the company is sure of success. The outcome of strikes has always been disastrous. The army of the unorganized is more powerful than the organized workmen, and it is not possible for one of the present organizations to stand out successfully against any railroad.

The proper course for the railroad men is to organize in one body and do away with the aristocracy in their ranks. The American Railway Union is founded on the principle that the best paid man in the service is nothing

---

† Published as "Eugene V. Debs: Labor's Eloquent Exponent at K of L Hall" in *Ft. Wayne Weekly Journal*, vol. 3 (January 25, 1894), 8.

more than an employee and the lowest paid man is also an employee of equal standing in the eyes of the company. There should be no aristocracy in labor's ranks. Just after the association of general managers was formed, a reduction of wages on the Louisville & Nashville road was commenced. Track men were cut as low as 67.5 cents per day. These reductions in wages are what produces the anarchists. The same reductions were made on a number of other systems, and the end is not yet, and reductions will become universal unless something is done.

The switchmen's strike at Buffalo was righteous and acknowledged so by all the brotherhoods, but they were unable to assist them. The militia lost the strike for the men, as it had done in a number of cases before. The strike on the Ann Arbor was defeated by the law in the hands of Judge [Augustus J.] Ricks. That was the most successful way yet tried. The latest was on the Union Pacific, where the receiver was appointed who secured injunctions against the employees' right to strike with his organization. There is no equality or justice in that. Courts are organized not to assist railwaymen, but to depress them. The only help is to unify and solidify our forces and in cases like this to strike and invite them to put us in prison together. If railway affairs are honestly administered, there would be no reduction or strikes. On the Northern Pacific and a number of other roads men do not make enough to pay board. Organizations are growing weaker and weaker day by day. At least 5,000 engineers and firemen are at present out of work. The policy of railway corporations for years has been to create a surplus in the ranks of labor.

The American Railway Union does not propose to mix up men indiscriminately, but to have branches composed of firemen, engineers, shopmen, etc. Each branch transacts its own business, and when properly organized their demands will be more readily acceded to, and [will thus] do away with strikes. The only thing for railwaymen to do is get together. For 30 years we have been organized, and every strike has added to the great army of scabs and cost the organization millions in money. Capital has profited by its disasters, but labor has had the reverse. We must unite the train service with the track, shop, and clerical forces, and until we do that we must expect defeat. We have arrived at the point where we must go forward or backward. We must keep step with progress. The railway companies have consolidated, but no consolidation has so far taken place among the railway brotherhoods. Let labor everywhere take a hopeful view of the situation. No matter how gloomy conditions are, I feel and know in a very short time there shall be an awakening, but until that time comes, things will grow worse. I do not claim that the American

Railway Union is perfect, but it is vastly better than the present organizations of brotherhoods. There is no secrecy, no oath or expensive initiation, dues, or insurance to keep up.

*   *   *

Arbitration[†]

February 1894

We have on our table *Transportation* for September 1893, in which appears the thoughtful article captioned "Arbitration as Applied to Railroad Corporations and their Employees," by Edward A. Moseley, secretary of the Interstate Commerce Commission.

Mr. Moseley is in a position to write instructively and entertainingly of railroad affairs. His position as secretary of the Interstate Commerce Commission enables him, in many matters, to be approximately correct, where others are left to wrestle with statements which, to put it mildly, are often vague, and so elastic that they can be twisted about in a way to suit a great variety of views and conclusions. Railroad employees will feel under obligation to Mr. Moseley for giving certain importance to their calling, which it has been the ambition of railway magnates to deny, especially at such times as the employees have had a grievance which they have desired to have removed by the said magnates.

Moseley recites numerous propositions relating to "combinations of capital" and "organizations of labor," stating that "they represent the two great interdependent and interacting forces of industry," and adds:

> Overwhelming power in the hands of the first means unbearable oppression to the other, while extreme advantage conferred upon the latter would, if unwisely used, inflict ruin upon the former. Each side is governed by the dominant motive of self-interest, and they should be placed and kept upon equal footing. To do this, full recognition of labor organizations is essential. A corporation which has brain and sinew for capital

---

[†]   Published in *Locomotive Firemen's Magazine,* vol. 18, no. 2 (February 1894), 135–139.

should be regarded as similar, in a legal sense, to a joint stock concern with a paid-up money capital. This much I believe is due to labor in any branch of industry.

The term "overwhelming power" we suppose means autocratic, absolute power—the power to grant, the power to withhold—and this power corporations possess in certain cases, or, if limited at all, it is only when labor organizations have interfered to check its sway. It is impracticable to parallel a money corporation and a labor organization. They are essentially dissimilar. They cannot be "placed and kept upon a similar footing," not even when "a corporation with brain and sinew for its capital" is pronounced, in a "legal sense," the equal of "a joint stock concern with a paid-up money capital." True it is that capital is unproductive without labor, and that, insofar as great industrial enterprises are concerned, labor is unproductive without capital, but such statements are the merest platitudes in the discussion of the comparative power of a capital corporation and a labor organization, or, if you please, a labor corporation. Mr. Moseley refers to Homestead, and Homestead confirms our position, vividly illustrates our idea. Say, for instance, the capital corporation of Homestead represented $10 million, and the labor corporation at Homestead represented 10,000 men of "brain and sinew." There are the two "corporations" side by side, dominated by "self-interest." The capital corporation possessed "overwhelming power," the corporation of "brains and sinew" in this contest had, in fact, no power at all, or if it had power, by exerting it did so to its own injury. True, it stopped the productiveness of capital, which, demanding neither food, clothing, nor shelter, subject to neither sickness, sorrow, pain, nor death, could retire, keep quiet, and wait while the labor corporation starved, froze, went naked, took sick, and died. What "extreme advantage conferred" upon the labor corporation could have inflicted ruin upon the capital corporation that would not have been equally ruinous to itself? And even suppose it had utterly wiped out of existence the Homestead mills, the comfort of Carnegie and Frick and those identified with them as capitalists would not have been marred, while the *stockholders* in the corporation of "brain and sinew" would have perished.

In discussing troubles arising between labor and certain capitalists—never between labor and capital—it is readily admitted that parties to the controversies are governed by "self-interest." This self-interest question presents widely different phases when discussed from points of observation occupied by a capital corporation and a labor organization. Mr. Moseley is well aware that the estimated value of the railroads of the United States represents not less than $4 billion dollars of *water*—of fraud. It is called "capitalization," and capital corporations perpetrate the frauds. Labor corporations exhibit to the world no such "self-interest." They have never demanded more than would afford their "stockholders" of "brain and sinew" a respectable living. Hence it is seen that on the one hand capital corporations are animated by a "self-interest" essentially different from that which characterizes labor corporations or organizations. Labor corporations carry no watered investments. Congress nor the states give them land. Their schemes to wreck and rob have not called for congressional legislation nor state legislation to put an end to their perfidies— they have only "brain and sinew," and it is Mr. Moseley's idea to legislate in such a way as to bring about an "equality of power and force" between the two corporations and thereby establish arbitration. He says:

> One is the full recognition of railway labor societies as corporations. The other is the settlement of disputes between railway employer and railway employees by means of compulsory arbitration between the men represented by their labor corporation as one party and the stockholders of the company represented by the railway corporation as the other party. We then obtain that *equality of power and force which compels* the essential requisites of friendly relation, respect, consideration, and forbearance.[7] Disputes between employers and employees can be satisfactorily adjusted only upon the basis of fair concession and mutual advantage. The strict rules of law are wholly inapplicable to such controversies, and so far the only plan which appears to offer a solution of the difficulty is arbitration. It is not conceded to be practicable to compel the parties engaged in productive enterprises to accept arbitration, but that objection loses all its force when it is proposed to limit it to those engaged in railway transportation.

There is associated with the term "arbitration" that which smacks of justice, equity, fair play; the same is true of courts established to administer justice evenhanded, but pity it is that courts are uncertain, so unreliable that men are advised to "keep out of court"—but there is this thing about judicial proceedings in courts of law—men may *appeal,* and the propriety of exercising the privilege is shown in the fact that the decisions of lower courts are often reversed, but if we understand Mr. Moseley, his idea is to have the decision of arbitrators *final.* He says:

> But so far as the settlement of disputes in which the public has direct interest is concerned, like those arising in the course of railway employment, Congress unquestionably has power to compel arbitration. The tendency of Congress to recognize labor associations has already been

shown. It is but a step further to provide that organizations of railway employees shall, when disputes arise with railway managers, file approved bonds with designated officials for and on behalf of the men; that they will abide by the decision of the board of arbitration; that the railway corporations shall likewise file similar bonds; and that awards made under such conditions shall be enforceable in the courts.

It does not require a *seer* to see at once that Mr. Moseley maps out a stupendous job. It may be true that Congress has the power to compel railroad employees to arbitrate, to single them out from all other classes of wage earners and rob them of their right to choose their own methods of settling their own grievances. Says Mr. Moseley: "It is not conceded to be practicable to compel the parties engaged in productive enterprises to accept arbitration, but that objection loses all its force when it is proposed to limit it to those engaged in railway transportation." Why it "loses all its force" Mr. Moseley does not inform the public, but it is easy to fathom the omission. When the railway corporation, being a "common carrier," oppresses its employees, and the employees quit work, the "common carrier" and the *public* are inconvenienced, hence it is necessary for Congress to pass a law providing that railway employees shall *not* quit work, but shall apply for arbitration and *remain* at work pending a decision. He says:

> Moreover, questions arising between employer and employee demand the most prompt method of settlement; and pending final settlement the relations existing at the time the dispute arose should be maintained and the parties should bear their grievances patiently during that period and rely upon just and proper revision and adjustment by the board of arbitration.

It is worthy of remark that when railway corporations have grievances against an employee they discharge him, or subject him to some penalty— *lay him off* for a period of time, which is simply a *fine* of so many dollars, but the *grievance* of the corporations against their men is that the men annoy the corporation with their grievances and insist upon sending their grievance committees to "headquarters" to obtain redress. This action, on the part of the employees, through their organizations has become so odious that the corporations desire the utter overthrow of the organizations, as has sometimes been accomplished. The organizations are thoroughly equipped to arbitrate, in compromise, to give and take, to settle every difficulty, but, as in the fuse of the Lehigh Valley corporation, the officials utterly refused to talk matters over with the officials of the organizations, President Wilbur contending that to make concessions would be, in effect, to abandon the control of the road to the organizations. To overcome this difficulty, organizations of railway employees are to be regularly *chartered* by Congress, the intimation being that when so chartered they shall be empowered to make contracts for the men who are members of the organizations, and this idea is emphasized by Mr. Moseley when referring to the "pecuniary" irresponsibility of individual members, which he suggests would be removed when the organization is empowered to "treat with the corporation," which, *boiled down,* means simply that the officials of an organization of railway employees shall have the authority to *hire out* the members of the organization, make all needed contracts for them—a species of chattel slavery that would decimate the organizations as if struck with the plague.

Manifestly, arbitration of a voluntary character is well enough, but the instant compulsory arbitration is suggested, manhood, citizenship, independence, and self-respect revolt. We have already, as has been suggested, the courts, all the way up from a justice of the peace to the silk-gowned body known as the Supreme Court of the United States, and we have laws enough, if they were woolen blankets, to keep the frigid zone warm. An arbitration court or courts, for to do any good there would have to be a multitude of them, would make a complex problem more complicated. A moment's reflection will confirm the conclusion. The statistician of the Interstate Commerce Commission informs the public that there are 171,503 miles of railroad track in the United States, controlled by 1,822 corporations, employing 821,415 persons. These employees, on lines sufficient to encircle the earth seven times, have a great number of grievances, and since Mr. Moseley says, "questions arising between employer and employee demand the most prompt method of settlement," it would seem advisable to have a Board of Arbitration for each railroad corporation, or 1,822 boards, ready to adopt "the most prompt method of settlement." If each Board of Arbitration consisted of three members then there would be spawned upon the country 5,446 arbitrators, or, if the Boards of Arbitration were to itinerate, their traveling expenses and hotel bills would be enormous; bills would peep o'er bills, and bills on bills arise, until there would be a revolt.

But there is another thing to be considered. Mr. Moseley suggests the giving of bonds by the organizations of railway employees to abide by the decision of the Board of Arbitration. To illustrate: Take a railroad, say of 1,000 miles, on which the firemen have a grievance; suppose there are on the road 20 lodges, or organizations, of firemen. Is it to be understood that each one of the 20 organizations is to give bond before arbitration can begin? The inquiry is pertinent—grows out of the arbitration question—or is it to he understood that the Grand Lodge of the firemen's order is to give the bond and be held responsible? If the latter idea is to be adopted, the Grand Lodge, if it had wings and could out-travel a homing pigeon, would not be able to respond to the demand. In a word, is the proposition, compulsory arbitration, as suggested by Mr. Moseley or any other gentleman, practicable?

Moreover, Mr. Moseley makes some suggestions which to our mind upset the superstructure. He seems to have an idea, after all, that there are insuperable difficulties in the way, found in the fact that the right sort of men to act as arbitrators are about as scarce as watermelons in Greenland. He says:

> To make arbitration effective and just, the arbitrators should be drawn from the vicinage and with particular reference to the particular case. A man who knows nothing about the work involved is not qualified to decide the question. When the matter in controversy involves how many hours a man should work, what pay he should receive, or any of the questions which cause dispute between the employer and the employee, those questions should be considered by men familiar with the particular employment under consideration as well as with the needs and situation of the employer. Such well-informed persons are to be found in every locality, and when questions arise between employer and employees they are best qualified to decide what concessions are fair and what will redound to the mutual advantage of the parties.
>
> As a rule, men who hold office for life or a defined term are unfit for such positions. A person, to be a good arbitrator, must be directly responsible in every case. Men who hold definite terms of office are placed in a position where they regard mankind as divided into classes, and they have, too often, but the instincts and sympathies of their "class." The ultraconservative man, the man whose whole interest lies in maintaining the present order of things, is prone to look through the closed window of his richly furnished apartment, and in this refracted light and perverted view to imagine that he sees in the workman passing by with blouse and dinner pail a member of "the dangerous classes." Arbitrators, on the other hand, should be men who know no class, but who represent the sovereign whole. The utmost publicity should be given to such awards, and to attain this end the law regulating arbitration might contain provision for a report by all boards of arbitration of the awards made by them to the executive head of the government and for the formal and official promulgation by him of all awards so made.

Anyone who will read the foregoing carefully will, we think, conclude that compulsory arbitration is not the way out of troubles between railroad employers and employees; that the scheme is largely visionary; that arbitration, well enough under certain conditions, would likely prove worse than valueless when made compulsory without the right to appeal.

Suppose the grievance of the employees should be opposition to a reduction of wages of, say, 10 percent. Arbitration is demanded. Thousands of the men are not organized, can give no bond, and are not, therefore, in the contest. They simply submit. Some of the employees receiving $3 and $4 a day accept the reduction. We will say the firemen demand a board of arbitration to sit in their case. Who are to be selected? According to Mr. Moseley, men "familiar" with the work, duties, and responsibilities of firemen, as also with "the needs and situation of the employer." In such a case about the best that could be done would be to have one fireman on the board, one railroad official, and one—anybody that the fireman and the official might select. The case is begun. The fireman says "to reduce his pay 10 percent, 20 cents a day, $60 a year, is to subject him and family to serious privations; that at his present wages he is barely able to live." The railroad corporation says "business is dull; that it pays no dividends, and that in reducing wages it is governed by necessities that cannot be overcome." The board takes the case and decides that the railroad corporation must be content with 5 percent reduction, and that the fireman must submit to a loss of $30 a year. The corporation is happy because it expected its demands to be reduced 5 percent, and therefore made the cut 10 percent. It has got what it expected in the case and is serene. It employs, say, 1,000 men, and by the cut makes a clear gain of from $30,000 to $75,000 a year. True, it may be said that because of arbitration some of the men, at least, saved 5 percent that otherwise would have been lost. This is assumption. It may be that with a strike and a tie-up in full view no reduction would have been demanded. Victories for the right have been gained in the past for courageous men who knew their rights and dared to defend them.

One of the hallucinations of the period is that the government is clothed with such absolute power that it can by statute provide employment for the idle, regulate wages, and do all other things that an autocrat may do. There is heard from many quarters a wild hue and cry in favor of a paternal government, such as exists in Europe, where the individual is lost sight of and the government overshadows everything, and compulsory arbitration is in that line: the term "compulsory" has that significance.

There are those who think that railroads should have at least a *semi*-military government, and that men should be *enlisted* for a term of years. Gods!

The military idea was illustrated at Homestead, Buffalo, and other localities. Still, scabs might enlist.

There are those who seem to be of the opinion that the relations existing between the government and the corporations, and between the government and the individuals, are practically the same, and that legislation, with equal propriety, may include both. There is, however, this difference: The government *creates* the corporation, but does not *create* the individual, and ours is a government of the people—of the individual. When the people become so degenerate as to passively submit to have their individuality wiped out, to be herded like cattle, no matter what plausible arguments are used to accomplish their degradation, the time will have arrived to sing again the old song addressed to the flag—"haul down that flaunting lie."[8]

T. V. Powderly and the Knights of Labor[†]
February 1894

For 14 years T. V. Powderly had been the general master workman of the great order of Knights of Labor, up to the time that he voluntarily laid down the trust at Philadelphia, and during the entire period Mr. Powderly gave his great abilities unstintedly to the cause of labor education. He had a lofty ideal. He believed in the vast mind forces, laying practically dormant, in the great body of American workingmen. This latent, unexerted force he sought to arouse, bring into action, unify, and harmonize for the good not only of labor but of society at large. Education was first, last, and all the time his theme, his inspiration. He was always in the van of the marching hosts. A pathfinder, he was forever blazing out new pathways to higher elevations. Never content with a slow, ambling, hesitating gait, he strode forward, for to his vision the goal was always in sight. And it should be said, without reference to the cohesiveness or the disintegration of the order of the Knights of Labor, Mr. Powderly won victories all along the line. He sent forth an army

---

†   Published in *Locomotive Firemen's Magazine,* vol. 18, no. 2 (February 1894), 143–144.

of new ideas, new forces, which are still on the warpath and are achieving ceaseless victories for the right.

Goldsmith said those who think govern those who toil, and Powderly's mission was to set toilers to thinking that they might govern themselves. There may be bleary-eyed croakers who are unable to discover the fruitage of the educational nuts Powderly had planted, but that does not count. They have taken deep root in thousands of minds, and although Mr. Powderly is no longer general master workman, he is not less an educator and a force and a factor in the conquering ranks of labor. In saying this of Mr. Powderly we institute no parallel between him and others who are engaged in the same laudable work. All honor to the courageous men as captains, lieutenants, or privates in the ranks of labor who have ideas, convictions, and the courage to express them. They are the salt of the earth. Living, they challenge the admiration of men whose good opinion is worth having, and, though dead, their great words and generous deeds are invincible.

The *Magazine,* without regard to organization, delights in commending men of the Powderly type. They are not infallible nor free from mistakes, because they are human, for human mistakes are within the realm of human remedies, and when made in the cause of human progress they are near of kin to truth and all manly virtues, and men are often to be beloved, if not canonized, for the enemies they have made. In the future, and in the near future, we, with thousands of others, will expect to hear Mr. Powderly's voice ringing along the lines of organized workingmen.

A Free Press†

March 1894

A congressman by the name of Hayes, credited to Iowa,[9] has introduced in Congress a bill to establish in the person of the postmaster general a censorship of the most odious character.

As the law now stands upon the statute books of the nation all needed

---

†   Published in *Locomotive Firemen's Magazine,* vol. 18, no. 3 (March 1894), 289.

protection is given, since indecent or immoral publications cannot be sent through the US mails without committing a penal offense. But this does not satisfy a set of long-eared and long- and short-haired cranks; they demand a censorship, by virtue of which the postmaster general may determine by his sweet will what is objectionable and should be cast out.

The law contemplated by the bill introduced by Hayes "would be," says the *New York Herald,* "an intolerable tyranny."

> A free press, answerable in the courts for any offense it may commit against law and morality, is the foundation of free government. A bill to create an arbitrary, ignorant, and partisan press censorship should receive short shrift at the hands of Congress. There is not even a plausible excuse for the suggestion of so monstrous a law. As was conclusively shown by a Senate report in 1882, there is law enough and to spare already on this subject. It is already a penal offense to send immoral or indecent publications through the mails. Whoever does so may be indicted, and upon conviction in the courts must go to prison for his offense. In a country of law and of orderly court proceedings this surely is enough. It would be an intolerable outrage for Congress to clothe the postmaster general or any other public officer with authority to supersede the courts, and without indictment, trial, or proof of any kind condemn men to shameful and ruinous penalties upon his own ignorant or prejudiced whim.

The views of the *Herald* the *Magazine* fully endorses, and we do not believe the bill introduced by Hayes will become the law of the land.[10]

The American Protective Association[†]

March 1894

The assumption upon which the APA, alias the American Protective Association,[11] is founded, is that the Roman Catholic religion is fraught with danger to American institutions, hence the further assumption that all men who believe in the religion taught by the Roman Catholic Church are the enemies of American institutions, and therefore, necessarily, are either embryo or fully developed enemies of our American form of government.

We recognize fully the difficulties of the task of banishing errors from the minds of bigots. We do not recall an instance in all history where, by the simple process of reason, argument, and common sense, success has attended such laudable efforts.

Nevertheless, it is true of the past that the influence of bigots has been reduced to the minimum—that their fangs have been extracted, their claws blunted, and the deadly poison secreted in the *glands* of the heart and soul neutralized to comparative harmlessness.

In the organization of the American Protective Association history repeats itself, but the astounding shame and infamy of the thing appears in its title. To call it "American" is to outrage all truth and decency. It is a blasphemous arraignment of the term "American," which from the foundation of the government has been a standing rebuke of all religious intolerance, expressed in the organic law of the nation as follows:

"Congress shall make no law respecting an establishment of religion or prohibiting the free exercise thereof."[12]

And, as a consequence, no state can make any law *respecting the establishment of religion or prohibiting the free exercise thereof.*

As a result, the states have, by their constitutions, following the example set by the great charter of *American religious liberty,* provided that "all men shall be secure in their natural right to worship Almighty God according to the dictates of their consciences,"[13] and that "no preference shall be given by law to any creed, religious society, or mode of worship,"[14] and that "no religious test shall be required as a qualification for any office of trust or profit."[15]

In such provisions we are permitted to contemplate the true glory that

†   Published in *Locomotive Firemen's Magazine,* vol. 18, no. 3 (March 1894), 280–282.

clusters around the name "American," and to make it play any part whatever in the damnable game of religious bigotry and persecution is infamous beyond the power of adequate characterization. It is the acme of devilishness. It is satanic without a redeeming qualification.

The founders of the American government were well advised of the dangers that would confront the people if bigots were left to exercise their infernal malignity toward those who differed with them upon the subject of creeds and worship. They lived in such close proximity to the colonial period of religious persecution that they could hear the necks of its victims snap as they swung off of the scaffold; they could hear the crack of the lash upon the backs of Quakers when they, at cart tails, were whipped from one town to another until the wilderness was reached, and they were left to perish, the victims of storms and the caressings of wild beasts. They saw colonial-established churches, imitations of European infamies, which banished, in the name of God, one class of worshippers that another class, more powerful, might with impunity riot in cruelties which the devil himself doubtless regarded as quite unnecessary for the glory of his kingdom, and they determined to establish an American policy which should effectually redeem America from the unspeakable horrors of a reign of bigotry. This, as we have recited, they accomplished when in the organic law of the nation they made America, at once and forever, the asylum of free religion.

In view of such facts of history, who can measure the astounding impudence and infamy of coupling with an organization established in the dark, in secret, for the avowed purpose of religious persecution, the name "American?"

What is the history of this APA? Those who have run it down are convinced that it originated with a gang of schemers whose sole object was to arouse dissensions in the ranks of organized labor. Everything else had been tried. Laboring men, members of organizations, particularly railroad employees, by turns had been cajoled and threatened, but the men stood firm, worked together in harmony, and added to their numbers. Then came the scheme to *bomb* their ranks with dynamite bigotry. The adroitness of the plot cannot be questioned. The fires of hell never burn more fiercely than when fanned by the breath of fanatics.

Regarding the history of the organization, we take the following from *Every Saturday*, published at Albany, New York:

> Between two and three years ago a conference was held in a certain office on Wall Street, which was attended by representatives of the Chicago and Rock Island Railway, the New York Central & Hudson River, the Chicago, Milwaukee & St. Paul, and numerous other railway companies, together

with representatives from several large rolling mill corporations and iron manufacturers generally, besides many miscellaneous trusts and combines.

The meeting was a strictly secret one and its object primarily to reduce the wages of the American workmen.

Numerous meetings of these same conferees were held at different places, the object always being the same. Fellow monopolists and corporation managers were frequently called upon to express their views and experience. These men were invited to come from various parts of Europe and Canada.

It was a gentleman from the latter country, a great railroad magnate, who formulated the idea upon which the committee was to work to bring about the desired result, viz., to reduce the wages of the American toiler.

The story goes that the invited guest from Canada was of the opinion that no way could be devised to lower wages until the powerful labor organizations were overcome; dissensions and dissolution must be forced into their ranks, and with their disruption accomplished it would be a very easy matter to lower the wages.

This very desirable end could be arrived at by instilling into their ranks a religious prejudice. "You know," said he, "they are nearly all honest, conscientious fellows, with little or no education, and they fear God and live up to their various ways of adoring Him."

He then went on to tell how they in Canada had a certain class of people who were pleased to be called Orangemen, and that they had an inherent dislike for Catholics and that the latter fully reciprocated in their hatred for Orangemen. All that was necessary to do in his country was to bring the two together and harmony would immediately give place to pandemonium.

These worse-than-devils concluded to act upon the Canadian idea. The railroads introduced a society and called it the American Protective Association (APA). Men were hired to boom the organization and do nothing else. Narrow-minded and prejudiced tools joined it, and the fight was on. Iron merchants did their share toward helping it along, and showed a preference for men whom it had succeeded in sucking in.

Here we have the underlying reasons set forth for the existence of such a nondescript organization as the APA. The reasonableness of the statement crops out in every line. The reduction of wages with railroad magnates is the supreme requirement—for every dollar of reduction goes to swell the dividends on watered stock—and if the organizations could be disrupted by the introduction of religious prejudices, or of discord in their ranks, a point would lie gained, all the more certainly since once light the fires of religious fanaticism and nothing short of a miracle can quench them. In this connection it is well for all labor organizations to understand the nature of the oath to which a member of the APA is required to subscribe to form any rational conception of the degradation to which he voluntarily submits, an oath which eliminates from its victim not only the nobility of Americanism, but every quality of manhood worthy of recognition, leaving the unfortunate creature with nothing to boast of except the depravity and malignity which in all countries and ages have made bigots the objects of unutterable loathing.

The oath is as follows:

> I do most solemnly promise and swear that I will use my influence to promote the interest of all Protestants, everywhere in the world; that I will not employ a Roman Catholic in any capacity if I can procure the service of a Protestant; that I will not aid in building, or in maintaining, by any resources, any Roman Catholic church or institution of their sect or creed whatsoever, but will do all in my power to retard and break down the power of the pope; that I will not enter into any controversy with a Roman Catholic upon the subject of this order, nor will I enter into any agreement with a Roman Catholic to strike or create a disturbance, whereby the Roman Catholic employees may undermine and substitute the Protestants; and that in all grievances I will seek only Protestants and counsel with them, to the exclusion of all Roman Catholics, and will not make known to them anything of any nature matured at such conferences; that I will not countenance the nomination, in any caucus or convention, of a Roman Catholic, for any office in the gift of the American people; and that I will not vote for, nor counsel others to vote for, any Roman Catholics; that I will endeavor at all times to place the political positions of this government in the hands of Protestants. (Repeat.) To all of which I do most solemnly promise and swear, so help me God. Amen.

We write to warn organizations of railroad employees against the infamous purposes of the APA. We write to tell them that once introduced into the organization their power to accomplish good for themselves forever vanishes. We write to enthrone everywhere throughout the boundaries of our favored land that true, lofty, and sublime Americanism, that regards men's religious convictions as sacred as life itself, and inextricably interwoven with the eternal and irrevocable rights of "Life, Liberty, and the Pursuit of Happiness." Once light the fires of religious fanaticism, and the lodge fire is at once and forever extinguished. The term "brotherhood" becomes a byword and fraternity would be everywhere proclaimed as a stupendous sham. Americanism is as opposite of bigotry as water is the opposite of fire, as truth is the opposite of a lie, or as eternal justice is the opposite of those wrongs which reduce men to the condition of slaves.

To read the oath taken by misguided members of the APA embodying, as it does, every ingredient of malevolence that makes unbridled bigotry a horror, and evinces such blind obedience to fanatical venom that civilization becomes savagery and Christianity the synonym of hate. We do not believe that the APA will be permitted, at the behest of the oppressors of labor, to wreck labor organizations, but it is "a pestilence that walketh in darkness,"[16] that it may destroy at noonday, and the only safety is in guarding the lodge from its blighting influences.

The Despotism of Dundy[†]

March 1894

Manifestly, labor has fallen upon evil times, or evil times, with crushing force, have fallen upon labor. It is between the upper and the nether millstones. It has been caught in the mill of some vengeful god and is being ground exceedingly small. The United States judges just now seem to be the gods with mills of modern invention, so constructed that a railroad employee can be reduced to slavery by a turn of a judicial screw, have his manhood, his self-respect, his independence, his sovereignty as a citizen, all eliminated in a twinkling. He is still left with his muscle, his capacity to work, but to live and breathe, with his heart beating time to the moanings of despair. To talk of liberty under such conditions is an insult to all things American. It would be a Christless shame to flaunt in the face of the slaves of Dundy,[17] Jenkins,[18] Fuller,[19] Ricks, and judges of their kidney, the star-spangled banner and ask them, as its stars and stripes floated out upon the winds of heaven, to sing the once cheering refrain,

> The star-spangled banner,
> O, long may it wave,
> O'er the land of the Free,
> And the home of the brave. [20]

The old flag no longer floats over the free, and the home of the brave has

---

†   Published in *Locomotive Firemen's Magazine,* vol. 18, no. 3 (March 1894), 278–280.

been, by judicial decrees, transformed into the hut of the pariah, the peon, the helot. The men on the Union Pacific, but yesterday freemen, today wear Dundy's collar, marked USA—branded, not yet on forehead or cheek or breast, but the hot iron of judicial authority has touched their souls and burned upon them ineffaceable scars.

It is possible there are feelings of resentment. The employees enjoy the luxury of memory. They doubtless think of the times when they were free, before Dundy damned them to degrading servitude at such wages as he deemed proper to award his serfs. These victims of Dundy's authority, who are fathers, remember the time when they gloried in the belief that, being free themselves, no taint of bondage attached to their offspring. Do they so believe now? Do they not know that Dundy's decree has manacled their hands, that they can use them only as he directs, fettered their legs, that they cannot get away—aye, fettered their tongues, that they dare not speak? Is that the condition on the Union Pacific? That is it. There is no exaggeration. An Omaha dispatch of January 28 [1894] says:

> The Union Pacific labor circles were stirred to the utmost depths today when the order of Judge Dundy, reducing wages on the system, was made public. All employees in every department are affected by the cut, which amounts to nearly 10 percent. The action of the court was not altogether a surprise, although most of the men thought the wage question would not be disturbed, but Judge Dundy went his brothers on the federal bench one better, and not only enjoined the men from striking, but cut their pay and *ordered them to work on at the reduced pay.*

We italicize a sentence just to call attention to the rapid strides the United States courts are making to multiply white slaves in the United States and the extraordinary feature of this slave-manufacturing business is that it particularly includes railroad employees who, in point of intelligence, education, character, and moral worth occupy, confessedly, advanced positions, and in regard to responsibilities stand in the highest position accorded the wageworkers of the country. And yet judges of the United States courts strike them down with a savagery as relentless as ever distinguished Portuguese slave hunters in the Dark Continent.

In view of such facts, what must be the damnable policy of the government of the United States? These satraps are the creatures, the spawn of the government. They are the parasites that fatten upon the revenues the government derives from labor. They are the trichina that riot in the muscles of the government hog. They are the rodents that are gnawing at the pillars of the liberties of the people and, while their work is going forward, the government, whatever that may be, much or little, looks on as unconcernedly as if the enslavement of American workingmen was of less consequence than the appointment of some hustler to a fourth-class post office.

In this warfare upon railroad employees there must be a malign purpose, known only to those whose interests demand lower wages of employees. The war waged by capitalistic corporations upon labor has this one thing in view, and only one thing, the reduction of wages, and when it is seen, as in the case of the Union Pacific, that wage-men are sandbagged by a United States judge, the conclusion is inevitable that the court and the corporation, in alliance, have decided to work the ruin of labor that the corporation may riot in wealth. It is the degradation of labor and the exaltation of the corporation, and if it be possible for the courts and the corporations, under cover of receiverships, to strike down the most manly and independent wageworkers of the country, the task of subjugating employees in other departments of industrial enterprises shall be comparatively easy.

In the great mining industries of the country, labor is on its knees. True, miners strike and protest while being subjected to ordeals of hunger, squalor, rags, and exposure, but the corporations, the plutocratic mine owners, permit them to writhe until exhaustion comes, then they go back to their underground tasks, wronged and robbed and still more degraded. The great family of ironworkers, as at Homestead, have felt the grasp of capitalistic corporations upon their throats, have resisted as does the prey in the coils of a serpent, to yield at last, when idleness and consequent want had done their work, a mass of mangled manhood, submitted to such terms as their masters might dictate, and thus the enslavement goes forward, but in no instance have men been rendered so debased and disgraced, humiliated and abject as the men on the Union Pacific by the autocratic orders of Judge Dundy. True it is that Jenkins and Fuller, Taft and Ricks, compelled men to stand and be robbed, but Dundy, in the language of the dispatch and the slang of the poker room, went all of his associates "one better" and, not content with reducing the wages of the men, chained them to the road, reduced them to rolling stock, and there they are, working, toiling, sweating, hoping perhaps that the day will come when the black-tongued plague which Dundy sowed in their midst will disappear and their rights as sovereign citizens be restored to them. We do not doubt that that day will come, since come it must if the ancient pillars of our liberties are to stand, come it must if the Republic is not to breed millions of Sampsons deprived of their eyes by judicial Dundys, and who, exasperated beyond endurance by corporate Philistines, grasp the pillars of the temple of our liberties and then, asking a just God to give them strength, wreck the superstructure, leaving it to others to build something in its place with the Dundy curse omitted.

But, omitting such figures of speech, however appropriate, we are constrained to inquire from whence comes this evolution of savagery? On the one hand we see the power of the state, the judiciary of the state, and the military force of the state in alliance with corporate greed to strike down labor, as in the case of Homestead. We see, as in the case of Buffalo, the state and the militia of the state in alliance with corporations to overwhelm labor with disaster, when labor was demanding that the power of the state should support its claims to fair dealing in strict accord with the statute of the state, which the corporations were openly, defiantly, and confessedly violating, demonstrating that states, their courts, and the standing armies are combined, in defiance of truth and justice, to enslave labor. The question ceaselessly recurs: why this governmental madness, this implacable hostility to labor—to the great army of workingmen? If such hostility is denied, we point to the records, to the facts, and to the conditions under which labor exists today—conditions which thoughtful men in every walk of life declare to be fraught with danger. Expressions of regard for labor, its prosperity and happiness could be quoted indefinitely, but when a United States judge, as in the case of Dundy, assumes autocratic power and goes "one better" than any other judicial miscreant in robbing men not only of their money but of their liberty, does any government protest? Not so much as an intimation of opposition to the infamous decree is heard.

What, then, must be the conclusion? This: The governments, state and national, look upon the wreck of the liberties of workingmen with composure. Such is the inevitable conclusion. What does it portend in the not far away future? Does it indicate peace and prosperity, love of law and respect for courts? Necessarily, nothing of the kind. What is the remedy? The ballot, an abandonment of old parties and their methods; the solid unification of workingmen for the purpose of securing, while they may, a peaceful solution of the problems which involve life, liberty, and the pursuit of happiness.

Here we call upon every patriotic workingman to urge forward the solidification of the hosts of labor to change the governmental policy toward workingmen. They ought not to be subjected to further degradation, humiliation, and outrage. The enslaving work ought to stop. It will stop. The times are ripe for resistance. The ballot, properly used, can work out for labor the needed reforms. The Dundys can be suppressed. Right and justice may be enthroned without a Sodom storm of fire,[21] but the storm can only be avoided by a timely resort to the ballot.

The Equality of Men and Women[†]

March 1894

The present is an age of reform, at any rate, of change. Antiquity long since ceased to command veneration—even what was esteemed good is pushed aside to make way for something deemed better, and there is a great host of crusaders whose purpose is to battle for the best. If this were all of it, the world would serenely contemplate progress and dream of perfection. But with all of our boasted progress and civilization, Christianity and knowledge, the vices and superstitions of the past are often reconstructed and made more offensive and are given a conspicuousness which, in earlier times, they could not enjoy.

Prominent among these vices and superstitions of which we read and which we are permitted to see and contemplate is the assumption of woman's inferiority to man. It does not matter that the world has experienced an age of chivalry; it does not matter that along the track of the centuries men have championed the cause of woman, called her an "angel" and applied other endearing titles to her, robed her magnificently and decked her with jewels of dazzling beauty, and paid her abject homage; it does not matter that women have been led to the altar and joined in matrimonial vows with all the pomp and ceremony the church could bestow; it does not matter that as wife she has been made mistress of the home, and as mother enshrined in the hearts of her children, and without whom there could be no home upon the earth; it does not matter that love is forever coining new words by which men are enabled to express their devotion and proclaim their vassalage to women. When the time comes to apply the test and determine the honesty of their professions of fealty, with scarcely an exception they are found ready to hurl at women the charge of inferiority to men. It is then that old and degrading wrongs and superstitions come into view, and then, swearing by their whiskers, mustache, and fists, tobacco and cigars, their muscle and avoirdupois, men swell to gigantic proportions of self-conceit and proclaim themselves superior to womankind—to mother, wife, and daughter, and like the "Oregon" hear no sound except their own boasting.[22]

It may not be difficult for the student to determine the whys and the wherefores of man's savage brutality toward woman—since the masculine has the larger share of muscle and physical power and can therefore subjugate the

†   Published in *Locomotive Firemen's Magazine*, vol. 18, no. 3 (March 1894), 282–285.

physically weaker sex, and as he finds enjoyment in the exercise of his power, the problem is easily solved. But why civilized, Christianized, educated, and sublimated men should contend that women are inferior to themselves, and continue to deprive them of the rights, privileges, and prerogatives men enjoy, constitutes one of the mysteries of this high noon of our civilization. At the first glance it would seem to have seen the mission of Christianity and the church to emancipate woman from the thralldoms of savagery and paganism, to have lifted her by divine power to ethereal elevations and to have enlarged her rights, rather than seek opportunities and excuses for abridging them. But it so happens that St. Paul, the great apostle to the gentiles, inoculated Christianity and the church with the virus of woman's inferiority, and from the days of Paul to the present, neither Christianity nor the church has sought to remove the stigma. It may be well to note the language of St. Paul in this connection, that the charge of misrepresentation, if made, may be speedily crushed, let it be understood that St. Paul claimed to be inspired, that is to say, to speak by divine authority. Let those who are capable grasp the proposition, and the reason why Christianity has evinced a relentless opposition to woman's equality with man is explained. St. Paul, in writing to Timothy, whom he called "my own son in the faith,"[23] said: "Let the woman learn in silence with all subjection."[24]

In this the great apostle would have women emulate the oyster and the slave. The oyster is silent, and the slave is both silent and subservient.

Again says the inspired apostle: "I suffer not a woman to teach, nor to usurp authority over the man, but to be in silence."[25]

Thus it happens in the year of "our Lord" 63, eighteen hundred and thirty years ago, the church began its relentless crusade against woman's rights, and as a general proposition has kept up the warfare for more than 18 centuries. In this connection it becomes interesting to note why St. Paul was animated by such hostility to woman. True, he was a bachelor, and probably had never known the ecstasy of "love's young dream,"[26] had never told to woman's ears his love beneath the light of the stars or the moon's pale beams, had never taken his sweetheart to church, riding double on a Judean donkey, but such were not the reasons that prompted him to degrade woman. His hostility reached back to Eden. He says: "For Adam was first formed, then Eve. And Adam was not deceived, but woman being deceived was the transgressor."[27]

Here we have the key that unlocks the Pandora box from which have escaped more ills to women all along the track of the centuries than there are stars in the firmament. But St. Paul felt the divine command to write to the Corinthian Christians something more on the woman question. Evidently the apostle had become alarmed on account of privileges granted the Corinthian Christian women, whereupon he wrote as follows:

> Let your women keep silence; for it is not permitted unto them to speak; but they are commanded to be under obedience, as also saith the law. And if they will learn anything let them ask their husbands at home; for it is a shame for women to speak in the church. [28]

The point we make is this: that the position taken by St. Paul, supplemented by the affirmation that he was inspired by God himself, to degrade women in the eyes of the Christian world fully accounts for the centuries of enslavement more or less cruel and crushing that has fallen to the lot of women throughout Christendom. Their inferiority to men breathes in every line of St. Paul's writings upon the subject, a display of bigotry and arrogance which, in the light of reason, is sufficient to make the world blush scarlet. Is it strange that under such tutelage woman has been regarded inferior to man, or that centuries of wrong have not had the effect to impair her mental faculties, and as is seen in millions of instances, make women willingly accept the foul charge of natural, inherent inferiority? Had the same maledictions been hurled at man instead of woman, who can so much as surmise results upon the masculine branch of society throughout all lands where Christianity is the dominating religion?

The "woman movement" in these latter days is, we do not doubt, of all social, human, and civilizing movements, the one of the most far-reaching and transcendent importance. We by no means underrate the herculean task that challenges the mind forces of the men and women who are engaged in the work of woman's enfranchisement. We do not belittle the power of bigotry and superstition, which in alliance asserts woman's inferiority to man and denies them the rights and privileges which men enjoy, and of which they boast. We know that the press and the pulpit, with here and there an exception, demand that women shall keep silent and wear their fetters submissively. But we see in spite of all opposition that women are achieving triumphs in all the walks of life that challenge intellectuality and high endeavor, which must make St. Paul, if permitted to observe human affairs, somewhat restive.

What do we behold? The institutions of learning, moss covered with antiquity, throwing wide open their doors and admitting women to lyceums as sacred as where Plato and Aristotle taught, and we see them coming forth equipped and holding as high aloft the blazing torch of learning and progress as falls to the lot of their masculine competitors.

And yet there are those who cannot refrain from resorting to science (so called) to demonstrate woman's inferiority. They proceed to weighing brains, and find that the brain-weight of women is about five ounces less than that of men—hence this inference that in the "higher levels" of intellectual work, women are not men's equals—though admitting that girls are superior to boys at school when equal advantages are enjoyed. The injustice of the estimate of inferior work in high intellectual levels is manifest, because at the very time when boys begin such work, girls are retired upon such laurels as they may have won. But now, as opportunities are afforded women to enter the lists of high endeavor, men are required to make the most of their endowments. In a word, inequalities are disappearing and, in the race to win prizes where the feminine and the masculine minds contend for the mastery, the proof is overwhelming that but for the centuries in which the dwarfing processes have been carried forward, women today, in creative thoughts, clear perceptions, and sound judgment, would bear off the non-desirable prizes. An eminent scientist who holds to woman's intellectual inferiority when all the facts are summed up is forced to admit woman's intellectual superiority in numerous instances, as for instance, the following:

> Reading implies enormously intricate processes of perception, both of the sensuous and intellectual order, and I have tried a series of experiments, wherein reading was chosen as a test of the rapidity of perception in different persons. Having seated a number of well-educated individuals around a table I presented to them successively the same paragraph of a book, which they were each to read as rapidly as they could, ten seconds being allowed for 20 lines. As soon as time was up I removed the paragraph, immediately after which the reader wrote down all that he or she could remember of it. Now, in these experiments, where everyone read the same paragraph as rapidly as possible, I found that the palm was usually carried off by the ladies. Moreover, besides being able to read quicker, they were better able to remember what they had just read—that is, to give a better account of the paragraph as a whole. One lady, for example, could read exactly four times as fast as her husband, and could then give a better account even of that portion of the paragraph which alone he had had time to get through. [29]

Other and numerous instances could be given showing not only that women are men's equals intellectually, but often their superiors—and that any inequality should exist we hold is chargeable to the fact that women nowhere at any time have ever enjoyed opportunities equal to those conferred upon men to demonstrate to a gainsaying world that their mental endowments qualify them to participate fully in all human affairs designed to elevate human beings.

We are fully convinced that the opposition to the complete enfranchisement of women has its foundation in superstitions as degrading as any that have ever cursed the world. One by one these false theories are disappearing—and step by step women are advancing in the acquisition of knowledge. In the science of education, they challenge competition and silence criticism. In the science of law and of medicine, they are winning renown. In the pulpit, their sermons evince that they can delve as deeply into the mysteries of theology as any masculine graduate of the divinity schools can boast. In the lecture field, they draw and win applause; on the stage, their admirers are a mighty host. In art and literature, they are achieving triumphs of which men might well be envious—but their enfranchisement can be celebrated only when they are permitted to grasp the ballot. Then their fetters will drop from around them, as did the shackles from 4 million slaves when Abraham Lincoln declared their emancipation.

To this it is coming, and the movement is mining momentum. Men talk about the ballot unsexing women—as well say that the crown has unsexed Victoria.[30] The ballot, as a weapon, is mightier than the sword, and women can wield it in the interest of peace and of purity—silence and submission have had their day—henceforth, agitation and aggressive warfare. Henceforth the shibboleth—"For Truth and the Right," and as the "eternal years of God" are pledged for the triumph of truth and right,[31] duty marks the way which will grow brighter until women in America stand forth emancipated by the conquering power of eternal justice.

Liberty and the Courts[†]
March 1894

The *Commoner and Glassworker,* in a recent issue, publishes the following:

> The general manager of the Northern Pacific Railway has discovered a new way to prevent strikes. He goes into the United States courts and has all the leaders in the movement arrested for "combining and conspiring to quit the service of the road." Upon this complaint an injunction is issued against each individual, and a failure to observe the court's order will land the offender in prison. It is the first order of the kind ever issued in the United States. The Northern Pacific is now in the hands of receivers. The difficulty arose out of reductions in wages. Should this action of the court hold good, the working classes will soon find all their rights and privileges as free men nullified, and they will be forced by due process of law to labor for just such compensation as receivers and courts deem proper and just to the government and stockholders, and the right of individual contract is void. It is difficult to distinguish between such action on the part of a republic and some of the old English laws of two or three centuries ago, which fixed both the wages and hours of the working people. Our boasted freedom is fast becoming a sham and mockery, and will hasten the entire dissolution of our present social conditions.

The foregoing is highly suggestive. The receiver of a railroad and a 3x4 United States judge in combination are able, it seems, to compel employees to hold up their hands while the aforesaid receiver and lodge put on the manacles and rivet them.

That the Northern Pacific Railroad should be in the hands of a receiver creates no surprise; that a receiver of such a bankrupt concern should exert his powers and authority to reduce wages that dividends may be paid on watered stocks and bonds is strictly in keeping with modern methods of piracy. Receivers are to railroad corporations what the jimmy is to expert safe examiners who, needing cash, smilingly and philosophically remark, in the language of P. M. Arthur: "If you can't get what you want, take what you can get." Corporations have no souls to be damned and are expected to wreck and rob, rob

---

[†]   Published in *Locomotive Firemen's Magazine,* vol. 18, no. 3 (March 1894), 275–277.

and wreck, in carrying forward their great enterprises designed to develop the resources of the country and give *éclat* to our Christian civilization. But hitherto it has been held that judges of courts, particularly United States courts, were, in all things relating to character, reputation, and justice, in a word, all things of good report among men, superior to corporations and their tools. True, there have been mean, depraved, despicable judges, vicious creatures, moral monstrosities entitled to receive "greater damnation" than falls to the lot of many other scoundrels, but the people generally, in fact, universally, in this country, have been taught to revere judges of courts. There has been an idea, widely disseminated, that as a last resort appeals to the courts for justice would not be disregarded, that the poor and the friendless, as certainly as the rich and powerful, would be heard and their wrongs redressed. Such has been the drift of opinion. If at any time in the past such conditions were based upon facts they have in these latter days become the most arrant delusions. True, it is written in the Bill of Rights that "Justice shall be administered freely, and without purchase; completely and without denial, speedily and without delay." But it has turned out that the Bill of Rights has proven to be, in ten thousand instances multiplied by ten thousand, a miserable fallacy, mockery, and deception; until it has come to be understood that the thing labeled "justice," to be "administered freely and without purchase," bears about as much resemblance to justice as a blue-tailed fly bears to a bald eagle. And as for justice being administered "completely and without denial," there are upon record ten thousand cases where maimed railroad men have been denied justice by courts, and where cruel denials have been administered to the widows and orphans of dead railroad men who were killed in the line of duty, by judges of courts where corporations demanded the sacrifice, and as for justice being administered "speedily and without delay," the records show that the declaration constitutes the prize sham of the age.

As a result of all this the reverence the people formerly entertained for judges and courts of justice is rapidly disappearing. It is widely believed, indeed it has become a settled conviction, that a poor man has about the same chance for justice in the courts of the country that a hummingbird would have in passing through the flames of Vesuvius to escape without having its wings singed, while the rich, the corporations, trusts, and all rascally combinations, by the magic of money have things as they want them, upon the principle, doubtless, that gave Jay Gould his astounding success, that when he "wanted a judge he bought him;" at any rate the fact is that judges and courts in the United States are no longer revered. Wigs and gowns and all the ancient flummery which made a judge appear to the populace as a creature of superior dust—porcelain as compared with brickbats—have lost their talismanic power, until the "ermined robes" of an average judge have no more significance than attaches to a ten dollar ulster, and United States judges in integrity and intellectuality rate fearfully near zero.

For this rapid depreciation of judges and courts there must be a reason, and it behooves the people to investigate until they ascertain the true cause. We do not imagine any very deep excavations will be required to develop a mine of ignorance and egotism of astounding richness. Surface indications are simply immense. The outcroppings of imbecility are quickly pointed out by schoolchildren. It is a rare circumstance to find a United States judge who is not afflicted with big-head and pig-head, a condition of vacuity and vanity, stupidity and stubbornness, arrogance and insolence, qualities which have become so common as to rarely create surprise, and yet it so happens that vast interests are committed to these judicial deformities, which may he determined, right or wrong, just as flipped coppers may come up heads or tails, as chance may decide, but if a railroad pass is dropped in the slot of the judicial machine, or something more weighty still, then justice throws her scales to the dogs, strips the bandage from her eyes, and breaks for the woods, but that particular judge proceeds to "hold court" and "issue decrees," just as if he was not under popular indictment for malfeasance in office.

Why this humiliating degeneracy? It is not difficult to answer the important query in consonance with an overwhelming weight of facts.

In the first place, political partisanship has, in numerous instances, contributed to the degradation of the judiciary. It has been, to some extent, a popular theory that a hidebound partisan, elevated to the bench, at once proceeds to burst his shell and transform himself into a sublimated creature, in whose makeup all the humps and depressions on his cranium indicative of meanness and malignity disappear, that an "itching palm" is no longer a source of trouble, and that the hinges of his knees are so readjusted that they will not respond when wealth and power demand crooked legs. Alas, experience has taught the people to discard such hallucinations, and to regard courts as deadfalls and judges as simply the manipulators of the triggers.

Judges being selected for their partisanship, for their familiarity with the machine, and as a reward for services, it follows, as a general proposition, that small potatoes are, as a rule, elevated to the bench, and the courts become, therefore, so many political machines, clothed with extraordinary powers and prerogatives. It is well known that in the scramble for nomination or appointment the supreme essentials of a judge—large ability, knowledge of the principles of law, unflinching honesty, tireless devotion to right and justice, are practically ignored and that candidates secure election or appointment because they have rendered a political party assistance in campaigns, rough and tumble fights for supremacy. True, it may be said that sometimes a qualified man is selected, but such incidents are exceptional. As a rule, judges of courts seldom rise above mediocrity, and often fall calamitously below it. Being men of small caliber, often mental midgets, what more natural than that they should bring courts into contempt by orders, rulings, and decisions which make jurisprudence ridiculous?

It is contended that lawyers of brains no longer aspire to be judges: (1) Because they can earn more money practicing law, and (2) because the office of judge, generally, has become odious rather than honorable, in which small men strut around, targets for the flings and jeers of the people, their decisions being largely in the nature of chuck-a-luck[32]—or, worse still, like a 25-number lottery, where the chances are 999,000 to 1 that you do not draw a capital prize, and about 200,000 to 1 that you draw no prize at all. If it were a fair game of chance, men might gamble for justice in the courts and curse their luck while heroically accepting defeat; but it has come to this, at last, that the rich—corporations and trusts, as in the case of the Union Pacific, the Northern Pacific, and the Ann Arbor affair—can obtain anything they want to help them crush the poor. Anything to the contrary is the exception—and only magnifies the rule. Occasionally, some distinguished scoundrel is lightly punished. In such a case, the press engages in flambeau reports which are of special service to rich rascals generally, because, in the midst of the glorification over the conviction of one miscreant, a thousand go scot-free, or to Canada.

Certain it is that throughout the land, judges and courts are regarded with ever-increasing suspicion and derision. Under the constitutions of states and the federal constitution, judges, as has been observed, are clothed with autocratic power. Note the creature called "judge" who, by a stroke of his pen, reduced sovereign citizens, employees on the Union Pacific and Northern Pacific, to slaves. Note the infamous rulings of Ricks and Taft in the Toledo affair. Such exhibitions of power are becoming alarmingly frequent, and the people believe they have discovered the reason why of them. With small salaries, venal judges will "make hay while the sun shines." Poor devils have nothing to offer for justice but gratitude, while the corporation can add to its thanks the coin of the realm—banquets, free passes, and luxurious palace cars. True, men may appeal from Pilate to Caesar—if they can give bond—in the absence of which they go down to silence and defeat, and as well might a sparrow protest against a cyclone, or a jackrabbit against a prairie fire.

The judiciary of the country, in the opinion of multiplied thousands, is the rodent that is gnawing at the foundations of the liberties of the country, and if the question is asked why so many mobs, regulators, white caps, popular uprisings in which Judge Lynch presides? The answer is generally—"Oh, damn the courts, they're no good."

Talk of dangers to the perpetuity of liberty and free institutions from ignorance, poverty, wealth, and its combination—the real danger lies in a venal, debauched, arrogant judiciary. Corporations are now chuckling over their victories achieved by pliant, weak, imbecile lickspittles "on the bench." The Union and Northern Pacific incidents ought to be convincing. They tell in "mournful numbers" what is in reservation for railroad employees. Chained to the corporation—subjected to the lash of general managers *et al.,* their condition may be better than that of old plantation slaves, "fo de war"—for as yet, we believe, they are not included in "blanket mortgages," nor listed as assets in watered stocks and bonds. As an initial step, they are simply chained to the tracks, to their machines, to pick, throttle, punch, switch, and brake, but as in the case of Job, how soon the devil will rob them of everything but their integrity, his "Honor," the judge, only knows—but the way things are moving, it ought not to be long before railroad employees will curse the day they were born, since to eat their hard-earned fare as a part of the rolling stock of a railroad is enough to create a widespread epidemic of suicide. Such calamities suggest the immortal words of Patrick Henry—"Give me liberty or give me death."

The Northern Pacific[†]

March 1894

To succeed in securing an honorable adjustment of misunderstandings between railroad corporations and their hard-worked employees is always a source of satisfaction.

The Northern Pacific railroad, from its inception down to the present, has been the one railroad goose that railroad wreckers and gamblers have plucked as often as a pin feather came in sight, or it has been the bleating sheep to be sheared as often as there was wool enough on it to pay for the shearing. It has been regularly plucked, sheared, and skinned by a gang of Christless whelps as often as they could secure enough booty to get up a big blowout at Delmonico's[33] or pay the bills of a trip to Europe, and when, as in the present case, the concern had been sandbagged and bludgeoned to an extent that a receiver and a United States court, a sort of an ox-and-ass team, was required to draw its breath, the receiver and the court combine to rob the employees that the old goose may replume herself for another plucking just to keep the gamblers and wreckers in pocket change and their wives and daughters in pin money.

The fellow, Judge Jenkins, ambitions of notoriety quite regardless of its character, doubled up his decrees in the interest of the corporation, seemingly desirous of making himself specially odious to railroad employees.

In the first instance, the Jenkins judge, sitting at Milwaukee, issued his autocratic order restraining the employees of the Northern Pacific railway company from going on a strike, or from damaging, interfering with, or injuring the property of the road in the hands of the receivers. It also contained the following prohibition, restraining the officers, agents, and employees of the receivers "from combining and conspiring to quit, with or without notice, the service of said receivers, with the object and intent of crippling the property in the custody, or embarrassing the operation of said railroad, and from so quitting the service of the said receivers, with or without notice, as to cripple the property or to prevent or hinder the operation of said railroad."

But the receivers becoming alarmed, they appealed again to Jenkins, who issued a second injunction directed to the officers of the various labor organizations, embracing the employees of the Northern Pacific by name, restraining

---

†   Published in *Locomotive Firemen's Magazine*, vol. 18, no. 3 (March 1894), 290–292.

them from conferring with, advising, or counseling the men to go on a strike, and restraining the men from striking or quitting the employment of the company or receivers, either with or without notice.

The action of this judicial snipe was so outrageous that action has been proposed in Congress to see if something cannot be done to curb his autocratic ambition, as will be seen by the following resolution, offered in the House of Representatives by Congressman McGann,[34] February 5 [1894]:

> *Resolved,* That the Committee on Judiciary of the House be and is hereby directed to make such investigation into all the matters and things herein alleged and report to the House whether or not the Hon. Judge Jenkins, judge of the United States Circuit Court of the seventh circuit, has therein abused powers or process of said court, or oppressively exercised the same, or has used his office as such judge, to intimidate or restrain the employees of the Northern Pacific railroad or the officers of labor organizations, to which said employees or any of them were affiliated, in the exercise of their rights and privileges under the laws of the United States; and if they shall find that said judge has abused the process of said court, as alleged, or oppressively exercised the powers of his office as judge of said court to the injury of the employees of said railroad and others, then to report whether such act or doings of said judge warrant the presentment of articles of impeachment therefor, and to further report what action, if any, should be taken by Congress to prevent a repetition of the conditions now laid by said order, and by an injunction upon railway employees on the said Northern Pacific road, those engaged on other roads, officers and members of labor organizations throughout the country, and all persons generally.

It may not be that the fawning corporation sycophant will be impeached, but that the Jenkinses, Dundys, Rickses, and Tafts will hear and feel something drop, calculated to curb despotic proclivities, we do not doubt.

At this juncture it is specially refreshing to note that all the United States judges are not of the Jenkins and Dundy stripe. This is made to appear in the columns of the *St. Louis Globe-Democrat* of February 11. Speaking of the extent of the jurisdiction of Jenkins it seems that inasmuch as the larger part of the Northern Pacific lies in the eighth judicial circuit, of which Judge Henry C. Caldwell is the presiding judge, it becomes necessary to institute proceedings in this, the eighth circuit, in aid of or ancillary to those originally instituted before Judge Jenkins at Milwaukee, in the seventh circuit. The jurisdiction of Judge Jenkins only extends to the western boundary of the state of Wisconsin. All of the Northern Pacific railroad from Duluth, in Minnesota, which runs through the states of Minnesota, North and South Dakota, and Nebraska and Colorado lies in Judge Caldwell's circuit, and it therefore became necessary to have Judge Caldwell endorse Jenkins. This Judge Caldwell refused to do. He is evidently not a corporation lickspittle, is not purchasable, and is withal a man of sterling convictions. He is reported as saying:

> If receivers should apply for leave to reduce the existing scale of wages, before acting on their petition I would require them to give notice of the application to the officers or representatives of the several labor organizations to be affected by the proposed change, of the time and place of the hearing, and would also require them to grant such officers or representatives leave of absence and furnish them with transportation to the place of the hearing and subsistence while in attendance, and I would hear both sides in person, or by attorneys, if they wanted attorneys to appear for them.
>
> The employees on a road in the hands of a receiver are the employees of the court, and as much in its service as the receivers themselves, and as much entitled to be heard upon any proposed order of the court which would affect the whole body of employees. If, after a full hearing and consideration, I found that it was necessary, equitable, and just to reduce the scale of wages, I would give the employees ample time to determine whether they would accept or reject the new scale. If they rejected it they would not be enjoined from quitting the service of the court, either singly or in a body. In other words, I would not enjoin them from striking, but if they made their election to strike I would make it plain to them that they must not, after quitting the service of the court, interfere with the property, or the operation of the road, or the men employed to take their places. A United States court can very readily find the means to effectually protect the property in its possession and the persons in its employ. I have in one or two instances pursued the policy I have indicated, and the differences were satisfactorily adjusted.

The *Globe-Democrat* says:

> To put the position of the two courts sharply: Judge Jenkins, in the seventh circuit, holds that he has power to restrain the officers of the labor organizations from ordering a strike and the men from going on a strike or from combining or counseling together for the purpose of inaugurating a strike. Judge Caldwell's action shows that he holds the power of the court to extend only to preventing the employees or anyone else from injuring or destroying the property in the hands of receivers, or by force or threats interfering with the men who are engaged in operating the

road. He does not, by his order, undertake to prevent them from going on a strike, or undertake to enjoin them from consulting together with reference to a strike, leaving that without inference by the court with the declaration that if any persons interfere with the property or men actually at work, either by violence, threats, or intimidation, he will then deal with them as lawbreakers.

Manifestly, Judge Caldwell is a man, while Jenkins is a mouse, and as a result, the order of the mouse is circumscribed within narrow limits—men are still men where Judge Caldwell rules—though they may be something quite different under the jurisdiction of Jenkins.

The troubles between the employees and the receivers of the Northern Pacific began in December. For a time, there was every indication that the federated orders had determined to make a stand for their rights; that whether pleading or protesting they would show Spartan courage. The various federated orders had their grievance committees marshaled in force. They met and deliberated, called for their grand executive officers, who responded regardless of time, distance, or expense.

The negotiations finally ended on February 10, when the following letter was addressed by Mr. E. E. Clark, chairman of the federated executives to General Manager Kendrick:

> Dear Sir:—
>
> As chairman of the federated board of representatives of your employees, I am instructed by them to inform you that in view of the present conditions they reluctantly accept the situation, and request that, agreeable to their expressed willingness, the receivers petition the court to ratify the amendments to the schedule on January 1, which have been agreed to by them in the several conferences which have been held in St. Paul and this city.
>
> In doing this, we express the hope that rapidly improving business and increased earnings will soon render it consistent for you to restore in whole or in part that which has been found necessary to hike from the men.
>
> Yours very truly,
> *E. E. Clark*

We regret that the men have had to accept the reduction while their hearts

> Like muffled drums, are beating
> Funeral marches to the grave.[35]

Furious Fanatics[†]

April 1894

We have been deluged with communications during the past few days in reference to the editorial on the American Protective Association which appeared in the March issue of the *Magazine*. A peculiar feature of this correspondence is that in every instance where the writer condemns our utterances, he does so anonymously. There is not an exception to the rule. Several of them demand that their communications be published, but in accordance with a well-known rule of the *Magazine,* they have all found their way to the wastebasket. The *Magazine* is avowedly in favor of fair play, and its columns are open to all sides of a question, but it does not under any circumstances publish anonymous communications.

The editorial alluded to contains the opinions of the editor, and he alone is responsible for them. He has no apology to make for such utterances. If the persons who criticize and condemn him have the courage of their convictions and desire a hearing, they can have it, and the *Magazine* is open to them, but they cannot be permitted to play the role of sneaks and shoot from ambush. Let them have the manliness to step to the front and give expression to their honest thought and, right or wrong, their course will challenge respect and admiration.

One correspondent, who addresses us as "Father Debs," demands retraction, and coupled with the demand there is a covert threat of assassination. An anonymous writer is, as a rule, a sneak, and a sneak is always a coward, and the coward who makes this threat is convincing proof of the truth of the article in question.

We care nothing about the American Protective Association except insofar as it is forced into labor organizations, is made to set brother against another, divide the membership, destroy the strength that unity confers, and reduce the whole mass of workingmen to the insufferable level of slaves. And that is what is being done with the APA, and we know it of our own knowledge. We do not speak upon hearsay. We know of scores of lodges, unions, and divisions that have perished all but in name under the blighting curse of such persecution, and if suffered to continue it is only a question of a short time when labor organizations will be exterminated as if by the ravages of a plague and then wages will go down to the starvation point, rights will be cloven down, and the sun of

---

[†]   Published in *Locomotive Firemen's Magazine,* vol. 18, no. 4 (April 1894), 396.

American labor will set in universal gloom. It is such calamities that we would avert, and this and this alone prompted us to sound the warning. We do not doubt there is bigotry and fanaticism on the other side. But one wrong does not justify another, and it will not do to follow a vicious example.

The APA, naturally enough, does not show its hand among the wealthy and influential—the ruling classes. As a matter of course, it does not disrupt plutocratic relations nor array corporations against each other—they have too much sense to be divided upon any such proposition. It is left for the poor devils who are already half starved and more than half enslaved to take each other by the throat and in the interest of their masters bring on their self-destruction. And, singular enough, not one in fifty of these insane bigots who are so exceedingly sensitive on the subject of religion could, to save his soul, repeat the ten commandments or the Lord's Prayer.

We are not and never have been Catholic.[36] We hate a bigot of one denomination as much as another. We have no choice of fanatics. They are found in all creeds and all denominations, and if they had their way the reign of the wheel and the rack and the thumbscrew would again be inaugurated, and the music of groans would fill the land.

Let us have done with persecution because of opinion's sake, and above all let us show ourselves possessed of hard sense enough to know that in introducing sectarian war into our labor organizations we are carrying out the designs of our masters to enslave and rob us.

Open Letter to Gov. Knute Nelson
in St. Paul, Minnesota†

April 23, 1894

St. Paul, Minn., April 23, 1894

To Hon. Knute Nelson,
Governor of Minnesota,
St. Paul, Minn.

Dear Sir:—

Replying to your communication of even date, which I have carefully noted,[37] I beg to say that the remaining members of the committee of the American Railway Union representing the employees of the Great Northern Railway Company will arrive in this city tomorrow, Tuesday morning, and with said committee is lodged the authority to meet the official representatives of said railway company for the purpose of negotiating a settlement of existing difficulties. The committee, promptly upon their arrival, will call upon President [James J.] Hill, of the company aforesaid, and seek by all means at their command to effect a settlement that will be just and satisfactory to all parties concerned.

Permit me to assure you that so far as the American Railway Union and its representatives are concerned, there is no disposition to continue the present unfortunate complications beyond the absolute necessities of the case; on the contrary, every effort which common justice and a prudent regard for the public welfare and the American spirit of fair play can suggest will be exhausted to reach an amicable adjustment.

Meantime, you may rest assured that so far as it lies in my power to prevent it, there shall be no violation of any law, state or national, on the part of the employees or their sympathizers, and trusting that a prompt resumption of traffic may follow the conference, I have the honor to subscribe myself,

Very truly, your obedient servant,
Eugene V. Debs,
President, American Railway Union

---

† Published as part of the article "Arbitration Advised," *St. Paul Globe,* April 24, 1894.

ARU Purposes and Procedures[†]

May 1894

In writing of the new order of railway employees known as the American Railway Union at so early a date in its history, only purposes in view can be set forth, and these, since the space at our command is limited, must be severely epitomized.

The value of organization need not be discussed. It is conceded. The present is an era of organization, of the unification of forces. Workingmen comprehend its essentiality and adopt it as a means of progress and protection. The American Railway Union is in full accord with such a plan of campaign.

Consulting the highest official authorities, the railways of the United States, Canada, and Mexico require about 1 million employees of various classes to carry forward their operations. Of these employees, to say that 150,000 are members of organizations would be a liberal estimate. This would leave 850,000 to be provided for, and the mission of the American Railway Union is to provide these unorganized employees with an organization which will meet every requirement.

It has been written that the present generation knows more than all former generations, because, knowing all that former generations knew, the present generation has added indefinitely to the general stock of knowledge; hence I hold that the American Railway Union, having before it the achievements of all other organizations, is in a position to take advantage of whatever may be deemed wise and advantageous, and to remedy the more glaring defects which are forced upon the attention of the students of labor problems.

The American Railway Union will seek assiduously to devise methods of economy in its management. The great body of wage-earners are poorly paid, and for organizations to indulge in extravagance of any description upon revenues extorted from the membership is wrong, the flagrancy of which increases the more it is investigated.

Salaries out of all proportion to abilities or services rendered are conspicuous among the crying errors that have crept into organized labor. To eliminate such imperfections and to introduce economical methods of management will

---

† First published in *Transportation,* circa May 1894. Reprinted as "The American Railway Union" in the *Railway Times,* vol. 1, no. 10 (May 15, 1894), 2.

have the attention of the American Railway Union in every measure proposed. Economy begets simplicity of machinery, while extravagance is the prolific parent of pride and ostentation, fundamentally at war with progress and the prosperity of those who are taxed to maintain the display. Multiplied thousands of workingmen, railroad employees, have joined organizations, which they have been compelled to abandon because of excessive taxation.

The American Railway Union will be protective in its policy, but it will advance upon the lines of error without issuing pronunciamentos filled with gasconade for the purpose of demoralizing the authors of wrongs; on the contrary, having boundless confidence in logic, truth, and common sense, and believing in the American idea of fair play, its striking machinery will be adjusted in a way to secure justice, if possible, without a resort to war, nor as a last resort will it declare war unless victory is assured insofar as all conditions can warrant such a result.

To accomplish its purpose the American Railway Union will avail itself of every means at its command to educate its membership out of old ruts and twilight environments into higher and smoother pathways and a broader light. It will institute a new order of diplomacy which, if concessions and compromises can smooth the corrugated brows of contestants, it will be done before and not after battles have been fought and untold sacrifices have been made, acting upon the principle that

> Peace hath her victories
> No less renowned than war.[38]

The American Railway Union will have the courage of patience and prudence and knowing the right will seek for it with becoming diligence, and will have the courage to stand firmly for it and by it when emergencies require action.

Government Control of Railroads and Employees[†]
May 1894

Persons calling themselves "nationalists," and others, perhaps, who choose some other designation, advocate the ownership and the management of the railroads of the United States by the federal government.

We are not, at this writing, inclined to discuss the financial aspect of the proposition; how, if the government should conclude to purchase the railroads, the money could be obtained to pay for them, but instead, to call attention of the readers of the *Magazine* to conditions that would most probably confront employees who would be required to operate the roads, a branch of the subject which does not seem to have attracted much attention, if, indeed, it has been broached at all by the advocates of government ownership of the railroads of the country.

It is eminently prudent to say that it is a question in which railroad employees are vitally concerned, and upon which their views should have due consideration. Nationalism, at least as applied to railroading, is paternalism, or wilder still, Bellamyism—an ism which dwarfs out of sight the individual, while it indefinitely expands government control to absolutism. It must be this, necessarily, since there is no appeal from the dictum of the government. The subject warrants exhaustive criticism, and the more it is investigated, the more urgent the analysis appears.

The value of the railroads of the country is now placed at $11 billion—or about five times the cost of the war of the rebellion—and the number of employees required to operate 175,223 miles of track of these roads, as reported December 31, 1892, approximates 1 million. In case the government should own and operate these roads, they would be practically consolidated into one great system, and the interests involved would be of such vast magnitude as would probably make it necessary to create another department of the government. To manage an establishment of such enormous proportions would require military discipline of the most rigid character, in which case employees *enlisted*—that would doubtless be required—they would at once come under laws and regulations of a cast-iron order from which, as has been observed, there would be no appeal.

---

†   Published in *Locomotive Firemen's Magazine,* vol. 18, no. 5 (May 1894), 468–470.

Here it becomes pertinent to inquire, first, in case of government ownership and management of the railroads, would the organizations of railroad employees as now constituted be tolerated? Is it to be presumed that immediately upon the passing of the ownership of the roads from the corporations to government all grievances would disappear, and a railroad employees' millennium would dawn? But suppose employees should insist upon maintaining their organizations with all of their grand officers and machinery for presenting grievances and ordering strikes, is there a man who entertains the idea that the government would for an instant permit the slightest interference with its orders and regulations? A moment's reflection discloses the preposterousness of such a conception. Employees might be permitted to maintain organizations of a beneficiary character to improve the moral, social, educational, and financial condition of their members, but the government would make all regulations relating to time and wages, nor would it for a moment distinguish between a scab and a union man; belonging to an organization would cut no figure at all, and as a consequence, organizations would at once be required to relegate all their machinery for protection to the limbo of forgotten things. As well expect enlisted soldiers in the regular army to maintain organizations for the purpose of criticizing orders of superiors, presenting grievances and proposing to strike if concessions were not granted. Indeed, under laws already in force, as interpreted by certain United States judges, it is questionable if railroad employees connected with the train service are any longer free men, the interpretation of the law being that they are a part of the rolling stock of the corporations, held to their places by the force of law.

With such facts in sight, is it not to be presumed that, under government control of the railroads, the first thing Congress would do would be to make laws concerning their management? Such a conclusion is not only logical, but inevitable. The laws thus enacted would doubtless confer upon a department, which the law would create, the duty of making rules and regulations for the management of the roads. The government, having become a "common carrier," would brook no delays—and employees would not be consulted any more than soldiers in the army are consulted about their movements. "Obedience" and "silence" would be the watchwords—and any infraction of the rules would be punished with military promptness and rigor.

With government control of the railroads, contracts between the government and the employees would be based upon law, with penalties attached of more or less severity, in which the punishment of recalcitrant employees would only be considered because, though the government might be in the wrong, there would be no process by which it could be arrested, tried, and punished, the government would be king—and the maxim is "the king can do no wrong," only the subject, the slave, the employee—hence the proposition for the government to control the railroads becomes a species of despotism, such as applies to the control of armies.

In the management of the railroads, the government would want about 1 million men. It is not to be presumed or assumed that the government would tolerate any happy-go-lucky policy relating to the required force to operate the roads. It would insist upon order. The trains must go their ceaseless rounds, day and night. What more natural than the inauguration of a system of enlistment for a term of years, during which the men, while permitted to die, would not enjoy the privilege of quitting, any more than soldiers in the regular army may throw down their muskets with impunity. Desert they might, but as desertion is a perilous business, employees once in the toils would probably prefer to serve out their time, rather than be hunted down by spies and detectives governments have in their employ.

Again, suppose an employee was discharged from the service as the lightest penalty the authorities could inflict, what would be the condition of the unfortunate? He would be practically branded as an outcast, blacklisted to an extent that he would not be permitted to enter the service again. True, he might be pardoned and reinstated, but the government, having absolute control, would doubtless prefer that such degraded employees should be warnings to others to obey orders and be silent.

As to the matter of wages, if the government should purchase and control the railroads, what assurance has labor that wages would be higher than at present? Indeed, what is there to inspire the belief that wages would not be reduced below their present averages? Manifestly, there is nothing upon which labor can hang a hope that its condition would be improved. If the purpose of the government should be to pay high wages and at the same time reduce the cost of transportation, there might be developed the fact that the business, like the post office department, was not a self-supporting enterprise, in which case appropriations would be required to meet deficits. If such a condition of things should occur, a cry would be heard demanding retrenchment and reform, and thus to avoid deficiencies wages might be reduced, in which event, what means of redress would be in sight for the employees? The grievance committee, even if one existed, would not chirp, and the coming together of grand chiefs and grand masters and grand lodges would be missionless. Neither strike, kick, nor boycott would be tolerated. Mass meetings and whereases would avail nothing, and all that would be left for the employee would be submission and silence.

Whatever else may be said of the government ownership of railroads, it is difficult to see in what regard the employee thereby would be benefited. We regard it quite too early to advocate absolutism in industrial enterprises. As matters now stand, there is quite enough of petty and pusillanimous czarism in shop, forge, factory, and mine and in the railroad service, and labor, we feel warranted in saying, does not clamor for more subjugation.

Objectionable Bosses[†]

May 1894

The strike in the Brooks Locomotive Works, Dunkirk, NY,[39] has now become so serious that an appeal has been made to Buffalo for state troops in case they may be needed. The beginning of the strike was caused a month ago by the refusal of the riveters in the boiler factory to work under certain contractors. President Hinman[40] declined to yield to the demands of the strikers, although 28 men from Philadelphia refused work upon learning they had been brought to replace strikers, and the workmen from Philadelphia at present secured are not able to venture safely outside the works. The lack of riveters had necessitated suspending labor in other departments, and now about 600 men are out of employment. Although the emergency may not arise, state troops at Jamestown and Buffalo are reported as being ready to move at a moment's notice.

The foregoing clipping from the *Railway Age* brings into prominence one of the causes which in numerous instances are productive of labor troubles.

It so happens that frequently proprietors of large industries select as overseers of their shops men who, though they may be in some regards competent, are in many other respects totally disqualified for the positions they hold. Pigheaded, bigoted, and arrogant, they conceive it to be their duty to play the role of guards in penitentiaries or bosses of convict laborers. Their ideas of discipline are not specially dissimilar to those practiced by overseers of Negroes in old "plantation times," and though the lash is not used, the attitude of the

†   Published in *Locomotive Firemen's Magazine,* vol. 18, no. 5 (May 1894), 473–474.

boss toward the men is that of a petty tyrant, and who, dressed in a little brief authority, exercises it in such a way as to earn the contempt and loathing of the men he seeks to control. He is no more fit for the position than hell would be for a powder magazine, or a chestnut burr for an eye-stone.

Whenever such men are placed in control of great industries, troubles, more or less damaging to the business, are certain to occur, and though they may not lead to open rupture—to a strike—they are certain to create conditions flagrantly in antagonism to the welfare of those who have their money invested in the industry. To secure the best work, workingmen must be treated as men and not as menials, as slaves; and when the overbearing methods of the boss can no longer be endured, a strike is inevitable and is just and honorable. Indeed, it is the last resort of men who have a spark of self-respect to assert their manhood. The principle involved is a dear one, and for its recognition workingmen have the right to resort to extreme measures.

The Labor Problem[†]

May 1894

We are by no means oblivious of the fact that the caption of this article is a somewhat antiquated chestnut—hackneyed to an extent that rarely falls to the lot of any industrial or economic subject within the realm of discussion, but does it follow, therefore, that the labor problem has been discussed to an extent and so exhaustively that it should be laid aside?

It so happens that notwithstanding a thousand pens and ten thousand tongues have been engaged in solving the labor problem, it still remains unsolved, and if we are to believe only a part of what we hear and see, the conclusion is inevitable that the labor problem, now, as peremptorily as at any time in the past, challenges men of the largest abilities to wrestle with the difficulties it presents.

There are those, insignificant neither in number nor mental grasp, who

---

[†]   Published as "The Labor Problem" in *Locomotive Firemen's Magazine,* vol. 18, no. 5 (May 1894), 470–471.

do not hesitate to affirm that the labor problem involves the perpetuity of the cherished institutions of the American government. It was a saying of the lamented Lincoln that this government "could not exist half free and half slave," that slavery or the form of government would have to be abandoned, and now the assertion is made that this government cannot exist with a contemptible minority of plutocrats and an overwhelming majority of proletarians, and the proposition is woven into the warp and woof of the labor problem.

No man who gives the subject a moment's serious thought has failed to observe on the part of the plutocratic class the attitude of employers toward employees. In certain cases, there is a mock solicitude for their welfare and repetition *ad nauseum* of the old Shakespearean saw, "There is a divinity that shapes our ends,"[41] that is to say, shapes the workingman's ends so that he can be driven into the mud and kept there, and on the other hand, shapes the ends of the rich employer so that regardless of winds and tides he is always on top, and booted and spurred, astride of the workingman, rides him whithersoever he will, always claiming that some "divinity" is responsible for conditions as they exist, that it is heaven's order and therefore any resistance only serves to fasten the fetters more securely, sink the workingman deeper in the mire, and lift the employer to higher altitudes of opulence and independence.

It is worthy of remark that of late it has become popular in certain quarters to inject into the labor problem about everything politicians wrangle over— such as government ownership of railroads and telegraph lines, the single tax, bimetallism, the initiative and referendum, and so on to the end of the chapter, including the transfer of labor organizations, rank and file, to some one of the political parties. By such a harum-scarum policy the real labor problem is practically lost sight of, however notorious the leaders in the scramble may become. To make things if possible still worse, Bellamyism is often hitched onto the labor problem, and thus vagary and hallucination, arm in arm, may be seen almost any day, blazing the way to some utopia where only so much labor is required to gather up and stow away the wealth.

We hold that primarily and fundamentally the labor problem involves *wages*—and that when wages are adjusted upon a basis of justice, the labor problem is practically solved. It was said by the Master in his sermon on the Mount, "Seek ye first the kingdom of God and his righteousness, and all these things shall be added unto you."[42]

That is to say, don't go roaming into the realms of discussion and waste your time and strength, but rather find the one thing needful and go for it with all your might and when found, grasp and hang on to it. Things of minor importance will come necessarily and inevitably and be added to your stock of valuables. Hence we infer that the supreme purpose labor should have in view is to secure just wages; and this obtained, all other things that labor needs will be added as certainly as that there is such a law as gravitation.

What are the other things to be added? Preliminary to giving an answer directly, we assume that money has power to secure the other things referred to. Money may not work miracles, but it does work wonders—and these wonders are seen on every hand—and hence we observe that the man who seeks for money and finds it adds indefinitely to his possessions—and the more money he secures, the greater is the number of things which go to make up the sum total of his assets. With the rich, it is called "income;" in the case of the workingman, it is called "wages." To those at all critically observant, it will be found that men with the largest incomes have the most of the things which go to embellish homes—and it requires a master of fine writing to describe the luxuries which their incomes command—and it is easy enough to mark the upward grade in surroundings from incomes of $3,000 to $3 million.

We have read, time and again, in the preambles of the constitutions of labor organizations that their purpose was to advance their membership morally, socially, and intellectually, all of which is well enough in its way, but which, omitting the supreme demand, wages, is of little consequence in the discussion of the labor problem.

We hold that the fundamental idea of labor organizations should be wages, precisely as with capitalists, the purpose is dividends, and with merchants, profits. Syndicates, trusts and monopolies, pools, also railroad corporations, are not organized for moral, social, and intellectual improvement of their members, but to make money, to improve their financial condition, and to this one thing they bend all their energies, and thus it should, in our opinion, be with labor organizations to obtain wages, the higher the better.

We urge the wage method of solving the labor problem because it alone can solve it. Workingmen everywhere, we refer to organized workingmen, demand just wages, their fair share of the wealth they create, and as we approach that point, workingmen become contented. The day a workingman receives what he believes to be just wages, with him the labor problem is solved and it never will be solved until just wages are secured. If this is true, and we challenge denial, why waste time and breath over minor questions? Why clamor for single tax? Why run mad over nationalism, another term for parentalism? Why resolve to go pell-mell into some newfangled political party? Why get hoarse over the initiative and referendum? Why not, on the contrary, unify, solidify, and federate to secure honest, fair, and just wages? And above all, why should labor writers and speakers be constantly repeating the stale platitude that "capital has rights as well as labor"? Capital will take care of its rights. It will never abdicate any right and, moreover, labor does not seek to wrest from capital any of its rights. It simply contends that capitalists shall no longer starve and degrade it by methods which have prevailed since history was rescued from fable. Labor is the investment, wages the dividend. With fair wages the labor problem is solved.

The St. Paul Victory: Speech in Terre Haute[†]

May 3, 1894

Gentlemen, My Friends and Neighbors:—

From the depths of my heart I appreciate and thank you for this demonstration of your confidence and respect. I had not the remotest idea that on my return to my native city such a magnificent demonstration awaited me.[43]

As a rosebud yields to the tender influences of a May shower, just so does my heart open to receive the expressions of gratitude and esteem from you, my friends and neighbors. [*Cheers.*] I have, as you are aware, just returned from the Northwest, the scene of trouble on one of the greatest railroad systems in the country. The contest on the Great Northern system has no parallel in the history of railroad trouble. From the hour the strike commenced the men were a unit; they stood shoulder to shoulder—engineers, firemen, brakemen, conductors, switchmen, and even the trackmen and freight handlers, who are generally first to suffer, stood up as one man and asserted their manhood. [*Cheers.*]

One of the remarkable features, very remarkable, in the contest, was the good feeling which prevailed during the 18 days of the strike, and the good feeling lasted during the trying and anxious hours of arbitration. I am glad, my friends, to be able to say to you tonight that in all these 18 days there was, from

---

†   First published as "At Home: Neighbor Debs, President of ARU Welcomed" in *Terre Haute Express,* May 4, 1894. Reprinted in the *Railway Times,* vol. 1, no. 10 (May 15, 1894), 1, 3.

one end of the Great Northern road to the other, not a single drop of human blood spilled. The American spirit of fair play was uppermost in the minds of the manly men who were involved in the trouble, and their fight for wages was conducted without rowdyism or lawlessness. [*Cheers.*] The reduction on the Great Northern Railway was without cause. In resisting it, the employees met solidly organized capital face to face, and man to man, and for 18 days not a pound of freight was moved, and not a wheel turned, with the exception of mail trains. As a result of this unification, this show of manliness and courage on the part of the employees, they gained 97.5 percent of what they claimed as their rights. The arbitration of the differences was entrusted into the hands of 14 representative businessmen of the Twin Cities, with Charles Pillsbury,[44] the merchant miller prince, as chairman. The preliminaries leading up to that memorable meeting of arbitration covered many weary hours, but once in session and facing the great question of wages of thousands of men, these 14 men—all of whom were men of capital and employers of labor—reached a verdict in one hour, a verdict for the employees, by which $146,000 more money will monthly be distributed among the deserving wage earners than would have been had they not stood up for what they knew to be justly theirs.

My glory, my friends, consists of the gladness which I know will be brought into the little cottage homes of the humble trackmen among the hills of the West. I can almost see the looks of gratitude on the faces of these men's wives and little children. In all my life I have never felt so highly honored as I did when leaving St. Paul on my way home. As our train pulled out of the yards, the tokens of esteem which I prize far more highly than all others was in seeing the old trackmen, men whose forms were bent with years of grinding toil, who receive the pittance of from 80 cents to $1 per day, leaning on their shovels and lifting their hats to me in appreciation of my humble assistance in a cause which they believe had resulted in a betterment of their miserable existence. [*Cheers.*]

The American Railway Union does not believe in force except in the matter of education. It believes that when agreements and schedules are signed there should be harmony between all. It believes and will work to the end of bringing the employer and employee in closer touch. An era of closer relationship between capital and labor, I believe, is dawning, one which I feel will place organized labor on a higher standard. When employer and employed can thoroughly respect each other, then, I believe, will strikes be a thing of the past. For as Mr. [James J.] Hill, president of the Great Northern, said to me at the conclusion of the arbitrating conference, "You have fought a good fight and I respect you." And I answered, "Mr. Hill, if this shall be your policy I will give you my word of honor that in the future your road will be engaged in no more such trouble as has just terminated."

This strike is not without its fruit and will result in much good all along the line. I hope to see the time when there will be mutual justice between employer and employees. It is said the chasm between capital and labor is widening, but I do not believe it. If anything it is narrowing down, and I hope to see the day when there will be none.

What has occurred tonight seems to me like a dream, a revelation. You are all too generous, noble, magnanimous, and my heart rises to my lips in receiving this demonstration from you, my neighbors, from the people of my home, where I was born and have grown from childhood to manhood. A look into the recesses of my heart only can show the gratitude I have no words to express. I can only assure you my eternal friendship and loyalty. With my heart on my lips I thank you, my friends—noble men, lovely women, and little children. Had I the eloquence of an Ingersoll I could not express the happiness, long life, and success I wish you one and all. Once more, with gratitude trembling upon my lips, I bid you all good fortune and good night. [*Great cheers.*]

First Speech to Striking Pullman Workers, Turner Hall, Kensington, Illinois[†] [excerpt]

May 14, 1894

I am with you heart and soul in this fight.[45] As a general thing I am against a strike, but when the only alternative to a strike is the sacrifice of manhood, then I prefer to strike. There are times when it becomes necessary for a man to assert his manhood. I am free to confess that I do not like the paternalism of Pullman. He is everlastingly saying, "What can we do for our poor workingmen?" The interrogation is an insult to the men. The question is not, What can Mr. Pullman do for us; it is, What can we do for ourselves?

†   As published in W. T. Stead, *Chicago To-day; or, The Labour War in America* (London: "Review of Reviews" Office, 1894), 177.

Under this system of paternalism in vogue, it is only a question of time until they own your bodies and have your souls mortgaged. It is a question that can be demonstrated to a mathematical society. In ten years more of this system, he will own your bodies and have your souls mortgaged. Pullman's pretended philanthropy makes this a question of emancipation. His specious interest in the welfare of the "poor workingman" is in no way different from that of the slave owner of 50 years ago. Remember that no power that can be devised will be neglected to divide you. But if you will follow Mr. Howard's advice, there is no power on earth to make this strike a failure. Division means defeat and disaster.

Remember that the American Railway Union would rather be defeated honorably than triumph in disgrace. We believe in evolutionary revolution. We prefer agitation to stagnation. The same process that makes a Pullman makes a thousand paupers. And the remedy is all in your own hands. We must change the conditions of affairs—not by force, but the right and intelligent votes of the toiling thousands.

Second Speech to Striking Pullman Workers, Turner Hall, Kensington, Illinois[†] [excerpt]

May 16, 1894

———

I believe a rich plunderer like Pullman is a greater felon than a poor thief, and it has become no small part of the duty of this organization to strip the mask of hypocrisy from this pretended philanthropist and show him to the world as an oppressor of labor. One of the general officers of the company said today that you could not hold out against the Pullman Company more than ten days longer. If it is a fact that after working for George M. Pullman for years you appear two weeks after your work stops, ragged and hungry, it only emphasizes the charge I make before this community, and Pullman stands before you a self-confessed robber. A rich man can afford to be honest; a poor man is compelled to be.

———

† As published in W. T. Stead, *Chicago To-day; or, The Labour War in America* (London: "Review of Reviews" Office, 1894), 177–178.

I do not believe in violent methods, but I do believe in telling the truth. The paternalism of Pullman is the same as the interest of a slaveholder in his human chattels. You are striking to avert inevitable slavery and degradation. Here is your father-in-law anxious about all his children. "You only owe me $70,000 for rent now, and I am not pressing you for payment!" Was there ever a greater public sham? All the time worried about your welfare and piling up millions in one of the great monopolies of the age, by putting his hands into your pockets. I differ from the gentleman who contends that Pullman's gift of $100,000 for a monument is a matter to be considered—it is too easy to be generous with other people's money.

Do you know what this man does with his conductors and porters? Do you know that they are forced to live upon the charity of the traveling public?

*   *   *

Charging exorbitant prices for his accommodations, lost to all sense of shame, he not only expects but depends upon the generosity of the people, who pay him the revenue upon which he waxes fat, to give his employees enough to live on. Only last month I went in a Pullman car over part of the western country. The conductor told me he was paid $30 a month, and had from this to board himself and support his family. The porter had $10 a month. Both were away from home two weeks at a time. That conductor asked me for money to buy him something to eat. This is the work of a great philanthropist.

When the officials of the Pullman Company believe they are going to reduce you to subjection in a week or ten days, they are making the mistake of their lives. This strike is going to be won, if it takes months, and it will be won because we are right.

Judge Caldwell and the Union Pacific Employees[†]
June 1894

When a man is summoned to give testimony in court, and takes an oath to tell the truth, any eulogy touching his veracity becomes a questionable compliment, an intimation that "the truth, the whole truth, and nothing but the truth" had been in peril, and that the witness had been, fortunately, rescued from the unpleasant dilemma to which perjurers are sometimes subjected.

It appears that Judge Caldwell entertains views relating to the duties of a judge quite in consonance with those which devolve upon a witness—he does not like to be eulogized nor thanked for being honest and upright—as is shown by the following incident:

> Chairman Vrooman of the B of LE thanked the judge for his decision, whereupon the judge, quick as a flash, replied: "No thanks are necessary, Mr. Vrooman, *when a court does its duty clearly, without fear or favor, it is not deferring of thanks.*"

These were words "fitly spoken," as beautiful and as valuable as "apples of gold in pictures of silver."[46] Judge Caldwell is evidently made of the right sort of material—a large percentage of iron and sand, with no intermixture of sawdust, putty, or *caoutchouc.*[47] Nevertheless, Mr. Vrooman is not to be seriously criticized for thanking Judge Caldwell for his celebrated decision, since every honest man in the country feels thankful for his verdict, for, notwithstanding it was not entirely unexpected, when it came it was phenomenal—a revelation that at once set a revolution in motion. Judge Caldwell's decision was eminently natural and rational, direct and honest, distinguished for its law and common sense, and justice to all parties.

In this connection it is pertinent to remark that it was these characteristics that created widespread surprise. We have remarked that a decision was expected in which something would be said differing from the decision of Judge Dundy, and workingmen entertained hopes that some relief would be granted them, that they would receive honorable recognition, and their rights receive some judicial consideration, but they had so often, of late, been the victims of brutal judicial bludgeons, wielded by other United States judges, in the interest of receivers and

†   Published in *Locomotive Firemen's Magazine*, vol. 18, no. 6 (June 1894), 588–589.

corporations, that they were unprepared for declarations from the bench which emancipated them from the degrading grasp of ignorant and rapacious receivers acting in the interests of men who held millions, evidences of debts, but in fact representing the most stupendous frauds ever perpetrated in this country.

Judge Caldwell, in treating this feature of the case, became morally heroic. He referred to the receivers, of whom four of the five were totally incapable of determining what wages employees should receive, and their opinions upon the subject were of no consequence, because they knew nothing about wage schedules, and while the judge expressed a prudent anxiety to have the road relieved of its financial embarrassments, he said, "to accomplish this desirable result the wages of the men must not be reduced below a reasonable and just compensation for their services. They must be paid fair wages, though no dividends are paid on the stock and no interest on the bonds." It is just here that Judge Caldwell puts some facts upon record, in such a way that ought to strike dumb those who are eternally defending corporations as models of honesty and lampooning labor organizations as the enemies of capital. Said the judge: "It is part of the public history of the country, of which this court will take judicial notice, that for the first $36 million of stock issued this company received less than two cents on the dollar, and that the profits of construction, represented by outstanding bonds, was $43,929,238.44." These two items represent $79,929,528.44, of which at least $35,280,000 was pure fraud. $43,929,328.44 was a trick in construction, also a fraud upon innocent stockholders and the government.

After all, we inquire, what is there remarkable about the decision of Judge Caldwell that it should awaken continental interest? Truth never changes; justice is eternal; inalienable rights are immutable. Judge Caldwell grasped them and wove them into the woof and warp of his decision—a triumph of the judiciary over the world, the flesh and the devil, corporation cussedness and capitalistic greed. That the decision was phenomenal, rare, exceptional, is of itself an arraignment of the courts of the country. Judge Caldwell, erudite, profound, and analytical, capable, abstruse; master of the technical in law and logic, like all great-minded men, states propositions which a wayfaring man can comprehend, and then, bringing the law of equity to bear upon the case, brushes aside subterfuges, sophistries, special pleadings, chicane, and every vulgar trick, and blazes a way through the jungle of jugglery that leads men out into the clear light of common sense, which is always good law. He pays no attention to the sinuous trails of serpents, the pathways of trappers, the little elevations where prairie dogs bark, but knowing the right way, he illuminates it by the search lights of justice and wins the gratitude of a nation.

Workingmen—railroad employees—have believed that they had rights that should be respected, but time and again corporations, aided by judges, had struck them down, until railroad employees were being taught that only fines and imprisonment awaited them if they asserted their rights, but Judge Caldwell came to their rescue and told them, told the country, corporations, and receivers that, "In this country it is not unlawful for employees to associate, consult, and confer together with a view to maintain or increase their wages by lawful and peaceful means any more than it was unlawful for the receivers to counsel and confer together for the purpose of reducing their wages. A corporation is organized capital; organized labor is organized capital. What is lawful for one to do is lawful for the other."

It was this right, which had been struck down, that Judge Caldwell restored, and in the reestablishment of which he took occasion to remind employees and employers that railroad receivers cannot abrogate contracts at their own sweet will; that they cannot "hang employees and try them afterwards;" in a word, that laws are made for employees as well as employers; that courts are established to administer justice, and not for the purpose of aiding and abetting wrong; that in the United States "the period of compulsory personal service, save as a punishment for crime, has passed," an intimation that the courts which have sought to visit upon railroad employees "the pains and penalties of the early English statutes" perpetrated a damnable outrage, for which they should be impeached and disgraced forever. In announcing that railroad employees are entitled to fair wages, that contracts shall be respected, that employees shall be paid though the payment of dividends, and interest on watered stocks and bonds is postponed, that employees have a right to organize and confer together in all matters relating to their welfare unmolested and unintimidated, we say, in making such announcements Judge Caldwell voiced eternal principles of right and justice, for which he is entitled to the gratitude of railroad employees and all the toilers of America.

The *Magazine* has a right to indulge in no little self-felicitation, because on numerous occasions since we have had control of its pages we have, in our way, advocated the principles laid down by Judge Caldwell in his masterly decision, and the decision absolutely vindicates the theories of law and justice we have advocated and maintained. The decision of Judge Caldwell is full of inspiration for workingmen to stand firmly by their organizations, and to be content only when they are awarded the fullest measure of their rights.

The Outlook of Labor†

June 1894

In every section of our broad land men, regardless of trade, calling, or profession are studying the outlook of labor—prognosticating, questioning, and reading the signs of the times. Capitalists, merchants, manufacturers, agriculturalists, politicians and statesmen, philanthropists and economists are profoundly interested in the outlook of labor. This is not surprising, since it is fundamentally true that when labor is prosperous general prosperity, happiness, and contentment prevail, and when adversities befall labor every interest feels the baneful consequences. If hitherto such facts have not been fully recognized, they are now admitted and their force fully comprehended by all thoughtful men, and they are daily coming into more pronounced conspicuousness.

Men laugh at the Coxey "commonweal" demonstration,[48] when in fact it would be difficult to find its parallel in grim, haggard, and dangerous characteristics. The calling together from all parts of the continent of a horde of men forced into idleness by no fault of their own, ragged, hungry, and homeless, seeking work or subsistence, levying contributions as they march, everywhere creating unrest and alarm, is a spectacle which no prudent citizen can contemplate with composure. It is a symptom of a national disease ceaselessly boding evil. It is organized poverty, an army of hungry, ragged men, always on the verge of despair, inviting recruits from the ranks of the wretched and forlorn wherever they are found. On all sides we hear it said that Coxey is a crank, that no good can come to him, to his army, or to others by this "commonweal" demonstration. The conclusion is correct, no good can possibly come from forced idleness, prolonged hunger, such shelter for men as is provided for beasts, and often no shelter at all. No good can come from bringing together from east, west, north, and south large bodies of men who, if not clothed and fed and sheltered, will find ways to obtain such essentials at any risk, because "hunger knows no law."[49] Coxey, though he will not extort from Congress the enactment of laws which operate to give the idle work, nor provide for them in any way, it is becoming painfully apparent that he has begun a movement well calculated to breed discontent and make it epidemic throughout the country, and just what results will follow no one can foretell. ·

†   Published in *Locomotive Firemen's Magazine*, vol. 18, no. 6 (June 1894), 590–591.

If an army of 100,000 enforced vagabonds should manage to reach Washington, they would constitute an object lesson such as the world never beheld since the Israelites marched out of Egypt through the Red Sea;[50] statesmen, politicians, philanthropists, educators, and divines could contemplate it and exclaim, "Here is one of the evidences of progress, religion, education, and civilization in a government of the people, by the people, and for the people. Here is seen the fruits of class legislation. Here is an exhibition of plutocracy, corporation, trust, monopoly, and robbery on the one hand, and poverty, hunger, squalor, and degradation on the other hand. Here are two exhibits in the great Columbian Fair No. 2, held in the capital of the nation, AD 1894. Look! By all the pagan gods in a pile, above the army of *citizen* vagabonds, without food, clothes, or shelter, floats the star-spangled banner, 'Old Glory!'"

We do not suppose Coxey will march into Washington a hundred thousand hungry, ragged, shoeless, hatless, frostbitten American citizens, but it will not be because there are not 100,000 idle work-seekers in the country, for there are millions of them, but enough will straggle into Washington to humiliate the nation—enough, as we have suggested, to make an object lesson for the study of statesmen, if any are found in the capital of the nation.[51]

In studying the outlook of labor the inquiry goes round, What are employers doing to improve conditions? The reply is, in some cases nothing, in others as little as possible, while almost invariably those who are doing anything in the way of giving employment, a reduction of wages in some form is insisted upon. In numerous cases the cut is direct, ranging from 5 percent to 25 percent, the average being fully 10 percent. If, however, the wages per day or per hour are maintained, the reduction is reached by reducing the number of hours per day, or the number of days per week, often equivalent to a direct cut of from 10 to 50 percent. Nor are these cuts of wages, direct and indirect, the only burdens imposed upon labor. In addition, there has been going on a ceaseless discharge of employees who are forced into idleness without an opportunity to earn any rate of wages.

In carrying out their program of reduction, employers claim in every instance that they are in the grasp of imperative necessities that cannot be avoided, the result of conditions they had no hand in creating, and which they can neither control nor modify. The facts seem to warrant such declarations. There is universal business demoralization—and what is being done is, as we have remarked, at reduced wages. It is not to be doubted that almost every form of investment in industrial enterprises pays, just now, small dividends or no dividends at all, and that in numerous cases operations are continued at a loss.

Be this as it may, labor in the United States is paying the severest penalties ever imposed upon it since the government had an existence, and there never was a time in the history of the country when the outlook of labor was more gloomy.

The inquiry goes round, When can a change in the outlook be expected? In reply, men well posted in dates and data say that the Panic of 1873, less serious than that of 1893, dragged along for six years, and that the country did not fully recover from its effects till 1879, hence no time can be named when the business depression now afflicting the country will disappear. Those who pretend to know whereof they speak, on the one side, contend that the mood of the country demanded the coinage of what is called the "seigniorage" silver in the treasury, and Congress enacted a law providing for such coinage of silver dollars, but the president, thrusting aside the action of Congress, interposed his veto, and that source of relief disappeared.[52] There are those who have clamored for sweeping reforms in tariff legislation proposing to relieve the people of intolerable burdens of taxation, but the party in power[53] wrangles and factionizes until all hope of relief in that direction disappears. Meanwhile the country suffers, and labor more than any other interest. Nothing can be hoped for from legislation, but during this period of suspense and uncertainty, confidence in the future is semi-paralyzed and the day of relief postponed.

Under such circumstances and in such conditions, what can labor do? Can labor set industrial enterprises in operation? Can labor, even if organized, obtain fair wages per day? Is not labor so conditioned, as a general proposition, that it must accept reduced wages or remain idle? Would a strike improve conditions? Such is the character of the questions with which labor is called upon to wrestle. If anyone has prudent advice to give, the present is a time when it will be patiently considered.

As we write, a case under our observation occurs. Carpenters demand 30 cents an hour. Contractors will pay 25 cents an hour. Carpenters refuse. Contractors remain firm. Pending the controversy, nine houses which were to be constructed are abandoned, and a contract to build a $150,000 block is in peril. Meanwhile carpenters are idle. Contractors refuse to consult unions and contract with individuals. Such are the facts disclosed. Conditions are abnormal. Labor leaders now have an opportunity to speak. What will they say? As the English say, "Hear! hear!"

The Union Pacific and the United States[†]

June 1894

There exists a certain class of writers and talkers whose business appears to be the defense of railroad corporations and managers at all times and under all circumstances, and they are never more impudent and blatant than when railroad employees protest against the outrages perpetrated by these corporation officials. It is a well-known fact, because it is an officially recorded fact, that the Interstate Commerce law had its origin in charges of outrages perpetrated by railroad corporations so enormous and so flagrant as to cause a universal protest and a demand for remedial legislation. It is not required that we should recite these indictments; they are known and read of all men, and include almost every form of duplicity and fraud known to our Christian civilization. Not only was Congress called upon to arrest the deluge of rascality, but state legislatures were implored to interpose and check, if possible, the rapacity of railroad corporations. And now we have authentic advice from Washington giving an outline of legislation to be enacted to punish the officials of the Union Pacific for a series of outrages perpetrated by them to defraud the United States government. The charges are of the most serious character and exhibit a degree of lawlessness which it is difficult to contemplate with composure.

The joint resolution submitted to Congress by Representative Boatner[54] of Louisiana, in its recital specifies numerous violations of law for the purpose of defrauding the government, such as "an attempted consolidation with the Kansas Pacific Railroad and the Denver Pacific Railroad and issued stock of the Union Pacific on this consolidation for $14 million. It is charged that afterward further stock amounting to $10 million was issued for the alleged purpose of making repairs, etc.; that the purchase of the two railroads by the Union Pacific was made by the directors, who were themselves stockholders in the Kansas Pacific and the Denver Pacific, while the president of the Union Pacific was at the time president of the Kansas Pacific; that dividends have been voted in violation of the acts of 1873 and 1878, not out of actual earnings and while the Union Pacific was still in default to the United States. These payments from 1873 to 1884 are stated to have been $27 million."

Specifications further recite that the directors of the Union Pacific paid

---

†   Published in *Locomotive Firemen's Magazine*, vol. 18, no. 6 (June 1894), 591–593.

"the interest on the first mortgage bonds of the Oregon Short Line Railroad Company, amounting to $4 million; that the directors, in violation of the law and their official duties, paid subsidies to the Pacific Mail Steamship Company amounting to about $1.4 million." The resolution arraigns the directors of the Union Pacific for numerous malfeasances, the purpose of which was to commit fraud and which were successful to a degree that demands prompt action on the part of Congress to protect the interests of the government, and the charge is specifically made that the directors of the Union Pacific "misappropriated and misapplied the property and funds" of the road, or in other words, embezzled and stole money which belonged to the United States, and that they should be compelled to restore the stolen property.

Let it be remembered in this connection that the men who are arraigned by Congress for fraudulent practices, mean duplicity, corruption, and business rottenness, are the men who, with the aid of United States judges, seek to make the employees of the road pay the penalties of their rascality. Is it to be presumed that such a gang of railroad wreckers as have had charge of the Union Pacific, and who have for years schemed to defraud the government and pocket the proceeds of their knavery, would hesitate to offer a United States judge, or any other judge, a bribe to aid them in their bunco business? And is it not infamously apparent that their hooks and traps have been successfully baited? Is it not visible to the naked eye that directors, receivers, and judges are moral lepers, as unclean as the inmates of pesthouses? When such monstrosities are clothed with power to impoverish workingmen, what remains of life worth the living? When by virtue of law wrongs are perpetrated and workingmen defrauded, hopes of redress may be entertained, because the law may be repealed or amended; but in cases where there is no law, when a United States judge, in the arrogance of absolutism, robs workingmen of wages and ties them to a machine, sentences them to hard labor, and fines and imprisons them for "contempt," what is there left of our boasted liberty and citizen sovereignty? In old abolition times, when the country was "half free and half slave," men pointed to the "star-spangled banner" and shouted, "Haul down that flaunting lie," but no slave owner in all of the "Sunny South" treated a "nigger" more contemptuously than the Jenkinses treat railroad employees. These ermined autocrats, these tsars, sultans, and shahs, don't care for law, though they are created by law, the theory being that they constitute a department of the government and are not amenable to law. And the query has gone the rounds of the press, "What are you going to do about it?"—a sneering equivalent of Vanderbilt's exclamation, "The public be damned."

The idea seems to prevail that United States judges are the pliant tools of corporations, whose supreme duty it is at the bidding of their masters to reduce workingmen to the condition of the dog under the wagon. To what extent railroad employees will play dog or dogs at the behest of ermined autocrats is as yet an unsolved problem, but we surmise it will be well for the peace of the country if courts are cautioned to be a little more careful in issuing their decrees. As yet the United States is not Poland, nor yet Ireland, though when a United States judge decrees that sovereign citizens shall not consult together about wages and welfare, under penalty of fine and imprisonment, Russia, Turkey, Persia, Ireland, and Poland, and every other country where men's rights have been cloven down and men are slaves, march in procession, bearing testimony of this degradation autocrats have secured for the masses, and the world looks on and sees the United States take its place at the tail end of the train.

Corporations, directors, and managers, as in the case of the Union Pacific and the Northern Pacific and other great systems of railroads, bring about wreck and ruin. Then a United States judge is appealed to, to strike down the rights of workingmen, and dire penalties are threatened if the decree is disobeyed. Thus, step by step, men are degraded and all too often accept their disgrace without protest.

But not all of them tamely submit. A readjustment is coming. We want it to come by righteous processes. We want it to come by the peaceful though often rugged roads of justice. We want it to come by the administration of honest laws, by unbribed, undebauched, and unimpeachable courts. We want it to come by the ballot, by legislation designed to promote the welfare of the nation, but come it will. It is coming. Men who are not deaf hear the cries of a thousand Johns in the wilderness[55] to make straight paths for labor's emancipation from the decrees of purchased judges, from the tortures of scheme-created poverty and wretchedness, from the curse of class legislation. It would be folly to fix a day for the readjustment. There will be signs, and we have them; there will be wonders, and we are having them; there will be portents, they are seen in all directions. The hope of all good men is that the readjustments may come as the sunshine and the shower come to make the earth beautiful and fruitful of blessings, but come they will, and men at the helm of the ship of state will be wise if they study the signs of the times.

Keynote Address to the First Convention of the ARU: Uhlich's Hall, Chicago[†]

June 12, 1894

Ladies and Gentlemen:—

I appreciate the honor conferred by the position I occupy on this occasion, because it affords me the great satisfaction of welcoming you as delegates representing the American Railway Union, in this, the first convention of the order—an organization of railway employees, called into existence by conditions vindicating its necessity, the rapid growth and power of which is phenomenal to an extent that has no parallel in the history of labor organizations anywhere, at any time, or on any continent; facts which, while well calculated to arouse honest exultation, impose upon us the gravest responsibilities.

This organization was launched upon the troubled seas of labor June 20, 1893, one year ago. If on that day there were doubts and misgiving, there were also stout hearts, hope, and a faith which was the "substance of things hoped for." There were a number of organizations in the field, but it was believed that there was room for one more, and hence the flag of the American Railway Union was unfurled to the breeze and the order began its first voyage of discovery and conquest.

On August 17, 1893, the first local union of our order was organized, and now, after a lapse of nine months and 28 days, we number 425 local unions and more than 100,000 members. Such growth in numbers, power, and prosperity was never before recorded of any other labor organization, and while we have a right to felicitate each other upon this wonderful development, it will be the part of wisdom to remember that our responsibilities have kept pace with our progress, and that as delegates and officers of this young but gigantic organization, we are charged with the duty of enacting organic laws bearing the impress of wisdom and patient investigation for its government.

[†]   Published as "The Address" in the *Railway Times,* vol. 1, no. 12 (June 15, 1894), 3. Also published in *American Railway Union, Proceedings, First Quadrennial Convention.* Chicago: 1894, 3–13.

A New Departure

The American Railway Union is not only a new organization of railway employees, but it is a new departure in the organization of this class of wage earners. We begin our career as an order with new formulas, new policies, new purposes, and new shibboleths. We start out with the declaration, for the truth of which there is overwhelming proof that in the towering, pivotal, and essential feature, that of *protection* against corporate power, all the organizations of railway employees hitherto known have been dismal failures.

In saying this, I must not be charged with being the enemy of the old organizations, nor must my utterances here be regarded as discourteous, for all railroad employees whose knowledge of the facts gives weight to their opinions know that the strength of my young and my mature manhood has been freely given to one of these organizations, and that I speak from a knowledge of facts obtained from years of study and familiarity with the workings of these organizations. To assume that because I discovered defects, because I point them out and bring them to the attention of my fellow workingmen, that I am, therefore, the enemy of the rank and file of these organizations, is a resort to questionable methods to obscure imperfections and to perpetuate inefficiency.

The American Railway Union found, on the day of its organization, a broad and inviting field for the display of its philanthropic energies. This field was entered and cultivated, and here today we are permitted to contemplate the abundant harvest that comes to us as a reward for work well done, and thousands of railway employees hitherto unsheltered by any organization, but who were left out in the cold to endure the pitiless storms of corporate power, vie with each other in repeating the plaudit, "Well done, good and faithful servants. You were faithful to your trust when local union No. 1 was born, and we now place in your charge 425 unions, and awaiting the deliberations of our representatives in the first convention of our order, we stand pledged to multiply our unions, until every neglected railway employee has a home beneath the sheltering flag of the American Railway Union." In all this magnificent work, in all the splendid triumphs that have fallen to the lot of the American Railway Union, it has simply minded its own business, neither directly nor remotely interfering with the business of other organizations.

Building the Organization

Appreciating the fact that in building an organization of railway employees it must, like a modern battleship, be built for war, we have determined to build upon that plan. If peace prevails, from a sense of prudence or fear, the ship may display her bunting, ride safely at anchor in port, exercise her crew or make trial trips to test sailing qualities, the ideal always prevailing that if war is declared the ship is ready for action. The American Railway Union is built upon this plan. It enjoys peace and prosperity. It indulges in no bravado, but at all times, and in all seasons, it is prepared to assert the rights of its members and to exhaust its resources in their defense.

It has been found that of all the organizations of railway employees hitherto constructed, not one was constructed for battle—not one had perfect armor plates. In every instance the plates were found to be full of what experts in naval architecture call "blow holes," cracks and imperfections to the extent that, when a corporation battleship or a fleet of these monsters delivered a broadside at labor's crafts when a battle was on, labor's navy went down with all of the grand commanders, crew, and petty officials on board.

Taught in the school of experience, the American Railway Union accepts no armor plates (especially those manufactured by Carnegie, Frick & Co.) with blow holes, open or "plugged." It has already demonstrated in its youth that it can win victories against powerful odds, that it can see the right and that it has the courage to defend the right, when others, looking through spectacles with "dollars of the daddies" for eyeglasses, could not see the right—when the grandest exhibition of their courage took the shape of orders from their boots, the headquarters of their hearts and courage, directing their members to submit to the wrong for the glory of the corporation and the goodwill of the watered stock and bondholders.

There is one thing far more deplorable than strikes and war. It is when men accept degrading conditions and wear collars and fetters without resistance. When a man surrenders his honest convictions, his loyalty to principle, he ceases to be a man. Decorate him with the insignia of office, robe him in purple and fine linen, give him a palace and let him feast his full on the choicest luxuries, and still he is a poltroon. Lazarus, as the gate of Dives, attended by vagabond dogs, expands to proportions as far above such a coward and sneak as Pike's Peak towers above the burrow of a prairie dog.

Wisdom, Work, and Peril

But, as I have intimated, this convention means serious work for the American Railway Union. Let it be remembered that the order is now on trial with a future of work and peril. The first great demand upon the delegates is conservative propositions for organic laws and unbroken harmony in deliberations. There is danger in extremes, and defeat lurks in discord, nor is this all; however paradoxical it may seem, there is, nevertheless, an element of danger in prosperity, and against this we will find it the part of wisdom to guard with sedulous care. Present conditions are fruitful of manifold defects and deficiencies, which are annoying and constitute grievances, which, while productive of injury and vexation, are far below the plane of gravity which demands any resort to extreme measures for redress or adjustment, and which, were this order to take cognizance, would be productive of continuous embroilment, and which would result in the discredit of the order. Industrial conditions are at present of a character which demands a constant exercise of the virtue of patience and forbearance when difficulties are encountered, which under other and more favorable conditions would demand the interposition of the order.

We meet in convention at a time when the business and industrial conditions of the country are most deplorable. Such prostration, paralysis, and widespread demoralization in financial, commercial, and industrial affairs were never before known in American history. It would be surprising if such conditions did not enter into the deliberations of this convention, and cool heads will be required to formulate declarations, which while giving expression to honest convictions at the same time steer clear of rocks and shoals and reefs, among which the ship of state is now sailing, or feeling its way.

In the first place, the country is full of men forced into idleness, which, as a general proposition, they did not create and cannot control. Banks break by the hundred, commercial establishments suspend operations, and railroads, representing more than a billion [dollars] of investments, are forced into the hands of receivers. These cyclonic disturbances fall with crushing force upon labor, which is powerless to resist their force to an extent which will lessen the burdens it is compelled to bear.

The Coal Miners' Strike

In the case of the strike of the coal miners, it may be said that they voluntarily abandoned their work, but it should be remembered that the purpose of the miners was as patriotic as ever prompted men to battle for a principle or to take up arms in defense of home, wife, and children. I do not doubt that this convention will devote time and consideration to the condition of the coal miners of the country. They have been despoiled and degraded. Toiling and starving, these men consolidated and struck for wages that would have the effect, in some measure, at least, to emancipate them from burdens that no American citizen should bear, and from the horrors of oppression which defy exaggeration. And yet, the wages these miners demand are so meager that the country is astounded at the exhibition of piratical greed which refuses the moderate demands of men who, having exhausted patience and endurance, concluded to strike.

The representatives of the American Railway Union, in convention assembled, will, I am sure, voice only sentiments of profound sympathy for the overtasked and underpaid coal miners of the United States, and give utterance only to words of unmitigated scorn and contempt for those who have oppressed them, and those who oppose their efforts to secure just pay for their exhausting and perilous work, regardless of the source from which opposition emanates. And this sympathy on the part of the American Railway Union is all the more natural and becoming because the ordeal which it passed on the Great Northern Railway was in many regards similar to that which now confronts the union coal mine workers of the country.

Gratitude is a most precious jewel in union labor's diadem, and the American Railway Union cannot afford to forget that in its struggle on the Great Northern the miners of that section of the country came to its rescue, not only with words of sympathy and cheer, but with even more substantial evidences that our demands were just, and I do not hesitate to believe that the time will come in the history of the American Railway Union—if, indeed, it has not already come—when coal miners strike for honest wages, no ARU man, in any capacity, will contribute to their defeat by hauling a pound of coal an inch mined by non-union labor.

The coal mine workers of the United States are confronted with a host of enemies and multiplied obstacles. There are convicts and scabs by the thousands; there are mine owners and operators, always and forever scheming to reduce wages, and who would reduce our civilization to the plane of Hottentots if thereby they could increase the size of their fortunes; there is railroad cash, court injunctions, marshals and deputy marshals with Winchester rifles, and, in addition, soldiers—federal and state—with shotted rifles and Gatling guns. Can they win against such odds? Three hundred thousand union mine workers may be compelled to dig coal, and at the same time dig their graves, and here, speaking for the American Railway Union, I bespeak for the coal miners your profoundest sympathy and your most serious consideration.

The men who resist tyranny in labor affairs are fighting the battles of workingmen now and in all future time. Humble, obscure, and unlettered they may be, but in their valor and sacrifices they are bearing testimony of divinity in human nature. Such battles are not less glorious than those of Thermopylae and Marathon,[56] though the orator and poet may not embellish them in eloquence and song.

Commonwealers

Another phase of the deplorable conditions in which workingmen find themselves involved is the organization of what is known as the "Coxey, or Commonweal armies," of which General Coxey of Ohio is commander in chief. There never was such a continental display of hopeless poverty since time began. Out of work, out of money, and without food, ragged, hungry, friendless, and homeless, these commonwealers began their march to the capital city of the nation while Congress was in session. It would require the genius of a Milton or a Dante to describe these Coxey armies. These wretched men heard to cry, "On to Washington!" and they responded, as did the Highland clans of Scotland when the sound of the pibroch[57] called them to battle. The proposition was to go to Washington and permit the lawmakers of the nation to see what congressional legislation had accomplished for workingmen, and to the call they

> Came as the winds come, when
>   Forests are rended;
> Came as the waves come, when
>   Navies are stranded.[58]

Faster and still faster they rallied as the bugle call echoed through the land. They walk, they ride, they float; the storms beat upon them, their tent the skies, their couch their mother earth, their pillows stones. Some fall by the way and are buried by their comrades, unknelled and unsung, to sleep their last sleep in unknown and forgotten graves. But the survivors press forward to Washington, and as they march, recruits start up from almost every center of population in all of the land, from mountain and valley, from hill and dale, from abandoned mine and silent factory, shop and forge—they come and tramp to the muffled drum—funeral march of their throbbing hearts. The cry is, "On to Washington," where on the marbled steps of the nation's capitol, in their rags and barefooted, they would petition Congress to enact laws whereby they might perpetuate their wretched existence by toil—laws that would rekindle the last remaining spark of hope, that their future would be relieved of some of the horrors of hunger and nakedness.

It is written that "hope springs eternal in the human breast,"[59] and it is also written that "hope deferred maketh the heart sick."[60] The hopes of the commonwealers have been deferred, aye, crushed, and lie dead at their feet, and the commonwealers are walking upon their graves. Congress has ears, but it will not listen to the tale of their woes; Congress has eyes, but it will not look upon rags and wretchedness; Congress has tongues, but they do not move when human woes demand words of sympathy and condolence.

The capital city of the nation has a patch of ground where the sun and rain produce grass, now known as "sacred grass," and Coxey and his fellow leaders are now languishing in prison because their unsanctified feet pressed the nation's "sacred grass," and over this "sacred grass" patch floats the nation's starry emblem of liberty and independence. Oh, my fellow representatives of the American Railway Union, were it possible for our

> Flag of the free heart's only home,
> By angel hands to valor given,[61]

to realize the deep degradation to which it has been subjected in the nation's capital, every star upon its blue field would be a *shooting star*, and every stripe upon its folds a whip of flame to scourge the miserable men who make the nation's ensign symbolize oppression instead of liberty. It would be strange indeed if this convention, composed of workingmen, should terminate its deliberations without making special reference to the commonweal armies whose foremost men are suffering imprisonment because their *sovereign* feet stepped upon the nation's "sacred grass."

Oh, my fellow workingmen, there must be no slavery in this land of "the star-spangled banner." There must be no cry go heavenward to make angels weep, nor hellward to make devils blush, from famishing men, women, and children, victims of a greedy and heartless capitalism that coins the life and soul of honest toil into dollars to swell its unholy possessions.

Cause of Labor Distress

This convention, I do not doubt, will deem it within its province to investigate somewhat the cause of labor demoralization throughout the country, and fortunately for the convention it has the right to adopt the language of President [Grover] Cleveland and declare that it is "principally owing to congressional legislation." I do not doubt the absolute correctness of the president's affirmation, and accepting it as true, the proposition would seem to be prudent that if legislation has brought upon the country the unparalleled curses which now afflict it, legislation ought to be sufficiently potent to remove the curses complained of, one of the rules which, like the machinery of a locomotive, ought to work both ways. But unfortunately for labor and for the country, the legislation now going forward at Washington, instead of affording relief, instead of lifting the burdens from the bent forms of laboring men and women, instead of dispersing clouds and dispelling gloom, it is adding indefinitely to the woes congressional legislation has inflicted.

Doubts and uncertainties are intensifying the unrest of the people. Instead of workingmen finding employment, the armies of the idle day by day are increasing. There are more rags fluttering on the bodies of Americans than can be seen elsewhere from the Congo forests to the home of the Laplanders, and that too in a land where decent clothing is a drug on the market. There is more hunger in the United States of America, where food is fabulously abundant, than can be found in any zone that belts the earth from the poles to the equator. There are more Lazaruses begging crumbs that fall from rich men's tables than angels ever beheld since the morning stars sang together, and there are more rich men like Dives, rolling in luxury and dressing in purple and fine linen, than statisticians have numbered.

I am not here to formulate plans of a partisan character to relieve the distress that has fallen to the lot of labor. I care nothing for parties as such, but as an American citizen, and assuming that President Cleveland told the truth when he charged that the business depression and demoralization and the brood of ills this legislation has spawned upon the country was principally owing to congressional legislation, I am free to assert that congressional legislation, radically different from what we have had, from what we are now having and are likely to have, must be had, and that speedily, if as a nation we are to have peace and prosperity.

This convention, representing as it does more than 100,000 workingmen, I do not doubt will deem it wise to give expression to its views upon matters of such commanding import.

I entertain an American regard for the ballot. I do not underestimate its power. I do not doubt that the time is at hand when wageworkers will combine and consolidate for the purpose of righting the wrongs legislators have brought upon the country by vicious legislation, and that this they will do under some banner, on some platform, and the declaration of some policy, which will, like a tide taken at the flood, lead to victory. To do this is to enter politics, and partisan politics.

Congressional legislation, which the president of the United States declares is principally responsible for our present national afflictions, was partisan legislation, enacted by political parties which, in dividing the spoils of success, have always given the turkey to the rich, and the turkey buzzard to the poor—to the workingman. If this policy is to be changed, it must be done by the ballots of workingmen emancipated from the parties, which, regardless of names and professions, are equally capable. Taking this view of the subject, I fail to discover any valid reason why this convention may not consider the propriety of an alliance on the part of workingmen of a party whose leaders, and whose platform and policy, is to have congressional and state legislation which will lift workingmen to a higher plane of prosperity rather than continue to contribute their support to the political parties which have shorn them as if they were sheep, and degraded them as if they were chattels.

Men Ambitious to Regain Their Former Standing

I take pleasure in calling the attention of this convention to a large body of men who have been members of some of the organizations of railway employees, but who, under the pressure of adverse circumstances, lost their standing and have been found in the ranks of non-union men. It is not required that I should catalog all the misadventures of these unfortunate men, or content that in all regards they are blameless, though investigation would doubtless disclose the fact that in a vast majority of cases they were the victims of adverse circumstances which they were utterly powerless to overcome, such as sickness, loss of employment, and hence inability to pay dues and "stand square on the books." The loss of their standing in the respective organizations has been, in numerous instances, the loss of friends and the loss of hope. Despondency took the place of courage, and as disappointments multiplied and wants pressed heavily upon them, it is doubtless true that in numerous instances they were induced, indeed compelled, by their necessities to accept wages which fixed upon them the insufferable stigma of *scabs* when, in fact, their better natures rebelled at such a classification.

I know that there are thousands of these men anxious to regain their position and honorable standing in the ranks of organized labor, and here the question arises: "What can the American Railway Union do to redeem such men from the ranks of non-union workingmen?" Thousands of these victims of misfortune are honest men and anxious of showing themselves such, and the American Railway Union may, with eminent propriety, adopt the splendid maxim that "While it is human to err, it is divine to forgive"[62] and extend to such men an opportunity to make good their professions of fealty to organized labor.

An Eight-Hour Day

Among advanced thinkers in the ranks of labor, the eight-hour day is regarded as the most important means of solving the labor problem. It is one of the propositions, the wisdom of which can be demonstrated with mathematical accuracy. The cry is that there are more men than there is work—and the affirmation is absolutely true, if men continue to work ten hours a day. There is just so much work to be done; hence if you reduce the number of hours constituting a day's work, you add to the number of men required to do the work; hence also, if 100 men work ten hours a day, it is equal to 1,000 hours; if the hours are reduced to eight, the number of men required to perform the job in one day would be 125, because 125 men working eight hours equals 1,000 hours. Therefore, if 5 million men working ten hours a day were to work only eight hours a day, the result would be that 1,250,000 idle men would find employment. It is a mathematical demonstration of an economic and philanthropic proposition which, could it be adopted throughout the country, would result in a harvest of untold peace, prosperity, and contentment.

There are numerous other blessings which would come to workingmen, and to society at large, were the eight-hour day universally adopted. Workingmen would have more hours for rest, more hours for study, more hours in their homes and with their families—in every instance a change of condition for the better, for the good of workingmen, for the good of society, and which could not fail of adding indefinitely to the power of our civilization to bless mankind.

The American Railway Union, I am persuaded, is in favor of the eight-hour day, and I suggest that it would be both wise and opportune for this convention to call a conference of all labor organizations to urge legislation to establish an eight-hour day in every department of labor and to keep alive the agitation upon the subject by voice, pen, and ballot until victory is achieved.

The Pullman Strike

The Pullman strike, in the town of Pullman and against the millionaire Pullman, began under the auspices of the American Railway Union on the 11th day of May [1894]. Pullman the town, like Pullman the proprietor, has a national reputation not specially unlike that which Carnegie, Frick, and Homestead enjoy. Whether Carnegie, Frick, or Pullman is the more intimate friend of his satanic majesty, he of the forked tail and cloven foot, it is needless to inquire. All of them go back to him on Sundays, but on working days, when the business is to rob and degrade working men and women, Pullman and the devil pull together at Pullman as merrily as "Buck and Bright," hitched to a harrow.[63] So devoutly has Pullman robbed the Pullman employees, so religiously has he cut down wages, so piously has he made his retainers economize so as to prolong starvation, so happily are the principles of Pullman blended with the policy of the proprietor of the lake of fire and brimstone, that the biography of the one would do for the history of the other, and not a change of a letter or a punctuation mark would be required by the severest critic.[64]

Pullman, as greedy as a horse leech, saw his employees losing strength, saw them emaciated, but he kept on sucking their life currents. It was work and poverty in Pullmantown, or Pullemdown, until, patience ceasing to be a virtue and further forbearance becoming treason to life, liberty, and pursuit of happiness, the employees determined to strike to better their condition. Pullman was very rich; his employees were very poor; but they concluded that the town of Pauperdom was better than Pullmandom and, in a moment of righteous energy, quit work, which simply gave Pullman, the plutocrat with a soul so small that a million of them could dance on the little end of a hornet's stinger, an opportunity, by refusing them fair wages, to suck their blood to the last drop and coin it for the gratification of his pride and the enlargement of his pomp.

The Pullman strike, as an object lesson, will, I doubt not, engage the attention of this convention. It is a terrible illustration of corporate greed and heartlessness and pharisaical fraud which for years has prevailed in this county, and which has created conditions in the presence of which the stoutest hearts take alarm.

National Ownership of Railroads

There are thousands of American citizens profoundly versed in economics who do not hesitate to affirm that the time is approaching when the government will be required *to own* the railroads, to prevent the railroads from *owning* the government. Accepting the figures of the census bureau at Washington that the wealth of the country is $65 billion, and accepting current valuation of the railroads of the country at $10 billion, it is sure that the railroads already own 15.38 percent of the entire wealth of the country—enough to dominate legislation by debauching legislatures and sending their tools to the United States Senate, where the olfactory organs of honest men are saluted by more stenches than Coleridge discovered when he visited Cologne.[65]

The question "How shall we pay the railroads?" is one that need not trouble the people until the ballots of the people demand that the government ought, for the general welfare, to own them; and the day the people decide the question, the way to buy the railroads will be made exceedingly luminous. Other countries have demonstrated the feasibility of national ownership of railroads, and the problem need not and ought not to deter those who believe in the practicability of the undertaking in the United States from giving the fullest and truest expression to their convictions. That it would be a great undertaking need not be questioned, but the American people are familiar with great undertakings, and when once resolved upon, bugbears and scarecrows will disappear. Some legislation might be required to squeeze out the water that constitutes about two-fifths of the estimated value of the railroads of the

United States, upon which the owners are extorting dividends from a patient and despoiled people, and by cutting down the wages of employees. With government ownership instead of schemes to enrich plutocrats, the policy would be to give dividends to the public in cheaper transportation, and honest wages to those who really operate the roads. The princely salaries of presidents, vice presidents, general managers, et al., would disappear, and employees, who now have their wages cut to make good losses in Wall Street, would be honestly and regularly paid, and this equitable distribution of receipts would work a revolution in the condition of railroad employees.

We are becoming familiar with the subject, and the more it is discussed the more practical and patriotic the scheme appears. The members of the American Railway Union have had abundant opportunities for knowing that the change of ownership of the railroads of the country, from corporations to the government, could by no possibility make their condition worse, but that, discussed from any and from every point of view, the change would be of incalculable benefit to them.

Membership of Women

The American Railway Union admits women to membership. There are thousands of women in the employment of the railroads of the country, doing work necessary to carry forward the great enterprise in which the railroads are engaged. That these women should be protected goes without saying, and the American Railway Union throws wide open its doors to receive them and will demonstrate its loyalty to them by maintaining that when a woman performs a man's work, she ought, in all justice, to have a man's pay.

The Strike on the Great Northern

The strike inaugurated on the Great Northern Railway began on April 13, 1894, and ended on the first day of May 1894, counting 18 days. The strike was an [exertion] of resolute men who refused the degradation incident to a reduction of wages below a decent living standard. The resistance of these men to the imposition of degrading wages was in all regards chivalric. They saw and clearly comprehended the importance of unity of opinion, purpose, and action, and took the necessary steps to secure all the benefits such unity could confer. They were in the right and realized that "Thrice is he armed that hath his quarrel just."[66] They did not underestimate the power of their foes, but sized them up, number and weight, in a way which demonstrated from first to last that the American Railway Union was the master of the situation. The battleground extended from St. Paul to the coast, involving the rights and wages of thousands of men. In every engagement the American Railway Union won decisive advantages. The ranks of the union were never broken, never dismayed, never faltered, and as an exhibition of fealty to right and justice, every day and continuously, the records of labor's struggle presents no parallel.

I would be unpardonably faithless to duty were I to fail to mention in this connection the valuable services rendered by employees of the Great Northern who, though members of other organizations, clearly saw that the American Railway Union was right, and with that splendid courage which dares to be true with conviction, contributed their full quota to secure victory, and this was done in defiance of orders designed to make them the friends of the enemies of labor.

Taken all together, a more notable victory has never been achieved in a railway affair in the United States or elsewhere. The success of the American Railway Union was complete—wages were restored, and all the men who engaged in the strike have been restored to their employment, a feature of the victory which can be said of no other extended railroad strike.

Conclusion

Delegates to the first convention of the American Railway Union, I welcome you most cordially, and salute you as brothers and coworkers of a great cause, the banding together of employees of every class on American railways.

The work of organization has been exceptionally arduous—a wide area of country has been traversed. The task has been herculean, but results are of a character which atone for all the exhaustive labor that has been bestowed. The fires of local unions are blazing on mountains, in valleys, and on plains. Phenomenal success so far has attended our efforts. The strides of the American Railway Union have been gigantic. It is rapidly encompassing the great Republic from ocean to ocean—from the lakes to the gulf. Wise legislation by the convention will bring to our order still greater and more marvelous triumph. Mistakes should be guarded against. The future of our order is largely in your hands. The eyes of all other labor organizations are fixed upon this convention. I do not doubt but we shall meet every reasonable expectation and perfect our organization, which will prove an enduring blessing to all classes of railway employees.

The forces of labor must unite. The salvation of labor demands it. The dividing lines must grow dimmer day by day until they become imperceptible, and then labor's hosts, marshaled under one conquering banner, shall march together, vote together, and fight together, until workingmen shall receive and enjoy all the fruits of their toil. Then will our country be truly and grandly free, and its institutions as secure and enduring as the eternal mountains.

If the union of labor's army is prevented or delayed by jealous leaders, let them step aside or be set aside. The one supreme demand of the hour is that railway employees shall get together. If they will do this, the officers of the American Railway Union will promptly and cheerfully retire to private life. Neither the honors nor emoluments of office will tempt them to stand in the way of unification an instant, and to test their sincerity, let the proposition go forth from this convention to all railway employees to meet upon common ground, and there unite forces for the protection of all. Such an army would be impregnable. No corporation would assail it. The reign of justice would be inaugurated. The strike would be remanded to the relic chamber of the past. An era of peace and goodwill would dawn. Let us do what we can to hasten the coming of that day.

The Race Line and the ARU:
Statement to the Convention[†]
June 18, 1894

It is not the colored man's fault that he is black; it is not the fault of 6 million Negroes that they are here.[67] They were brought here by the avarice, cupidity, and inhumanity of the white race. The father of our country was an owner of slaves. Bind down the white race for centuries and their intellects would become stunted, their refinement would disappear.

If we do not admit the colored man to membership, the fact will be used against us. I am not here to advocate association with the Negro, but I am ready to stand side by side with him to take his hand in mine and help him whenever it is in my power.

[†]   Published as "Draws a Race Line: Question of Color Before the American Railway Union" in *Chicago Tribune*, vol. 53, no. 170 (June 19, 1894), 12.

The Coal Miners' Strike[†]

June 1894

All things considered, the strike of the coal miners of the United States is proba-bly the most serious event in industrial affairs that ever occurred in this country.[68]

In the onward march of invention, steam power is employed almost uni-versally; coal has practically displaced wood as fuel, and as a result, wherever a locomotive puffs and whistles on the 200,000 miles of the railroads of the country, or wherever a stationary engine is located, coal is in demand as a fuel. Nor is this all. Beyond the limits of natural gas, in all the great cities and most important towns, coal is used for domestic purposes, and thus coal becomes a universal fuel—an article of prime necessity the importance of which cannot be exaggerated.

A person at all thoughtful need only to survey the field of enterprises in which coal is used to generate steam to be convinced that to cut off the supply of coal, or to materially reduce the quantity mined, must be attended with incalculable disasters to business, disasters so overwhelming in their sweep as to arrest the wheels of progress and the march of civilization.

According to the census report, there was mined in the United States, in 1889, 65,723,110 tons of bituminous coal, and 35,863,230 tons of anthracite coal—a total of 101,586,360 tons, and it is safe to say that now the annual product of the mines is not less than 150 million tons, and to say there are 300,000 men employed in mining this annual output is an exceedingly conservative estimate.

In this brief outline it is seen that in itself the coal mining industry ex-pands to vast proportions, and when we consider how intimately and indissol-ubly coal is associated with all the great industrial enterprises of the country, the mining industry expands to such proportions of interest and importance that it is practically impossible to grasp sums total.

If we were to introduce arguments relating to cause and effect, we are in-clined to the opinion that no other industry in this country is productive of an amount of wealth approximating that which can be traced directly to the labors of the coal miner; and the inquiry is naturally suggested: Does the miner, even in a remote degree, share in the benefits which his arduous vocation creates? That he does not is universally conceded.

[†]   Published in *Locomotive Firemen's Magazine,* vol. 18, no. 7 (July 1894), 682–683.

If the investigator goes to the anthracite coal fields of Pennsylvania for facts and proof, he will be forced to the conclusion that in no land beneath the sun, in no era of the world's history, has human depravity had a more satanic exemplification than in the afflictions which the proprietors of the Pennsylvania anthracite coal mines have studiously and continuously visited upon coal miners; and coal proprietors everywhere throughout the country, with exceptions as rare as angels' visits, have pursued the same degrading, defrauding, hunger-panged policy. The world has known the enormity of the evils complained of. The story in all its haggard features has repeatedly been told. The miserable victims of "man's inhumanity to man" have occasionally rebelled, only to be forced into submission by hunger, cold, and nakedness. Living but one remove from the condition of wild beasts, they lived and toiled and died, the victims of cruelty, poverty, and degradation such as have cursed no civilized land under heaven.

But, and America ought to be thankful for the fact, coal miners have not become so debased that they would no longer protest, and under the leadership of men who knew the right and dared maintain it, the miners organized to demand justice, and all ordinary efforts having failed to secure redress, at least 150,000 men resolved to cease digging coal until they secured fair wages for their work. This organization is known as the United Mine Workers.

The cause of the strike now in full blast was the reduction of wages in certain districts, where the prevailing price at the beginning of the reduction was 79 cents a ton, and the cut proceeded until prices were reduced all the way from 38 to 60 cents a ton, netting a man from 50 to 75 cents a day.

The resistance to this piratical policy began by local strikes, but no benefit resulted, and there came the order for the members of the United Mine Workers to quit; and as we write not less than 150,000 men are idle, demanding 70 cents a ton as a uniform rate for digging a ton of coal; and no man who is at all familiar with the subject will charge the miners with making an unreasonable demand.

We have indicated the great importance of coal as a fuel, and this fact has prompted proprietors to put forth superhuman efforts to replace the miners who are striking, by men who, regardless of right and justice, are willing to accept such wages as the proprietors offer. The regular miners, who are contending for simple justice, are disposed to resist the employment of such men, and as we write, news comes of battle and blood—of dead and wounded, and the outlook is full of peril.

Already the premonitions of a coal famine are widespread and unmistakable. In numerous instances, railroads have felt its grasp and have reduced the number of their trains. From every direction information comes that factories have had to suspend operations, and the declaration is made that unless the miners at an early day resume work, the condition of business will be of a character so deplorable as to defy exaggeration. Every branch of business will, to a greater or less extent, be involved. Ten thousand engines will stand still, and a million employees will be added to the ranks of the idle—and all because 150,000 or 200,000 miners absolutely declare they are robbed, degraded, and starved that mine owners may grow rich upon their unrequited toil.

What is to be done?

It is the old, old question. If the miners can hold out, the operators will be compelled to pay them fair wages; and since the alternatives are work and starve, or be idle and take the chances, the indications are that the latter choice will be made, and if it is, the duration of the struggle cannot, in the nature of things, be long protracted, and the miners will win a notable victory, all the more certain because their demands are just.

We predict a victory for the mine workers. In saying this we are not unmindful of the sacrifices the mine workers are making, but we believe the interests at stake demand that the struggle shall be carried forward until the nation shall learn also, by sacrifice, the fact hitherto disregarded, that the nation's boasted wealth and progress, civilization and all its attendant blessings, depend primarily upon the toiling masses, and that justice to them, whether resulting from legislation, arbitration, or striking, is the basis of national prosperity. Experience may be, and often is, a dear school, but if the nation will learn in no other school, then let the test come, as come it will, and the sooner it comes the better it will be for all concerned.

Declaration at the ARU Quadrennial Convention Regarding a Potential Pullman Boycott[†] [excerpt]

June 22, 1894

———

I believe that every delegate in this room has full power to act, or he would not have been sent here. You should reach out now and strangle this monster Pullman—not Pullman the man, but Pullman the corporation. If you were to cut that heartless, soulless, grasping, grinding monopoly open this minute, not one drop of human blood of sympathy or feeling would come out. If you got anything from its veins, it would be something in the nature of mayonnaise sauce.

We should act at once. To defer action is useless. Some will say that we are not strong enough. We will say that we are not strong enough. We will never be stronger if we do not prove our strength today.

Speech on the Forthcoming Pullman Boycott to a Mass Meeting of Railroad Workers in Chicago[‡] [excerpt]

June 25, 1894

———

I have perfect confidence in the America people and believe that they will uphold us in this fight.[69] Their shibboleth is fair play. There is not a breath of free air in Pullman, nor is there a man, woman, or child who touches his soil who can be called free. These people are starving not because they will not work, but because they may as well starve idle as at work. There are no cowards in

———

†   Wire service report of the Associated Press, published as "A Pullman Boycott" in the *Los Angeles Times*, vol. 13, (June 23, 1894), 2.

‡   Published as part of the article "Boycott Is On Today" in the *Chicago Tribune*, vol. 48, no. 177 (June 26, 1894), 8.

the American Railway Union. Heretofore we have been on the defensive. Now they have invited us into a battle, and we accept the challenge.

The American Railway Union has had just 11 struggles, and it has won them all. The Pullman strike will make an even dozen. If, however, by any frightful fate the American Railway Union should be defeated in this strike, let me tell you that it will not be the end. There is not a man in the American Railway Union that can be bought, sold, or bribed. I appeal to the people in this country to stand by us, for our fight is just.

Telegram to Labor Leaders Announcing the Launch of the Pullman Boycott[†]

June 26, 1894

June 26, 1894

A boycott against the Pullman Company to take effect at noon today has been declared by the American Railway Union.[70] We earnestly request your aid and cooperation in this fight of organized labor against a powerful and oppressive monopoly. Please advise if you can meet with us in conference, and if not if you will authorize someone to represent you in this matter. Address: 421 Ashland Block.

***Eugene V. Debs**,*
President

[†]   Published in *In the Circuit Court of the United States, Northern District of Illinois: United States of America, Complainant, vs. Eugene V. Debs et al., Respondents: Proceedings on Information for Attachment of Contempt.* Chicago: 1894; 62–63.

Statement on the Strike to the *Chicago Tribune*[†]
June 27, 1894

We do not wish to interfere with the trains that are already made up. To stop their making up is our object, and that we will do tomorrow. The switchmen are with us and will obey the orders that we issue tomorrow morning.

Our object is primarily to prevent the running of Pullman cars over the great through lines. If we can bring them to terms, we will have no trouble with the smaller roads. The roads we are after are the Illinois Central, the Northern and the Southern Pacific, the Santa Fe, the Chicago & Great Western, and the Wisconsin Central.

Statement on the Strike to the *Chicago Inter Ocean*[‡]
June 27, 1894

We shall not attempt to cut Pullman cars out of trains, but we shall do all in our power to prevent them from being placed in trains. In this I speak for the order, but I cannot say what some of the more excited sympathizers throughout the country may do. I do not think that a Pullman car will leave Chicago today.

Roads in the hands of receivers will cut no figure with us. We have the same right with those lines that we have with others.

We do not intend to resort to violence under any circumstances, and if violence is attempted against the property of any railroad company, we will send our own men to protect that property.

Our men will quit, and if their places can be filled, all right, we have no objections, but we shall do all in our power to peaceably prevent the running of Pullman sleepers.

[†]   Quote appearing in the article "Boycott to Be in Force Today" in the *Chicago Tribune,* vol. 53, no. 178 (June 28, 1894), 2.

[‡]   Quote appearing in the article "Knights of Labor to Aid" in the *Daily Inter Ocean,* vol. 23, no. 96 (June 28, 1894), 3.

Speech to a Mass Meeting of Illinois Central Railroad Workers on the Pullman Strike, Fischer's Hall, Chicago†
[excerpt]
June 27, 1894

These are stirring times.[71] *[Applause.]*

This is a fight in which there is no doubt as to the right and wrong side. On one hand is a corporation endeavoring to starve thousands of workmen; on the other are workmen trying to get bread enough for their families. Every laboring man within the sound of my voice knows in which direction his duty lies. The American Railway Union will spend its last cent to aid them in this fight.

The American Railway Union is the only labor organization not prevented by its constitution from helping any class of railway employees. We must stand closer together. Our only hope is in union and organization; the hope of the corporation is the creation of dissensions and divisions. The American Railway Union is the one broad organization that covers all branches of railway labor. To hell with the law of any labor organization that prevents men from protecting themselves in their rights. Those who are not with us are against us. Do your duty and be true to yourselves, and we will win.

---

†   Published as part of the article "Debs Makes a Bombastic Speech" in the *Chicago Tribune*, vol. 53, no. 179 (June 28, 1894), 8.

Message to the Railway Employees of America[†]
June 29, 1894

Chicago, IL, June 29 [1894]

To the Railway Employees of America:—

The struggle with the Pullman Company has developed into a contest between the producing classes and the money power of the country. This is what Lincoln predicted at the close of the Civil War, and it was this reflection that gave the great emancipator his gloomiest forebodings. We stand upon the ground that the workingmen are entitled to a just proportion of the proceeds of their labor. This the Pullman Company denied them. Reductions had been made from time to time until the employees earned barely sufficient wages to live, not enough to prevent them from sinking deeper and deeper into Pullman's debt, thereby mortgaging their bodies and souls, as well as their children's, to that heartless corporation.

Up to this point, the fight was between the American Railway Union and the Pullman Company. The American Railway Union resolved that its members would refuse to handle Pullman cars and equipment. Then the railway corporations, through the General Managers' Association, came to the rescue, and in a series of whereases declared to the world that they would go into partnership with Pullman, so to speak, and stand by him in his devilish work of starving his employees to death. The American Railway Union accepted the gauge of war, and thus the contest is now on between the railway corporations united solidly upon the one hand, and the labor forces upon the other. Every railroad employee of the country should take his stand against the corporations in this fight, for if it should be lost, corporations will have despotic sway, and all employees will be reduced to a condition scarcely removed above chattel slavery; but the fight will not be lost. The great principle of American manhood and independence is involved. Corporate power, drunk with its own excesses, has presumed too far upon the forbearance of the American people, and notwithstanding a subsidized press (to which there are many notable and noble exceptions), public sympathy is with the striking employees,

†   Published in the *Railway Times*, vol. 1, no. 13 (July 2, 1894), 2. Republished in the *Railway Times*, vol. 1, no. 16 (August 15, 1894), 1.

who are merely contending for the right of their fellow toilers to receive living wages for their work.

I appeal to strikers everywhere to refrain from any act of violence. Let there be no interference with the affairs of the companies involved, and, above all, let there be no act of depredation. A man who will destroy property or violate law is an enemy and not a friend to the cause of labor. The great public is with us, and we need only to maintain a dignified, honest, straightforward policy to achieve victory. Let it be understood that this strike is not ordered by myself or any other individual; nor is the strike inaugurated anywhere except by consent and authority from a majority of employees themselves.

Neither is this a fight simply of the American Railway Union. The question of organization ought not to be raised, but every man who believes in organized railroad labor and its battles for his rights and those of his fellow men. I have faith in the great body of railway employees of the country and am confident they will maintain an unbroken front in spite of any opposition that may be brought to bear against them. I am perfectly confident of success. We cannot fail.

E. V. Debs

Conditions[†]

July 1894

The optimist may be satisfied with conditions and the pessimist may lament over what he deems the misfortunes of mankind, and if the pessimist seeks to remedy the affliction, whatever it may be, he is the better man of the two, but if he is content to murmur, bewail, and croak, then the optimist is the more lovable character. There are certain untoward conditions which, being productive of great mental or physical distress, cannot be contemplated with composure, so independent of human agency that they are termed "acts of God." It would be an easy task to catalogue some of them as, for instance, earthquakes, cyclones, the calamities attending overflows of rivers, death-dealing thunderbolts, storms

---

[†]   Published in *Locomotive Firemen's Magazine*, vol. 18, no. 7 (July 1894), 678–680.

at sea, when navies go down, railroad wrecks which neither care nor foresight could prevent, and many other kindred and inscrutable dispensations. In such cases it were folly to complain. There is no remedy. The best that can be done is to consult experience and science for the purpose of reducing results in the line of death and destruction to the minimum.

Men possessed of common sense do not, while contemplating disasters of the kind mentioned, sit down and growl on the one hand, content with the theory that all things are for the worst, nor, on the other hand, fold their hands and smilingly assert that things are ordered for the best. On the contrary, they take a hand in ordering and adjusting affairs to the extent, at least, of confronting nature with appliances designed to modify the disastrous consequences of conditions they did not create, as, for instance, build strong ships to battle with storms at sea, set up lightning rods to catch thunderbolts, build low, one-story houses when living within a seismic territory, and thus we could indefinitely point out how men on the alert, in a measure, at least, may modify results when conditions productive of disaster are beyond their control.

But there are conditions brought about by human agencies, many of which are fruitful of calamities of wider sweep and more direful consequences than those which are credited to a mysterious providence. And it is such conditions that men are required to consider, because by giving them special examination ways and means may be found to change them and create other conditions calculated to promote the welfare of individuals and communities.

In this connection it becomes eminently prudent to inquire regarding the condition of our country. It is blessed beyond the power of hyperbole with food products. Our granaries are full to repletion, and we seek constantly for foreign markets in which to dispose of the surplus. In this we have a condition that even a pessimist must approve and admire, and an optimist may shout with some show of propriety, "I told you so; all things are done for the best." Certainly, it was the order of nature to create the soil, to send the sunshine and the rain, and it was the order of a largely redeemed human nature from savagery to plow, sow, cultivate, and harvest the products. Usually, however, we credit such a condition to Providence, and to such a conclusion we are not disposed to offer objections further than to say, "in creating them, God and man are in alliance."

But while we are indulging in thanksgiving for such boundless stores of food, we are confronted by a condition which silences rejoicings. Multiplied thousands of our people, men, women, and children, are in the grasp of hunger, premonition of famine. What of such a condition? It is purely a condition brought about by human agencies. There is no mysterious Providence in any sense responsible, and hence it becomes possible for human agencies to diminish the sufferings of the people, and these are being employed; but to abate the distress caused by the conditions is not sufficient, the supreme demand being to prevent the recurrence of such national calamities.

In surveying the field of battle, for such it is, where the idle, the impoverished, the ragged, hungry, and homeless, have struggled for life, men, stouthearted and strong-nerved, confess to sensations akin to despair. To relieve the universal distress, to provide for the destitution seen on every hand, appears a work so herculean that only the power of a miracle-working God is equal to the task, but as the condition was created by man, man must work out of it or succumb to the indescribable curse, and if experience—and since the new world was discovered it never taught a more terrible lesson for the benefit of workingmen—will not suffice to redeem men from the bondage of error when by the fiat of their sovereign will it may be done, then the time is at hand to write the epitaph of a government by the people, of the people, and for the people.

Men who discuss remedies for conditions productive of disaster inquire relative to the cause of the calamity. The president of the United States, after collecting all the facts available by the government, called Congress in extraordinary session to change deplorable conditions. Banks were failing by the hundred, industrial enterprises were closing their doors, money became phenomenally scarce, disaster after disaster followed fast and followed faster, wreck and ruin was seen on all sides, and the president said the condition was owing to "congressional legislation." That was the cause assigned by the chief magistrate of the nation, and the legislation which was selected to bear the anathemas of the nation was the famous and infamous "Sherman bill," which simply provided for the purchase of a certain amount of silver bullion, for which the government issued in payment silver certificates which entered into the currency of the country. It was charged that the "Sherman bill" caused undue exportation of gold, and with this the hue and cry began.

The arraignment of Congress upon the charge of being responsible for the calamities under which the country for a year past has suffered is an indictment of the people, of popular government in all of its branches, since it is the theory of our government that the people are sovereign, and have such laws and such administration of the government as they desire. But this may be said: If the people find themselves betrayed by their representatives, they may displace them for others who are not knaves, and in this way so far as legislature is concerned, change conditions or prevent the recurrence of calamitous conditions; but everything depends upon the intelligence, courage, and integrity of the people.

In discussing the deplorable condition of business affairs it will be profitable to keep prominently in mind President Cleveland's declaration that the cause is "congressional legislation." We do not doubt the president's averment, hence we affirm that Congress has betrayed the people. The president's indictment includes the two great parties that have for years controlled congressional legislation, and these two great parties, corrupt to the core, are now asking the people to still further trust them. They closed the mills and the factories throughout the great mining regions; they closed the silver mines as if by a decree of Jehovah. They created a condition in finance which paralyzed business of every description and filled the land with idleness and all the indescribable woes which idleness inflicts, and now they appeal to the victims of their perfidy and treachery for a new lease of power, that congressional legislation may proceed in the old ruts, and in the old ruts it is proceeding.

Bearing in mind the declaration of the president, charging present conditions upon congressional legislation, men naturally turn to Congress for relief and are required to contemplate spectacles of wrangling, duplicity, and perfidy which leads to the conclusion that conditions are to be made still more disastrous. Senators are charged with using their information for successful gambling in stocks, and an investigation is to probe the charge to find the depths of congressional rottenness. The great body of the people have lost all confidence in congressional integrity. The hope which animated the nation when Congress assembled, that conditions would be changed for the better, has practically faded out of sight. Business demoralization continues. The army of men forced into idleness is not diminished; the fangs and pangs of hunger are doing their work; tramps multiply. Those who have work are confronted with demands for a reduction in wages; poverty goes down to deeper depths. There are more rags, more riots, but no reform, and still Congress yields only Dead Sea fruit, and the conclusion is forced upon all thinking men that parties as they exist cannot create better conditions and will not supply remedies for the disasters which the president says are the result of congressional legislation.

If the ballot is to change conditions, if the ballot is to prevent the recurrence of such conditions as now afflict the country, it is time that workingmen should renounce their bondage to the old parties, to find or found one whose representatives in Congress shall so legislate that no president from this time forthwith and forever shall be required to say that the country is in the grasp of appalling calamities as the result of "congressional legislation." Will workingmen be taught by experience? Will they heed admonitions such as present conditions voice in thunder tones? We shall see.

"All We Ask Is Fair Play":
Message to the Public†

July 5, 1894

To the Public:—

So many misleading reports have been given currency in reference to the great railroad strike now in progress that I am prompted, in the interest of justice and fair play, to give the public an honest, impartial statement of the issues involved and the facts as they actually exist. My purpose in this is to have the great American public—the plain people—in every avenue of life, conversant with the situation as it really is, that they who constitute the highest tribunal we know may pass judgment upon our acts—condemn us if we are wrong and uphold us if we are right.

First of all, let it be said that the Pullman employees who struck May 6 last did so entirely of their own accord.[72] Their action in so doing was spontaneous and unanimous. They simply revolted against a series of deep-seated wrongs of long standing, and no power could stay them. It has been charged, and the charge has been widely accepted, that they were induced to strike by their "leaders" and labor agitators; that if left alone they would have remained at work. The charge is wholly untrue. The fact is that the officers of the American Railway Union used all their influence to pacify the employees and advised them repeatedly not to strike, but to bear patiently their grievances until a peaceable settlement could be effected. To the truth of this statement the employees themselves will bear willing testimony.

But the grievance of the employees, men and women, had become so aggravated, so galling, that patience deserted them and they abandoned their employment rather than submit longer to conditions against which their very souls rebelled. Whether they were right or not, let only those judge who comprehend the conditions under which these faithful employees toiled and groaned. Let us avoid sentiment. The bare facts will suffice, and they are haggard enough to excite the sympathy of every good citizen, rich or poor, employer or employed. The Pullman Company, be it understood, owns the town of Pullman, owns the houses, the homes of employees, controls the light and

---

† Published as "To the Public" in the *Railway Times,* vol. 1, no. 14 (July 15, 1894), 3.

water and other necessaries of life, and wages are so adjusted to living expenses that in a large majority of cases the employees are barely able to support their families. Proof overwhelming can be furnished. One instance will suffice. At the time they struck, the employees were in arrears to the Pullman Company $70,000 for rent alone. Wages had been repeatedly reduced, but rent and other expenses remained the same. At this rate it would have been a question of a short time only until the employees would have been hopelessly involved in debt—mortgaged soul and body to the Pullman Company.

The employees, from the beginning, have been willing to arbitrate their differences with the company. That is their position today. The company arrogantly declares that there is nothing to arbitrate. If this be true, why not allow a board of fair and impartial arbitrators to determine the fact? At this point we appeal to the public as to whether the position of the Pullman Company or the position of the employees is entitled to the sanction of the public conscience. If the employees were to assume the position of the Pullman Company and defiantly declare they had nothing to arbitrate and arbitrarily demand unconditional surrender as the only basis of settlement, they would merit the condemnation of the public, and it would certainly and swiftly fall upon them with crushing severity.

Committee after committee waited upon the officials of the Pullman Company with a vain hope of effecting a settlement. They were willing to make concessions, to compromise in the interest of peace. All their advances were repelled. The company was, and is, unyielding as adamant. Finally, June 12, the delegates of the American Railway Union, representing 425 local unions of railway employees located on the principal lines of American railways, met in convention in Chicago. The Pullman trouble had been discussed at their local meetings. Many of the delegates came instructed. The grievances of the Pullman employees were taken under consideration. Two separate committees were sent to the officials. Not the slightest satisfaction could be obtained. As a last resort the delegates by *unanimous vote* determined that unless the Pullman Company would agree to do justice to their employees within five days, the members of the order would decline to haul Pullman cars. This action, be it remembered, was not taken until the strike had been on six weeks, and every conceivable effort to obtain redress had failed because of the obstinacy of the company.

Up to this point the trouble was confined to the Pullman Company and its employees. How, then, did the strike extend to the railways? Let the answer be given in accordance with the facts. The day before the order of the delegates declining to haul Pullman cars went into effect, the General Managers'

Association, representing the principal western railways, met and passed a series of resolutions, declaring in substance that they would uphold the Pullman Company in its fight upon the employees, that they would haul Pullman cars, and that they would stand together in crushing out the American Railway Union. The resolutions in question were published in the city papers and can be referred to in substantiation of this averment. It will thus be seen that the railway companies virtually joined forces with the Pullman Company, went into partnership with them, so to speak, to reduce and defeat their half-starved employees. In this way the trouble was extended from line to line, and from system to system, until a crisis had been reached. The business of the company is demoralized to an extent that defies exaggeration. To say that the situation is alarming is entirely within the bounds of prudent statement. Every good citizen must view the outlook with grave concern. Something should, something must be done. The American people are a peace-loving people—they want neither anarchy nor revolution. They have faith in their institutions, they believe in law and order, they believe in good government, but they also believe in fair play. Once aroused they will not tolerate arbitrary and dictatorial defiance, even on the part of an alliance of rich and powerful corporations.

What can be done to dispel the apprehension that now prevails and restore peace and confidence? The American Railway Union, by whose authority and on whose behalf this statement is made, stands ready—has from the beginning stood ready—to do anything in its power, provided it is honorable, to end this trouble. This, briefly stated, is the position the organization occupies. It simply insists that the Pullman Company shall meet its employees and do them justice. We guarantee that the latter will accept any reasonable proposition. The company may act through its officials or otherwise, and the employees through their chosen representatives. Let them agree as far as they can, and where they fail to agree let the points in dispute be submitted to arbitration. The question of the recognition of the American Railway Union, or any other organization, is waived. We do not ask, nor have we ever asked, for recognition as an organization. We care nothing about that, and as far as we are concerned it has no part in the controversy. Let the officials deal with the employees without reference to organization. Let the spirit of conciliation, mutual concession, and compromise animate and govern both sides, and there will be no trouble in reaching a settlement that will be satisfactory to all concerned. This done, let the railway companies agree to restore all their employees to their situations without prejudice, and the trouble will be ended. The crisis will thus be averted, traffic will resume, and peace will reign. The railways are not required to recognize the American Railway Union. This has never been asked, nor is it asked now.

If there are those who discover in this statement a "weakening" on the part of employees, as has been so often charged, when an exposition of the true attitude of our order was attempted, we have only to say that they are welcome to such solace as such a perverted conclusion affords them. We have been deliberately and maliciously misrepresented, but we have borne it all with an unwavering faith that the truth will finally and powerfully prevail. We firmly believe our cause is just, and while we hold that belief we will not recede. If we are wrong, we are ready to be convinced. We are open to reason and to conviction, but we will not be cowed or intimidated. Were we to sacrifice the multiplied thousands of wageworkers who have committed their interests to our hands and yield to the pressure of corporate power, we would be totally unworthy of American citizenship.

It may be asked what sense is there in sympathetic strikes. Let the corporations answer. When one is assailed, all go to the rescue. They stand together; they supply each other with men, money, and equipment. Labor, in unifying its forces, simply follows their example. The corporations established the precedent. If the proceeding is vicious and indefensible, let them first abolish it. In this contest, labor will stand by labor. Other organizations of workingmen have themselves felt the oppressive hand of corporate capital. They will not be called out, but will go out. And the spectacle of Mr. Pullman, fanned by the breezes of the seashore, while his employees are starving, is not calculated to prevent their fellow wageworkers from going to their rescue by the only means at their command.

A few words in reference to myself, although ordinarily I pay no attention to misrepresentation or vituperation, may not be out of place, not because of myself personally, but on account of the cause I have the honor to in part represent, which may suffer if silence is maintained while it is assailed with falsehood and malignant detraction. I shirk no responsibility, neither do I want credit to which I am not entitled. This strike was not "ordered" by myself, nor by any other individual. I have never "ordered" nor "called" anybody out. Under the rules of the American Railway Union, members can only strike when a majority of their number so decide. The vote of the delegates in this instance was unanimous. And wherever men struck, they did so of their own accord. I have simply served the notice after the men themselves had determined to go out. This is the extent of my authority, and I have never exceeded it. My alleged authority to "call" or "order" out has been made the pretext on which to assail me with every slander that malignity could conceive. So far as I am personally concerned detraction cannot harm me, nor does it matter if it could. I do not amount to more than the humblest member of our order—perhaps not as much. Fate or fortune has assigned me a duty, and, no matter how trying the ordeal or severe the penalties, I propose to perform it. The reflection that an honest man has nothing to fear sustains and comforts me in every hour of trial.

In closing, let me repeat that we stand ready to do our part toward averting the impending crisis. We have no false pride to stand in the way of a settlement. We do not want "official" recognition. All we ask is fair play for the men who have chosen us to represent them.

If the corporations refuse to yield and stubbornly maintain that there is "nothing to arbitrate," the responsibility for what may ensue will be upon their heads, and they cannot escape its penalties.

Eugene V. Debs

Telegram to ARU Local Leaders on Status of the Pullman Boycott[†]
July 6, 1894

July 6, 1894

C. S. McAuliff,
Milwaukee, Wis.

We have assurances that within 48 hours every labor organization in the country will come to our rescue.[73] The tide is on, and the men are acquitting themselves like heroes. Here and there one weakens, but our cause is strengthened by others going out in their place. Every true man must go out and remain out until the fight is won. There must be no halfway ground. Our cause is gaining ground daily, and our success is only a question of a few days. Don't falter in

---

[†]   Published in *In the Circuit Court of the United States, Northern District of Illinois: United States of America, Complainant, vs. Eugene V. Debs et al., Respondents: Proceedings on Information for Attachment of Contempt.* Chicago: 1894; 88.

this hour, but proclaim your manhood. Labor must win now or never. Our victory will be positive and complete. Whatever happens, don't give any credence to rumors or newspaper reports.

Eugene V. Debs

Warning to All Striking Employees[†]
July 6, 1894

To All Striking Employees:—

In view of the report of disturbances in various localities I deem it my duty to caution you against being a party to any violation of law, municipal, state, or national, during the existing difficulties. We have repeatedly declared that we respect law and order, and our conduct must conform to our profession. A man who commits violence in any form, whether a member of our order or not, should be promptly arrested and punished, and we should be first to apprehend the miscreant and bring him to justice. We must triumph as law-abiding citizens or not at all. Those who engage in force and violence are our real enemies. We have it upon reliable authority that thugs and toughs have been employed to create trouble so as to prejudice the public against our cause. The scoundrels should be in every case made to pay the full penalty of the law.

I appeal to you to be men, orderly and law-abiding. Our cause is just, the great public is with us, and we have nothing to fear.

Let it be borne in mind that if the railroad companies can secure men to handle their trains, they will have that right. Our men have the right to quit, but their right ends there. Other men have the right to take their places, whatever the opinion of the propriety of so doing may be.

Keep away from railroad yards, or rights of way, or other places where large crowds congregate. A safe plan is to remain away entirely from places where there is any likelihood of being an outbreak.

The railroad managers have sought to make it appear that their trains do

---

†   Published as "To All Striking Employees" in the *Railway Times,* vol. 1, no. 14 (July 15, 1894), 3.

not move because of the interference of the strikers. The statement is an unqualified falsehood, and no one knows this better than the managers themselves. They make this falsehood serve their purpose of calling out the troops.

Respect the law, conduct yourselves as becomes men, and our cause shall be crowned with success.

Eugene V. Debs

"The Situation Is More Favorable Today": Interview with the *Chicago Daily News*[†]

July 6, 1894

The situation is more favorable today than at any time since the trouble began. This is true because of the unanimous action of all labor organizations, showing that they are in sympathy with the American Railway Union's cause.

It is now a certainty that all men who labor or who sympathize with labor are going to be with us. We are to hold a popular mass meeting at Battery D,[74] where representative men not connected with the union will make addresses, in which Gov. Altgeld will be supported in his position, and it will be urged that federal troops be removed.

In California $10,000 has been raised by popular subscription to help on the fight.

At a meeting Sunday [July 8] delegates from labor organizations will meet and take some action.

[†]   Published as "Debs on the Situation" in *Chicago Daily News*, vol. 19, no. 160 (July 6, 1894), 10.

Open Letter to President Grover Cleveland[†]
July 7, 1894

Chicago, Ill., July 7 [1894]

To the Hon. Grover Cleveland,
President of the United States,
Executive Mansion, Washington, DC

Dear Sir:—

Through a long period of depression, enforced idleness, and low wages, resulting in widespread poverty and in many cases actual starvation, the working people have been patient, patriotic, and law-abiding, and not until the iron heel of corporate tyranny was applied with the intention to subjugate the working people to the will of arrogant monopolies did they make any effort to stay their oppressors. The Pullman strike was not declared until the employees of the Pullman Company were driven to the verge of starvation, their entreaties spurned with contempt, and their grievances denied a hearing. No refusal to handle Pullman cars was declared by any railway employee until all propositions looking toward arbitration and conciliation were rejected by the Pullman Company. Notwithstanding the facts set forth above were known to the public and the national authorities, you have seen fit, under the guise of protecting the mails and federal property, to invoke the service of the United States Army, whose very presence is used to coerce and intimidate peaceable working people into a humiliating obedience to the will of their oppressors.

By your acts, insofar as you have supplanted civil and state authorities with the federal military power, the spirit of unrest and distrust has so far been augmented that a deep-seated conviction is fast becoming prevalent that this government is soon to be declared a military despotism. The transmission of the United States mails is not interrupted by the striking employees of any railway company, but by the railway companies themselves, who refused to haul the mails on trains to which Pullman cars were not attached. If it is a criminal interference with the United States mails for the employees of a railway company

---

† Published in the *Railway Times,* vol. 1, no. 14 (July 15, 1894), 4.

to detach from a mail train a Pullman palace car contrary to the will of the company, then it holds true that it is the same criminal interference whenever a Pullman palace car is detached from a mail train in accordance with the will of a railway company while said mail train is in transit. The line of criminality in such case should not be drawn at the willingness or unwillingness of railway employees, but at the act itself, and inasmuch as it has been the common practice of railway corporations to attach and detach from mail trains Pullman palace cars at will, while said trains are in transit and carrying the mails of the United States, it would seem an act of discrimination against the employees of the railway corporations to declare such acts unlawful interference with the transmission of the mails when done by employees with or without the consent of their employers.

In view of these facts we look upon the far-fetched decision of Attorney General Olney, the sweeping un-American injunctions against railway employees, and the movements of the regular army as employing the powers of the general government for the support and protection of the railway corporations in their determination to degrade and oppress their employees.

The present railway strike was precipitated by the uneasy desire of the railway corporations to destroy the organizations of their employees and make the working people more subservient to the will of their employers; and as all students of government agree that free institutions depend for their perpetuity upon the freedom and prosperity of the common people, it would seem more in consonance with the spirit of democratic government if federal authority was exercised in deference to the rights of the toiling masses to life, liberty, and the pursuit of happiness. But, on the contrary, there is not an instance on record where in any conflict between corporations and the people the strong arm of the military power has been employed to protect the working people and the industrial masses from the ravage and persecution of corporate greed. But the measure of character has been in the line of declaring the corporations always good and in the right and the working people always bad and in the wrong.

Now, sir, we pledge to you the power of our respective organizations, individually and collectively, for the maintenance of peace and good order and the preservation of life and property, and will aid in the arrest and punishment of all violators of the civil and criminal laws of state and nation. In the present contest between labor and railway corporations, we shall use every peaceable and honorable means at our command consistent with the law and our constitutional rights, to secure for the working people just compensation for labor done and respectable consideration in accordance with the inherent rights of all men and the spirit of republican government. In doing so we appeal to all the liberty-loving people of the nation to aid and support us in this most just and righteous cause.

[American Railway Union,]
by Eugene V. Debs,
President

Order of the Knights of Labor,
by J. R. Sovereign,
General Master Workman

The Situation†

circa July 7, 1894[75]

On Friday, May 19 [1894], the employees of the Pullman Palace Car Company, at Pullman, struck against a reduction of wages, tyranny, and degradation, and the strike has steadily progressed until it has attained continental proportions.[76]

It is not the purpose of this article to recite incidents of the strike, but rather to point out the reasons why the strike has led to present conditions, with such reflections as the subject suggests.

Let it be said at the start that the Pullman employees never, at any time, objected to the rapid increase of Mr. George M. Pullman's great wealth, though his multimillions represented very accurately the amount he had, by financial legerdemain, abstracted from them. What they wanted, and the utmost they demanded, was fair wages and honorable treatment.

The employees of the Pullman Palace Car Company, like the great mass of their fellow toilers, preferred to submit to extortion and injustice as long as the wrongs could be borne rather than interfere with the plans of the company or

---

†   Published in *Locomotive Firemen's Magazine,* vol. 18, no. 8 (August 1894), 760–762.

create any disturbance. The testimony that such is the distinguishing trait of the great body of American workingmen is overwhelming.

There is not a strike on record which, upon investigation, does not disclose the fact that labor had been cruelly wronged, and the wonder has been that American workingmen could be induced to bear the outrages inflicted upon them so long and so patiently.

In writing of the situation, it were supreme folly to so much as intimate that workingmen have been unmindful of the losses and sacrifices incident to the adoption of extreme measures to maintain their rights. They have comprehended more fully than others the bitterness of the ordeal they would be required to pass in vindicating their manhood and their just demands, and the strikes which have occurred, whether success or defeat attended them, have, in every instance, added indefinitely to the glory of the sturdy manhood of American workingmen.

No one questions the declaration that a strike is quasi war, not necessarily sanguinary, though now and then blood and carnage have told the terrible penalties labor has paid in its efforts to obtain the privilege of living as becomes American citizens.

For the strike now on, as we write of the situation, George M. Pullman is responsible. It is becoming awfully tragic, and history will declare, when peace is restored, that it had its origin in the venality, despotism, and oppression of George M. Pullman. He is the author of the present situation. He began years ago to lay the foundation of his autocracy at the town of Pullman. This fact is vividly shown in an editorial article in the *Chicago Herald*. That paper says:

> In advance of the inevitable trial, Mr. Pullman will do well to consider certain facts. He has set up in the town of Pullman a modern satrapy—a survival of medieval feudalism repugnant to the thought and spirit of the 19th century. He has endeavored to combine a great industrial establishment with a hodgepodge jumble of Bellamy socialism and Russian autocracy. He has attempted to revive in America an institution that has not been seen since the fifteenth or sixteenth century.
>
> How well the experiment has succeeded he himself can testify. Satisfactory at first, like all things novel, the "model town" has degenerated. The "thousands of happy, contented, well-paid workers" have been transformed by degrees into sullen, discontented strikers—justified, unhappily, in their sullenness and discontent. The wheels are idle, the chimneys of the mills stand smokeless.

Does Mr. Pullman feel justified in continuing the strike? Granting that he may defeat his striking employees this time, does he care to invite another and another—and yet another—inevitable so long as wrong conditions exist? These are the conditions he should consider carefully, and any true friend—if he has one—will advise him as to their answer.

He should subdivide his town and sell lots to anyone who will buy. He should abolish the system of overseers and inspectors and quasi spies. He should enfranchise his men and make them freemen instead of feudal retainers. He should come down from his ducal throne and take his place among Americans as an American. He should become a democrat instead of an autocrat; a benefactor rather than a slave driver. He should be a man.[77]

In the foregoing the reader has a graphic pen picture of George M. Pullman. In his "Russian autocracy," his sub-autocrats and "quasi spies," we have the origin of the strike and the cause of the present situation, aided by the railroad managers combined to perpetuate the strike regardless of the cost of money and blood.

The policy of George M. Pullman to rob his employees is characteristic of the man. His insatiable thirst for money is not confined to his piracies upon his employees, but extends to the public, and his methods of robbery are so much like those of an outlaw as to make them a subject of congressional investigation. As a consequence, Senator John Sherman[78] of Ohio introduced a resolution to investigate George M. Pullman's piracies, and the resolution was adopted by the United States Senate, the purpose of the resolution being to put an end to Pullman's plunderings of the public.

In an interview published in the *St. Louis Globe-Democrat,* Senator Sherman took special pains to point out the infamies practiced by George M. Pullman, and among other things said:

> I regard the Pullman Company and Sugar Trust as the most outrageous monopolies of the day. They make enormous profits and give their patrons little or nothing in return in proportion.[79]

Senator Sherman gives George M. Pullman a certificate of character so infamous that the government proposes to clip his claws and restrain his rapacity. He is probably the first plutocrat made rich by plundering employees and the traveling public to be subjected to investigation and punishment for his crimes, and yet this rogue receives the aid of railroad managers, who form an alliance with him that they may perpetuate his piracies and reap a percentage of the plunder.

This fact brings into view the question of sympathy on the part of labor organizations for the oppressed and robbed Pullman employees.

This sympathetic feeling has had much to do in creating present conditions. This purpose of workingmen to aid their fellow toilers when in trouble, a trait of human nature worthy of the highest eulogy, is almost universally denounced by the press of the country, while the action of railroad managers is commended. Such exhibitions of high consideration of Pullman and his pals and brutal denunciation of workingmen who have by words and deeds shown sympathy for the Pullman employees, is a feature of the situation which has tended to aggravate conditions. The men who sympathize with their fellow men in distress are those who are animated by the spirit of Christ, and those who denounce them and malign them for such exhibitions of brotherly feeling, without which the world would be transformed as if by Jehovah's decree into a hell, are the Pharisees, the canting hypocrites, who "devour widows' houses," and for a "pretense, make long prayers," and who, therefore, as Christ said, are entitled to "special damnation."[80] These "whited sepulchers,"[81] these plutocrats and their sycophantic parasites—fleas in the hair of the Pullman dog—do not complain of sympathy when one corporation or a dozen corporations combine with the Pullman corporation and express their profound sympathy for Pullman, though they see the four thousand victims of his rapacity reduced to suffering.

We do not write of the situation to approve or to extenuate violence. We deplore such incidents of strikes. The *Locomotive Firemen's Magazine* has never, since it passed under our control, applauded a wrong. It has been our purpose to enthrone and uphold the right. But there has never been a strike of any notable proportion that deeds of violence, more or less deplorable, have not occurred. Why? Is it because men are depraved? Is it because men are brutified? By no means. Admitting that a strike is war presupposes resisting forces—power confronted by power. Strikes are always based upon a principle; exceptions confirm the rule. Labor demands fair wages; it strikes against oppression, poverty, squalor, degradation, and all the numberless woes that oppression, injustice, and tyranny inflicts. The enemies of labor, those who oppose the workingmen, are those who rob them, and the conscienceless gang of boot-lickers who hope to profit in some way by their fealty to power. In good old colony times, when the king imposed the tea tax, brave men, disguised, boarded a ship loaded with tea and threw the entire cargo overboard. The king and his Tories protested, and out of such acts of heroic defiance came the Revolutionary War, and from out of the war came the American republic. Where labor has triumphed in a strike society has always been benefited, and where the strike was lost society has always been the loser. Why? Because society is profoundly interested in the preservation of manhood, independence, and prosperity of the masses, while plutocrats, governed only by their greed, look only to their own interests, which they hold are promoted by the degradation of labor, because with that degradation wages go down and their piracies become the more profitable.

Under such circumstances it is not only not strange but natural that in the contention for supremacy by the forces of right and the forces of the wrong, deeds of violence should sometimes occur. It is human nature—it is history, and history will repeat itself until the day of darkness comes for our land, when plutocrats are supreme, or think themselves supreme. Before an amazed country, the preliminary acts of a mighty tragedy are being acted, and it were well to let the curtain fall.

The condition of the country is becoming hourly more momentous. The camps are all astir, where drums beat the long roll and the bugles call to arms. The president of the United States, the commander in chief of the army and the navy, is concentrating his battalions in various places. When a semi-savage queen had been dethroned in the interest of good government and of civilization, the president became so profoundly stirred that he sent a private commissioner to feel the pulse of the old queen and report to him how matters stood; but when four thousand Pullman employees were being ground to dust between corporation millstones, the commander in chief goes a-fishing, and at the call of courts concentrates soldiers of his standing army, à la tsar, at various points with the orders to fertilize American soil with the blood of American workingmen. As we write, the work of bloodletting has begun, and the street gutters of Chicago are running red with blood.[82]

The situation is one of terrible significance. The country is alarmed. More than one-half of the continent is involved, and the army of the idle is increasing. George M. Pullman's greed, depravity, and despotism, aided by the alliance of railroad managers, have brought about conditions of peril from the contemplation of which bold men turn away.

As we conclude the article, it must be said that the situation is full of premonitions that the worst has not been reached. There are no encouraging symptoms. The outlook is in all directions disheartening. Around the horizon and overhead naught but storm clouds meets the vision. The vivid flash of the lightnings of anger accompanied by the sullen, deep-toned mutterings of human voices mingled with the explosions of powder bode only evil. But, regardless of the outcome, it will be written that George M. Pullman and his confederate despoilers of labor were responsible.

Statement to the Press While Awaiting Release on Bail in Chicago[†]

July 10, 1894

We have been placed under arrest to answer to an indictment found against us by the federal grand jury, in which we are accused of conspiracy to commit and of committing offenses against the United States by obstructing and interrupting the mails of the country.[83] Our bail has been fixed at $10,000. Since I have been brought here I have been informed officers of the court have gone to our headquarters in the Ashland block and taken my personal correspondence and some of the records of the ARU. I do not know by what right this act has been committed. It seems to me to be an infamous outrage.

Not only did they take my personal effects and papers, but carried with them my unopened mail. I have never heard of that before in this country. In Russia, and not out of that country, have such things been done. It seems like the act of the tsar of Russia instead of the act of a free country. The seizure was made by an officer of the court and a post office official. I am not running a lottery and cannot understand under what laws the post office authorities are a party to the seizure of my private mail. It is an outrage, and you call this a free country. It seems to me not to be compatible with the stars and stripes. It is no longer a question of right in this country, but a question of force, and absolute force at that.

[†]   Wire service report, as published in *Lincoln Journal Star*, vol. 13, no. 246 (July 11, 1894), 8.

Proposal to the General Managers' Association from the Board of Directors of the ARU[†]

July 12, 1894

Chicago, July 12, [1894]

To the Railway Managers

Gentlemen:—

The existing troubles growing out of the Pullman strike having assumed continental proportions, and there being no indication of relief from the widespread business demoralization and distress incident thereto, the railway employees, through the board of directors of the American Railway Union, respectfully make the following proposition as a basis of settlement:

They agree to return to work in a body at once, provided they shall be restored to their former positions without prejudice, except in cases, if any there be, where they have been convicted of crime.[84]

This proposition looking to an immediate settlement of the existing strike on all lines of railway is inspired solely by a purpose to subserve the public good. The strike, small and comparatively unimportant in its inception, has extended in every direction until now it involves or threatens not only every public interest, but the peace, security, and prosperity of our common country. The contest has waged fiercely. It has extended far beyond the limits of interests originally involved, and has laid hold of a vast variety of industries and enterprises in no wise responsible for the differences and disagreements that led to the trouble. Factory, mill, mine, and shop have been silenced, widespread demoralization has sway. The interests of multiplied thousands of innocent people are suffering. The common welfare is seriously menaced. The public peace and tranquility are imperiled. Grave apprehensions for the future prevail.

This being true, and the statement will not be controverted, we conceive it to be our duty as citizens, and as men, to make extraordinary efforts to end the

†   Published in *In the Circuit Court of the United States, Northern District of Illinois: United States of America, Complainant, vs. Eugene V. Debs et al., Respondents: Proceedings on Information for Attachment of Contempt.* Chicago: 1894; 102–103.

existing strike and avert approaching calamities whose shadows are even now upon us. If ended now the contest, however serious in its consequences, will not have been in vain. Sacrifices have been made, but they will have their compensations. Indeed, if lessons shall be taught by the experience, the troubles now so widely spread will prove a blessing of inestimable value in the months and years to come.

The difference that led up to the present complications need not be discussed. At this supreme juncture every consideration of duty and patriotism demands that a remedy for existing troubles be found and applied. The employees propose to do their part by meeting their employers halfway. Let it be stated that they do not impose any condition of settlement except that they be returned to their former positions. They do not ask the recognition of their organization, or of any organization.

Believing this proposition to be fair, reasonable, and just, it is respectfully submitted with the belief that its acceptance will result in the prompt resumption of traffic, the revival of industry, and the restoration of peace and order.

Respectfully,
Eugene V. Debs, President,
G. W. Howard, Vice President,
Sylvester Keliher, Secretary,
American Railway Union

Correspondence with P. M. Arthur, Chief Engineer of the B of LE†

July 14, 1894

---

(1) Debs to Arthur, July 14, 1894

The executive committee of the American Railway Union authorized President Debs to send the following dispatch to Chief Arthur, of the Brotherhood of Locomotive Engineers, Cleveland, Ohio:

Chicago, July 14

The newspapers quote you as having issued an official order to your members requiring them to work with scab firemen, or anyone the companies may employ. It is also reported to us, on what seems reliable authority, that you are issuing letters of recommendation to engineers for the purpose of filling positions vacated by the strikers. In other words, that you are supplying scabs to take the places of striking engineers. We desire to do you no injustice, but wish to be advised of the facts in the case. We are now making history, and do not wish to put any man on record improperly. An early answer will much oblige.

By order of the board of directors, American Railway Union,

E. V. Debs

℘

(2) Arthur to Debs, July 14, 1894

Cleveland, O., July 14

To Eugene V. Debs, President, ARU, Chicago:—

I have advised the members of the Brotherhood of Locomotive Engineers, when called upon, to attend strictly to their own business as engineers, and be ready to run their engines whenever it could be done with safety, regardless of whom the companies employed to fire the engines. I have not issued any letters

---

† Published as part of the article "Obligation vs. Amalgamation" in *Locomotive Engineer's Monthly Journal*, vol. 28, no. 8 (August 1894), 741. Not included in J. Robert Constantine's three-volume collection of Debs's letters.

of recommendation for members of the B of LE to take the places of strikers. I have advised members of the B of LE that they were at liberty to take the places of any of the members of the Brotherhood who quit contrary to the laws of the Brotherhood, but not to take the places of any of the members of the American Railway Union who had quit by order of that organization.

P. M. Arthur

Brothers and Friends, the ARU Asks the Helping Hand[†]

July 15, 1894

In the prolonged contest now on between corporate greed and tyranny on one hand and all labor on the other, fortune placed the ARU in the place of honor—in the front rank.[85] Backed by the endorsement of unified labor, it must not be allowed to fail. It is your fight as well as ours.

Our modest dues, owing to enormous membership, were fixed to meet running expenses and meet ordinary exigencies. But the long drawn-out contest, involving necessarily constant calls on the reserve fund, has pushed us financially to a point that we must call on our reserve lines and all true friends of liberty and justice for support. The ARU needs money, needs it badly and at once. What can you do, brothers? If you can help us, remit to Sylvester Keliher, Secretary ARU, 421 Ashland Block, Chicago, Illinois. Someday when any of our sister organizations have to bear the brunt, call on us with a certainty of reciprocation.

Fraternally submitted to all of our friends and sympathizers.

For the American Railway Union,
Eugene V. Debs, *President*
Sylvester Keliher, *Secretary*

---

†   Published in the *Railway Times*, vol. 1, no. 14 (July 15, 1894), 1.

Statement to the Press from Cook County Jail[†]
July 17, 1894

Well, this means a few days of rest and quiet at least.[86] I have not had much rest for over a month and I am badly in need of it.

No, sir, we shall not give bonds. Our bonds are $3,000 each, but we would not give bonds if they were five cents each.

We are not posing as martyrs, neither do we ask for sympathy. All I have to say about our arrest today is that matters have come to that point in this free country when it is held to be a crime to advise a man what to do when he seeks your advice. We are guilty of no crime unless the simple expression of an opinion is a crime. We are not responsible for this strike. Pullman is responsible for it.

To the American Public[‡]
July 22, 1894

Headquarters, American Railway Union,
Cook County Jail, Chicago,
July 22 [1894]

To the American Public:—

It is almost universally conceded that the Pullman Company, through oft-repeated reductions of wages, excessive rents, and many other causes, has grievously wronged its employees, and, whatever may be said about the great railway strike which resulted in consequence of such grievances, the arbitrary refusal of said

---

†   Published as "Debs Goes to Jail" in *Indiana State Sentinel,* July 25, 1894, 6.

‡   As published in *In the Circuit Court of the United States, Northern District of Illinois: United States of America, Complainant, vs. Eugene V. Debs et al., Respondents, Before Honorable William A. Woods, Circuit Judge, etc.: Proceedings on Information for Attachment for Contempt.* Chicago: Bernard & Hornstein, Printers, n.d. (1894), 50–52.

Pullman Company to submit to arbitration in any form (even to decide the question if there was anything to arbitrate) is proof positive that said company had no faith in the justice of its cause and fears the disclosures that are certain to result from an honest investigation, and in view of the heavy loss entailed upon the country, such obstinacy on the part of the Pullman Company is deserving of the severest condemnation.

The Pullman Company makes the plea that it is asked of them that they shall run their works at a loss. The statement is absolutely false. What was asked was arbitration, and this would have resulted in even-handed justice. The Pullman Company has robbed its employees, and an investigation would have disclosed a state of affairs which would have horrified the nation. This is why arbitration was refused. It is notoriously true that the Pullman Company pays its conductors and porters such paltry wages that they are obliged to depend upon the public to support them. Yes, this rich and powerful corporation virtually compels the public to pay the wages of its sleeping-car employees, and, this notwithstanding, extortionate rates are charged for sleeping-car accommodations.

We propose that the Pullman Company shall be brought to justice, and this in a way that will not necessitate a strike with its attendant ills. It may be suggested that this should have been thought of before the great strike was inaugurated. In that case little, if any, attention would have been paid to the appeal we are about to make. As one of the results of the strike the company is aroused, and any proper appeal will command attention. The Pullman Company [is] still defiant, and as cruel to its former employees as it is indifferent to the public weal. It is determined to starve its employees into submission. As remorseless as a man-eating tiger, it waits complacently until their last penny is gone, and they are thus forced to crawl back into their heartless, oppressive employ. The spectacle is well calculated to make men and angels shudder.

Shall the Pullman Company have the support of the public in carrying out this hellish policy? Shall the public be a party to the starvation and degradation of the more than four thousand employees, men and women, whose only crime is that they ask living wages? We believe—indeed, we know—what the answer will be. We have faith in the American people. They uphold justice; they love fair play; and now in the name of justice and fair play we appeal to the great American public, to every good man and every good woman, not to ride in a Pullman car until the Pullman Company does justice to its employees. Let the cars run absolutely empty. No friend of labor, no friend of humanity would occupy a seat or berth in a Pullman car. Let this policy be inaugurated, and we will then see how long the railroad companies will be bound by their contracts, as they have induced the public to believe, to haul Pullman cars.

We propose to continue this strike against the Pullman Company through good and evil report and without regard to consequences until justice shall be done. There will be no surrender. We will use every available and lawful means to press the contest. Dungeons shall not daunt us. The struggle is for humanity and against the most cruel tyranny, and unless we are deaf to every impulse of mercy and fellow feeling, must be crowned with success.

Think of the Pullman employees as your own sisters, brothers, children. If you have any doubt as to the outrages of which they have been the victims, we refer you to the Rev. W. H. Carwardine,[87] Pullman, Illinois, a gentleman of the highest character and standing who has long been a close student of the conditions at Pullman and is able to speak from personal observation and experience.

Persons desiring to contribute money or supplies to Pullman employees will please forward same to David V. Gladman, treasurer, Pullman, Illinois.

It is requested that all papers throughout the land favorable to labor, to justice, to humanity, copy this statement in full and keep it standing as long as possible.

Earnestly appealing to the great public to aid us in this unequal contest between a rich, powerful, arrogant, and defiant corporation and its famishing, half-clad employees, and relying with implicit faith upon the powerful triumph of the right, we subscribe ourselves,

Very respectfully yours,

Eugene V. Debs, President
George W. Howard, Vice President
Sylvester Keliher, Secretary
L. W. Rogers, Editor, Railway Times

Labor Strikes and Their Lessons[†]

Late July 1894

The times in which we live demand plain, straightforward, heroic talk; subterfuge is cowardice. There should be no evasions, no concealments, no masks, no idol worship, no spectacular parade of effete theories of government, no advocacy of Russian tactics in dealing with serfs, and no Sultanic or Satanic practices in determining the rights of the workingmen.

Fortunately, or otherwise, as men view the subject, we live at a time when the "labor problem" is before the country for debate and solution. Those who enter the argumentative arena must come equipped with arguments based upon cause, with logic keen as a Damascus blade and as penetrating and as quieting as a federal bullet or bayonet.

The labor problem is the problem of problems now before the country. In another publication I took occasion to say that the labor problem involves the consideration of a number of problems, but they all go to make up the one problem as certainly as that air is composed of oxygen, nitrogen, and carbon. Suppose the subject for discussion be taxation? All taxes are paid by labor. Suppose it be revenue? All revenues are derived from labor. Suppose it be wealth? All wealth is the creation of labor. Is the question building cities? Only labor makes them possible. Is it clearing away the wilderness? They would remain as God planted them but for labor. Is it a question of food? Famine would be universal only for labor. But for labor no keel would cleave the waves nor locomotives speed along their iron tracks. The warehouses would stand empty, factories would be silent, ships and docks would rot, cities would tumble down, and universal ruin would prevail. These are economic truths, like the azoic rocks upon which the world is built; they are the verities upon which civilization, progress, and the hopes of the world are based.

In this connection I quote the language of Hon. Stephen B. Elkins,[88] late secretary of war, who, referring to labor agitation at the time, said:

[†]   Published in John Swinton, *Striking for Life: Labor's Side of the Labor Question: The Right of the Workingman to a Fair Living* (New York: Western W. Wilson, 1894), 315–326. This book was reissued as *A Momentous Question: The Respective Attitudes of Labor and Capital* (Philadelphia: Keller Publishing Co., 1895). Swinton signs the foreword of this book "July 1894," thereby dating this contribution.

I am, with others, to some extent, an employer of labor. I take a deep interest in the labor question. To my mind it rises in importance above all others. * * * The question presented by the present labor agitation is both industrial and social, and concerns not the capitalist nor the wage-receiver exclusively, nor the one more than the other, but the whole body of society and the state itself. It involves a great principle, in the presence of which individual interests become insignificant. No question more serious or of graver importance ever came before the American people, and upon its right settlement may not only depend the future of society, but ultimately the fate of the great republic. [89]

I reproduce the language of Mr. Elkins to demonstrate the invulnerability of the proposition that the labor problem, in its present importance and far-reaching influences, towers above all other problems; that in its settlement, if justice hold sway, the "gates of hell" will not prevail against the "great republic," but if, in the solution of the labor problem, justice is bribed or bludgeoned into silence by the weapons of rapacity, and spoliation forever wielded for the discomfiture of labor, ultimate consequences will not be contemplated with composure.

The lessons taught by strikes are to be studied with reference to causes as well as effect, if the purpose in view is to find remedies for the ceaseless unrest in the ranks of labor, culminating all too often, perhaps, in strikes.

Every strike of workingmen of which the public has taken cognizance has had its origin in wrongs and rank injustice; but, if we are to believe the common press reports, strikes result from pernicious influences exerted by "labor agitators," "walking delegates," men of small capacities devoted to making mischief, and that but for them labor would be contented and prosperous. Manifestly, such assumptions are false, manufactured for base purposes, and are therefore unworthy of more consideration than attaches to puerile mendacity; and yet it will not be gainsaid that such utterances, designed to obscure the truth, have been potential in poisoning the public mind and in bringing about conditions which have indefinitely increased the burdens and ills which have afflicted labor to an extent that in many instances defies exaggeration.

Sane men, seeking for the truth, whether identified with labor organizations or standing aloof from them—men interested in the public welfare—men whose incomes are not dependent upon the spoliation of wage earners, will hesitate long before accepting as conclusive the *ex parte* arraignment of labor agitators as the cause of strikes. They will reason that the widespread unrest everywhere prevailing in the ranks of labor must, of necessity, have a more logical cause; that agitation is but an expression of grievances which, having been borne to the limit of endurance, are forced at last upon public attention, the *dernier ressort*[90] often being the strike, and when it comes it has its lessons, which communities, states, and nations are required to study. To dismiss them with a sneer as the mere effervescence of agitators, the froth of fanatics, the vagaries of cranks no longer answers the demand. The lessons which strikes force upon public attention are of such a serious character that at last the government of the United States has determined to delve for causes, to find the poisoned fountains from which labor grievances flow, at least in one instance, in which the strike has stirred the nation to profounder depths than has hitherto been credited to any labor upheaval.

Taking into consideration my environments, reticence with regard to the great strike of the American Railway Union—sometimes spoken of as the "Pullman strike"—might in some quarters be deemed a virtue, but as it has taught the nation a mighty lesson I know of no reason why I may not be heard upon the subject.

I do not use these pages for self-defense. I neither seek nor crave notoriety. I am neither passive nor defiant. With convictions intact and manhood unabashed, I view the past of my life with composure and await developments unmoved.

I write of the lessons of the strike, their immediate influence, with such reflections relating to the future as, reasoning from cause to effect, may suggest. If we as a nation are to have an era of justice to labor, in which the alarm bells of strikes are to be heard no more, no one will hail the advent of peace and goodwill with more enthusiasm than myself. But I do not believe, nor do I think it can be shown, that strikes have been an unmixed evil to labor, to society, or to the state.

The tongue of history does not proclaim that strikes have been uniformly or mainly abortive. On the contrary, history teaches that much, great, and permanent good has resulted from strikes. The time is largely within the memory of men now living when employers exacted *12, 14,* and, in some instances, *16* hours as a day's work. Men demanded a reduction of hours of toil, but the demand was conceded only after years of struggle, accompanied with strikes and attended with many sacrifices incident to resistance, such as idleness and want. But the men were heroic, patient, and persistent, and though they suffered in contending for a principle embodying right and justice, they bequeathed to American workingmen a ten-hour day—indeed, a nine-hour day—rescuing from the grasp of employers at least five hours a day for rest, for recuperation, for home, for mental and physical improvement, and society is all the better for the victory won by the time-strikes of workingmen. The inordinate greed, the mercenary instinct of human nature were overcome by strikes oft repeated, and, though sometimes lost, were ultimately successful. Nor has the demand for a still less number of hours for a day's work ceased.

There are in the field a host of labor agitators who are demanding that eight hours shall constitute a day's work. The federal government, in response to agitation, has yielded to the demand. States have passed eight-hour laws with *provisos* which practically nullify contemplated benefits, but the work of agitation and education proceeds. There have been eight-hour strikes attended with sacrifices and inconveniences, idleness, and the ills which idleness entails, but the work goes bravely on and victory is in sight.

In this contention for a reduction of hours it is admitted that society is largely the beneficiary, because every movement which emancipates men from mental and physical exhaustion inures to the welfare of the homes of working-men, and therefore to the well-being of the state.

As a general proposition, I think the statement will not be seriously questioned that a large majority of the strikes have had their origin in disagreements relating to wages, nor do I hesitate to affirm that the general policy of employers has been to secure the largest possible number of hours for a day's work at the least possible rate of wages. I refer to the rule—that there are notable exceptions goes without the saying, and these exceptions students of labor questions grasp with eagerness and give them the widest possible publicity, because they serve as an exemplification of what may be accomplished when men who employ labor and capital are animated by a desire to deal justly and not avail themselves of conditions to make themselves rapidly rich by methods which bear a striking resemblance to piracy.

Omitting many causes of strikes, which will readily occur to the minds of those at all familiar with labor troubles, I repeat that the bedrock cause of the strikes which have from time to time aroused public attention has been wages; and if there are those who deny the affirmation, they will find it difficult to supply proof to maintain their position, and therefore the lessons taught by strikes are eminently and preeminently of an economic character. They relate to the well-being of a vast number of men, currently estimated at 17 million. If they are underpaid, if they are the victims of injustice, if of the wealth they create they do not receive such a share as enables them to live above the level of squalor and remote from the boundary lines of degradation, in consequence of which they strike for better conditions, public opinion should be concentrated more upon the causes and less upon the effects of the strike, because upon the removal of the cause rests the only hope for peace, and such would be the case if public opinion were not largely manufactured by agencies which wealth, and not weal, creates and controls.

In the United States there are reasons for maintaining that the wage-question has more significance and importance than in any other country, growing out of the fact that the wage earners of the United States are bona fide citizens, clothed with all the prerogatives of citizenship. They constitute a part, and a very large and important part, of "we, the people." They are not opposed to the government, to its laws, nor to its flag. They are not anarchists, and though badgered and buffeted as members of the great army of labor, they are, nevertheless, by constitution and statute, sovereign citizens, and when they strike it is that their food, clothing, and shelter may be such as become American citizens; and this lesson is always taught when they strike for rights, the denial of which deprives them of liberty, of the means of pursuing happiness, and of life itself; since when wages will not sustain life, mendicancy and vagabondism, even worse than death, ensue. The idea is fully expressed in the following lines by an unknown author:

> Know, autocrats, aristocrats!
>   All men with sounding titles!
> Whose hands have wrung with demon's grasp
>   The pauper's shrunken vitals—
>   *Man* has awakened in his might,
>   He knows the wrong, he knows the right!
>   *We* say it! *We* the people!
>
> There was a time when ignorance
>   Fell with a leaden weight
> Upon "the mass"—ye call'd it thus—
>   The mass felt then but hate!
>   But now we wake to know our might.
>   We know the wrong, we know the right!
>   *We* say it! *We* the people!
>
>   *   *   *
>
> God did not say that some should starve
>   While others cloy with pleasures;
> He did not constitute a class,
>   The keepers of his treasures!
>   It has seem'd thus before, but light
>   Has shown the burden'd what is right!
>   *We* say it! *We* the people!

He never said that any man
   Was born to rule another.
But told us that we each should treat
   Our fellow as our brother.
      And now, awakening in our might,
      We mean to have it so—'tis right!
        We say it! *We* the people![91]

There are a number of lessons taught by the strike which the obstinacy of the Pullman Palace Car Company forced upon its employees and upon the country. To grasp them in their entirety is not an easy task; to catalog and classify them in a way to enable the general reader to realize to the fullest extent the wrong and injustice they teach demands a process of analytic and synthetic discussion for which I shall not ask space.

On the one hand, a great corporation, rich to plethora, rioting in luxuries, plutocratic, proud, and powerful, and yet mean and mercenary to an extent that compels hyperbole to sit dumb in the presence of piracies decked out in the robes of paternalism and philanthropy—a corporation adept in chicane and duplicity reduced to a science—in possession of land, habitations, water, light and fuel, mills and machinery, thus controlling the lives and liberties of at least 25,000 human beings, men, women, and children, becomes an object lesson which the nation is now required to study.

On the other hand is seen an object lesson of a different type. It is not a picture of houses and lands, lawns and landscape, "sacred grass," violets and rose trees, sparkling fountains and singing birds, and an atmosphere burdened with the aroma of flowers, but of human beings living amidst such surroundings and toiling for a pittance doled out to them by their employers—as a Heber[92] might say: "Where every prospect pleases," and only man is wretched, where sunken eyes and hollow cheeks speak of poniard-pointed hunger pangs, where childhood has lost its joyousness and motherhood its hopes, and where strong men bow like reeds before tempests which drive them to despair.

As an object lesson, the condition of the Pullman employees before the strike is worthy of serious consideration. Unable to shelter themselves, unable to feed themselves, unable to clothe themselves, the Pullman employees were made to realize their hapless and helpless condition, where the power on the throne ordered all their ways and reduced them to a point of destitution which required them to sit upon their coffins and contemplate a lingering death by starvation. It is assumed that labor agitators brought about the Pullman strike. Is it not, on the contrary, the fact that the Pullman employees, having been despoiled to the limit of endurance, by the exercise of their volition decided to strike? And that too upon the hypothesis that, whatever might happen, their condition could not be made worse. This being the fact, verified by overwhelming testimony, does it not become the public, the courts, and the government, in studying the lessons of the strike, to probe for causes, and then determine if the effects were not as logical as in any case of cause and effect within the entire domain of human affairs?

The cause of the strike was brazen heartlessness, cruelties that touched the vitals of innocent toilers untainted by crime, obedient to law, seeking to maintain their families by their work, and striking only when robbed by processes as relentless as footpadism. The cause being cruelty—a crime as infamous as ever made a human heart its hiding place, a crime that makes its perpetrator a monster while it blasts the hopes of its victims—ought to be productive of resistance, and such resistance ought to command the approval of every honest patriotic American.

The great lesson of the Pullman strike is found in the fact that it arouses widespread sympathy. This fellow feeling for the woes of others—this desire to help the unfortunate; this exhibition of a divine principle, which makes the declaration plausible that "man was made a little lower than God," and without which man would rank lower than the devil by several degrees—should be accepted as at once the hope of civilization and the supreme glory of manhood. And yet this exhibition of sympathy aroused by the Pullman strike is harped upon by press and pulpit as the one atrocious feature of the strike. Epithets, calumny, denunciation in every form that malice or mendacity could invent have been poured forth in a vitriol tide to scathe those who advocated and practiced the Christ-like virtue of sympathy. The crime of the American Railway Union was the practical exhibition of sympathy for the Pullman employees. Humanity and Christianity, undebauched and unperverted, are forever pleading for sympathy for the poor and the oppressed. In all the tomes of civilized literature those who search for expressions and periods indicative of man's primal innocence, of hope for his deliverance from base desires, his emancipation from vice, inherited or acquired, of faith in an eternity of happiness, find them embodied in emanations flowing from sympathetic souls that have been loyal to God, to truth, and to justice; true to convictions, true to duty, however fierce the ordeal their fidelity may have required them to endure.

In studying this lesson of the Pullman strike, men, sturdy men, who know the right and dare maintain the right, have had occasion to note to what an extent the love of "filthy lucre" has debauched the press of the country—not all of it—no, for in all of the cities of our boasted civilization, our marts of money and trade, there have been publications that could be neither intimidated nor debauched. Invective, scurrility, and maledictions have done their utmost, and yet those courageous advocates of the right ceaselessly thunder into the public ear the dangers of despotism, warnings which will be remembered and treasured all the more certainly if the passing cyclone of passion shall have obliterated for a time the landmarks of liberty, and by arbitrary methods shall have secured that dangerous peace which comes to nations in the red track of bullets and bayonets, or is found behind the iron doors and bars of bastilles.

The strikes, while they have taught the country that sympathy remains in the breasts of thousands, have impressed upon all the fact that others prefer to nurse selfishness as cold as ice, and hate as hot as old Nebuchadnezzar's fiery furnace[93] and as relentless as death; and, by a strange perversion of mind and morals, there are those who predict national health, happiness, and prosperity from those who imperil the security and peace of the state by their rapacity, in alliance with the victims of their spoliations, who, at least, debased to the level of coolies and peons, accept degradation without resistance.

But there is a lesson taught by the Pullman strike, the study of which affords a glimmer of hope and satisfaction. It has taught the nation to place an honest estimate upon George M. Pullman. It has dragged the wrecker of homes and hopes from luxurious abode and sentenced him to the pillory for life, where he will feel the pelting storms of the scorn of men, women, and children who have been the victims of his villainy.

Again, the lesson taught by the Pullman strike has forced upon the chief magistrate of the Republic the fact that there is a pressing necessity for investigation; that labor demands other than military methods to mold its destiny. It has taught the nation that American workingmen ought not to be subjected to Russian methods, unless it has been determined to reduce them to serfs and their homes to huts and lairs. The fact that a commission has been appointed, clothed with federal power, to investigate the causes leading to the Pullman strike, is encouraging; and if, peradventure, such results should be obtained as shall ultimately elevate labor and emancipate workingmen from corporation slavery, and permit them to rejoice in all the fruitions of liberty, then, in that case, history will record the fact, regardless of present verdicts, that in the organization of the American Railway Union there was a "divinity that shaped its ends," and an inscrutable Providence directing its acts. Should such be the verdict, such the outcome, those who may be called upon to suffer for the good they have accomplished will be consoled and strengthened by the reflection that, innocent of riot, rapine, and blood, they were instrumental, in alliance with other forces, in ushering in an era when employer and employ shall learn war no more; when the last bullet and bayonet, sent upon their mission of death, have drawn from the hearts of oppressed workingmen their last libation to redden the altars of American liberty.

A Military Era[†]

August 1894

Away back, some six or seven hundred years before the dawn of the Christian era, Isaiah, the prophet, with a prophet's vision, saw, or thought he saw, a time when the nations would "beat their swords into plowshares, and their spears into pruning hooks," when "nation would not lift up sword against nation," and when they would "learn war no more,"[94] and some six hundred years after Isaiah's prophetic words Christ was born, and the angels filled the world with rapture when they sang, "Glory to God in the highest, and on earth peace, good will toward men."[95] It would scarcely be becoming to so much as intimate that Isaiah was the victim of hallucination, but so far, though 24 centuries have come and gone since he saw the disappearance of swords and spears, the nations are still learning war, and if here and there swords have been transformed into plowshares and spears into pruning hooks, it has been because more effective death-dealing weapons have been available, and instead of "on earth peace," as the angels proclaimed, the war spirit has dominated the world, and never more completely than at present. Indeed, the present may very properly be regarded as a military era.

We have no desire to write of the military establishments of European nations—all Christians except a handful of Turks, and all trusting to guns instead of gospel, to powder rather than to prayer to carry forward our Christian civilization. We are particularly interested in the military affairs of the United States. True, as a nation, in our infancy we were rocked in a war cradle, and the music of the nursery was supplied by fife and drum, the scream of bullets, and the bursting of bombs. There were blood and carnage all the way from

†   Published in *Locomotive Firemen's Magazine,* vol. 18, no. 8 (August 1894), 764–765.

Boston to Charleston. There was a Continental army with Washington at its head, and yet when the war was over and England retired from the fray, the Continental army disappeared as if by enchantment. There was no war spirit in time of peace, because peace hath her victories as renowned as war, indeed, far more renowned. Again, in 1812–15, when troops were required, the people, who are the government, supplied them, and when peace was declared, everything bearing the appearance of war vanished. Again, in 1860–65, the people responded, saved the union, and this done, soldiers became citizens.

Standing armies are a menace to liberty, hence, as a nation, we do not want one, and will not tolerate such a machine to aid the schemes of heartless, ambitious men. But at this particular juncture ceaseless efforts are made to infuse the American people with what is called a "war spirit." True, there is no war, nor a probability of war, but there are thousands, soft-shelled lads, dudes, and donkeys, who are persuaded by men of small caliber who are ambitious to wear swords and parade for the delectation of hoodlums, to enlist in what they call the "home guard," the "state legion." This would be innocent enough were it not for the fact that these military nincompoops are the creatures of designing men, corporation plutocrats and mine owners who, by the aid of high state officials, can use the troops to perpetuate such outrages as their greed may require.

The press, as is usual, comes to the rescue and advocates more troops, better equipments, better guns with longer range, that death may be more certain. They say the times demand greater military power, but a military power is autocratic, it is despotic, cruel, heartless, murderous, bloody, and the only power which can reduce freemen to slaves. Why is there such a clamor for the establishment of such a power in the United States of America? Where are the enemies of our "God-favored country?" Who are these enemies? What is their character? What are their implements of warfare? These are pertinent questions. They go to the marrow of conditions. They sink down into the soul of the nation like lead in still waters. What answers are made to these interrogatories? They come from every direction, north and south, east and west, from center to circumference. The enemies to be killed by the military power are the workingmen of the country. They are found in our mines. They dig coal, iron, lead, zinc, quicksilver, copper, silver, and gold. The enemies of the country are found at the blazing, roaring forge.

They are in all the factories where wheels move by steam power or water power; they are along all of the 500,000 miles of land and water transportation; peaceful, patient, industrious, they constitute the power that moves the world.

Their implements of warfare are the pick, the hammer, the engine, the ten thousand and one tools with which workingmen build all the monuments that mark the country's progress and glorify our civilization. To subjugate such enemies is the high ambition of the plutocrats who clamor for troops. Steadily by degrees these enemies are being subjugated by the standing armies of states and of the nation. The dance of death and degradation goes merrily on. The sublime purpose of the war spirit now sought to be aroused is the reduction of the wages of workingmen and working women. To reduce wages builds up fortunes on the one hand, and on the other hand scoops out a deeper degradation for the wretched victims of the military power. The work is going bravely on. Every year the law forges fresh manacles for labor, and now the suggestion is that additional power shall be given the military arm; that it shall be larger and have a more devilish grasp; that it shall be stronger that it may strike a more death-dealing blow. To increase the military power, to whom do the plutocrats and their fawning, lickspittle press propose to appeal? To workingmen—and "tell it not in Gath, publish it not in the streets of Askelon,"[96] these plutocrats and their aiders and abettors expect to recruit their armies from the ranks of workingmen. Since time began such an insult was never offered free men. And now the question arises, how do workingmen treat the unspeakable insolence and indignity? To hear the reply is enough to make all the pagan gods retire from the business, enough to make a brass dog tuck its tail between its legs and howl, for it is a fact that workingmen, black, white, and yellow fall into line in this military force and go forth to shoot workingmen whose crime is that they resist degradation.

The theory that ours is a "government of the people, by the people, and for the people," was once well founded. A change has come. We cling to the shadow, but the substance is disappearing. We have the shell, but a military serpent has about sucked its last remaining liberty-sustaining principle. The government is rapidly becoming a military despotism. Laws are made to enrich the few and enslave the many, and the military arm, already powerful, is to be made more potent to trample upon justice, crown and enthrone the wrong, bludgeon truth to silence, and exile right.

The crisis is here. It is possible for workingmen to aid their enemies by joining the military, or they may by their ballots make for themselves a destiny of freedom.

Legislation[†]

August 1894

It will be conceded, we assume that legislation is the means by which governments exist and are perpetuated: legislation, signifying lawmaking, a legislator is a lawmaker, one clothed with legal authority to make laws—hence absolute rulers are legislators, their decrees are laws. Absolutism in government has not been popular hitherto in the United States. We boast of a government by the people, we talk of the sovereignty of the citizen, and yet, whether a law is made by an autocrat, a congress, or a legislature matters little, it has precisely the same end in view and reaches it; by the autocrat, with terrible directness, by a limited monarchy and a democracy, by a more circuitous route, but in at least three objective points, results are the same. All the autocrat can do, or the extreme of his power, is to take (1) life, (2) liberty, and (3) property, and the mildest government on the face of the earth, regardless of name, can do and does the same things. We are not discussing processes, but results. In the instances cited, autocracy and democracy do precisely the same things. The case admits of neither sophism, technicality, nor special pleading: the facts are as stated, and in both cases the claim set up is the supremacy of law.

In the United States, the people discuss legislation. Here we have a free press and free speech; here, the people, excepting always office-holders, parasites, lickspittles, and all the fawning crew of bootlickers, are not afraid of officials, from a coroner who sits on a corpse to a president; the people have a fad that these officials are simply servants, not masters, and yet these servants (?) in Congress and legislatures enact laws as infamous as ever disgraced an autocracy. The machinery constructed by the government by the people crushes and grinds and kills and robs, just the same as a government by a tsar, sultan, or shah, as we have remarked, with a little more circumlocution, but ultimately reaching the same result.

Let it be understood that we are not defending autocracy, nor aristocracy, nor any other -ocracy, except democracy, the supreme will of the people, but it is nevertheless true that when legislation crushes an individual, it does not matter to him or her whether he or she is the victim of the decree of an autocrat or of a law enacted by a body chosen by the people. If the life of a man is taken,

---

† Published in *Locomotive Firemen's Magazine,* vol. 18, no. 8 (August 1894), 762–763.

what matters it to the victim who ordered his death? After the halter, the axe, or the bullet has done their work, subsequent proceedings no longer interest the victim, but between sentence and execution the condemned may, if he regards his sentence unjust, engage in very serious reflections, however unprofitable they may be. If the subject of an autocrat, having no voice in the government, he will not accuse himself of having had any agency whatever in bringing about his doom, and the same would be true if the despot had deprived him of his liberty or his property, having had no voice in shaping the laws under which he suffers, he could not reproach himself for any dereliction of duty, he simply had to submit in silence to death, slavery, and poverty as his master might choose. But in a government like ours, if by the operation of law calamities overtook and overwhelmed him, he could not submit without realizing that in some measure he had been the author of the misfortunes of which he complained. He had lived in a land where the people were the sovereigns, in a land where ballots determined everything, and if he voted for vicious men and continued to vote for them, he would be regarded in a measure, and a very large measure, the author of the calamities he bewailed, and would be entitled to precious little sympathy.

To this it has come. Legislation is largely accountable for the national ills which are now of such a formidable character as to excite universal alarm, and the people who have been choosing vicious representatives are primarily responsible for every vicious law upon the statute books; blinded by partisan fealty, the people have for years pursued a course which has at last produced a crop of bitter fruits, and the end is not yet to be seen. Men see the frowning cloud and the vivid flash of the lightning, and they hear the deep toned mutterings of the thunder, and when any suggestion is made by workingmen that a different class of representatives are required to enact wise and just laws, and to repeal vicious and odious statutes, a subsidized press and bribe-cursed and debauched men cry out, "politics, politics," as if there was some other way out of the darkness into the light, some other way from peril to safety other than politics, something superior to the ballot wielded by honest, conscientious men. But there is no other method of relief that comports with our system of government. If our liberties are to be maintained, if our institutions are to be perpetuated, it must be done by a free, untrammeled ballot, and men must be in politics if they vote at all, and when men can be persuaded to vote for honest men pledged to honest measures, plutocrats will cease to rob, will cease to have at their beck and call the armies of the states and of the nation to aid them in their piracies upon labor, and they will have a judiciary which, under ermined robes, will cease to hide an untold amount of infamy.

Probabilities and Possibilities[†]

August 1894

There was never a period in the history of labor when probabilities and possibilities were so entangled in men's minds as at present. The most astute are unable to map out a pathway to any goal, near or afar, and the problems which confront the most thoughtful are becoming every day more complex and stubborn.

Men write and reason only to increase confusion. Facts are so pliant that probabilities degenerate to possibilities and suddenly become improbabilities, if not impossibilities, when it is found necessary to change front, choose some new road, and pursue it until again confronted with obstacles which will not yield, and then things proceed while affairs grow worse by degrees and rapidly assume conditions which are admittedly full of peril.

What are the probabilities for the future of labor? Are they of a character warranting the conclusion that its condition will improve, or that it will be less prosperous than at present—in a word, become worse? Scanning the situation as a mariner surveys the skies, what probabilities are discovered? Are not all probabilities merged into possibilities? Do men say this or that is probable, or that it is possible? Take, for instance, the question of wages. What is probable? Is it likely that present rates of wages will be maintained? Is it presumed that wages will decline? Is it to be expected that wages will advance? In discussing such propositions, if probabilities are about equal, then they are contradictory and disappear to give place to possibilities or to chance, and everything is at sea—deep sea, where there are no soundings, or navigators of the labor ships are sailing amidst treacherous currents and perilous surroundings.

Discussing probabilities, we mention arbitration, sometimes thought to be a panacea for labor troubles, a desideratum, the one thing needful to take wrong from the throne and place it upon the scaffold. Arbitration is as old as the eternal hills. It is primal, has been in vogue since prehistoric men disagreed about flints and furs. Arbitration fills the bill sometimes. To arbitrate presupposes that one of the parties demands more than simple justice requires, and that concessions must be made by one party or both. There are advocates of arbitration who are so much in love with the theory that they would eliminate the voluntary feature and introduce compulsory, arbitrary arbitration,

---

[†]   Published in *Locomotive Firemen's Magazine*, vol. 18, no. 8 (August 1894), 765–768.

according to statute, which is not arbitration in fact, or as the term is generally understood, but rather a court to hear and decide arbitrarily, with penalties attached to enforce decisions. It goes for little, or for nothing at all, to contend that such arbitration settles the disputed points. To say that a settlement thus arrived at is better for labor is to intimate that labor needs a guardian created by law to take charge of its interests and determine what is best for it. And here the question arises, is it probable that working men will submit to such an arrangement and surrender their right to determine for themselves what methods shall be adopted to protect their interests? We think the probabilities are not in the direction of compulsory arbitration, though there is a possibility of such a thing. It would doubtless happen that a corporation would cut down wages to an extent that organized labor would revolt. In such a case the compulsory arbitration law would doubtless compel the aggrieved organized workingmen to submit to the reduction of wages or appeal to the arbitration law for redress.

Suppose the rate of wages was $1.25 per day, and the corporation cut it down to $1? Organized labor would seek to show that $1 a day was insufficient wages, but if the corporation would come in and show it could have all the men it wanted at that price, what would the arbitrators be likely to decide? Would they say the corporation should pay $1.25 a day, when the proof was that they could hire men to do their work for $1 a day? True, organized labor might show that the men offering to work for convict prices were *scabs*, but the corporation would insist they were men, capable to perform the labor required, in which case the arbitrators would be in a dilemma, and their decision, if it had any effect at all, would be the creation of a wage scale. Is it probable or even possible that workingmen will, by their votes, encourage such a scheme? That non-union men may favor such an arrangement, it is both possible and probable, but it ought not to be either probable nor possible for union workmen to place in the hands of any set of men the determination of wages, upon which their lives, their liberties, and their happiness depend. The probable ought to be that workingmen will not build scaffolds for their own immolation. Why should it be possible for a body of organized workingmen to place in the hands of one man the power to annul the will of a majority of their number when authoritatively expressed? Such a thing beggars all ideas of the probable and enthrones the wrong in human affairs, and places the right on the scaffold, which makes the most hopeful doubt, begets distrust where there should be confidence and the most courageous halt in their advance. This thing of conferring autocratic power and surrendering in advance ought to stand in the catalogue of possibilities. It ought to be classed with the impossibilities.

Federation of labor organizations has been for years the battle cry, and a federation that would proclaim labor invincible when contending against its foes is a possibility, just as it is possible for a time to come when the lion and the ox will eat straw together from the same stack, when the ox will forget that it has horns and the lion will cease using its paws, but to class such things as probabilities, or even possibilities smacks of hallucination. Why? Because in the present condition of what is called "human nature," the class rises superior to the cause, and each for all and all for each does not exercise sufficient sway to create a probability, nor even a possibility that any sort of a federation is at hand which will make an ironworker, for instance, the champion of the rights of a cigar maker, and thus on through the entire list of trades. These are glowing theories *ad infinitum* and *ad nauseum,* but when an emergency arises, men survey a desert where not even a cactus, nor a sprig of sage grass of the practical appears. Worse still, perhaps, federation is used just as the devil quotes scripture,[97] to beguile its votaries and make conditions worse. Federation is possible. We have it now, and have had it for years past and gone, and men who are at all thoughtful, in surveying the field and contemplating results, are reminded of the "barren fig tree" with an abundance of foliage and no fruit. Is it probable that this sort of federation is to go on forever? Certainly, it is possible. Men now, as in the past, are wedded to idols, and the difference between worshipping a stock or a stone and a form of federation that is inefficient is scarcely apparent.

Is it probable that something better will come? Is it possible for workingmen to suggest an improvement upon federation? We do not doubt it. We suggest consolidation of trades and callings. We mean one government, one constitution, one supreme law, one flag, one shibboleth— *"labor omnia vincit."* [98] With this consolidation labor organizations become invincible. Are there any precedents calculated to encourage and inspire confidence? Assuredly. On every page of authentic history there are examples of the conquering power of the consolidation of forces, and a government becomes contemptible in the eyes of all nations where it is either incapable or neglects to protect its humblest citizen against outrages perpetrated by any other sovereignty. Is it probable that labor will consolidate its forces, and thus make it possible to protect even one of its members against outrage?

The verdict of the world, long since rendered, is that a nation never expands to greater or sublimer proportions than when, with its consolidated power, it redresses the wrongs inflicted upon *one* of its citizens, and an example or two furnished by the United States of America illustrates our idea. Some years ago, a subject of the emperor of Austria came to the United States and simply declared his intention to become an American citizen. Soon after he visited his native land and was arrested, his American citizenship was ignored, and he was required to do military duty for a government he had renounced. An American battleship was in an Austrian port, and its commander having learned that Martin Costa, the American citizen referred to, was in that city, demanded his release and that he should promptly be sent on board of his ship and be placed under the protection of the American flag. The authorities hesitating to obey the order, the battleship was brought broadside to the city and her decks cleared for action. Her guns were shotted, and then came the order, "Send Martin Costa, the American citizen, on board my ship or I'll bombard your city." It was enough. The American citizen was rescued. The name of an obscure man was given to history. The right was vindicated. American citizenship was made to mean something, and American power and prestige was something more than sounding brass.[99]

Again, an utterly unknown American citizen was wrongfully imprisoned by the authorities of Mexico. His liberation was demanded by the American government. Mexico hesitated. Then came an exhibition of power on the Mexican border, and the peremptory order to release the American citizen. It sufficed, and the prison doors swung open, and the prisoner was free. The incidents related were premonitions of war in the event the humble and obscure American citizens had not been surrendered. These were exhibitions of consolidated power to resist wrong and oppression, and the world applauded. In labor affairs, consolidated power on the part of organizations would achieve the same results, by different methods. There would be no military display, no bugle calls to sanguinary strife, but the power exerted would not be less potential in securing beneficent results. When a corporation oppressed a wiper, a trackman, or a shopman, his case would at once concentrate upon it the consolidated power of the organizations. If it were a railroad, the demand would be made to remove the burden from the humble worker, and a refusal would hush to Pompeiian silence the industry. True, there would be inconvenience, but justice would demand the sacrifice, the wrong would be taken from the throne and placed upon the scaffold, and he would be a degenerate American who would not rejoice over such a victory.

It is possible to consolidate. It is possible to enthrone the right. It is possible to be true and brave and honest. What are the probabilities? We think they are cheering. We believe the outlook is hopeful. We fancy we see the dawning of a better day for labor in every field of toil. Men are learning to analyze errors and to eliminate them, and possibilities are becoming probabilities.

Entrenched errors are hard to dislodge, but with consolidation of the forces of labor such notable victories would be won for the right that men would wonder as they contemplate the dreary road labor has traveled to reach, at last, the goal of success.

Populist Advice[†]

August 1894

When it comes to striking at the polls, we know the people will be with us. It will be a contest by the money power, by which this country has been absolutely ruled for so many years. Havemeyer goes into the United States Senate and dictates what duty shall be on sugar, and all the people combined cannot stop him.[100] Let a poor man go to Washington to protest, and they arrest him for treading on the grass.[101]

I am Populist and am in favor of wiping both the old parties out so they will never come into power again. I have been a Democrat all my life, and I am ashamed to admit it. I want every one of you to go to the polls and vote the Populist ticket. What we are trying to do is to make a job worth something. As it is, there is little difference in financial condition between the men who have and those who have not jobs.

[†]   Excerpt from a speech, published as "Debs' Advice" in *People's Voice* (Wellington, KS), August 10, 1894, 8.

Testimony to the United States Strike Commission†
[excerpt]
August 20, 1894

August 20, 1894, Eugene V. Debs, being first duly sworn, testified as follows:

Commissioner [Carroll D.] Wright[102]*: State your name, age, residence, and oc-cupation.*

Eugene V. Debs: Eugene V. Debs, 38; Terre Haute, Indiana; am at present president of the American Railway Union and editor of the *Locomotive Firemen's Magazine.*

Commissioner Wright: How long have you been president of the American Railway Union?
Debs: Ever since it was instituted, June 20, 1893.[103]

Commissioner Wright: Are you a railroad man or understood so to be?
Debs: Yes, sir. I was actively engaged in the railroad service at the time I became a member of the railway employees' organization.

Commissioner Wright: In what branch of the railway service?
Debs: I served as a painter and locomotive fireman.

Commissioner Wright: How long did you serve in those capacities?
Debs: About four and one half years.

Commissioner Wright: We would like to have you state, Mr. Debs, in your own way, in narrative form, the history of the present strike, so far as you know it from your own knowledge; that is to say, what led to the strike or boycott, and what was done by the American Railway Union, or its directors or members, in their official capacity. In this statement please cover the ground as fully as you can, but as briefly as possible.
Debs: In the early part of May last year I received at my home in Terre Haute, Indiana, a telegram from Vice President Howard, of the American Railway Union, who is located here, notifying me that there was a probability of

---

†   Published in *Report on the Chicago Strike of June–July, 1894, by the United States Strike Commission, Appointed by the President July 26, 1894, Under the Provisions of Section 6 of Chapters 1063 of the Laws of the United States Passed October 1, 1888, with Appendices Containing Testimony, Proceedings, and Recommendations.* Washington, DC: Government Printing Office, 1895; 129–180.

a strike on the part of the Pullman employees who were members of the union. I immediately wired him, authorizing him to act as president of the union, assuming the duties of my office on account of my inability to be there, but to do all in his power to prevent a strike.

Commissioner [John D.] Kernan[104]: *Have you got these telegrams, or copies of them?*

Debs: There is a clerk in the office now, in the absence of Mr. Howard, looking up the telegram I sent him, and I will introduce it before this commission.

Commissioner Kernan: Does that refer generally to the documents which you are speaking of in the course of your testimony?

Debs: Yes, sir. The American Railway Union had been involved in a strike on the Great Northern road in the latter part of April [1894], and at a meeting of the officers of the union we concluded that many of our members might possibly be flushed with the triumph of that strike, and if we were not extremely careful we would be precipitated into other disturbances. We concluded it would be best, if it was possible, to keep out of any trouble whatever, for the time being at least, and I was particularly anxious at that time to avoid any strike if it was possible to do so. On the morning of May 11 I received a telegram from Mr. Howard informing me that the employees had struck. Shortly after that I came to the city of Chicago. I went to Pullman in person and made a personal investigation of the conditions existing there, in order to satisfy myself as to the justice or injustice of the action taken by the employees. I was obliged to go to St. Paul, and on my return I again stopped at Pullman and continued the investigation. I met the employees in person, both men and women, and I became satisfied that the conditions under which the employees there were obliged to work fully justified them in the course they had taken.

I found that the wages and the expenses of the employees were so adjusted that every dollar the employees earned found its way back into the Pullman coffers; that they were not only not getting wages enough to live on, but that they were daily getting deeper into the debt of the Pullman Company; that it was impossible for many of them to leave there at all, even if they were disposed to quit to try and better their condition. Many of them told me personally that the conditions were very objectionable to them, but there was no escape for them. Wages had been reduced, but the expenses remained the same, and no matter how offensive the conditions were, they were compelled to submit to them. After I heard those statements I satisfied myself that they were true, and I made up my mind, as president of the

American Railway Union, of which these employees were members, to do everything in my power that was within law and within justice to right the wrongs of those employees.

In the meantime, I found that every effort was being put forth on the part of the employees, as well as the representatives of the organization, to induce the Pullman Company to submit to arbitration. We had succeeded in settling the trouble on the Great Northern by arbitration. We had absolute faith in the justice of our case. We were confident that any fair and impartial board of arbitrators would decide in favor of the employees. The Pullman Company, through its officers, refused positively to entertain any proposition coming from any source looking to the arbitration of the difficulties. They maintained the position that there was nothing to arbitrate. While I am on this subject of arbitration I desire to say that after the trouble broke out, we then proposed that they select two representatives and that two representatives be selected by the judges of the court, and they four select the fifth representative, to decide as to whether there was anything to arbitrate.

*   *   *

On June 9 the delegates representing the American Railway Union, 465 local unions and about 150,000 employees, in round numbers, met in first quadrennial convention in the city of Chicago. In due course of the proceedings, the matter of the Pullman trouble came up for consideration. The convention resolved itself into a committee of the whole to hear reports of committees and to take such action as in their judgment was deemed best to protect the interests of the suffering employees. And just here I would like to have the gentlemen of the board understand that all of the meetings of the American Railway Union were publicly held, with open doors—the first time in the history of American railway employees' organizations.

*   *   *

The result of the consideration of the convention was the appointment of a committee, consisting in part of Pullman employees that were delegates and in part of delegates who were not Pullman employees.

That committee was authorized to call upon Mr. Wickes,[105] the vice president of the company, and ask him if he would not agree to arbitrate the difficulties existing between the company and the employees. Mr. Wickes notified the committee that he would meet no kind of a committee except a committee of his own employees. We then substituted Pullman employees for the remainder of the committee, so that the committee was composed wholly of employees of the Pullman Company. Before the committee left the hall, I, as president, instructed that committee not to go to the Pullman Company as representing the American Railway Union or any other organization. I said, "Waive that question entirely, if the organization is objectionable; we are perfectly willing to waive that and treat with Mr. Wickes as employees of the company and in that capacity." The committee returned with the information that Mr. Wickes absolutely refused to make any concession looking toward the arbitration of the difficulty. The matter was then referred to a special committee, who were authorized to recommend to the convention such action as in their judgment was necessary to be taken. The committee went into session and recommended that if the Pullman Company refused to concede anything looking to the arbitration of this difficulty within five days, that the delegates resolve that they would refuse to haul trains to which Pullman cars were attached . . . Under the rules of the American Railway Union, the majority rules in all instances and in all things. No strike can be inaugurated except by a majority of the men who are involved, nor could any strike action be taken by delegates except by the majority of the body. The delegates, by instruction from Vice President Howard and myself, went to the bodies that they were authorized to act for, the several unions; they were authorized to communicate with the unions they represented by telegraph and report the result to the convention. Most of the delegates did so, and in every instance, so far as I know, they were authorized by their several unions, in meeting assembled, to stand by the Pullman employees even to the extent of refusing to haul Pullman cars. After the committee had reported a vote was taken, and the vote was unanimous in favor of the adoption of the report, that providing, as I have said, that after the lapse of five days if the Pullman Company refused to arbitrate, that the members throughout the country refuse to haul Pullman cars.

Commissioner Wright: Five days from the 21st of June?
Debs: Yes, sir. That vote, as I say, was adopted unanimously with not one dissenting voice. Delegates had heard the reports of all the committees. Many of them had gone to Pullman in person, had met the employees and satisfied themselves of the justice of the position of the employees, and they were so thoroughly imbued with the justice of the claims of the employees, and they felt it, as a sense of duty binding upon them, to stand by those employees in their struggle for their rights, so the voice was unanimous; a very remarkable proceeding in a matter of such great importance as that, involving as it did the situations of all those delegates and their constituents.

*   *   *

In two instances the reductions that had been made by the railroad companies were restored, one by the power of the American Railway Union on the Great Northern on the first day of May, last. A reduction of wages amounting to $146,500 a month, according to the figures of President Hill, was made there. The American Railway Union organized and combined within its organization all classes of employees, and it made a stand for the restoration of that $146,500 a month, and the restoration was made on the first day of September through arbitration. Practically everything was conceded, and the board of arbitration itself, composed of representative businessmen of the cities of St. Paul and Minneapolis, say that our disposition was fair.

*   *   *

The employees on the other roads felt, in view of this fact, that their wages had also been unjustly taken from them. On the Union Pacific, where the men were reduced 10 percent in their wages, Judge Caldwell—the gentlemen of the board will doubtless remember his scathing arraignment of the methods that were in operation there, and the policy of the managers that had made such a reduction under such circumstances. The employees on other roads felt that if upon the Union Pacific, where Judge Caldwell ordered the reductions restored, and upon the Great Northern, where the board of arbitrators agreed that the reduction had been unjustly made, if that was true upon those two systems it was equally true on other systems and lines of railway that were, at least, in as sound a financial condition, and that they made their reductions seemed taking advantage of the unfortunate condition of the times, and not because they were compelled to make them by their financial condition. This created unrest in the ranks of the American Railway Union.

The employees had, to a large extent, lost confidence in the other railway brotherhoods, who had failed, in a single instance, to successfully resist these reductions that were gradually being made all over the country, and all of the delegates, therefore, came to the meeting of the railway union with the hope and expectation that the railway union would do something to restore their wages and to protect them in their rights and wages as employees. This is the reason that they were so ripe to espouse the cause of the injured Pullman employees. This prompted their action fully as much as the grievances of the employees. While the injuries and grievances of the Pullman employees appealed to their sense of justice and to their sense of duty for redress, these further grievances of their own made the matter more binding upon them, and wrought them up to that point where they felt it a duty as binding upon them to do everything in their power to protect the Pullman employees, as well as their constituents, who had sent them to the convention. The vote, as I have said, was unanimous. There was not one dissenting voice. In this there was no purpose on the part of the delegates to interfere with traffic, but the primary purpose was, if possible, to cut off the Pullman cars so as to cut off the Pullman revenue, and thereby compel the Pullman Company to arbitrate its troubles with these employees.

Commissioner Wright: Mr. Debs, you have stated, I think, that your people advised against the Pullman strike which occurred on the 11th of May?
Debs: Yes, sir.

Commissioner Wright: Yet you have stated that their grievances appealed to your sympathy with such force that you were bound in your brotherhood to protect the Pullman employees?
Debs: Yes, sir.

Commissioner Wright: Then why did you advise against the strike which occurred on the 11th of May?
Debs: I advised against the strike, as I stated, in the earlier part of May, before I knew anything about the condition. I was at Terre Haute. Mr. Howard wired me there was a strike probable. As we had just gotten through the Great Northern strike, and as I knew about the condition at Pullman, wired back and said, "Do everything in your power to prevent any strike from being inaugurated at this time."

*   *   *

Commissioner Wright: Now, inform us what the action of your union would have been at this convention, relative to a general strike, had it not been for the existence of the Pullman strike. In other words, was the policy of the union affected, in your mind, by the Pullman strike, to force an issue peremptorily or otherwise?
Debs: No, sir; I would answer your question in this way. There would have been no trouble with the railway companies had it not been for the Pullman trouble. The delegates regarded it as an inauspicious time for the inauguration of a strike for any purpose on account of the depressed condition of the country, but the grievances the delegates and their constituents had already suffered at the hands of the railway companies aggravated the condition, and wrought them up to a point to at least espouse the cause of the Pullman employees at the time the convention met.

Commissioner Wright: The general strike or boycott, then, was not contemplated?
Debs: No, sir.

Commissioner Wright: Was a general strike or boycott brought to an issue at that time by the grievances at Pullman?

Debs: Yes; and it was this, the grievances of which they had already suffered, that ripened them or prepared them.

Commissioner Wright: In other words, the strike at Pullman precipitated that?
Debs: Yes, sir.

Commissioner Kernan: It would be incorrect to say that the cause of the strike was the grievances, of the various kinds, that the railroad employees had?
Debs: Yes, sir.

Commissioner Wright: Now, another matter. As to the motion which was unanimously passed by your convention, as I understand it, on the 21st day of June, declaring that unless the grievances at Pullman were adjusted within five days a general boycott would be declared against roads hauling Pullman cars; was this resolution served upon anybody officially or otherwise, either in writing or verbally?

Debs: By the convention?

Commissioner Wright: By the convention of its officers?

Debs: No, sir; it was not served on the railroad companies, but it was left with the representatives of each road to serve that notice. There was no action taken on the part of the convention peremptorily, for the reason that the American Railway Union was not regarded with favor by the railway companies. As a general proposition they had done everything to retard its growth; they had refused it recognition and refused to have any dealings with it in any way, shape, or form. It has always been customary for railroad managers, as a general proposition, to accord free transportation to the officers of the various railway brotherhoods for the good they are supposed to do in the way of improving the condition or efficiency of the men. Such courtesies as other organizations have always received have been denied to the American Railway Union. They have even refused to answer its communications or to recognize it in any way whatsoever; and the convention felt, as I am persuaded, that any notice of this kind would simply be ignored by the railway companies.

*   *   *

Commissioner [Nicholas E.] Worthington[106]: Was there any public notice in the papers given of such action by the convention?
Debs: Yes, sir; in all of the papers.

Commissioner Worthington: And reporters and others were present when the convention took action?
Debs: Yes; at my request as president of the union. Some of the delegates

wanted to go into special or executive session. I arose in my place, and I said, "We want to have everything done in the broad, open light of day," and I asked the convention to allow the representatives of the press to remain, and they did so, and they did remain.

Commissioner Worthington: As a matter of fact, every road in Chicago was doubtless informed of this action through the published dailies of this city?
Debs: Yes, sir.

*   *   *

Commissioner Wright: About that time the general managers of the Chicago terminal lines—that is, the General Managers' Association—adopted certain resolutions declaring that they would resist the boycott which you proposed to order on the 21st of June. Do you know when those resolutions were adopted?
Debs: Yes, sir.

Commissioner Wright: When?
Debs: On the 25th day of June. They were published on the 25th day of June. When they were adopted I don't know, but presumably the evening before; but they were published on the morning of the 25th day of June.

Commissioner Wright: Four days after your action?
Debs: Yes. I don't know whether I should state here that in connection with these resolutions it was currently reported that the managers resolved at that meeting, though it is not published, but it is currently reported that they did resolve to exterminate the American Railway Union; that they had seen from the Great Northern victory that it was a menace to the railroad companies of the country, and it was the purpose to crush the American Railway Union in its incipiency. That is not published, but it was currently reported, and the information came to us from a source that seemed reliable.

*   *   *

Commissioner Wright: What was the strength of your union at that time—say the 21st of June?
Debs: In round numbers, about 150,000 members.

Commissioner Wright: Did you consider that the union was strong enough for a general strike?
Debs: Yes, sir; we considered that the union was strong enough to meet every expected demand.

*   *   *

Commissioner Wright: Take up your narrative now from the 21st of June.
Debs: Pursuant to the order of the convention, practically the order of the

150,000 employees composing the union, because it was taken by the delegates by authority of their several unions—and I would like to emphasize this point, for the reason that it has been repeatedly claimed and it has been the source of a great deal of prejudice, I think, to our cause, that the president of the union ordered the strike, that the president of the union was a self-appointed individual and ordered the strike—I would like to have that point understood, that the strike was practically ordered by the rank and file of the membership of the order; that is, the delegates acted by their express authority and instruction. I admit that when the reports came in from these committees, and from what I knew myself, that I was ready, as the president of the union, to sanction such action. I do not wish to shirk any responsibility for my act as the president of the union. I gave my hearty concurrence to the movement. I did not order it, however, nor did I have any voice in ordering it; but if I had had a voice in ordering it, I should have ordered it.

On the 26th day of June, pursuant to the order of the convention, the employees began to refuse to haul Pullman cars. The officers of the American Railway Union established temporary headquarters at Uhlich's Hall. They were very careful to instruct the men, or to advise the men, rather, in our advisory capacity, not to take this action anywhere unless it was sanctioned by the majority of employees and they felt strong enough to make it effectual. We said it is not wise for a few men to create trouble, and not to strike unless it is sanctioned by a majority of the employees, and unless it was certain that the employees of the body will stand by you in so doing. The committees came from all yards and from all roads to confer with us. The switchmen, for instance, would send a committee to us, and we would authorize that committee to act for that yard or for that road, and that committee would then go to that yard and take charge of the affairs, serve notice upon the men, and keep them in line, and above everything we advised them to do everything in their power to maintain order and prevent violence.

All of the meetings were held in the city of Chicago, and there were a great many. All of us were addressing from two to six meetings a day, and all the meetings that were held were held with open doors. We did not hold a secret meeting during the entire trouble, not one. We held meetings in close proximity to all of these yards and all of these roads, and all of the employees and the general public were there. We did not hold a meeting but what we admonished employees under all circumstances to maintain order. We said we want to win as becomes men; we want to win as becomes law-abiding citizens; we have got a right to quit in a body, and our right ends there; the railroad companies have the right to employ men to take our places, and their rights begin there, and we have no right to interfere. We are on record as saying that in our published documents and our public statements that were very widely circulated through the press. The records show that that was the case with all the committees that called upon us and in all the meetings that were held.

*   *   *

Commissioner Kernan: It is said some inflammatory telegrams were sent, either by you or by your authority; how is that?

Debs: Yes, I understand it is alleged certain telegrams were sent; but there was no telegram sent by my authority of an inflammatory character.

Commissioner Kernan: Have you not heard of any that were sent by your alleged authority?

Debs: None that were inflammatory, as I understand the term.

Commissioner Wright: A certain "buy a gun" telegram;[107] *was that sent by you?*

Debs: I can explain that if the gentlemen of the board desire an explanation.

Commissioner Wright: Yes, we do.

Debs: At the time the convention was held there was a young man, a delegate from Butte, Montana, by the name of L. P. Benedict. He was a typewriter and stenographer in the office of the auditor of the Montana Union Railway. He was made assistant secretary during the convention, and he was found to be so competent that he was employed as our regular stenographer and typewriter. When the trouble began there were thousands of telegrams and communications pouring in, and it was impossible for me to see them all personally, because I was at many of the mass meetings, and with committees, and going to different cities and addressing meetings, and things of that sort, so that it really was impossible for all these telegrams that were coming in to receive my personal notice. So then the work was attended to by various members of this board.

This young man Benedict answered by instruction of the board some telegrams, and in other cases, where the board was all absent, he answered the telegrams himself. Telegrams, when he had answered others of a kindred character, he would answer without instructions. This "buy a gun" telegram was sent to his superior, in whose employment he had been at Butte, Montana, who wired him to know something about the conditions. It was an expression that they had used themselves, between themselves, a playful expression, "Save your money and buy a gun." It was telegraphed to that superior, who understood the expression, and who wrote a letter that I can produce here. This official of the Montana union writes in here and exculpates Mr. Benedict, who sent the telegram. I had no notice of it; did not know anything about it until I saw it published in the papers. It is merely a playful expression they used out in Montana.

Commissioner Wright: Will you file that letter with the commission?
Debs: Yes, sir.

Commissioner Wright: This particular telegram was not signed by you?
Debs: This telegram was sent over my signature, for the reason that all telegrams were sent over my signature on account of my having a half frank.

Commissioner Wright: But not signed by you?
Debs: No, sir; not signed by me. I never saw the telegram and never knew it was sent until I saw it published in the Chicago papers, until after the indictment was found.

*   *   *

Commissioner Wright: Now go on with your narrative.
Debs: The employees, obedient to the order of the convention, at once, on the 26th, refused to haul Pullman cars. The switchmen, in the first place, refused to attach a Pullman car to a train, and that is where the trouble began, and then when a switchman would be discharged for that they would all simultaneously quit, as they had agreed to do. One department after another was involved, until the Illinois Central was practically paralyzed, and the Rock Island and other roads in their turn. Up to the first day of July, or after the strike had been in progress five days, the railway managers, as we believe, were completely defeated. Their immediate resources were exhausted, their properties were paralyzed, and they were unable to operate their trains. Our men were intact at every point, firm, quiet, yet determined, and no sign of violence or disorder anywhere. That was the condition on the 30th day of June and the first day of July.

Commissioner Kernan: The five-day notice expired when?
Debs: The five-day notice expired on the 26th day of June. Notice was issued on the 21st day of June. It is at this point that the intervention of the courts was sought. Now, if you gentlemen would like to have my opinion as to the cause that resulted in our defeat, I will be glad to make that statement, but it is merely my opinion.

Commissioner Wright: It is the facts we are after, and then your conclusions by and by.
Debs: Very well. On the second day of July I was served with a very sweeping injunction that restrained me, as president of the union, from sending out any telegram or any letter or issuing any order that would have the effect of

inducing or persuading men to withdraw from the service of the company, or that would in any manner whatsoever, according to the language of the injunction, interfere with the operation.

*   *   *

That injunction was served simultaneously, or practically so, by all of the courts embracing or having jurisdiction in the territory in which the trouble existed. From Michigan to California there seemed to be concerted action on the part of the courts in restraining us from exercising any of the functions of our offices. That resulted practically in the demoralization of our ranks. Not only this, but we were organized in a way that this was the center, of course, of operations. It is understood that a strike is war; not necessarily a war of blood and bullets, but a war in the sense that it is a conflict between two contending interests or classes of interests. There is more or less strategy resorted to in war, and this was the center in our operations. Orders were issued from here, questions were answered, and our men were kept in line from here.

At the time I was served with this injunction, all of the officers at all of the points at the headquarters or terminals of all of these roads were served with a similar injunction restraining them all from sending any telegrams or from discharging the functions attached to their several offices. Following the issuance of that injunction a few days, I have forgotten the exact date, a special grand jury was convened for the purpose of examining into my conduct as president of the American Railway Union in connection with this trouble. The grand jury was in session very briefly, but found a bill upon an information that was filed, and I was ordered to be arrested. A warrant was issued and placed in the hands of a United States marshal for that purpose. On the 7th day of July, if I am not mistaken, I was arrested and brought before the court, and my bond was fixed, with my three official associates, Mr. Howard, vice president; Mr. Rogers, editor of the *[Railway] Times,* and Mr. Keliher, our secretary, we were simultaneously arrested and we were placed under a joint bond of $10,000. Very shortly after this there was an attachment issued for an alleged contempt of court, upon information that I had, as president, violated the injunction issued by Judges Wood and Grosscup.

Commissioner Wright: That is, the injunction served on you on the second day of July?

Debs: Yes. As soon as the employees found that we were arrested and taken from the scene of action, they became demoralized, and that ended the strike. It was not the soldiers that ended the strike; it was not the old brotherhoods that ended the strike; it was simply the United States courts that ended the strike. Our men were in a position that never would have been shaken under any circumstances if we had been permitted to remain upon the field, remain among them; but once that we were taken from the scene of action and restrained from sending telegrams or issuing the orders necessary, or answering questions; when the minions of the corporations would be put to work at such a place, for instance, as Nickerson, Kansas, where they would go and say to the men that the men at Newton had gone back to work, and Nickerson would wire me to ask if that were true; no answer would come to the message, because I was under arrest, and we were all under arrest. The headquarters were demoralized and abandoned, and we could not answer any telegrams or questions that would come in. Our headquarters were temporarily demoralized and abandoned, and we could not answer any messages. The men went back to work, and the ranks were broken, and the strike was broken up by the federal courts of the United States, and not by the Army, and not by any other power, but simply and solely by the action of the United States courts in restraining us from discharging our duties as officers and representatives of the employees . . .

Commissioner Worthington: What was that date?

Debs: On the 7th of July, as I remember it, representatives of certain officers of the law, acting under the authority of the federal officials, raided our headquarters and seized our books and papers and my private unopened correspondence. The clerks remonstrated with the authorities, but they listened to nothing, but insisted upon bundling up everything there was about the office and taking it away out of the place to the office of the federal prosecutor. I want to say, in justice to the court, to Judge Grosscup, that the next morning he sent for me and explained that this action had been taken without authority, and he ordered the papers restored—my personal papers.

Commissioner Kernan: What officers did it?

Debs: I understand officers acting under the instructions and by the authority of the then-prosecuting attorney, Mr. Milchrist, and the postal authorities.

*   *   *

On the second day of July, the day upon which the injunctions were served upon me, as I remember, I am not positive about that date, General Miles came to Chicago in charge of the Federal troops or regular soldiers. It was stated in the press of the city of Chicago on the second day after General Miles's arrival, and especially those papers that were defending the corporations, so I assume the reports were correct, that upon General Miles's arrival in the city of Chicago he repaired to the headquarters of the General Managers' Association. He was in consultation with the general managers, and the next day he was quoted as saying in the press that "he had broken the backbone of the strike." So far as I know, General Miles has never denied either statement.

Now, it seems to me, if I am permitted to make an observation, that General Miles was vulgarly out of place when he made such a statement. In the first place, it was highly improper for him, as an officer of the federal government, to go to the general managers, who were a party to this controversy. It would have been just as proper for him, in my judgment, to have visited the headquarters of the American Railway Union and gone into confidential consultation with the officers of that organization as it was for him to go to the general managers' headquarters and meet in private confidential consultation with them. On the next day it was reported in an interview that was widely published in the Chicago newspapers defending the corporation that he had said he had "broken the backbone of the strike." It was believed his mission here was to preserve and maintain order, and not to take an active part in the strike, nor to defeat the strike, any more than he was to come here to defeat the railroad corporations. But the fact is, he was in active alliance with the general managers, not only to maintain order, but to suppress the strike. That was his real mission in Chicago.

*   *   *

At this time we realized that we were not only confronted by the railway managers, but it had resolved itself into a conflict in which the organized forces of society and all the powers of the municipal, state, and federal governments were arrayed against us. We then said we did not start out to antagonize the government nor to make a war against the government, but simply started out in an issue with the railroad corporations, and now that this was assuming such alarming conditions, such grave proportions, and innocent people were suffering, we said, "We will declare this strike off upon the simple condition that the railway managers put our men back to work." That was about the 6th day of July, if I am not mistaken, at the time the strike was at its very worst—at its zenith.

Commissioner Wright: Was that notice served on the managers?

Debs: We held a meeting of the board and said, "We will declare this strike off, in consideration of the fact that it has assumed such threatening phases; that for the public good, if for no other consideration, we will declare this strike off." The board was unanimous in its conclusion, and a document was prepared which said substantially this, that we had been appealed to by the citizens, by letter, and by telegram, from every conceivable source; from the West, where fruits and other perishable freights were spoiling, and from men whose private interests were suffering, who were in no way involved in the original controversy, and the pressure became so great that we said, "It is our duty to declare the strike off."

Commissioner Kernan: How did you get authority to declare the strike off?

Debs: I will explain that. When the board met, we were daily in consultation with the committees representing the various roads centering in the city of Chicago, which was really the strike center. Every day the committees came to receive their instructions and to make their reports. When we became satisfied that things were assuming too serious a phase, and that a point had been reached when, in the interest of peace and to prevent riot and trouble, we must declare the strike off, we advised with those committees. We gave it out as our opinion to the men, through the committees, that the strike had better be declared off, if we could do so honorably. The men agreed, without a dissenting voice that I heard, from every source and from every road, that they were willing to declare the strike off, if they were allowed simply to go back to work. It was in the crisis when everything was at stake, where possibly it might have eventuated in a revolution. We said, "We feel satisfied, from the authority we have already received from all the men we can possibly reach, and from all the roads, we feel justified, in view of this crisis, in making this proposition and speaking for the rest who cannot possibly be reached—who are too remote to be reached." It was a time for action, as we believed, and prompt action at that.

We then prepared a document, in which we proposed that we would declare the strike off on condition that they would take back the employees. We said, "We do not ask you to recognize our organization; we do not ask you to recognize us; we simply say that this matter has become so serious that we ought to be patriotic enough to declare it off, and we are willing to meet you halfway by declaring it off, by advising our men to go back to work at once, if you will simply take them back. We tried to get Mr. Gompers and a committee representing the American Federation of Labor and affiliated trades to present that document to the general managers. Mr. Gompers and his associates, representing their affiliated orders, had been called here and were holding a meeting at the Briggs House. Mr. Howard, the vice president, and I attended the meeting and laid the entire matter before them, upon which they went into session. They agreed to present the document, but they desired that in presenting this document, I, as president, should accompany them to the general managers, which I did not feel inclined to do, because I knew I was very offensive to the general managers, and that no good could possibly come from any action in which I would have a part. I did not decline to do so because I hesitated on account of any reception that might be accorded me, but on account of the matter of expediency purely. We then went and called upon Mayor Hopkins.[108]

Commissioner Wright: You had not completed that statement. What did Gompers do?

Debs: I did not accept their proposition to present this statement. They agreed to do it in consideration of my going with them, as president, but we did not see fit to accept that condition. So we declined the proposition, but we considered it best to go to Mr. Hopkins, who was then the chief magistrate of the city and in a neutral position, where he could with propriety serve in that capacity. We called upon Mr. Hopkins, and he said he would very willingly deliver that proposition to the managers. Mayor Hopkins called upon Alderman McGillen,[109] who had been active as an alderman in introducing a resolution looking to the arbitration of the Pullman difficulties, and in giving other valuable aid to the cause. We invited Alderman McGillen, and they two presented this proposition, and met at the headquarters of the general managers to present it. It was currently reported that the general managers received an intimation that such a proposition would be made. The fact of this proposition being contemplated had been published in the press. It was reported that the general managers had received information that it was to be delivered, and they hastily withdrew. This I do not know of my own knowledge, but I give it to you as it was currently reported.

This I have from Mayor Hopkins himself. Mayor Hopkins and Alderman McGillen called and met Mr. St. John and afterwards Mr. Egan, chairman of the General Managers' Association. They declared that they would accept no proposition whatever signed by Mr. Debs or his associates; that they did not recognize them and would have nothing whatever to do with them. Mr. Hopkins then said, You cannot afford, in such a critical time as this, to ignore as fair a proposition as this. The time has come when this trouble has got to be settled in one way or another. These men make an absolutely fair proposition. They are willing to go back to work, to resume the traffic and end all this trouble, if you will simply put them back to work. Then Mr. Egan said, "Why, we are getting along all right, and we will operate our roads without these men." His honor, Mayor Hopkins, said, "If that is the case, I will withdraw the soldiers, if you are operating your roads." To which Mr. Egan at once protested, and said, "Oh, no, we have got to have the soldiers." Then Mr. Hopkins said, "You have got to do something." Then Mr. Egan said, "We will call a meeting of the board of managers and see what they will do, but we do not believe they will do anything." The result of their action was that they sent the document back, not with any answer, but simply saying they would not accept any proposition coming from that source. So the document was practically returned unopened.

Commissioner Wright: Did Mayor Hopkins report to you all you have now stated, on his return?

Debs: Yes. All of this was reported to Mr. Howard and myself and Mr. Sovereign, grand master workman of the Knights of Labor, who happened to be here at that time. The document came back to us with the announcement that the officials absolutely would do nothing looking to a settlement of this trouble; not only that they would not reinstate the men, but they would not consider the proposition. They would consider no proposition, and this confirmed the belief I had which was warranted by what had already occurred, that the general managers did not want to settle this trouble, but wanted to exterminate the American Railway Union, in accordance with the resolution they had adopted at their private meeting, as was currently reported at the time. They wanted no kind of a treaty. They wanted to accept no kind of a proposition or any negotiations looking to a settlement of the troubles. They wanted to crush and annihilate the American Railway Union at whatever cost to the public.

Commissioner Wright: You say that from general information?
Debs: Yes.

Commissioner Wright: Not from any statements made by the Railway Managers' Association to you?

Debs: No, sir; we have tried to get documentary evidence verifying this conclusion, but we have not succeeded. Our telegrams were all public property. They were all produced in the courts, published in all the papers. Every telegram we sent that was of any consequence was given to the public, but we have not been able to get a single telegram that passed between the general managers and Attorney General Olney. If we could get these telegrams there would not be any question about our being able to produce some testimony that would verify the other testimony here—that which is not already substantiated by proof.

Commissioner Worthington: I think you stated the date when this communication was sent to the General Managers' Association, and when the reply was received; if not, will you please state it now?

Debs: The communication or proposition was delivered about 11:30 in the morning, and we received the answer about 4 that afternoon on the same day; I think that was the 7th day of July.

*   *   *

Commissioner Worthington: Was the reply in writing?

Debs: No, sir; they would not make any reply in writing. They sent a messenger to Mayor Hopkins and informed him that these men they would have absolutely nothing to do with; but, on account of his being the mayor, and on account of his being able to afford them certain protection that they were very seriously in need of, out of courtesy to him they would deign to tell him that they would have nothing to do with the proposition; but if it had not been for that they would have ignored him as well as the committee.

*   *   *

Commissioner Kernan: What, if anything, did you do to ascertain whether your men were concerned in violence, and have them report it to you?

Debs: We did that through our committees; our committees called at headquarters every morning, and the advice was renewed for them to guard the company's property, if they went near it at all, and to apprehend anyone that might be caught destroying property. That instruction was given again and again to the several committees that called at headquarters. We knew that if there was trouble, if there was disorder and riot, we would lose, because we knew enough by experience in the past that we had everything to lose by riot and nothing to gain. We said the man who incites riot or who engages in disorder is our enemy, and we have got to be the first to apprehend and bring him to justice; so we called upon our men and advised them, urged them to do everything in their power to maintain order, because we felt and knew if there was perfect order there would be no pretext upon which they could call out the soldiers or appeal for the intervention of the court, and we would win without a question of a doubt; that it was only by disorder that we could possibly lose, and that disorder was not a part of the policy of the American Railway Union any more than if there was a Fourth of July celebration here tomorrow and some drunken riot should occur and somebody got killed, no more than that would be a reflection upon the patriotic participants in that celebration.

The American Railway Union stands by its suffering members, as every fair-minded man will admit is commendable. They knew that public sympathy was with them up to that point, and they knew how likely it was that something might be done by the rabble to destroy that sympathy.

I admit that on account of the natural excitement that prevailed there was turbulence and disorder, and perhaps riots, although never to the extent that was represented by the press. No one sought harder or with more persistency to curb it and stop it than did the officers of the American Railway Union. I state that as a positive fact, susceptible of overwhelming proof.

Commissioner Wright: Did the officers of the American Railway Union protest against the employment of military forces to prevent rioting and violence?

Debs: They protested against the introduction of federal troops before the local and state authorities had been appealed to. Mayor Hopkins himself admitted, and it is a matter of record, that there was nothing here warranting the introduction of federal troops. It was that that aroused, aggravated, and angered the men and caused the trouble that subsequently ensued.

Commissioner Wright: But you did not protest against the employment of local troops?

Debs: No, sir; not in the least.

Commissioner Worthington: In that connection, Mr. Debs, I would like to ask you whether, so far as you know, the first acts of violence or destruction of property occurred before or after federal troops were brought here?

Debs: My best recollection is they occurred after the Federal troops were brought here. The real serious trouble that occurred, occurred afterward. There might have been some minor disturbances before, but nothing that would not have occurred in the ordinary course of affairs.

Commissioner Worthington: How long after the federal troops were brought here was it before the state troops were ordered?

Debs: I am not certain, but very shortly after the federal troops were brought here, the state troops were ordered out. The police force had already been enlarged. I do not know whether it would be proper to say it, because the police will say it for themselves, but they reported to me in person, a great many of them, that the men were perfectly law abiding, that they had not the slightest trouble with them.

Commissioner Wright: What action did your union take during the trouble here concerning the employment of men not members of your union?

Debs: We treated them as if they were members, insofar as we were able to control them, assured them we would give them the same degree of protection that we gave our own members in the event of our succeeding, and what we expected to do if we succeeded was simply to restore the men to their positions. We assured these non-union members that we would protect them, so far as restoring them to situations, the same as we did our own members. But, of course, we had no control over them. We could not expel them or punish them.

Commissioner Wright: Did you attempt to intimidate them to prevent them from working?

Debs: No, sir.

Commissioner Wright: Is that the policy of your union to do so?

Debs: No, sir; never.

Commissioner Wright: Is it the policy of the union to avoid that?

Debs: Yes; it is the express policy of the union, as has been expressly stated in one document I issued, a copy of which has been filed with the board, in which I declared, as president of the union, that it was the policy of the organization that there should be no intimidation. That our men had a right to quit, and there their right absolutely ceased. The other men had a right to take their places, and they had no right to interfere, and if they did they must expect to be punished, both by the union and the civil authority.

Commissioner Wright: Mr. Debs, has the action of the 21st of June ever been officially annulled?

Debs: Yes, sir.

Commissioner Wright: When?

Debs: A convention of delegates was called on the second of August, representing unions in the strike territory. The purpose of that meeting was to have the delegates thoroughly understand the situation. There was no longer any confidence in telegraphic reports, or even in letters, because it is alleged that a great many letters that were written—whether the charge was properly made or not, I do not know—but it was the belief among many of our members, and it was declared by them, they had written letters that never reached their destination; that they could not rely upon the telegraph. We knew all our telegrams were given to the authorities and general managers, and so the convention was called for the second of August, and that was in session two days. We heard reports from each delegation in regard to the trouble in his section, and then it was decided inasmuch as the strike had been inaugurated by a vote of delegates, predicated upon the vote of the members themselves, that the strike could only be declared off in the same way. It was then agreed that each system should be authorized to declare the strike off by a majority vote of that system. We then adjourned, and the delegates returned to their respective homes and held a meeting.

In almost all places except certain points on the Santa Fe system the strike has been declared off, annulling this action of the 21st day of June.

Commissioner Wright: What is the policy of your union relative to the older brotherhoods and your relations to them?

Debs: The relations are not, from an official standpoint, friendly, unfortunately. I have been and am now connected with one of the old organizations, the Brotherhood of Locomotive Firemen, which I joined the 27th of February, 1875. I became grand secretary of that organization and editor of their magazine on the 18th day of July, 1880, and I still edit their magazine. In the 14 years I have served in that organization I never had a candidate nominated against me, or a vote cast against me. In September 1892, I was unanimously reelected and I resigned; but by the unanimous voice of the delegates, they refused to accept my resignation. I then got up in my place and stated I was no longer in harmony with their methods, with their purposes.

Commissioner Kernan: Did you state why?

Debs: I said the railroad companies, and in order to show I was not animated by any selfish consideration, the convention offered me, by a unanimous vote, the right to fix my own salary. They voted me, by the unanimous voice of the delegates, $2,000 to go to Europe on a vacation, and that is lying in the treasury yet, as I have never touched it and never intend to. They offered me anything within their gift to remain a member of their organization, and I said I could not consistently remain an officer of that organization, for the reason I was not in harmony with their methods and purposes, under the existing conditions, and those conditions were that the Brotherhood of Locomotive Firemen embrace both engineers and firemen. That organization has a membership of about 26,000 members, and there are about 12,000 engineers in that number. A man joins the organization as a fireman; in the course of time he becomes an engineer. By his association among the firemen he feels a natural friendliness for his early associations. Some others, promptly upon becoming engineers, join the Brotherhood of Locomotive Engineers, and so there is a spirit of rivalry between those two organizations, on account of the engineers being divided, part of the order being locomotive firemen and part of them locomotive engineers. That has resulted to the detriment of those two organizations on a number of roads I could cite, where the firemen demanded a certain schedule and the engineers insisted they did not want that, and it would reach a point where they would threaten to take each other's places.

I knew we could never develop any strength or power with such a condition of affairs as that, and I saw no hopes for a better condition. The same condition precisely exists between the Order of Railway Conductors and the Brotherhood of Railroad Trainmen. The trainmen do everything they can to retain conductors in their own ranks and keep them from going into the conductors' organization, and that results in friction between the Order of Railway Conductors and Brotherhood of Railroad Trainmen; that same friction existed between the Brotherhood of Trainmen and the Switchmen's Mutual Aid Association. On the Chicago and Northwestern road in May 1892, the Brotherhood of Trainmen, through their officials, went into partnership, so to speak, with the officials of the Northwestern road, and they discharged every switchman, about 400 in number, from their service so as to destroy the Switchmen's Mutual Aid Association, and the Brotherhood of Railroad Trainmen filled their places. That work was going on all over the country. The members of one organization conspiring against the members of another organization, simply because of their being members of rival organizations.

Conditions were becoming worse every day. I was the first to speak in favor of the project of federation. Immediately after the Burlington Strike, in 1880, I said, "We have been defeated because we are not strong enough; I have always believed we ought to unify the entire service; we are without the power the officials exhibit; when we so unify we can strike," and we succeeded in organizing such a federation, composed of representatives of these various organizations, with the exception of the engineers and the Order of Railway Conductors, when the trainmen conspired with the Northwestern officials to displace the switchmen because they belonged to a rival organization. I then at once took my stand with the switchmen and it resulted in disrupting the federation. At the next associated convention held at Cincinnati, I stated my reasons for refusing to remain in the locomotive brotherhood. I said, "It is not a question of salary, but a question of conviction." I am in this position; this class organization is simply perpetuating what I conceive to be a mistake, as Professor Ely said the other day, the strict trade organizations have served their purpose, the conditions have changed; there used to be hundreds of small railroads in operation, but they have been merged with and absorbed by the great corporations; there has been a consolidation of the interests of corporation, whereas the employees, on the other hand, have been dividing their forces in rival organizations.

I said, "I want to entirely give up my official connection with this organization in order that I may be in a position to do what little I can toward unifying all the railroad employees and harmonizing them for their mutual good. I have no feeling against the railway brotherhoods; I have no cause to have any. I founded the Brotherhood of Railroad Brakemen, now the Brotherhood of Railroad Trainmen; organized the first union, paid its first expenses, and did much toward making it a national organization. I did very much to make the Switchmen's Mutual Aid Association a national organization, as the records will show. I have no personal feeling against these different organizations, but simply believe they have served their purposes and are no longer adapted to the conditions now existing. While the railroad corporations have been consolidating their interests, getting closer together, we have been getting further and further apart, and have been so busily engaged in making war upon each other that we have lost sight of the real purpose of consolidation, and we will all in time become victims of the corporation; they can reduce wages or take any advantage they desire and we have to submit." It was because I could not get consolidated action . . .

Commissioner Wright: Your policy, then, is to consolidate, absorb, all railroad interests so far as employees are concerned?

Debs: Not to consolidate, the purpose is unification; we declare that we do not insist it shall come through the American Railway Union; we declare we are willing to resign our official positions at once.

Commissioner Wright: That is, you will abandon your association for the sake of a unified one that will comprehend them all?

Debs: Yes; we will resign our positions. The railroad employees in this country are ready to unify now and work together, instead of being used to work against each other, but the hostility of the leaders of these various organizations makes unification impossible. Now, we have said and say now, we will resign our official positions at once, sever forever our relations with labor organizations if other leaders will do the same, and let these employees come together and select their own leaders.

* * *

Commissioner Wright: Come back to the conference at the Briggs House and relate briefly how that originated, at whose instigation, etc.?

Debs: During the progress of the strike we were in receipt almost daily of assurances, written and oral, from the members of other trades organizations that they were in hearty sympathy with the American Railway Union in its struggles. Several of them, notably Thomas I. Kidd, general secretary of the machine woodworkers, proposed that they call a meeting of the representatives of the various trades unions for the purpose of devising ways and means to aid us in our struggles.

This meeting was not called at our suggestion or at our solicitation, but was a voluntary act on the part of sympathizing trades unionist representatives. A preliminary meeting was held and the matter of coming to the aid of the American Railway Union was discussed, and then it was agreed to set a meeting for the following Sunday—the date of this meeting I have forgotten, but it was on the day President Cleveland issued his first proclamation—and to invite the representatives of all other organizations to attend that meeting to see what could be done. The officials of the American Railway Union attended that meeting by invitation but took no part in the meeting except to give their views. I was called upon as the president of the railway union by the meeting to state my views as to what should be done. I said, in substance: "Gentlemen, it would be presumptuous for me to offer this body any advice; you are all representative labor men; you have all had experience in such troubles as this; you understand your relations to the American Railway Union; you understand your duty, if you have a duty to yourself, to your constituents, and the cause you represent; do what you believe to be your duty. I have no advice to offer." The tenor of the remarks made by my colleagues was the same. We neither encouraged nor discouraged them from taking part in the trouble.

Previous to this, however, I had conceived the idea of inviting to a conference all of the officials of all the labor organizations in the country. I invited the chief officers of each of the railway brotherhoods, Mr. Arthur of the engineers, Mr. Sargent of the firemen, Mr. Wilkinson of the trainmen, Mr. Barrett of the switchmen, Mr. Powell of the telegraphers, Mr. Clark of the conductors, Mr. Gompers of the American Federation of Labor, Mr. Sovereign of the Knights of Labor, and others. All of them believed that it would be well to have a conference of labor representatives. The invitation was ignored by all of the railway brotherhoods, except in the case of Mr. Sargent, who sent as his representative the grand secretary and treasurer and the vice grand master. Mr. Sovereign, of the Knights of Labor, came of his own accord. Mr. Clark, of the conductors' organization, said he had business in Chicago and would probably be here; if so, he would call, but he never called. Mr. Arthur, Mr. Wilkinson, and the rest ignored the request to meet in conference. Mr. Gompers wired, in substance, that he was with us in sympathy, but he could not possibly come to Chicago at that time. At the meeting held on Sunday evening, which was composed very largely of representatives of organizations affiliated with the American Federation of Labor, of which Mr. Gompers was the head, the representatives passed a resolution not only inviting Mr. Gompers to come to the city of Chicago, but insisting upon his coming—those who were members of his own organization.

Mr. Gompers answered he would come as requested, and he came, together with all the chief officers of all the organizations affiliated with the American Federation of Labor. Mr. Gompers called on me in person the afternoon that he arrived, and invited Mr. Howard, our vice president, and myself to appear before their meeting that evening. We attended that meeting and found, I think, 28 representatives there of the various trades unions affiliated with the American Federation of Labor, some not affiliated with that organization. Upon our entering the hall I was introduced by Mr. Gompers and asked to make a statement to the meeting of all the causes that led up to this strike, and I did so as briefly as I could. At the close of my statement a number of questions were asked by Mr. Gompers and others, which I answered; and at the close of the examination Mr. Howard and myself withdrew from the conference, they remaining in session in secret conference, as I am informed, until the next morning. What took place at that conference I do not know of my own knowledge. I only know from what Mr. Gompers said to me in a personal interview the next day. Does the commission wish to hear that?

*   *   *

Commissioner Wright: State what Mr. Gompers told you if you desire.

Debs: I was going to make this statement. I had said to the conference, "We have no request to make or advice to offer; do what you believe you should do under the circumstances." Then Mr. Gompers asked me what I would do if I were in his place. I said, "Now, understand, I am speaking for no one but myself, but I would make an injury to one in the cause of labor the concern of all. My theory has always been and is now that labor ought to stand by labor, and if I were you, in your place and you in mine, I would muster all the forces of labor in a peaceable effort to secure a satisfactory adjustment of our grievances, even if we had to involve all the industrial industries of the country."

The next day Mr. Gompers called on me in person, accompanied by P. J. McGuire, vice president of the American Federation of Labor, and we had a personal interview lasting 30 or 35 minutes, and Mr. Gompers said the conference was thoroughly in accord with us; that there was no opposition whatever, except on the part of two representatives of the old brotherhoods who were there, and so far as I was concerned they spoke of me in the highest terms, but they were opposed to the American Railway Union, believing it was designed to absorb their organization, but that the conference was wholly in sympathy with the American Railway Union, believing it was right in its struggles, but had reached the conclusion, after long and serious deliberations, that it was not advisable at this time to take an active part in the trouble, informing me, however, they had voted $500 as a contribution to our legal defense fund, and were going to open subscriptions and receive money to provide a legal defense for us; that each and every member felt we were right in this contest; that we ought to be supported; that we ought to win; but did not believe that it was advisable for them to involve themselves in the trouble at that time. Mr. Gompers's assurances to me were in the highest degree assuring so far as our methods, our policy, our purposes, and our attitude were concerned, and he assured us the full measure of sympathy and support that his organization could give.

* * *

Commissioner Wright: Have you any further statements to make with reference to the narrative of events occurring here in Chicago during the recent troubles? I ask that before going on to another subject.

Debs: Yes, sir: I would like to say something with reference to the treatment of this matter by the press. I want to say that from the very beginning of this trouble the American Railway Union in its purposes and all its acts has been very grossly misrepresented by some of the leading newspapers of the city of Chicago. Interviews were printed which were not had at all. I want to relate one instance that came under my personal observation which was published here at the time, but may not have been noticed, to show to what extent we were made the victims of a capitalistic press. I think it is a matter the people ought to understand. We have had no way of contradicting falsehoods that have been told about us in the way of counteracting the vicious impression created by false reports.

At the time of the Briggs House meeting, a reporter on the *Chicago Tribune* named Legwig came to me, in the presence of two witnesses, and said, "I have just been discharged." I said, "What for?" He said, "They had me before the grand jury and wanted me to swear to an interview I had with you, and because I would not commit perjury they discharged me." He then showed me an interview—I had had an interview with him, but it was so perverted and distorted in the paper that I did not recognize it as the same interview. He and several other reporters came to me in confidence, and two other members in confidence, and asked us not to have any feeling against them, because after the copy passed from their hands it went into the hopper and came out in a way that made us say things that never were said, and which they were not at all responsible for. We were made to say the most ridiculous and vicious things imaginable that went through the Associated Press, and then the press of the country generally made editorial attacks upon us predicated upon those alleged interviews. The press of Chicago had hired falsifiers, and I can prove it, men to manufacture reports calculated to bring us into bad repute in this community and throughout the country.

Commissioner Wright: Was this confined to papers representing the side of the railroad, or to both sides of the controversy?

Debs: I think in the main they were inclined to papers representing the railroads. There were other papers that were fair, such papers as the *Chicago News* and the *Chicago Record;* they did not favor either side, they were absolutely impartial, they told the truth. Interviews we had with reporters on those papers were correctly reported. The *Chicago Dispatch,* the *Chicago Mail,* the *Chicago Times* espoused the cause of the strikers and took our side of the case. I am speaking of such papers as the *Herald, Inter Ocean, Tribune, Journal,* and *Post.* Now, for instance, when I left here to go home it was reported and it went over the Associated Press wires, and I found over 300 letters at my home in Terre Haute in regard to it, that I left here in a Pullman car and waved my adieus from a Pullman car. Then all the press in the country said, "When will you fellows stop following that humbug who appeals to the public not to patronize Pullman cars and then rides away in one himself?" Now, I did not do that. I have not set foot on a Pullman car since the 11th day of May, 1894. The press all over the country published that I was riding about in Pullman cars. What was the purpose? It was to arouse the prejudice of the public against me because I happened to stand for labor, to destroy the confidence of labor in me, to set me up as a huge fraud and humbug. Then they published that when the train that I was in arrived at Danville, an angry railroad striker accused me of being responsible for the loss of his job and struck me. There was not a word of truth in that statement. These are two instances of thousands of statements published all over this country, for no other reason except to prejudice the minds of the public against the officers of the American Railway Union.

                    *   *   *

Commissioner Worthington: One other question bearing on the incident of the strike, if I comprehend your statement as to the extent of the strike. It was only to the non-handling of Pullman cars?

Debs: Yes, sir.

Commissioner Worthington: Suppose that on one of the roads that were using Pullman cars a train was made up that did not have a Pullman car on it, did it extend to not working on that train?

Debs: No, sir; the trouble did not extend to that, but a little statement is necessary on that point. Where they were not hauling Pullman cars, it was not intended to inaugurate the strike. There was a definite understanding on that point, but at cities, for instance, like St. Louis, Indianapolis, and other large points, the switching is done by associations; the switching facilities are so arranged that they form a kind of a combination and their relations are so intimately interwoven that when you involve one company you necessarily involve all the rest. At Indianapolis the switchmen struck, including those upon roads where Pullman cars were not handled, but they were involved because they worked in the same yard, used the same track, and it was almost impossible to avoid it; then when it came to putting new men in the switchmen's places the men said they would not work, which involved other roads where Pullman cars were not hauled. One notable instance of that was the Big Four system, where no cars were involved. I do not believe that road would have been involved in the strike at all if it had not been for the fact they had reduced the wages of their employees 10 percent and there was universal dissatisfaction on that system on that account. There was no intention of involving any company that did not haul Pullman cars.

Commissioner Worthington: For interference with any train that did not have Pullman cars attached?

Debs: Yes; that is right. We shall prove on our hearing in court that we agreed to haul mails upon certain roads, agreed to supply men to haul the mails, but that the company refused their services unless the Pullman cars were attached. There are many cases where the railroad companies absolutely refused to haul the mails and were responsible for the delay of the mails because they had formed an alliance with the Pullman company and would not haul the mails or anything else unless the Pullman cars were attached. They alleged they had a contract with the Pullman company that made it obligatory upon them to haul those cars, but they published everything else and never published those contracts.

*   *   *

Commissioner Worthington: You believe generally in the enforcement of law?
Debs: Yes, sir.

Commissioner Worthington: And in the enforcement of proper authority supported by sufficient force to make the law operative?
Debs: Yes, sir.

Commissioner Worthington: It is no part of the object of the American Railway Union in any way to unlawfully resist the authorities, either state, municipal, or federal?
Debs: No, sir.

Commissioner Worthington: You have given considerable thought to this labor question and the best means of preventing strikes or settling difficulties?
Debs: Yes, sir.

Commissioner Worthington: State in a general way what you think is the best to be done in order to avoid strikes and settle the differences that occur between employees and employers, especially where quasi-public corporations are employers.
Debs: Well, there are two ways. One way, of course, of averting a strike is by submitting, by adopting the policy of the old railway brotherhoods that are now existing. Their policy is a submissive one and has been for some time. Nowadays, under their regime, when a railroad manager reduces wages— for instance, he proposes a 20 percent reduction when he only intends a 10 percent reduction, and then compromises on a 10 percent reduction—and submitting in that way averts the strike.

As long as the brotherhood or organizations are non-resisting—that is to say, as long as they submit to whatever may be imposed upon them in the way of reduction—as a matter of course, there will be no strike, but the tendency of wages will be down constantly. That is the mystery of all these organizations. They have gradually succeeded in getting certain schedules under conditions, however, that no longer exist, but whatever they secured in the line of concessions was secured by the power of organized effort. There have been some strikes which have always and everywhere been disastrous to the organizations that participated in them. They have lost thousands of members, men have lost their places, and they have been taxed millions of dollars to keep up strike machinery that never did protect the members. It was this that brought us to the conclusion that if we could unify all the railroad men of the country, or practically do it, we would represent a power that, prudently directed, would be a means of averting strikes. We said, even if the railroad companies could defeat us, it would be such an expense and such a disastrous undertaking for them that if we were organized upon that basis they would agree to settle troubles amicably rather than allow us to go on a strike. That was the hope. If that had not been the hope and belief of the founders of the American Railway Union, that institution would never have been born. We find under the present condition that even if we should be able to unify all of the railroad men of the country it would be impossible to win a strike, because, in the first place, all of the organized orders of society are against the strike.

All of the powers of government are against a strike. For instance, as long as a strike does not inconvenience anybody and bears no indications of succeeding no one cares anything about it, and as a general proposition they just dwindle out to nothing, and except the men who lose their places nobody knows or cares anything about it; but when a strike causes public inconvenience—and a railroad strike inevitably does that—as soon as a strike reaches that point where it gives evidence of being successful, other forces are brought into operation that are, and properly so, impregnable. Since the trouble on the Ann Arbor road—that was the starting point—where Judge Ricks and Judge Taft rendered the first decision in this new field of jurisprudence, from that time until this, whenever there has been a strike, as soon as the point is reached where inconvenience is being caused, then the courts are appealed to and injunctions are served that practically paralyze the organization. Under the existing conditions, if all the railroad men in the country were organized within one brotherhood and acted together, it would be impossible for them to succeed.

*   *   *

Commissioner Worthington: Don't you think that if arbitration in the form of conciliation before a strike occurred was compulsory that, in a great many instances, strikes would be averted?
Debs: No, sir.

Commissioner Worthington: Do you think if an arbitration had been had with the Pullman Company, for instance, and a certain decision arrived at, that the Pullman employees would have been disposed to accept it, or, in other words, not have struck after a fair arbitration?
Debs: Yes, sir; I believe that.

Commissioner Worthington: Could not there be legislation that would have compelled the Pullman Company to arbitrate, and would not such an arbitration have averted that strike?
Debs: In answer to that proposition, let me say I do not believe any good could possibly come from compulsory arbitration; that seems to me to be a contradiction of terms; arbitration to have the desired effect should be mutual and voluntary. If a railroad company is compelled by law to submit to arbitration, it is safe to say that a verdict or result, whatever it may be, and more especially if it is adverse to the railroad company, will not be very agreeable to them, and they will not feel any kinder toward their employee. My idea is to secure harmonious relations, there must be kindness and mutual confidence as a basis. In compulsory arbitration that is the relation that will bind an employer and employee together; force them to maintain that relation and it will not be either pleasant or satisfactory. I really think on the whole the condition of the employee would become worse instead of better, and I believe more harm than good would come out of compulsory arbitration.

*   *   *

Commissioner Kernan: Have you any doubt that if public opinion had been directly informed as to the entire situation the strike would probably have been averted and that you would have succeeded in your just demands?

Debs: I believe that is true.

Commissioner Kernan: Don't you think that if before a strike was inaugurated there was a law requiring a tribunal to sit as this one is now doing and investigate all the facts and hear all the parties that that would be a very efficient means of enlisting public opinion and enlisting its sympathies upon the side of right?

Debs: Yes, sir; but everything depends upon the board. If it were this board I would unhesitatingly say yes.

Commissioner Kernan: After giving the answers you have, why is it you take the position that nothing can be done as a relief worth trying, except government ownership of railroads?

Debs: I believe that is the logical conclusion. My idea is to make a reform positive and complete at once; in place of traveling along slowly inch by inch to reach the same destination.

Commissioner Kernan: Is it not a very seriously debated question whether government ownership of railroads is in the end beneficial to the companies that have it?

Debs: I confess it is a very serious question. There is no doubt in my mind, though I do not claim, of course, to have fathomed it in all its details and effects.

Commissioner Kernan: Assuming that the fact is that government ownership of railroads results in poor service and higher rates than ownership by individuals or private corporations, what effect would that have upon your views?

Debs: It does not have that effect where it has been tried.

Commissioner Kernan: But assuming it does, that an examination of the history of the question shows that result, how would that affect your judgment?

Debs: I should not favor it if the conditions were to be worse than they are now. I only favor it on condition it might be reasonably demonstrated that the conditions were to be decidedly improved.

Commissioner Kernan: You think it ought not to be adopted unless it would not only benefit labor, but also give the public better service and at more reasonable rates?

Debs: Yes, sir. I believe that is the only way discrimination will ever be abolished.

Commissioner Kernan: Do you not see that the acquirement of railroads by the government would involve very great friction, and unless it was actual confiscation upon terms laid down by the government, would require a long time to adjust?

Debs: Yes, sir.

Commissioner Kernan: In the interim, therefore, what are your views as to how we had better meet the situation and attempt to assuage the present condition?

Debs: Leaving aside the question of ultimate government ownership?

Commissioner Kernan: Yes, as one that is, under the circumstances, so far remote and difficult to bring about that it will take some time, at least, to deal with that question. Without that remedy, what would be your views in that aspect of it?

Debs: My views are that if the administrative department of the government were right, there would be no further legislation required than that we already have to prevent such outbreaks as we have had here. It is the perfect confidence with which the railroads depend upon the powers of society and of the government to come to their rescue that prompts them to trample underfoot the rights of their employees with impunity and do many other things which, if they were left to fight their own battles, they would not do. But they know when they are in conflict with their employees they can with perfect confidence rely upon the strong arm of the state government and national government to come to their rescue, and this is what inspires them to do many things that result in trouble which they would not. We, as the American Railway Union, have always said at every step we have taken that we wanted the public to know what we were doing. We have not a secret connected with our organization. We do not hold a secret meeting; we have not a grip, sign, or password, for the reason we have said such mysteries destroyed the confidence of the people in our work, and we want to do everything and let the whole world know we will not do anything that is wrong or that we are ashamed of.

We have always said we were in favor of arbitrating every difficulty. Every proposal we have made in that direction has been rejected with scorn. We have nothing to look forward to to defend us in times of trouble. We have only got a number, and a limited number, of poorly paid men in our organization, and when their income ceases they are starving. We have no power of the government behind us. We have no recognized influence in society on our side. We have absolutely nothing but the men who begin to starve when they quit work. On the other side, the corporations are in perfect alliance; they have all of the things that money can command, and that means a subsidized press, that they are able to control the newspapers, and means a false or vitiated public opinion. The clergy almost steadily united in thundering their denunciations; then the courts, then the state militia, then the federal troops; everything and all things on the side of corporations. When the authorities are called upon to intercede in troubles of this kind, do they ever ask labor a question? Never. They always go to where capital sits in council and there receive their orders, as I view it—do what they command shall be done.

We have had a great many conflicts in this country between capital and labor. We know by experience and by the truth of history that in a great many of those conflicts, the workingmen were right. We know that their wages were unjustly reduced and their rights trampled down. When and where did the militia ever come out and take its stand on the side of labor, to prevent the workingmen's being robbed and degraded? Never. Whenever and wherever they have been called out, it was always to take their place on the side of the capitalist. They have gone into partnership with the oppressors of labor to crush labor. If there was a perfect sense of duty and justice prevailing at the proper places, they would not have to exercise their powers as they now do, always with the one purpose of crushing the workingmen. They could enforce the demands of justice without any additional legislation on the subject, in my opinion; but the moneyed power, it seems to me, is potential enough to control all this machinery, and will be able to do it with the additional legislation that you propose, in my opinion.

Commissioner Worthington: Would it not be able to do it to a still greater extent if the government owned the railroads, because it would have more employees under the government to be reached politically?

Debs: Not to the same extent, in my opinion, for the reason if the government owned the railroads the people would have a citizen interest in those railroads.

Commissioner Kernan: How about the poor man that was laboring in some outside employment or unable to get any labor at all; would he not necessarily grow to regard the railroad employees as members of a favored class?

Debs: That carries me several steps further. He also is a victim of a wage system which I believe in abolishing entirely.

Commissioner Wright: Do you believe there is no solution of any of these troubles under the present industrial system?

Debs: No, sir; that is my candid conviction.

Commissioner Kernan: Then government ownership of railroads is only an expedient; it is not a final solution after all?

Debs: It would be a final solution so far as the railroads are concerned, but not of other matters.

Commissioner Kernan: Then would government ownership of all trades and property follow as a solution of the other?

Debs: I believe in a cooperative commonwealth as a substitute for the wage system.

Commissioner Wright: Another name for state socialism?

Debs: No, sir; I do not call myself a socialist. There is a wide difference in the interpretation or definition of the term. I believe in a cooperative commonwealth upon the principles laid down by Laurence Gronlund. You may have read his works. I believe that is the rational solution of the whole question. We recognize the main features of state socialism. I can say in relation to the wage system that in my judgment—I am studying this question and I want much more light than I have got; I am in need of much more, and speak for nobody but myself—but I am impressed with the conviction that the social and industrial conditions will grow worse instead of better, so long as the wage system remains in vogue. If a man is obliged to depend upon another man as to whether he shall work or not, he is a slave.

Now, with the introduction of labor-saving machinery—and that is a misnomer, in my judgment, of labor-displacing machinery—and unrestricted foreign immigration, we now have the spectacle of ten wage workers who have families depending upon their support competing for the same job of work. There are not jobs enough to go around, and the result is a great many men out of work. They are bidding against each other—as a matter of course we all believe, as we say we do, in the freedom of contracts, and during this late trouble all of the papers, or the principal papers, in the country, said, "We have to maintain that principle if we have to do it with shot and shell, Army and Navy—that a man can work for anybody he chooses to work for and for any figure that may be agreeable between them." I deny any such proposition as that—

Commissioner Wright: Just there, do you mean to say that nine men out of every ten are out of employment?

Debs: No, sir; not on the whole. I meant to say that was the case in many parts of the country.

Commissioner Wright: I understood you to say that ten men were bidding against each other for one job, which but one could get.

Debs: I meant to apply that locally. I was out in Colorado and saw that condition there; I did not mean that that is the condition in the whole country.[110] Professor Ely says that we have 3 million able-bodied paupers in this country, and I regard him as good authority on that subject. We have men bidding and compelled to bid by their necessities, having families dependent upon them, and they have to work, and they bid against each other, and the man who bids the least gets the work, and the others are out of work. Now, I have said, I deny men have a right to do that; no matter what may be said about the freedom of contract under our Constitution, no man has a right to sell himself into slavery; no man has a right to do that; and yet that is what it amounts to if a man agrees to work at unliving wages, and that is precisely what they do—what the wage system compels them to do.

I am not opposed to immigration; on the contrary, I think under proper restrictions there is room for millions of people to come to this country to be good citizens, but that undesirable element of immigration of which this country has been made the dumping ground, brought here at the behest of corporations in the state of Pennsylvania, for instance. As an example, a few years ago in the state of Pennsylvania miners were getting from $4 to $6 per day and were enabled to live as becomes American citizens. Then the operators combined, sent their agent to Europe, and imported the most vicious element of European countries, men who are working today at from 40 to 65 cents per day; men who did not live in huts or in hovels, but in holes in the ground, like animals, displacing the miners who lived as becomes American citizens and educated their children so they might be in a condition of intelligence to perpetuate free institutions. And then a great many people wonder where the Coxey Army comes from. Now, with all this element that comes in here to compete against our own labor, displacing as they have done a vast number of workingmen, together with the improved machinery that has done away with the services of thousands of men, competition is bound, in my judgment, inevitably to degenerate into perfect slavery, if it does not already exist.

Commissioner Kernan: Then, I understand, you favor some restriction of immigration, so as to prevent an undesirable element from coming in and competing in the way you suggest?
Debs: Yes, sir.

*   *   *

Commissioner Kernan: Is it not your position that not only railroad employees, but all employees who work for hire, ought in a strike of the kind we have just passed through stand and support the striking organizations?
Debs: Yes, sir; I will give you my reason for that.

Commissioner Kernan: I want to ask one question that is in my mind. If a condition existed in the country like that, would it not be exceedingly dangerous to the peace and welfare of the country?

Debs: I do not believe it would be as dangerous as it is now, for the reason if labor was as thoroughly organized as we contemplate, the men who control capital would be more considerate of the rights of labor.

Commissioner Kernan: Look at the question from your standpoint and see what the result would be if carried out in that direction; would not the result be that the men must reach the conclusion that we must try to devise some way of at least providing temporary expedients and remedies rather than permit things to go to such an extreme?

Debs: I don't know; that depends upon circumstances some. I think where there is an ill, it is well in place of applying expedients . . . and out of that will come a better condition. It seems to me if we were so thoroughly organized, we could very promptly stop the whole machinery. It would stop on the very spot by abolishing the wage system, and that is what I desire.

Commissioner Kernan: Is it not quite likely that the human nature of such an organization would lead it to become tyrannical and as unjust as those resisting it?

Debs: Yes; I believe human nature is about alike on each side.

Commissioner Kernan: That is an objection, then, in the direction which you suggest?

Debs: I think not, for the reason that impelled us to organize the American Railway Union. I believe a little power is dangerous. I believe that organized labor is much more tyrannical, much more dangerous to society and to itself with a little power than if it had more power. For instance, take 100 switchmen—I only refer to the switchmen to illustrate the point because all railroad men are practically alike—and organize 10 or 12 of them, and you will have a strike in 15 minutes. They want to demonstrate their power, and the probabilities are that the company will do something to provoke them to strike, or encourage them at least; but suppose all of those switchmen are organized, suppose the great body of railroad men were organized, and more prudent counsel will prevail; the organization will be more conservative, and the chances for strike largely reduced.

Commissioner Kernan: Instead of permitting this unification to go forward in the present way, what would you say in regard to having it done in the same way unification of capital is permitted—by incorporate charters, where legal restrictions could be asserted for the protection of the members?

Debs: There would be this difficulty: Railroad companies are managed by a board of directors. The board can meet in a small room and transact their business expeditiously; they can do as they please, and there is more or less business of a private character connected with all large enterprises. Nine men on a board of directors may control thousands of miles of roads and thousands of employees. There are no police to interfere with them, nobody disturbs them; they meet in secret and do their work, transact their agreements. On the other hand, the interests of labor are not committed to the hands of three or four men; thousands of them who have not had the early advantage of an education, who are ignorant and suspicious, some of whom are vicious, and they are more difficult to control; everything they do has to be done in public. If they hold meetings to prepare to strike, instantly the police stand ready to pounce down on them and disperse them. It is a force that cannot be controlled. The force of capital is controlled by educated, trained men, experienced men; they handle interests of a much greater magnitude, and in that way can do it much more effectually and expeditiously.

Commissioner Kernan: Why could not all the provisions that you refer to be preserved in a charter and sufficient elasticity be given to it to preserve the features you now have and get provisions added by which the organization would be recognized as a legal body and act as such?

Debs: I don't know but that would be a good idea. But the trouble is to get the railroad men to harmonize. They are in rival organizations now, that is the misfortune of it, and what one favors the other blindly opposes.

Commissioner Kernan: Looking at it fairly, is it not true that, after all; in the present condition of labor, its disadvantages you speak of are caused not only by the antagonism of corporations and capital, but also by the inability it has heretofore displayed to organize itself and unite upon wise and temperate lines?

Debs: Yes, sir; I admit that.

* * *

Commissioner Worthington: I receive the impression from the statement you made that if labor was unified as we have been speaking of it here this afternoon, it would be followed by the abolition of the wage system, in your judgment. Did you intend to be understood in that way?

Debs: I do not know that I intended to be understood just that way. I meant, in the first place, that these troubles could be reduced, as it seems to me, to a minimum, if the forces are unified; and then it was suggested that there would be something popping all the time if we were to go to each other's rescue. Then I said if it brought on a condition under which we were to be continually in turmoil, that would result in the abolishment of the wage system.

Commissioner Worthington: The state of turmoil in consequence of labor would abolish the wage system, not the unification of labor.

Debs: That is what I meant to say. If labor were thoroughly unified and able to secure what it believes to be its due it might be well enough satisfied with the wage system, but I do not believe that is possible with our present human nature.

*   *   *

Commissioner Wright: What has been the effect of the recent troubles on the membership of the American Railway Union?

Debs: I believe the American Railway Union is stronger today, numerically and in every other way, than it ever was since its organization. We are adding to our membership every day.

Commissioner Worthington: Is it not a fact that the men constituting the volunteer militia as a general thing are workingmen—wage earners?

Debs: Yes; very many of them.

Commissioner Worthington: Is there anything further you desire to state?

Debs: I believe nothing now.

Commissioner Wright: If there are any representatives present of the Rock Island or Illinois Central Railroad companies who desire to cross-examine Mr. Debs, they have the opportunity now.

[No response. Witness excused.]

The Limit of Endurance[†]
September 1894

Everything has its limits except space and eternity, provided they can be called things. The mind and all of its wonderful faculties: thought, imagination, hope, fear, and aspirations, all operate within certain boundaries. It may be said that time should be included with space and eternity—perhaps so; it is not essential since we absolutely know nothing of either. True, for convenience we divide and subdivide time and space, but eternity is beyond our grasp, and we

---

† Published in *Locomotive Firemen's Magazine,* vol. 18, no. 9 (September 1894), 877–879.

let it alone. And time and space, though we talk about seconds and centuries, of inches and miles, we find as we proceed that all limits vanish, and we turn our attention to things which have limits, and determine as best we may what their limits are. Life has its limits, our years are numbered—three score and ten is the limit;[111] millions fall short of it, a few go beyond it. The luxuries of wealth have their limit; the privations of poverty have their limit. Human joys and human sorrows have their boundaries. Crime and cruelty, virtue and vice operate within certain restrictions fixed by human depravity, or human probity, regardless of any particular form of government. In a despotism the autocrat determines limits; in a democracy the people exercise that power; in either case it is human willpower, not divine power, and, it being human power that prescribes limits, it becomes possible for human power to change the limits, to broaden or contract them.

As to the limit of human endurance, history is full of examples, in reading which the mind either expands with rapturous delight or evinces unutterable scorn and detestation. Slavery is an old-time institution. What were the conditions before the flood we are not advised, but as human slavery includes the sum total of human depravity, we do not doubt that the giants—for there were giants, we are told, in those faraway times—subjugated those of less power and brought about that condition of wickedness which prompted the Creator to declare He would annihilate the race; the limit of sin had been reached as also the limit of Jehovah's patience, but his wrath was modified to the extent of saving one man and his family, Noah, all others were drowned as if they had been so many rats.[112] Again we find, according to the record that divine as certainly as human endurance has its limits, as, for instance, the cruelties inflicted upon the Israelites in Egypt.[113] These cruelties became so continuous and flagitious that in the councils of the Almighty that vengeance took the place of patience. The grievance committees of the oppressed Israelites were repulsed by Pharaoh, à la Pullman, until all heaven cried, "Shame!" just as all the Pullman employee pointed their fingers at Pharaoh Pullman and held him up to the scorn of all workingmen of America whose chicken hearts and white livers had not taken refuge in their boots. Outside of heaven there was no sympathy for the Israelites when Moses ordered the strike, and in dealing with it, God, who was first, last, and all the time on the side of Moses, the great labor agitator, did not consider in the slightest degree the inconvenience His methods would bring upon the innocent people of Egypt. To subdue Pharaoh the people suffered every plague, and there were nine of them fell upon the people with the same terrific force that they fell upon Pharaoh. It was Jehovah's way of managing a strike, and as the strike proceeded, Jehovah's wrath burned with a fiercer fury, until, to bring Pharaoh to terms, the firstborn in every family of the Egyptians was slain in a night, then while all Egypt was rapt in mourning, while every family was wailing, while the embalmers were at work making a mummy in every Egyptian home, the limit of endurance was reached, and Pharaoh consented to let the enslaved Egyptians go, and suspend brickmaking for a time; but he had no sooner consented than he relented and followed the fugitives and met his Red Sea defeat. Ultimate limits of divine and human patience had been reached, and the right won a victory.

Since that epoch in the history of labor, numberless Pharaohs have arisen to oppress, rob, and degrade the world's toilers and put to the test human endurance, and in millions of instances the limit has been reached, and the victims of oppression have gone down to death, unknelled, uncoffined, unshrouded, and unsung; and still the Pharaohs and the Pullmans and the corporations and the courts and the armies are driving men to the uttermost limits of endurance. In doing this, the pulpit comes to the rescue, and recites Paul's direction to Titus "to be subject to principalities and powers," and "obey magistrates,"[114] which, had it been followed by the patriots of '76, there would have been no Declaration of Independence, there would have been no great American republic, a new nation would not have been born, and "the flag of the free heart's only home"[115] would never have waved over "the land of the free and the home of the brave."

We would have remained the subjects of King George and would never have known the inspiring thrill of manhood sovereignty. But the limits of human endurance had been reached, and Patrick Henry condensed it all into a sentence when he said: "Give me liberty, or give me death."[116] Then the patriots of the colonies struck for liberty, regardless of inconveniences, sacrifices, death, and desolation. Property was destroyed, the laws of England were set at defiance, and after an eight-year struggle, victory perched upon the standard of Washington. King George and his armies were driven away, a price was set upon Washington's head, there was treason in his camps, but France, looking on, said liberty is a good thing, the cause of Washington is just, and from sheer *sympathy* joined in the strike and helped to win a victory. Indeed, without such sympathy the struggling Continental Armies might have gone down in defeat. And yet thousands of workingmen whose vital interests are involved, under the leadership of a Tory press, declaim against sympathy as if it were a crime.

The question arises: Will the time ever come in America when the toiling masses will declare that decreased wages and consequent poverty and degradation have reached the furthermost limits of endurance? Already such conditions have been reached by multiplied thousands, and other thousands are yearly being drawn down to death in the maelstrom of corporate greed. Here and there they appeal to their fellow toilers as fate bears them on toward the verge of the vortex for help, for sympathy, telling them they too are approaching by steady steps to the engulfing whirlpool, but a hireling press and armies of degenerate men tell them their fears are groundless and their protests criminal, and other thousands of their fellow toilers, eating the crumbs which fall from rich men's tables, moral and mental deformities, rattle their chains and chuckle as they see men straggle, as they hear them protest, and by forces they cannot withstand [are held] to silence.

Men talk of hard times, of commercial, financial, and industrial demoralization, and while they talk and scheme, the corporations rob their victims and the limit of human endurance is reached, and trouble begins. The toilers are ostracized, the rich only have influence, they pursue their victims to the uttermost limits of endurance and when they turn upon their pursuers the government brings out its judicial and its military machines, injunctions cover the land like shrouds, marshals swarm like bees in June, troops shoot and stab, the innocent and the guilty pour out their life blood, and the proclamation goes forth: "Quiet reigns." The government for the corporation, of the corporation, and by the corporation triumphs; the government for, of, and by the people, ceases to be—no, not that exactly—"Freedom's battle once begun stands numberless defeats."[117] The champions of the poor may be imprisoned, perish in dungeons, starved and exiled until their bones fill all the valleys, but at last the genius of liberty shall breathe upon the dry bones, and as in the prophet's vision the world shall see rise up an army, greater than all standing armies of potentates and plutocrats, an army equipped with moral and with physical power that shall bear down and sweep away all opposition and win a victory for labor, the fruition of which shall last until the sun is cold.

An Appeal to Labor†

September 1, 1894

Men and Brothers:—

The Pullman strike, under the auspices of the American Railway Union, has created an issue which, while it has resulted in the arrest and indictment of the officers of the American Railway Union, places on trial, as never before, organized labor of the country. In other words, the trial of the officers of the American Railway Union is absolutely the trial of organized labor.

The Necessity for Funds

In the coming trial, every thoughtful member of labor organizations will appreciate the fact that labor will be confronted by organized railroad capital, representing billions.

Against this formidable array of money, and the power of money, stands organized labor on trial, because the organization known as the American Railway Union unfurled and flung to the breeze the banner of resistance to wrongs which, the more they are contemplated, the more monstrous they appear.

The defense of the American Railway Union officials, which is but another way of stating the fact that organized labor is to be defeated, requires money, and a large amount of money, to enable organized labor to grapple with organized capital and maintain successfully its standing before the tribunals, where, by the fiat of the court, it is to plead.

The Amount Which Should Be Raised

In making this appeal to organized labor, and the friends of organized labor throughout the land, I do not hesitate to aver my belief that *$100,000* should be contributed.[118] The amount, at first glance, may seem large, but it dwindles to insignificance when the magnitude of the issues involved are considered.

What Are the Issues?

I answer: the eternal right of workingmen to organize; to demand their rights; to resist oppression; to confer together in all matters relating to their welfare;

---

†   Published in the *Railway Times,* vol. 1, no. 17 (September 1, 1894), 1.

and finally, as the last resort, to strike. These unalienable rights are in peril. The American Railway Union voiced them and championed them, and when they were attacked, corporations cheered and sustained by the money power, the American Railway Union protested, proposed peaceable adjustments, and, failing in all propositions, finally gave its endorsement of the strike, which is impressing upon the national mind the fact that wrongs must be redressed if peace and prosperity are to succeed the storm.

For this defiant and patriotic attitude of the American Railway Union, in the interest of organized labor and the welfare of the country, its officers have been indicted, and with them there will be a trial of organized labor. In the contemplation of ultimate verdicts, the few men who have been indicted, as compared with the thousands whose interests are involved, are of comparatively little consequence. If the verdict of the jury stays the hand of vengeance, if corporate power is humbled by the fiat of justice, if the indicted defenders of workingmen's rights go forth free to proclaim that law and liberty are still in alliance, then in that case organized labor will take on new strength and courage, drooping hopes will revive, and faith in the perpetuity of free institutions will stretch forth its hands to grasp the fruitions of labor redeemed by the genius of justice. If, however, the money power of corporations shall be able to debauch jurors, if the verdict dooms the men to prison who dared, when labor pleaded for the reinstatement of its rights, to stand forth, regardless of consequences, in the van of the conflict, then in that case the doom of organized labor is sealed.

The Battle Is On

The corporate enemies of organized labor, with all the appliances and equipments of war, are scheming for strategic advantages, and the preliminaries of the battle are seen in every direction. To meet them and thwart their schemes, money is required. In making this appeal for contributions to the defense fund, I am not playing the role of mendicant. I simply say that, in the persons of the indicted officials of the American Railway Union, the rights of organized labor are indissolubly linked. No power can disunite their destiny. Hence, such contributions as may be made are for the emancipation of organized labor from aristocratic, plutocratic, and corporate thralldoms, the contemplation of which fills the mind with alarm.

Only those who are deeply imbued with the conviction that the rights of organized labor are in peril are asked to contribute, and if these give a fraction, even a tenth of one day's income, I do not doubt we shall be able to send out, all over the width of the land, Perry's immortal dispatch: "We have met the enemy, and they are ours."

Eugene V. Debs,
President, American Railway Union

(Friendly papers please copy.)

Separate Organizations Can Never Succeed: Speech to the Seventeenth Convention of the B of LF, Harrisburg, Pennsylvania[119]

September 13, 1894

Worthy Grand Master and Brothers:—

I address this body from a point of right and justice; I never go where I am not wanted, and I will leave it to a majority here to decide if I am to be heard. I understand that an effort has been made to bar the door against me, and if this effort is sustained by this body, I will retire. I have heard that I was to be deposed as editor of the *Magazine,* that my resignation has been accepted. I also hear that my character has been attacked. I came here to respond to all charges and innuendos affecting my character. I leave it to you whether I shall be heard in my own defense or not.

*   *   *

I thank you all for this courtesy. I realize there are those who are opposed to me. There are those who are opposed to giving me an opportunity to be heard on my own behalf.

Two years ago, we met in Cincinnati. After 12 years in the service of the brotherhood, I went there to resign and not to accept anything. My resignation was unanimously refused. I told those delegates that I did not agree in policy with the Brotherhood of Locomotive Firemen; I told them that I did not want the *Magazine,* but the delegates insisted.

†   Published without title in *Journal of Proceedings of the Fourth Biennial Convention (Seventeenth Convention) of the Brotherhood of Locomotive Firemen: Held in the City of Harrisburg, Pa., September 10, 11, 12, 13, 14, 15, 17, 18, 19, and 20, 1894.* Terre Haute, IN: Moore & Langen, 1894; 499–505.

They told me, "Let us have your name in connection with the *Magazine,* for it will be helpful." If I made a mistake in accepting this position, the responsibility is shared by you. I accepted the position as editor of the *Magazine* on three stipulations: First, that I should not be a grand officer; second, that I should not be the manager of the business connected with the *Magazine;* and third, that my salary should not exceed the sum of $900 per year. The committee insisted on paying me $3,000 per year, and I accepted $1,000.

At that time I had concluded that the brotherhood was a failure as a protective organization, and I have not changed that opinion. I believe that everyone should have a right to his opinion and a right to express it. I believe that the protective features of the brotherhood are not a success, but I have been accused of saying more.

In all my life I have never directly, or indirectly, injured the Brotherhood of Locomotive Firemen. I have never said to a member that he should leave the brotherhood. I have never said it here or anywhere else. I have always advised firemen to stay with the brotherhood. That's what I said, and I defy anyone to contradict it. The dream of my life has been to unify the railroad men of this country. Under existing conditions all railway organizations of the country cannot cope with the railway corporations. The Great Northern made a reduction of from 10 to 60 percent. This reduction was made by James Hill because he knew that he could make this reduction on account of the condition of organized labor. All the organizations submitted to it because they knew that they could not possibly win a strike. But the American Railway Union resisted it; the men united and stood together. They struck and stayed out 18 days and had their wages restored. I claim that this was a positive vindication of my position and shows that railwaymen ought to cooperate. It has been charged that the sympathetic strike is absolutely criminal, but I claim that it is not.

You can never succeed with the men divided in separate organizations. If engineers have a grievance, the firemen will have none. An injury to one should be an injury to all. It is wrong to be separate. The corporations do not take this view of it; when a road becomes involved in a strike, the other roads, the newspapers, the banks, and all the rest come to the rescue. I only wish that labor might follow the example set by capital. That is the only way you will ever protect yourselves. I do not believe that a strike to be successful must be supported by public sentiment. I care nothing about public sentiment. Public sentiment hanged John Brown. I haven't forgotten that public sentiment supported slavery for years. If organized labor has a mission, it is to make war on public sentiment that makes these conditions possible. What are brotherhoods going to do to relieve this calamity? What are any of these organizations going to do to relieve this calamity? I do not believe that this brotherhood will move the country upward in one hundred years.

They accuse me of saying many things against you. Here is what I have said: I regard the average lodge meeting of the Brotherhood of Locomotive Firemen a farce. They go and remain until 12:00 and 1:00 at night engaged in some foolish initiation. What do they do? The lodge room should be a schoolroom. When they go home, they should read books on the subject of finance, land, and rights of labor. Intelligence is what is required; ceremonies give no returns.

It is said that I have attacked the beneficiary features of your organization. I say to you, no man should be compelled to carry insurance, whether he can or not. You say that you must protect your widows and orphans. You have expelled thousands of widows and orphans—you have expelled three or four thousand members per year. I said so at San Francisco. When their last dollar is gone, they are expelled. Who provides for their widows and orphans? You claim that you practice charity. There is no charity in it. A member pays for everything he gets, and he can get just as good investments in any insurance company.

I have said that I do not believe in your federation. One man has the power to paralyze all organizations. Suppose you have federated the Brotherhood of Locomotive Engineers, the Brotherhood of Locomotive Firemen, the Conductors, the Brakemen, and Switchmen on the Santa Fe. Suppose you have a grievance and all vote to strike. The grand officers meet, and if a single one objects there will be no strike. His voice outweighs all. No man should be vested with such autocratic authority. A 10 percent reduction means millions of dollars a year and thousands of dollars per month and a railway company can afford to buy one. I am accused of being in bad company; my associates may not be right, but I think they will compare very favorably with Wilkinson and Arthur. Mr. Wilkinson had 425 switchmen discharged and furnished men to take their places. I do not wish to say anything against Arthur here. He is the worst enemy of labor today. He is the owner of a paper that fights labor; he is the director of a bank, and the railways endorse him; and they say that I am the opposite. No man can be a friend of a corporation and a friend of labor. A railway official may be friendly with you personally, but he is subservient to those above him. I am one of those who believe that no railroad man gets too much wages; there are many not getting enough.

In May 1893, 27 general managers formed a protective association. I have a report of that meeting. They have banded themselves together to fight labor. In cases of trouble all are to go together, all assessments prorated; the corporation is supplied with men, money, and machinery. They declared at their meeting that if they acted in concert they could reduce wages. They began on the L&N;[120] they took in the ETV&G[121] and then the "Big Four."[122] One after another they reduced wages, a few at a time. Then the Union Pacific and Northern Pacific, and then the Great Northern. That's where we stopped it. The Chicago & Great Western was ready to reduce wages but stopped then and there. Their purpose was not to arouse all at the same time. The General Managers' Association had books printed giving uniform wages so that they could say that they could pay no more than other lines. Then they would make more reductions until they had their men down to the level of slaves.

If class organizations had been equal to requirements, they should have resisted these reductions. The others do not act in good faith with you in your plan. The "Big Four" had no cause to reduce wages, and if all had been organized no reduction would have taken place. On the Union Pacific it was Judge Caldwell and not the organizations that saved the reductions. He said that while the road was in the hands of the court, the road must pay the old wages [even] if no dividend was paid. If it had not been for Judge Caldwell, wages would have been reduced. The millionaires must have their dividends, must have their share even though you starve. If the men on the Great Northern had depended on your class organizations, that money saved to the employees would have been pouring into the coffers of the stockholders. Some men say times are hard. I admit that. I admit there are hard times—but there are fewer trains and they limit their expenses to their revenue, yet they reduce wages.

Not long since there was a railway official in Chicago that spoke to me. He said, "Debs, now is the time to make the master stroke of your life. If you will recommend that the men accept these reductions now, you will put the companies in a position to restore wages when business improves."

I said to him, "Your road has been doing an overwhelming business in the last 60 days, why do you not increase wages? Did you ever voluntarily increase the wages of your employees on account of increased business?" He did not remember that he ever had. When times are hard they reduce your wages, yet when prosperity comes they are not willing to increase wages. Within recent years, conditions have changed. Railroad companies are getting close together, but when the men get in trouble, others take their places. They have you quarrel over religion and politics. The officials endorse the APA,[123] and that is evidence to my mind that it is destruction to you. During the late trouble I had a talk with a private detective who was once a brotherhood man and had sympathy for their cause. He told me of something that occurred in one of the general managers' meetings. Mr. St. John, a general manager, got up and said, "You can't handle that man Debs, you can't handle the ARU. We must crush him and the ARU. He did not say anything about crushing the other organizations."

You talk about class organizations. You have no class organizations.[124] Wilkinson told me that he had 500 firemen in the Trainmen's. You have no class organization. Poll this convention and you will find a very large number here who are engaged in other departments. There is no strictly class organizations. I have seen wipers[125] that belonged to the B of LE. Why not have an organization to represent all? There are 12,000 engineers, I believe, in the Brotherhood of Locomotive Firemen. I believe you have 26,000 members; this would leave 14,000, and you must take into consideration the 5,000 more who are hostlers, in other branches of the service or out of business entirely. There are 40,000 firemen in Canada, the United States, and Mexico. If, after 21 years, you have succeeded in organizing 10,000, at that rate you will have the firemen organized in 60 years. You are spilling them out as fast as you are taking them in. You have expelled 3,000 per year; this, with the withdrawals, is simply suicide.

I have said that no brotherhood ever won a strike. Recall and name the strikes of the brotherhoods. You were defeated on the CB&Q,[126] on the Ann Arbor, the Lehigh Valley, and on the Elevated road.[127] You have never won a strike. The companies are opposed to your coming together. The companies know you would be better off. The companies make little concessions to you so as to bind you up in contracts so that you stand idly by while they crush others.

You talk about your insurance. The protective features of your organizations are the main thing. That is what puts money in your pockets, and with money in your pockets you can buy insurance. Without protection, your brotherhood is a failure. Will you tell me if there is a road in the country where the brotherhood could protect you from a 10 percent reduction of your wages? Conditions have changed; centralization is the order of the age, and because I have tried to centralize labor I have been condemned. I admit I have ambition. I have worked for the ARU for $75 per month and have not collected that. I was elected president of the ARU on the 12th day of June [1894]. I wanted to retire from official life; I tendered my resignation; I told them I would help them, but as a member. They would not allow me to retire. Has Mr. Arthur ever tendered his resignation? The labor organizations would unite today but for the grand officers. I make you this proposition, I and my associates, my colleagues, will resign if the other grand officers will resign. Will Mr. Arthur, Mr. Wilkinson, or Mr. Clark accept this proposition? Yet they say I am selfish.

I want you to unify; it doesn't matter how much you unify, you can wipe out the name ARU, but you must unify. When you make contracts for firemen, make contracts for all. Give the wiper justice, the engineer, give justice to all.

Railway corporations use one organization to defeat another. You say, "We can't break our contracts;" do they break their contracts? Did the Lehigh break its contract with the men? On the Great Northern the ARU strived to obtain justice, and the brotherhoods did everything to defeat us, but we won. In the late strike of the ARU, members of the brotherhood took their places and in many instances took their own brothers' places. Who profited? It was a righteous strike; I can prove that it was a righteous strike. The railway companies relied on the brotherhoods. I make the prediction that Mr. Arthur will never order another strike. He knows that for every man that would strike, there are 40 ready to take his job. I do not approve of this, but it is a fact. When there is a strike, thousands of men will flood in that direction. I am not criticizing you, I am only telling the truth. The officials are independent and would reduce wages but know that for a while yet conditions will be feverish.

I want to ask you this question: Why do you strike as a last resort, why a last resort? The courts would enjoin you and your grand officers, no messages could be sent. Grover Cleveland would send soldiers to put bullets into hearts. If you did strike, then wouldn't it be suicide? They would have plenty of men to take your places. The corporations have no use for you. They persecute you when you attack wrong. When the officers tell you that the brotherhoods are all right, don't believe it because they say so. I could have the favors of the railway officials if I wanted them. I don't ride on passes; this is the irony of fate, for it was I who first procured an annual pass for a grand officer.

In all probability I will never appear at a firemen's convention again. I joined the Brotherhood of Locomotive Firemen at the age of 19 years. I was appointed grand secretary and treasurer by the then grand master, Brother F. W. Arnold. When I received this appointment, I did not seek the position. I was city clerk of Terre Haute with bright prospects in other channels. Brother Sam Stevens came to see me three different times and begged me to accept the position. He said, "You can save the brotherhood." When I took charge the brotherhood was bankrupt, the publishers of the *Magazine* were pressing a bill for $1,800 for the printing of the *Magazine*. I gave a note for this amount. Some said there is no use to build up the brotherhood, you will be robbed again. There were unpaid beneficiary claims; I secured them all myself. When I tell you this, I do not want your sympathy; I tell you this so that you can see if I am as selfish as what has been said against me here. I paid $1,000 out of my salary of $1,500 to pay beneficiary claims. At the convention, the brother-hood was demoralized. I went from room to room and begged them to remain true—but another year and I would guarantee the brotherhood would be out of debt. At Buffalo, I subscribed $60 out of my own pocket.[128] I worked that year as I never worked before—it was slavery. For six years I knew no Sunday. I used my salary as city clerk; I worked one year for nothing and paid out $800 for the brotherhood. The second year, I drew $1,500 and paid out $1,300 for clerk hire. This left me $200. The third year, I received $2,000 and still paid clerk hire. In 1884, I received $2,000 and clerk hire. I had no passes. I packed my grip and went out to work for the brotherhood, was put off of trains and did the best I could to get over the roads. The first seven years, I never drew one cent for expenses. Every dollar I drew went into lodge meetings. When I was appointed grand secretary and treasurer, I was also editor of the *Magazine* without compensation until 1880. From 1886 to 1890 I received $500 per year. At San Francisco I received $1,000 per year.[129]

The brotherhood began to grow, to expand at all times. Since I was con-nected with this organization, I defy any man to question my integrity offi-cially. I put up the money for the brotherhood. When I did this my friends said "no," but I had faith in its future. When the CB&Q strikers needed money, I furnished $29,000 on my personal name. At the last convention, six months' absence and $2,000 was given me, but I did not touch it. Is that evidence of my being selfish?

During the latter years I have been well paid, but I could have made more in other callings. The American Press Association offered me the general man-agership. There are some who find fault because my sister and brother are in the Grand Lodge office.[130] When I called to my assistance my sister, she was teaching school at $75 per month; my brother first worked for $10 per month. No one will ever charge that he has ever defaulted. Of the millions of dollars he has handled, he has accounted for every dollar.

From first to last, my heart has been with the brotherhood. I have made mistakes, perhaps. I have the courage of my convictions. I say what I think. I have taken different views, different sides. My popularity began to wane at San Francisco because of the position I took against the beneficiary feature of the brotherhood. But at Cincinnati,[131] my popularity reached its zenith. I have served 12 years in an official capacity and have never had a vote cast against me, nor a nomination against me.

Now I want to say a few words about the lodge that I am a member of at Terre Haute. I am told that a member of that lodge is here carrying clippings of newspapers, criticisms of me by the venal press. I did more for that lodge than that man can in a century. When the 1877 strike came, that lodge went down in a crash. For two years I went to the hall every meeting night, even though there was no one there. I paid the hall rent. I held up members when short of funds. For a period of ten years I probably missed six meetings, but I confess I seldom visit them now. I am opposed to such imitations. I saw men walking around with a rope around their necks and other senseless doings, and I was opposed to it. I went home and read books.

I have been lied on by the press *[Brother Debs here read a clipping from the Harrisburg paper]*. The *Chicago Herald* and other Chicago papers were hired especially to coin lies about me. Interviews were distorted, and when a reporter went before the Commission of Investigation they asked him if he wrote a certain interview. He said yes. They asked him if I had said those things and he said no, here is what Debs said, and he pulled his shorthand notes from his pocket. This reporter was discharged from his paper.

With all of their accusations, they have never accused me of being on the side of corporations. I spent eight days in the Cook County jail; I went there as a protest against inhumanity. What the outcome will be I do not know. They have 600 charges against me. I am charged of being guilty of conspiracy.

If it had not been for my wife, my aged father, and mother I would not have made a defense. They could have sent me to prison, to the scaffold. Would a selfish man do this? If the truth is ever known, it will be shown that I tried to prevent that strike. But was the strike a failure or no? What does that greatest authority on labor subjects say? What does John Swinton[132] say? He says the strike was not lost; that the strike has done more for the cause of labor than anything ever before. Read *The Arena*.[133] The strike may be condemned, but it was as righteous a strike as ever was.

I want to speak in a hall somewhere, where those who do not want to hear me do not have to come. I will then tell you all about that strike. It was not a strike; it was a spontaneous upheaval. I was not responsible for that strike. There has got to be something done in a short time. If there is nothing done, the French Revolution will be repeated. Carroll D. Wright says there are 3 million idle people in this country. The country is paralyzed and the idle on the verge of starvation. We say, wait until times get good, get prosperous again. There is not an intelligent man who doesn't know that this panic was premeditated. People this winter will go hungry; they will go shivering through the winter clad in rags. Clothing cheaper than ever, but labor in rags. Is it a want of the necessaries of life? Are the labor organizations doing anything?

This panic has been a banker's panic. The poor man's money has been withdrawn, making gold the standard. Are labor organizations doing anything to restore silver to the people? If we could but destroy the money monopoly, land monopoly, and the rest of them, all would be different. You say labor organizations do not discuss politics. I would have labor to unify at the polls and vote for an independent People's Party. Some say politics mean destruction to labor organizations, but the reverse is the fact. There are questions I would like to see labor interest themselves in. Their conditions are like a cancer; you can cover it with a poultice, but the cancer continues to spread. You must apply the knife and root it out if you expect relief.

I will not take up any more of your time. I will say to you individually and collectively, I wish you well. I have done my duty as I understood it. If any person attaches any blame for what I have done, I will accept it like a man. I hope that I have given some evidence that I did the best I could. If the *Magazine* has not met all requirements, the fault lies elsewhere. I made up my mind that nothing would be said about the ARU in its columns. I said nothing about the Great Northern in the *Magazine*. If I have made mistakes, I believe that you will grant justice. I assure you that you will always have my cordial support, and if you will do what I believe should be done, you will unify the railway labor of the country. Some plan will present itself. I shall always be found on the side of labor. If we differ, let us honestly differ. I wish we had more faith in each other than in the past.

I have this for the men who know me and believe in me: I hope my hand may be paralyzed and my eyes blinded if ever I do aught against labor. About the rest that my enemies have said about me I have nothing to say. I am too busy to spend much time about personal and individual quarrels, but I do not hesitate to meet any living man, and if there is any here who would say aught against me, I am here to defend myself. From the depths of my heart, I thank you and wish you prosperity.

Altgeld and Pullman†

October 1894

For a number of years, the town of Pullman has been regarded as a sort of a paradise, an Eden, where the "thorny stem of time" was continually blossoming
and producing the most delicious fruits that labor ever gathered and garnered.
Descriptions of Pullman became revised editions of "Baxter's Saints' Rest."[134]
Painted or modeled, Pullman appeared a fairyland, and George M. Pullman,
in white robes, playing angel, was forever singing:

> Here bring your tools and skill,
> Here rent my houses,
> Labor has no sorrows
> Pullman cannot heal.

And, sure enough, men flocked to Pullman with their wives and children,
their tools and their skill; they rented Pullman houses, burned Pullman gas,
drank Pullman water, and became Pullman slaves.

George M. Pullman grew fat faster and faster until he bloomed into a
multimillionaire. The more millions he secured, the meaner he became. Pullman gradually lost its paradisiacal pretensions and became more like a poor
farm—a penitentiary or slave pen. Wages were reduced, clothes became rags,
food scarce, rent high, and hence debt, destitution, and despair transformed
Pullman into a sort of a hellhole, where George M. Pullman personated his
royal forked tailed highness to a dot. With true satanic genius he gave his slaves
the choice to work or starve, or work and starve. In either case, starvation was
their fate, and starvation has come. Fully 8,000 men, women, and children in
Pullman are in the grasp of famine.

Governor Altgeld, having been made aware of the deplorable condition of
George M. Pullman's late employees, issued the following proclamation to the
people of Illinois, and especially to the citizens of Chicago:

> There is great distress growing out of the want of food in and around the
> town of Pullman. More than a thousand families, or in the neighbor-
> hood of 6,000 people, are utterly destitute—nearly four-fifths of these

---

†   Published in *Locomotive Firemen's Magazine,* vol. 18, no. 10 (October 1894), 975–
977.

are women and children. The men have endeavored to get work, but were unable to do so. * * * As a rule the men are a superior class of laboring people—industrious, capable, and steady, and some of them have worked for the Pullman Company for more than ten years. Those who have been given work can get food, but are still in such an impoverished condition that they cannot help their neighbors if they would.

The relief society is unable to get more supplies. On last Saturday it gave to each family two pounds of oatmeal and two pounds of cornmeal, and, having nothing left, it suspended operations, leaving the people in an absolutely helpless condition. The County Commissioners of Cook County, as overseers of the poor, have rendered some assistance, but, owing to limited appropriation, they can furnish relief but for a short time. We cannot now stop to inquire the cause of this distress. The good people of this state cannot allow women and children by the hundred to perish of hunger. I therefore call upon all humane and charitably disposed citizens to contribute what they can toward giving relief to these people.

The governor has also called on the commissioners of Cook County to do all in their power in the matter.

The foregoing reads like a wail from India or Russia. It informs the world that Pullman is famine-cursed and that help must come speedily if Pullman's slaves are to be rescued from death by starvation. Governor Altgeld telegraphed George M. Pullman regarding the condition of his former employees, as follows:

It is claimed they struck because, after years of toil, their loaves were so reduced that their children went hungry. Admitting that they were wrong and foolish, they had yet served you long and well, and you must feel some interest in them. They do not stand on the same footing with you, so that much must be overlooked. The state of Illinois has not the least desire to meddle in the affairs of your company, but it cannot allow a whole community within its borders to perish of hunger. The local overseer of the poor has been appealed to, but there is a limit to what he can do. I cannot help them very much at present, so, unless relief comes from some other source, I shall either have to call an extra session of the legislature to make special appropriations or else issue an appeal to the humane people of the state to give bread to your recent employees. It seems to me that you would prefer to relieve the situation yourself, especially as it has cost the state upwards of $50,000 to protect your property and as both state and the public have suffered enormous loss and expense on account of disturbances that grew out of the trouble between your company and its workmen.

The millionaire, true to his cold-blooded nature, remained silent and passive. Governor Altgeld became heroic, and having made a personal inspection
of Pullman homes, addressed a letter to the conscienceless author of the horrible discord, in which he said:

> I examined the conditions at Pullman yesterday, visited even the kitchens
> and back rooms of many of the people. I learn from your manager that
> last spring there were 3,260 people on the payroll. Yesterday there were
> 2,220 at work, but over 600 of these are new men, so that only about
> 1,000 of the old employees have been taken back, thus leaving over 1,000
> of the old employees who have not been taken back. A few hundred have
> left. The remainder have applied for work, but were told that they were
> not needed. These are utterly destitute. The relief committee has exhaust-
> ed its resources. It seems to me your company cannot afford to have me
> appeal to the charity and humanity of the state to save the lives of your
> old employees. Four-fifths of those people are women and children. No
> matter what caused this distress, it must be met.
>
> If you will allow me, I will make this suggestion: If you had shut
> down your works last fall when you say business was poorer you would
> not have expected to get any rent from your tenants; now, while a dollar
> is a large sum to each of these people, all the rent now due is a compar-
> atively small matter to you. If you will cancel all rent to October 1 you
> would be as well off as if you had shut down. This would enable those
> who are at work to meet their most pressing wants. Then, if you cannot
> give work to all, work some half time, so that all can at least get some-
> thing to eat for their families. This will give immediate relief to the whole
> situation, and then by degrees assist as many to go elsewhere as desire to
> do so, and all to whom you cannot give work. In this way something like
> a normal condition could be reestablished at Pullman before winter, and
> you would not be out any more than you would have been had you shut
> down a year ago.

To this letter Governor Altgeld received a reply from George M. Pullman,
declining to contribute to the suffering people in his town, and the governor
therefore dismissed him, substantially, as follows:

> I see that your company refuses to do anything toward relieving the situ-
> ation at Pullman. If you will make the round I made, go into the houses
> of these people, meet them face to face, and talk with them, you will be
> convinced that none of them had $1,300 or any other sum of money a
> few weeks ago. It is not my business to fix the moral responsibility in this

case. There are nearly 6,000 people suffering for want of food. They were your employees, and four-fifths of them are women and children. Some of these people have worked for you more than ten years. I assumed that even if they were wrong and had been foolish, you would not be willing to see them perish. I also assumed that, as the state had just been to a large expense to protect your property, you would not want to have the public shoulder the burden of relieving distress in your town. As you refuse to do anything to relieve the suffering in this case, I am compelled to appeal to the humanity of the people of Illinois to do so.

The foregoing is only an outline of a corporation campaign against enslaved and starving men, women, and children of unparalleled greed and satanic cruelty. We introduce a mere synopsis of Pullman's rapacity and depravity, to preserve the record, and exhibit George M. Pullman before the world as one of the meanest monsters the country has produced.

An Era of Bloodhoundism[†]

October 1894

"Down South," when a "nigger" commits a crime and runs away, the first thought is to put bloodhounds upon his track. Some "niggers" evade the hounds. The hounds lose the scent, and the "nigger" goes free, at least for a time. "Up North," things are transpiring which suggest the bloodhound tactics in vogue "down South." When workingmen arouse the ire of the railroad magnates by resisting oppression, spoliation, and degradation, having no faith in the ordinary methods of repressing wrong, the magnates fly to the federal courts, which promptly issue injunctions, which in every essential particular are as arbitrary and as despotic as ever emanated from a tsar or a sultan, and to compel obedience, selections are made from the rabble and criminal element to play the rule of deputy marshals, and armed with pistols, they are put upon the track of workingmen, à la bloodhounds hunting "niggers," to capture or to kill as their

---

†   Published in *Locomotive Firemen's Magazine,* vol. 18, no. 10 (October 1894), 977–978.

brutal instincts may dictate, and when these official hounds do not suffice, these federal officials, paid from revenues created by labor, "touch the button," and the land swarms with troops, ordered out by state and federal authorities, and then the plutocratic class and their lickspittles, the press vermin, that riot in the hair and intestines of corporations, applaud such bloodhoundism.

Reverend John Snyder, in the *St. Louis Globe-Democrat,* in the list of "Timely Topics," which he discusses, refers to the act of President Cleveland in sending federal troops to Chicago, an act which has been uproariously endorsed by both houses of Congress. Mr. Snyder professes to have "unbounded confidence in Mr. Cleveland's honesty and patriotism, and large admiration for his wisdom and statesmanlike qualities;" nevertheless, he believes that Governor Altgeld of Illinois, in his acts and protests, "is nearer the spirit and purpose of the constitution than the president." He offers a lame apology for the course pursued by the president, and adds:

> But history shows that nations have seen their rights gradually melt away under just such pleas of pressing necessity. Besides, there is no evidence that such an emergency had arisen as the president seemed to assume. The state of Illinois was abundantly able to cope with the conditions, even though the moving or detention of the United States mail was a question at issue. The danger has already passed, and as serious as it was, it never assumed such proportions as justified the denial of the clearly implied right of the state of Illinois to protect the interest of its citizens without federal interference; and a bad precedent has been established. The very heart and core of our governmental system is found in state autonomy. Take that away and we become simply an unwieldy and inelastic mass which will slowly drift into a centralized and bureaucratic despotism. We fought the war of 1861 to destroy the notion that this union could be legally dismembered: not to cancel or obscure the plain, constitutional right of state sovereignty. Mr. Altgeld may be an anarchist and a blatherskite, but I solemnly believe that when this hour of natural human passion has passed away, his protest to the president's action will be regarded as sound in logic and strong in its adherence to the spirit of constitutional law.

In analyzing the foregoing, it is easy to see that the writer believes President Cleveland to be a usurper who has violated the Constitution and has established a dangerous and an alarming precedent, which has only to be followed and reenacted as often as the creatures of federal preference may demand it, to ultimately establish a despotism upon the ruins of the Republic. That their executive outrages are perpetrated in the interest of the rich is shown in every stage of the proceedings. In the name of law and order, law is struck down, the will of a despot is substituted, and though quiet may be established by bullets and bayonets, it is not *order* but oppression, submission *par* necessity, with a proviso to be thrown off when conditions promise a glimmering chance for the downtrodden to break their yokes and chains—a policy fruitful of protests and inflammatory appeals, calling always for more troops and other equipments to maintain a government which was once the government by, of, and for the people, which found its support, strength, and glory in the intelligence, prosperity, and sympathy of the masses, but which now in its legislative, judicial, and military departments is a government by, of, and for the plutocratic class from which the masses are turning with loathing. This condition of things is treated with levity and scorn. The courts issue decrees, and fine and imprison men without trial, and when men protest, chief executives, with the vengeance of savages, institute bloodhound tactics and hunt down those who dare resist, as bloodhounds pursue "niggers" "down South," and this is done beneath the starry folds of the national flag, and men are expected to sing:

> Long may it wave.
> O'er the land of the free and the home of the brave.[135]

No sane man can contemplate present conditions with composure. The whole country is volcanic. There is a hot breath of discontent rising from the throats of millions of oppressed men, like smoke from active volcanoes, and the country is in the grasp of alarms, and federal and state bloodhoundism will not make things better.

A Larger Standing Army[†]

October 1894

There is now a demand, made by certain military gentlemen who wear shoulder straps and who are fed from the public crib, for a larger standing army. It has been suggested that there should be a military post in every state, where at least a thousand soldiers should be stationed and held in readiness for serious work.

In looking over the field, men inquire: What is the necessity for a larger standing army? Are there any enemies in sight, foreign or domestic? Is there a probability of an invasion from Mexico or Canada? No replies are made to these queries, and still the demand is made for a larger standing army, more federal troops. It is understood that corporations of the Pullman and Homestead stripe, coal operators and railroad magnates and other employers of labor, favor the increase of the federal army, and it is just here that the secret leaks out. The patriot is the man who reduces wages, and the enemy to be shot down is the man who resists spoliation. The plutocrat believes in powder, ball, and bayonet. He has observed their quieting effects. Every workingman killed for clamoring for fair wages helps the piratical employer amazingly. The circumstance, while it intimidates workingmen, emboldens the pirate—assures him of security and impresses him with confidence in the strength of the government, and the act is wildly applauded. If Europeans so much as intimate that ours is not a strong government, the president, the general in command, and the corporations point proudly to battlefields where workingmen lie stiff and cold in their bloody rags, and ask what European government can improve upon the spectacle. Europe looks, and acknowledges the *corn*,[136] and joins in with American plutocratic patriots in singing our national anthem, "The Star-Spangled Banner."

The president orders out the federal troops. Having been a hangman, he has the required nerve to do his duty when a murderer is to be hanged or a workingman shot. On such occasions he expands to the largest proportions of a tsar, sultan, or shah, and yet there is something connected with the business which seemingly troubles his waking and sleeping hours. Possibly dead men visit him in his dreams and show him their wounds, flaunt their bloody shirts

---

[†]   Published in *Locomotive Firemen's Magazine*, vol. 18, no. 10 (October 1894), 974–975.

in his face, call his attention to their gloomy homes, introduce him to their starving wives and children, and bother him so much that Congress comes to his aid and passes resolutions applauding his military orders. It does not matter that the Congress which endorses the military exploits of the president is the target for the scorn and contempt, the flings and jeers of the country, imbecile and incapable to an extent that defies characterization—bribed and debauched, vulgar and venal until all the people cry out: Shame! It is the Congress fitted by nature and acquirements to vote that the military remedy for labor troubles is just the thing, and the plutocratic corporations cry the louder for a larger standing army. The enemy to be subdued is labor.

At the same time, while the demand is being made for a larger standing army, governors of states and military gentlemen of small caliber are demanding a larger "home guard," more state troops, greater military efficiency. If it is asked why this demand, the reply is that labor is becoming dangerous. It will not be degraded and robbed to please the corporation, but as that is just what the military machine is for and nothing else, the corporation insists upon more state troops. If, however, the active state militia is to be increased, the recruits must come chiefly from the ranks of labor, and workingmen, in the event of becoming a part of the military machine, will be required, if ordered, to shoot down their fellow workmen. If they, however, do not want to join in that sort of work, they can easily avoid it by refusing to enlist.

In this connection an incident at Pullman has special significance. It was reported by the Associated Press as follows:

> The sensation of the day at Pullman was the refusal of Company M of the First Infantry to eat at the same table with non-union workmen. At 1:30, Lieutenant Bowra marched Company M up to the big mess tent that stands on the lawn behind the Hotel Florence. There the company was left in command of Sergeant Cook. When the company came to break ranks at the tent entrance they were indignant to see two tables within filled with non-union employees of the Pullman company. The workmen were a part of the new force hired today. They had been smuggled in with the soldier boys on the apology that they were afraid to go home for dinner.
>
> As the practice had been tried in a smaller way last week, to the distaste of the company, the soldiers were prepared for decisive action. William Byrnes, a member of the company, stepped into the entrance and said: "As volunteer soldiers, the men of Company M are here to see that the laws of Illinois are obeyed. I am not aware that it is soldierly or that

discipline compels us to do what we feel is unpatriotic and not worthy of gentlemen. My scruples demand that I shall not associate with scabs. I refuse to sit with them at the same table."

There was an outburst of applause from Byrne's comrades, and Sergeant Cook marched the company across the street and broke ranks.

"We will not enter that tent," a dozen privates said, "till we are assured that all non-union workmen are to be kept out."

The workmen were finally marched out and the company marched in, receiving the assurance that they will hereafter have the mess tent to themselves.

The foregoing has been widely commented upon by the press, the point being made that a soldier on duty is not expected to have any views of his own; being a part of an unthinking machine, he is simply to obey the orders of his superiors, shoot, stab, hew down, and trample upon those he is told are the enemies of the state, and eat his grub without having anything to say about his surroundings. The Pullman incident is, therefore, in the line of rebellion, mutiny, grave insubordination, but it sharply defines the deep-seated hostility of state troops to scabs—men who are willing to accept such degrading wages as corporations choose to offer. Taking this view of the subject, the Pullman incident is a note of warning that plutocratic employers will do well to heed, since it is indicative of still graver incidents of insubordination on the part of state troops recruited from the ranks of workingmen.

Open Letter to a Milwaukee ARU Member
on the Results of the Election†

November 16, 1894

Yours of the 10th received.[137] Of all the interviews I have seen, Governor Altgeld's is the only one that correctly states the causes that led up to the political revolution this fall. The Democratic administration, in its implacable hostility to labor in the interests of trusts, combines, and corporations, as demonstrated during the [Pullman] trouble last summer, is what did the business. There were, of course, other causes, but this was the main, central, pivotal cause of democracy's "knockout."

You did well at Milwaukee and through the whole Northwest, and I heartily congratulate you. The People's Party is here to stay, and in two years more will be fully equipped for the national contest. The Democratic Party will never get into power again while you and I live. It had its golden opportunity, it surrendered to and did the bidding of the money power, and the people of this generation will not trust it again. I expect nothing from the Republican Party. It is notoriously the party of plutocracy, and the goldbugs[138] will shape its policy and dictate its legislation. The People's Party is the only party in which all the reform elements can unite and pull together. We have all got to put in our best efforts, and now is the time to begin.

Give McAuliffe, Archibald, and all the boys my cordial regards. They made a heroic fight, and I glory in their pluck.

Yours faithfully,
Eugene V. Debs

---

† From a wire service report, as published in the *Decatur Herald*, vol. 15, no. 36 (November 17, 1894), 1.

Denial of News Reports Alleging Hostility Toward Samuel Gompers[†]

November 26, 1894

It is totally untrue that I am to fight President Gompers in the coming convention, or that the American Railway Union is to attack the American Federation of Labor.[139] Whatever difference there may be relating to policy, principles, or methods between the two organizations, they enjoy each other's confidence and respect, and the American Railway Union will do nothing, either through its officers or otherwise, to mar or jar such harmonious relations.

The American Railway Union harbors no resentment: It stands for the solidarity of all labor, and if in the course of events the American Federation of Labor in any conflict it may have with the autocratic power requires the aid (not the vapid, meaningless thing called "sympathy and moral support," but the active and actual reinforcement) of the American Railway Union, it shall be freely given so far as it lies in my power to give it.

Statement to the Press on the Decision Finding ARU Leaders Guilty of Contempt[‡]

December 14, 1894

I am a law-abiding man and I will abide by the law as construed by the judges. But if Judge Woods's decision is law, all labor organizations may as well disband.[140] According to him, every strike is conspiracy and unlawful.

Even if our wages are reduced 30 percent and two or more of us decide to quit rather than submit to the reduction, we are guilty of conspiracy. Of

---

[†] Wire service report, as published as "A Denial from Debs" in the *Decatur Herald,* vol. 15, no. 44 (November 27, 1894), 5.

[‡] Wire report, published as "Debs Says There Was No Evidence" in *Buffalo Evening News,* vol. 29, no. 55 (December 15, 1894), 1.

course, he says, strikes are all right if they are peaceful, but who can tell when violence will follow? We warned the men to respect property rights and even to keep off the right of way of railroad companies. Judge Woods intimates that this advice was given for the effect it would have on the public and that the strikers were not expected to heed it. What right has he to draw such an inference? There is nothing in the evidence to support it.

Notes

1. Edward Atkinson (1827–1905) was the inventor in 1886 of a slow cooker that enabled quantities of food to be prepared with a minimal energy input, akin to the principle of the modern Crock-Pot.

2. John Jacob Astor (1763-1848) a merchant, fur trader, and real estate speculator, was one of the wealthiest men of his era.

3. Debs spoke to a gathering of about 600 railroad workers along with ARU vice president George W. Howard at a meeting at Hirzel's Hall, Terre Haute. A list of 201 charter members for a new ARU lodge was the result. The material quoted here is an extract of Debs's complete report.

4. Reference is to the August 1892 Buffalo switchmen's strike, a two-week stoppage against three railroads which was defeated following the commitment of 8,000 members of the state militia to restore order.

5. The Evansville & Terre Haute Railroad.

6. William Riley McKeen, Sr. (1829–1913) was a native of Vigo County, Indiana, who made a career as a banker and railway investor. He was an initiator of the Terre Haute & Indianapolis Railroad in 1867, which became part of the Vandalia line three years later.

7. An early statement of the concept of "countervailing power" popularized by economist John Kenneth Galbraith (1908–2006).

8. "On the Flag" was a poem associated with Horace Greeley and the radical abolitionist movement circa 1860, which included the words, "Haul down that flaunting lie! / Half-mast the starry rag; / Pollute not freedom's sky / With hate's polluted flag."

9. Walter I. Hayes (1841–1901) was a Democrat elected to four terms in the House of Representatives from Iowa's Second Congressional District. He was a member of Congress from 1887 to 1895.

10. According to the *Los Angeles Times* of March 4, 1894, the bill proposed by Rep. Hayes, in the tradition of the Alien and Sedition Acts of 1798, would give to the postmaster general "the power to exclude from the mails all publications of an immoral nature and also those which criticize the administration or any of its acts." Hayes's 1894 proposal foreshadowed the Sedition Act of 1918, wielded with effect against radical opponents of the Wilson administration's military campaign in Europe.

11. The American Protective Association, established in Iowa in 1887, was the leading nationalist and nativist political organization of the 1890s, a mass movement standing transitionally the Know Nothing movement of the 1850s and the second Ku Klux Klan of the 1920s. A secret society making use of ritual patterned after the Masons, the APA was staunchly anti-Catholic and sought removal of loyal Catholics from employment in schools and positions of public trust, as well as immigration restrictions curbing Catholic entry. The group was strongest in the Midwest and the Northeast, with a paid membership exceeding 100,000 by 1894. It abruptly declined after its failure to exert influence in the election of 1896, barely surviving the nineteenth century.

12. First Amendment to the United States Constitution.

13. Constitution of Oregon (1859), Article I, Section 2.

14. Second constitution of Indiana (1851), Article I, Section 4.
15. Second constitution of Indiana (1851), Article I, Section 5.
16. From Psalms 91:6.
17. Elmer Scipio Dundy (1830–1896) of Nebraska was appointed to the federal bench in 1868 by President Andrew Johnson.
18. James Graham Jenkins (1834–1931) was appointed US district court judge for the Eastern District of Wisconsin by President Grover Cleveland in 1888.
19. Melville Fuller (1833–1910) was chief justice of the US Supreme Court from 1888 until his death in 1910. He was appointed to the post by Grover Cleveland in 1888.
20. "The Star-Spangled Banner" (1814) by Francis Scott Key (1779–1843) originally contained four verses. Debs quotes the concluding lines of the second verse here.
21. Allusion to Genesis 19:24–25.
22. Allusion to "Thanatopsis" (1817) by William Cullen Bryant (1794–1878).
23. 1 Timothy 1:2.
24. 1 Timothy 2:11.
25. 1 Timothy 2:12.
26. Allusion to "Love's Young Dream," from *Irish Melodies No. IV,* by Thomas Moore (1779–1852).
27. 1 Timothy 2:13–14.
28. 1 Corinthians 14:34–35.
29. George J. Romanes, "Mental Differences of Men and Women," *Popular Science Monthly,* vol. 31 (July 1887), 385.
30. Victoria (1819–1901) was queen of Great Britain from 1837 until her death. She was the mother of nine children.
31. Allusion to "The Battle-Field" (1837) by William Cullen Bryant: "Truth, crushed to earth, shall rise again; / The eternal years of God are hers."
32. A wager game played with dice.
33. Delmonico's was popularly regarded as the finest restaurant in New York City.
34. Lawrence E. McGann (1852–1928), a Democrat, was a two-term member of Congress from Chicago.
35. From "A Psalm of Life," by Henry Wadsworth Longfellow (1807–1882).
36. Debs's mother, however, was raised a practicing Catholic.
37. Knute Nelson (1843–1923), a Republican, was governor of Minnesota from 1892 to 1895, when he became a US Senator. Nelson's letter to Debs, seeking information on the Great Northern Railway strike and broaching the subject of whether arbitration would be possible for its expeditious settlement, appears in Constantine (ed.), *Letters of Eugene V. Debs, Volume 1,* 62–63.
38. From "To the Lord General Cromwell" (May 1652) by John Milton (1608–1674).
39. The Brooks Locomotive Works was established in November 1868 and remained in continuous operation until its purchase by the American Locomotive Company in 1904. The final locomotive from its Dunkirk plant was produced in 1929.
40. Marshall Littlefield Hinman (1842–1907) was named president of the Brooks Locomotive Works in February 1892.

41. From *The Tragedy of Hamlet, Prince of Denmark* (c. 1602), act 5, scene 2.
42. Matthew 6:33.
43. The evening of May 3, 1894 marked a personal high point in the political life of Gene Debs. Following the successful conclusion of negotiations with the Great Northern Railway after an 18-day strike, a labor struggle which gained national attention, Debs was greeted at the railroad station in Terre Haute as a conquering hero, with deafening cheers from a crowd at the train station, complete with a brass band. The assemblage made their way to the Terre Haute House Park, where Debs gave this speech.
44. Charles A. Pillsbury (1842–1899), former member of the Minnesota State Senate and namesake of the Pillsbury Company, played a critical role in mediating an end to the strike.
45. Debs spoke to Pullman workers in the neighboring railroad town of Kensington, Illinois, at Turner Hall—strike headquarters, where daily public meetings were held.
46. Allusion to Proverbs 23:11.
47. Unvulcanized natural rubber.
48. Jacob S. Coxey, Sr. (1854–1951), an ambitious Ohio Populist politician, led a national march of unemployed workers to Washington, DC, in the wake of the 1893 economic meltdown. This group of protesters, which sought expanded public works spending to guarantee jobs, was formally known as the "Commonweal of Christ" and popularly nicknamed "Coxey's Army." The campaign began March 25, 1894 in Massillon, Ohio, and culminated on May 1 when Jacob Coxey and his charismatic top lieutenant, Carl Browne (1849–1914), were arrested before Coxey could deliver a speech from the Capitol steps.
49. English proverb.
50. Allusion to Exodus 14.
51. Approximately 500 were on hand to finish the march to Washington with Coxey.
52. "Seigniorage" is the difference between the sum of the intrinsic value of metal in a coin plus its manufacturing cost minus its face value—the "profit" derived by the issuing entity. Issuance of silver dollars containing a lesser value of rare metal vis-à-vis the amount of gold in a gold dollar would have generated additional government revenue, funds allowing an expansion of relief spending.
53. The Democratic Party controlled the 53rd Congress, elected in November 1892. It was swept out in a landslide in November 1894.
54. Charles Jahleal Boatner (1849–1903) was a Democrat first elected to Congress in November 1888.
55. Allusion to Matthew 3.
56. The battle of Marathon was fought in 490 BC and was won by the citizens of Athens, who turned back the invading Persian force of King Darius I (550–486 BC). The battle of Thermopylae followed in 480 BC, in which about seven thousand Greek defenders managed to defeat the massive invading Persian force of King Xerxes I (518–465 BC).
57. A form of martial music played by bagpipes.

58. From the song "Pibroch of Donuil Dhu" (1816) by Sir Walter Scott (1771–1832).
59. From "An Essay on Man" (1734) by Alexander Pope (1688–1744).
60. Proverbs 13:12.
61. From "The American Flag" (posthumously published, 1835) by Joseph Rodman Drake (1795–1820).
62. This maxim originates from a couplet in the poem "An Essay on Criticism" (1711) by Alexander Pope (1688–1744): "Good nature and good sense must ever join; / To err is human; to forgive, divine."
63. Reference is to the left (buck) and right (bright) oxen in a yoke, who were frequently given these as call names.
64. The allusion to Satan is meant to mock George Pullman's popular reputation as a generous patron of church construction.
65. Allusion to the poem "Cologne" (1834) by Samuel Taylor Coleridge (1772–1834).
66. From *Henry VI,* by William Shakespeare.
67. On June 18, 1894, the first convention of the American Railway Union spent a full day debating a provision in the organization's constitution limiting membership to those "born of white parents." A motion to strike the clause spurred protracted debate on the matter. Debs spoke in favor of the proposal to remove the ARU's "whites only" provision. The proposal to eliminate the offending words failed on the morning of June 19 by a roll call vote of 100–112, thereby limiting ARU membership to whites only.
68. In response to a heavy round of wage cuts associated with the Panic of 1893, on April 21, 1894, a strike of bituminous coal miners was launched by the United Mine Workers of America, who demanded a return to wage rates prevailing on May 1, 1893. A total of 180,000 miners in Pennsylvania, Illinois, Ohio, West Virginia, and Colorado stopped work in connection with the eight-week action, which came to an unsuccessful conclusion in the last days of June. Although published in the July issue of *Locomotive Firemen's Magazine,* this article clearly predated the 1894 American Railway Union strike.
69. According to reports elsewhere in the press, this evening mass meeting in Chicago, addressed by president Debs, vice president Howard, editor Rogers, and ARU directors James Hogan and M. J. Elliott, among others, responded enthusiastically to calls for unity in the boycott against the Pullman Palace Car Company, with speakers emphasizing to the switchmen in attendance their pivotal role in the forthcoming labor conflict.
70. This telegram was sent to the following: Samuel Gompers, president of the American Federation of Labor, Clinton Place, NY; J. R. Sovereign, general master workman of the Knights of Labor, Des Moines, IA; G. W. Perkins, president of Cigar Makers' International Union, Chicago, IL; J. D. Stevenson, grand chief of the Brotherhood of Railroad Carmen, East St. Louis, IL; Miles W. Barrett, grand master of the Switchmen's Mutual Aid Association, Chicago, IL; Walker V. Powell, grand chief of the Order of Railroad Telegraphers, Vinton, IA; John McBride, president of the United Mine Workers, Columbus, OH; E. E. Clark, grand chief of the Order

of Railroad Conductors, Cedar Rapids, IA; Peter M. Arthur, grand chief of the Brotherhood of Locomotive Engineers, Cleveland, OH; Frank P. Sargent, grand master of the Brotherhood of Locomotive Firemen, Terre Haute, IN, and S. E. Wilkinson, grand master of the Brotherhood of Railroad Trainmen, Galesburg, IL.

71. About 250 striking Illinois Central Railroad men attended the morning meeting at Fischer's Hall, located at 82 Lake Street in Chicago.

72. Debs gets the date of the Pullman strike wrong here. The walkout at the Pullman works began in the morning hours of May 11, 1894, following an all-night meeting at Turner Hall in nearby Kensington, Illinois. See Lindsey, *The Pullman Strike,* 122–123.

73. In a post-strike interview Debs acknowledged authorship of this telegram, which was transmitted to about 40 local strike committees of the ARU, 22 of which were on the Santa Fe Railroad system.

74. Battery D was a massive National Guard field artillery armory built in 1880 near the lakefront in Chicago, on the corner of Monroe Street.

75. Although only published in the August 1894 issue of *Locomotive Firemen's Magazine,* this article on the Pullman strike was clearly written during the first part of July.

76. Debs again gets the starting date of the Pullman Strike incorrect. The walkout took place on May 11, 1894.

77. This *Chicago Herald* editorial was reprinted in other papers on July 5, 1894, indicating that it was probably first published on July 4.

78. Republican John Sherman (1823–1900) was secretary of the treasury under Rutherford B. Hayes and attempted to toe a compromise position between free coinage of silver and the advocates of the gold standard, generally favoring the latter. He was named secretary of state by William McKinley in 1897, remaining at that post until the spring of 1898.

79. Sherman made the remarks in Washington, DC, on June 30, 1894, in the context of a query as to whether the Interstate Commerce Commission had the right to regulate rates of sleeping cars.

80. Allusion to Mark 12:40 and Luke 20:47.

81. Allusion to Matthew 23:27.

82. Rioting began in Chicago on July 5 and ran for several days.

83. At 4:30 p.m. on Tuesday, July 10, after about three hours of deliberation, a federal grand jury returned indictments against ARU leaders Eugene V. Debs, George W. Howard, Sylvester Keliher, and L. W. Rogers for conspiracy to obstruct the US mail. The four officers were arrested around 5 p.m. and held for several hours before being released on bail of $10,000 each, set by Judge Peter S. Grosscup. While the officers were detained, a deputy US marshal and the chief inspector of the Chicago postal division raided the office of the ARU and filled a mail sack with records, letters, circulars, and telegrams. Personal mail was later returned to Debs and his associates; telegrams and official documents were used in building the case against them.

84. According to Samuel Gompers, writing in the July 1905 issue of *The American Federationist,* this document was produced by Debs and his associates sometime prior to a three-hour meeting of American Federation of Labor leaders held in Chicago on

the morning of Thursday, July 12. Debs, Howard, and Keliher initially sought that the document be presented to the Railway Managers' Association by Gompers, the AF of L president recounted.

85. This appeal may have been written by Sylvester Keliher, who published it over Debs's signature for reasons of authority.

86. This statement was made during a brief interlude while Debs was awaiting preparation of his cell at Cook County Jail following his arrest on contempt of court charges. Four officials of the ARU were jailed in two adjoining cells of the "debtors' department," with Debs and George W. Howard sharing one cell and Sylvester Keliher and L. W. Rogers housed in the other.

87. William H. Carwardine (1863–1929) was the pastor of the First Methodist Episcopal Church of Pullman, Illinois. An adherent of the social gospel and committed supporter of the People's Party, Carwardine wrote a sympathetic account of the 1894 labor conflict, *The Pullman Strike,* for the Unitarian-cum-Populist publisher Charles H. Kerr & Co.

88. Stephen B. Elkins (1841–1911) was secretary of war from 1891 to 1893, during the administration of Republican Benjamin Harrison.

89. From a speech delivered by Elkins to fellow Republicans at Columbia, Missouri, June 3, 1885.

90. "Last resort." This is a rare instance of Debs, the son of French immigrants, dropping a French phrase into his writings.

91. This radical egalitarian poem was contributed anonymously to the weekly New York political magazine *Yankee Doodle,* vol. 2, no. 50 (Sept. 18, 1847), 238. Debs silently omits the third and fourth stanzas from this six-stanza work.

92. Apparently a reference to poet Reginald Heber (1783–1826).

93. Allusion to Daniel 3:16–22.

94. Isaiah 2:4.

95. Luke 2:14.

96. From 2 Samuel 1:20.

97. Allusion to *The Merchant of Venice* (c. 1597) by William Shakespeare, act 1, scene 3: "The devil can cite Scripture for his purpose. / An evil soul producing holy witness / Is like a villain with a smiling cheek, / A goodly apple rotten at the heart."

98. "Work conquers all." A phrase from *Georgics,* book 1 (29 BC), by Virgil (70–19 BC).

99. The Martin Costa affair took place in late June and early July of 1853.

100. Henry Osborne Havemeyer (1847–1907), a New York industrialist, was a sugar refiner who organized an American sugar refiners' trust in 1887.

101. Allusion to the treatment meted out to Coxey's Army leaders Jacob S. Coxey and Carl Browne on May 1, 1894, when a prepared speech that was to be delivered from the Capitol steps was short-circuited by police on the basis of such a charge.

102. Caroll D. Wright (1840–1909), a progressive from Massachusetts, was the first US Commissioner of Labor. In the summer of 1894 Wright chaired the three-person federal commission appointed to investigate the Pullman strike.

103. The ARU was actually launched at an organizational meeting held in Chicago on

February 9, 1893, attended by 24 people. A follow-up three-day organizational conclave that heard and approved the report of the ARU's constitutional committee was held in Chicago at the Hotel Greene from April 11 to 13 of that same year. In accordance with this constitution, provisional officers and directors of the organization were elected at the session of April 12, which was the actual date Debs assumed this mantle.

104. John Devereaux Kernan (1844–1922) was a lawyer from Utica, New York, who was the son of former Democratic United States senator Francis Kernan (1816–1892).

105. Thomas H. Wickes, Sr. (1848–1905) was second vice president of the Pullman Parlor Car Company and in charge of the company's operating department at the time of the strike.

106. Nicholas Ellsworth Worthington (1836–1916) was a lawyer and a Democratic member of Congress from 1883 to 1887. He was elected a circuit court judge for the Tenth Judicial District of Illinois in 1891, serving in that capacity until his retirement in 1915.

107. During the Pullman strike, an inflammatory telegram sent above Debs's was extensively reported in the press, intimating that the ARU had planned July strike violence. The telegram in question reads in full: "General managers are weakening. Chicago is becoming paralyzed. If settlement don't come in forty-eight hours paralysis will be complete. The fur will fly before long. Ice and potatoes out of sight now. Tell Effie I am safe and well. Save your money and buy a gun. —E. V. Debs."

108. John Patrick Hopkins (1858–1918), a Democrat, was mayor of Chicago from 1893 to 1895.

109. John McGillen, an ally of Governor John Altgeld, was the powerful chair of the Cook County Democratic Central Committee during the 1890s.

110. Richard T. Ely (1854–1943) was a pioneer labor historian and economist who wrote and taught for nearly three decades at the University of Wisconsin.

111. Allusion to Psalms 90:10.

112. Allusion to Genesis 6–8.

113. This and the following alludes to Exodus 7–15, *passim.*

114. Reference to Titus 3:1: "Put them in mind to be subject to principalities and powers, to obey magistrates, to be ready to every good work."

115. From "To the American Flag" (1819), by Joseph Rodman Drake (1795–1820).

116. Patrick Henry (1736–1799) made the famous utterance in a speech to the Second Virginia Convention in March 1775.

117. Apparently Debs's own adage, adapted from *The Giaour* (1813), by George Gordon Byron (1788–1824): "For Freedom's battle once begun, / Bequeathed by bleeding sire to son, / Though baffled oft is ever won."

118. By every indication, only a tiny fraction of this amount was ever raised.

119. Debs was not a delegate to the Brotherhood of Locomotive Firemen's 17th National Convention, held in Harrisburg, Pennsylvania, although he remained a member of the organization until leaving on December 15, 1895. He therefore had to receive the dispensation of the delegates to address the body—a matter of some controversy owing to the tense relations between the ARU and the B of LF in the aftermath of the failed Pullman strike.

120. The Louisville & Nashville Railroad, first chartered in Kentucky in 1850.
121. The East Tennessee, Virginia & Georgia Railway, constructed during the 1850s.
122. Nickname of the Cleveland, Cincinnati, Chicago & St. Louis Railway, formed by merger in June 1889.
123. The American Protective Association, an anti-Catholic secret society established in 1887.
124. In this context: organizations dedicated to one exclusive craft.
125. A low-level engine maintenance worker.
126. The Chicago, Burlington & Quincy Railroad, a name first utilized in 1856.
127. That is, the New York Elevated Railroad.
128. The Buffalo (5th) convention of the B of LF was held in September 1878.
129. The San Francisco (15th) convention of the B of LF was held in September 1890.
130. Debs's sister Eugenia ("Jenny") and brother, Theodore, were paid office employees working for Debs.
131. The Cincinnati (16th) convention of the B of LF was held in September 1892.
132. John Swinton (1829–1901) was editor and publisher of *John Swinton's Paper,* a weekly labor newspaper, and author of a contemporary book on the Pullman strike.
133. *The Arena* was a liberal intellectual monthly published from 1889 to 1909 by Benjamin Orange Flower (1858–1918).
134. Reference to *The Saints' Everlasting Rest* (1650), by Richard Baxter (1615–1691).
135. "The Star-Spangled Banner" (1814), by Francis Scott Key (1779–1843) was originally written with four verses. The penultimate line of the second verse reads: "'Tis the star-spangled banner, long may it wave."
136. "Acknowledge the corn" is a nineteenth-century slang expression meaning "to admit the truth."
137. The date and recipient of this letter, an individual who was said to have been granted permission to reprint the contents, is not indicated in this wire service report. The secretary of the Milwaukee ARU lodge was William Hogan.
138. Advocates of a restricted monetary output based only in gold and gold-backed money, which would have the effect of preserving the wealth of creditors at the expense of borrowers.
139. This statement, made to an unnamed Milwaukee correspondent, was released in reply to an Associated Press story asserting that Debs would fight against American Federation of Labor president Samuel Gompers at the forthcoming Denver convention of the AF of L.
140. William Allen Woods (1837–1901) was a federal judge of the Seventh Circuit Court of Appeals, the Northern District of Illinois. Woods spent the better part of a month working on a decision in the case of the leaders of the American Railway Union, who were charged with contempt of court for violating a judicial injunction against striking in the Pullman affair. Following two continuances, Woods's 60-page decision was rendered on December 14, 1894, with the ARU officials declared guilty of contempt of court. Debs was sentenced to six months in county jail as most culpable, with three-month sentences handed out to his codefendants. Ten days were allowed for appeal before execution of sentence.

1895

Accused of Every Crime but Selling Out:
Speech at St. Paul, Minnesota†

January 4, 1895

There are people who believe that this republic will go down in gloom. I am not one of the number.[1] I have faith in the intelligence of the masses. We are here tonight to discuss the causes leading up to the great railroad strike of last summer. There may be some here who do not believe in what is known as the labor strike. Let me tell you that there has not been a victory won in the interest of liberty or patriotism in this republic that has not been won by a strike. The battle of Lexington was a strike against British oppression, and the Rebellion was a strike against slavery. When it is a question between submission to injustice and going out on a strike, I'll take the strike every time, and "by the eternal," as old Andrew Jackson said, "I'll take the consequences."

I have been accused of every crime on the calendar, but I have never been accused of selling out. Had I catered to the General Managers' Association, I might have had the respect of everybody but myself. I am no respecter of public opinion. Public opinion is the creation of the press—and in alluding to the press I make no personal allusion to the gentlemen connected with the press. For mendacity and malignancy, the St. Paul press has to render an account of itself. Oh, Lord! Do you see this red book? *[Holding up a pamphlet.]* It is published by the General Managers' Association and is made up of editorials from the newspapers of the country condemnatory of the great strike and the officers who had charge of it. The object of the publication is to terrorize railway employees.

[He then read an extract from the pamphlet, charging him with murder.]

I never knew a liar who could conceive of such a thing as an honest man. I propose to stand by my own acts and take responsibility of them; and if that takes me to the gallows, I shall meet it like a man. I propose to retain the respect of and keep on good terms with Debs.

[He then read from a book written by Rev. Mr. Carwardine relative to conditions that existed at Pullman previous to the strike.][2]

Let it be understood that at Pullman there is not a thing that is now owned by the Pullman Company, not even a freeman. I made a personal examination

---

†   Published as "Debs Was Eloquent" in the *St. Paul Globe*, vol. 18, no. 5 (January 5, 1895), 8.

of the condition of the Pullman employees previous to the strike, and the conditions I found there it is beyond my power to describe. They were practically destitute. And no wonder, for, according to the report of the investigating commission, they were charged 30 percent more rent than is paid anywhere else in Illinois. That man Wickes is a monster who ought not to be tolerated on American soil. Not because of the treatment of his employees, but because in suing for divorce in Chicago the other day his wife testified that he had kicked and otherwise brutalized her. And a man who will kick his wife is unfit to live on American soil.

The speaker went into the history of the origin of the strike, relating the circumstance of the decision to strike unless the wages were improved, and the subsequent discharge of the committee that waited on the management.

Mr. Pullman seemed astonished at the audacity of the men to send a committee to him, and asked if he had not been a father to his employees. Well, the Lord deliver me from such a father. I would rather be an orphan. *[Applause.]*

A little girl, whose father was in the employ of the company 15 years, was told after the death of her father that if she desired to continue in the employ of the company, she would be expected to sign a contract to allow a certain portion of her wages to be retained each month until a debt of $65 due from her father was liquidated. This is a fact that was proved before the commission.

Mr. Debs then told of the steps that were taken to settle the trouble by arbitration.

The only reason the officials of the company refused to accept was because they realized that if they did, a condition of affairs would be disclosed that would place them in the pillory. It has been charged that I ordered the strike. The truth of the matter is that I never had a voice in the matter at all. I did not have a vote, because I was presiding over the convention, which was composed of 400 delegates representing 150,000 railroad men.[3] The convention ordered the strike. If there is nothing in a sympathy strike, then the brotherhood of man is a myth. There never was a strike that was not a sympathy strike.

The railroads claimed to be under contract to haul Pullman cars, but you never saw one of these contracts published. The fact is, they were not under any obligation to haul Pullman cars, but the General Managers' Association met, it decided that the roads would have to haul Pullman cars, and it would stand by Mr. Pullman, and that it would exterminate the ARU. The last proposition they have been glad to sublet about a week later.

The speaker then quoted from an editorial published in the Chicago Herald at the time, showing, he claimed, that the General Managers' Association was doing the very things that have been branded as a conspiracy when done by labor organizations.

The Northern Pacific is the one corporation goose that has been plucked every time there is a pinfeather in sight. Its blood was sucked by the officers until it had to be placed in the hands of receivers and wages reduced. Then, when the men refused to accept, Judge Jenkins restrained them from striking. Judge Jenkins, who sat on the bench when I was convicted the other day—Judge Jenkins, who, if justice were done him would be wearing stripes—and you will notice that before I get through I am liable to be guilty of contempt of somebody's court, and if I were not I should be guilty of contempt of myself—Judge Jenkins restrained the employees of that road from striking, but he did not restrain the receivers from reducing wages. If that is justice, then farewell to liberty in this country in spite of our applause for the American flag and "The Star-Spangled Banner."

Have you notice that none of the roads in the General Managers' Association have reduced wages since the big strike? No, the atmosphere is a little hazy, and it is not healthy to make reductions just now. But just as soon as the atmosphere clears a little, the program will be carried out. There was not a thing in the actions of those who went out in that great strike that I would change if I could. They acted manly in defense of their rights, and were in no wise responsible for the violations of law that resulted. The time will come when the men who participated in those strikes will be proud of it. The truth is not known yet, and they can afford to be patient. I believe with [William Cullen] Bryant that "Truth crushed to earth will rise again." If the United States government had kept its hands off, the railroads would have made terms with the men.

The General Managers' Association saw it was defeated and set fire to its own cars. If the employees had burned cars, is it not reasonable to suppose that a Pullman car or two would have been burned? But not all the general managers desired was a conflagration, and old boxcars answered the purpose. A lot of thieves and thugs and cutthroats were sworn in as deputy United States marshals on the pretense of protecting property, and these in many instances destroyed more property than they saved. Captain Palmer, of the fire department, told me that when the department went to put out the fire in the railroad yards he saw a man cutting the hose. He slugged him, and when he was picked up a United States marshal's badge was found on him. If any ARU men set fire to cars, why don't they produce one of them? Just one. They cannot do it. Not an ARU man set fire to a single car. It was not to their interest to do so, but it was to the interest of the general managers to do so.

According to the newspapers, I ought to go to the gallows. Well, I invite John M. Egan, the president of the General Managers' Association, to mount the gallows side by side with me. Everything has been said to poison the public mind. They have even said, "Debs is insane." Well, I hope I am, if they are sane.

Mayor Pingree of Detroit,[4] a man in every sense of that word, a man prompted by noble impulses, visited Chicago, and on calling on Mayor Hopkins, said: "Great heavens, mayor, I thought Chicago was all in flames." The newspapers actually made it appear that the strikers were going about with torches laying everything in ashes.

The speaker then severely criticized the newspapers in their attitude toward the strikers and their chase for sensational matter about himself ever since. He declared that John M. Egan knew that Chicago and Cook County would have to pay him for every rickety car that was burned in the effort to arouse public sentiment against the strikers.

There was not an iota of trouble as far as the public peace was concerned, until the federal troops were called out by the president of the United States, Grover Cleveland, in violation of the constitution.

"What could you expect from a hangman?" yelled a voice from the gallery, and the house went wild.

No president ever had such a rebuke administered to him as did Grover Cleveland last November. It was not a rebuke from the Democratic or Republican party, but from the American people.

There is no escaping from the doctrine of Judge Woods that the men who ordered the strike are responsible for the crime that followed. All I insist on is that the same doctrine be applied to the General Managers' Association which forced the strike. The trouble is that our judicial machinery is constructed to catch minnows and let whales slip through.

When the leaders were arrested, the emissaries of the railroad companies got in their work, and what was a well-disciplined, orderly body of men became chaotic, and began returning to work. This was how the railroads triumphed. It was simply a case of the United States government entering into partnership with the railroads to starve into submission their employees. I shall stand by this proposition though they send me to prison for life. Had General Miles gone to the strikers for his orders on the calling out of the troops, what a howl would have gone up. But he went to the General Managers' Association, and after the strike was ended they feasted him. Why not? He boasted that he had broken the backbone of the strike. But the time may come, before I have completed my work, when General Miles may wish he was less zealous in aiding the railroads to defeat their employees. He forced men to work at the point of a bayonet at Chicago. That was never done in Russia, but it was done under the stars and stripes.

Mr. Debs then spoke in the strongest terms against the proposition to increase the standing army to 100,000, predicting the decay of the Republic if ever it is accomplished. The remainder of his speech was largely an appeal to workingmen to study and think for themselves, and not have to depend on leaders for knowledge as to what they should or should not do. He was roundly applauded at the close.

Address to the American People:
A Manifesto from Woodstock Jail[†]
January 8, 1895

McHenry County Jail, Woodstock, Ill., January 8, 1895

In going to jail for participation in the late strike we have no apologies to make nor regrets to express. We go to jail not like quarry slaves, but sustained by the consciousness that we have done our duty. No ignominy attaches to us on account of this sentence. I would not change places with Judge Woods, and if it is expected that six months or even six years in jail will purge me of contempt, the punishment will fail of its purpose.

Candor compels me to characterize the whole proceeding as infamous. It is not calculated to revive the rapidly-failing confidence of the American people in the federal judiciary. There is not a scrap of testimony to show that one of us violated any law whatsoever. And if we are guilty of conspiracy, why are we punished for contempt? This question will continue to be asked with ever-increasing emphasis.

I would a thousand times rather be accountable for the strike than for the decision.

The ridicule of the press that we are "posing as martyrs" will not deceive the people. We all have homes and loved ones, and none of us are here by choice. We

---

[†]   Published as "Address to the American People," the *Railway Times,* January 15, 1895, 2. An extract of this manifesto was widely published in wire service reports in editions of January 9.

simply abide by the arbitrary action of the courts. There is a higher power yet to be heard from. No corporation will influence its decision. Our cause is that of conscientious liberty, and we have an abiding faith in the American people. We accept our lot with becoming patience and composure. We can afford to wait.

So far as I am concerned, I feel that when all the circumstances are considered, it would only have been disgraceful if we had so acquitted ourselves as to have kept out of jail. Our enemies are entitled to all the comfort they can extract from our imprisonment, and our friends have no concern.

Questions of great and grave importance are up for decision. Great principles involving the liberty of the citizen are at stake. Out of all this, good will come. There is one fundamental, bedrock principle—that the American people will never suffer to be sacrificed. It may be menaced, as it now is, but when the high court, "we, the people," have passed final judgments, its enthronement will be fixed and secure for all time.

We are by chance the mere instrumentalities in the evolutionary processes through which industrial slavery is to be abolished and economic freedom established. Then the starry banner will symbolize, as it was designed to symbolize, social, political, religious, and economic emancipation from thralldom of tyranny, oppression, and degradation.

Eugene V. Debs

Our First Great Need[†]

January 16, 1895

McHenry County Jail, Woodstock, Ill., January 16, 1895

Labor has fallen on troublous times. All the forces of society and all the powers of government are arrayed against workingmen. The mills of oppression are steadily grinding, and the lot of the average workingman is scarcely one remove above slavery. What shall be done to check this vicious, demoralizing tendency

---

[†]   Written for *Cooperative Age*. Reprinted in the *Railway Times*, vol. 2, no. 6 (March 15, 1895).

of the times? I answer: Let us get together and pull together for the good of all. There is no other hope for salvation. As long as workingmen vote the same ticket, their masters vote they must expect to be doomed to slavery. When will workingmen have the good sense to follow the example of capitalists and vote together, and vote *their interests?*

At present, the grand army of labor is divided and torn into factions and fractions, whose high purpose, it seems to be, is to destroy one another. Let us break up our hostile camps, eschew all *-isms,* banish dissension, and shoulder to shoulder march to the polls and take possession of the government in all its departments. Let us do this first, and do our quarreling, if we must quarrel, afterward. Until we do this, capitalism will rule with iron hand, and the courts and armies will enforce its decrees. The lot of the toiler will become worse and worse until the very dead line of degradation will be reached and the starry banner of the republic, whatever we may say about its waving "over the land of the free and the home of the brave," will simply symbolize the triumphant reign of the money power and the enslavement of the common people.

It would help us little to improve (if such a thing were possible) the present competitive wage system. It is essentially a system of spoliation. There is not a redeeming feature to it. Every thoughtful man knows it is maintained by the overmastering greed of the ruling rich. Nothing less than the complete overthrow of the grinding, degrading, pauperizing conspiracy against wageworkers will answer the demand. Why should one man work like a galley slave to keep another in luxurious idleness? Every man is entitled to all he produces with his brain and hands. The night of wage competition is dark, but the dawn of cooperation is near at hand. Let us get close enough together to hear each other's heart throbs. Let us unite in harmonious cooperation, and the day of deliverance is near at hand.

The Political Lesson of the Pullman Strike[†]

March 1895

The lessons taught by what is known as the Pullman strike are manifold. They are industrial, financial, and commercial lessons, and naturally, as the component elements of air or water, blend and constitute a political lesson which all men of intelligence are now studying with profound solicitude. Contemplating the strike from such a point of observation, it may be regarded as a national blessing rather than a national calamity.

It may not be impossible to discuss political questions without reference to political parties, but such is not the American habit. Political parties are the natural result of free speech, and while there is even a remnant of this right remaining in the country, men will divide and group themselves into parties. To deprecate political parties involves hostility to free speech and the abandonment of all hope of reform.

The Pullman strike has aroused national solicitude. It has vividly defined political issues. If on the one hand it has made prominent the power of the government by the use of such instrumentalities as its courts and armies, it has on the other hand given, if possible, more conspicuousness to conditions, which injunctions, however despotic, and bullets, however quieting, cannot, in the nature of things, improve; but which, under the application of such Russianized methods, must proceed continually from bad to worse, until revolution rescues free institutions from the grasp of corporate anarchism, or they lie crushed and dead in the python coils of a triumphant despotism.

I do not overcolor the situation. As I write, national scorn is concentrated upon Congress, where the sugar trust and the whiskey trust, by the persuasive power of money, humiliated the American people in the presence of the nations,[5] and now we behold the party responsible for the abandonment of right, truth, justice, and all things of good report among men, with an impudence sufficiently brazen to make the devil himself blush for what the president terms perfidious dereliction of duty, asking the American people to renew its lease of power.[6] In doing this, the party that won eternal infamy by yielding to the power of the sugar trust and the whiskey trust arraigns the other great party for having been guilty of legislating in the interests of trusts

---

†   Published as "Political Lessons" in the *Railway Times,* vol. 2, no. 5 (March 1, 1895), 1.

and corporations for more than 30 years, and against the interests of the people, and what is more important still, it introduces irrefutable testimony to sustain the indictment.

The Pullman strike has, in connection with other agencies, served the important purpose of attracting attention to chronic delinquencies of the two old parties, and is impressing upon the mind of multiplied thousands of voters the necessity for another political party.

Afro-American chattel slavery was the national curse and crime which a half century ago burned into the American conscience the necessity for a new party. Agitators who fanned the divine spark into a flame were pelted with storms of vulgar epithets, scurrility, and maledictions, to the extent of the resources of the English language. They were confronted with mobs, driven from platforms, and free speech was cloven down; the courts were invoked and decisions rendered which even yet are regarded as monumental infamies, and all along those gloomy years the government, in all of its departments, kept high advanced the national ensign symbolizing liberty, but at the same time floating above slave pens and slave blocks, slave whips and shackles, making the United States darker than the "Dark Continent," and extorting the cry "Haul down the flaunting lie!"

The agitation proceeded. The demand for a new party became yearly more pronounced; the signal fires of reform burned fiercer and higher; men rallied to the new standard and the new party, which had its origin in agitation, mobs, riots, and death, and finally overwhelmed all opposition and in 1860, after 40 years of struggle, was victorious, and, later on, amidst the smoke and carnage of war, and at a fearful cost of life and money, 7 million slaves stood forth unfettered and free, and the stars and stripes for the first time in 86 years floated over a land in which there were no slaves.

Since that period of vanquishing wrong and the enthronement of the right, a system of wage-slavery has been introduced. Warmed into life in the womb of greed, and fostered by laws and legislation as unholy as that which legalized slave stealing and the breeding of human beings like swine for the market, it has gained power and prestige until wage-slaves, under the domination of the money power, acting through trusts, syndicates, corporations, and monopoly-land stealing, capitalization, railroad wrecking, bribery, and corruption, defying proper characterization, we are confronted with conditions bearing the impress of peonism, infinitely more alarming than was African slavery in its darkest days.

Under such circumstances, what, I ask, is more natural within the entire realm of human duties than that wage-men should organize, agitate, and strike for their rights?

The Pullman strike, confessedly more far-reaching in its sweep and significance than any other struggle the continent has witnessed, will pass into history as having been the one thing needful to arouse the nation to the perils which the money power has spawned upon the country.

The American Railway Union, having from the first discountenanced violence and deplored the destruction of property, may, I think, suggest that the Pullman strike, notwithstanding such unfortunate features, has its compensations. No one will deny that the Pullman strike has aroused the government from its stupor to a sense of its obligations to ascertain the cause of the phenomenal disturbance, and the work of investigation, once begun, the hope and the belief may be entertained that it will be prosecuted until foundation infamies are discovered and dragged forth for the enlightenment of those who, in the absence of such information, find it profitable to apply the epithet of "anarchist" to those whose courage created the necessity for investigation, which, if honest and thorough, as indications warrant, the inevitable conclusion will be reached that men who strike against starvation wages and for the protection of those who are dependent upon them against corporate and plutocratic spoliation represent the true American spirit and courage which, once destroyed by the rapacity of heartless employers of the Pullman stripe, aided by United States courts and United States troops, would foreshadow calamities which it would be difficult to exaggerate. If, through the agencies of investigation and legislation, the curse of wage-slavery disappears, or is so modified as to produce greater contentment in the armies of labor, fruitful of the hope that at no distant day full emancipation shall be secured by wise legislation, the American Railway Union will expand to colossal proportions of organized philanthropy such as the ages have not witnessed, because the lesson it will have taught legislators and courts, presidents and governors, and men in command of military machines is that the majesty of truth and justice, rather than the tyranny of injunctions, aided by the persuasive power of powder, must preserve our free institutions if they are to be perpetuated. Never since the colonies were rescued from the grasp of King George has man's capacity for self-government been so confessedly on trial as in these closing years of the century. Thoughtful Americans are adopting the views expressed by Lord Macaulay,[7] that Americans are not qualified to perpetuate the government the fathers founded. On every hand is heard applause when a court, in the spirit of a tsar, lays its hands upon workingmen, and as whim may dictate, deprives the victims of its authority of property and liberty, and rejoicings, rising to paeans, are heard when in obedience to military commands wage-men demonstrate, as they fall bleeding and gasping, that ours is a "strong government." Macaulay thought that we should be able to preserve a government and civilization, but that liberty would be sacrificed.

Under the reign of the two great parties that have dominated the government, many years will not be required to fulfill Macaulay's prophecy—indeed, only a semblance of liberty remains when courts and the military put forth their unrestrained power. Such facts are taught by the lesson of the Pullman strike, but, fortunately, still other lessons are inculcated, among which is the lesson that the time has come for a new party to take the reins of government and bring it back to pristine purity, and that now is the time for workingmen and all who are animated by the spirit of patriotic devotion to liberty to unify to perpetuate the liberties of the people, to the end that government by the people, of the people, and for the people may not perish from the earth.

"The Liberty We Enjoy Is a Hollow Mockery": Message to the People[†]

March 1, 1895

March 1, 1895

Memory is not dead. We recall the heroic deeds of our forefathers who pledged life, honor, and property to secure liberty for themselves and for future generations. In recalling their heroism, their sacrifices, and their sufferings Americans must be as dead as Egypt's embalmed mummies if their hearts do not beat responsive to the holiest and sternest passions that ever burned and glowed in a freeman's heart.

Those immortal patriots founded a government of equal rights. They abhorred kings. They trampled upon crowns. They broke scepters and forever exiled a titled nobility and aristocracy from the land, and, accepting the revelation that "God is no respecter of persons," they proclaimed the eternal truth that all men are "created equal," and to give their fiat enduring force they, "the people," crowned themselves by divine right sovereign citizens and took the ballot as a symbol of their sovereignty.

Since that august period, more than one hundred years have come and gone, and what is the legacy they have left for the present generation? On the one hand, we are invited to survey the material progress of the nation, and the facts challenge the imagination to paint a more glowing picture of triumphs over all opposing forces. The march of the nation westward, following the star of empire, has all the glamour of fiction. The carving of the vast domains into separate territories and their transformation into states and bringing them into the federal union under one flag is the wonder of the world.

I should like to dwell upon such evidences of national prosperity. An American born, to eulogize the greatness, the power and prosperity of my country would be in strict accord with every high and ennobling aspiration of my mental being. But 200,000 miles of railroads, mines, factories, forges, great cities, forests and farms, standing armies, navies, gold and silver, banks, trusts, syndicates, plutocrats, do not, all combined, constitute a state—only

---

[†] Published as "Debs to the People" in the *Coming Nation* (Tennessee City, TN), March 30, 1895.

men who know their rights and, knowing, dare to maintain them however great the sacrifice.

Our nation's physical greatness nor its fabulous wealth constitutes its glory, nor yet its schoolhouses nor its churches. If amid splendid triumphs of what the world calls progress the wageworkers of the country are oppressed, robbed, degraded, shot down like vagabond dogs and imprisoned like felons, driven from decent habitations and forced into dens which wild beasts would not inhabit, then our civilization is savagery. Fair it may be to contemplate from certain points of observation, but it is nevertheless a whited sepulcher, under whose captivating exterior exist abominations of which, if heaven takes cognizance, the eternal God must again repent that he made man at all.

Here, with the ballot; here, with constitutions framed for the protection of all, are daily perpetrated acts of despotism of unparalleled enormity, except perhaps in lands where the lives and liberties and the property of the people are in the hands of a tsar, a sultan, or a shah. And it is also true that in the United States acts of tyranny are perpetrated which demonstrate that appeals to courts and legislatures for justice are as unheeded as when a storm-beaten wayfarer appeals to a blizzard for protection.

Fellow workingmen, the outlook is appalling. Never since the minions of King George shot down the minutemen at Concord has liberty been in as great danger as now. Indeed, the liberty we enjoy is a hollow mockery. Workingmen have no liberty. The plutocratic corporation, the autocratic judge, who enacts law by injunction and enforces it by deputy marshals armed with pistols and clubs and supported by troops with shotted guns, have banished liberty from the land. Workingmen are simply tolerated if they remain silent and do the bidding of their masters. If, under the tortures of hunger and nakedness, despair provokes protest, the injunction, the club, bayonet, and bullet enforce submission, and this work of enslavement goes steadily on.

I speak as a victim, from a dungeon tomb, as one who loved his fellow man and dared raise his voice to mitigate the pangs of famine in a suburb of hell known as Pullman, and all over this once favored land men are imprisoned or are driven into idleness and vagabondage, blacklisted and exiled because they had the courage to teach trampled hearts to feel the curses that their plutocratic masters were heaping upon them. If, as it is said, the darkest hour of night is just before the dawn, then, fellow workingmen, the dawn ought to be near at hand—or do the enemies of labor contemplate a still darker hour before the first ray of light heralds relief and bids us hope? To what further increase of the armies of wretchedness do the corporations demand? To what deeper degradation are workingmen to descend to gratify the greed of the venal corporations and those who aid them in their piracies? To what greater depths do those who rob labor desire to plunge their barbed iron into the quivering souls of workingmen, that they may coin the tortures of their victims into dividends on watered stocks and bonds? Will workingmen cease to protest? Will the injunction and the prison, the blacklist and hunger, robbery and degradation, teach them submission? Will the bayonet and the bullet, the club and the blood that follows the blow, teach American workingmen how to starve and die that plutocrats may fare sumptuously every day? It has been done. The crime has been committed under the stars and stripes and is being repeated every day of the year. History repeats itself. How often shall such history be repeated in this land? How long shall the United States of America stand before the nations of the earth with the boastful lie of liberty in its throat, while corporation, court, and armies have multiplied thousands of men in the dust beneath their despotic hoofs?

The answer is not difficult. While workingmen use their ballots to enthrone men in power who are their enemies, the work of degradation will proceed. When workingmen conclude to use their ballots to elect to office neither plutocrats nor the fawning parasites of plutocrats, then, and not till then, will emancipation day dawn. There are dangers ahead. To aver them I appeal to the workingmen of America to abandon, at once and forever, the old political parties, to unify and cast their votes for a party whose every battle cry is "justice to labor," a party that is pledged to righteous laws and a righteous administration of justice.[8]

Eugene V. Debs

The ARU's Fight Is for All Humanity:
Speech at the Fargo Opera House, Fargo, North Dakota[†]

March 6, 1895

Ladies and Gentlemen:—

First of all, permit me to thank the reverend gentleman who has just presented me from the very depths of my heart for his beautiful words, which I appreciate far beyond the power of language to express.

There are many thousands of our people who view with apprehension and alarm the widespread unrest that pervades our social, industrial, and political system, and taking counsel of their doubts and fears, they arrive at the conclusion that the prophecy of Macaulay is about to be fulfilled, that "self-government is to be an administrative failure," and that the sun of our republic is to set in universal gloom.

I am not of that number. Having faith in the ever-increasing intelligence of the masses, I am persuaded that the grand old ship of state, with her precious cargo of human hopes and aspirations, will breast all of the billows and weather all of the storms, and finally safely reach her destined port.

I admit that the immediate outlook is not rich with promise, and yet there is a hopeful view to be taken of the situation. The feudal system gave way to the competitive system, which in my judgment is now in the throes of dissolution, and the competitive system has to give way and fall into the cooperative system. We have met tonight for the purpose of speaking of the more important phases of the late great strike, the greatest industrial upheaval of modern times.

If there are those present (as I do not doubt there are) who know me only as I have been described in the papers, and who are therefore prejudiced, I ask them in all fairness to dismiss that prejudice and give me the benefit of a fair and impartial hearing. In what I shall have to say tonight, it will be my purpose, as it has always been my purpose, to present the issues fairly, to see an injustice upon one side as quickly as upon another, and to do equal and exact justice to both.

---

†   Published as a pamphlet, *Verbatim Report of the Lecture Delivered by Eugene V. Debs at Opera House, Fargo, ND, March 6, 1895.* Fargo, ND: TLPU/Independent Publishing Co., n.d. (1895). Specimen in the Indiana State University Debs pamphlets collection bears a handwritten inscription by Debs on the cover reading, "(Taken by a boy and full of errors: E. V. D.)."

First of all, let it be understood that the Pullman Company is capitalized at $31 million, according to their own statement. They have an undivided surplus of $25 million. The company of Pullman own the town of Pullman absolutely. There is not an inch of free soil there, nor is there a free man, woman, or child—a species of serfdom that, if known, would horrify the world.

Preliminary to what I shall have to say, let me introduce the words of a clergyman, Rev. Carwardine, for two years a resident minister in Pullman, a gentleman of unimpeachable integrity, widely known and as widely respected. There is an introduction to his book by another minister of the gospel who made a visit to Pullman, the Rev. Mr. Driver,[9] and he says that this book is filled with facts, for which facts the author is not responsible. If sometimes the author's spirit flames with indignation, let it be remembered that it is against heartless tyranny and in defense of long silent and outraged innocence. The author means neither to minify nor magnify. He has not fallen into misrepresentation. The statements can all be verified again and again. In his work Mr. Carwardine says: "The great trouble with this Pullman system is that it is not what it pretends to be. It is a civilized relic of European serfdom."

We all enjoy living here because there is an equality of interest, and we have a common enemy, the company, but our daily prayer is, "Lord, keep us from dying here." An eminent writer in *Harper's Monthly* in 1884, on Pullman, declared that at that time, ten years ago, its great faults were:

> Bad administration in respect to the employment, retention, and promotion of employees. Change is constant in men and officers, and each new superior appears to have his own friends, whom he appoints to desirable positions. Favoritism and nepotism exist; natural dissatisfaction, a powerful prevalence of petty jealousies, discouragements of superior excellence, frequent change of residents, and an all-pervading feeling of insecurity.[10]

The writer further declares that it is not an American idea. It is a species of benevolent feudalism, and as to its morals, the writer says: "The prevailing tendency at that day was the desire to beat the company."

It is generally agreed that the maximum average wage paid at the time of the strike was $1.85. As to the lowest wages, it is difficult to average. The wages are paid every two weeks. Two checks are given to each employee—one a rent check, the other a paycheck. Wages are paid at the bank. When they go to the bank, they receive their two weeks' pay, the half month's rent is taken out, and the paycheck is cashed. The scenes enacted at the bank during last winter were pitiable. Not only was the current rent urgently demanded, but back rent was asked for under circumstances in many cases entirely uncalled for.

After deducting rent, the men invariably had only from one to six dollars or so, on which to live for two weeks. One man has a paycheck in his possession of two cents after paying rent. He has never cashed it, preferring to keep it as a memento. He has it framed. Another I saw the other day for seven cents. It was dated September 1893. The man had worked as a skilled mechanic for ten hours a day for twelve days and earned $9.07. He keeps a widowed mother and pays the rent, the house being in his name. His half month's rent amounted to $9. The seven cents was his, but he has never claimed it. Another employee had 47 cents coming to him on his paycheck, and then was asked if he would not apply that on his back rent. He was indignant. He replied: "If Mr. Pullman needs that 47 cents worse than I do, let him have it." He left it.

These instances might be indefinitely multiplied. Let me recite one that came under my personal observation. There was a young woman working there under the name of Jennie Curtis. Her father died last August a year ago indebted to the company $65 for rent. The next day after the funeral the young woman was notified that if she expected to continue in the service of that company she would be expected to sign an agreement to pay to the company in installments the $65 owed by her father at the time of his death.

She told me that after making the payment of the regular installment, there was not enough left to supply herself and the little brother and sister with the necessaries of life, and she had to depend upon the charity of the neighbors. These instances might be multiplied indefinitely.

A child born at Pullman is born in a Pullman house, is rocked in a Pullman cradle, is educated in a Pullman school, attends a Pullman church, works, of course, in a Pullman shop, and when at last death (sometimes the poor man's best friend) has wrung from the unfortunate victim the last despairing sigh, he is wrapped in a Pullman shroud, placed in a Pullman casket, drawn in a Pullman hearse to a Pullman cemetery, and buried in a Pullman grave. That is the story of a human life at Pullman. The wages are so adjusted to each other that in some way every dollar earned by the employees finds its way back into the coffers of the Pullman Company.

During the year preceding the strike, the wages were reduced three times, and under the last reduction there was not enough left to supply the necessaries of life. They were patient to a degree that defied exaggeration, and I say here tonight that no man with a heart throbbing in his bosom could have gone to Pullman and made investigation without coming away in sympathy with the strikers.

While there were three reductions in the wages of these employees, there was no reduction in the rents. The testimony was given by a number of real estate experts that the rents at Pullman were from 25 to 40 percent higher than they were in any of the adjoining towns. The claim was made by the company that they were obliged on account of the depression of the times to make some reduction. They did not make the reductions on account of the depression of the times, but they did make them to crush out their competitors, because they could have their work done for nothing. For the item of rent the employees were in debt to the company at the time of the strike $70,000.

They were getting deeper and deeper into the debt of the Pullman Company every day, and they realized that it was only a question of time until they should be mortgaged body and soul and their children and their children's children to the Pullman corporation forever.

For taking part in this strike I have been condemned by a great many people and I have lost the respect of a great many others, but I have kept my own. I have been true to myself. Before I conclude my arguments, I know I shall be able to convince you that those men, in striking for their rights, did only as you would have done, had you been similarly oppressed.

The Pullman Company is one of the wealthiest on the continent. It increased its capital from 1883 to 1889, a period of six years, $12 million—or $2 million a year. There never has been a reduction, even to the fraction of a percent, in their dividend. Regularly they have declared their dividend, adding yearly to their capital. They had no excuse for grinding their old and trusted employees into the dust. They did it simply because they thought they had the power to do it, as remorseless as a conflagration. They did not hear the music of groans and sighs at Pullman.

The employees of the Pullman Company did not want to strike. Mr. Carver Dean said they did everything that honorable men could do to avoid a strike. At last they appointed a committee and called on the officials of the city of Chicago and Mr. Pullman happened to be there. Mr. Pullman, let me say, who poses before the world as a philanthropist, is the veriest hypocrite, and I propose to strip him of his mask and let you see him as he is. When his employees came to this meeting his conscience (if he had one) must have smitten him, and he thrust his hand into his pocket and he assumed the expression of a Pharisee as he said, "Have I not been a father to you?" When the committee told it to me I said, "The good Lord deliver me from that kind of a father. I had a good deal rather take my chances on being an orphan."

Then he said, "I will investigate your grievances," and then for the first time they saw a glimmer of hope. They said, "At least our grievances will be investigated by the officials, and there is a bare possibility that justice may be done." And the very next morning the committee were discharged. That is the way in which the Pullman Company kept faith with its employees; it had promised to investigate and then discharged the committee.

That day every man, woman, and child withdrew from the service of the company, and I honor them for it. I am not unmindful of the fact that a great many people are opposed to [use of] the strike. I confess that I am myself, but on account of the overmastering greed of some corporation, the time comes now and then when you have got to choose between a strike and degradation, and when that time comes, I believe in striking with all the force at my command, and then I feel as Jackson did about it, "By the eternal, I will take all the consequences of my acts." And when my case is called, they will not have to issue a bench warrant. I will be there to toe the mark of duty. I will not take my private car and leave for the seashore, as did Pullman.

I would remind you here tonight that we live under a striking government; that there is not a star nor a stripe in the American flag that does not tell of a strike. At Lexington, where the shot was fired that was heard around the world, at Concord, and all along that track of gloom and glory, there was one continuous succession of strikes for liberty and independence, and had it not been for the magnificent courage and patriotism of the revolutionary fathers in striking for their rights, we would have been British subjects tonight instead of sovereign American citizens.

Every inch of progress that has been made in this world was made by virtue of a strike, and the revolutionary fathers were not only strikers, but they were a class of boycotters, and so were the revolutionary mothers as well. You have often heard the boycott spoken of as a crime. The revolutionary fathers put the boycott on tea, and they did not only boycott, but they destroyed property as well. They went down to Boston Harbor and made a teapot of it, and the revolutionary mothers said, "Amen, we will go without our tea."

There were Tories who said Washington was a dangerous demagogue, but now the schoolchildren honor his memory. The difference between a demagogue and a demigod is only about a quarter of a century. A good many people say, "We must maintain law and order." Well, suppose Washington and Jefferson and Franklin and Paine had been for law and order. They trampled the law underfoot with impunity in as holy a cause as ever prompted men to action in this world.

I am for law and order myself, but I want it to be the right kind of law, and I want it enforced against all people alike. The trouble has been in this country that our judicial nets have been so adjusted as to catch the minnows and let the whales slip through. If the metropolitan press of this country had been published in the days of Washington, they would have denounced these grand patriots. They were denounced by the weak and by those who said, "Why don't you let well enough alone? You will bring trouble upon the country if you continue in lawlessness and riot and bloodshed." And then those patriots expanded to the proportions of freemen and said, "If there has got to be war in order to get independence, let it come now, that our children may enjoy the blessings of peace." There were those who thought an agitator was perfectly disreputable, but it was simply a question of agitation or stagnation.

I am an agitator. I do not blush when I admit it. I am going to do all that is in my power to change conditions. They do not suit me. I do not see how any man with a heart throbbing in him can be satisfied with the conditions as they are now in this country. There are those who say, "Let well enough alone." If this is well enough, what could be bad enough? Progress is born of agitation. The men who agitate pay the penalties, and some of the penalties they pay are misrepresentations. They are misrepresented by those who cannot conceive of a pure, disinterested motive. The motives of the men who incur all these penalties and who invite social condemnation are as far above the motives of their detractors as the stars are above the rolling prairie.

I know there are those who believe with Walpole that "Every man has his price." Walpole was a scoundrel and had his price, or he never would have conceived that infamy.[11] But there are men in this world who have not got their price; there are men who are pure and incorruptible; there are men who cannot be influenced by all the wealth of the corporations, nor can they be silenced by all the penalties that may attach to them. Those men are the "salt of the earth," as Christ said, the light and the hope of this world. I have made up my mind long since that I am going to be true to myself.

Many people say that we ought to consult public opinion, do not do anything that shocks society. Let me say to you tonight in all candor that I have not the slightest faith in public opinion as a guide. As a general proposition, public opinion is wrong. I admit that it gets right in the course of three thousand or four thousand years, but that is too long for an ordinary mortal to wait. It was public opinion that kept up the infamous institution of slavery for years. It was public opinion that put Wendell Phillips (as noble a heart as ever beat "betwixt us and the mercy seat") in the pillory in his native town and spat upon him. It was public opinion that committed those monstrous outrages against Harriet Martineau, as noble a woman as ever breathed.[12] She was to go to Ohio and make speeches against slavery, and the people arose and said that if she put her foot on Ohio soil they would strangle the life out of her body.

It was public opinion that murdered John Brown, because he was tender and humane enough to say that property in man is a crime. Wendell Phillips was born with a silver spoon in his mouth. He belonged to the aristocratic classes. He could have been universally respected, he could have been a social lion, but he preferred to speak out against an institution that fired his noble soul with indignation. He ostracized himself. Society closed its doors in his face and poured its filth upon his head, but he stood erect; he had the courage of his convictions. However severe the alternative, he did not falter in his God-given mission, and he lived long enough to see the inhuman institution of slavery destroyed.

Had Phillips and Garrison and all the rest of their coadjutors been silent, had they believed in law and order, had they feared to incur the abuse that comes from agitating (especially when the old institution is the subject of attack), the institution of slavery would have been upon our soil yet, would pollute the free atmosphere of the republic.

It is precisely so with the working people of this country. Admitted or not, as you feel about it, but the fact is that the industrialists of this country are in serfdom; are in bondage from which there is no escape for the individual except possibly through the back door of suicide. Is the fact a haggard one? So much the worse for our much-vaunted civilization. But I do not take a gloomy view of the future. I believe with Fitch that the common people of this country are beginning to think for themselves.

In the past they have been satisfied to do their thinking by proxy, but they are now beginning to do something for themselves. The working people are the hope of the future. It is here, under the flag of the 44 stars, that workingmen are beginning to ask why it is that they must press their rags still closer lest they jostle against the silken garment which their fingers have made; why it is that they must walk weary and shelterless in the shadow of homes that they have erected but may not enter.

Workingmen are beginning to think, and they will soon begin to act; they will not beg for their rights, but they will take them, not in lawlessness, not in pillage and riot, but in a lawful manner. They will take them by the power of the ballot, the weapon that "falls as lightly as the snowflake falls upon the sod, yet executes a free man's will as lightning does the will of God."

They are theories of the people because of centuries of oppression and toil and martyrdom, and they know that the people of a free country will hear that cry, because here labor is the king; the conservator of all capital. Labor makes the forest monarch fall low unto the earth and seizes the monster and transforms it; labor smites at the adamantine doors of vast treasure chambers, and shall not workingmen carry their own? Who shall doubt it? When the mariner passing over the tropic seas looks for relief, he turns his eyes to the southern cross, and as midnight approaches, the southern cross begins to bend, and the stars begin to change their places, and the Almighty marks the passage of time on the heavens. Let labor everywhere take heart of hope, for the cross is bending, and the midnight is passing, and "Joy cometh in the morning."

Here let me remind you (returning to the subject) that the Pullman employees never asked the Pullman Company to do anything but to submit their trouble to arbitration. I believe, as they believe, in the American principle of arbitration, and if a man will not submit to it, it is evidence that he has no faith in the justice of his cause.

The employees simply said, "Let us arbitrate," and the company said, "There is nothing to arbitrate," and Mr. Pullman (who has a happy faculty of getting away when he is wanted) went to the seashore until his old and trusted employees should be starved back into his employ on his terms. We made this proposition. We said, "Let the Pullman Company select two representatives, let the judges of the Circuit Court appoint two representatives, and let these four appoint a fifth. We will not ask for a representative on the board at all. Let that board of five decide if there is anything to arbitrate, and if that board decides that there is nothing to arbitrate, the employees will go back to work.

But the company insisted that it did not have anything to arbitrate for two reasons: The first was that they knew that no five men could have been found in the city of Chicago who would not have decided in favor of the employees. There was another more important reason. They knew that if such an investigation would have been made, a state of affairs would have been disclosed that would have horrified the world. That was why they were opposed from first to last to the question as to whether there was anything to arbitrate.

The delegates of the ARU met in convention on the 12th day of June, and many of the delegates visited Pullman in person. I went there myself. I could not believe the report of the horrible conditions at Pullman. I went there twice; from home to home, from hovel to hovel, I met the wives of some of the employees and the wives of some of them I did not meet, because they did not have clothes to make them presentable.

I saw children suffering hunger and in rags, the most pitiable spectacle I ever saw in my life, more rags than I have ever seen before, anyhow. The delegates visited there, and their hearts were touched. It could not be otherwise, and they said, "We will make a final effort to adjust this trouble." They appointed a committee and asked the Pullman Company if they would not give their employees a hearing, and they dismissed them without consideration. They went a second time and were treated with disdain and contempt.

The mayor and city council of Chicago visited them, but all of their efforts were unavailing; the Pullman Company stood stubborn as adamant. Then the committee said, "If the Pullman Company refuses to show any disposition to adjust this difference with their employees, then we, as members of the American Railway Union, will not join in the wrong." So they decided by the vote of 425 delegates.[13]

You hear that I am responsible for the strike. I did not even have a vote in ordering the strike, but 425 sturdy men, after having exhausted every effort that kindliness could suggest, voted without a dissenting voice to refuse to handle Pullman cars if the Pullman Company did not show some disposition to treat with its starving employees. I cordially endorsed the action of the delegates. They could not have done otherwise without having been cowards and apostates. The Pullman employees were members of their organization; they were their brothers and their sisters; they were the victims of conditions which they could not avoid or control.

It was the duty of their brothers to go to their rescue and they did it, and I am proud of it, and when all the truth is known, they will not be obliged to blush for their conduct. But before I go into this part of the argument, I want to show you that there were other influences in operation that justified the action of these delegates. I hold in my hand a clipping from the *Chicago Herald* of May 5, 1893, six weeks before the American Railway Union was instituted.[14] The *Chicago Herald* cannot be charged with being unduly friendly with labor organizations. The three great papers of Chicago were against us and burdened the wire with falsehoods.[15] The *Chicago Herald* says in regard to the Managers' Organization: "Setting forth the reasons as given by the General Managers' Association for forming an organization, a principle of which, that in case of a strike on any one road which was a member of the association, caused by a reduction of wages which was shortly to be put into effect one line at a time, the other roads would force their employees into a combination for the purpose of quelling the strike or else compelling them all to go out on a sympathetic strike for mutual protection."

If a sympathy strike is a crime and conspiracy, as has been held, and if the Managers' Association has been organized to force sympathy strikes, I ask you, "Who are the conspirators?"

The 26 railroads centered at Chicago combined through their general managers with two great purposes in view: first, to reduce wages all over the country, and second, to put those who protested on the blacklist and forever bar the doors against them. This institution was formed prior to the organization of the ARU. Shortly after this institution was organized, reduction of wages began all over the country. I have here another report that I desire to read. Here is a copy of the original reduction made very shortly after this Managers' Association was perfected: which acquainted the employees of a reduction of 15 to 33.3 percent in their wages, reducing the wages of section men and helpers in freight and roundhouses, etc., as low as 67.5 cents per day.

I submit it is not possible for a man to provide for his wife, to rear his children as becomes an American citizen, on 67.5 cents a day. He cannot live in a cottage (I know because I saw); he is compelled to live in a hovel such as a vagabond fox would not inhabit. He has got to subsist upon food that is not fit for a human being, and he is compelled to allow his children to grow up in ignorance because he does not get wages enough, notwithstanding he works hard and faithfully every day in the month to buy clothes to make his children presentable, and his children, by the force of circumstances of which they are the victims, are compelled to grow up ignorant, and a great many of them drift into crime.

The foundations of this republic rest in the virtue and intelligence of the people. If multiplied thousands of workingmen are ground and crushed to an extent that they cannot educate their children, what a change a few generations will produce; and I want to say that the foundations of the Republic will rest very insecurely then.

Let me call your attention to the fact that no two railroads reduce wages at the same time; they do not care to arouse too many employees at once and call public attention to the reduction. These reductions occurred every two weeks or so. They came up into the eastern part of the country and took in some of the railroads there, and then came to this part of the country. They took in the Chicago & Eastern Illinois road, then they took in the Northern Pacific (and, by the way, let me say that the Northern Pacific is the one corporation goose that has been plucked every time there has been a pinfeather in sight).

When some of these corporations have a courageous, manly body of men working for them, and they are afraid that a reduction will result in a strike, they avoid reducing the wages and go on and wreck the road. After they have wrecked the road, they apply for a receiver, and then the court grants the receivership; then the court, on due application, orders a reduction of wages, and after the reduction has been ordered, there is another order issued restraining the men from quitting the employ of the company. Jenkins did not, however, issue an order restraining the company from discharging the men, and it's a mighty poor rule that won't work both ways.

No, that did not occur in Russia. That was here, under the stars and stripes. I addressed a meeting in the home of Judge Jenkins the other night at Milwaukee, and I said if justice were done him he would be wearing stripes and pounding rocks, and if that is contempt of court he is entitled to make the most of it. The other day he sat on the bench, and the court crier said, "God save this honorable court." I said, "Amen. I do not know of any power this side of the Almighty that could save it."

That Northern Pacific reduction was a case of the court holding the men up while the corporation went through their pockets. But the reduction did not stop there. The Great Northern fell into line, but it did not last long there, because once in the history of labor the men had the sense to unify their forces. That was all that saved them. By the power of unified effort, they succeeded in making a settlement that was perfectly amicable and perfectly satisfactory, so far as I know, to all concerned.

At the same time that there was a reduction on the Great Northern, there was a reduction ordered on the Chicago & Great Western, to take effect later. As soon as the men quit the Great Northern, this road decided that the atmosphere was not favorable for a reduction, and notwithstanding the fact that the reduction was ordered, it was not made, nor has it been made from that day to this.

Then a reduction was ordered on the Union Pacific, but they had a judge there who was an upright man, and his name commands my respect. I refer to Judge Caldwell. After exposing the rascality of the management and showing that if the property was honestly managed, it could have paid its employees honest wages, he said, "There will be no reduction on this system if not another dollar is paid on the watered stock." There was no reduction, not because the corporation was not desirous of making it, but because between the corporation and the employees there was a judicial Gibraltar. If there were more judges of that character in the country, there would be more confidence in the courts.

So, when the delegates met, they were employed on roads, some of which had already made a reduction and others were going to make them, according to the carefully arranged program of the General Managers' Association, and when these delegates saw the horrifying conditions at Pullman, they said, "We might as well strike and starve as work and starve; we would at least preserve our manhood."

The strike began on the 26th day of June. In just four days the Managers' Association was completely defeated. The American Railway Union was triumphant. There was, as the records show, not the slightest disorder or law-lessness up to that time. The Managers' Association saw they were defeated and something had to be done to rescue them from that dilemma, and something was done. The cars began to burn. I want to prove to you tonight that they were not burned by the members of the American Railway Union, nor by their sympathizers. There was no escape for the general managers except by the torch of their emissaries, and I want to prove to you that it was done by their emissar-ies. The American Railway Union had everything to lose by arson, by riot, and by lawlessness, but the railway companies had everything to gain. They could then apply for an injunction. They could then arrest and imprison the leaders.

I made this statement in Chicago the other night in the presence of four thousand people, and a gentleman was in the audience who bore testimony to it. Captain Power, a high official in the fire department of the city of Chicago, came to me and said, "Debs, when the cars were burning and I was trying to put out the fire, I found a man trying to cut the hose, and I struck him and found that he was a deputy United States marshal, and was employed by the General Managers' Association."

We had 80 witnesses at Chicago, and among them high officials in the police and fire departments, to testify as to who lighted the fires and incited the riot and was responsible for the lawlessness. There is an official report on file in the office of the mayor of Chicago, signed by two policemen who were deputized to clothe themselves in citizen's dress and find out who were setting fire to the boxcars in Chicago, and at midnight they saw two men who had lighted a match and were about to set some cars afire, and they arrested them and found that they were both deputy United States marshals in the employ of the General Managers' Association. The gentlemen were there who testified to it under oath, but they did not get the chance to testify. While we could have continued the trial, and were anxious to continue the trial, and could have le-gally continued the trial, they refused to listen to any proposition under which the trial might have been continued.

The true conspirators will be known. Just now we are the conspirators, but there will be a shifting of the scenes, and the gentlemen who a little while ago waited in perfect composure for us to go to the penitentiary may go there themselves before we get through with them.

The American Railway Union believes in the supremacy of the law. The American Railway Union is composed of manly American citizens. They be-lieve in and are at all times ready to uphold our institution, and if the old flag were assailed, if Old Glory was in peril, I do not hesitate to declare that no body of men would go to the front more quickly and more valiantly than the men who make up the American Railway Union, and not only them, but the workingmen of the country generally, because they are the men who do the fighting when there is any fighting to be done.

I wonder if Mr. Pullman could say as much for himself? I presume he would be a good deal like Mark Twain was at the time of the late unpleasantness. He said, "I propose to suppress this rebellion if it costs every one of my wife's relatives." He would be patriotic by proxy. He would be a hero at very long range. No, the ARU is not responsible for the violence that was committed at Chicago. The ARU did everything within its power to preserve order, to maintain the law, to prevent bloodshed; but on the 30th day of June, when all of the roads were paralyzed, (simply because the men in a body withdrew from the service of the company) when that time came, and the general managers realized that they were defeated and that the ARU had compelled them to make some terms looking to a satisfactory adjustment of the existing trouble, they saw there was only one way in which defeat could be turned into victory; they had 4,200 deputy marshals sworn in, and the chief deputy marshal who swore them in, more than 2,000 of them, testified under oath that many of them were the toughest-looking men he ever saw. They were dragged from the slums of the city of Chicago, clothed with United States authority, their pockets were filled with money and they were given a knowing look, and they went among the men who were congregated about, and then the trouble began.

They were the men who commenced all the trouble, and just as soon as the trouble began and the wires were burdened with the information that Chicago was in flames and under the rule of a mob, the law-abiding citizens said, "We must suppress that mob, and preserve rule and order." I am constrained to say that everything was peaceable, and the only evidence of riot was the presence of the militia, which had been called out.

We wanted no trouble. The Managers' Association wanted trouble; that was their only escape, and they did not hesitate to employ the means that were required to relieve them, if they had to resort to bloodshed. "Truth crushed to earth will rise again." Let me ask you, if the members of the ARU had been led by a malicious motive, if they had been bent on destroying property, is it reasonable to suppose that they would have destroyed just one Pullman palace car? They were in the yard, they were just as easy of access, but there was not one of them destroyed. They were too expensive. The fire always originated in out-of-service hospital cars, which were not worth more than $25 apiece. They served the purpose of a conflagration, and that was all that was required.

They reasoned that Cook County would be legally responsible for every car destroyed. They would not lose anything by the conflagration but would be reimbursed in full. However, they have not yet brought their suit for damages, and I apprehend that they are not going to bring any suit.

In the late trial there was sufficient to induce them to change their minds. When they bring these damage suits against the city of Chicago, they want to put on a tire escape equipment. The city of Chicago is loaded with evidence to show that they destroyed their own property, or at least that it was destroyed by thugs and thieves in their employ, and they are going to show that many of them are now in the service of the company. They do not want any damages. There will be no suits brought; they have changed their minds very considerably the last few days. They did not know that they were going to be called on the witness stand, and they were . . . the worst scared lot of managers I ever saw, and they were afflicted with a chronic lapse of memory. I know that a general managership is a position that is extremely exacting, but I did not know that it had such a demoralizing effect upon the mental faculties. Let me relate a little instance. We had five general managers on the stand. Three days before the strike occurred, the general managers met and the Pullman Association with them, and they formed an association. Mr. Wickes, the vice president of the Pullman Company, was there, and on account of the secret proceedings which took place, the meeting was called an emergency trial. This was on the 24th day of June.

Five of the general managers were put on the stand and asked what Mr. Wickes of the Pullman Company was there for, and not one of them could remember. One of them did say that Mr. Wickes was there to tell them he had nothing to say. I know what he was there for, and so do you. He was there for the purpose of perfecting the partnership between the General Managers' Association and the Pullman Company. The General Managers' Association did not want the Pullman Company to settle. One word from the general managers would have been sufficient to compel the Pullman Company to arbitrate its differences with its employees, but that word was not spoken.

I will tell you why the General Managers' Association went into partnership with the officials of the Pullman Company to starve their employees to death. I know whereof I speak. We had a detective or two of our own. The General Managers' Association had viewed with great alarm the rapid development of the ARU. They said, "This unification is going on all over the country. They have succeeded on the Great Northern. If this is permitted to go forward, it will not be long before they will have a voice in regulating wages," and that was just what the general managers did not want to see. Their interest is in keeping the ARU divided and quarreling among themselves, and they have been very successful at it, I must say.

They understood the strength of the ARU. They thought they could snuff it out like a candle. When the trouble commenced, the injunctions were issued. As a matter of course, it is a very easy matter to demoralize a well-disciplined system of working men. Take away their leaders and persuade them that all the well-organized forces of society are against them, and their defeat is accomplished. The ARU had no friend. The ARU stood by and for itself. I mean to say in that immediate vicinity. I know that here and there was a noble soul who had the courage to speak out and to invite abuse because of speaking out, but as a general proposition all the powers were against it.

It was a struggle that a body of workingmen were making for all humanity. They were fighting the battle that you will have to fight in a few years. Am I an alarmist? Let me read the words of another agitator. See what he says on the subject. You all know him, and you will not malign him, either. His name is Abraham Lincoln. You applaud him now, but they did not applaud him then. In 1864 the labor organizations made him an honorary member, and he wrote a letter in honor of this, and this is what he said:

> I see in the near future a crisis approaching that unnerves me and causes me to tremble for the safety of my country. As a result of war, corporations have been enthroned and an era of corruption in high places will follow, and the money power of the country will endeavor to prolong its reign, working upon the prejudices of the people until all wealth is aggregated in a few hands and the republic is destroyed. I feel at this moment more anxiety for the safety of the country than ever before, even in the midst of war.[16]

He saw with prophetic vision what the future had in store. When he wrote that letter, he was denounced for it. He was maligned for being an agitator, but he spoke from the fullness of his patriotic heart, and if you do not believe that the prophecy has been entirely fulfilled, you will believe it before the lapse of many more years. The world is not just. It is a long way from being generous. I admit that we are making a little progress, but it is like a painted ship on a painted sea, impossible to tell whether we are moving at all; but I believe we are moving in the right direction.

To return to the subject: Injunctions were issued by the courts to restrain us from doing our duty, to demoralize our men, to defeat the cause of labor and make the cause of corporations triumphant. What is an injunction? It is a law made by a judge. If you violate that injunction you are tried by that same judge, and in the federal court there is no appeal from that injunction. It does not matter whether the injunction is valid or not, you are compelled to obey it, and if you violate it you are arrested and sent to jail for contempt of court, so that every federal judge can be a tsar.

You are not punished for committing a crime, but for contempt of court. I said when I was sentenced, "I am glad I am compelled to be guilty of contempt of such a contemptible court, or else I would have to be guilty of contempt of myself." I want to see the time come when our judicial tribunals will stand for justice.

When I was in jail at Chicago, I had for a fellow prisoner a young boy 22 years of age. He had just been married a short time, lost his situation through no fault of his own, and he could not find work. His wife thought she could find something to do, but she did not have clothes enough to make herself presentable. In leaving his cottage and going toward the city, he often passed a secondhand store, and he saw an old secondhand coat swinging in the breeze that was used for a sign. He passed it and thought of his wife, and one day, when he thought no one saw him, he stole it, but as a matter of course he was arrested and given 12 months in jail.

A short time ago there was a shortage of $2 million in the Santa Fe Railroad. Mr. Reinhart was president; he was the responsible official.[17] He did not plead "not guilty." He was permitted to resign. He lives in Boston. He basks in the smiles of the aristocrats there. He is a social lion. Everybody doffs his hat in his presence. He is a colossal scoundrel. He ought to have gone to the penitentiary for 20 years, but he was not even arrested. He was not enjoined. He was not punished for contempt of court. He is a rich man. The poor man who stole the coat was friendless. We have a law for the rich and another law for the poor. If I had about two hours' time I would demonstrate it to you.

The poor man who stole a coat because his wife was suffering went to jail for 12 months. He did not have the money with which to buy justice. In many of the courts of our country, justice is for sale to the highest bidder. I have a faculty for giving the promptings of my heart, and some people like me for it and some don't, but it does not matter to me. That boy stole a coat, and in doing so he only responded to the promptings of his heart; he simply was obedient to the dictates of his feelings. I want to say that if I had been in his place and had tramped all the streets in search of work, and my wife wanted a coat and I could not get it for her honestly, I would steal it, and it seems to me that if a perfectly honest judge dispenses justice, Reinhart, the president of the Santa Fe Railroad, would be in the penitentiary, and the boy who stole the coat would be promoted.

Do you notice that there are no injunctions issued against corporations? Injunctions are exceedingly convenient instrumentalities to be employed when workingmen resist reduction and degradation. We have a law on the statute books called the Anti-Trust Law. Senator Sherman said that this law was never intended to be used against the workingmen. Do you know of any trust that has been suppressed by it? They have grown more rapidly since that was made a law than before. When the great strike was organized last summer, it was discovered that that was the very law to be used against the workingmen, and they used that law with which to crush the workingmen.

So far as its effect upon trusts is concerned, it is not perceptible, I think, not visible to the eye. When workingmen strike to resist injustice, then it is found that they have combined in restraint of trade and are punishable by fine and imprisonment, or death; but the injunction serves another purpose. This has become a government by injunctions. I said at the time I was arrested, "If I and my colleagues had violated any law, let us be tried by a jury of our peers, and if we are guilty we will go to the penitentiary." They knew that there was no jury that would convict us, but they had to put us into jail. How did they do it? They issued an injunction. If you have never read it, you ought to get a copy of it. I could not have avoided violating that injunction unless I would have died right suddenly after it was served on me. Only a corpse would have escaped conviction of contempt of court for the violation of that injunction. I know there are a great many people who wish I were one.

That injunction restrained me from writing a letter, sending a telegram, holding a conversation with any of the employees of any of the railroads. I think it even intended to restrain me from holding communion with myself. I was persuaded, for a time at least while I was thinking about the matter, that I had better not be indiscreet enough to think aloud lest someone should hear me and report me, and I should be guilty of contempt of court.

I called on two of the leading lawyers of the city, and they said, "Proceed as you have been doing; you have been leading a perfectly lawful life." I took their advice and got six months for it, but I am not sorry for it. I have nothing to regret. I said at the time, "If it is six months or six years, or the rest of my natural life, it will not cause me to flinch a bit."

This injunction struck down every citizen's right, and I could not help being in contempt of that order without being in supreme contempt of myself. I said, as between the court and myself, "I will stand by Debs and take the consequences." Then they sent men down to my home at Terra Haute, Indiana, where I was born and reared and lived all the days of my life, to find out what they could ascertain in regard to my character that would be useful in evidence.

Terre Haute is a city of 38,000 population, and after they had scoured that place, called on all the ministers and lawyers and the city officials, they came back and said they could not find a soul to testify against my character. I do not believe there is a man, woman, or child in Terre Haute but will testify to my being an honest man. These statements would not be in good taste but for the fact that the capitalistic press of this country has deluged me with mis-representation and slander. They sought to destroy utterly my influence, and they sought to do it by having the people of this country believe that I was a monster of depravity.

I could have their favors if I desired them. I could have the opinion of being a gentleman, instead of an agitator and a revolutionist. I could bask in the smiles of the general managers of this country, but I do not desire or expect their favors. My duty lies in another direction. They are merely employees themselves. They are obedient, and compelled to be obedient, to the money power above them. They do as they are compelled to do. They have no right to have a heart. They have got to be men who are made of cast-iron, and if any one of them shows any tendency of having a heart and humanity within, they remove him and put an iron man in his place who does as he is ordered to do. In our days, if a man becomes the general manager of one of these railroad corporations, he has got to extinguish the last spark of humanity that glows or burns within his breast.

The time will come in the very near future when many of the people who have taken their position against us will find out that they themselves are in danger; they will find that they are confronted by the very power that has for the time being crushed us.

There is a centralization going forward in this country that is a menace to the Republic, by processes that will not bear investigation. The wealth of this country is centralizing in a very few hands. The process is exceedingly rapid. In proportion as this century goes forward, pauperism increases throughout the land. In the history of no country is there a record of such an accumulation of wealth as that which has taken place in this country in the past 50 years.

The multimillionaires are multiplying and so are the mendicants. The pal-ace and the hovel go up side by side. No trouble about the resources of this country. No trouble about wealth. There is no excuse for the conditions that now prevail. They are traceable in direct line to the powers that are gained over the people, and unless something is done to resist their operations, the Repub-lic will be destroyed.

I am not an alarmist, but I believe it is time to offer a cry of warning. The cry will go up, "He is a demagogue." I accept the compliment. From that standpoint I am a demagogue and expect to be. For the past ten years, when a man has had the courage to protest against wrong in high places, the cry of "anarchy" goes up, but that loses its force. The people are beginning to see the gravity of the situation that confronts them. There has got to be a change, and a very radical change.

In these small western places you may not appreciate the necessity for it, but go to the centers of population, to Chicago, New York, or San Francisco, and see what wretchedness, what squalor, what poverty and degradation prevail there. It is increasing day by day in exact ratio as the wealth of the country centralizes in a few hands. Rapidly we are approaching that period in our history where we will have but the two classes, the rich and the extremely poor. The working people of this country are getting poorer and the rich richer, and what we call the middle classes of this country are going to disappear entirely.

Labor-saving machinery was designed to be a blessing to the world, but on account of the greed of the corporations, it is getting to be a curse. We no longer have the shoemakers and the village blacksmiths and the small stores in the large cities. They have all disappeared. You have the great stores and the great enterprises, everything running to trusts. You simply have the trust and the employees. A man has got to have an immense capital to start in business. Immense capital is required to carry forward the industrial enterprises of the times, all of which has the tendency to enslave the people of the country. I believe the time has come when we should see the situation precisely as it is. It does no good to try and deceive ourselves. Sooner or later the haggard truth will confront us. Better prepare for what I conceive to be the inevitable.

As a matter of course, I cannot lose faith in the destiny of the Republic. I am so constituted that the more the obstacles multiply, the greater my will and determination. I cannot become despondent, nor can I surrender. I know there are thousands of men when the time comes who will be equal to every duty that the hour may impose upon them, with perfect faith that everything will come right in the end, and that the very influences that are in operation that now seem dangerous will be found favorable to the cause of emancipation.

It was said in the days of the Coliseum by the Romans that "When falls the Coliseum, Rome will fall, and when Rome falls, falls the world." I prefer to say that when the American home falls, falls the Republic, and when the Republic falls, the greatest and brightest light that ever passed through the pathway of progress goes out forever.

Ruskin says the nation lives in the cottage.[18] That used to be true, but it is no longer true. There is a large proportion of the nation that lives in hovels, holes, and dens. It ought to live in a cottage.

I believe that the most beautiful and elevating influences of the world are in the home. I love to cultivate the cottage, the hearth, and the fireside. It must be admitted that workingmen have not always been true to themselves. They have not taken advantage of the opportunities given them. Every workingman ought to have a library in these days of cheap literature; ought to expand his mental horizon and improve his mind. I know of railroad men who would rather sit around the roundhouse and tell about "runs" that never have been made nor ever will be. I have said that no man ever went to the penitentiary in this world who spent his leisure hours at his fireside. This is the one source of enjoyment that I possess. I have one of the loveliest homes in the world. My father and my mother and my wife and my sisters and my brother are all there, and no matter how trying the ordeal may be, that is the one place where I can go where I am always welcome.

Every workingman, no matter how humble his home may be, can make it blossom with affection. I can see no more touching picture than the working-man returning to his home and seeing the light at long range, and as he enters the door feeling the hearty welcome that is accorded him, to see him draw up his chair to the fireside and read to his wife, and cultivate the graces of home, and wake up strengthened and refreshed in the morning.

I wish the workingmen of the country would pay more attention to the homes. Be true to the home and the home will be true to you. Spend your leisure time there. Take up a book and make up your mind to study it and learn something more than that that is required to perform your work and furnish you with the necessaries of life. Try it for 12 months and you will thank me for the suggestion. I know whereof I speak.

Workingmen must hew out their own way to emancipation. If the work-ingmen would be free, they themselves must strike the blow, and every man must free himself. You cannot be freed by proxy. Every man has got to solve the labor problem and solve it for himself. There is no darkness but ignorance. A workingman who is ignorant and dependent is in slavery. The very instant that he begins to take advantage of his surroundings, that very instant he begins to solve the labor problem and hew out his way to emancipation.

Those who think must govern those who toil. I want the workingmen of this country to mix some thought with their toil. I want them to follow the light of their own judgment. I for my part had rather depend upon my own judgment and go wrong than to go right following someone else. We do not need labor leaders. Let every man cultivate self-reliance; depend upon himself. If we do that right along, we will have a race of sturdy men who will be freemen.

If we would be really free, we should strike the shackles of bondage from the women of our country. We are not unmindful of women. We decorate them with rare jewels, but we keep them in political serfdom. Let us decorate them with that rare gem, political equality. If they do not choose to exercise this power, it is for them to decide. That time is coming in the very near future, and you will not be willing to admit that you opposed it. If a woman has not got a right to vote, where did we get ours? And if women have not got a right to vote, we are not quite civilized. We are making a little progress. I believe all the signs of the times are sure, and I believe that after a while the world will be fit to live in.

We have too much cupidity and selfishness. Men ought to have noble aspirations. This struggle, this continual conflict, each for himself, each willing to trample over the prostrate body of his fellows just to supply the material necessities of life, is continually going on. I want to see conditions under which we will do more to cultivate the intellect, the heart, the soul, the family relation, the home; when we will be less greedy, less selfish, nearer just than we are now.

I believe some progress is being made in that direction. I believe the day is coming when the workingman shall stand as free and independent as any in the land, and when he shall be rewarded for his toil of brain and hand.

> A labor day is coming, when a workingman shall stand,
> As free and independent as any in the land;
> When he shall be rewarded for his toil of brain and hand,
> For the Right is marching on.
>
> A labor day is coming, don't you hear the grand refrain,
> Rounding through the country from the Golden Gate to Maine,
> That workingmen are free, having broken every chain?
> For the Truth is marching on.
>
> A labor day is coming, when Truth shall hold full sway,
> When Justice full enthroned, like the noontide god of day,
> Shall set no more forever, for its coming let us pray,
> For the Right is marching on.
>
> A labor day is coming, when our starry flag shall wave,
> Above a land where famine no longer digs a grave;
> Where money is not master, nor a workingman a slave,
> For the Truth is marching on.[19]

There are those who seek to discourage. There are those who seek to dishearten the men who are trying to reform the world. There are those who have no sympathy with the movement that is designed to make conditions better. To use a phrase: "They are not in it." This makes me think of a line that I saw the other day about one of those selfish men who was not in it:

> They built a church at his very door—
>   He wasn't in it.
> They brought him a scheme for relieving the poor—
>   He wasn't in it.
> Let them work for themselves as he had done,
> They wouldn't ask help from any one
> If they hadn't wasted each golden minute—
>   He wasn't in it.
>
>   *   *   *
>
> A carriage crept down the street one day—
>   He was in it.
> The funeral trappings made a display—
>   He was in it.
> St. Peter met him with book and bell;
> "My friend, you have purchased a ticket to—well,
> The elevator goes down in a minute."
>   He was in it.[20]

My friends, I hope some of the words I have uttered have found their way to your hearts. I know there are those of you who disagree with me, yet I am one of those who believe that men and women can differ honestly and yet grasp each other's hand in genuine friendship.

In all the forests there are no two leaves that are just alike, nor two grains of sand on all the seashore that are just alike, and among all these myriads of minds there are no two working alike. We can disagree, and yet we can respect each other. Speak the truth. Speak the facts. I know that you will draw your own inferences, and when the final verdict is rendered, I have no doubt it will be on the side of right and justice.

I believe I know what my duty is, and in my humble way I am going to try and fulfill it. I have sympathy for the struggling men and women of the country, and I am going to do what little lies in my power to ameliorate their condition. Every man who is in the right, whether he is black or white, if he is doing his level best, is my brother, and I am going to do what little I can to improve his condition and to contribute to his happiness.

With you, I hope that the dawn of a better day is near at hand, and I have faith that the night of slavery is on the wane, and the dawn of the day of emancipation is near.

Permit me to thank you, not with my lips merely, but from the depths of a grateful heart, for the patience and the kindness with which you have listened to me, and whether you agree with me or not, I bid you one and all good night, Godspeed.

The Solidarity of Labor[†]

May 1895

In mere physical enterprises the age in which we live laughs at impossibilities. The ancient alchemists sought to transmute base metals into gold. In this they were not successful, but their labors and discoveries laid the foundation of scientific chemistry, the value of which it is impossible to overestimate. Living today they would suffer all the odium that attaches to cranks, visionaries, vagarists. They were dreamers and with patience and sincerity sought to realize their visions. Did they work in vain? By no means. Chemistry is their monument and the old alchemists are immortal and all nations are their beneficiaries.

We talk of the fatherhood of God. Is that a vagary? A mere freak of fancy? If so, it is better to dismiss it. It is fashionable to refer eloquently to the brotherhood of men. Is that another hallucination unworthy of consideration by men of brains? If so, let it also be remanded to the limbo of forgotten myths. Galileo, several centuries ago, became satisfied that the earth moved. It was a fact, but the monks of the Inquisition said it was a lie and made the old mathematician and astronomer recant to save himself from torture. Thus it is seen that along the track of the centuries, verities and vagaries have intermingled until in their separation it is found that in a vagary there is an element of fact, and in a fact, an element of vagary, and about the best that can be done under the circumstances is to find whether truth or error preponderates.

[†]		Published as "Labor: Is Its Solidarity Impossible of Realization?" in the *Railway Times,* vol. 2, no. 9 (May 1, 1895), 1.

In discussing the solidarity of labor, I am not without certain data that serves as a foundation for those who believe that its consummation is within the boundaries of the possible. There is such a thing as human fellowship, and solidarity means fellowship, fraternity, mutual sympathy, interest in each other's welfare, and in seeking to bring about solidarity in the ranks of workingmen it must be apparent that only their highest good is sought.

Is solidarity practical? Every labor organization in the country demonstrates that it is not a mere theory, that it is not speculative, that it exists and is accomplishing good results. These organizations seek to cultivate fellowship and to establish fraternal obligations; to bring their members into active sympathy with each other, creating bonds of union promotive of their welfare; hence, solidarity is not a hallucination. We see it in operation in every hand. This being true, I make the point that it is possible to bring all organizations of workingmen into one household of faith. What obstacles are there in the way that may not be overcome by the enlightening influence of education? I know of none, not one. I see science and invention have encircled the earth with electric wires and made the orient and the occident neighbors; I have seen science and invention issue their mandates and in obedience to their command, rivers and chasms are spanned, mountains are tunneled to make straight the pathway of transportation upon which the iron horse of civilization travels, and I conjecture, however herculean the task may be, that it is possible for the divinities of education, common sense, and self-protection to so shape events that workingmen will ultimately see that their interests demand solidarity.

It should be understood that solidarity is the enemy of faction and the champion of unity. There is one supreme demand of labor, and that is unification. Labor factionalized is labor impotent. The enemies of labor appreciate this imbecility and profit by it. They unify for victory and achieve it. Labor sails in a hundred small crafts in seas where plutocratic devilfish abound, and there is not an instance on record where one of these labor crafts challenged resistance that the plutocratic devilfish with their prehensile arms have not dragged them down to defeat, and, being equipped with the means of obscuring their motives if not their acts, have managed to make labor pay all the penalties and endure all the odium consequent upon defeat. I assume that common sense will ultimately overcome these prevailing errors and that labor, by the invincible power of solidarity, will be prepared to successfully resist plutocracy.

I have repeatedly declared that in the absence of solidarity it is folly for men to strike against the wrongs inflicted upon them by their employers, and if labor had the solidarity of its enemies, everything bearing the stamp of righteousness would be secured, because the exhibition of power would be so overmastering that resistance would be madness.

I am profoundly impressed with the conviction that solidarity is the last and only hope of labor. There must be, of necessity, an *ultima Thule,* the farthest limit of labor's endurance of wrong. There must come a time when labor will make a final effort to resist encroachments upon its rights. My forte is not bombast. I formulate no rhetorical periods to captivate the populace, but I do evoke the genius of American citizenship to bear witness that the work of degradation now going forward will not be permitted to proceed forever nor until labor, deprived of its eyes and shorn of its Sampson locks, becomes the sport of its enemies.

What is it that today menaces the tranquility of society and the stability of the government? To name the contingency of a foreign war is an idiocy. The imprisonment of an ex-consul at Madagascar, the shots fired by a Spanish gunboat at an American ship in Cuban waters, or England's novel method of collecting debts of Central and South American republics, are simply contemptible. Indian wars are all of the past—what then? The one thing that affrights is the condition of labor. The corporation, trust, and capitalistic Shylocks, by processes more infamous than Shakespeare's Jew adopted to glut his vengeance,[21] pursue a policy of starvation, degradation, and death. I speak by the card—neither sickness, starvation, nor death could curb the "cruel devil" that dominated George M. Pullman. Carnegie, the "blowhole" thief and hypocrite, who first robbed his employees and then, to kill them, provided electricity, scalding water, and Pinkertons; and the General Managers' Association, pursuing workingmen with a blacklist as deadly as a cobra's fang, have brought about, with the aid of infamous legislation, a condition which is everywhere arousing alarm.

Lincoln said this government could not exist "half free and half slave." Can it exist half starved and half well fed? Can it exist half degraded and half exalted?

I propose the solidarity of labor; that by peaceful methods labor problems may be solved for the peace, glory, and perpetuity of the government as founded by the patriotic fathers. I would have labor vote one way to emancipate labor and save the Union, as Union soldiers shot one way to save the Union and emancipate the slaves. And over all and above all, I would write, as old Job wanted to write, "with an iron pen and lead in the rock forever,"[22] this motto: With solidarity, the rights of labor can be secured.

New and Old:
The Dead Past Must Bury Its Dead[†]
May 1895

Trust no future how'er pleasant,
Let the dead past bury its dead,
Act—act in the living present,
Heart within, and God o'er head.

—Longfellow[23]

The poet took no stock in the past and quite as little in the future. He was for the new; the old was dead. The "living present" occupied his attention. His "psalm of life" occupied his attention. His "psalm of life" embodies the true philosophy of life. The idea is to act, and we can act only in the "living present." The past is gone, the future is not born, there is no tomorrow, a moment gone is past forever; the wheels of time roll forward. Time has no back-action machinery, no brakes. The speed is arranged and there is no change. If human affairs get out of order, the time for repairs is the present; neglected, they grow worse. That is the law eternal and immutable. Men who do not act in the living present are as useless as clods, practically dead. He who is going to act tomorrow never acts; he dreams and rusts and decays.

> To-morrow is that lamp upon the marsh, which a traveler never reacheth. To-morrow, the wrecker's beacon, wily snare of the destroyer.[24]

Of all the mistakes of life, none are more disastrous than to postpone acts which should be performed today until tomorrow. The present is preeminently practical. The human faculties, mental and physical, were never in all the ages past aroused to such activity as now. The truth was never in such imperative demand. Wrong was never more fiercely denounced, never were the boundary lines between justice and injustice, right and wrong, more vividly displayed, and yet there are men who have potato eyes and cannot see them. They do not act, human infirmities, scarcely responsible, they must be classed with the feeble-minded and dismissed, and only an inscrutable God knows why they exist.

[†]   Published in the *Railway Times*, vol. 2, no. 10 (May 15, 1895), 1.

We hear it said that history repeats itself; we ask is it true, and answer yes and no. We do not suppose that we are to have repeated the monarchies and empires of the past or its mythologies and pagan rites, but since like causes produce like effects, we affirm that superstitions of the present, like superstitions of the past, will be productive of degradation, physical and mental. If despotism in the past enslaved the ignorant and cowardly, it will repeat itself in the present and is now before our eyes repeating itself.

It is not required to designate by name or character the despot. Whether his title be tsar, sultan, or shah, king or emperor, a senate, a legislature, or a president, a combination of plutocrats, corporations, or a money power, mere names are immaterial—the condition is the supreme question and the condition has come. It is steadily growing worse. History is repeating itself. The old is valueless except for examples. They are not dead, nor buried. Truth is imperishable. Deeds are their own eternal monuments. We speak well of the dead only when the dead are worthy of commendation. In this we follow the line mapped out by the Bible. It spares no man, however exalted.

Bryant said, "Truth crushed to earth shall rise again."[25] The metaphor is false. Truth was never crushed to earth. In no contest was it ever maimed or crippled; always erect and fully panoplied for the battle, it awaits the call of its votaries. Truth hates a coward—the fawning bootlicker and rod-kisser—the man who accepts chains and slavery rather than a martyr's crown. There was never a coward in the marshaled armies of truth, nor a man who failed to act.

> New occasions teach new duties;
> Time makes ancient good uncouth;
> They must upward still and onward,
> Who would keep abreast of Truth.[26]

Somewhere, sometime in the dim past, the rust-covered old, the seeds were sown that were to produce a harvest of liberty. We believe the seeds took deeper root in American soil than elsewhere in all the earth. It has been the nation's boast; we have chanted it in song and made it the woof and warp of a thousand eulogies. We now say it is menaced by a money power in the hands of depraved and conscienceless men who are determined to reduce American citizens to slavery, to poverty, want, and degradation, a condition in which history will repeat itself. The "living present" must bear testimony that a crisis has come and that gloom is deepening over the land. Manifestly the time has come to decide and to act, "hear within and God o'erhead."

In all the ages, there was never a nation that flourished and fell in which the men who toiled had the right to shape their own destinies by the power of the ballot; that crowning glory was reserved for the toilers of America, and yet here wage-slavery is rapidly increasing while thousands of wage earners stand with "mute lips apart"[27] and refuse to act; doubt, hesitate, wrangle, and divide while, as in the past, their enemies rivet their chains more firmly.

The old supplies no such instances of human degeneracy. The past had its slaves, but they were not responsible for their degradation. When American liberty is buried, American freemen, degenerate beyond the power of expression, will have dug its grave.

> Once to every man and nation comes the moment to decide
> In the strife of Truth and Falsehood, for the good or evil side.[28]

And that time has come to the workingmen of America. It is the "living present." If they act in view of the perils that confront them, if now they grasp the "iron helm of fate,"[29] if now they rise and expand to the full stature of freemen, if now they wield their ballots in the cause of liberty, they will have erected a monument as imperishable as truth and grander in its proportion than any of the seven wonders or seven thousand wonders which mark the track of the centuries.

"Every Federal Judge Now Constitutes a Tsar": Statement to the Press on the Supreme Court's Verdict†

May 27, 1895

I know only of the decision as it appears in the evening dispatches, and, assuming that it is correctly reported, it appears the case was not decided on its merits, but that it was found that the circuit court, having final jurisdiction, its act was not reviewable by the Supreme Court, and therefore the writ [of habeas corpus] was denied.[30] I expected a favorable decision, but I am not disappointed. After the decision by that tribunal upon the income tax bill I am not at all surprised to see the decision of the lower court affirmed in our case.

---

†   Published as "Scores the Supreme Court" in *Chicago Record*, May 28, 1895.

Both decisions are absolutely in the interest of the corporations, syndicates, and trusts, which dominate every department of the federal government, including the Supreme Court.

Jefferson's prophecy is being literally fulfilled. The "sappers and miners," as he denominated them, are at work undermining the federal fabric. States' rights are practically eliminated, while the right of a citizen to a trial by jury of his peers as vouchsafed by the Constitution is broken down. Every federal judge now constitutes a tsar. The decision of the Supreme Court has crowned them and given them autocratic sway. They can now issue any kind of injunction restraining any man from doing anything, and then deprive him of his liberty after simply going through the farce of a hearing before the same judge issuing the injunction. Railroad corporations may now reduce wages and enforce any kind of conditions upon their employees without fear of resistance. If employees see fit to quit, they can be put in jail for exercising this prerogative. And this infamous outrage has now the judicial sanction of the Supreme Court of the United States.

It is notoriously true that the people of this country, except a small minority that are direct beneficiaries of such monstrous perversions of justice, have no confidence in the Supreme Court. Not only this, but the criminal autocrats have no confidence in each other. To substantiate this, it is only necessary to read the scathing arraignment by Justice Harlan[31] of his judicial associates. I shall abide by the decision with perfect composure, confidently believing that it will hasten the day of the public ownership, not only of the railroads, but of all other public utilities. I view it as the death knell of the wage system. In the long run this decision will prove a blessing to the country.

"Even in Defeat Our Rewards Are Grand":
Circular Letter to Members of the ARU[†]

June 1, 1895

Terre Haute, Ind., June 1, 1895

Sirs and Brothers:—

A cruel wrong against our great order, perpetrated by William A. Woods, United States circuit judge, has been approved by the United States Supreme Court, and from under its shadow I address this communication to you; but though prison walls frown upon myself and others whom you chose as officials, I assure you that neither despondency nor despair has taken the place of the courage which has characterized our order since the storms of persecution first began to beat upon us. Hope has not deserted us. Our faith in the future of our great order is as strong as when our banners waved triumphantly over the Great Northern from St. Paul to the coast. Our order is still the undaunted friend of the toiling masses and our battle cry now, as ever, is the emancipation of labor from degrading, starving, and enslaving conditions. We have not lost faith in the ultimate triumph of truth over perjury, of justice over wrong, however exalted may be the stations of those who perpetrate the outrages.

The Storm and the Battle

I need not remind you, comrades of the American Railway Union, that our order in the pursuit of the right was confronted with a storm of opposition such as never beat upon a labor organization in all time. Its brilliant victory on the Great Northern and its gallant championship of the unorganized employees of the Union Pacific had aroused the opposition of every railroad corporation in the land.

To crush the American Railway Union was the one tie that united them all in the bonds of vengeance; it solidified the enemies of labor into one great

---

[†]   Originally published as a circular letter to members of the ARU, an excerpt of which
       was widely reprinted in the press. Republished as "Proclamation: By the President of
       the American Railway Union" in the *Railway Times*, vol. 2, no. 12 (June 15, 1895),
       1. Reprinted as "Proclamation to the ARU" in *Debs: His Life, Writings, and Speeches*
       (Girard, KS: Appeal to Reason, 1908), 291–295.

association, one organization which, by its fabulous wealth, enabled it to bring into action resources aggregating billions of money and every appliance that money could purchase. But in this supreme hour the American Railway Union, undaunted, put forth its efforts to rescue Pullman's famine-cursed wage-slaves from the grasp of an employer as heartless as a stone, as remorseless as a savage, and as unpitying as an incarnate fiend. The battle fought in the interest of starving men, women, and children stands forth in the history of labor's struggles as the great "Pullman Strike." It was a battle, on the part of the American Railway Union, fought for a cause as holy as ever aroused the courage of brave men; it was a battle in which upon one side were men thrice armed because their cause was just, but they fought against the combined power of corporations which by the use of money could debauch justice, and, by playing the part of incendiary, bring to their aid the military power of the government, and this solidified mass of venality, venom, and vengeance constituted the foe against which the American Railway Union fought labor's greatest battle for humanity.

Rewards and Penalties

What has been your reward for your splendid courage and manifold sacrifices? Our enemies say they are summed up in the one word: "defeat." They point to the battlefield and say: "Here is where the host of the American Railway Union went down before the confederated enemy of labor." They point to the spot where Miles's serried soldiery stood with drawn swords, tramping steeds and shotted guns to kill innocent men whose only crime was devotion to wretched men and women, the victims of Pullman's greed. They designate the places where the minions of a despotic judge, the thieves and thugs, taken from Chicago slums, transformed into deputy marshals and armed with clubs and pistols, went forth to murder indiscriminately and to arouse the vengeance of the people by incendiary fires, and they point to the General Managers' Association, the Nero of the occasion, whose pitiless enmity of labor would have glorified in widespread conflagration rather than permitted a strike in the interest of famishing men, women, and children, to have succeeded; and such disasters, say the enemies of labor, are the rewards of the courage of the ARU men, a courage as invincible as was ever displayed by Spartans, and which makes Pullman's Labor Thermopylae to live in history as long as the right has a defender in the ranks of American workingmen.

Brothers of the American Railway Union, even in defeat our rewards are grand beyond expression, rewards which come only to brave men, the consciousness of noble deeds performed in the holy cause of labor's emancipation.

Cowards, the fawning, sycophantic poltroons of power, never knew the thrills of joy that reward the heroes of battles fought in the interest of the oppressed.

> Once to ev'ry man and nation comes a moment to decide,
> In the strife of Truth and Falsehood, for the good or evil side.[32]

The American Railway Union did decide. It espoused the cause of justice. It furrowed the land deeper with its plows of truth and courage than had fallen to the lot of any other labor organization since time began, and the seeds of emancipation which it sowed broadcast are germinating, and a new era is destined to dawn upon labor.

Sons of Brutish Force and Darkness

True it is that the "sons of brutish force and darkness," who have "drenched the earth with blood," chuckle over their victories. They point to the blacklisted heroes of the American Railway Union, idle and poor, and count upon their surrender. Their hope is that our order will disband; that persecution, poverty, and prison will do the work. These gory-handed enemies of our order expect to put out our lodge fires, silence our battle cries, disrobe ourselves of courage and manhood, permit them to place their iron-shod hoofs on our neck and sink us to fathomless depths of degradation and make the American Railway Union the synonym of all things the most detestable.

Can They Do It?

In the presence of prison doors and prison bars and weary months of incarceration, I answer a thousand times, NO! In the grasp of despotic power, as infamous and as cruel as ever blackened the records of Russia, I treat with ineffable scorn the power that without trial sends me and my official associates of the American Railway Union to prison. I do not believe, nor will I believe, that my brothers, beloved of our great order, will throw their courage away and join the ranks of the enemy while their comrades, the victims of worse than Russian vengeance, are suffering in prison.

In Russia

In Russia, the land of the autocrat, liberty is unknown. In that thrice-damned country liberty and justice, free speech and free press, and trial by jury are banished, and a trail of blood and tears from the palace of the despot to prison and to death, made by men and women whose only crime is a desire for freedom, tell their doom; and yet in Russia imprisonment, torture, and death only increase the ranks of men and women who cry, "Give me liberty or give me death."

In Russia, the victim of autocratic displeasure is denied a trial by a jury of his peers. William A. Woods carries out the Russian practice. In Russia the doomed man or woman is arraigned before the supreme despot or one of his numerous satraps. Truth, justice, mercy are forever exiled, hope disappears, and only words of satanic cruelty are uttered. Age, sex, character, innocence, name, and condition count for nothing. It is enough to know that the brave soul yearned for freedom, and the penalty of exile, imprisonment, torture, or death is inflicted, and it has come to this at last in the United States of America, that the law of injunction is the will of a despot, and by the exercise of this Russian power American Railway Union officials go to prison, and the hope is that by the exercising of this power the American Railway Union will be crushed.

Stand by Your Order

In this supreme juncture I call upon the members of the American Railway Union to stand by their order. In God's own good time we will make the despot's prisons, where innocent men suffer, monumental. We will link them with the legends and lore of labor's struggles to be read by our children and our children's children when Bartholdi's goddess of liberty with her torch enlightening the world has succumbed to the ravages of time.

> Count me o'er earth's chosen heroes—they were souls that stood alone,
> While the men they agonized for hurled the contumelious stone,
> Stood serene, and down the future saw the golden beam incline
> To the side of perfect justice, mastered by their faith divine,
> By one man's plain truth to manhood and to God's supreme design. [33]

Yours fraternally,
Eugene V. Debs,
President

Statement to the Press While Awaiting
Recommitment to Jail[†]

June 7, 1895

———————

I don't mind serving out the sentence so much as the delay on my work for the ARU.[34] I will take my desk and all things necessary to my office work with me. I have a large trunk packed with these already. It will be necessary for me to have a stenographer with me also to handle my correspondence.

As near as I can figure it, I can reduce my sentence to about five and one-half months, which will let me out about November 1.[35] So it is not such an awful thing after all. The only objection I have to it is the inconvenience and injustice of the sentence.

Cooperation Not Competition:
An Interview with the *Cincinnati Enquirer*[‡]

June 26, 1895

———————

I never took a more hopeful view of labor's future than now. The deadline of wretchedness and degradation has almost been reached. Avarice and cupidity are as they have ever been, totally blind. As insatiate and remorseless as a conflagration, they pursue and devour. They make no concession. Their sway must be absolute. The slave power had it a third of a century ago. The money power has it today. History will repeat itself.

There is an invisible yet a mighty mustering of the forces of labor going forward. They are doing some powerful thinking. When the supreme hour is

———————

†   Wire service report datelined Terre Haute, as published in the *Fort Wayne Daily News*, vol. 22 (June 7, 1895), 1.

‡   Published in *the Cincinnati Enquirer*, June 29, 1895, original title unknown. Reprinted as "Not Despondent: E. V. Debs and His Fellow Prisoners in Woodstock Jail" in the *Railway Times*, vol. 2, no. 14 (July 15, 1895).

struck they will instinctively and spontaneously unite their tremendous forces and hew out their pathway to emancipation. The time is not quite ripe yet. A few more federal troops, a few more injunctions, a few more jail sentences, perhaps another Supreme Court stab-hole in the Constitution, and the reign of might will end and that of right begin.

Effect on Politics

"What effect will it have upon the coming presidential election?" Mr. Debs was asked:

It will, in my opinion, have the effect of tremendously increasing the vote of the People's Party, and if that party's convention is composed of wise, liberal, and patriotic representatives, and they formulate a platform upon which the great mass of reformers—be they socialists, single taxers, trade unionists, or whatnot—can unite and harmonize, they will, in 1896, take at least second place, and in 1900 at the latest, sweep the country. The Democratic Party as a national organization is dead beyond resurrection and will never see power again in this generation. The Republican Party is the party of the money power and will make a desperate fight to maintain supremacy. The future contests will be between this party and the People's Party; the one the party of the rich—the classes—the other the party of the poor—the masses. In this fight the people will win. There is today an overwhelming majority against both the old parties. It is only required to unify this opposition, and the good work is going bravely forward.

The Silver Question

"Will silver benefit the question of labor?"

To a limited extent, and this only for an inconsequential period. I am for free silver as a means to an end. The free coinage of silver would, in my opinion, relieve somewhat the present stringency and stimulate to activity our industrial enterprises, but the great world of labor, which involves all there is of worth to the world, will not be regenerated by the free coinage of silver or any other metal. The money sharks will manipulate silver just as they do gold, and with the same results to labor.

Cooperation

Cooperation is the *ultima Thule* of social agitation. The philosophy of cooperation is rational, humane, and all-embracing, and I subscribe to it without reservation. The trend is toward the cooperative commonwealth. It is the hope of the world. Vested iniquity will contest every inch of its progress, but it will come as certain as the dawn. The competitive system has had its day; it has blotted out all the stars of hope, filled the world with groans, and reduced humanity to slavery. The strong have devoured the weak. All the highways of the centuries are strewn with the bones of the hapless victims. Competition is the mother of selfishness and greed. Competition develops the fangs, not the souls of men. Competition is fit only for the social degeneracy of savages and beasts. Competition has spawned a brood of vices which have filled our highways with tramps, our asylums with insanity, our prisons with crime, and the whole land with unspeakable woe; and the verdict of an awakened public conscience will relegate it to the relic chamber of the barbarous past. Mutualism, cooperation, which contemplate the "brotherhood of man," will come as certain as the earth revolves upon its axis, soon after the sun of the twentieth century lights the world.

Strikes

"Do you still believe in strikes as a means to success?"

No, sir! But I would not totally abolish the provision for them. The dread of a strike has a powerful restraining effect upon that class of employers who regard their employees as so many chattels or cattle. Abolish the strike, and workingmen are totally helpless. Forced to choose between a strike and degradation, I would strike if I stood alone. I would not disrobe myself of my manhood; I would scorn to strip myself naked of my independence. I don't like strikes any more than I like war. Are the American people ready to abolish war?

I don't take much stock in arbitration. If it is "compulsory" it is vicious in principle, and if it is voluntary it can't be enforced. I have a notion that under any kind of an arrangement the rich employer would get the turkey and the poor employee the buzzard, just as it is in many of our courts. Still, while the competitive system lasts, I am willing to give it a fair trial. I am willing to admit that boards of arbitration have done some good, and I shall not discourage any effort made to extend to its utmost limit the scope of its usefulness as a factor in preventing or adjusting labor difficulties.

Concerning Governor Altgeld, Mr. Debs says the Illinois executive is the staunchest, ablest, and most courageous friend of labor in the United States, and he would make him president.

Mr. Debs says he doesn't want a pardon:

Jail life may have a demoralizing effect upon its victims, but we shall not degenerate to an extent that we would accept our liberty on any such condition. We are content to serve our full time. Some of these days the sentence of the assassins of constitutional liberty will be pronounced, and there will be no appeal from it.

The injunction law is utterly infamous. It stabs to death the "Goddess of Liberty" and crowns and scepters the harlot of despotism. It is the last resort of tyranny.

Duty of the Church?

"What should be the stand of the church with regard to the labor question?"

Squarely on the side of labor. That was the doctrine of Christ. But the church has never been for labor and never will be until labor triumphs, and then the church will be its staunchest supporter. Wendell Phillips declared the church was the foe of the abolitionists and the strongest supporter of slavery. It has always been so. The church is on the side of power, right or wrong, and every honest minister will admit it. It is supported by and is the main support of the money power, and the minister who is great enough and self-sacrificing enough to preach Christ soon preaches himself out of the pulpit.

Liberty's Anniversary[†]

July 1895

Sitting in Woodstock Jail, behind prison bars, and permitting my fancy to have free rein, what more natural than to contemplate the resounding acclamations of a great nation celebrating the anniversary of the birthday of liberty? What more natural than to commune with the dead, who, when living, in the spirit of heroism expanded to the full stature of patriots and dared all things, battles, wounds, imprisonment, confiscation, and death, to secure liberty for themselves and their posterity.

But in the midst of such ardent admiration of the men who wrested the scepter from England's proud monarch and secured for the American people

---

[†]   Published in *The Twentieth Century* (New York), July 4, 1895. Reprinted as "In Prison: Fourth of July Reflections Upon the Advance of Despotism" in the *Railway Times,* vol. 2, no. 14 (July 15, 1895), 1.

the priceless boon of liberty, I am compelled to ponder present conditions and ask myself, "What remains of the liberty thus secured for the American people? Why celebrate the 'birthday' of American liberty when liberty itself lies cold and stiff and dead, stabbed to death by nine gowned and ermined men, who, if they have any mission connected with the affairs of the American people, it is to forever stand guard over their constitutional and unalienable rights."

It has been regarded as a patriotic duty for Americans, on the Fourth of July, to apostrophize liberty and to select from the vocabularies of all languages eulogistic words to describe its value and its glory, and when words failed to express those essential attributes of liberty which made life itself an inferior blessing, bonfires have blazed, cannons have belched their thunder, banners have waved, drums have throbbed, and bugle blasts have called the people to assemble and rejoice together over God's inscrutable decree in bestowing upon Americans blessings denied to all other peoples, kindreds, and tongues since time began. Nor do I doubt that on this anniversary such exhibitions will be repeated, but it will be a hollow mockery. The stage will be gorgeous with scenery for the play of liberty, but liberty will be absent—only its ghost will appear, only its "canonized bones" will be present; only its skeleton jaws will move to tell American slaves that the supreme "funeral directors" have buried it in a potter's field without so much as a slab to mark its resting place.

And yet the farce will proceed, and orators will be found to bombard the air to convince the people that in the nation's grand march across the continent and in its physical achievements, the *ultima Thule* of its destiny has been reached. If liberty is referred to at all, it will be to emphasize the plutocratic doctrine that a government of the people, by the people, and for the people and constitutional guarantees of liberty are as so many vagaries, and that a strong, centralized government is what the Fathers designed and should be established upon the ruins of the Republic, and that the Constitution itself, ceasing to be a guarantee of the liberties of the people, should be eventually so construed that one man, robed, crowned, and sceptered as a judge, combining the characteristics of caitiff and satrap, could, as whim might influence him, strike down every constitutional right of the citizen and send him to prison.

I am familiar with the often-quoted maxim:

> No man e'er felt the halter draw,
> With good opinion of the law.[36]

It has been said of every martyr from the first time that a thumbscrew was ever applied by the Inquisition. It was said of every victim broken upon the wheels, disjointed upon the rack, or burned at the stake. It has been a handy excuse for tyrants in all ages and is as current now as when the beasts of bigotry first lapped the innocent blood of their victims.

I know with what gusto corporations and their ermined sycophants and all their brood of degenerate creatures regard the imprisonment of the officers of the American Railway Union, and yet it is not law nor the administration of law that called forth our protest, but the abrogation of all laws and the substitution of ironclad despotism. Innocent men, untainted by crime, we appealed to the courts and to the Constitution for protection, for guaranteed rights. We appealed as American citizens to the Supreme Court of the nation. As well might we have appealed to so many man-eating tigers in an African jungle. Our destiny was imprisonment, and it tells the story of the final triumph of Russian methods of government in the United States of America. For my associates and myself, I may say:

> Of all the work my hand hath wrought
>   Beneath the sky,
> Save a place in kindly human thought,
>   No gain have I.[37]

And yet, when, on the morning of the Fourth of July, the effulgent glories of the sun gild my cell, and when his softer evening rays invite to meditation, my thoughts must turn upon conditions which give the lie direct to the old-time American boast of liberty and independence. The law of injunction, a despotic decree, is the death knell of liberty as once enjoyed by the American people. That myself and associates in prison happen to be the victims of the unspeakable outrage in no regard emphasizes my abhorrence and detestation of the traitorous grasp of power by which the atrocious crime against the liberties of the people was perpetrated. I would have demanded for the most brutal, base-born, and red-handed criminal a trial by an impartial jury, under due forms of law, and would have punished him only by the fiat of a verdict legally obtained, but in the case of myself and associates, we behold American citizens, charged with no crime, and without indictment or trial, branded as criminals and sent like galley slaves to prison by one man who, arrogating to himself the authority of lawmaker, judge, and jury, plays the role of tsar and sends whom he will to prison, as the Russian despot sends men to Siberia, to prison or to death, as it suits his caprice.

The question may be prudently asked: What remains worth saving of the liberties of Americans? I answer—the ballot. It is a powerful weapon if the American people can be persuaded to unify and wield it in defense of their rights and their liberties. True it is that the people have slept while their enemies, "working like gravity," have stolen the most valued jewel from their crown of sovereignty. Can it be recovered, or is it entirely lost? It required eight years of a bloody, cruel, and devastating war to secure it, and thousands of brave souls perished in the patriotic conflict. If the anniversary of the Fourth of July is devoted to arousing the American people to a realization of their great misfortune, if they will resolve to regain their liberties by renewing the pledge of the Fathers to perish or conquer, then Woods and Woodstock Jail may stand in the future monumental infamies, from which the people may go forth as did the revolutionary heroes from the infamous edicts of King George to regain their lost liberties—and all along the lines of the hosts of the common people, the victims of plutocracy and their corrupt agencies, should resound again the battle cry that was heard from Lexington to Yorktown: *"Give me liberty or give me death!"*

The Coming Workingman[†]

July 1895

    Yet thus to pass away!—
To live but for a hope that mocks at last—
To agonize, to strive, to watch, to fast,
    To waste the light of day,
Night's better beauty, felling, fancy, thought,
All that we have and are—for this—for naught.[38]

I have read of the coming billionaire, of the pomp and circumstance that will attend him and of the power that he will exercise. A man with a thousand millions. Why not? Men of 300 millions are already here, and $300 million earning 6 percent interest would in something over 55 years earn a billion. It is therefore not only possible but highly probable that by AD 1947, the billionaire will bloom. I challenge any man to suggest why the promised billionaire will not come, and I challenge any man to exaggerate the power that he might wield in human affairs.

---

†   Published in the *Coming Nation*, whole no. 113 (July 13, 1895), 2.

If it be possible, and this is conceded, within the next 25 years, for a man with $300 million by the simple process of interest to become a billionaire, it is one of the simplest sums in arithmetic to show what would be the amount controlled by the heirs of men who today represent fortunes ranging from $5 million to $200 million during the period named, 55 years.

What is the tendency of money today? Is it not consolidation, aggregation? The unification of vast sums to control the business enterprises of the country? Does anyone deny the tendency? Do not all intelligent people see it, know it, and admit the truth of the proposition that wealth is combining for the purpose of exercising absolute control over the industrial and commercial enterprises of the country? By such assertions, do I deal in vagaries? Is not the element of absolute truth so large as to startle men who are students of cause and effect, who are capable of looking beyond the present and of pointing out results if present methods go forward undisturbed?

The growth of wealth is by processes as silent as the ebb and flow of the tides, and the processes of consolidation are equally quiet. There is no blast of trumpets, no speechmaking, no parades, no banners bearing devices; all is calm and serene, and the world knows what has been done only when the announcement has been made that capitalists have combined to control this, that, or the other great industry which employs labor and fixes prices. Already the name of trusts are legion; they are steadily increasing. It is now seen that trusts are controlled by men who are less than millionaires, running up the scale until millionaires are included, and when a great industry combining all the smaller industries in any one line of business forms a trust, then labor is at its mercy, and when was it known that a trust possessed the element of mercy?

Such things are the *avant-couriers* of the coming billionaires and thousands of millionaires. I do not doubt that there are thousands in the ranks of labor who are studying the signs, who are noting the drift of events. If the indications are that there is a coming billionaire, is there anywhere a token of the coming workingman who will be able to unify labor in a body more invincible than a Roman phalanx? I do not apprehend that labor is so stolid as not to be apprehensive of the coming crisis. If in this estimate of the foresight of labor I am correct, then, indeed, it behooves labor to earnestly inquire if the coming workingman is to be on hand when the crisis comes.

I do not doubt the coming workingman will be found at the right time, provided labor is willing to consolidate its forces.

So far, labor has been fruitful of leaders, but unfortunately these leaders, with rare exceptions, even if exceptions can be found, are not seeking to unify the hosts of labor for any trial of strength with the billionaire and his forces. They are not seeking the federation of all the labor forces to meet the "impending crisis." Manifestly, labor must have, where organized, a number of officials. The lodges constituting a national, international, or a continental order must have officials. There must also be a supreme power, a head for such an organization, very much after the style that an army is officiated, from a corporal to a commanding general. The real trouble, as I view the situation, is to solve the problem of unifying labor organizations so that there shall be one superior commander like Washington or Grant, who shall command the forces when the time comes to meet the billionaire and in all conflicts that may occur under the combined forces of the millionaires who are now "moving upon the works" of labor. It is a military maxim, "in peace prepare for war," but for labor, in the language of Patrick Henry, "there is no peace" nor truce except for that class of labor which submits to aggression and meanly wears fetters and descends to degradation without protest. No man will ever be found in their ranks to resist the boss of labor on any field when the stake is "life, liberty, and the pursuit of happiness."

Where, then, are we to look for the coming workingman upon whom organized labor will concentrate its hopes in the coming struggle? The answer must be, in the ranks of organized labor.

I have said there are numerous "labor leaders." We hear of them often, we see them occasionally, but do we see them or hear them rising above petty ambitions, fraternal jealousies, expanding to intellectual proportions that pass beyond the boundaries of orders, proclaiming the eternal truth that the hope of labor depends upon the unification of the hosts of labor? In the ranks of the millionaires, awaiting the coming of the billionaire, supremacy in leadership is easily arranged. The man with the most money controls; he is awarded no title; his money talks, and his reign is undisputed. Labor cannot proceed upon the money basis. It must choose a leader, if it wins a final victory, who, coming from the ranks, must be able, by virtue of his mind forces, his intellectual equipment, his identification of labor, his conscience and his courage, his self-abnegation and profound solicitude for the welfare of others, to secure the confidence of all.

Can such a man be found? Is such a man a possibility? I do not hesitate to believe he can be found and will be found. I am forced to admit such belief to avoid the admission of the dying alchemist, that after all the hopes of labor, its struggles and sacrifices, death comes before victory and all come to "naught." What shall be the signs of the coming of such a man? Shall there be seen another burning bush, and from the midst of the flames shall there come again a voice calling upon another Moses to be a leader of the oppressed?[39] The present is not a time of miracles. I look for no manifestations of Jehovah's disapproval of the reign of the millionaires, except that which shall come from the intellectual advancement of the hosts of labor and the development of that courage which, trusting in the right, dares fight for its supremacy.

American voters have the ballot and with it can achieve victories of a grandeur exceeding the Red Sea catastrophe.[40] At their command are schools and books and opportunities for the marshaling of mind forces to promote their own welfare such as the world never beheld. This advancement, I think, will continue until labor appreciates the value of unification, and then will come the time for the selection of a leader who will be more than a match for the millionaires in the contest of the coming billionaire.

Success and Failure[†]

July 1895

There is a tide in the affairs of men
Which, taken at the flood, leads on to fortune;
Omitted, all the voyage of their life
Is bound in shallows and in miseries.

—Shakespeare[41]

Suppose I start out by naming some of the essentials to success? Is the response, name them? I comply and jot down the following: education, industry, frugality, integrity, veracity, fidelity, vigilance, sobriety, and charity; these things I hold are essential to success in life. What about failure? I do not suppose there is anywhere to be found those who start out in life to achieve failure and yet, as certainly as the excellencies of character which I

---

†   Published in *Minneapolis Times,* undetermined date in July 1895. Reprinted as "From Woodstock: President Debs and Secretary Keliher Write for the *Minneapolis Times*" in the *Railway Times,* vol. 2, no. 14 (July 15, 1895), 2.

have named are essential to success, their opposites will bring failure and all the woes which failure entails.

The opposite of education is ignorance; of industry, slothfulness; of frugality, wastefulness; of integrity, dishonesty; of veracity, falsehood; of fidelity, treachery; of vigilance, carelessness; of sobriety, inebriety; and of charity, miserliness, heartlessness, and unforgivingness.

The question arises, what is success in life? The answer is likely to be, in a majority of cases, securing wealth, getting rich, and I am convinced that the thing we call "public opinion" renders the same verdict. I have named certain traits of character as essential to success in life. It may be well to scan them closely; this done, the reader might count over such millionaires as occur to his mind and ask, does the world credit them with the possession of the virtues named? With reference to some of the essentials, the reply will doubtless be affirmative, as, for instance, education, industry, frugality, vigilance, and sobriety will be accorded the man who has secured wealth; but what of integrity, veracity, fidelity, and charity? Can it be said that success in life has been achieved if the possessor of wealth, however vast and dazzling, is dishonest, false, treacherous, and venal? After all, is not such a life a failure?

It is just here that the lamentable fact appears that the possession of wealth to thousands, though knowing the methods, condone the dishonesty, leaving to the elect few the herculean task of championing those virtues without which, no matter what outward surroundings may be, the final verdict must be, when an appeal is taken to the higher court of eternal justice, that the mere possession of wealth does not constitute success in life; that life may be the saddest of failures though its possessor inhabits a palace as resplendent as if it were built of diamonds, though the luxuries of all climes supply his board, and his robes for costliness rival those of earth's proudest potentates. Do such reflections satisfy the great majority? Scarcely. To say that is to arraign our Christian civilization and force into the shade all those excellencies of character which, when possessed, make life a success though the man is as poor in worldly goods as was Lazarus when only vagabond dogs constituted the charity commission in the city where he starved.

An incident transpired at Omaha during a session of the quadrennial conference of the Methodist Episcopal Church which is worthy of note as illustrating popular views of what constitutes success in life.[42] In that great conference, made up largely of Christian ministers, there came up the question of "capital and labor," and a movement was made to determine where the church stood upon the question. A resolution was introduced by Rev. Thomas

Hanlon[43] demanding that the church in all matters concerning "capital and labor" should plant itself squarely on the side of labor, and in advocating the resolution said:

> The laboring classes are drifting away from the church. Our church is made up of women, to a large extent. The men are drifting away from it. We must take a stand on this great question affecting labor and capital. The church has been too much inclined to lean toward the interests of capital.

In the foregoing, the Rev. Mr. Hanlon arraigned the church for leaning toward the interests of "capital," aiding thereby the inculcation of the idea that the possession of wealth is the standard whereby to measure success in life. To what extent the church has lent its influence in the direction pointed out by Mr. Hanlon cannot be estimated, but it may be asserted that the church, the school, and the press have been in alliance to make the mere possession of wealth the standard by which to ascertain the measure of success a man has secured. That this is the popular conviction and verdict it is folly, I am persuaded, to deny. But is it a rational conviction? Is it a verdict based upon principles that can stand the test of investigation? When the announcement is made, "he died poor," are survivors to conclude that necessarily the life of the dead man was a failure?

What's an Educated Man?

The phrase "an educated man" is taken to mean one who has obtained a collegiate education, a university education, but it so happens that comparatively few of the men who have laid the foundations of the present millionaire fortunes in the United States were graduates of such institutions of learning. John Jacob Astor, Commodore Vanderbilt, and Jay Gould may be cited as cases in point, and the list could be extended indefinitely. It follows, therefore, that the term "educated" as one of the essentials of success in life, even in accumulation of wealth, need not mean that higher education to which I have referred. The younger generation of millionaires, the inheritors of wealth, need not be considered, since insofar as the possession of money demonstrates success in life, it matters not whether they were born blind, deaf, and dumb, or idiots; and about all that can be said of some of them is that what little intellect they possess is distinguished by its prehensile quality enabling it to grasp and "hold on," though in numerous instances the feeble-minded progeny of millionaires are without this quality and once in possession of wealth, they sow it to the wind and in due time reap the whirlwind, and then failure becomes conspicuous.

Dismissing popular verdicts and public opinion, more frequently wrong than right, in estimating success in life, it will be profitable to note instances of splendid success in which money at no time played a conspicuous part; instances in which "higher education" was not a factor, but in which industry, integrity, fidelity, and frugality were the prime essentials.

I am not required to occupy space to furnish an extended list of those sometimes called "self-made men," nor do I deem it necessary to make reference to ancient history for examples. What is wanted is one colossal figure, one splendid specimen; the reader will readily recall others until the catalog bears down all opposition.

Abraham Lincoln answers my purpose. No land, no century, not nation, tribe, or kindred, since the tribes sought to build a tower to heaven in the plains of Shinar,[44] has produced a man who, whether patrician or plebeian born, secured grander success than tell to the lot of Abraham Lincoln, whose early life was one of poverty and squalor but who, nevertheless, expanded to such sublime proportions that the world is full of his fame. Compared with him, what of the Rothschilds, Vanderbilts, Astors, and Goulds? Our vocabulary is utterly bankrupt in words whereby comparison can be instituted. Molehills to mountains will not answer the demand. Let the world reverse its conclusions—wealth and a collegiate education are not necessarily essentials to success in life, and the success achieved by Abraham Lincoln is conclusive on such points.

But why, it may be asked, go in search of exceptions for examples of success in life? The query is pertinent. It demands attention. I admit its commanding significance. The successes in life are found in richer abundance along the highways of endeavor where the world's toilers pass to and fro from their tasks. In contemplating the subject, the humble home expands to a palace. A few years ago, a few humble workingmen laid the foundation of the great labor and industrial organizations which today are national, international, and continental. Without money, with limited education, without influential friends, like—

> The men who rounded Peter's dome
> And groined the aisles of Christian Rome,

they built better than they knew.[45] They achieved success. It does not matter that their work has not secured monuments of granite or brass. It does not matter that their names are not themes for song and story. Not at all. I do not discuss such rewards. They fall to the lot of the few. I simply assert the fact that these apostles of social and industrial emancipation achieved success. I do not know whether they are living or dead. If living, their possession of worldly goods may to some indicate a failure. Not so; their work was a triumph which forever makes failure stand back.

Mordecai and Haman

Who has not read the legend of Mordecai and Haman?[46] The former poor, obscure, and unhonored, sitting at the king's gate; the latter proud, powerful, jealous, and revengeful. The king, restless, sleep flying from his eyes, calls for the "Chronicles" and bids his attendant to read. Finally the name of Mordecai is reached in connection with some service he had performed for the king. Immediately the question, has Mordecai been rewarded? The answer was no. His enemy, Haman, had prepared a gallows upon which to hang him. Presto! Mordecai, the Jew, had achieved success. Haman was a failure. Mordecai was rewarded with honors and Haman was hung on the gallows he had erected for Mordecai. It was one incident in the life of Mordecai that achieved success and forever redeemed his life from failure. At long intervals kings and courts and rulers reward success in life, but in millions of instances no note is made of the victory.

There are in our country ten thousand humble homes where the father is industrious and temperate, the mother frugal and patient, and the children obedient. In such homes there is only a common school education, but there is integrity, frugality, and affection. Each day brings its trials, its conflicts, its serious problems, and each day brings its victories, its successes. There is little money, just the wages of the toiling father and the ceaseless devotion of a mother who never grows weary. It is in such homes that labor organizations have their invincible devotees and which, in the fullness of time, are to demonstrate that organized labor is a success.

Of failure, who shall be the judge? Who knows? Once upon a time a poor widow, under a benevolent impulse, pushed her way through the moneyed throng and aided the fund to the extent of "two mites," about four mills of our currency.[47] The contribution attracted the attention of Jesus Christ and then and there he gave the poor widow immortality.

Again, in securing success in life, an unknown tramp, plodding his way along a railroad track, discovered a broken rail. He immediately went back to flag an express train and prevented a disaster. His life, though his dead body fills a pauper's grave, was a splendid success. With W. W. Story, let us join him in his song:

> I sing the hymn of the conquerer, who fell in the Battle of Life,—
> The hymn of the wounded, the beaten, who died o'erwhelmed in the
>   strife;

Not the jubilant song of the victors, for whom the resounding acclaim
Of nations was lifted in chorus, whose brows was the chaplet of fame,
But the hymn of the low and the humble, the weary, the broken in heart,
Who strove and who failed, acting bravely a silent and desperate part;
Whose youth bore no flower on its branches, whose hopes burned in
   ashes away.
From whose hands slipped the prize they had grasped at, who stood at
   the dying of day
With the wreck of their life all around them, unpitied, unheeded, alone,
With Death swooping down o'er their failure, and all but their faith
   overthrown.

While the voice of the world shouts its chorus,—its paean for those who
   have won;
While the trumpet is sounding triumphant, and high to the breeze and
   the sun
Glad banners are waving, hands clapping, and hurrying feet
Thronging after the laurel-crowned victors, I stand on the field of defeat,
In the shadow, with those who are fallen, and wounded, and dying and
   there
Chant a requiem low, place my hand on their pain-knotted brows,
   breathe a prayer,
Hold the hand that is helpless and whisper, "They only the victory win,
Who have fought the good fight, and have vanquished the demon that
   tempts us within;
Who have held to their faith unseduced by the prize that world holds on
   high;
Who have dared for a high cause to suffer, resist, fight,—if need be, to
   die."

Speak, History! who are Life's victors? Unroll thy long annals and say,
Are they those whom the world called the victors—who won the success
   of the day?
The martyrs, or Nero? The Spartans, who fell at Thermopylae's tryst,
Or the Persians and Xerxes? His judges or Socrates? Pilate or Christ?[48]

Open Letter to the State Convention of the People's Party of Texas†

July 17, 1895

McHenry County Jail, Woodstock, Ill., July 17, 1895

L. Calhoun, Chairman, [etc.]
Fort Worth, Tex.

My Dear Sir:—

I am in receipt of your esteemed favor of July 1 [1895], requesting me to write a letter to be read on the occasion of the Populist state rally, to be held at Fort Worth on the 5th, 6th, and 7th of August.

You say: "Knowing that you cannot come, I am requested to write you and urge you to write a letter to the people, laboring men especially, of Texas, to be read on one of the days of the meeting."

You speak a gloomy truth when you say, "Knowing that you cannot come." All the people of the entire state of Texas—farmers, mechanics, professional, business, railroad, and laboring men—should know why I and my associates cannot be present at the grand rally of Populists at Fort Worth.

I am profoundly in sympathy with the policy and principles of the Populist Party of the United States,[49] and it would be a source of great satisfaction to meet and hold converse with the courageous and patriotic people of Texas, who are marching to certain victory under the banners of populism.

My heart is in the emancipating cause championed by the Populist Party, and as the Supreme Court nor any of its subordinates has, as yet, enjoined its pulsations, it beats in approval of every measure advocated by the Populist Party, and until the sentence of imprisonment inflicted by a petty autocrat expires, I must be content to send my greetings, as I do now, to my political friends in council.

While I am committed unequivocally to "free silver," I regard the political shibboleth of little consequence, as compared with that other battle cry,

---

†   Published as "Letter from Debs" in *Fort Worth Daily Gazette*, vol. 19, no. 245 (August 7, 1895), 8. The letter was read to the assembled delegates at the People's Party's convention at Fort Worth during the evening session on August 6.

"free men"—and I am persuaded that the Populist Party of Texas, and of the country, includes both as fundamental essentials to American independence and progress.

It becomes eminently vital at this juncture of our national affairs that a third political party should be organized, since any dispassionate survey of the past and every honest analysis of the present conditions emphasizes the haggard truth that the two old parties, the Democratic and Republican parties, have brought the country to the verge of ruin.

In calling a special session of the 53rd Congress, Mr. Cleveland declared that the wreck and ruin which has come upon the country was "owing chiefly to congressional legislation," and this arraignment being true, any expectation of relief from further congressional legislation by either of these old parties will result in disappointment and added disaster.[50]

The Republican Party was arraigned before the bar of public opinion for its plutocratic policy. It was charged with high crimes and misdemeanors against the great body of the American people, and the people, with united voice, rendered a verdict of "guilty," and wrested from it the scepter of power, and the Democratic Party, with banners blazoned with declarations of reform, with Grover Cleveland at its head, came into power.

It would be a gross falsification of history to suppress the fact that the people generally placed great confidence in the Democratic Party. It had won distinction as the party of the people, and as uncompromisingly hostile to plutocrats and all tribes and gangs that prey upon the substance of the people. It was widely remarked by those who watch the every varying moods of the people in political affairs that their rebuke of the Republican Party in 1892 was irrefutable proof that the people had determined to have honest government, that legislation in the interest of trusts and banks, whose policy of plunder constituted a colossal sham, should no longer hold the country in its grasp.

This popular upheaval was justly regarded as a demonstration of the people's capability for seeing the trend of national politics, and of their power to apply the needed remedies. But when it was found that the Democratic Party had become as thoroughly debauched as was the Republican Party, that it, too, was dominated by the money power, that it was no longer worthy of trust and confidence, what was the humiliating spectacle presented for the nation's contemplation? The Republican Party, expelled from power in 1892, with all the odium of its treason to the people still clinging to it, unwashed and unrepentant, is placed in power in 1894.

It was under such conditions that the Populist Party developed its great strength, and upon its success depends the welfare of the country.

The Populist Party fully comprehends the fact that in the coming battle for honest government, it is to fight the money power of the country—a power which will brook no restraint. Without a soul to be saved or damned, it plays the role of priest and pirate with equal duplicity, and always with the same end in view. It debauches the press to secure its designs and compels the pulpit to offer prayers and invoke heaven's benediction upon its piracies.

It sets up its idols in congressional and legislative halls, and bribes its spineless vassals to worship them.

It enters what was once the most august judicial tribunal the world has ever known, accomplishes its nefarious purposes, and retires, leaving the temple of justice reeking with more stenches than Coleridge discovered in the city of Cologne, while the people wonder by what power, human or divine, it can be deodorized.

The money power enters the White House by the front door and compels the president of the United States to issue gold bonds, that the Rothschilds and Shylocks, foreign and native, may riot upon wealth wrung from American toilers—and when these toilers seek to resist oppression, degradation, starvation, and slavery in a way that has been the glory of the American name, the money power, like a Russian autocrat, orders out the standing armies of state and nation in all the pomp and circumstance of war. Workingmen are quieted by the persuasive power of bullets, powder, and bayonets, and blood drained from their veins stains the earth, which but for them would be a desert. And this is done under the folds of our starry banner, triumphantly waving over the land of the plutocrat and the home of the slave.

This is the power that the Populist Party has got to fight in coming campaigns and all hope of success centers in the ceaseless bombardment of its strongholds, its banks, its trusts, its corporations, and its combines, its press, and every other covert from behind which it seeks to perpetuate its existence.

The farmers of the country are profoundly interested in the contest. The money power in unnumbered ways filches from the profits of their toil and, controlling market and transportation, compels them to part with their products at a loss, and this done, it stands ready with a mortgage which ultimately transfers home, land, forest, and field, and every movable thing to its engulfing maw.

The millions of men and women engaged in gainful occupation, from the sweatshops of the great centers of population to the plowman turning the furrow, all, regardless of name or occupation, cannot prosper while vicious legislation permits the money power to levy tribute upon them to an extent which barely permits them to live, while it drives millions into the ranks of the idle, to be fed by charity or to subsist by crime.

When you invited me to write a letter to be read at the great Populist rally, because "knowing I cannot come," you condense into five words a state of affairs in the United States, in the presence of which exaggeration becomes a meaningless term.

I will not be present because a petty United States judge, in defiance of every constitutional guarantee of the liberty of the people, has thrust myself and associates into prison, a despotic exercise of power as infamous as ever sent a liberty-loving Russian to Siberian mines, to prison, torture, or to death.

This act of despotism, extending as it does far beyond myself, tells the people the gloomy truth that an autocratic centralized power has been established, and that under its sway the constitutional guarantees of the liberties of the people have been struck down. Believing that the mission of the Populist Party is to restore the lost liberties and reestablish a government by the people, by the all-pervading power of the ballot, my voice goes forth from my prison to cheer on the Populist hosts of Texas and the country, and with an unfaltering faith in the ultimate triumph of the party, I bid all who march beneath its banners, Godspeed!

Yours faithfully,
Eugene V. Debs

Slaves and Cowards[†]

July 1895

The great mass of American workingmen are in abject slavery. A few realize it and protest; still others realize it and are content; while countless numbers of them are totally indifferent as to their condition, and oblivious of their surroundings, and if they are one degree above the beast of the field, or give one thought to anything, they give no appreciable evidence of it. Still, my heart goes out in sympathy. I always think they are as good as they can be.

They are the victims of centuries of greed, centuries of tyranny and plunder, and if they are sunk to the level of total depravity, the blame is not with them. They have got to be lifted and educated and redeemed. The process is slow and painful. Thousands of them are satisfied to crawl and grovel, and will resist any attempt to lift them out of the mire into the sunlight. If my jail life will help, I have no objection to being shorn of what little liberty I enjoyed. The future is getting molded and fashioned in the present, and I have perfect faith that it will be brighter and better.

I wish no political nomination in '96, nor at any other time. I want nothing from the people—I simply want them to do something for themselves. I care nothing about empty honors. Besides, I don't know that there is any particular glory in being president of a nation of slaves and cowards.

[†]   Published in *San Diego Vidette*, July 25, 1895, page unspecified. Copy in *Papers of Eugene V. Debs* microfilm edition, reel 10.

Prison and Pardon:
Open Letter to William C. Endicott, Jr.[†]

July 27, 1895

Woodstock, Ill., July 27, 1895

Hon. William C. Endicott, Jr.,
Attorney in Charge of Pardons,
Department of Justice,
Washington, DC

Dear Sir:—

I beg to acknowledge the receipt of your notice in the matter of the "application for pardon of Eugene V. Debs, *et al.*" and to say that I was not aware that such an application had ever been made. Neither I nor my colleagues ever signed or authorized such an application or had any knowledge whatsoever upon that subject. Will you kindly oblige me by sending me the application or a copy thereof and letting me know by whom the same was filed? It is an utter surprise to us, for we never desired nor contemplated asking for a pardon. The Department of Justice, so called, refused us justice and we scorn its mercy. I speak for all my colleagues as well as myself when I say we would all rather rot in jail than enjoy our freedom by the clemency of those who sentenced us.

Thanking you for your kindness and hoping to hear from you soon, I am,

Very truly yours,
Eugene V. Debs

[†] Published as part of the article "Prison and Pardon" in the *Railway Times*, vol. 2, no. 16 (August 15, 1895), 1.

"The Old Brotherhoods Are Disgraced or Dead": From a Circular Letter of the ARU†

August 1, 1895

We do not hesitate to say that so far as the old brotherhoods are concerned, they are either disgraced or dead, or both. They were active allies of the railroad corporations in crushing workingmen in the great [Pullman] strike. Murder will out. Their treachery to labor will bear its own fruit. They cannot escape the consequences of their treason. Organized labor has repudiated them, and many of the corporations, having used them as tools to do their dirty work, have no longer any use for them. Their schedules are abolished, their wages are reduced, and their members who were most "loyal" to the company last summer [1894] are being discharged right and left without cause. They are cowed and intimidated. They dare not move hand or foot. They are reaping what they have sown.

A member of the ARU may be without a job and in hard straits, but he need not be ashamed to look his fellow men in the face. It is an honor to be an ARU man, and it will be more and more an honor when history records all the truth regarding that memorable conflict. On the Soo line[51] the engineers and firemen are engaging in a disgraceful quarrel, and the other orders are more or less implicated in it. It is due wholly to class selfishness and class prejudice, which are fostered by class organization, and which will exist as long as class organization endures.[52] And yet they talk about federation! As if any man of sense could be caught by such idiotic twaddle! As well talk about federating fire and powder.

On the Cotton Belt[53] the schedule of the telegraphers has been summarily abolished. Just now the papers are filled with reports that the ORT,[54] backed by the Cedar Rapids Federation, will tie up the Cotton Belt, and that the strike will extend over the entire Gould system.[55] Let us see! We predict that there will not be any strike. The truth is, the old orders could not inaugurate a

---

†   Published as part of the editorial "Let Us Have Peace" by W. S. Carter in *Locomotive Firemen's Magazine*, vol. 20, no. 2 (February 1896), 127. Reference made and excerpts quoted in *Locomotive Engineer's Monthly Journal*, vol. 29, no. 9 (September 1895), 807–808, which intimates Debs's authorship. No surviving copy of the original document is known.

strike. Their own members, realizing that it would mean suicide, would refuse to obey the order, and they could not call out a corporal's guard. Thousands of their own former members are swarming all over the country, waiting "to get a crack at them."

The ARU is for all organized labor, and will never prostitute itself to the base purpose of forming an alliance with railroad corporations to crush and defeat and imprison and starve workingmen, members of another organization.

The "grand" officers of the old brotherhoods, in their secret meetings,[56] condemn the ARU and malign its officers, but *they dare not meet them on the platform.* In their official organs they allude to the ARU by cowardly innuendo. They talk about a "rival" organization and its "emissaries," but they lack the manliness to name either. They well know that these "emissaries" are simply trying to open the eyes of the railroad men to the fact that the old brotherhoods are robbing them—taking large sums of money from them for which they do them no earthly good, but on the contrary keep them in a state of helplessness, under the easy control and subjection of the railway companies. The federation, so called, makes it impossible for the organizations to use what little power they do have, and that is why the railroad officials "wink the other eye" and encourage the old brotherhoods, give their grand officers free passes and the members abundant taffy. It is the old case of "the spider and the fly," that men of brains clearly see and well understand. The grand officers of these orders are very courageous behind barred doors. They paw the earth in denouncing the ARU. Will they meet the officers of the ARU on the public platform in the presence of the railroad men of the country? When the members of these brotherhoods tell you what their grand officers said, ask them if their grand officers, individually or collectively, will meet a single representative of the general union before an open meeting of railroad men. We will soon be out of jail and open to engagements, and if one or more of these gentlemen can be induced to meet us and we do not wipe him or them from the face of the earth, we will agree to retire from the labor field. This is a fair proposition. Let the railroad men of the country hear both sides and then decide which organization stands for labor and which is in league with the corporations to perpetuate their slavery.

Let words of good cheer be voiced all along the line. We will soon again be on the field of action. The skies of the future were never so bright as now. Every true man will do his full duty.

Yours fraternally,
Eugene V. Debs,
President

Sylvester Keliher,
L. W. Rogers,
James Hogan,
R. M. Goodwin,
M. J. Elliott,
William E. Burns,
Board of Directors

Labor Omnia Vincit[†]

August 5, 1895

McHenry County Jail, Woodstock, Ill., August 5, 1895

I would hail the day upon which it could be truthfully said, "Labor conquers everything," with inexpressible gratification. Such a day would stand first in Labor's Millennium, that prophesied era when Christ shall begin his reign on the earth to continue a thousand years.

The old Latin fathers did a large business in manufacturing maxims, and the one I have selected for a caption of this article has been required to play shibboleth since, like "a thing of beauty and a joy forever,"[57] it came forth from its ancient laboratory. It is one of those happy expressions which embodies quite as much fancy as fact.

The time has arrived for thoughtful men identified with labor—by which I mean the laboring classes—to inquire, what does labor conquer? Or what has it conquered in all the ages? Or what is it now conquering?

If by the term "conquer" is meant that labor, and only labor, removes obstacles to physical progress, levels down mountains or tunnels them, builds

---

[†] First published in a Labor Day program of indeterminate title. Boston: Central Labor Union, Sept. 1895. Reprinted in *Debs: His Life, Writings, and Speeches* (Girard, KS: Appeal to Reason, 1908), 253–255.

railroads and spans rivers and chasms with bridges, hews down the forests, digs canals, transforms deserts into gardens of fruitfulness, plows and sows and reaps, delves in the mines for coal and all the precious metals; if it is meant that labor builds all the forges and factories, and all the railroads that girdle the world and all the ships that cleave the waves, and mans them, builds all the cities and every monument in all lands; I say if such things are meant when we vauntingly exclaim, "Labor conquers everything," no one will controvert the declaration, no one will demur—with one acclaim the averments will stand confessed.

But with all these grand achievements to the credit of labor, how stands labor itself? Having subdued every obstacle to physical progress, what is its condition? The answer is humiliating beyond the power of exaggeration, and the aphorism "Labor omnia vincit" becomes the most conspicuous delusion that ever had a votary since time began.

It will be well for labor on Labor Day to concentrate its vision on the United States of America. The field is sufficiently broad and there are enough object lessons in full view to engage the attention of the most critical, and it will be strange indeed if the inquiry is not made. What has labor conquered up to date in the United States? The inquiry is fruitful of thought. What is the testimony of the labor press of the country, corroborated by statistics which defy contradiction? It is this, that the land is cursed with wage-slavery—with the condition that labor, which, according to the proverb, "conquers everything," is itself conquered and lies prostrate and manacled beneath the iron hoofs of a despotism as cruel as ever cursed the world.

To hew and dig, to build and repair, to toil and starve, is not conquering in any proper sense of the term. Conquerors are not clothed in rags. Conquerors do not starve. The homes of conquerors are not huts, dark and dismal, where wives and children moan like the night winds and sob like the rain. Conquerors are not clubbed as if they were thieves, shot down as if they were vagabond dogs, nor imprisoned as if they were felons, by the decrees of despots. No! Conquerors rule—their word is law. Labor is not in the condition of a conqueror in the United States.

Go to the coal mines, go to the New England factories, go to Homestead and Pullman, go to the sweatshops and railroad shops, go to any place in all of the broad land where anvils ring, where shuttles fly, where toilers earn their bread in the sweat of their faces, and exclaim, "Labor omnia vincit," and you will be laughed to scorn.

Why is it that labor does not conquer anything? Why does it not assert its mighty power? Why does it not rule in Congress, in legislatures, and in courts?

I answer, because it is factionized, because it will not unify, because, for some inscrutable reason, it prefers division, weakness, and slavery, rather than unity, strength, and victory.

Will it always be thus unmindful of its power and prerogatives? I do not think so. Will it always tamely submit to degradation? I protest that it will not. Labor has the ballot. It has redeeming power. I write from behind prison bars, the victim of a petty tyrant. My crime was that I sought to rescue Pullman slaves from the grasp of a monster of greed and rapacity.

I think a day is coming when "Labor omnia vincit" will change conditions. I hear the slogan of the clans of organized labor. It cheers me. I believe with the poet that

> A labor day is coming when our starry flag shall wave,
> Above a land where famine no longer digs a grave;
> Where money is not master, nor the workingman a slave—
> The right is marching on.[58]

Eugene V. Debs

Open Letter to the *Evansville Tribune*[†]
August 8, 1895

McHenry County Jail, Woodstock, Ill., August 8, 1895

Editor, *Evansville Tribune:*

I write by request of Miss Blanche Johnson, special correspondent for the *Tribune,* who assured me on behalf of the obliging publisher that my friends in Southern Indiana will be pleased to hear how I am getting along and what my plans are for the future.

It is now 77 days since I and my seven colleagues began to serve our sentence for contempt of Judge Woods's court. Just why the distinguished judge singled me out for special favors by giving me six months while he deemed three months sufficient for the rest can only be accounted for upon the hypothesis

[†] Published as "Retrospective and Prospective" in *Evansville Tribune* (Indiana), August 19, 1895.

that my contempt for his judicial highness was twice as great as that of my good and faithful fellow prisoners and, if they do not object, I am willing it should rest upon that ground. Candor compels me to admit, however, that the ameliorating influence of time has not diminished my scorn for the court of Indiana's far-famed "block" signal judge,[59] and if I had to serve a sentence measured by my contempt for that judicial satrap, the remaining years of my life would hardly make a good beginning. I haven't forgotten, and I'm not going to forget, that Judge Woods, at the behest of the railroad organizations, enjoined us from doing many things we never intended to do and never did do, and some things we had a constitutional right to do, and then sentenced us to jail without a trial, in exact accordance with the program of his plutocratic masters. The injunctions were issued for that very purpose. We have violated no law, we have committed no crime, we have never been charged with any offense, have never been tried, and yet we occupy felons' cells, and for this Judge William A. Woods is alone responsible. He did the bidding of the corporations even to the extent of abrogating the right of trial by jury and strangling to death civil and constitutional liberty—and without engaging in bravado I wish to serve notice on that ermined gentleman that the day will come when he will stand at the bar of the American people and answer for his crime.

My colleagues leave here on the 22nd instant, in time to [address] the score or more unions that are waiting, and participate in the festivities of Labor Day, which, I am persuaded, will be celebrated with more than ordinary éclat this year.

On the first day of our incarceration we organized the "Cooperative Colony of Liberty Jail" and adopted a code of rules which have been rigidly observed through the whole period of our confinement, and to this fact I attribute the excellent health we have enjoyed and the great amount of work we have been able to perform. We rise at 6:00 sharp each morning. At the ring of the alarm bell Inspector Elliott calls 6:00 at each door, and in 15 minutes we are all required to be bathed and dressed and in the jail yard ready for exercise. We are then under command of Colonel Hogan, who puts us through the military drill. We have but two guns, one of which, an old army musket, the sheriff carried through the Civil War, and the other, a wooden one, made by Secretary Keliher, who is an experienced woodworker. After this we are put through a squad drill and then follows a turn at punching the bag, dumbbells, elastic exerciser, handball, etc., until 7:30 breakfast is announced. At 8:00 sharp we are in the jail corridor, which constitutes our study room and workshop, and from that hour until 12:15, noon, there is perfect silence and each member is at his study or correspondence. From 12:15 to 1:00 rest and exercise are taken and then dinner is announced. From that hour until 5 is devoted to reading, study, and correspondence. From 5 till 6:30 we are put through a rigorous course of exercising and then supper is announced. After supper and until 8:00 we enjoy a social chat at rest and then the debate of the evening begins on some subject announced the previous evening. The debating academy is under the tutelage of Professor Rogers, who in years that are gone divided time between the pedagogue and the railroad brakeman. The debate lasts an hour and a half, or, until 9:30, then preparation is made for retiring and at 10:00, by the stroke of the bell, every "contempt"-ible one of us is required to be in bed, and woe unto him who chirps or breaks the stillness of the sleeping hours. This is our program 16 hours a day and seven days a week.

Of course, our reading embraces the principal social and economic works, fiction, history, poetry, and other branches of research and study.

There is a ceaseless torrent of correspondence [which] pours in here from every quarter of the globe. Resolutions of sympathy by thousands have been sent in by all classes of people, including farmers, mechanics, miners, laborers, sewing girls, newsboys, bootblacks, etc. In addition to the work we do ourselves, we have a stenographer and typewriter who is kept busy early and late with correspondence. We also have innumerable demands for interviews and articles from newspapers and magazines and have lately contributed to *The Arena,* the *Cincinnati Enquirer, St. Louis Post-Dispatch, St. Louis Chronicle, Chicago Journal, St. Paul Globe, Minneapolis Tribune,* and many others.

The American Railway Union has renewed its youth. It is springing full-fledged into the arena again. Judge Woods and the General Managers' Association made a monumental mistake in putting our officers in jail and blacklisting and exiling our members. There is something in the breast of a freeman that rebels against tyranny. Thousands of men have been made staunch members of the ARU by being driven to the verge of starvation for having belonged to it. The order is today growing at a rate that exceeds all expectations, and the day is near when it will be infinitely more powerful than ever before.

I propose to remain with the American Railway Union until every obstacle has been overcome and it is rich and powerful in numbers and resources, and then I propose to resign my office and give my attention to the unification of all workingmen and workingwomen in one great organization whose purpose shall be their social and industrial regeneration by means of a united ballot. The scheme may seem chimerical, but it is perfectly feasible and no power on earth can prevent it. There will be such subdivisions as may be necessary in the large variety of trades and conditions that will be represented, and it will be under the supervision, not of a "chief" or "master" or other potentate, but of a labor congress, elected from the ranks by direct vote of the members. Space forbids detail. It is enough to say that the workingmen and women will unify their forces and hew out their way to emancipation.

Workingmen have been the slaves of corporations and women have been the slaves of both. Under the "new order" the wife will walk the highlands of equality by the side of her husband, and they will together enjoy the enrapturing vision of a land redeemed from a form of slavery that has darkened all the ages since old father Adam played the role of sneak when he said: "She gave me of the tree and I did eat."[60]

Eugene V. Debs

The People's Party's Situation in 1896[†]
early August 1896

McHenry County Jail, Woodstock, Ill.

If I were to base conclusions relating to political conditions in 1896 upon the decision of the people in 1894, I should be quite positive that the Republican Party would carry the country by a sweeping plurality. But in late years there appears to be a determination on the part of the people to break away from old alliances, and no political seer feels competent to forecast conditions in the immediate future.

During the past 25 years the old parties found it an easy matter to formulate platforms and bring their followers into line. The platforms were constructed to catch the unthinking masses, and this done, they were promptly relegated to the limbo of useless lumber. But a new era has dawned. The spider's song to the fly has been overworked.

Men can no longer be bought in "blocs" and delivered on election day. The spoils of office have been greatly reduced by civil service regulations; besides, the masses have advanced and the herds of "dumb driven cattle" are no longer driven to the polls to be voted by the bosses. Such things have brought about conditions that have changed the aspect of political affairs.

---

†   Published as "The Situation in 1896" in *Batavia Sentinel* (Iowa), August 9, 1895.

The imperative duty of constructing platforms is even now giving the old parties vast vexation.

The Democratic Party had a platform in 1892. It was plausible. The people accepted it as an honest expression of principles and policy. The party turned traitor to professions and met the fate of Ananias, its prototype.[61]

The Republican Party reads its doom if it follows the Democratic example.

Both of the old parties are split upon the money question, and no dodging or hedging will be tolerated.

Out of the entanglement of bimetallism, monometallism, gold standard, silver standard, double standard, and single standard, they will be required to state explicitly their principles and their policy, and there is no way to escape. They will find that the people mean business.

I refer to such things merely to show the complications of the political situation.

Relying upon current comment, the Democratic Party is dead. The statement is scarcely correct. The Democratic Party is not dead but disgraced, equivalent to death. Those who are trying to whitewash it find it difficult, and to make the situation as bad as possible, it has, insofar as Grover Cleveland and his officeholders are concerned, fallen into line with the Republican Party on the money question, and in 1896 we may see the Republican Party swallow what is left of the party of Jefferson, Jackson, *et al.*

To make it still more difficult to forecast "results in 1896," I point to the Populist Party.[62] It has been called into existence by the voice of millions of men formerly acting with the two old parties. It is young, strong, aggressive, and enthusiastic.

It demands reform in every department of the government. It demands the free and unlimited coinage of silver. It denounces the debauching alliance between the government and the national banks and demands that the still more shameful and corrupting alliance between the government and the Rothschilds, the rapacious shylocks, whether foreigners or natives, be dissolved. It would wrest the scepter of power from trusts, corporations, syndicates, and every combination of plutocrats regardless of name, and reestablish a government by the people.

This party has become a standing menace to plutocracy. It confronts and denounces its schemes everywhere.

The farmers, cajoled and cheated, poor and penniless, with their possessions shingled all over with mortgages, have determined to abandon the old parties.

The workingmen who think are everywhere aroused and are asserting their manhood, determined to no longer be victimized by political parties which, after their votes are cast, regard them as so many swine.

What will this party do in 1896? Who can tell? If it fulfills its mission, it will hold the balance of power in the next Congress and will dictate legislation. If not strong enough to enact its reform measures into laws, it will be strong enough to arrest infamous legislation by either of the two old parties. Standing by the right, yielding never a jot or tittle of its reform principles, the people will endorse its fealty to the welfare of the nation, and with the new century it will come into possession of the government.

With all the light I can command and reasoning from cause to effect, and from effect to cause, I predict a vast increase of the Populist vote in 1896 and an overwhelming victory for the party in 1900.

Eugene V. Debs

Term Half Over: Interview with the *Chicago Chronicle* at Woodstock Jail[†]

August 22, 1895

I don't think I will be lonesome, although of course I will miss the boys at first.[63] But I have work to do, lots of it, and I know they will be doing their work, and that will help me to stand it. Then, you know, my wife is here and will be back and forth most of the time.

*   *   *

We have a great work before us and we are going at it at once. For myself, it will take about two weeks for me to catch up on my correspondence. I get letters, hundreds of them, from all kinds of people, and they tend to show that there is something in the American which makes him side with the underdog when it has been abused too much. I see that in my own little case. There is a trend of popular feeling in our favor right along . . .

What we intend to do is to build up the American Railway Union and make it the strongest organization in the country. There are 880,000 railroad

---

[†]   Published as part of the article "Labor Leaders Set Free: Imprisoned ARU Directors Released at Woodstock" in *Chicago Chronicle,* August 23, 1895.

men in the country, and I know that seven-eighths of them are with us. But they do not speak their minds, attend meetings, or join the union for fear of the blacklist. The General Managers' Association has declared that no man who took part in the strike or who joins our union can work in this country, and it passes the blacklist around, although there are a few laws against conspiracy, which, it seems, are intended only for labor unions, not managers' unions.

We are going to get around the blacklist simply by having a secret union. There will be no public meetings. No one will know who joins it, and the man who denounces it to the company's agents may be a director. By January 1 [1896] we will have agencies in all the principle cities of the union. Burns will work in Chicago. Goodwin is going to Winona, and from there he will work out to the West. Keliher will establish headquarters in Minneapolis, which is his home. Rogers is going to Pueblo, Colorado, Hogan to Ogden, Utah, and Elliott will work in the East. It is a gigantic task, but with the help of our friends we will succeed. Each district supervisor will have a lot of assistants, who will go to the houses of the men who desire to join and there enlist them in the union. It is the only way to overcome the system of espionage under which we constantly work.

I will doubtless be released from this place on November 20, as that will make 180 days of service. As soon as I get out I will go to Terre Haute, and I expect it will take me a month or more to straighten up affairs in the business office of the union. About January 1 I will start on a tour of the country, speaking and organizing unions. I would not attempt a consolidation, merely a unification, a harmonizing. In all matters of general concern, the labor unions of the country should be united—the general purpose of all is the same. It should be easy to make arrangements for all to work in conjunction, and I think that the labor leaders of the country will get together and formulate a plan of [action].

Change in Public Mind

It is marvelous how public sentiment is changing. Had we done in 1886 what we did last year, we would have been executed. But the execution of the anarchists, whom we call anarchists for want of a better name, although they are not anarchists, taught the people a lesson. To the hanging of those men we owe our lives, and people are just beginning to see what a monstrous act that hanging was. Years from now, a hundred perhaps, there will be more monuments to those men who were hanged because they raised their voices in indignation against police invasion of the people's rights to assemble peaceably in mass meeting. Those things grow upon the people slowly. John Brown was hanged in 1859, but now his name is honored and revered, and a hundred years from now it may be placed beside that of Lincoln as the original emancipator of the Negro.

Governor Altgeld, I think, is the greatest governor in the United States, although I have never seen the gentleman. His act in pardoning Schwab, Fielden, and Neebe showed him to be a brave man.[64] He has the ability of a statesman and the courage of a true man. His friends advised him that he was courting political death, but he was brave enough to do it for right's sake.

I do not regret the time I have spent in jail, nor do any of the boys. It has been well and profitably employed, and I do not look forward to three months more of imprisonment with any misgivings. I shall keep to the old schedule of working 16 hours a day and I have enough matter promised to papers and magazines to keep me busy for a long while. Besides, my wife will be here quite often, and Sheriff Eckert makes it as pleasant as possible.

Pleads for Prisoners

*   *   *

There is one thing that should be changed—that is the way they hold court in these country districts. Twice a year court convenes to try any persons who may be in jail or out on bail. Now, suppose a poor fellow is arrested on complaint of someone for stealing an old coat or a loaf of bread. He is bound over to the criminal court, and if he has no friends and cannot give bonds he must go to jail. Now, if the court has just adjourned, if it is the day after court, that man, whom the law presumes to be innocent until a case is proved, must stay in jail here six months awaiting trial. Think of it! My God! It is awful. That is a sentence in itself, and, if after being locked up on prison fare for six months he is not guilty or if no one appears to prosecute, what redress has he? None. Deprived of his liberty on a mere suspicion, locked up six months or for three or four months, because he is poor and has no friend to sign a bond! And this is the land of liberty and freedom! In Japan, where we send missionaries, the courts sit all the time. This system is wrong, hideously wrong. There should be a plan of taking the prisoners to where the court is sitting or some other way beside locking them up for months without a trial. In Chicago, of course, the volume of business causes delay, but here there is no court, no judge, no hope for months.

*   *   *

Open Letter to Jacob S. Coxey[†]

August 25, 1895

In surveying the field of politics, corruption is seen on every hand, and as a result there has gone forth a resounding call for reform.[65] To anticipate any change whatever from either of the old parties is the culmination of political idiocy. They differ only in name. Their policy is, in every important proposition, essentially the same. Both are dominated by the money power, and both are equally debauched by its influence.

The present administration is probably the most infamous that has ever cursed the country. It is a moral and political malformation. From the vilest deputy marshal with a club and a gun to the Buzzards Bay partner of the Rothschilds,[66] it is one blended mass of indescribable political villainy. The people have repudiated it by a storm of scorn, which finds adequate expression only in the term "cyclone." The Democratic Party, incapable and corrupt, full of false professions, detested and scorned throughout the land, is as dead as a mummy and embalmed in its own slime. There is no resurrection for it unless the people after all should decide that it is better than the Republican Party.

In one regard it may be said that the Republican Party, steeped to its eyes in infamy, is superior to the Democratic Party, because it does not hesitate to boldly champion every measure calculated to enlarge the power of plutocrats, while the Democratic Party makes profession of loyalty to the people, to which it turns traitor in the supreme hour of trial.

In this supreme emergency, what is the rational course to be pursued by men who would purify the government and once more have a government of the people? There is but one answer: It is to come out boldly for the People's Party to rally under its banner and support its candidates at the polls. There is absolutely no hope of reform that does not center in the supremacy of the People's Party.

It is impossible to either cleanse or deodorize the two old parties. They constitute the Augean stables in which is accumulated an amount of filth and corruption in the presence of which exaggeration is impossible. The corporations debauch the courts, and the courts respond by declaring statutes designed

---

†   Published as "Debs' Fiery Letter" in *Chicago Record,* vol. 15, no. 205 (August 26, 1895), 1.

to make them contribute to the support of the government from their stolen wealth unconstitutional.[67] The corporations appeal to the courts for injunctions that they may the better enslave workingmen and at once they spread out over the land, and thousands of moral deformities from the slums, with clubs and guns, swarm the highways to do the bidding of judicial tsars. The corporations appeal to Grover Cleveland, a trained hangman, whose statesmanship is symbolized by a halter, a shotgun, and a fishhook, and sudden as lightning from a storm cloud the army comes with shotted guns to shoot workingmen with as little concern as if they were savages away from their reservations. The corporations appeal to a pliant judge, whose robes are as spotted as leopard's hide, for a decision to send innocent men to prison without a trial, and promptly prison doors swing open to receive the victims of despotic power.

These haggard truths, sounding the death knell of liberty, demand of the people an unconquerable determination to place a party in power pledge to sweeping reforms, and there is but one party upon which the people can center their hopes, and that is the People's Party.

It would afford me immense satisfaction to be present at the gathering in Lake View, but Tsar Woods, in the interest of corporations and in defiance of my constitutional rights, has deprived me of my liberty, and I must remain a prisoner until my sentence expires. In the meantime, as I have opportunity, I shall not fail to voice my convictions that the hoped-for reforms must come through the supremacy of the People's Party.

Open Letter to W. L. Rosenberg[†]

August 31, 1895

Woodstock, Ill., August 31, 1895

W. L. Rosenberg, Esq.,
Editor, *Cincinnati Tageblatt,*
1346 Walnut Street, Cincinnati, O.

My Dear Sir:–

I beg to acknowledge receipt of your favor of some days ago and also your note of inquiry of the 28th instant [August 28].[68] Pardon my seeming remission, I have been so overwhelmed by correspondence and so besieged by visitors that I have hundreds of unanswered letters before me. I have carefully read all you say and beg to assure you that, in the main, I fully concur in your views. You are perfectly right in what you say about my name in connection with the presidency. I am not only free from political aspiration, but do not want any political office whatever.

I am doing what little I can to emancipate my countrymen from degrading conditions. I realize that this can only be done by total abolishment of the wage system and the introduction of that infinitely more rational, just, and humane system which contemplates the cooperation of all for the good of all.[69] I also agree with you that a definite platform of principles must be formulated and that this must be supported by a thoroughly organized sentiment on the part of those who are working to bring about the changes so greatly needed in our social and industrial conditions.

The first thing in order is to unify all classes and schools of reformers, formulate a platform on which all can meet. Then pledge the support of all to the platform and the men chosen as its representatives, and in this way we shall be able to win at the polls and usher in the better day. I wish my friends to omit all mention of my name in connection with the presidential or other nomination and to devote all their time and energies to unifying and solidifying the reform sentiment.

Thanking you for your kindness and candor, I am,

Yours very truly,
Eugene V. Debs

---

†   Published as "Correspondence with Debs" in *Labor* (St. Louis), September 14, 1895.

The Pullman Strike After One Year[†]

September 1895

The American Railway Union did not receive much public notice till the big strike occurred on the Great Northern system, April 13, 1894. The wages of all the employees on the system had been reduced from 10 to 40 percent, aggregating, according to the statements of the officials of the road, $16,000 a month. The old brotherhoods acquiesced in the reduction because, as is assumed, they felt themselves unable to cope with the powerful corporation. At this juncture our policy of united action, which distinguishes the American Railway Union from the brotherhoods, came into boldest prominence. Under the auspices of the new order all the employees, from conductors and engineers to wipers and callboys, in every department, quit the service of the company. This was an innovation which attracted attention in all parts of the country. The employees were jubilant, and the railroad companies were alarmed. The strike lasted 18 days, and on May 1 it was settled by arbitration and practically everything contended for by the men was conceded.

To show the fairness of the order it need but be stated that the board of arbitration was composed of 21 millionaire merchants and manufacturers of Minneapolis and St. Paul. Every man on the board was an employer of labor, and yet we did not hesitate to commit all our interest to their hands.

Start of the Pullman Strike

A few days later, on my return to Terre Haute, I was informed by the vice president [George W. Howard] that the Pullman employees who were members of our order had serious grievances and threatened to strike. I immediately advised him to do all in his power to avert a strike, and this he did, as the employees themselves testified to the United States Strike Commission. Their wages had been repeatedly reduced, but their rents and other fixed charges remained the same, and notwithstanding they were putting in full time, they were getting deeper and deeper into the debt of the Pullman Company every day. At the time the strike occurred on May 11 [1894], they were indebted to

---

[†]   Published as "Debs States the Case" in *Chicago Chronicle*, September 1, 1895, 21–22. Reprinted as "History: Graphic Pen Picture of the Great Pullman Strike" in the *Railway Times*, vol. 2, no. 18 (September 16, 1895), 1, 7.

the Pullman Company for the one item of rent alone $70,000.

We felt that the victory on the Great Northern would have a tendency to stir to action men on other roads, and that in some places there might be undue eagerness to strike. We were especially anxious, for the good of the order, to prevent any further strike, feeling that we could secure justice by arbitration, as had been done on the Great Northern, with the difference that the difficulties would be arbitrated before instead of after the strike, and in pursuance of this policy everything possible was done to restrain the Pullman employees from striking. They acted on the advice of Vice President Howard, until an incident occurred which precipitated the strike without his knowledge or the knowledge of any other officer of the order.

Breach of Faith Charged

The committee which had charge of the employees' grievances had secured an interview with Mr. Pullman. He promised that these grievances should be investigated. The following morning three members of the committee were laid off. This resulted in the spontaneous stoppage of work, and the great Pullman strike was on. There was a deliberate breach of faith on the part of the Pullman Company, and it was resented by the employees laying down their tools and leaving the shops.

It will thus be seen that the charge so often made, that the strike was instituted by labor agitators, is utterly false and absurd. Shortly after the strike occurred I was called to St. Paul, and I stopped over at Pullman to make a personal investigation.[70] I visited the houses of the employees and talked with them in person, as also with their families, and found a condition of affairs there which no language can describe. It was perfectly clear that the employees had been methodically plundered. They had been ground to atoms between the upper millstone of reduction and the nether millstone of extortionate living expenses. Some of the employees apologized to me for not being able to introduce me to their families, as their wives had not clothing enough to make themselves presentable. The money I had in my pocket I gave away in charity, and I had to borrow money in Chicago to take me to St. Paul. I am entitled to no credit for this, for I would have a heart of stone had I left with a dollar in my pocket. That awful spectacle of squalid wretchedness, hungry children, and poverty indescribable was well calculated to sow in any human breast the seeds of the greatest strike the country has ever known. And all of this, be it remembered, at a time when, according to the sworn statements of Pullman officials, there was a surplus of $25 million in the vaults of the Pullman Company.

Power of the Company

The fact was established before the Strike Commission that rents at Pullman were fully 25 percent higher than elsewhere. An enormous profit was derived from the water supply received from Chicago. While no order compelling employees to deal in Pullman stores was issued, it was well understood that failure to do so was not in the interest of the employee. Pay day came every two weeks, and the rent money was deducted whether a dollar remained for the family or not. There are checks still in existence ranging from 2 cents upward representing two weeks' work. The debt of the employees to the company represented an unbreakable bond of slavery.

Many people have asked why the employees did not leave the place if these conditions prevailed. The answer is they could not leave because they were virtually mortgaged to the Pullman Company. Living expenses exceeded wages, and the indebtedness grew larger day by day. Many employees were thus working for the Pullman Company for less than a bare living. Instead of having a little over at pay day there was a deficit, and the employee found himself in a condition of slavish dependence from which there was no escape.

Purpose to Crush Competition

It has been contended that the Pullman Company accepted contracts at losing rates for the sake of keeping its employees at work. This contention is not supported by the facts. It is admitted that losing contracts were accepted, but the purpose was to crush out competition, and this could be effectually done because the Pullman Company was getting a large part of its work done practically for nothing. The loss on the contracts was more than balanced by the excessive rents and other forms of extortion.

The Pullman Company was chartered in 1867 with a capital of $1 million. It increased in six years, from 1883 to 1889, from $13 million to $25 million, or an average of $2 million a year. In 1894, when the strike occurred, it had increased its capital stock to $36 million, and on this enormous capital it paid a quarterly dividend of 2 percent, amounting to $3,880,000 per year. With this showing, aside from financial considerations, the employees were smarting under numerous petty grievances which, combined, amounted to insufferable despotism. The indignities put upon them by petty bosses were outrageous. It is but just to Mr. Pullman to say that he was probably in utter ignorance of many of the wrongs his employees suffered. In what I have to say here I do not discuss Mr. Pullman personally. I deal with the general policy of the Pullman Company in relation to its employees.

Nothing to Arbitrate

On June 12, 31 days after the employees struck, the regular convention of the American Railway Union met in Chicago. That convention would have been held if the Pullman strike was never heard of. It had been ordered for that date and was not by any means called especially to consider the Pullman strike. It was composed of about 425 delegates,[71] representing in round numbers 125,000 railroad men. One of the matters which came up early in the convention was the grievances of the Pullman employees. A committee was appointed to investigate and called on the officials to see if an amicable adjustment could not be effected. Mr. [Thomas H.] Wickes of the Pullman Company objected to the committee because it was partly composed of others than Pullman employees. Another committee was at once appointed, consisting solely of Pullman employees, and they were told by Mr. Wickes that the company would run its business to suit itself; that it had nothing to arbitrate. In the meantime, Mr. Pullman went east to spend a period at the seashore.

A great many delegates visited Pullman to make a personal investigation. All came back impressed with the magnitude of the wrongs done the employees and resolved that something must be done at once to rescue the unfortunates from such a tyrannical and pauperizing condition. The convention was not disposed to act hastily. Every effort which could be conceived was put forth to end the trouble. There was no desire to extend it. When it was seen that the Pullman Company would entertain no proposition looking to a settlement, it was proposed by some delegates that it was then their duty to their suffering brothers and their families at Pullman to refuse to handle Pullman cars. This sentiment found immediate favor. In my speech before the convention I appealed to the delegates, in view of the unfortunate industrial condition of the country to pursue a conservative course. I said:

> There is a danger in extremes, and defeat lurks in discord. Nor is this all. However paradoxical it may seem, there is nevertheless an element of danger in prosperity, and against this we will find it the part of wisdom to guard with sedulous care. Present conditions are fruitful of manifold defects and deficiencies, which are annoying and constitute grievances which, while productive of injury and vexation, are far below the plane of gravity which demands any resort to extreme measures for redress or adjustment. Industrial conditions are at present of a character which demands a constant exercise of the virtue of patience and forbearance when difficulties are encountered, which under other and more favorable circumstances would demand the interposition of the order.

It will be noted that decisive action was not taken until the eve of adjournment, and this action was confined exclusively to Pullman cars. There was no intention to stop trains, to quit work in shops, or to do any other thing except not to handle Pullman cars. I can cite scores of instances where men proffered their services to haul the mails and other trains, but in each case the offer was declined in accordance with the policy agreed upon, that unless Pullman cars ran all traffic should stop.

One word from the General Managers' Association would be sufficient to compel Pullman to settle with his employees. This word was not uttered. Why? Because the General Managers' Association courted the opportunity to clash with the ARU. When the delegates decided not to handle Pullman cars, the General Managers' Association held an emergency meeting. Mr. Wickes, Pullman's chief in command, was present. It is a little singular that when these general managers were put upon the stand in the conspiracy trials last January, not one could remember the object of that emergency meeting or why Wickes was here.

The resolutions adopted by the general managers about this time clearly defined their policy. They resolved, among other things, that Pullman cars should run. In other words, they would back the Pullman Company in starving its employees to death, while at the same time they would wipe out the American Railway Union. The triumph of the union on the Great Northern when it was but ten months old had alarmed them. They viewed its marvelous growth with grave apprehension. They probably thought it would be comparatively easy, since they were solidly united, to crush out the American Railway Union at so early a stage of its existence. They greatly underestimated the power and extent of the order. I have it upon good authority that they felt perfectly able to snuff out the order without much more difficulty than if it were a candle.

Sufficient Notice Given

The delegates, it should be observed, gave five days' notice in regard to the handling of Pullman cars, and the action was unanimous. This remarkable feature of the proceeding should not escape notice. In that entire body of 425 delegates, on the whole the most intelligent body of railroad men I have ever seen, there was not a single one who dissented. They were so strongly imbued with the wrongs and sufferings that had been borne by the people of Pullman that their sense of humanity prompted them to the action they took. Upon this point the most conservative, who are found in all bodies, were radical. They could do nothing less without forfeiting all claim to human sympathy.

In the annals of the world there is no sublimer exhibition of self-sacrifice. They esteemed 14,000 starving men, women, and children of more consequence than the running of a few palace cars. Their action requires no apology from me or from anyone else. As Professor Herron,[72] the eminent theologian, said: "The time will come when they will stand monumental in history for their love and devotion to their fellow-beings."

It may be well at this point to introduce the report of the United States Strike Commission. It is still fresh in the minds of the people. It declared, after exhaustive investigation, that the employees had been grossly mistreated; that the officers of the ARU were opposed to the strike; and that the General Managers' Association was not only an unlawful but a dangerous body. A question of grave import is, what was the policy of the order in reference to the railroads and to the public?

Obedience to Law Counseled

No scintilla of evidence has ever been introduced to show that any violence or infraction of the law was at any time contemplated. In all the addresses issued I counseled obedience to the law, and my associates did the same. We believed, as we still believe, that men had a lawful right to quit work. More than this we never claimed. If the companies could operate their trains, their right to do so was never questioned. That there was violent interference to some extent is not denied, but it has never been traced to the ARU. There was abundant opportunity to do so during the conspiracy trials, but the prosecution utterly failed to make a single point.

For the first few days after June 26, when the railroad strike began, everything was peaceable and orderly, and not until the railroad companies began to swear in deputy United States marshals by the thousand was there serious trouble. Four thousand of these were sworn into service at the request of and paid by the railroad companies. Just let me quote from the official report of Chief of Police [Michael] Brennan:

> Another source of annoyance to the department was the conduct of the deputy United States marshals. These men were hastily gathered, largely from the scum and refuse of the lowest class of the city's population. While there were honest men among them, a large number of them were toughs, thieves, and ex-convicts. There were also some strikers sworn in. Several of these officials were arrested during the strike for stealing property from railroad cars. In one instance two were found under suspicious circumstances near a freight car which had just been set on fire. They were

dangerous to the lives of citizens on account of their careless handling of pistols. They fired into crowds of bystanders when there was no disturbance and no reason for shooting. Innocent men, women, and children were killed by these shots.

I aver that nearly all the rioting, car burning, and lawlessness generally is traceable to this source. The facts overwhelmingly support the averment. The railroad companies had everything to gain, the employees everything to lose. If the employees, because of hostility to Pullman, had been bent on the destruction of property, why did they not destroy palace cars instead of stock cars? The query is exceedingly pertinent. When the rioting began and cars were fired, public sympathy, which is all-powerful, turned against the strikers, and that instant their cause was lost.

From the riot to the injunction is but a step. From the injunction to jail is but another step. In this way it is quite easy to defeat a strike. Until violence began, the strikers were triumphant, and this would have been the ending but for the deputy marshals who incited the trouble, which was deemed sufficient to justify the interference of the courts, the jailing of the leaders at every point, the calling out of the army, and the breaking up of the strike. As a matter of course the ARU never started out to antagonize the government. It is singular, however, that in no single instance in the history of the Republic have the authorities ever interfered on the side of workingmen. When their great powers have been invoked, it has always been in support of the corporations and on the side of property against human life.

Clamor for Prosecution

There was a general clamor for the prosecution of the leaders of the strike. The corporations insisted that the conspiracy should be punished to the full extent of the law. In due course of time the officers of the ARU were indicted for conspiracy. It was deemed a very easy matter to convict them and send them to the penitentiary.

The trial began January 24 [1895]. All of the evidence of the prosecution was presented to the jury. The defense then began to tell its story, and as the tale was unfolded a perceptible change was visible on the faces of the jurors. The tide was rapidly turning against the prosecution. An unconditional acquittal became painfully apparent. There were scores of witnesses yet to testify, and the truth, the whole truth, was about to be disclosed. At this supreme juncture the only real misfortune befell us. A juror was taken ill. The defense sought by all the means at their command to have the trial continued. They agreed to wait till the juror got well or to continue with 11 jurors or to subpoena another, or to do anything else to reach a verdict. The prosecution strenuously refused to proceed. They were ignominiously defeated and knew it. It would not do to have such a verdict go on record. It would be in ghastly conflict with the sentence of Judge Woods, which committed us to jail upon practically the same issues.

Since the trial I have received authoritative proof that the jury was practically unanimous in the opinion that there was no case. It is most unfortunate for us that this verdict was not put on record, but this does not lessen the moral effect of the vindication.

Exonerated by the Commission

The United State Strike Commission had exonerated us and had put the corporations in the pillory.[73] A jury of our peers, after hearing all the evidence, would have found us not guilty, and yet we languish in jail, not for having committed crime, but for alleged contempt of court. By two duly constituted bodies we were tried and our cause investigated, and in each case the verdict was equivalent to acquittal, and yet we occupy felons' cells.

In the face of this I do not see how any fair-minded man can avoid the conclusion that constitutional rights in this country are nothing more than a hallucination.

Reverting again to the strike, it should be borne in mind that the Pullman Company set at defiance the whole city of Chicago. An appeal was made to the city council, and that body appointed a committee to call on the Pullman Company to ask them to consent to arbitration. This committee, of which Alderman [John] McGillen was chairman, was authorized to make this proposition: that the Pullman Company should select two representatives, the judges of Cook County two more, and these four [select] a fifth, to inquire into the matters as to whether there was anything to arbitrate, and if this board found there was nothing to arbitrate, the employees agreed to return to work in a body. The employees did not even ask to have a representative on the board. The Pullman Company rejected the proposition with scorn.

Suppose the Pullman Company had made the same proposition and the employees had spurned it. What would have been the public verdict? Would not the whole country have condemned the strikers? Then what must be the enlightened public verdict in relation to this company? The Pullman Company were afraid to have that investigation made. They knew that if it were made there would be disclosed a state of affairs that would have horrified the country. I wish to state that all through the conspiracy trials Judge Grosscup acted with eminent fairness. He seemed desirous to get at the real facts and to have even-handed justice meted out.

What the Decision Means

As to the effect of the adverse ruling of the Supreme Court resulting in our imprisonment, it will in its ultimate result have the same effect upon the money power that the Dred Scott decision had upon the slave.[74] Stripped of all extraneous matter, the decision means that workingmen, while ostensibly having the right to organize, have not the right to exercise the legal functions of organization. In other words, they are compelled to submit to any conditions their employers may impose, because if they quit in concert and such cessation of work results in the interruption of the mails or interferes with interstate traffic, the fact of the workingmen having united is construed as conspiracy, and they are held accountable by the court for all acts of omission or commission that may result. The effect of this will be to destroy the usefulness of organization insofar as the fundamental, pivotal object, which is united resistance, is concerned.

Judge Trumbull[75] says: "The doctrine announced by the Supreme Court in the Debs case, carried to its logical conclusion, places every citizen at the mercy of any prejudiced or malicious federal judge who may see fit to imprison him."

Knowing this, railroad employees will certainly not quit work if any judge can by the injunction process declare them guilty of contempt and put them in jail for three to six months. The workingmen of the country realize the gravity of the situation. The dangerous encroachments of the federal judiciary are now more clearly comprehended since Judge Woods committed us to jail and the Supreme Court declined to review the decision, claiming that the lower court had complete and final jurisdiction.

Trial by Jury Denied

So far as my colleagues and myself are concerned, the imprisonment is of little or no consequence; so far as the principle involved in our incarceration is concerned, it amounts to everything, for the reason that if the right of trial by jury can be abrogated in the case of one citizen and he can be arbitrarily thrust into jail, so can all others. And hence every safeguard of our much-vaunted civil rights is destroyed, and no citizen is secure. Some of the most eminent jurists of the country declare that the constitution has been violated and that a federal judge, district or circuit, can now enjoin any man from doing anything, lawful or unlawful, and lock him in jail, guilty or not guilty. He issues the injunction, hears the evidence, pronounces the sentence, thus constituting himself judge, jury, plaintiff, and executioner. Between this man, who in respect to the liberty of the citizen has supreme power, and the tsar of Russia, there is not the slightest difference. In each case the citizen is the helpless victim of autocratic whim or caprice.

When all the people fully comprehend the situation, they will act. There is a higher [judge than] the Supreme Court, and someday the court will find itself at the bar of the tribunal of We, the People.

Example of the Corporations

On this proposition all labor harmonizes. Every trade union in the land has declared itself, has cried out against the monstrous assumption of power by one man. When I am again allowed my rights as a citizen I intend to take up the great work where I laid it down. We hope to bring about a unification of labor, a harmony between unions, for all are working to the same end. In seeking thus to combine all classes of labor, we simply follow the example set by the corporations. We feel that if they had the lawful right to combine their tremendous power to reduce wages, to blacklist employees, the latter had the same power to unify their forces for mutual protection. If such a combination is unlawful, if the courts construe it to be a conspiracy and against public policy, then let the corporations who initiated the proceeding abolish it. The one necessitates the other. On our part we acted purely in self-defense. What possible hope would the employees of any road or system have against such a colossal alliance as is represented in the General Managers' Association? They would be ground to atoms.

And therefore the work must go on. But to avoid the spies and sneaks who fatten on the misfortunes of the toilers and who are quick to report the name of every man who joins an association to better his condition, the work will hereafter be carried on in secret. No engineer need know whether his fireman is a member of the ARU. And it will be spread until it becomes the strongest union in the world, for there are 800,000 railroad men eligible. Every man who served his term in this county jail is now a worker in the field, stronger and better equipped for the fight than if he had not been here. We will carry on the work, even unto the end.

I have had ample time for retrospective reflection, but had I to do it again I would not change my course in the slightest degree. I did what my head prompted and my heart approved, and I have no regrets. I would do all I did and as much more as I could on the same lines if a hangman's noose instead of a felon's cell confronted me. The losses, the sacrifices, and the sufferings incident to the strike will dwarf into insignificance in comparison with the monumental blessings which will flow from it when the last chapters shall have been written.

Open Letter to the 1895 Labor Day Celebration in Terre Haute[†]

September 2, 1895

In responding to your request, I am disposed to recite a page of what all Christendom proclaims "sacred history."[76]

There existed some 2,500 years ago a king clothed with absolute power known as Darius, who ruled over the Medes and Persians.[77] He was not a usurper, like William A. Woods, the United States circuit judge. Darius was royal spawn. All the people in Darius's empire were slaves. The will of the king was absolute. What the king said was law, just as we find in the United States of America, that what a United States judge says is law. Darius, the Persian despot, could imprison at will. The same is true of Woods, the despot.

Do I hear an exception? Allow me to support my indictment by authority that passes current throughout the Republic. Only a few days ago the venerable Judge Trumbull, one of the most eminent jurists and statesmen America has ever produced, wrote these burning words:

> The doctrine announced by the court in the Debs case, carried to its logical conclusion, places every citizen at the mercy of any prejudiced or malicious judge who may think proper to imprison him.

This states the case of the officers of the American Railway Union in a nutshell. They violated no law, they committed no crime, they have not been charged, nor indicted nor tried, and yet they have been arbitrarily sentenced and thrust in jail, and what has happened to them will happen to others who dare protest against such inhumanity as the monster [George M.] Pullman practiced upon his employees and their families.

More than 2,500 years have passed to join the unnumbered centuries since Darius lived and reigned, and now in the United States we have about fourscore Darius despots, each one of whom may at his will, whim, or pleasure imprison an American citizen, and this grim truth is up for discussion on Labor Day.

It will be remembered that during the reign of Darius there was a gentleman

---

[†]   Published as "Debs to His Home Folk" in *Chicago Chronicle,* September 23, 1895, 5. Reprinted as "Terre Haute: Labor Day at the Home of Eugene V. Debs" in the *Railway Times*, vol. 2, no. 18 (September 16, 1895), 2.

by the name of Daniel whom the king delighted to honor. The only fault that could be found with Daniel was that he would not worship the Persian gods, but would, three times a day, go to his window, looking toward Jerusalem, and pray. This was his crime. It was enough. The Persians had a religion of their own. They had their gods of gold, brass, clay, stone, wood, anything from a mouse to a mountain, and they would not tolerate any other god. They had, in modern parlance, an "established church," and as Daniel, like Christ, would not conform to the Persian religion, "the presidents of the kingdom, the governors and the princes, the counsellors and the captains," or, as in these latter days, the corporations, the trusts, the syndicates, and the combines, concluded to get rid of Daniel, and they persuaded Darius to issue an injunction that no man should "ask a petition of any god or man for 30 days save of thee, O king!"[78] and the king, à la Woods, issued the decree. But Daniel, who was made of resisting stuff, disregarded the injunction and still prayed as before to his god. Daniel was a hero. In the desert of despotism he stands forever.

> As some tall cliff that lifts its awful form
> Swells from the vale and midway leaves the storm,
> Though round its breast the rolling clouds are spread,
> Eternal sunshine settles on its head.[79]

But the bigots triumphed for a time. The king's decree must stand and Daniel, as a penalty for prayer, must be cast into the lions' den, and the bigots, the plutocratic pirates and parasites of that period, thought that would be the end of Daniel. They chuckled as in fancy they heard the lions break his bones and lap his blood. They slept well and dreamed of victory. Not so with the king. He knew he had been guilty of an act of monstrous cruelty, and in this the old Persian despot was superior to Woods. The king could not sleep and was so pained over his act that he forbade all festivities in his palace. In this he showed that he was not totally depraved.

The king had a lurking idea that somehow Daniel would get out of the lions' den unharmed and that he would overcome the intrigues of those who had conspired to destroy him. Early in the morning he went to the mouth of the den. Daniel was safe. His god, unlike the Supreme Court, having found Daniel innocent of all wrongdoing, locked the jaws of the lions, and Daniel stood before the king wearing the redemption crown of truth more royal than a princely diadem. Then the king, who had been deceived by the enemies of Daniel, the sycophants and vermin of power, gave his wrath free rein and had them cast into the lions' den, where they were devoured by the ferocious beasts.

History repeats itself. I am not a Daniel, but I am in jail by the decree of an autocrat. I appealed from one despot to a whole bench for justice, and the appeal was unheeded. I and my associates were innocent. There was no stain of crime on our record, but neither innocence nor Constitution was of any avail. To placate the money power, the implacable enemies of labor, we were sent to prison, and here alone, contemplating the foul wrong inflicted on me and my associate officials of the American Railway Union, with head and heart and hand nerved for the task, I write this letter to be read on Labor Day to friends and neighbors in the city of my birth.

It is not a wall of despondency nor despair. The cause for which I have been deprived of my liberty was just, and I am thrice armed against all my enemies. To bear punishment for one's honest convictions is a glorious privilege and requires no high order of courage.

No judicial tyrant comes to my prison to inquire as to my health or hopes, but one sovereign does come by night and by day with words of cheer. It is the sovereign people—the uncrowned but sceptered rulers of the realm. No day of my imprisonment has passed that the bars and bolts and doors of the Woodstock jail have not been bombarded by messages breathing devotion to the cause of liberty and justice, and as I read and ponder these messages and grasp the hands of friends and catch the gleam of wrath in their defiant eye and listen to their words of heroic courage, I find it no task to see the wrath of the sovereign people aroused, and all opposition to the triumphant march of labor consigned to oblivion, and as an earnest of this from every quarter come announcements that the American Railway Union is growing in membership and strength, destined at an early day to be, as it deserves to be, an organization which by precept, by example and principle, will ultimately unify railroad labor in the United States and make it invincible.

There is a mighty mustering of all the forces of labor throughout the country. Labor is uniting in one solid phalanx to secure justice for labor. When this time comes, and coming to it peacefully, I hope, no judicial despot will dare to imprison an American citizen to please corporations. When this time comes, and coming it is as certain as rivers flow to the sea, bullion and boodle will not rule in Congress, in legislatures, and in courts, and legislators and judges and other public officials will not be controlled, as many now are, by the money power. There is to come a day, a labor day, when from the center to the circumference of our mighty republic, from blooming groves of oranges to waving fields of grain, from the pine lands of Maine to the Pacific coast, the people shall be free, and it will come by the unified voice and vote of the farmer, the mechanic, and the laborer in every department of the country's industries.

I notice in your letter that you say, "We have been unable to get a representative labor speaker for our Labor Day celebration," and here let me say that on Labor Day all men who wear the badge of labor are "representative speakers"—not "orators," perhaps, as the term is accepted to mean, and yet orators in fact, from whose lips fall "thoughts that breathe and words that burn;"[80] coming warm from the heart, they reach the heart and fan the zeal in a great cause into a flame that sweeps along like a prairie fire. It has been the good fortune of labor to produce from its ranks men who, though unlearned in the arts of oratory, were yet orators of the highest order, if effect instead of fluency is considered. It is the occasion that makes the orator, as it is the battle that makes the veteran. Mark Anthony said, "I am no orator, like Brutus," but when he showed Caesar's mantle to the populace of Rome and pointed to where the conspirators' dagger had stabbed Caesar, the oratory of Brutus paled before his burning words. And every man, however humble he may esteem himself, may on Labor Day hold up the Constitution of the United States and point to where the judicial dagger stabbed liberty to death and make the people cry out for the enthronement of the constitution—and Terre Haute has a hundred such orators.

I write in the hurry and press of business. Before me are a hundred letters demanding replies. I pass them by to respond to an appeal from my home, and in fancy as I write I am with you. I am at home again. My father, bending beneath the weight of years, salutes me. My mother, whose lullaby songs nestle and coo in the inner temple of my memory, caresses me, her kiss baptizes me with joy, and as if by enchantment—

> And years, and sin, and manhood flee
> And leave me at my mother's knee.[81]

In this mood I write, with the hope that the celebration at Terre Haute will inspire renewed devotion to the interest of labor, and with a heart full of good wishes I subscribe myself

Yours fraternally,
Eugene V. Debs

The Outlook for 1896:
Interview with the *St. Louis Chronicle*[†]
September 13, 1895

Views upon the presidential election in 1896 must, of course, be largely conjectural and take the form of hypothesis. "Ifs" and "buts" must be introduced, not to obscure convictions or conclusions, but rather to emphasize them.[82]

The minds of the people have not, of late years, been so greatly perturbed upon political issues as at present. The two old parties, like ships storm-driven toward a rock-bound coast, are trying to find safety from wreck.

The Republican Party, hopeful of success by the demerits of the Democratic Party rather than any merits of its own, evidently believes a victory in 1896 is in sight, while no one who surveys the field dispassionately regards the Democratic Party of sufficient strength to capture a single state of the Republic, regardless of who may be its candidates.[83] The Republican Party, equally corrupt and untrustworthy, is more adroit. Confessedly the party of trusts, corporations, and every piratical combine known to the country, it boldly flaunts its flag, and the great boodlers of the nation rally to its standard. If it wins in 1896 it will be a notable victory of the money power; and if the signs of the times are worthy of attention, they force the conviction that whatever the money power has accomplished in the past in debauching the press and in levying contributions to win elections by the corrupting power of money, will be as one to 16 compared with what it will do in 1896.[84]

There is still another possibility to be considered relating to the presidential election of 1896. The Republican Party and the Democratic Party are on the money question practically one. The goldbugs dominate both and declare that at all hazards the gold policy must be maintained.[85]

Goldbugs Under One Banner

The Democratic Party being irretrievably wrecked, nothing remaining in sight but Cleveland and his officeholders and defeat in 1896, what more natural than that Democratic goldbugs should go over en masse to the Republican goldbugs

---

[†]   Published as "What Debs Says: About Parties and the Presidency in 1896" in *St. Louis Chronicle*, Sept. 13, 1895.

and join in the fight against Democrats, Republicans, and Populists, whose rugged patriotism and integrity are pledged to rescue the government from the hands of American plutocracy?

Hitherto John Sherman has stood for all that is vile and corrupting in the financial affairs of the country—the archfoe of the masses and the trusted friend of the money power. But now Grover Cleveland has vaulted into prominence and out-Shermans Sherman, and instead of seeking to rescue the country from deplorable conditions created by Sherman and the Republican Party, doffs his presidential cap and climbs into the Republican bandwagon and scowls at every Democrat who dares oppose his treason to Democratic principles, while he sends forth his cabinet ministers—Carlisle[86] and the rest—to bring Democrats into the Republican fold.

This is the last nail to be driven into the Democratic coffin before its burial in 1896; and this done, the Democratic Party passes away as did the old Whig Party. Such being the trend, what of the outlook in 1896?

Plutocracy vs. the People

There are millions of men in the two old parties who will no longer be dominated by the money power. They see distinctly that the end is widespread ruin. The break is ostensibly on the financial question—on the one side the Rothschilds and on the other the American people. In other words, the Plutocracy vs. the People. The term "Rothschilds" is accepted to stand for all that is odious and infamous in American finances, and free silver for all signifies redemption from foreign control of the American monetary system.

I have not the time to state nor have you the space to print the far-reaching reforms that would follow in the wake of the free coinage of silver. It would annihilate the dominating power of the plutocracy. It would divorce America from the corrupting alliance with foreign Shylocks and sharks and make the United States, financially, an independent nation, and open up the way for reforms which the People's Party is pledged to inaugurate.

The disintegration and death of the Democratic Party simplifies the situation, since it emphasizes the fact that in 1896 there will be but two parties, practically, in the field—the People's Party and the Republican Party.

Principles, Not Men

If it be accepted that goldbug Democrats will combine with goldbug Republicans to win a goldbug victory in 1896, then as a corollary the free silver Democrats and free silver Republicans will combine with the People's Party to save the government from still greater disaster than has already been inflicted by the rule of the money power.

Making such allowances as are required for the tenacity of men, their disinclination to abandon longstanding associations, it is evident that millions of men are prepared to renounce their allegiance to the two old parties and swing into line under the Populist flag, and this being true, the People's Party has only to formulate a platform embodying the reforms which the people demand, a platform upon which all classes of reformers can unite to sweep the country.

In this contest it does not matter who the Republicans nominate, Harrison, McKinley, or Reed.[87] They all stand for the same odious policy and are equally obnoxious.

The People's Party

The People's Party stands for reform. It is preeminently an American party. It is the party of the common people of all classes, including the farmer, the mechanic, the laborer, the businessman, the professional man, and all those whose love of country is greater than lust for gold. It is the party of those who believe the people should rule, and to this party the patriots of America are rallying as in 1861 they rallied to the standard of the Union.

Current Topics
The New Woman, Bicycles, Bloomers[†]

September 1895

The New Woman

We hear much nowadays about the "new woman." The theme is an inviting one. It breathes of a "good time coming," when woman shall be at least the equal of man. And the Lord knows this is not claiming much for her. For, as millions of

---

†   Published in the *Cleveland Plain Dealer,* unspecified date, September 1895. Original title unknown. Reprinted as "Current Topics: Debs Discusses the 'New Woman,' the 'Bicycle,' and 'Bloomers'" in the *Railway Times,* vol. 2, no. 19 (October 1, 1895), 1.

men are slaves, so millions of women are the slaves of slaves. In respect to woman, man has not risen above animal creation. He is the stronger and therefore rules; and woman only has what he has seen fit to "allow" her. Conceal it as we may, the haggard fact stands forth that men have by virtue of superior strength kept women in bondage. Of course, I totally dismiss dresses and diamonds and dainties. I discuss the inherent, inalienable right to "liberty and the pursuit of happiness." In our country, the ballot makes the sovereign. Withhold it and slavery follows. Men have with instinctive fealty to their sex assumed and exercised all authority, and woman's sphere has been limited to meek submission.

The "new woman," I am persuaded, will take her place side by side with man in the great struggle for social, economic, and intellectual emancipation. She will no longer be disenfranchised by her sex. She will have an equal chance from the start and will invade every domain in which brains and pluck and energy compete for the world's prizes. She will scorn to be the petted plaything of society. She will be no more masculine nor less "modest" than now. She will more than ever grace and beautify the home by the witchery and magic of a woman's love. She will go out by herself when she chooses to do so, and her release from the guardianship we now force upon her will be all the protection she will require. She will marry, not to escape the vulgar gossip of a soulless society, but to please herself; and love born of moral and intellectual equality will be the only consideration. She will command the homage of man, and hand in hand they will travel life's journey together.

My mother is advanced in years, but I am proud to believe her to be the best type of "new woman." My wife and sisters have all the crowning glories of the "new woman." In our family there is no superiority of sex. There is no authority, and none is needed. The home under the sweet and tender influences of the "new woman" will be radiant with love and joy.

The Bicycle

The mission of the bicycle is greatly underrated. Human ingenuity, in evolving the bicycle, has given man a mighty boon. It is to play a great part in the world's affairs. It is to liberate millions from the thralldom of foul atmosphere, squalid and filthy apartments, and all the multiplicity of debauching and demoralizing conditions that make the lives of workingmen and women in manufacturing and commercial centers a continuous curse. It is to be an important factor in depopulating cities and building up the country.

It will be a mighty leveler upward and downward. The bicycle will attack the fabulous value of city real estate, distribute population, lower rent, close up the tenement den, and extinguish the sweatshop hell. It will free the inhabitants of cities from the fetid odors their overcrowded conditions generate and pour a perpetual flood of fresh air upon the race. As a matter of course working people will have them, and the man who trudges to his daily toil will be an object for a relief commission.

The limits of an interview will admit only the merest glimpse of the possibilities of the bicycle. The great health-giving advantages of fresh air and exercise will by the fiat of the bicycle be the heritage of the race. The bicycle, not the medical profession, will triumph over disease. The wheel is on the trail of consumption and will overtake and vanquish the remorseless destroyer. Men and women and children will all ride the bicycle, and the enrapturing panorama of nature will no longer be forbidden glories to most of the race.

Of course, the bicycle is yet in embryo. The wheel of the future will revolve to suit man's fancy and the variety, design, and capacity will be practically without limit. And when monopoly and special privilege are abolished, the bicycle may be purchased for a song and will be within the reach of all. The world will yet revolve on wheels.

Bloomers

The "bloomer question" should be solved by the sex that wears them in a way to suit themselves. Men of sense will hail with satisfaction any change in the woman's dress in which health and comfort shall be in harmonious alliance with elegance and style. Women know a thousand times better than men what they should wear, and I regard it as presumptuous and impertinent for men to meddle in such affairs. If men wanted to wear bloomers they would wear them, nor would they ask the consent or consult the views or desires of women. It should be understood that women are the equals, not the wards of men, and in their own affairs they have the right to suit themselves.

For myself, I confess to a liking for bloomers. They seem cool and comfortable, and there is something about the air of the girl who wears them that reminds me of the Declaration of Independence. They are immodest only to the immodest. I have immense admiration for women who have the audacity to fly in the face of antiquated "forms" and "usages." With iconoclastic courage they shock the prudes of both sexes and pave the way of higher elevations and loftier attainments. Mrs. Annie Jenness Miller[88] is one of the really great women of the century.

"In Unity There Is Strength":
Open Letter to the *Chicago Evening Press*†
September 23, 1895

Theodore Parker[89] said, "The books that help you most are those that make you think the most," and, insofar as thinking is concerned, circumstances are like books. A circumstance that makes one think is valuable in many ways. Just now there are numerous circumstances which have forced a whole country to "thinking," and none more intensely than that portion dependent upon wages for subsistence. The present is the time for workingmen to think. Goldsmith wrote that "those who think govern those who toil." The thought power and the money power govern the world. These two powers in alliance command the military power, and this trinity of powers bears down all opposition. Exceptions are few and far between, and when found strengthen the rule.

In the United States it may be said that a new army of thinkers has entered the field. This army, as yet untrained and undisciplined, is sufficiently vigorous to create disturbances in the old currents and tides of thought that have ruled the country, particularly in industrial affairs.

Undeveloped Brains

These new thinkers, with rare exceptions, though possessed of independence and courage, have not as yet got their mental powers under full control; hence, though thinkers and toilers, they are still the victims of those who think more methodically. This is not strange. They are only partially emancipated. They repeat in a sort of an idle way, "In unity there is strength," but when unity is proposed they lose sight of the conquering philosophy of the maxim and split up into factions and furnish the world with the paradox that their boasted strength is weakness; and their organizations, instead of scouring victories, invite disaster. Such circumstances are fruitful of thought. Capable men say there must be readjustments, new departures. We have followed this trail far enough. We need not retrace our steps, but we must get out of the jungle. We must advise other thinkers that we are capable of organizing a campaign of victory.

---

† Published as "Debs Writes a Long Letter" in *Chicago Evening Press*, vol. 15, whole no. 4473 (September 23, 1895), 2. Debs wrote a regular series of weekly articles for this paper during his final months of incarceration.

How shall this be done? What is the new departure required? I do not regard such questions as abstruse. On the contrary, they simply suggest the maxim "In unity there is strength," and impress upon all who think at all the imperative character of the demand to unify forces for the simple purpose of securing victory, not for one, but for all. And it is just here that the circumstance comes into view that victory for all is the one thing about which labor organizations have thought little and cared less. There have been few victories over envies, jealousies, and selfishness. Every organization for itself and "the devil take the hindmost" has wrought its debasing work until at last corporations entertain feelings toward organizations scarcely one remove from contempt. Organizations in numerous instances aid in defeating organizations, and the circumstance is not only fruitful of thought but of serious doubt as well. If unification cannot be secured, then why continue the struggle? Why court defeat and humiliation? Far better disband, blow out all the lodge fires that have ever been lighted, and go back to unorganized chaos. If, as is seen every day, men are to continue to abandon the right for a "mess of pottage" and accept the ultimatums of those known to champion the wrong, why longer, with banners befouled with blotches of cowardice and degeneracy, advertise to the world that organization is a sham and a delusion possessing less protective power than so many herds of wild asses?

Higher Organizations

Such circumstances confront organizations of workingmen with startling defiance. Can they be overcome? If, for example, the 900,000 railroad employees of this country cannot, by virtue of their thought power, be brought into harmonious alliance, then their doom is fixed, irrevocably decided. Is that to be the conclusion? Not yet. What is the supreme demand? Unification of thought— oneness of purpose—one grand central idea: Justice to the humblest worker. We must get away from the duke and baron curse in labor organizations, the aristocracy of $4 a day which beats down the man who gets but $1 a day and keeps him in the ranks, as financiers would say of debased coin, something subsidiary, weak, dependent, and forever wearing the stamp of inferiority. Is it possible to get out of su:ch a degrading rut? I think so. But to accomplish a purpose so elevating and disenthralling, the thought of the organizations of workingmen must be of a higher and a bolder type than now prevails.

In writing upon such topics, it is always my purpose to be practical, and I can conceive of nothing more in the line of practical thought relating to the future of labor than for workingmen to unify their power. Simple organization does not now and never will answer the demand. Nonunion men are too numerous; alienation is too rampant. There is, therefore, a demand for leaders broad enough and unselfish enough to grasp the situation and secure unity. This done, the way is clear; omitted, and the fate of organization is sealed.

Myron Reed and Labor Unification[†]

September 28, 1895

Woodstock, Ill., September 28, 1895

Reverend Myron Reed,[90] of Denver, Colorado, is one of the greatest ministers in America. As a divine he is immensely practical and has become justly celebrated for his epigrammatic style of preaching. He is a man of sturdy honesty and unquestioned courage. He tells the truth without fear or favor. He does not cater to wealth nor compromise with hypocrisy. Mr. Reed makes no pretensions to oratory in the ordinary acceptation of the term. In this regard he is as unlike Talmage as a gray eagle is unlike a lightning bug.[91] No matter what his subject may be, Mr. Reed handles it very much after the style that a blacksmith handles iron. He hammers it into usefulness, makes something out of it that the people want. As, for instance, in discussing labor questions, he is quoted as saying:

> But let labor be organized. Let the hands and the feet and the whole body obey the head. Let there be no paralyzed hand. Why did the revolutionary war last for seven years? Because it was fought by 13 colonies, one jealous of the other, generals jealous one of the other. Gates plotted against Washington.[92] If you have a load that it requires 13 horses to pull, you will not pull it by putting on three and working them till they are discouraged, and then try seven and then five. You want the 13 at one time, heads looking one way, traces straightened, each horse well into his collar. Then gee a little and yell.

†   Published in *Erie Graphic,* unknown title and date. Reprinted as part of "Labor Literature: Eugene V. Debs on a Variety of Live Topics," the *Railway Times,* vol. 2, no. 21 (November 1, 1895), 3.

The foregoing remarks are eminently characteristic of Rev. Myron Reed. They embody real wisdom, the true philosophy of the labor question. Every word weighs a pound. With proper organization workingmen can solve the problem; without it they are powerless. It is the difference between strength and weakness, victory and defeat. To a certain extent, workingmen comprehend the difference between organization and disorganization, between an army and a mob. But the organization of labor, so far, has not secured anticipated benefits. It seems difficult to get organizations in line to pull together. The reason of this is, I surmise, entirely in consonance with human nature, though directly in conflict with human interests. Human nature seems to have had for its policy, from the first, "Every man for himself and the devil catch the hindmost," while human interests would rescue, if possible, the hindmost from the grasp of the cloven-footed enemy. As soon as organization is so perfect that it secures all workingmen their rights, whether skilled or unskilled, seeking the welfare of the masses as certainly as the classes, the then 13 or 1300 organizations will pull together whatever load fate may impose, and the time will have arrived to "gee a little and yell." Till then organizations may "gee and haw," but the corporations will only pile on more burdens and chuckle as they see them, as at present, stuck in the mire listening to the advice of a certain labor leader who smilingly tells them, "If you can't get what you want, you must take what you can get."

The American Railway Union is unifying the railroad employees throughout the country. They realize that the railroad companies, insofar as labor is concerned, are solidly allied. No *class* organization exists among them.[93] They comprehend the power of perfect unity. If railroad employees would secure the benefits of organization, fair wages, and such treatment as becomes *men*, they have got to follow the example of the corporations and *get together*. They can never do this by organizing and maintaining separately the various classes. These can be maintained within one organization, as in the case of the American Railway Union, but when separately organized, class jealousies are aroused which make harmony impossible and reduce all to helplessness.

When the railroad men of the country and workingmen generally comprehend the necessity of closing up the ranks, getting together and pulling together, they will emancipate themselves from the thralldom of injustice.

"Stand Together": Open Letter to W. W. Williams, Editor of *Quincy Labor News*[†]

October 5, 1895

Woodstock, Ill., October 5, 1895

W. W. Williams,
Editor, *Quincy Labor News*

Dear Sir:—

* * *

As for the nomination for the presidency, with which you do me the honor to associate my name, I am not a candidate and cannot accept such honors even if tendered to me. There are many and cogent reasons why I should decline to hold public office or be a candidate for public honors or emoluments.

I only regret that the draft upon my time is so constant and excessive to give me little leisure to keep abreast of the procession of stirring events which now engage the attention of the American people and especially men of thought in the ranks of organized labor.

My prison bars deprive me of active participation in affairs which command my solicitude. Were I deprived of my liberty for crime, had I been adjudged guilty of a misdemeanor or a felony by a jury of my peers, under due process of law, rights guaranteed by the Constitution to every grade of criminal known to the code, I would have suffered in the silence becoming such law breakers. But to be imprisoned for no crime whatever, to be deprived of my liberty when there is no stain upon my innocence, to be arrested, sentenced, and imprisoned as if I were a Russian subject, is at once as flagrant an act of despotism as was ever committed.

Aside, however, from all personal considerations, the infamous invasion of my liberty and the liberty of my associate officials of the American Railway Union touches every workingman on the continent, and was designed to intimidate them and to force them into submission to their employers.

It is this alarming condition of things which appeals to the workingmen of the United States. In vain will it be for them to entertain the thought that

---

[†]   Published as "From E. V. Debs" in *Quincy Labor News*, October 12, 1895.

they are not the victims of despotic power should they arouse the hostility of the corporations which employ them.

These corporations run the judicial and military machinery of the government, which will tolerate no manifestations of that freedom and independence which were once the glory of our people.

In surveying the field, I fail to discover any hope for the toilers, the wage slaves of the United States, excepting in their unification; and this accomplished, I behold at no distant day their emancipation.

I am not a visionary. It is my habit to deal with verities. I know the processes of evolution require time. Education is not achieved in a day. I am satisfied the trend is right and as I survey the field, my confidence gains strength and vigor.

The American Railway Union stands forth as a sublime test of moral courage. Traduced, defamed, and persecuted, it does not falter. Beaten down, it rises again. Having the best interests of labor at heart and based upon the truth, it becomes invincible, and all over this fair land men of courage are rallying to its standard. The battle does not frighten them. Corporations and courts do not intimidate them, nor defeats discourage them. With them an injury to one is not only the concern of all but an injury to all. They will never close their eyes and ears to the cries of distress, and no power beneath the stars can silence their tongues when the liberties of their fellow workers are invaded.

To the workingmen who read your valuable paper, I would say, *Stand Together*. Permit no artificial lines to separate you. No matter under what flag you rally, the flag of units should wave triumphantly over all.

Unified, solidified, working together and voting together, you can conquer. Divided and fractionalized, your doom is sealed.

Eugene V. Debs

The Mind's Workshop[†]
October 10, 1895

Woodstock, Ill., October 10, 1895

We are constantly reading of the products of the mind, and in all our working hours, with never a moment's omission, we are confronted with the achievements of the mind in tangible forms too numerous to be cataloged or classified. We read of the efforts of the mind, the triumphs of the mind, and the treasures of the mind. We have textbooks devoted to what is called "mental philosophy," and still when the question is asked, "What is the mind?" no man can answer. As well expect by reaching out to feel the stars. Defying explorations and investigations, the profoundest thinker of the age may discuss learnedly the operations of the mind, but when required to define "mind" he is as incapable of solving the problem as were the cavemen of prehistoric times.

It is conceded that the brain is the seat of the mind, and we know that the head is where the brain is located. In other words, the head is the mind's workshop, where it carries forward all of its vast and mysterious operations; and of the billions of heads created since the "beginning," no two have been alike, and the difference in the mind's machinery by which it carries forward its enterprises is greater than any dissimilarity discovered in the construction of heads from that of an idiot to that of the profoundest philosopher that ever commanded a world to listen when he expounded the heights and depths of wisdom. Milton said:

> The mind in its own place and in itself,
> Can make a heaven of hell, a hell of heaven.[94]

The mind's "own place" is the head, and while men talk learnedly of the head, no man has ever seen the mind performing its operations. Churchill wrote that:

> Within the brain's most secret cells
> A certain Lord Chief Justice dwells.
> Of sov'reign pow'r, whom One and All,
> With common Voice we *Reason* call.[95]

But it so happens that comparatively few brains can boast of a "Lord Chief

---

[†]   Published in *Columbus Press*, unspecified date. Reprinted as part of "Labor Literature: Eugene V. Debs on a Variety of Live Topics" in the *Railway Times*, vol. 2, no. 21 (November 1, 1895), 5.

Justice" or any other distinguished jurist or philosopher worthy the name of "Reason," or any other faculty of similar characteristics; and still it is held that by proper mind culture, begun in youth and carried forward to mature age, every brain, if it does not finally have a "Lord Chief Justice" to preside over the mind, may possess some less distinguished dignitary to guide and direct the mind and enable it to achieve usefulness.

In numerous instances, those who have written of mind culture and mind development make little note of physical training, discarding the idea that a healthy body is required, as a general proposition, to secure a healthy mind. True it is that instances are on record where minds of exceptional vigor have inhabited the brain of men whose physical powers were abnormally weak, and that on the other hand, men of great physical development remain all their days in mental childhood, instances which go far to prove that mental training had little to do with physical drilling and discipline, and that the mind's development was dependent upon conditions apart from food, air, exercise, and other health-giving accessories. Sir Isaac Newton is referred to as ranking low in his studies until, aroused by the insults of a fellow student, he resolved to achieve supremacy. Adam Clarke is another illustration of stupidity, who excited ridicule until his dormant faculties were aroused, when he outstripped his fellow students and won immortality by his mental achievements.[96] Of Napoleon it has been said by those who knew him best that in his boyhood he exhibited none of those masterly qualities which enabled him later to burst like a volcano upon Europe, overthrow thrones and kingdoms, and exhibit himself as one of the master spirits of the world. It is to be inferred that such men have healthy bodies, and that they possess healthy brains, without which their names would not adorn the pages of history.

Nor is it to be overlooked that within the realm of mind achievements writers are constantly referring to such ancient worthies as the Greek philosophers, poets, and sculptors—to ancient orators—as also to men of modern times, such as Shakespeare, Milton, and others of great renown, while little or nothing at all is said of men who, being neither philosophers, poets, nor warriors, have led on the pioneer hosts of civilization and redeemed a part of the world at least from savagery, and who are yet to make all the wildernesses bloom and reclaim the desert wastes, if such work is ever performed.

Look at the schools of the period, and what does the world behold? Reference is made to those colleges and universities where a youth is taught that the highest achievement of the mind is to translate a Greek or a Latin poem or to learn his piece and "spout" it in the presence of a bald-headed committee and receive a blue ribbon as a reward.

On the other hand, what is said of the brawny brainworkers who in ten thousand shops are carrying forward the enterprises of this wonderfully practical age? Little or nothing at all. If there could be instituted an intellectual tournament in which a graduate of the university and a graduate of, for example, the Baldwin Locomotive shops were to appear to demonstrate which of the two minds had achieved the largest development, the scene would be singularly unique. The graduate of Rockefeller's Standard Oil University[97] would possibly have for his subject "Was Adam Originally a Rag Baby?" The committee would listen with profound attention to the Standard Oil University graduate. There would be ringing applause as the "rag baby" theory was extolled or denounced, and the graduate would leave the stage with tokens of boundless appreciation. Now comes the graduate of the Baldwin Locomotive Works. As he emerges from behind the screen a locomotive follows. Then they stand side by side, and the locomotive builder simply says, "I built this wonderful machine." Does he receive the blue ribbon? By no means. The "rag baby" orator is at once pronounced the most intellectual. The committee observes nothing in the building of a locomotive to be compared with the achievement of the graduate of the Standard Oil University, who is invited to a banquet while the graduate of the Baldwin Locomotive Works retires to reflect upon modern ideas of brains and mind development.

For centuries there have been what is called the "learned professions"—law, theology, and medicine. Possibly theology should have precedence, as the priests have dominated all others. Under the shield, medical quackery has flourished until schools (?) have multiplied to an extent that the term "learned" has become practically meaningless. Nor are things essentially different in theology, and the world is confronted at last with so many "right" ways and "wrong" ways that thousands are discarding the teachings of "learned" professors. As for law, while there remain certain recognized landmarks of justice and equity, it is found that of all the delusions and snares that have cursed the world, law supplies by far the greatest number. Hence it may be said that after all, mind development, except in the practical affairs of life, has not advanced since the days of Adam, and strange as may appear, the graduates of colleges who profess to know it all are as determined now as when the ancients consulted their oracles to ignore all mind development except in cases where they consent to apply the stamp of their approval. As a result, the shop is a thing of contempt in the estimation of the college, and though the shop can display more mind development in a year than the college can in a century, the world runs after colleges and shouts its praises, and the shop chimes in to swell the laudations.

Conditions†

October 14, 1895

In European and Asiatic countries, conditions relating to different classes of people excite little concern as compared with the United States. Here the most impoverished as well as the most affluent have the ballot. Here all are sovereign citizens and eligible to the highest official stations in the government. In European and Asiatic governments such rights and privileges are unknown; the one or two exceptions to the rule need not be mentioned since they do not, in the liberty of their citizens, parallel the rights and prerogatives conferred by our constitution and laws.

In referring to the essential differences in conditions, it is proper to observe that in the one case centuries of despotism have created acquiescence. The rich rule and are content; the poor obey, and their obedience has been so long and so cruelly enforced that like "dumb, driven cattle"[98] they submit. In the United States we have by constitution and laws the reverse of such conditions. Here we started out upon what was deemed an eternal truth, that "all men are created equal." We discarded titles and inherited prerogatives. All were clothed with divine right to rule. At the polls the poor and rich met on a level. Here we swept away everything resembling caste. The pomp and pride and arrogance of a titled nobility and aristocracy we tabooed. In a word, we started out with a nation of free men. More than 100 years have elapsed since we began teaching the doctrine of equality before the law. These lessons have been woven into the fiber of American thought, into our laws and literature, into our national songs and anthems. The fathers fought and bled for the truths they embody, and multiplied thousands have died for them. Here, and only here, every man counts one, and no man counts more than one.

Are We Losing Our Birthright?

The question arises, are we insensibly drifting toward conditions which exist in less favored lands? And are we relaxing our hold upon our birthrights? Are we using our dearly bought rights and prerogatives in a way that shall eventually wrest them from our grasp? Is American liberty in peril? What is the condition

---

†   Published as "Debs Fires a Shot" in *Chicago Evening Press,* October 14, 1895. Reprinted in *Appeal to Reason* (Kansas City, MO), whole no. 9 (October 26, 1895), 3.

of the rich, and what is the condition of the poor? Without exaggeration, in words of truth and soberness, what is the trend of affairs? The rich are growing richer. Fortunes amount skyward. We have produced an aristocracy of wealth requiring extravagant speech to describe. Our millionaires are counted by thousands. They constitute a money power which has developed barbaric sway. It has grasped every source of production and every means of transportation. It controls the ballot and dictates legislation. It blotches federal and state statutes. It debauches judges and jurors. It bribes congressmen, senators, and state legislators, and to build higher its mountain of wealth it turns footpads on all the highways of labor and robs those who toil and live by wages. Such are the conditions on the one hand. No one denies it whose opinion is not debauched.

What are the conditions of the poor in the United States? I challenge the record for a denial of the averment that in no land beneath the skies are conditions more deplorable, and President Cleveland, in his message to Congress, declared that these conditions are the result of "congressional legislation." Here the poor are becoming poorer. Here squalor and degradation are spread out over a continent of food products in fabulous abundance; and in sight of bursting granaries men, women, and children starve. What is to be seen more harrowing in Europe, in the land of the Orient?

Crisis Is Near at Hand

Can these conditions be perpetuated? If so, by what means are they to be permanently established? If we admit that they ought to be perpetuated, no change in the means which have created the calamity need to be made. I do not believe present conditions can be made perpetual. I do not believe the means that have been employed to bring about present conditions are to continue. I believe a crisis is near at hand. I believe that the debauching, crushing, degrading money power will be required to take its hooves off the prostrate millions—who are evincing a mighty unrest. I do not doubt that armies and courts and all the machinery the money power can command will be brought into the contest. I do not doubt that there will be traitors in the camps of those who are loyal to the eternal principles of justice, as there were Tories in 1776. But there is to come a battle of ballots, possibly a battle of bullets and bayonets, when truth shall triumph because "the eternal years are here."[99]

I take no stock in the "decline and fall of Rome" theory. History, in that regard, will not be repeated in the United States of America. The American people are not like the Romans. A century of freedom, instead of centuries of slavery and oppression, will bring forth fruits when the final struggle comes different from anything that ever ripened in the fierce heat of battle. Loyal to law and obedient to its mandates, the time is coming when "we, the people" will declare that bowed forms, as slaves' garb, huts, and peonage are not American, and that the laws and system which create such abominations are not American, and then will come another reconstruction period, and, phoenix-like, Liberty, rejuvenated, will come forth from the ordeal to live and flourish and bless the world.

Regarding Finances:
Letter to the Directors of the ARU[†]

October 29, 1895

Woodstock, Ill., October 29, 1895

Official Letter to Directors

Dear Sirs and Brothers:—

I am under the necessity of addressing you in regard to the finances of the order. Prior to leaving here it was agreed at a meeting of the directors that each should keep, in the moneys advanced him, within the revenues that came to the General Union through his efforts. I have just had a financial statement made which shows that, including the amounts advanced on leaving here, a total of about $1,100 has been advanced to the directors and that not to exceed $200 in all has been received by the General Union since their leaving here, as a result of their efforts.

Of course, I realize the great difficulties under which the directors are working and I have no complaint to make, but under the circumstances I am compelled to ask that as far as possible each director support himself during the next two or three months, or until the financial condition of the order is

[†] Mimeographed typed document in Special Collections Department, Indiana State University, Terre Haute, through gift of Marguerite Debs Cooper. Not included in Constantine (ed.), *Letters of Eugene V. Debs: Volume 1.*

such that we can again meet our obligations. At this writing there is not only not a dollar in the treasury, but I shall have to make a loan to meet the bills and expenses due on November 1. It is proper that I should say that Brother [Martin J.] Elliott's work has brought very nearly enough revenue to cover amounts advanced him, but others have not succeeded in having any money at all forwarded to the General Union. In this crisis I wish to help all in my power, but I feel I must have the help of all in bearing the burden. I also take it for granted that members of the board expect me to see to it that the agreement above referred to is carried out. The prospects in the near future are very bright, and I feel that we shall soon reach safe ground.

With best wishes, I am as ever,

Yours fraternally,
Eugene V. Debs

The Aristocracy of Wealth[†]
October 30, 1895

Woodstock, Ill, October 30, 1895

The world is called upon to contemplate several kinds of aristocrats, a human being "who is overbearing in temper or habits, a proud or haughty person," and who, if by any freak of fortune obtains place and power, becomes to the extent of such power, an autocrat, a pompous, overbearing person, who—

> Dress'd in a little brief authority
> Plays such fantastic tricks
> Before high heaven as makes the
> Angels weep.[100]

In the United States of America, the founders of the government, having not only holy horror but an unmitigated contempt for aristocracy and autocracy, provided in the fundamental law of the Republic that "titles of nobility"

---

† Published as "Debs on Aristocracy" in *Chicago Mail–Evening Press*, vol. 14, whole no 4509 (November 4, 1895), 2.

should never be granted. They comprehended fully the vulgar ambition of certain degenerate creatures in the form of men, who above all things desired titles of nobility that they might strut and parade before the common people as persons who, by virtue of titles, were separate and apart from them, above and superior to them, having a right to direct and control them, and while by the constitutional interdiction these contemptible poltroons cannot be made dukes "and a' that," they take advantage of wealth or position to play the role of what Josh Billings[101] called "damphools"[102] just the same as if they had been decorated with titles and were under the law permitted to "lord it" over their fellow mortals who had not climbed the aristocratic pole and made themselves as ridiculous as the fabled monkey.

As the years speed by and colossal fortunes multiply, the country witnesses the steady increase of the untitled aristocrats who propose to shape the destinies of the masses and who have succeeded in their designs to an extent that well-founded alarm exists in every section of the land.

The aristocracy of wealth is now as well established in the United States as is the aristocracy of blood in any European country, and the laws as they exist confer upon this aristocracy unlimited power to compel labor to do its bidding or accept the penalties of disobedience, which include idleness and all the untold ills of which idleness is the prolific parent.

It is universally admitted as an economic axiom that labor creates all wealth, but it so happens that the power which wealth creates never accrues to labor; on the contrary, this wealth, the product of labor, secured by others under the operation of laws piratical in purpose and practice, is made the most implacable foe of labor that exists in the world. And there can be found no more notable instances of this damnable outcome than are presented in the Homestead and Pullman domination of the aristocracy and autocracy of wealth, fostered, guarded, promoted, and protected by what is called law—and what is true of law in Pennsylvania and Illinois is true in every other state of the American union.

The aristocracy of wealth has everything its own way, and constitutions and laws are so framed that the men who create wealth have no rights except to accept what they can get, and if this morsel subjects them to poverty and degradation there is no redress for them. The laws of the state and the power of the state, civil and military, are on the side of the aristocracy of wealth, and there is no appeal.

It is true that workingmen, by their ballots, could change such outrageous conditions, but there are leaders (?), heaven save the mark, steeped to their eyes in partisan prejudices and jealousies, who cry out that workingmen must "steer clear" of politics, as if there was something in politics that would or could lead them into conditions still more deplorable. Thus it happens that there are labor leaders who are playing into the hands of the aristocracy of wealth and helping on the subjugation and degradation of labor.

The question arises just here, is organized labor engaged in creating still another class of aristocrats and autocrats; men who, wearing certain titles and occupying certain positions, do the very things which preeminently distinguish the autocrats of wealth, when the supreme demand is that labor shall unify its forces in order that infamous laws may be repealed and infamous decisions reversed, without which all labor organizations are helpless and all workingmen in slavery, while the aristocracy of wealth proceeds with slight deviations and inconveniences in carrying out its policy of spoliation?

It is high time that organized labor should learn the power and the imperative necessity of a unified ballot of all who work for their daily bread without regard to color or sex. It is also high time that allegiance to parties which make laws for the protection of capitalists and the subjugation of labor should be abandoned, and that men should be found to enact and administer laws for the equal protection of labor, which creates all capital and carries forward all the industries of the world.

In this unification of labor forces for the amelioration of conditions by constitutional and lawful methods, such as are contemplated in political action, there is no need of interfering with trade unions or any of the numerous social and industrial organizations or encroaching in the slightest degree upon their province or functions. On the contrary, labor organizations would be indefinitely strengthened by such a policy. The proposition is so self-evident as to require no argument for its elucidation.

Until that time comes, capitalism will be in power and have absolute control. Capitalism will make the laws and administer them, control the army, bribe the press, silence the pulpit, and workingmen will pay the penalty of their ignorance and stupidity in abject slavery.

Eugene V. Debs

Letter to Thomas J. Elderkin in Chicago[†]

October 31, 1895

Woodstock, Ill., October 31 [1895]

Thomas J. Elderkin,
President, Trade and Labor Assembly,
Chicago, Ill.

Dear Sir and Brother:—

Your favor of the 20th inst. [October 20, 1895] in reference to the reception to be tendered my colleagues and myself upon my release and the condition upon which the Trade and Labor Assembly of Chicago will participate therein has been received and noted.

I quote from your letter as follows:

> Some say you advocate the abolishment of trade union theories, while others declare you are still a friend and strong advocate of trade unions. The question of a demonstration by the Trade and Labor Assembly upon the occasion of your release from jail November 22, rests upon your position toward trade unions, for if you still believe trade unions are adequate for the emancipation of the workingmen the Trade and Labor Assembly will cheerfully join in the demonstration.

Permit me to decline in advance any "demonstration" on the part of persons whose sentiments are represented in the foregoing proposition. If the Trade and Labor Assembly of Chicago can afford to make such a proposition, I cannot afford to consider it. For 21 years I have been defining my "position" in relation to trade unions, and on all proper occasions I have given full, free, and unequivocal expression to my views, but I must respectfully decline to do so for a consideration, even though that consideration be in the form of a reception upon my release from a jail in which I have served a sentence of six months for my fealty to the principles of the very trade unions which now propose to interrogate me as to my "position" in relation to their interests.

[†]   Published as part of Stephen Marion Reynolds, "Life of Eugene V. Debs" in *Debs: His Life, Writings, and Speeches* (Girard, KS: Appeal to Reason, 1908), 42–44. Not included in Constantine (ed.), *Letters of Eugene V. Debs: Volume 1.*

The statement that I am or ever have been hostile to trade unions and that I am advocating or intending to advocate their "abolishment" is too palpably false and malicious to merit an instant's contention. There is, of course, a purpose in having this question raised at this time, but it is difficult for me to conceive that it emanates from a Trade and Labor Assembly. If it had its origin in the General Managers' Association or some kindred body, it would be in consonance with the fitness of things and I should readily understand it.

Permit me to say, therefore, that the proposed reception is in no sense a personal affair. I understand it to be tendered in recognition of the principles involved in the illegal and unjust imprisonment of my colleagues and myself, and as voicing abhorrence of, and protest against, judicial despotism in the United States, which constitutional rights are cloven down in the interest of corporate wealth.

I have not asked for a reception and I am sure I have no ambition to be the guest of anyone who finds it necessary to place me on the witness stand and interrogate me as to whether I am his friend or his enemy, especially after serving six months in jail for advocating his rights and defending his interests. To make myself perfectly clear, if there are those who have any doubt as to my "position," then, so far as I am concerned, I advise them to take the safe side and stay away from the intended reception.

The charge that I have "changed my views" in regard to trades unions, which, as I am informed, prompted the action and attitude of your assembly, is simply a pretext which will serve the purpose for which it was designed if it creates dissension, arouses a sentiment unfavorable to the reception, and makes of that occasion a dismal failure. The reason for this is so apparent that it will readily suggest itself. I admit that my views are subject to "change," but not of the legal tender variety.

I beg to assure you that no discourtesy is intended, although if the Trade and Labor Assembly had intended a deliberate affront it could not have adopted a method better calculated to serve that purpose than by attempting to pillory me in public at this time on the question of my allegiance to organized labor.

I have the honor to subscribe myself, with best wishes.

Yours fraternally,
Eugene V. Debs

"The Policy of the Great Northern Is Dishonest and Disreputable": Statement to the Associated Press[†]

November 4, 1895

The policy of the Great Northern Company in relation to its employees is totally dishonest and disreputable. For several months a scheme has been in operation to disrupt the American Railway Union, notwithstanding the solemn pledge of President [James J.] Hill that no employee should be interfered with on account of his connection with the organization. The strike of April 1894 resulted in an agreement between the company and the union, which was effected May 1, under the auspices of a local board of arbitration composed wholly of merchants and manufacturers, and of which Charles A. Pillsbury was chairman. Tremendous reductions, ranging from 10 to 40 percent, had been made by the company, and these were restored by the board. From that day to this the company has not lived up to its agreement one hour. Competent and trustworthy employees have been discharged again and again for no other reason than that they belonged to the union.

President Hill chafed under the verdict of the board. He smarted under defeat. His imperious will brooks neither restraint nor opposition. That he secretly resolved to exterminate the union there is not the slightest doubt. A few months ago I went over the entire system and I know whereof I speak. There have been so-called readjustments which have invariably resulted in reductions of wages. I can prove to the satisfaction of any honest man that the company has broken faith with its employees in the most flagrant and shameless manner. President Hill gave his word of honor that he would always hear any grievance his employees might have, either through themselves or anyone they might select to represent them. He made this declaration in the presence of the board of arbitration, and Mr. Pillsbury will bear testimony to the fact; not only this, but I have it in writing over his own signature. Yet, notwithstanding this, he refused in a cold-blooded manner to give audience to a duly constituted committee appointed by his employees

---

[†]   Published as part of the article "Great Northern" in the *Railway Times*, vol. 2, no. 22 (November 15, 1895), 3.

to simply ask him to carry out the company's agreement which the men had accepted in good faith.

This is how much value James J. Hill places on his honor. He makes the excuse that some of the committee are not now in the service of the company. As a matter of fact, the intimidating policy of the company has overawed the employees so that they fear to serve on a committee. They know that service on a committee means certain discharge. Hence they have submitted until their condition is one of slavish fear and subjection. Whether the employees strike or not will be determined by themselves. I am unable to foretell their decision. Directors [Sylvester] Keliher and [Roy] Goodwin, in conjunction with the board of mediation, are on the ground, and I have faith in their judgment and will approve their course whatever that may be. According to my advices the Great Northern Company has already begun the hiring of thugs and ex-convicts at various points.

Let me say that unless the feeling among the people along the Great Northern system has changed since last spring, something more than a strike may develop if James J. Hill's policy of duplicity, dishonesty, and subjection forces the men to abandon their employment. I know that the farmers and shippers and the people generally in that section are thoroughly aroused. They comprehend the situation perfectly and are wholly in sympathy with the wronged employees.

Liberty:
Speech Delivered on Release from Woodstock Jail at Battery D, Chicago[†]

November 22, 1895

Manifestly the spirit of '76 still survives. The fires of liberty and noble aspirations are not yet extinguished. I greet you tonight as lovers of liberty and as despisers of despotism. I comprehend the significance of this demonstration and appreciate the honor that makes it possible for me to be your guest on such an occasion. The vindication and glorification of American principles of government, as proclaimed to the world in the Declaration of Independence, is the high purpose of this convocation.

Speaking for myself personally, I am not certain whether this is an occasion for rejoicing or lamentation. I confess to a serious doubt as to whether this day marks my deliverance from bondage to freedom or my doom from freedom to bondage. Certain it is, in the light of recent judicial proceedings, that I stand in your presence stripped of my constitutional rights as a freeman and shorn of the most sacred prerogatives of American citizenship, and what is true of myself is true of every other citizen who has the temerity to protest against corporation rule or question the absolute sway of the money power. It is not law nor the administration of law of which I complain. It is the flagrant violation of the Constitution, the total abrogation of law and the usurpation of judicial and despotic power, by virtue of which my colleagues and myself were committed to jail, against which I enter my solemn protest, and any honest analysis of the proceedings must sustain the haggard truth of the indictment.

In a letter recently written by the venerable Judge Trumbull, that eminent jurist says: "The doctrine announced by the Supreme Court in the Debs case, carried to its logical conclusion, places every citizen at the mercy of any prejudiced or malicious federal judge who may think proper to imprison him." This is the deliberate conclusion of one of the purest, ablest, and most distinguished judges the Republic has produced. The authority of Judge Trumbull upon this

---

[†]   Published in the *Chicago Chronicle*, November 23, 1895. Reissued as a pamphlet by
      E. V. Debs & Co. as part of the Progressive Thought series, vol. 1, no. 1 (January
      1899).

question will not be impeached by anyone whose opinions are not deformed or debauched.

At this juncture I deem it proper to voice my demands for a trial by a jury of my peers. At the instigation of the railroad corporations centering here in Chicago, I was indicted for conspiracy and I insist upon being tried as to my innocence or guilt. It will be remembered that the trial last winter terminated very abruptly on account of a sick juror. It was currently reported at the time that this was merely a pretext to abandon the trial and thus defeat the vindication of a favorable verdict, which seemed inevitable, and which would have been in painfully embarrassing contrast with the sentence previously pronounced by Judge Woods in substantially the same case. Whether this be true or not, I do not know. I do know, however, that I have been denied a trial, and here and now I demand a hearing of my case. I am charged with conspiracy to commit a crime, and if guilty I should go to the penitentiary. All I ask is a fair trial and no favor. If the counsel for the government, alias the railroads, have been correctly quoted in the press, the case against me is "not to be pressed," as they "do not wish to appear in the light of persecuting the defendants." I repel with scorn their professed mercy. Simple justice is the demand. I am not disposed to shrink from the fullest responsibility for my acts. I have had time for meditation and reflection and I have no hesitancy in declaring that under the same circumstances I would pursue precisely the same policy. So far as my acts are concerned, I have neither apology nor regrets.

Dismissing this branch of the subject, permit me to assure you that I am not here to bemoan my lot. In my vocabulary there are no wails of despondency or despair. However gloomy the future may appear to others, I have an abiding faith in the ultimate triumph of the right. My heart responds to the sentiments of the poet who says:

> Swing back today, O prison gate,
> O winds, stream out the stripes and stars,
> O men, once more in high debate
> Denounce injunction rule and czars.
> By Freedom's travail pangs we swear
> That slavery's chains we will not wear.
>
> Ring joyously, O prison bell,
> O iron tongue, the truth proclaim;
> O winds and lightnings, speed to tell
> That ours is not a czar's domain.
> By all the oracles divine

We pledge defense of Freedom's shrine.

O freemen true! O sons of sires!
O sons of men who dared to die!
O fan to life old Freedom's fires
And light with glory Freedom's sky.
Then swear by God's eternal throne,
America shall be Freedom's home.

O workingmen! O Labor's hosts!
O men of courage, heart and will;
O far and wide send Labor's toasts
Till every heart feels Freedom's thrill,
And freemen's shouts like billows roar
O'er all the land from shore to shore.[103]

"Liberty" is not a word of modern coinage. "Liberty" and "slavery" are primal words, like good and evil, right and wrong; they are opposites and coexistent.

There has been no liberty in the world since the gift, like sunshine and rain, came down from heaven, for the maintenance of which man has not been required to fight, and man's complete degradation is secured only when subjugation and slavery have sapped him of the last spark of the noble attributes of his nature and reduced him to the unresisting inertness of a clod.

The theme tonight is personal liberty; or, giving it its full height, depth, and breadth, American liberty, something that Americans have been accustomed to eulogize since the foundation of the Republic, and multiplied thousands of them continue in the habit to this day because they do not recognize the truth that in the imprisonment of one man in defiance of all constitutional guarantees, the liberties of all are invaded and placed in peril. In saying this, I conjecture I have struck the keynote of alarm that has convoked this vast audience.

For the first time in the records of all the ages, the inalienable rights of man, "life, liberty, and the pursuit of happiness," were proclaimed July 4, 1776.

It was then that crowns, scepters, thrones, and the divine right of kings to rule sunk together and man expanded to glorious liberty and sovereignty. It was then that the genius of liberty, speaking to all men in the commanding voice of eternal truth, bade them assert their heaven-decreed prerogatives and emancipate themselves from bondage. It was a proclamation countersigned by the Infinite—and man stood forth the coronated sovereign of the world, free as the tides that flow, free as the winds that blow, and on that primal morning when creation was complete, the morning stars and the sons of God, in anthem chorus, sang the song of liberty. It may be a fancy, but within the limitless boundaries of the imagination I can conceive of no other theme more appropriate to weave into the harmonies of freedom. The Creator had surveyed his work and pronounced it good,[104] but nothing can be called good in human affairs with liberty eliminated. As well talk of air without nitrogen, or water without oxygen, as of goodness without liberty.

It does not matter that the Creator has sown with stars the fields of ether and decked the earth with countless beauties for man's enjoyment. It does not matter that air and ocean teem with the wonders of innumerable forms of life to challenge man's admiration and investigation. It does not matter that nature spreads forth all her scenes of beauty and gladness and pours forth the melodies of her myriad-tongued voices for man's delectation. If liberty is ostracized and exiled, man is a slave, and the world rolls in space and whirls around the sun a gilded prison, a doomed dungeon, and though painted in all the enchanting hues that infinite art could command, it must still stand forth a blotch amidst the shining spheres of the sidereal heavens, and those who cull from the vocabularies of nations, living or dead, their flashing phrases with which to apostrophize liberty, are engaged in perpetuating the most stupendous delusion the ages have known. Strike down liberty, no matter by what subtle and infernal art the deed is done, the spinal cord of humanity is sundered and the world is paralyzed by the indescribable crime.

Strike the fetters from the slave, give him liberty, and he becomes an inhabitant of a new world. He looks abroad and beholds life and joy in all things around him. His soul expands beyond all boundaries. Emancipated by the genius of liberty, he aspires to communion with all that is noble and beautiful, feels himself allied to all the higher order of intelligences, and walks abroad, redeemed from animalism, ignorance, and superstition, a new being throbbing with glorious life.

What pen or tongue, from primeval man to the loftiest intellect of the present generation, has been able to fittingly anathematize the more than satanic crime of stealing the jewel of liberty from the crown of manhood and reducing the victim of the burglary to slavery or to prison, to gratify those monsters of iniquity who for some inscrutable reason are given breath to contaminate the atmosphere and poison every fountain and stream designed to bless the world?

It may be questioned if such interrogatories are worth the time required to state them, and I turn from their consideration to the actualities of my theme. As Americans, we have boasted of our liberties and continue to boast of them. They were once the nation's glory, and, if some have vanished, it may be well to remember that a remnant still remains. Out of prison, beyond the limits of Russian injunctions, out of reach of a deputy marshal's club, above the throttling clutch of corporations and the enslaving power of plutocracy, out of range of the government's machine guns and knowing the location of judicial traps and deadfalls, Americans may still indulge in the exaltation of liberty, though pursued through every lane and avenue of life by the baying hounds of usurped and unconstitutional power, glad if when night lets down her sable curtains, they are out of prison, though still the wage-slaves of a plutocracy which, were it in the celestial city, would wreck every avenue leading up to the throne of the Infinite by stealing the gold with which they are paved, and debauch heaven's supreme court to obtain a decision that the command "thou shalt not steal" is unconstitutional.

Liberty, be it known, is for those only who dare strike the blow to secure and retain the priceless boon. It has been written that the "love of liberty with life is given" and that life itself is an inferior gift; that with liberty exiled life is a continuous curse and that "an hour of liberty is worth an eternity of bondage." It would be an easy task to link together gilded periods extolling liberty until the mind, weary with delight, becomes oblivious of the fact that while dreaming of security, the blessings we magnified had, one by one and little by little, disappeared, emphasizing the truth of the maxim that "eternal vigilance is the price of liberty."[105]

Is it worthwhile to iterate that all men are created free and that slavery and bondage are in contravention of the Creator's decree and have their origin in man's depravity?

If liberty is a birthright which has been wrested from the weak by the strong, or has been placed in peril by those who were commissioned to guard it as Gheber priests watch the sacred fires they worship,[106] what is to be done? Leaving all other nations, kindred, and tongues out of the question, what is the duty of Americans? Above all, what is the duty of American workingmen whose liberties have been placed in peril? They are not hereditary bondsmen. Their fathers were free born—their sovereignty none denied, and their children yet have the ballot. It has been called "a weapon that executes a free man's will as lighting does the will of God." It is a metaphor pregnant with life and truth. There is nothing in our government it cannot remove or amend. It can make and unmake presidents and congresses and courts. It can abolish unjust laws and consign to eternal odium and oblivion unjust judges, strip from them their robes and gowns, and send them forth unclean as lepers to bear the burden of merited obloquy as Cain with the mark of a murderer.[107] It can sweep away trusts, syndicates, corporations, monopolies, and every other abnormal development of the money power designed to abridge the liberties of workingmen and enslave them by the degradation incident to poverty and enforced idleness, as cyclones scatter the leaves of the forest. The ballot can do all this and more. It can give our civilization its crowning glory—the Cooperative Commonwealth.

To the unified hosts of American workingmen fate has committed the charge of rescuing American liberties from the grasp of the vandal horde that have placed them in peril, by seizing the ballot and wielding it to regain the priceless heritage and to preserve and transmit it without scar or blemish to the generations yet to come.

> Snatch from the ashes of their sires
> The embers of their former fires,
> And he who in the strife expires
> Will add to theirs a name of fear
> That Tyranny shall quake to hear.[108]

Standing before you tonight reclothed, in theory at least, with the prerogatives of a free man, in the midst of free men, what more natural, what more in consonance with the proprieties of the occasion, than to refer to the incarceration of myself and associate officials of the American Railway Union in the county jail at Woodstock?

I have no ambition to avail myself of this occasion to be sensational, or to thrust my fellow prisoners and myself into prominence. My theme expands to proportions which obscure the victims of judicial tyranny, and yet, regardless of reluctance, it so happens by the decree of circumstances that personal references are unavoidable. To wish it otherwise would be to deplore the organization of the American Railway Union and every effort that great organization has made to extend a helping hand to oppressed, robbed, suffering, and starving men, women, and children, the victims of corporate greed and rapacity. It would be to bewail every lofty attribute of human nature, lament the existence of the golden rule, and wish the world were a jungle, inhabited by beasts of prey, that the seas were peopled with sharks and devilfish, and that between the earth and the stars only vultures held winged sway.

The American Railway Union was born with a sympathetic soul. Its ears were attuned to the melodies of mercy, to catch the whispered wailings of the oppressed. It had eyes to scan the fields of labor, a tongue to denounce the wrong, hands to grasp the oppressed, and a will to lift them out of the sloughs of despondency to highlands of security and prosperity.

Here and now I challenge the records, and if in all the land the American

Railway Union has an enemy, one or a million, I challenge them all to stand up before the labor world and give a reason why they have maligned and persecuted the order. I am not here to assert the infallibility of the organization or its officials, or to claim exemption from error. But I am here to declare to every friend of American toilers, regardless of banner, name, or craft, that if the American Railway Union has erred, it has been on the side of sympathy, mercy, and humanity—zeal in a great cause, devotion to the spirit of brotherhood which knows no artificial boundaries, whose zones are mapped by lines of truth as vivid as lightning, and whose horizon is measured only by the eye of faith in man's redemption from slavery.

I hold it to have been inconceivable that an organization of workingmen, animated by such inspirations and aspirations, should have become the target for the shafts of judicial and governmental malice.

But the fact that such was the case brings into haggard prominence a condition of affairs that appeals to all thoughtful men in the ranks of organized labor and all patriotic citizens, regardless of vocation, who note the subtle invasions of the liberties of the American people by the courts, sustained by an administration that is equally dead to the guarantees of the Constitution.

It is in no spirit of laudation that I aver here tonight that it has fallen to the lot of the American Railway Union to arouse workingmen to a sense of the perils that environ their liberties.

In the great Pullman strike the American Railway Union challenged the power of corporations in a way that had not previously been done, and the analyzation of this fact serves to expand it to proportions that the most conservative men of the nation regard with alarm.

It must be borne in mind that the American Railway Union did not challenge the government. It threw down no gauntlet to courts or armies—it simply resisted the invasion of the rights of workingmen by corporations. It challenged and defied the power of corporations. Thrice armed with a just cause, the organization believed that justice would win for labor a notable victory, and the records proclaim that its confidence was not misplaced.

The corporations, left to their own resources of money, mendacity, and malice, of thugs and ex-convicts, leeches and lawyers, would have been overwhelmed with defeat, and the banners of organized labor would have floated triumphant in the breeze.

This the corporations saw and believed—hence the crowning act of infamy in which the federal courts and the federal armies participated, and which culminated in the defeat of labor.

Had this been all, the simple defeat of a labor organization, however disrupted and despoiled, this grand convocation of the lovers of liberty would never have been heard of. The robbed, idle, and blacklisted victims of defeat would have suffered in silence in their darkened homes amidst the sobbings and wailings of wives and children. It would have been the oft-repeated old, old story, heard along the track of progress and poverty for three-quarters of a century in the United States, where brave men, loyal to law and duty, have struck to better their condition or to resist degradation, and have gone down in defeat. But the defeat of the American Railway Union involved questions of law, constitution, and government which, all things considered, are without a parallel in court and governmental proceedings under the constitution of the Republic. And it is this judicial and administrative usurpation of power to override the rights of states and strike down the liberties of the people that has conferred upon the incidents connected with the Pullman strike such commanding importance as to attract the attention of men of the highest attainments in constitutional law and of statesmen who, like Jefferson, view with alarm the processes by which the Republic is being wrecked and a despotism reared upon its ruins.

I have said that in the great battle of labor fought in 1894 between the American Railway Union and the corporations banded together under the name of the "General Managers' Association," victory would have perched upon the standards of labor if the battle had been left to these contending forces—and this statement, which has been verified and established beyond truthful contradiction, suggests the inquiry, what other resources had the corporations aside from their money and the strength which their federation conferred?

In replying to the question, I am far within the limits of accepted facts when I say the country stood amazed as the corporations put forth their latent powers to debauch such departments of the government as were required to defeat labor in the greatest struggle for the right that was ever chronicled in the United States.

Defeated at every point, their plans all frustrated, outgeneraled in tactics and strategy, while the hopes of labor were brightening and victory was in sight, the corporations, goaded to desperation, played their last card in the game of oppression by an appeal to the federal judiciary and to the federal administration. To this appeal the response came quick as lightning from a storm cloud. It was an exhibition of the debauching power of money which the country had never before beheld.

The people had long been familiar with such expressions as "money talks," "money rules," and they had seen the effects of its power in legislatures and in Congress. They were conversant with Jay Gould's methods of gaining his legal victories by "buying a judge" in critical cases. They had tracked this money power, this behemoth beast of prey, into every corporate enterprise evolved by our modern civilization, as hunters track tigers in India jungles, but never before in the history of the country had they seen it grasp with paws and jaws the government of the United States and bend it to its will and make it a mere travesty of its pristine grandeur.

The people had seen this money power enter the church, touch the robed priest at the altar, blotch his soul, freeze his heart and make him a traitor to his consecrated vows, and send him forth a Judas with a bag containing the price of his treason; or, if true to his conviction, ideas, and ideals, to suffer the penalty of ostracism, to be blacklisted and to seek in vain for a sanctuary in which to expound Christ's doctrine of the brotherhood of man.

The people had seen this money power enter a university and grasp a professor and hurl him headlong into the street because every faculty of mind, redeemed by education and consecrated to truth, pointed out and illumined new pathways to the goal of human happiness and national glory.

The people had seen this money power practicing every art of duplicity, growing more arrogant and despotic as it robbed one and crushed another, building its fortifications of the bones of its victims, and its palaces out of the profits of its piracies, until purple and fine linen on the one side and rags upon the other side defined conditions as mountain ranges and rivers define the boundaries of nations—palaces on the hills, with music and dancing and the luxuries of all climes, earth, air, and sea—huts in the valley, dark and dismal, where the music is the dolorous "song of the shirt"[109] and the luxuries rags and crusts.

These things had been seen by the people, but it was reserved for them in the progress of the Pullman strike to see this money power, by the fiat of corporations, grasp one by one the departments of the government and compel them to do its bidding as in old plantation days the master commanded the obedience of his chattel slaves.

The corporations first attacked the judicial department of the government, a department which, according to Thomas Jefferson, has menaced the integrity of the Republic from the beginning.

They did not attack the supreme bench. A chain is no stronger than its weakest link, and the corporations knew where that was and the amount of strain it would bear. How did they attack this weakling in the judicial chain?

I am aware that innuendoes, dark intimations of venality, are not regarded as courageous forms of arraignment, and yet the judicial despotism which marked every step of the proceedings by which my official associates and myself were doomed to imprisonment was marked by infamies, supported by falsehoods and perjuries as destitute of truth as are the Arctic regions of orange blossoms.

Two men quarreled because one had killed the other's dog with an axe. The owner of the dog inquired, "When my dog attacked you, why did you not use some less deadly weapon?" The other replied, "Why did not your dog come at me with the end that had no teeth in it?" There is an adage which says, "Fight the devil with fire." In this connection, why may it not be intimated that a judge who pollutes his high office at the behest of the money power has the hinges of his knees lubricated with oil from the tank of the corporation, that thrift may follow humiliating obedience to its commands?

If not this, I challenge the world to assign a reason why a judge, under the solemn obligation of an oath to obey the Constitution, should, in a temple dedicated to justice, stab the Magna Carta of American liberty to death in the interest of corporations, that labor might be disrobed of its inalienable rights and those who advocated its claim to justice imprisoned as if they were felons.

You may subject such acts of despotism to the severest analysis, you may probe for the motive, you may dissect the brain and lay bare the quivering heart, and, when you have completed the task, you will find a tongue in every gash of your dissecting knife uttering the one word "pelf."[110] Once upon a time a corporation dog of good reputation was charged with killing sheep, though he had never been caught in the act. The corporation had always found him to be an obedient dog, willing to lick the hand of his master, and declared that he was a peaceable and law-abiding dog; but one day upon investigation the dog was found to have wool in his teeth and thenceforward, though the corporation stood manfully by him, he was believed to be a sheep-killing dog. The world has no means of knowing what methods corporations employ to obtain despotic decrees in their interest, but it is generally believed that if an examination could be made, there would be found wool in the teeth of the judge.

I do not profess to be a student of heredity, and yet I am persuaded that men inherit the peculiarities of the primal molecules from which they have been evolved. If the modern man, in spite of our civilizing influences, books, stage, and rostrum, has more devil than divinity in his nature, where rests the blame?

Leaving the interrogatory unanswered, as it has been in all the past, it is only required to say that men with the ballot make a fatal mistake when they select mental and moral deformities and clothe them with despotic power.

When such creatures are arrayed in the insignia of authority, right, justice, and liberty are forever in peril.

What reasons exist today for rhetorical apostrophes to the constitution of the Republic? Those who are familiar by experience, or by reading, with the pathways of the storms on the ocean will recall recollections of ships with their sails rent and torn by the fury of the winds, rolling upon the yeasty billows and flying signals of distress. Clouds had for days obscured sun and stars and only the eye of omnipotence could tell whither the hulk was drifting—and today the constitution of our ship of state, the chart by which she had been steered for a century, has encountered a judicial tornado and only the gods of our fathers can tell whither she is drifting. True, Longfellow, inspired by the genius of hope, sang of the good old ship:

> We know what Master laid thy keel,
> What Workmen wrought thy ribs of steel.
> Who made each mast, and sail, and rope,
> What anvils rang, what hammers beat,
> In what a forge and what a heat
> Were shaped the anchors of thy hope![111]

But the poet wrote before the chart by which the good old ship sailed had been mutilated and torn and flung aside as a thing of contempt; before Shiras "flopped"[112] and before corporations knew the price of judges, legislators, and public officials as certainly as Armour[113] knows the price of pork and mutton.

Longfellow wrote before men with heads as small as chipmunks and pockets as big as balloons were elevated to public office, and before the corporation ruled in courts and legislative halls as the fabled bull ruled in a china shop.

No afflatus, however divine, no genius, though saturated with the inspiring waters of Hippocrene,[114] could now write in a spirit of patriotic fire of the old constitution, nor ever again until the people by the all-pervading power of the ballot have repaired the old chart, closed the rents, and obscured the judicial dagger holes made for the accommodation of millionaires and corporations, through which they drive their four-in-hands[115] as if they were Cumberland gaps.

Here, this evening, I am inclined to indulge in eulogistic phrase of liberty because once more I am permitted to mingle with my fellow citizens outside of prison locks and bars.

Shakespeare said:

> Sweet are the uses of adversity,
> Which, like the toad, ugly and venomous,
> Wears yet a precious jewel in his head.[116]

I know something of adversity, and with such philosophy as I could summon have extracted what little sweetness it contained. I know little of toads, except that of the genus judicial, and if they have a precious jewel in their heads or hearts it has not fallen to my lot to find it, though the corporations seem to have been more successful.

The immortal bard also wrote that

> This our life, exempt from public haunt,
> Finds tongues in trees, books in running brooks,
> Sermons in stones, and good in everything.[117]

If to be behind prison bars is to be "exempt from public haunt," then for the past six months I may claim such exemption, with all the rapture to be found in listening to the tongues of trees, to the charming lessons taught by the books of the running brooks and to the profound sermons of the stones. There is not a tree on the Woodstock prison campus, or nearby, to whose tongued melodies or maledictions I have not in fancy listened when liberty, despotism, or justice was the theme.

The bard of Avon, the one Shakespeare of all the ages, was up to high-water mark of divine inspiration when he said there were those who could find tongues in trees, and never since trees were planted in the garden of Eden has the tongue of a tree voiced a sentiment hostile to liberty.

Thus, when in prison and exempt from judicial persecution, the tongues of trees as well as the tongues of friends taught me that sweets could be extracted from adversity.

Nor was I less fortunate when I permitted my fancy to see a book in a running brook as it laughed and sang and danced its way to the sea, and find that on every page was written a diviner song to liberty and love and sympathy than was ever sung by human voice.

And as for the stones in Woodstock prison, they were forever preaching sermons and their themes were all things good and evil among men.

In prison my life was a busy one, and the time for meditation and to give the imagination free rein was when the daily task was over and night's sable curtains enveloped the world in darkness, relieved only by the sentinel stars and the earth's silver satellite "walking in lovely beauty to her midnight throne."[118] It was at such times that the "Reverend Stones" preached their sermons, sometimes rising in grandeur to the Sermon on the Mount.

It might be a question in the minds of some if this occasion warrants the indulgence of the fancy. It will be remembered that Aesop taught the world by fables and Christ by parables, but my recollection is that the old "stone preachers" were as epigrammatic as an unabridged dictionary.

I remember one old divine who, one night, selected for his text George M. Pullman, and said: "George is a bad egg, handle him with care. Should you crack his shell the odor would depopulate Chicago in an hour." All said "Amen" and the services closed. Another old sermonizer, who said he had been preaching since man was a molecule, declared he had of late years studied corporations, and that they were warts on the nose of our national industries— that they were vultures whose beaks and claws were tearing and mangling the vitals of labor and transforming workingmen's homes into caves. Another old stone said he knew more about strikes than Carroll D. Wright,[119] and that he was present when the slaves built the pyramids; that God Himself had taught His lightning, thunderbolts, winds, waves, and earthquakes to strike, and that strikes would proceed, with bullets or ballots, until workingmen, no longer deceived and cajoled by their enemies, would unify, proclaim their sovereignty, and walk the earth free men.

Oh, yes, Shakespeare was right when he said there were sermons in stones. I recall one rugged-visaged old stone preacher who claimed to have been a pavement bowlder in a street of heaven before the gold standard was adopted, and who discussed courts. He said they had been antagonizing the decrees of heaven since the day when Lucifer was cast into the bottomless pit. Referring to our Supreme Court he said it was a nest of rodents forever gnawing at the stately pillars supporting the temple of our liberties. I recall how his eyes, as he lifted their stony lids, flashed indignation like orbs of fire, and how his stony lips quivered as he uttered his maledictions of judicial treason to constitutional liberty.

But occasionally some old bald-headed ashler,[120] with a heart beating responsive to every human joy or sorrow, would preach a sermon on love or sympathy or some other noble trait that in spite of heredity still lived even in the heart of stones. One old divine, having read some of the plutocratic papers on the Pullman strike and their anathemas of sympathy, when one workingman's heart, throbbing responsive to the divine law of love, prompted him to aid his brother in distress, discussed sympathy. He said sympathy was one of the perennial flowers of the celestial city, and that angels had transplanted it in Eden for the happiness of Adam and Eve, and that the winds had scattered the seed throughout the earth. He said there was no humanity, no elevating, refining, ennobling influences in operation where there was no sympathy. Sympathy, he said, warmed in every ray of the sun, freshened in every breeze that scattered over the earth the perfume of flowers, and glowed with the divine scintillation of the stars in all the expanse of the heavens.

Referring to the men and women of other labor organizations who had sympathized with the American Railway Union in its efforts to rescue Pullman's slaves from death by starvation, the old preacher placed a crown of jeweled eulogies upon their heads and said that in all the mutations of life, in adversity or prosperity, in the vigor of youth or the infirmities of age, there would never come a time to them when like the Peri grasping a penitent's tear as a passport to heaven,[121] they would not cherish as a valued souvenir of all their weary years that one act of sympathy of the victims of the Pullman piracy, and that when presented at the pearly gate of paradise, it would swing wide open and let them in amidst the joyous acclaims of angels.

From such reflections I turn to the practical lessons taught by this "Liberation Day" demonstration. It means that American lovers of liberty are setting in operation forces to rescue their constitutional liberties from the grasp of monopoly and its mercenary hirelings. It means that the people are aroused in view of impending perils and that agitation, organization, and unification are to be the future battle cries of men who will not part with their birthrights and, like Patrick Henry, will have the courage to exclaim: "Give me liberty or give me death!" I have borne with such composure as I could command the imprisonment which deprived me of my liberty. Were I a criminal; were I guilty of crimes meriting a prison cell; had I ever lifted my hand against the life or the liberty of my fellow men; had I ever sought to filch their good name, I would not be here. I would have fled from the haunts of civilization and taken up my residence in some cave where the voice of my kindred is never heard. But I am standing here without a self-accusation of crime or criminal intent festering in my conscience, in the sunlight once more, among my fellow men, contributing as best I can to make this "Liberation Day" from Woodstock prison a memorial day, realizing that, as Lowell sang:

> He's true to God who's true to man; wherever wrong is done,
> To the humblest and the weakest, 'neath the all-beholding sun.
> That wrong is also done to us; and they are slaves most base,
> Whose love of right is for themselves, and not for all their race.[122]

Shall the Standing Army
of the United States Be Increased?[†123]

December 1895

In proposing an increase of the standing army in his late interview at Washington, General Miles simply gives expression to his own well-known views and to the views of his predecessor, General Schofield.[124]

Since the strike in the summer of 1894, both have insisted that the peace and security of the country demanded a large increase in the standing army.

There are those who will agree with these renowned military chieftains, but they are decidedly in the minority. The American people, generally speaking, do not like standing armies, and are not inclined to cultivate the military spirit.

To come directly to the point, what is the purpose of General Miles in having the army increased?

Let us be perfectly frank in answering the interrogatory and avoid all ambiguous terms. General Miles says we have to anticipate "internal dissension" and be prepared for it. What is meant by "internal dissension?" The general does not leave us in doubt. He means labor strikes, though he does not like to use that term.

In plain language, the object is to overawe workingmen who resist corporate greed and rapacity by organized effort and, if need be, allay their hunger pangs and silence their protests with bayonets and bullets. There is no other internal dissension in sight, and the Hayes-Tilden incident[125] is introduced simply as the ghost in the play, to arouse the nation to the frightful possibilities that are in store for it if the army is not increased.

Let it be understood that when the army is called out to interfere in labor disputes it is always for the purpose of subjugating and defeating the workingmen in the interests of capitalism. This has been the unvarying rule, and there is no exception to it. It does not matter that the employers were cruel, tyrannical, and dishonest. It does not matter that the employees had been the victims of greed and piracy and had been reduced to starvation and goaded into desperation—the one duty of the soldiery has always and everywhere been

†   Published in *New York Journal,* unspecified date, December 1895. Reprinted as "More Soldiers: Shall the Standing Army of the United States Be Increased?" in the *Railway Times,* vol. 3, no. 1, (January 1, 1896), 1.

to overwhelm them with force; shoot holes in their emaciated bodies and drain their veins with bayonet thrusts, that a soulless corporation might without resistance gorge itself with the profits of their unrequited toil.

There is still another purpose in having more federal soldiers, and that is to entirely prevent what General Miles is pleased to call "internal dissension."

How is this to be done?

Easily enough. The soldiers are to be quartered near the centers of population where large bodies of workingmen are employed, and their very presence, with their murderous machine guns and their Krag-Jørgensen rifles,[126] will overawe and intimidate workingmen, sap them of their manhood, and reduce them from the dignity of American citizens to the unresisting submissiveness of swine and sheep.

What then? The corporations may proceed with the barbaric sway to cut down wages to the starvation point, and number their employees as ranchmen brand their steers, as is already being done in the large mills in Illinois and Wisconsin, and impose such other conditions as they may see fit, and the workingmen have only to suffer and submit in silence. Victims of industrial piracy, they have only to work their lives out in wretchedness and despair that their masters may gorge themselves with all the luxuries of all climes, and if they attempt to resist the outrage in the way that has been the glory of the nation, the army is promptly ordered out with shotted guns to teach them by the quieting effect of bullets obedience to their masters.

This is the purpose, and this is the only purpose General Miles has in demanding an increase of the standing army. It is strongly intimated that President Cleveland will urge the passage of such a bill in his message to Congress.

I do not doubt it in the least. It would be in perfect consonance with the plutocratic policy of his administration. But will the people, the great mass of liberty-loving American people, accept a policy which contemplates the subversion of their liberties and ultimately the overthrow of the Republic?

That the proceeding, if unchecked, will culminate in a military despotism no man capable of reasoning from cause to effect can doubt. For the workingman it means a bayonet at his back to keep him at his task under such conditions as his master may impose, and he may contemplate the spectacle at his leisure. I maintain that there is neither necessity nor excuse for an increase in our army, and that such an increase would be antagonistic to the spirit of the Constitution and at war with free institutions.

Large standing armies and liberty do not go together. They do not thrive in the same soil. One or the other must give way.

In his farewell address Washington, the father of his country, in alluding to the American people, said:

> They will avoid the necessity of those overgrown military establishments, which, under any form of government, are inauspicious to liberty, and which are to be regarded as particularly hostile to Republican liberty.[127]

Here we have it on the authority of Washington himself that overgrown military establishments are particularly hostile to republican liberty, and no true patriotic American citizen doubts it. It is not to resist foreign invasion, nor to defend against external violence, that the army is to be increased. There is no danger in that direction. It is purely because of "internal dissension," which General Miles deems inevitable, knowing that the commercialism of the times which now operates through monopolies, syndicates, and trusts, is grinding millions of workingmen to atoms, and driving other millions to idleness and desperation. It is not surprising that syndicates cause "internal dissension," but he makes a great and grave mistake if he thinks he can allay trouble by being provided with soldiers enough to murder the hapless victims of man's inhumanity to man.

In these days men do not strike without good cause. If the public could and would stop long enough to examine into the cause of labor disturbances, the results would be far different, and there would be far fewer strikes; but the public has neither time nor inclination to hear the woes of the suffering people. The powers of government and society are against them. The press, as a rule, maligns and misrepresents them. The pulpit is silent. The courts, the army, and nearly all officials are against the half-famished and wholly desperate victims of brutal corporate capital. In the treatment of the poor the doctrine of Christ is wholly ignored. The people see only the riot, and then they are ready to approve and applaud the killing of workingmen by armed soldiers, who are themselves supported by the profits upon the unpaid toil of their victims.

The people do not know, nor do they seem to care to know, that back of this riot, and leading up to it, is a long train of abuses and wrongs which are borne in silence until submission is no longer possible, and that then only do the poor wage-slaves abandon their employment and seek redress of their grievances.

General Miles says: "We should have a military organization capable of protecting life and property against internal attacks." In a time of profound peace this is a sad commentary on existing conditions. From whence are these attacks to come? From the lawless, criminal elements of society? There is not a state in the Union that is not amply able to protect itself against the vicious classes. I doubt it there is a governor in the Union who will assert the contrary. The state militia in the several states is and will be equal to every requirement, and this is in harmony with the American theory of government, save of those who favor a large standing army, who approve the course of President Cleveland in ordering federal troops into a sovereign state in defiance of the Constitution, and in utter disregard of the protest of the governor and of the local authorities. This is despotism pure and simple.

As for the rioting at Chicago during the Pullman strike, and the subsequent bloodshed, it occurred only after the arrival of the federal troops. This is a fact of easy verification. Had there been no federal interference, had affairs been left in control of state and municipal authorities, I doubt if a single life would have been lost or any serious damage to property have occurred.

I do not wish to unnecessarily sound any alarm bells, nor am I desirous of being sensational, but if the money power and its emissaries want to precipitate a fierce and bloody revolution in the United States of America, it cannot more certainly accomplish its design than by increasing the standing army. This will be the initial step toward the cataclysm. The American people are patriotic and peace-loving, and if only half-fed and half-clothed they will be content. If disturbance and turbulence are threatened there is a cause for it, and rather than prepare to murder the unfortunate victims, it would be a thousand times more humane, more to our credit and honor, and more in consonance with our much-vaunted Christian civilization to honestly seek to remove the cause.

Instead of General Miles's program I would have the labor unions in every city and town in the country organize, equip, and maintain a uniform rank, let them drill and learn all the movements and maneuvers of military action, let them bear arms and know how to handle them.

Why not?

The suggestion is strictly in accord with the letter and spirit of the Constitution. They are the mainstay of the republic. They have fought and will have to fight all her battles. With the workingmen of the country trained and equipped for action, the peace and security of the Republic would be assured.

The Ways of Justice[†]

December 1895

We hold these truths to be self-evident—that all men are created equal,
that they are endowed by their Creator with certain inalienable rights;
that among these are life, liberty, and the pursuit of happiness.

—Declaration of Independence

It has been held that in the political institutions of the United States there are two fundamental facts recognized—the sovereignty of the people and the equality of conditions. It is held by eminent jurists that these facts are original, perfect, and uncontrollable.

In the formation of the government under which we live, certain rights of the individual are surrendered, but never an inalienable right, never the right of life, liberty, and the pursuit of happiness.

To invade such rights, to strike them down, is despotism pure and simple.

It does not matter by what method such rights are abridged or destroyed; it does not matter under what circumstances the rights are murdered or who the assassin may be; it does not matter whether a vandal court, a savage, or a sultan perpetrates the crime, nor by what juggling lies are clothed in robes of truth, nor does it matter what high officials surround the bier upon which a dead right is borne to its grave, or what Mark Anthony orations embellish the funeral, the occasion simply celebrates the death of rights essential to freedom, and when they cease to exist, though drums may beat and banners wave and eloquent tongues glorify law, the three cardinal rights—life, liberty, and the pursuit of happiness—lie dead in the presence of the people, and the "sovereignty of the people" and the "equality of conditions" go down together.

It is not to be expected that a despotism is to be proclaimed from the housetops and that the rights of the people are to disappear as when earthquakes swallow down cities. The approach of the calamity will be insidious.

[†]   Published as "Roasts the Courts: Eugene V. Debs Discusses the Ways of Justice" in *The Barbour County Index* (Medicine Lodge, KS), vol. 16, no. 32 (December 25, 1895), 1. This piece was reprinted with identical plates in a number of People's Party–supporting newspapers as if syndicated to that channel.

The subtle and treacherous enemies of liberty will inject into some law a provision to be vitalized at the proper time and made the weapon of those who espouse the cause of wealth against labor.

Such restrictions are largely within the boundaries of facts now in course of development, and provisions which are claimed to answer the demands of the friends of despotic power are said to exist in what are known as the Interstate Commerce law and the anti-trust law, which, as they are interpreted by the courts, uproot and scatter to the winds the right of railroad employees to decide for themselves whether they will continue or abandon work, as they may elect, because, forsooth, this work is of a "public" or "semi-public" character, and hence the public, more properly the government, under the laws which the government enacts, at once reduces the employee to a servitude that must inevitably, unless all sense of liberty and independence is crushed and dead, result in revolution.

One of the astounding phases of the controversy now going forward, involving the inalienable rights of citizens, is the autocratic power exercised by the courts. It is difficult to find words for the proper characterization of this power. In such discussions it becomes necessary to refer to the debasing methods by which certain mental and moral infirmities find their way to the bench and are permitted to don the robes of office. They are often the creatures of a corrupt appointing power and are selected because of their willingness to do the biding of those who are able to pay the price of their treason to justice. Having gained notoriety as corporation lawyers, their study and ambition having been to find law for the protection of the iniquitous practices of corporations, they go upon the bench to continue their corporation practice, until men who have the means are disposed to follow the example of Jay Gould, who said: "When I want a judge I buy him."[128] This debauchery of courts has reached a pass that a majority of the people regard courts, their orders, and decisions with profound suspicion and contempt; and this debauchery, this stupidity which distinguishes certain judges, creates in the public mind a continually intensified scorn, because the people behold in such things only the mockery of justice. They see a petty tyrant called a judge issuing dynamite orders designed for the destruction of the rights of workingmen and their organizations.

The practices of corporations to despoil workingmen are never so much as hinted at; only the rights of corporations to throttle, gag, crush, and degrade their employees receive attention. It was useless to attempt to obscure the facts. Sophisms and chicane have had their day, and it is seen that an effort is being made by the courts to subject employees to conditions such as in former days aroused men to denounce the starry ensign of the nation as a "flaunting lie."

It is held in certain quarters that the courts are not deciding "that strikes are always and everywhere illegal, but only that striking must be done in such a way as not to perpetrate an arbitrary and grievous wrong upon the public." A strike of railroad employees engaged in the train service necessarily and always subjects the public to inconvenience, which is called "a wrong," hence the intimation of the courts and the conclusion of corporations that since quitting employment on the part of employees perpetrates this "wrong," this inconvenience to the public, they shall not abandon their employment. But the courts do not intimate that it would be a "public wrong" or a public inconvenience for corporations at their pleasure to discharge one or 100 employees, or to reduce them to starvation wages and degrade them to peonage, hence it will be observed that neither the courts nor the corporations care a straw for the fundamental fact of "equality of conditions," which, once destroyed, no matter by whom, the ship of state, like a disabled ship at sea, drifts wherever the wind of chance and fate may drive it.

Are we to wait until every shackle is riveted? Are we to insist on crying "peace" when the shotted orders of courts, deadly as bursting bombs, render men as speechless as if they were dead? I ring no alarm bells when there is no danger approaching. I simply invite workingmen to contemplate the shadows of events, as fraught with danger as when Patrick Henry proclaimed: "Give me liberty or give me death."

Let it be understood that the old landmarks are being rapidly obscured, destroyed, forever obliterated. The autocracy of courts, defining by legal jugglery the rights of workingmen, the rights of corporations, and the rights of the people and the equality of conditions, and lobby-made law by debauched votes strike right and left and always at the rights of workingmen. They are shearing from Samson's head his locks of power; they are seeking to make him blind to their purposes; they laugh at his calamity and mock at his fear, but it were better to desist, better to be just, else the labor Samson may sometime grasp the pillars of the temple of despotism in America and reestablish the "sovereignty of the people" and the "equality of conditions" upon its ruins.

Notes

1. This speech, lasting two hours, was delivered by Debs at 8 p.m. to a packed house at Market Hall in St. Paul. It was one of his final public appearances before he and his ARU associates were jailed in Woodstock, Illinois, on January 8.

2. William H. Carwardine, *The Pullman Strike* (Chicago: Charles H. Kerr & Co., 1894). Carwardine (1855–1929) was a Methodist minister with a parish in Pullman, Illinois, who became an active public advocate on behalf of the strikers, authoring this sympathetic volume.

3. There were actually about 225 delegates and substantially fewer than 150,000 paid members of the ARU.

4. Hazen S. Pingree (1840–1901) was a Republican politician who was mayor of Detroit from 1889 to 1897. Pingree is regarded by historians as a progressive reformer.

5. Debs alludes to the passage of a Democratic Party–sponsored tariff bill that protected the high prices and profits of the monopolized sugar industry and the favorable treatment of the whiskey trust in a receivership action presided over by federal judge Peter S. Grosscup.

6. That is, the Democratic Party.

7. Thomas Babington Macaulay (1800–1859) was an English Whig politician and widely read historian.

8. That is, the People's Party, the so-called "Populists."

9. John Merritte Driver (1857–1918) was a Methodist Episcopal minister who presided over a congregation at Prairie, Illinois.

10. Richard T. Ely, "Pullman: A Social Study," *Harper's Monthly Magazine,* vol. 70, whole no. 417 (February 1885), 463.

11. The remark, attributed posthumously to a 1734 speech by British prime minister Robert Walpole (1676–1745), is today generally regarded as a misquotation ascribed to him by his enemies.

12. Harriet Martineau (1802–1876) was a British author and lecturer on matters of history and political economy.

13. While there were about 425 locals of the ARU at the time of the June 1894 convention, according to a listing of delegates by name in the union's official organ, *The Railway Times,* issue of June 15, 1894, there were actually about 206 delegates in attendance at the opening of the convention on June 12. Moreover, a roll call vote showed about 220 delegates present one week later when the convention decided making "white parents" a condition of membership. While it is possible that some delegates voted additional mandates, in no case were there actually 425 delegates present at the ARU's "First Quadrennial Convention."

14. Debs here repeats the myth—made permanent on the organization's official seal—that it was founded on June 20, 1893, at a mass meeting at Uhlich's Hall in Chicago. As we have seen, the ARU was actually established, its officers elected and its constitution drafted, during a series of meetings in February and April 1893, with a declaration of principles published April 16.

15. The *Tribune,* the *Daily News,* and the *Inter Ocean.*
16. According to a 2014 investigation by David Mikkelson for the website Snopes. com, this is a fraudulent Lincoln quotation that first gained mass traction during the election of 1896. The quotation's false modern pedigree is traced to inclusion of a forged letter, among other pieces of Lincoln apocrypha, by the "sloppy compiler" Archer H. Shaw in his 1950 *Lincoln Encyclopedia.*
17. Joseph W. Reinhart (1851–1911) was only briefly at the helm of the Santa Fe Railroad, serving as president from December 1893 until August 1894.
18. John Ruskin (1819–1900) was an English artist and social critic who espoused the ideas of charity and cooperation.
19. "A Labor Day is Coming" (1889), by J. B. Maynard.
20. "He Was Finally 'In It'" (1894), author unknown. A frequently reprinted humorous poem, apparently first published in the Masonic magazine *The American Tyler,* vol. 8, no. 21 (June 30, 1894), 496.
21. Shylock, a Jewish loan shark, was a fictional character in Shakespeare's *The Merchant of Venice* (c. 1597), and is remembered for having guaranteed a loan made to a merchant with a pound of flesh from next to his heart, and for having gone to great lengths to attempt to collect his due when the loan was defaulted.
22. From Job 23:23–24.
23. Stanza from "A Psalm of Life" (1838) by Henry Wadsworth Longfellow (1807–1882).
24. Two lines extracted from "Of To-morrow" (1837) by Martin Farquhar Tupper (1810–1889).
25. From "The Battle-Field" (1837) by William Cullen Bryant (1794–1878).
26. From "Stanzas on Freedom" (1843) by James Russell Lowell (1819–1891).
27. Another phrase from Lowell.
28. Opening lines from Lowell's hymn, "Once to Every Man and Nation" (1845).
29. Another phrase from Lowell.
30. This statement was issued by Debs from his home in Terre Haute on the evening of May 27, 1895.
31. John Marshall Harlan (1833–1911) was an associate justice of the Supreme Court appointed by President Rutherford Hayes in 1877. He remained on the bench until the time of his death.
32. Couplet from "The Present Crisis" (1844) by James Russell Lowell (1819–1891).
33. Additional lines from "The Present Crisis" by Lowell.
34. The report indicated that Debs was spending his free time on the morning of this interview on ARU business, including editing the forthcoming issue of *The Railway Times.*
35. Debs was jailed again on June 12, 1895, to serve the rest of his uncompleted six-month jail sentence for contempt of court. He was released on November 22.
36. From *McFingal: A Modern Epic Poem; Or, The Town-Meeting* (1775), by John Trumbull (1750–1831).
37. From "My Soul and I" (1846) by John Greenleaf Whittier (1807–1892).

38. Stanza from "The Dying Alchymist" (1830) by Nathaniel Parker Willis (1806–1867).
39. Allusion to Exodus 3:1–15.
40. Extension of the Moses metaphor, alluding to Exodus 14.
41. From Shakespeare's *Julius Caesar* (1599), act 4, scene 3.
42. The convention was held in Omaha in May 1892.
43. Thomas O'Hanlon, Sr. (1832–1912) was the longtime president of the Pennington Seminary in Pennington, NJ.
44. Reference is to the tower of Babel described in Genesis 11:1–9. Shinar is the Old Testament name for Mesopotamia.
45. Adapted from a stanza of "The Problem" (1847) by Ralph Waldo Emerson (1803–1882).
46. The tale is told—in a very different way than Debs recounts the story—in the biblical book of Esther.
47. The story of the widow's mites is told in Mark 12:41–44 and Luke 21:1–4. A mill is one-tenth of one cent.
48. "Io Victis" (1883) by William Wetmore Story (1819–1895).
49. Actually, the People's Party of the United States—"Populists" being a nickname for its members. Debs consistently misnames the party throughout this letter.
50. The special session of the Fifty-Third Congress was convened August 7, 1893, and ran through November 3. The message Debs cites was delivered by President Grover Cleveland to Congress on August 8. In it, Cleveland asserted that the nation's worsening financial crisis was "principally chargeable to congressional legislation touching the purchase and coinage of silver by the general government." Debs's use of Cleveland's anti-free silver remark in this context seems disingenuous.
51. Colloquial name of the Minneapolis, St. Paul and Sault Ste. Marie Railroad (MStP&SSM), principal American subsidiary of the Canadian Pacific Railroad. The name derives from the phonetic spelling of "Sault."
52. By "class," Debs means "craft."
53. Colloquial name of the St. Louis Southwestern Railway (SSW), a line running from St. Louis through Arkansas and into Texas.
54. The Order of Railroad Telegraphers, a craft brotherhood established in June 1886.
55. During the last week of July 1895, the cancellation of the wage schedule of the telegraphers on the Cotton Belt was announced, to go into effect July 28, with a strike threatened in response, thus providing a tentative date for this document. No copy of the original circular letter has as yet surfaced.
56. Lodge meetings were generally closed gatherings, limited to members, although the form of organization of the railway brotherhoods was open, not underground.
57. Opening line of "Endymion" (1818), by John Keats (1795–1821).
58. Concluding stanza from "A Labor Day is Coming" (1889) by Col. J. B. Maynard. The poem apparently was first delivered as conclusion to a speech by Maynard to a Knights of Labor picnic in Indianapolis on September 2, 1889. Debs reprinted an excerpt of this speech in the October 1889 issue of *Locomotive Firemen's Magazine,* page 868. Maynard was a member of the Brotherhood of Locomotive Firemen from Indianapolis.

59. Block signaling is a railway safety procedure limiting one train to each "block" of track at a time, a menial task performed by flagmen before the advent of automatic signaling. The precise meaning of Debs's epithet is unclear.

60. Allusion to Genesis 3:6.

61. Acts, chapter 5, tells the tale of Ananias and Sapphira, who lied about the price realized for land they had sold to apostles of the church, keeping part of the proceeds for themselves. The pair were then both struck dead by supernatural forces for their deceit.

62. That is, the People's Party.

63. This interview was conducted in Woodstock Jail at the time of release of Debs's fellow ARU officers—Sylvester Keliher, Louis Rogers, William Burns, Roy Goodwin, James Hogan, and Martin Elliott—who had been sentenced to terms of three months for contempt of court, as opposed to the six months given to Debs.

64. Illinois governor John Altgeld pardoned Oscar Neebe, Samuel Fielden, and Michael Schwab, the surviving labor leaders railroaded in the Haymarket affair, on June 26, 1893.

65. This letter was read by Jacob Coxey at a rally held at Fountain Grove, Illinois, on August 25. The site was isolated, described as being "in the agricultural districts of Chicago" and "reached by going as far as possible on the streetcar lines, walking a mile through cabbage patches and a bean yard, and between two chicken coops." While attendance at the gathering was understandably sparse, according to a news report Coxey's reading of Debs's letter was "lustily cheered" by the assembled "single-taxers, socialists, People's Party men, and all."

66. President Grover Cleveland maintained a "Summer White House" at Agawam Point in the Buzzards Bay community of Bourne, Massachusetts, located on Cape Cod.

67. In 1895 in the case of *Pollock v. Farmer's Loan & Trust Company,* the Supreme Court of the United States found in a 5-4 decision that the income tax on interest, dividends, and rents which was part of the 1894 Income Tax Act was unconstitutional. This decision would not be made moot until the adoption of the 16th Amendment of the Constitution in 1913.

68. Wilhelm Ludwig "William" Rosenberg (1850–193X) was national secretary of the Socialist Labor Party of America from 1885 to 1889. Rosenberg was associated with a Midwestern political action–oriented faction of the party that squabbled with a New York–based trade union–oriented faction, with the latter ultimately gaining control of the party apparatus and deposing Rosenberg in an 1889 split. In his own open letter to Debs, Rosenberg wrote: "The mind of the people has first to be revolutionized before 'success' can be accomplished. A political movement . . . has to be carefully prepared and worked up, and must, at all events, be controlled but by an overwhelming majority of wageworkers. The less success is promised and preached, the surer the success. From this standpoint it would be but a failure if you would run as candidate for the presidency and do it not as a Labor ticket, according to press rumors. In your place, I should advise all hasty friends of yours to abstain from any such course before a definite platform, backed by political labor organizations, is drafted and adopted by the majority of such political organizations."

69. This represents an early declaration by Debs of general acceptance of socialist principles.
70. Debs made public speeches to striking Pullman workers on May 14 and 16, 1894.
71. Debs here repeats that there were 425 delegates at the June 1894 "First Quadrennial Convention" of the ARU. A published list of attendees as well as the recorded count of a recorded vote during the gathering makes clear that there were more like 225 delegates gathered to represent the approximately 425 locals of the ARU.
72. Rev. George D. Herron (1862–1925) was an endowed professor of "Applied Christianity" at Iowa College (today's Grinnell College) from 1893 until his forced resignation in 1899. He was an active speaker on behalf of the Socialist Party of America during its formative years befor emigrating to Europe and becoming a social patriot during World War I.
73. The United States Strike Commission was appointed July 26, 1894, and its final report transmitted by President Cleveland to Congress on December 10 of that year.
74. The Dred Scott decision was a March 1857 ruling of the United States Supreme Court by a vote of 7-2 declaring that a slave residing in a free state was not entitled to his freedom and that the Missouri Compromise of 1820, which declared as free all American territories west of Missouri and north of latitude 36°20', was unconstitutional.
75. Lyman Trumbull (1813–1896) was a former US senator from Illinois, credited for writing the 13th Amendment to the Constitution banning slavery in the United States.
76. In honor of Labor Day 1895, a parade was held on the morning of September 2 in Terre Haute, followed by activities at the Vigo County fairgrounds in the afternoon, including an address by Senator Daniel W. Voorhees. A crowd estimated at 10,000 was in attendance. The regular order of speakers was suspended after repeated calls from the audience for the reading of this letter to the gathering by the jailed Gene Debs, to which the chair of the event acquiesced.
77. The story of Darius appears in the biblical book of Daniel, chapters 5, 6, and 9.
78. Daniel 6:7.
79. Stanza from "The Deserted Village" (1770), by Oliver Goldsmith (1728–1774).
80. Definition of "poetry" by English poet and historian Thomas Gray (1716–1771).
81. Couplet from "Better Moments" (1827), by Nathaniel Parker Willis (1806–1867).
82. This interview was conducted at the McHenry County Jail in Woodstock, Illinois, in conditions that the interviewer found to be "stifling and almost unbearable."
83. Democratic candidate William Jennings Bryan, the fusion nominee of the People's Party, ultimately carried 22 of the 45 states, limited to the South and the silver-mining states of the West, although losing handily in the electoral college.
84. Allusion is to the fixed 16:1 value ratio of silver to gold advocated by "free silver" advocates of the period.
85. Bryan was an outspoken advocate of expanding the money supply through the unrestricted coinage of silver.
86. John G. Carlisle (1834–1910), a conservative Democrat from Kentucky, was speaker

of the house from 1883 to 1889 and secretary of the treasury during the second Cleveland administration.

87. Thomas Brackett Reed (1839–1902), of Maine, was speaker of the house from 1889 to 1891 and again from 1895 to 1899. He actively sought the Republican nomination for president in 1896 but was defeated by William McKinley.

88. Anna "Annie" Jenness Miller (1859–1935) was an author, magazine editor, and prominent public speaker on the topic of women's clothing reform. Her name is most closely associated with the development of non-restrictive undergarments and the design of specialized clothing for physical activities. Miller's pioneering magazine was the New York monthly *Dress*.

89. Theodore Parker (1810–1860) was a prominent Unitarian minister and public supporter of the abolitionist movement.

90. Myron Reed (1836–1899) was a prominent Congregationalist minister who ran as a Democrat for Congress in 1886. Reed later turned to Christian Socialism and was elected head of the Brotherhood of the Cooperative Commonwealth, an organization dedicated to the establishment of socialist colonies in the West.

91. Rev. Thomas DeWitt Talmage (1832–1902), a Presbyterian minister, lecturer, and writer, was one of the best-known American religious figures of the nineteenth century.

92. General Horatio Gates (1727–1806) is best known for commanding rebel troops to victory over the British at the Battle of Saratoga in 1777.

93. That is, no set of craft-based subcategories ("classes") effectively dividing railroad labor into hierarchical strata.

94. From *Paradise Lost* (1667), by John Milton (1608–1674).

95. From *The Ghost* (1762), by Charles Churchill (1731–1764)

96. Adam Clarke (c. 1761–1832) was a British theologian who, over the course of 40 years, compiled a six-volume, 6000-page biblical commentary that served for decades as one of the fundamental documents of Wesleyanism.

97. Common epithet of the day for the University of Chicago, beneficiary of the philanthropic largesse of Standard Oil founder John D. Rockefeller, Sr. (1839–1937).

98. Allusion to "A Psalm of Life" (1838), by Henry Wadsworth Longfellow (1807–1882).

99. Allusion to "The Battlefield" (1837), by William Cullen Bryant (1794–1878).

100. Adapted from *Measure for Measure* (1604) by William Shakespeare (1564–1616).

101. Josh Billings was the pen name of Henry Wheeler Shaw (1818–1885), a humorist who frequently wrote in idiomatic slang.

102. Damn fools.

103. The source of this poem has not been determined.

104. Allusion to Genesis 1:1–4.

105. Although this maxim is sometimes attributed to Thomas Jefferson, current scholarship indicates that he never used the phrase.

106. Archaic pejorative for "Zoroastrian," derived from the Persian word for "infidel."

107. Allusion to Genesis 4:15.

108. From *The Giaour* (1813) by George Gordon Byron (1788–1824).

109. Title of an 1843 poem by Thomas Hood (1799–1845) that memorialized the wretched conditions faced by an exploited seamstress.

110. Dishonest riches.

111. From *The Building of the Ship* (1870), by Henry Wadsworth Longfellow (1807–1882).

112. Reference to Supreme Court associate justice George Shiras, Jr. (1832–1924), who flipped his vote to opposition in an 1895 case involving the constitutionality of the income tax, thereby voiding the measure in a 5-4 vote. It would only be with the ratification of the 16th Amendment to the Constitution in 1913 that a federal income tax would again be made possible.

113. Reference to J. Ogden Armour (1863–1927), a multimillionaire meat-packer.

114. Literally "Horse's fountain," a sacred spring from Greek mythology said to have been located on Mt. Helicon, where it had been formed by the hooves of Pegasus. Those who drank of its waters were said to have received poetic inspiration.

115. Four-horse coach.

116. From *As You Like It* (1599), Act 2, Scene 3, by William Shakespeare (1564–1616).

117. From *As You Like It,* Act 2, Scene 1.

118. From "Diana" (1830), by Rev. George Croly (1780–1860).

119. Caroll D. Wright (1840–1909) was the first US Commissioner of Labor and headed the 1894 congressional committee investigating the Pullman strike.

120. Block of stone.

121. Apparently a reference to a fable from Persian mythology, "peris" being mythical fairies.

122. From "On the Capture of Certain Fugitive Slaves Near Washington" (1845), by James Russell Lowell (1819–1891).

123. This article was written at the request of the *New York Journal,* a Hearst newspaper, which sought to juxtapose an alternative view to a piece contributed by commanding general of the US Army Nelson Miles advocating expansion of the size of the standing army of the United States.

124. Gen. John McAllister Schofield (1831–1906) was Nelson Miles's predecessor as commanding general of the US Army, holding the post from 1888 until the end of September 1895.

125. The 1876 election between Rutherford B. Hayes and Samuel Tilden was one of the closest and most controversial in American history, with Democrat Tilden failing to win election by the margin of a single electoral vote and barred from victory by the machinations of a specially created election commission. To reduce the level of civil unrest, a deal was brokered in which Republican-sponsored Reconstruction was ended in the South, ushering in a new era of right-wing white hegemony throughout the region.

126. The Krag-Jørgenson was a Norwegian-designed bolt-action rifle, manufactured by Springfield, that was the standard long-arm of the US Army from 1892 to 1903.

127. Washington's farewell address, actually an open letter to the citizens of the United Staes, was published September 17, 1796.

128. This appears to be either a slight misquotation or a paraphrase. The original Gould statement has not been successfully located.

1896

Consolidation[†]

January 1896

The spirit of the times, the signs of the times, and the trend of affairs in finance, commerce, manufactures, transportation, and industry are in the line of consolidation, solidification, combination, or union, as contradistinguished from individual effort.

However much we may sign for the "good old times," they will return no more. A new era has dawned. Old things have passed and are still rapidly passing away. An epoch confronts the business of the country that dates new departures, and an ironclad necessity, which will admit of no modification, demands that men fall into line and conform to new conditions.

Men, generally, have exceedingly crude conceptions of the extent to which the work of consolidating great industrial enterprises has gone forward. Since 1880 the movement, gathering impetus constantly, is attracting and demanding more and more attention.

A census bulletin relating to the manufacturing interests of the country names a number of industries which show a large increase of capital invested. To secure such results consolidation was the means resorted to, the organization of trusts by capitalists by virtue of which they control capital, product, and wages.

What is true of manufacturing establishments is true to a still greater extent in the management of the railroads of the country, and the fact is authoritatively stated in the reports of the Interstate Commerce Commission. In the year 1891, when the total mileage of all the railroad tracks of the country was given at 216,140 miles, 42 corporations controlled nearly one-half of the total mileage, and now a much larger percentage of the mileage is in the hands of a still less number of corporations.

It is needless to discuss the reasons for this work of consolidation. We simply know it is going forward, and that as it proceeds the consolidated roads acquire greater power to dictate terms to their employees; and the fact, known and read of all railway employees, forces upon them for consideration the question as to what measures ought to be adopted whereby fair wages and just treatment may be secured and maintained. It is the old question, and however

---

[†]   Published in the *Chicago Press and Journal,* unspecified date, January 1896. Reprinted in the *Railway Times,* vol. 3, no. 2, (January 15, 1896), 1.

assiduously and conscientiously men may consider it, there seems to be no escape from the use of means, long in vogue, whereby the right may achieve victories for those who demand it and are willing to defend it.

I do not doubt that there may be large improvements in methods on the part of railroad employees to meet the new emergencies created by the consolidation of railroad corporations, and the first and most vital requirement is for them to consolidate.

Let it be understood that federation is not consolidation. The consolidation of railroad corporations is not the confederation of railroad corporations. It is not a dozen, more or less, of corporations, each with its retinue of officials, meeting at stated times for consultation and to define a policy. On the contrary, the consolidated corporations have one head, one controlling power, which decides and acts. The various roads become a "system," with one president, whose acts are not dependent upon the views of some other president, and whether the system has 1,000 miles of road and 3,000 employees, or 10,000 miles of road and 30,000 employees, the decrees of the consolidated concern are equally potential and effective.

It is supreme folly to disguise the purpose which the railroad corporations have in view by consolidation. It is not to promote the moral, intellectual, and social condition of any man or body of men. Neither philanthropy, charity, nor benevolence is considered. The one purpose is to make money and enlarge profits. Such is the supreme demand, and consolidation is found to be a trump card in every game the system plays with the public or with its employees. In dealing with the public, the system emulates the independence of William Vanderbilt and declares, "The public be damned," and in dealing with employees the same laconic expletive is employed.

It is not required to dwell upon the subject or berate the corporations for adopting consolidation as a means of promoting their financial well-being. On the contrary, it is entirely natural that they should consolidate. They are wise in their day and generation. To say that corporations are unscrupulous is to repeat an old chestnut which makes the average reader weary. To say they have no soul, care nothing for decalogues and theological maledictions, is to repeat ad nauseam the stalest of criticisms. Denunciatory harangues do not alter the fact. Railroad corporations exist for the purpose of accumulating a surplus of cash for their owners, and they are not particular about methods; the testimony in courts and in Congress is overwhelming.

In view of such facts the question arises, what should be the policy of employees of railroads? In one direction we hear it said they should federate;

again we are told they should arbitrate, and from others we hear it said that if they "can't get what they ask for, they should accept what they can get and be quiet." Federation, arbitration, and submission have all been tried. Results are before the country. There is one other means for railroad employees to try to escape squalor and degradation, and that is unification, consolidation—to meet consolidation by consolidation—to resist the power enthroned in corporate consolidation by the power enthroned in unification of employees to secure and maintain justice, to make honest toil produce such dividends as will secure decent American conditions for the home, the family, wife, and children.

Consolidation in railroad employment is the climax, the chief good, the *ultima Thule* of organization. It takes in all. It constitutes a fraternity which redeems the saying "the brotherhood of man" from derision and contempt. It banishes the pestiferous dogma of a labor aristocracy, a loathsome disorder nursed by mental infirmities until labor, weakened by its growth and repulsiveness, finds that health and vigor can be regained only by asserting and maintaining the truth that the welfare of all railroad employees, regardless of classes and wages, demands equal consideration and protection.

The various classes and occupations in the railway service could still be maintained intact, and in all matters affecting any particular class or occupation exclusively, the employers engaged in the class so affected would have entire jurisdiction. But in matters affecting the common interests of all, or in the adjustment of a righteous complaint, the whole body of employees are at all times prepared for prompt and united action. This fact in itself would guarantee employee immunity from many wrongs of which they now complain.

Everything else has been tried, and as everything else has practically failed to secure the benefits sought to be obtained, all should be not only willing but earnest advocates of consolidation as the last resort of railroad employees to enthrone the principle of "each for all and all for each."

"Better to Buy Books Than Beer":
Speech at Music Hall, Buffalo, New York[†]
January 15, 1896

It has been said that centralization and combination is the watchword of this age. The centralization of wealth, the amassing of stupendous fortunes in the United States in the last half century, is without parallel in the history of nations. In the march of progress, we now count millionaires by the thousands and mendicants by the millions. We have passed the point referred to by the poet when he said:

> Ill fares the land, to hastening ill a prey,   .
> Where wealth accumulates and men decay.[1]

I do not wish to appeal to prejudice or to arouse passions. I wish simply to show that accumulated wealth in this country has created a power that not only dominates every part of the government but is a menace to the very safety of the Republic itself.

There are thousands of intelligent people who oppose labor organizations because they resort to the strike. They think it is not a nice thing because the horrid unions order strikes. As a general proposition, I am opposed to strikes. In my opinion, a strike is in the nature of a calamity, but now and then there comes a time when men must make a choice between strike and degradation, and when that time comes I favor the strike with all the power at my command. *[Loud applause.]*

One hundred years ago Patrick Henry said, "Resistance to tyranny is obedience to God."[2] On that principle we justify the strike. Every star in the flag of our Union stands for a strike. The shot fired at Lexington which was heard round the world was a strike. Were it not for that shot, we would be British citizens today instead of sovereign Americans. There were those who were willing to accept colonial dishonor, but there were sturdy men who would not surrender rights at a sacrifice of manliness, honor, or patriotism. Washington, Franklin, Paine, and Jefferson—all were agitators.

---

†   Published as "Strong and Mild: Eugene V. Debs Delivered an Intelligent and Forcible Address at Music Hall," *Buffalo Evening News,* vol. 11, 2nd ed., (January 16, 1896),
     1. This imperfect stenographic account checked to and combined with another published as "Full House: Music Hall Crowded to Hear Mr. Debs' Address," *Buffalo Enquirer,* January 16, 1896, 6.

I lay no claim to infallibility as to labor organizations. Their actions sometimes are rash, impetuous, and ill-advised. But I believe that the condition of the workers of this country has been infinitely improved because of organized labor. And in organizing, the workmen simply emulate the example of their employers. Railroads combine for mutual protection. General managers meet and decide to reduce wages. They determine the conditions of employment. That is called a conference. Railroad employees unite to resist the reduction. That is called a conspiracy. The difference between a conference and a conspiracy is the difference between a railroad manager and a section hand. *[Laughter and applause.]* If employers of labor and corporations have the right to combine, laborers have precisely the same right. It is more than a right, it is a duty, failing in which the laborers will be ground to atoms.

In our day, every department of the government is dominated by the money power. This is not the statement of an agitator, unsupported by extraneous testimony. It was only the other day that Senator Vest of Missouri[3] said that the United States Supreme Court had surrendered to the money power. The most startling proof of that assertion comes from the court itself, in its decision on the income tax, a measure designed to place the burden of taxation where it belongs. When the Supreme Court found the income tax law to be unconstitutional, its decision was a usurpation of the functions of Congress. I venture to say that if that law placed $60 million of taxation upon the shoulders of the poor, it would not have been found unconstitutional.[4] *[Applause.]*

The money power is in absolute control of the United States. It has invaded the Supreme Court. It has invaded the church. It dictates legislation. It is the absolute master of the situation. It sometimes seems to me that the lust for gold has eaten the heart out of our civilization.

Judge Trumbull said the other day, "Any federal judge can imprison any American citizen at his own sweet will." I charge that in so far as the federal courts' relations to labor are concerned, it is despotism pure and simple. I solemnly protest against a form of government by injunction. *[Loud and continued applause.]*

Such procedure undertook to restrain us from doing what we didn't intend to do, and then jailed us for not doing it. The judge constitutes himself judge, court, and jury. When the injunction was served on me, in order to show my good faith, I sought the advice of two of the best lawyers in Chicago. They told me to proceed in the course I had been pursing. I was within my constitutional rights. I was doing what any citizen had a right to do. I took their advice and got six months for it. *[Cheers, redoubled with laughter.]* I did not think it was a laughing matter.

What is the effect of the injunctional process? An injunction has all the force of law. It is not an enactment of Congress. It is not the will of the people expressed through its representatives. It is an order of the judge. An injunction is the arbitrary decree of a despot. In Russia there is nothing which excels it.

Are the railroads ever restrained from reducing wages? On the Northern Pacific Railroad, the employees were told if they stopped work, they were guilty of contempt of court. If you can legally restrain men from quitting the services of a railroad, it follows as a logical conclusion that you can restrain railroads from reducing wages.

The nets of justice are so adjusted as to catch the minnows and let the whales slip through. We do not ask the courts to help us, but we do ask them to allow us to help ourselves. The railroad managers were permitted to combine to lower wages, and then to employ thugs and ex-convicts as deputy marshals to instigate riots, destroy property, and create public sentiment adverse to the strikers. Then it was an easy matter to overwhelm them. The public press, or a good part of it, fertilized public opinion by misrepresentation, falsehood, and other means, and upon reading what was published, businessmen said, "That man Debs ought to be hanged." If the facts were as represented, I ought to have been. These are the newspapers which reach the whole people. The labor press is read only by laboring men.

Strikes are not always right, but as a general proposition they are. Only the other day, Professor George Herron said the time would come when we would take a backward look and pronounce the Pullman strikers sublime heroes.

In these times of hunger pangs, workingmen do not give up their positions to accept idleness and poverty without good cause. The world is unjust, and it is a long way from generous, but it is growing a little better every day. Will the workman always draw his rags closer to him in order not to touch the silken garments he has made? Will his nostrils always be tickled by the odor of banquets which he has spread but cannot taste? Will he always scan palatial residences which he has erected but may not enter? No, not always. Working-men are beginning to think. Soon they will begin to act. Not much longer will they supplicate for their rights, but they will take them, not by violence, not by lawlessness, but by a united ballot.

> A weapon that comes down as still
>   As snowflakes fall upon the sod;
> But executes a freeman's will
>   As lightning does the will of God;
> And from its force, nor doors nor locks
> Can shield you;—'tis the ballot box.[5]

Shall not labor come into its own? I do not doubt it.

Judge Dundy of Omaha sent a tramp to prison the other day for life for stealing a cent from a mail carrier.[6] The same judge sent Mr. Mosher, a bank president, to jail for two years for stealing $2 million from his depositors.[7] What was the difference between the tramp and the banker? Two million dollars.[8]

In many courts, justice is a purchasable commodity. I ask no special privileges for the poor, but I do ask that they be allowed to stand side by side with the rich. Why should riches shield rascality any more than poverty? If a poor man commits a crime, punish him. If a rich man commits a crime—punish him. *[Applause.]*

When I was in jail in Chicago *[laughter]* there was a fellow prisoner of mine who was serving a year for stealing a coat worth $2. He stole the old secondhand coat under as noble an impulse as ever entered the breast of man. His wife was nearly famished. She had not a coat on her back. He had no work. He had no means of buying a coat. The secondhand dealer had many secondhand coats. So he took one. The coat was not worth a dollar. But this is the question: Did that man go to jail because he stole the coat, or was it because he had no money? I don't hesitate to declare that if I had exhausted every honest means to get a cloak for my wife, I'd get one, if I had to steal it, before I'd let her die for the want of it. *[Loud applause.]*

The Santa Fe Railroad, under the management of its president, Mr. Reinhart, was $7 million short in its accounts. Yet Mr. Reinhart lives in Boston in social clover up to his ears. He committed a crime to which grand larceny is a glittering virtue. Yet he is not in jail. Why not? Because he is rich. The courts, very many of them, are not designed to punish the rich. I don't make this charge indiscriminately against all courts, remember.

What is the reason for this condition of affairs? It is because the corporations name the judges. It is almost impossible for a man to get on the federal bench without the support of the corporations. And when he gets there, he naturally belongs to the corporations.

Unfortunately for the country, there are thousands of workingmen who are the victims of conditions they did not create. We have not a government by the people so long as the best half of the people are disfranchised. I believe in political equality. We are not quite civilized so long as we deny to women the right to vote. It is her right to decide whether she wants to vote or not. Our laws place women on a par with idiots, criminals, paupers, and Indians. If women have not the right to vote, where did we get the right? Many of our social and economic ills will never be cured until we get equal suffrage. Women have more honor than men. They have more intelligence. You couldn't buy a woman's vote with a drink of whiskey. Every magnificent man has had a magnificent mother. Most anybody will do for a father.

I don't believe that industrial problems are to be solved by force. I want to see the time when the workingman will make better use of his leisure hours. Let the workingman cultivate the beautiful graces of the home and fireside. There are no bad influences at the fireside. Better to buy books than beer. I want to be candid enough to say that I have tried both. *[Laughter.]*⁹

Goldsmith says that those who think must govern those who toil. I want the workingman to mix some thought with his toil, cultivate self-reliance, and do himself what he can to solve the labor problem. Capital is doing just the same as you would do if you were in its place. The workingmen should have home libraries. Five dollars will buy a good many books these days, and 50 cents will make a fair start. Get a primer on economics and learn a little every night. Keep up the study for a year and see if you have not done much to better your condition. Learn to depend upon yourselves, for it is not necessary to be rich in order to be a man.

If you want to be respected, begin by respecting yourself. A man without an ambition and who does not want to amount to anything is the cheapest commodity on earth. If you want to be certain to have a great many friends, be sure not to need one. Save $1 a week, or as much as you can. No man has so sure a situation as the man who has something in the bank. He is the last man to be discharged. Everybody is your friend then and ready to help you.

I believe the wage system, which is only another name for the feudal system, must disappear. Machines are displacing men. There is only one remedy—that is for each man to work fewer hours and give the rest a chance. If four hours' work a day will clothe and feed the world, let four hours be a day's work. Some changes must be made. Some monopolies must be taken over by the people. The United States is the only civilized country that does not own its telegraphs. What is true of the telegraph is true of the telephone. It is true of railroads. The people should own them, or they will own the government. They asked me in Chicago if I believed in government ownership of railroads. I replied that I preferred it to railroad ownership of government. All these changes will come with education. That is the lever that will lift up all into the light. The middle classes in this country are fast disappearing. Soon there will be but two—the extremely few, who are the extremely rich, and the extremely many, who are the extremely poor.

I've lost the respect of many persons, but I've managed to keep my own. People say I ought to be influenced by public opinion, but when I reflect that it was public opinion that kept alive the institution of slavery, I'd rather be excused. Public opinion is invariably unreliable. Public opinion has sanctioned every great outrage which has ever been perpetrated. Every few hundred years public opinion gets right, but that is too long for anybody to wait. The minority is usually right.

I propose to keep on good terms with myself. I would hate to be like the man who woke up in his room one night and exclaimed, "My god, there is nobody in this room."

Every great reformer has been under the ban of public opinion. Washington in his day was called a demagogue. Today he is a demigod. The difference between a demagogue and a demigod is but a century. Christ, who taught the redeeming doctrine of mutual love, perished on the cross. Every reformer who has loved humanity better than himself has perished as a martyr. I hope to see the time come when the world will be civilized to the extent that it will permit a man to be true to himself. I hope to see the time when a man who is honestly trying to better conditions will be appreciated before he is dead and turned to dust for 100 years.

Every man who is trying to be right and is trying to do right is my brother. If we had more justice, we could get along with less charity. Charity is humiliating, charity stunts. An employer who gives his men 50 turkeys performs a commendable act, but I don't want to get my turkeys in that way. The form of charity that gives a Christmas turkey to each employee is more degrading than the pennies dropped into the hat of a beggar. What the workingman wants is a charity that will enable him to help himself.

Centralization and the Role of the Courts:
Speech at Germania Hall, Cleveland†
January 18, 1896

Ladies and Gentlemen:—

It has been said that centralization and combination are the master spirits of this age. The truth of the statement is so self-evident as to require no argument to strengthen or support it. The centralization of wealth in the United States of America during the last half of the nineteenth century is without a parallel in the history of the nations, and in the conquering march we now number the millionaires by thousands and the mendicants by millions, and the power conferred by centralized wealth defies proper characterization. The old maxim that "Knowledge is power" might very properly be amended by adding "But wealth is omnipotent." Centralized wealth dominates every department of the government of the United States. *[Applause.]* The voice of centralized wealth is potent in the halls of legislation *[applause]*, has invaded the church, and has absolute sway in all the affairs of man. This is not the charge of a wild-eyed anarchist, an irresponsible agitator, but of men of acknowledged standing in the affairs of the nation.

Only the other day in the United States Senate, Senator [George Graham] Vest of Missouri very broadly intimated that the United States Supreme Court was susceptible to corruptible influences. *[Applause.]* But the most startling arraignment of the Supreme Court, once the most august tribunal in the civilized world, originates in the court itself. A little while ago the court rendered its decision upon the income tax law, a law designed to place the burden of taxation where it properly belongs, upon those best able to bear it. *[Applause.]* The law was declared to be unconstitutional. When that decision was rendered, three of the gentlemen constituting that court gave their dissenting opinions. Justice [Edward D.] White,[10] in his opinion, used the following language:

---

†   Published as "Eugene V. Debs to the Workingmen of Cleveland" in *Cleveland World*, vol. 7, no. 147 (January 19, 1896), 3. Excerpt reprinted with incorrect attribution to Nashville as "Debs to the Slaves" in the *Coming Nation*, whole no. 160 (June 13, 1896), 2. An unattributed excerpt of this speech republished as "The Role of the Courts" in Jean Y. Tussey, ed., *Eugene V. Debs Speaks* (New York: Pathfinder Press) 1970, 50–52.

The injustice of the conclusion points to the error of adopting it. It takes invested wealth and reads it into the Constitution as a favored and protected class of property . . . whilst it leaves the occupation of the minister, the doctor, the professor, the lawyer, the inventor, the author, the merchant, the mechanic, and all the various forms of industry, upon which the prosperity of the people must depend, subject to taxation.[11]

Justice [John M.] Harlan used the following language:

The changes contemplated from the prayer of this matter are little less than revolution. Such a decision cannot have any other effect than of arousing much indignation among the freemen of the country. It cannot be regarded otherwise than as a disaster for the country.[12]

A Serious Charge

Here we have it upon the high authority of one of the Supreme Justices that this decision places disaster upon the country. Justice [Henry B.] Brown said the decision involved "nothing less than a surrender of the taxing power to the moneyed class." Johann Most never made a more serious charge upon an American institution.[13] One of these justices declares that this decision of the Supreme Court reads invested wealth into the Constitution of the United States; another, that it is little less than a revolution, and another that it is a surrender to the moneyed class. As a matter of fact, corporate capital dictates the appointment of federal judges. It is next to impossible for a lawyer, however great his attainments, to reach that high position unless he is on good terms with the corporations of this country. *[Applause.]* The decisions of the Supreme Court have almost uniformly been against the common people, and especially against the workingmen of the country. I undertake to say that if the income tax law had imposed a burden of $60 million upon the poor people it would not have been declared unconstitutional. *[Applause.]*

I am not here tonight to appeal to your passions, to arouse your prejudices or incite the populace, but to call your attention to matters of such serious import in our social, our political, our industrial affairs, as to challenge the thoughtful consideration of every patriotic citizen. There are multiplied thousands of people in this country who view with apprehension and alarm the widespread unrest that prevails in our social and industrial affairs, and taking counsel of their doubts and fears, they arrive at the conclusion of Macaulay, believing it about to be fulfilled: that self-government is a failure and that the sun of our Republic is to set in universal gloom. I am not of that number. Believing as I do in the largely increasing intelligence of the masses of our people, I am persuaded that the grand old ship of state will breast all the billows, weather all of the storms, and finally safely reach her destined port. *[Great applause.]*

As for the workingmen of the country, I am persuaded that upon these great questions they are thinking more seriously and more intelligently than they have ever thought before.

Will Take Their Rights

I agree with Fitch, and it is only here under the flag of 44 stars, where the workingmen are beginning to ask why it is they must press their rags still closer lest they jostle against the silken garments that their fingers have fashioned, and why it is they must offend their hunger with the odor of banquets they have spread but may not taste, and walk weary and shelterless in the shadow of the palaces they have erected but may not enter. Workingmen are beginning to think—they will soon begin to act! They shall not make longer supplication for their rights, but they will take them; not in lawlessness, in disorder, in crime, but in lawful, orderly manner will take them; they will take them by virtue of a united ballot *[applause]*—the weapon that comes down as silently as the snowflakes fall upon the sod, yet executes every man's will, as lightning does the will of God. And they hear the cries of people weary of centuries of oppression and tyranny, and the child of martyrdom, and they know a free people of a free country will answer that cry, because where labor is prophet or priest or king, the greater the concentration of all wealth, government, and civilization.

It is labor that heats the iron ore and seethes it in paths of fire, and rolls and hammers and tempers it into the brightest blade and the ponderous rail. It is labor that gathers the white fleece and transforms it into thousands of articles of beauty and use; labor that seizes the green-plumed forest monarch and bids him fall low upon the earth and sees his huge form sink under the saw, until the vast forests change into materials for home; labor that hammers at the doors of earth's chambers, bids them roll back upon their hinges—and shall not workingmen come into their own? Who shall doubt it?

The Midnight Passing

When the mariner sailing over the tropic seas looks for light, he turns his eye toward the Southern cross burning luridly above the tempestuous ocean, and as midnight approaches, the cross begins to bend, the whirling oceans change their places, and the Almighty marks the passage of time upon the dial of the universe. Though no bell may toll the glad tidings, the lookout knows midnight is passing, and relief and rest are close at hand. Let labor everywhere take cheer and hope, for the cross is bending, and midnight is passing, and "joy cometh in the morning."[14] *[Great applause.]*

There are those who, while admitting that our industrial affairs are seriously out of joint, claim that it is possible to quiet the discontent of the workingmen by force. The other day in the city of Washington, General Miles was interviewed and declared that on account of threatened internal dissension he believed it necessary we should have a standing army of at least 75,000. When I read the interview, it appeared to me Washington said something upon that subject. I looked up his farewell address and found he had declared against standing armies on American soil. *[Applause.]* I looked up Jefferson upon that subject and I found that he said precisely the same thing in a little different way. And then I said that standing armies and liberty do not thrive in the same soil. *[Applause.]* One or the other must give way, and it is usually liberty. The theory of General Miles is that we shall have soldiers enough to mass near the centers of population so that when discontented, wronged, oppressed, and often plundered workingmen resist injustice, they may be murdered.

Question of Humanity

In my judgment, what is called the labor problem is now the question of humanity. It touches at a very vital point of human society, involves the welfare and prosperity and happiness of all the people. It is not confined to the workingmen of the country merely; it has passed beyond the lines of labor, and we find that among professional men, among businessmen, among all classes of thoughtful, patriotic citizens, there is a disposition to find out what is wrong with our industrial affairs and apply the proper remedy.

And just here let me remark in this connection that workingmen have not been half true to themselves. *[Applause.]* They have not taken advantage of such opportunities as they have enjoyed. Believing as I do that for the solution of this question we rely largely, if not entirely, upon intelligence, I feel that the workingmen, those most directly, most vitally interested, should study this question in all of its phases; devote their leisure hours to the study of economic questions relating to food and clothing and shelter, and all other phases of this great problem. I said to the railroad men yesterday, at Olean, New York, that a great many of them were satisfied to sit in the roundhouse in their overalls and tell stories about runs that had never been made in the world and never would be made. *[Laughter and applause.]* I want to see them change their lodge rooms into schoolrooms.

Goldsmith [wrote some time ago]:

> For just experience tells; in every soil.
> Those that think must govern those that toil.[15]

Workingmen have done no thinking except by proxy. *[Applause.]* I want them to rely on their own thinker; I want them to cultivate self-reliance, to depend upon themselves.

Good Advice

A large number of workingmen have opportunities and fail to take proper advantage of them. In a few years they will find that they themselves are doing very much in the line of solving the labor problem. I want them to do some of it, to add a little something to the stock of their knowledge and heighten their intelligence. Do something in the line of self-improvement. Spend leisure hours at home. The labor problem is not going to be solved in the saloon. *[Applause.]* I can think of no more beautiful picture than that of a workingman who, returning home, finds the beacon light shining at the window; he takes his supper, then draws up his old armchair to the fireside, converses with his wife, plays with his children. The man that does that is doing something to solve the labor problem. *[Applause.]*

I admit there are many thousands of workingmen in the country who have no opportunities. From them I expect nothing; they have got to be helped; they are the victims of circumstances they did not create, that they have had no power to control. As I said before, there are between 3 and 4 million workingmen out of employment, traveling from city to city in search of employment that cannot be found. There are those, I say, who are victims of circumstances. There are workers who are willing and anxious to work, but there is no work to be found. In my opinion . . . there will come a time when there will be a change in the condition.

The Cheapest Commodity

Have you ever given serious thought of the condition of a man out of employment and expecting to find it? Have you ever put yourself in his place? Take a man with a good situation. He loses his place through no fault of his own; he looks all about Cleveland, he goes up and down the street and cannot find work—no one will give him an instant's attention. For in these latter years of the nineteenth century the cheapest commodity of the world is human flesh and blood. *[Applause.]* He leaves Cleveland, goes to the nearest place, and does not succeed, and before he realizes it he is 500 miles away from home. His last dollar is gone, he is a stranger among strangers—his clothes become seedy. At long range he can see his little cottage home, his wife in distress, his children crying for bread; he becomes embittered against society and it rankles in his breast, and in that mood it is but a few steps until he becomes a tramp by choice, and from there on it is but a few steps into crime.

I have made the contention that 90 percent of the criminals of this country could under proper conditions be redeemed. *[Applause.]* Most of them find their way to jail because they are poor. *[Applause.]* Poverty is made to bear all of the burdens; if they had the money they could employ a lawyer, the lawyer would make a defense, they would not be convicted. *[Applause.]* I don't hesitate to declare that in some of our courts, justice is a purchasable [commodity]. *[Applause.]* Not long ago, Judge [Elmer S.] Dundy sent a tramp who assaulted a mail carrier and took one cent from him to the penitentiary for life. The same judge sent [C. W.] Mosher, the Lincoln, Nebraska, bank wrecker, who robbed his depositors of $1 million, to the penitentiary for two years. *[Applause.]* What was the difference? A million dollars. *[Applause.]*

In Jail with Debs

When I was in jail at Chicago, *[applause]* I had a fellow prisoner who was serving a 12-months' sentence because he had stolen a secondhand cloak for his wife, valued at $2. I heard his story and verified it by the facts. He had been out of work for six months. He tramped around looking for work in vain. He passed the secondhand store and saw an old cloak swinging in the breeze that they were using for a sign; he took it for his wife, he thought of her sitting in her desolation. He was arrested, and it took five minutes to send him to jail for 12 months. The question that occurred to me was: Was he sent to jail for stealing the cloak or because he had no money? *[Applause.]* After I heard his story I said to myself, had I been in his situation, had I done my level best to get a cloak honestly for my wife, and she had gone in need of one, I would get a cloak honestly or otherwise if there was a cloak anywhere in the world. *[Applause.]*

Here is a man serving a 12-months' sentence who is not a criminal at heart. There is no self-accusation manifest in his conscience. He was dictated by as humane a motive as ever a man had in this world. His crime was a virtue and entitled to commendation. *[Applause.]* He was the unfortunate victim of circumstances, of an unfortunate condition, and should be entitled to the compassion of society. But he went to jail. and when a man goes to jail there is no escape for him except possibly through the back door of suicide. *[Applause.]* Society, as it is now constituted, doesn't allow a man who is identified with the criminal classes to redeem himself. Put a man in jail, release him, no one will give him work, nor a word of encouragement. He is exiled. No one knows him, society closes all of its doors in his face, abuse is heaped upon his head, and he is placed back in the jail and falls several degrees lower and finally he graduates from petty larceny to homicide. *[Applause.]* If it seems to you in the nature of an exaggeration, investigate for yourself.

Thankful to Judge Woods

I have to be thankful to Judge [William Allen] Woods *[hisses]* for one thing; I am thankful for having been in jail and to know something of the condition of the inmates. I understand now they are entitled to our sympathy, and I propose to do what little lies in my power to correct conditions under which these people are made criminals. *[Applause.]* Then there are those who are placed in the extremity of begging, but if a man is naturally bright, he will not beg. If I had the choice between begging and stealing, I am not sure, I am not certain, but I think I would keep my self-respect and steal. *[Applause.]*

Have you ever thought of the extreme humility of a strong, able-bodied man who is a supplicant for charity? Just think of it. It humiliates a man, disgraces him; his self-respect deserts him. No matter how good a man he may be, when he is in that condition long enough he is divorced from his manhood and he becomes an abject creature or a criminal. He is in the position that the poet wrote about a long time ago:

> See yonder poor o'er-labored wight,
>   So abject, mean, and vile,
> Who begs a brother of the earth
>   To give him leave to toil;
> And see his lordly fellow-worm
>   The poor petition spurn,
> Unmindful, though a weeping wife
>   And helpless offspring mourn.
> If I'm designed yon lordling's slave,
>   By Nature's law designed
> Why was an independent wish
>   E'er planted in my mind?[16]

The interrogatory has not been answered and may not be answered. Certain it is that a great many American workingmen are in that position today, when the opportunities are increasing and established in the large centers of population, and while this is going forward, while millions are out of work, unable to find work. We have shops and mills and factories in which women and children toil for 12 and 16 hours a day. *[Applause.]* Upon this subject Frances Willard,[17] one of the noblest of her sex, *[applause]* says:

> There are millions of men and women in Great Britain and America who would gladly work, but the pitiless, restraining hand of invention and monopoly hold them back, so that an opportunity to earn their bread by the sweat of their brow is already fought for as strenuously as men in former times fought for their lives . . . Under this procedure of resistless competition men are ground into dust by a heavier heel than old-time tyrannies could boast, and they seek forgetfulness in those indulgencies whose hallucinations deteriorate body and soul.[18]

Fifty Cents a Day

I met James Gist at Chicago the other day. This gentleman is very familiar with machine work and gives much attention to these matters. He had just returned from Kalamazoo, where he made some investigation of a large furniture factory. He found that men were at work who had worked there for ten years, six days a week, for $3—50 cents a day. Just think of a man working ten hours a day for 50 cents and having a wife and three or four children depending on him for support! He said he went through the factory and saw girls working at some of the machines 13 years of age, and on some of their hands were four of the fingers missing. Oh, what a state of affairs in a community! What a vile calumny upon our Christian civilization!

The struggle is fierce enough and sharp enough if a child is equipped for the battle of life. But just think of the children of these men out of employment, or these men who have employment at 50 cents a day, who are compelled to grow up without education. They do not have a home. John Bright[19] once said that the nation should live in a cottage. It should be so, but it is no longer so in this section of the country. They cannot live in a home; they cannot live in the home they inhabit; it is not fit for a dog to inhabit. The children are reared in such an environment. No education, no moral influence, and after they get old enough and drift into crime, as some of them inevitably do, because we are all creatures of our circumstances, then society imprisons them or hangs them.

Now, I have made the declaration that wealth dominates every department of our affairs—great aggregation of wealth. Even the man of ordinary means is being forced to the wall. Dun's reports show that last year we had in this country over 13,000 commercial collapses, aggregating more than $172 million. In this morning's dispatches I read Dun's report for last week of 396 failures. The failures going forward in the United States at the rate of 66 a day—just think what this means! Think of this bankruptcy, ruin, disaster, suicide . . .

Feeling the Pressure

But this process of centralization is going steadily forward. The middle classes are beginning to feel the pressure. One product after another is being monopolized. The tendency is to syndicates and trusts and combines and monopolies. In 1890 there was a law enacted designed to restrain the formation of trusts.[20] It had no effect and never can have any effect. The trust is the legitimate product of the present industrial system. We are rapidly approaching that condition when there will be in this country two classes separated by a very wide chasm— the few who have all the wealth, and therefore all the power, and the great masses of the people who are in subjection. Call this a republic if you will, but there is not an element of real republicanism in it. *[Applause.]*

I have said and say again there can be no civil liberty with industrial slavery. Long since we achieved our political independence, but we will not be free until we have achieved economic liberty. *[Applause.]* Something is being done in that direction every day. The theory is, according to Lincoln, in this country we have a government of and by and for the people. He said, to use his own language, "Liberty before property, or men before the dollar."[21] We have lived to see his words accepted literally—not, however, in the way he intended. We see the man before the collar, but upon his knees, crouching, supplicating for the dollar, and for permission to live, and it is only a theory we have in the words "of the people, by the people, and for the people."

We will never have a government of the people until we enfranchise woman and give her political equality. *[Applause.]* It is not for the want of regard, but we have a misconception as to the rights of womanhood. A woman has every right we have, and if she has not got a right to vote, where did we get ours? Whether she wants to vote or not is a question for her to decide and not for me. I am one of those who believe that a great many ills that afflict the body social and industrial can be eradicated when woman enjoys political freedom and equality. *[Applause.]* And why not? There is not a rational argument that can be made against the proposition. Denying woman the right of political equality, it is simply the crime of animal force—superior strength. Woman has much more honor than men as a general proposition. *[Applause.]* You could not buy her vote with a drink of whiskey. *[Laughter and applause.]* We decorate her with jewels but keep her in political subjection. I want to see the time come when we will decorate her with that rarest of all gems, political equality, and then men and women will walk the highland side by side enjoying the rapturous vision of a land without a slave. *[Applause.]* I believe, with Col. [Robert] Ingersoll, who once said that every magnificent man had a magnificent mother—almost anybody will do for a father. *[Laughter.]*

Restraining Workingmen

We now pass to some further matters in which labor has a very profound interest. I refer to the increasing tendency of the courts to restrain workingmen from asserting the power which organization confers upon them. We have arrived at a point where workingmen, especially those employed on railroads, are compelled by court decree to work for such wages and under such conditions of employment as the corporations may see fit to impose. When the managers meet together for the purpose of reducing wages, the newspapers inform us that they held a conference. When the workingmen combine for the purpose of resisting the reduction, they call it a conspiracy. *[Laughter and applause.]* Now, the only difference between a conference and a conspiracy is the difference between a railroad president and a section hand. If courts are justified in restraining workingmen from acting in concert to resist reduction in wages, then why are they not justified in restraining corporations from cutting wages? *[Applause.]* It is a poor rule that, like a locomotive, does not work both ways.

Here is an editorial that appeared in the *New York World* upon that point:

> More dangerous and menacing than any strike is the carefully laid plan for bringing about the intervention of the federal government on the side of the railroad. Such an injunction as that drawn by two corporation attorneys and granted by Judges Grosscup and Woods is a monstrous invasion of the people's rights. If operating a railroad is a public service, and railroad men are public servants in any sense that can justify federal control of their acts, then the federal government must not only protect the railroad companies against the employees when there is a quarrel between them, it must also protect employees in all their rights and privileges as public servants. It must guarantee them reasonable hours of service, fair wages, reasonable vacations, and all other guarantees that it gives to others in the public service.

Employees Chained

Not long since the Northern Pacific road passed into the hands of a receiver—and the Northern Pacific is the goose that has been plucked wherever there was a feather in sight—just after that there was a petition filed to reduce the wages of employees. At the same time there was a petition filed to restrain employees from striking. The court granted both orders, so that their wages were not only reduced under the guardianship and protection of the government, but they were prevented from quitting the service of the company under penalty of being guilty of contempt of court. Those railroad employees by virtue of those orders were chained to that corporation and made a part of its rolling stock. It was a case of the government of the United States holding up a body of workingmen while a corporation went through their pockets. *[Laughter and applause.]*

On the Union Pacific system, they made a reduction of wages and applied for a similar order, but there was an honest judge there—Judge [Henry Clay] Caldwell. *[Applause and cheers.]* Judge Caldwell expands to the proportions of an honest and upright judge, and I pay him the humble tribute of admiration and respect. Judge Caldwell said, "Before this reduction is made, I propose to call the employees into court and give them an opportunity to be heard." He called in the officials and he asked them to show the reason why the wages should be reduced, and he called in the employees and he heard their testimony, and when the hearing was closed, he said, "This reduction shall not be made." And he declared that if that property had been honestly managed, there would be no necessity for reduction of wages, and he said, "There shall be no reduction here if not another dollar is paid in the form of dividends to the owners of the road." It is this that inspires the confidence of the people exactly as in the other case it destroys it. I believe it was Choate who said that it is not so important that our courts are pure as that the people shall believe them to be pure.

And He Got Six Months

In our own case in Chicago an injunction was issued at a time when the American Railway Union had its great struggle for human rights, and they were triumphant in restraining myself and my colleagues from doing what we never intended to do and never did do, and then we were put in jail for not doing it. *[Applause and laughter.]* When that injunction was served on me, to show that I acted in good faith, I went to two of the best constitutional lawyers in the city of Chicago, and I said: "What rights, if any, have I under this injunction? I am a law-abiding citizen; I want what is right. I want you to examine this injunction and then advise me what to do." They examined the injunction. They said, "Proceed just as you have been doing; you are not committing any violence; you are not advising violence, but you are trying to do everything in your power to restrain men from the commission of crime or violating the law." I followed their advice and got six months for it. *[Laughter and applause.]*

What does Judge Lyman Trumbull say upon that subject? Judge Lyman Trumbull is one of the most eminent jurists the country has produced. He served 16 years in the United States Senate; he was chairman of the Senate Committee on the Judiciary; he was on the supreme bench of the state of Illinois; he has held all of the high offices, but he is a poor man. There is not a scar nor a blemish upon his escutcheon. No one ever impugned his integrity. What does he say about this subject? To use his exact language, he says: "The decision carried to its logical conclusion means that any federal judge can imprison any citizen at his own will." If this is true, it is judicial despotism, pure and simple, whatever you choose to call it.

When the trials were in progress at Chicago, Mr. George M. Pullman was subpoenaed to give some testimony. Mr. Pullman attached his car to a New York train and went East, and in some way the papers got hold of the matter and made some publication about it, and the judge said that Mr. Pullman would be dealt with drastically. In a few days Mr. Pullman returned, and he went into chambers, made a few personal explanations, and that is the last we heard of it. Had it been myself, I would have to go to jail, that is the difference.

Another Case

Only a little while ago Judge Hanford[22] cited Henry C. Payne[23] of the Northern Pacific to appear before him to answer certain charges, and he went to Europe, and he is there yet. Will he go to jail on his return? Of course not. Why? The reason suggests itself. If it were a railroad striker, he would be in Woodstock instead of Berlin.

Governor Altgeld, in many respects the greatest governor in the United States, says: "The precedent has now been established, and any federal judge can now enjoin any citizen from doing anything and then put him in jail." Now, what is an injunction? It has all of the force and vital effect of a law, but it is not a law in and by the representatives of the people; it is not a law signed by a president or a governor; it is simply the wish and will of the judge. A judge issues an injunction [and] serves it upon his intended victim. The next day he is arrested. He is brought into the presence of the same judge. Sentence is pronounced upon him by the same judge, who constitutes the judge and court and jury, and he goes to jail and he has no right of appeal. Under this injunctional process, the plain provisions of the Constitution have been disregarded.

The right of trial by jury has been abrogated, and this at the behest of the money power of the country.

What is the effect upon workingmen and especially railway employees to bind them to their tasks? The government goes in partnership with a corporation; the workingmen are intimidated. If there is a reduction of wages, they submit; if unjust conditions are imposed, they are silent. And what is the tendency? To demoralize, to degrade workingmen until they have reached the very deadline of degradation.

And how does it happen and why does it happen that corporations are never restrained? Are they absolutely law-abiding? Are they always right? Do they never transgress the law, or is it because the federal judges are their creatures? Certain it is that the united voice of labor in this country would be insufficient to name a federal judge.

Money in the Courts

If all the common people united and asked for the appointment of a federal judge, their voice would not be heeded any more than if it were the chirp of a cricket. Money talks. Yes, money talks. And I have no hesitancy in declaring that money has even invaded—or the influence, the power conferred by money has invaded—the Supreme Court and left that august tribunal reeking with more stench than Coleridge discovered in Cologne, and left all the people wondering how it was ever to be deodorized. There is something wrong in the country. The judicial nets are so adjusted as to catch the minnows and let the whales slip through, and the federal judge is as far removed from the common people as if he inhabited another planet. As Boyle O'Reilly would say:

> His pulse, if you felt it, throbbed apart
> From the common pulse of the people's heart.[24]

They are not in touch with the common people. Their people, their social environment, is altogether influenced by wealth. It enters into their very being. They are not answerable to the people. Jefferson declared more than a century ago that they would enlarge their powers and encroach upon the citizens until finally they would be a menace to the Republic, and the prophecy has been literally fulfilled, and the encroachment will continue as long as the people will continue to submit. Despotism is a condition of nonresistance by the people to the encroachment of tyranny and to the exact extent that people will submit, their rights will be encroached upon, and at last they will be in complete subjection.

I do not believe, however, that the spirit of '76 has been entirely extinguished. I believe that in the due course of time American manhood will assert itself. A great many people cry out against labor organizations—denounce the strike, condemn the strikers. They do not know, nor do any of them care to know, that back of the strike there is an almost interminable succession of wrongs. If there is a railroad strike and a man is stopped in his journey, he damns the strikers.

Troubles of Their Own

The public has no time to inquire into these wrongs that are gnawing at the base of society. They have got troubles enough of their own in this age of sharp competition. They know nothing about the condition of the great masses of people. They only know there is something wrong when their pocketbooks or their finances are touched, and then their verdicts are almost invariably against the striker. These are unfortunate conditions. A great many people say: "I have no use for strikers; they riot; they create disorder." But of the organization, but for the strike, American workingmen would be infinitely worse off than they are. *[Applause.]*

Jefferson once said: "God have mercy on us if we ever reach a point when the American has no longer that spirit of resistance to tyranny," and Patrick Henry said that resistance to tyranny is obedience to God. *[Applause.]*

It sometimes becomes the choice between tyranny and degradation, and when that time comes I believe in a strike. As a general proposition I am opposed to them. But there is a condition worse than being out of employment, and that is being out of manhood. I would rather be out of work than to be a spineless, crawling creature on the face of the earth. I propose to keep on good terms with myself if I have nothing to do. I am not going to be in the condition of the fellow who looked in the glass and turned away in disgust, saying, "I know that fellow very well." I am not going to be in the predicament of that fellow who, when about to wake up in the night, said: "My God! There is nobody in this room!" *[Laughter.]*

Here again tonight let me remind you, my friends, that we live under a striking government. At Lexington, where the shot was fired that was heard round the world, and from Concord clear to Lexington, there was one continuous succession of strikes. Against what? Against tyranny and oppression. For what? For liberty, for independence, and had it not been for the magnificent courage and patriotism of the fathers in striking for their rights, we would be British subjects tonight instead of sovereign American citizens. I want to see the spirit of resistance increased.

A century ago there were Tories, and we have them among us still— those who wanted peace at any price, who were willing to accept degrading conditions, willing to be humiliated, willing to sacrifices the colonial honor, their integrity, their manhood. And they said so to Washington and Franklin and Jefferson and Paine and the rest of those anarchists and demagogues and agitators. *[Applause.]* Washington was called a demagogue in his day; he was vilified as no other president of the United States ever was. He is a demigod today. The difference between a demagogue and a demigod is about a century. There were those who appealed to them and said, "If you continue this agitation, it will result in war and bloodshed." Then they said, "If we have got to have war to achieve our independence, let us have it now, that our children and our children's children may enjoy the blessings of peace." They were not merely strikers and law-breakers, but they resorted to violence and to riot and the destruction of property. Hancock and his compatriots did not hesitate to dress up as Indians and go down to Boston Harbor and dump the tea into the harbor. It is a good thing that Judge Woods didn't preside in that day. *[Laughter and applause and a voice: "Or Judge Ricks."]*

Mothers Also Strikers

And then what about the revolutionary mothers? They were not strikers—they were boycotters. They said, "We will not drink another drop of imported tea." They were filled with that sublime spirit of resistance that gives liberty and independence and all other things of good report among men. Precisely so with the labor organizations of our day. The labor organization is a product of tyranny and oppression. If all employers of labor had always treated their employees fairly and justly paid them in even-handed measure and value for their toil, there would not be a labor organization on the face of the continent, not one. *[Applause. A voice: "Nor a millionaire."]*

In organizing, labor simply emulates the example of capital, and all it is asking for today is just a fair chance. It doesn't ask for any special legislation; it doesn't ask for any privileges or favors; all it asks for is an equal, even chance at life. The capitalists are all combined—they act in unison and harmony in all matters touching their interest, and in this regard they are immensely in advance of the workingmen, who are often divided into factions, so busy in waging war upon one another that they have no time to do anything for the common good.

But as I say, we are making progress, and the universal unrest and discontent that pervades the country is to me the most cheering sign of the times. And if under present conditions the workingmen are content, I should be without a hope, and in all the horizon of the future I should not see one star. But unrest precedes agitation; agitation means education; education means emancipation.

Sometimes when I strain my vision just the slightest it seems to me that I can see the first faint glimpse of the dawning of a better day. *[Applause.]*

Walpole Lied

But there are those who denounce those engaged in this sort of agitation as demagogues and cranks and impostors, and they do not hesitate to declare that the men who are officially connected with the various organizations of the day never rise above self-interest. They believe, with Walpole, that every many has his price.[25] A scoundrel cannot possibly conceive of an honest man; no man can rise above his own conception.

When Walpole made that declaration, he lied. He had his price, or he never would have conceived of that infamous falsehood. There are men in the world above corrupting influences, and you find them in every walk of life. They are the men who are the salt of the earth and the light of the world and who are to hew the way to freedom.

And there are those who have no patience with any man who is identified with any kind of a reform. They frown upon every effort that is made in that direction. They have neither time nor inclination to listen to a word that may be said in that direction. I read about one of them the other day. They built a church at his very door, but he wasn't in it. They brought him a scheme for relieving the poor, but he wasn't in it. "Let them work for themselves and take care of their money as I have done," he said. But a hearse went up the street one day, and he was in it, and the funeral trappings made quite a display—and he was in it. St. Peter met him with book and bell: "Well, my friend, let me see your ticket . . . Your elevator goes down in a minute." *[Laughter.]*

Solved by Intelligence

Now what are we going to do about it? As I have already said, I am in favor of education. I believe in the uplifting, the emancipating, and the sublimating power of intelligence. These questions are to be solved by intelligence. I admit that it is a big question. In my judgment no man, not even the tallest intellect, can define a social system for the future. A social system is a matter of growth, of evolution, of development. It is growing every day; every hunger pang is helping it forward; every trust is doing something in that direction. *[A voice: "They are digging their own graves."]* Yes, they are digging their own graves, and they will fill them before long.

There are some phases of the question, however, that are perfectly simple and easy of comprehension and easy of adjustment. For instance, why do we not take possession of the telegraphs of our country? We are the only civilized nation on the face of the globe that does not own its own telegraph system. The United States and four or five tenth-rate republics in South America are the only countries in the world where the telegraph is operated for private profit instead of for the public weal. If I sent a telegram from here to California, I have to pay ten cents a word. In England you can send a telegram any distance for a cent a word, and the telegraph is more than self-sustaining. The Western Union Telegraph Company is capitalized for $100 million, and the very best authorities inform us that we can duplicate the system for $25 million. They have declared dividends as high as 400 percent upon their investment. Their employees are the worst-paid employees in the country. An operator used to be considered a skilled artisan and used to get fair wages; a great many of them are now working for from $20 to $25 a month. Men are being displaced and children put in their places. The great American people are compelled to pay extortionate prices for communicating with one another.

This ought to be a function of government—the telegraph ought to be operated in the interest of the people. And why not? What objection can possibly be made to it? Just imagine the advantages that would flow out from government ownership of telegraphs. The telegraph system would be indefinitely improved. We would send 20 messages where we send one now. We would want more lines, more employees, and a better service and a reduced cost. But we continue to permit a monopoly to take possession of and control this all-important function of our government.

Buy the Railroads

What is true of the telegraph is true of the railroads. *[Applause.]* A great many businessmen say these railroad strikes are disastrous and a menace to public business, to the business interests of the country. What are we going to do to avert them? Just take possession of the railroads and the question is solved. But they say, "We cannot afford to buy the railroads." That admission is a fatal one. Do you mean to tell me that the 70 million of our population cannot afford a luxury that a few people, a handful, indulge in? I don't believe that; I don't believe there is anything on American soil that the American people cannot afford to own. And the railroads would not be such an expensive investment after you had the water squeezed out of them.

Secretary Cobb of the Santa Fe investigating committee said the other day that there was not a railroad company in the United States that was not violating the Interstate Commerce law every day of its existence. They have forms of secret rebates, of which the favored shippers get the advantage. When they made an examination of the affairs of the Santa Fe system, they found that $7 million had disappeared. Mr. [Joseph] Reinhart was president of the company. He was permitted to retire. He is in social clover today up to his ears. Wealth, like charity, covers a multitude of sins. And what was done about it? Nothing. The great trusts and combinations have their secret branches.

There is specific charge made on the Northern Pacific system by Brayton Ives against the receivers.[26] There was no attention paid to it. They are the favored classes who enjoy the benefits of that discrimination that is prohibited by the Interstate Commerce law, and when it comes to a matter of travel, the rich men ride on passes, the middle classes have mileage, and poor people pay full fare.

And I am one of those who believe in going still further. I have arrived at the conclusion that as long as a vestige of the wage system remains, there is no escape from these slavish conditions. *[A voice: "There you touch anarchism."]* The machine has invaded every department of activity. It is displacing men by the thousands and tens of thousands, and the machine is said to be designed to bless the world. The machine is becoming more and more perfect every day, and it to a large extent reproduces itself.

People Own the Machine

I have just received a telegram from London saying that a typesetting machine has been perfected that sets the type of 20 compositors. If that be true, what is to become of the compositors of the country? Some people say, let them go into other occupations. But the workingmen are becoming more numerous and the places to work are becoming less. In the march of invention, machinery is to do the work of the world, and when that time comes the man who owns the machine will be the master of the world. I want the people to own the machines. *[A voice: "There is socialism for you."]*

As long as a workingman is compelled to work for such wages as his employer will allow him, under such conditions as his employer may impose, he is a slave. Call him a sovereign American citizen if you will, but he is a slave. Put yourself in that position *[a voice: "We are there now"]* and see if that is not literally true. Not only this, as long as men are competing with each other for a place to work, and the number of competitors is steadily increasing, the tendency of wages will be downward, and it will continue downward until the starvation point is reached. *[A voice: "It is there now."]* And no matter how humane or how just or even how generous the employing classes may be, that is a fact in the nature of things, and the steady reduction of wages is inevitable.

Now, I agree entirely with the worthy chairman of the evening when he says that we want to reduce the number of hours that constitute a day's labor. *[Applause.]* The rights of a single individual are as sacred as the rights of all the rest combined, and if there is a single man in the Republic who is denied the right to exchange his toil for the necessaries of life, there is slavery in our country. *[Applause.]* With 3 or 4 million others out of work, with a vast number of others who are working for a miserable pittance, we still find that in some of the factories, mines, mills, and shops of the country, men, women, and children are working from 12 to 16 hours a day.

There is no trouble about wealth or resources. We have them in fabulous abundance. What we want is a more equitable system of distribution. We want all men to have a fair chance in life. That was the theory of the government when it was founded. We don't want any privileged or any favored classes. We want no special privileges accorded by legislation or otherwise; but we do want to remove the handicap and give men an equal chance and an equal opportunity.

Four Hours a Day

Now, then, I am one of those who believe that if four hours a day will do the work of the world, let four hours constitute a day's work. *[Great applause.]* It does not matter to me what you call it. I believe in it. I want work for all men. In the city of Cleveland, there is a given amount of work to do and a given number of men to do it. Put them all to work and they can do it in about four or five hours a day, and it will be done just as well, if not better, than it is being done now.

We are sometimes told that the country is suffering from overproduction. There was never such a thing in the world. Give every man in Cleveland a good suit of clothes tonight and there won't be anything left in the stores; and fill all their stomachs and the grocers will have to send in more orders.

When men are out of work—and there are millions in that condition—they don't consume anything, they subsist upon charity. They have no money with which to buy anything, and in that exact proportion consumption lessens. Others are remanded to idleness. With improved machinery, they can turn out coal enough in three or four months to meet the demands of the market for a year. They run the mines three or four months, and then there is a lockout until the men are compelled to come back on any terms the company may affix. Mr. [John D.] Rockefeller took possession of the key of a very important storehouse of nature and said, "Whoever wants oil must pay tribute to me." He fixes the price of oil absolutely and you have got to pay his price, and he pays his employees wages fixed by himself and his corporations. There is no appeal from his decisions.

Now, I don't see what right a man has to station himself at a storehouse of nature and take possession of what was designed for the use of all mankind. *[Applause.]* And then Mr. Rockefeller increases, as he did last year, the price of kerosene from 20 to 40 percent and makes about $40 million by the operation. Then he gave the University of Chicago $3 million, and the whole world applauded. A great many people said, "Behold the modest philanthropist." I am not inclined to indulge in harsh names. I don't discuss Mr. Rockefeller personally—if we were in his place we would probably do as he is doing. He gives the University of Chicago $3 million—a mere pittance. I have a high appreciation of the educational institutions of our country, but I wouldn't want to get my education in such an institution. *[Applause.]* There is not an element of philanthropy in it. What would you think of a Jesse James University *[laughter]* or of a Captain Kidd College? The methods differ in kind as well as degree. Mr. Rockefeller and his corporations are enabled to extort these vast sums of money from the American people by legal processes compared to which grand larceny is a glittering virtue. I want it so that all the people will take possession of the oil fields and then build their own university. *[Applause.]*

Making Headway

But, I say again, we are making a little headway. The resistance is increasing. The opposition intensifies every day. There is a healthy public sentiment abroad; it is acquiring new force every day; it is beginning to crystallize. We are much in the position of the Republican Party in 1858, when Lincoln made his great speech at Chicago. There were a million and a half men who had already voted for reform. They differed about a great many propositions. Some were in favor of the total abolition of slavery, some others wanted conditional abolition, but they were all for reform. They were united upon one thing only, and that was upon what they didn't want. Lincoln made his great speech and he said, "Be patient and do not falter now, because we are to succeed in the near future."[27] And two years after, notwithstanding they were then torn into factions, two years afterward that reform sentiment swept the country, and slavery was extirpated from our soil. *[Applause.]*

Precisely so with the reform sentiment of this day. We differ about a great many matters simply because none of us comprehend them clearly. But we are getting new light. We want still more light; we all have the same end in view, but we are traveling upon different lines. But that there is to be a radical change in our social, in our industrial system in the near future, I have not the slightest doubt. Lincoln said, "You can fool all of the people some of the time, and some of the people all of the time, but you can't fool all the people all the time."[28] And if the immortal emancipator were still living, he would be on our side in this great contest. *[Applause.]* His startling prophecy is being fulfilled.

You remember that Jefferson said, "We want a government in which there shall be no extremely rich and no extremely poor."[29] We have them both. And Lincoln said that there was every indication of the development, the expansion of the money power that should subvert and destroy the liberty of the people. But the very factors that apparently threatened society are factors in the revolutionary processes that are to bring on the better day.

I am one of those who believe that what we call the wage system, that is to say the feudal system, that is to say the slave system, is in the last throes of dissolution. And I believe that we are getting together in a little closer touch. I believe that men fraternize more than they did a little while ago. They are becoming more tolerant of one another's views; they are beginning to reason together in a spirit of true humanity; they are beginning to take an inventory of their resources; they are beginning to map out the lines of progress; they are mustering the reform forces. And to me it is perfectly clear that in the very near future they are to vote their way from bondage to emancipation. *[Applause.]*

Lowell said:

> They are slaves who fear to speak
> For the fallen and the weak;
> They are slaves who weakly choose
> Hatred, scoffing, and abuse,
> Rather than in silence shrink
> From the truth they needs must think;
> They are slaves who dare not be
> In the right with two or three.[30]

A Broader Humanity

Lowell also said, "He is true to God who is true to man."[31] And we agitators are simply asking for a broader humanity. We are believers in the brotherhood of man. It does sometimes seem as if the lust for gold has eaten the heart out of humanity; that in this mad pursuit of the almighty dollar we forget the better and nobler things of life.

When the question is asked how much a man is worth, do we allude to integrity and intelligence and benevolence and kindness, and all those beautiful qualities that dignify and glorify men? Not at all. We have reference to the amount of money he controls. Money is of vastly more importance than manhood. Men are weighed according to their possessions, and if you would tell me how much money a man has got I can almost determine what degree he marks on the social thermometer.

But in the world of labor the conditions are changed, and there is every reason why we should look confidently on the future. The splendid prophecy of Burns will yet be fulfilled; in the world of labor at least we are beginning to estimate men according to their character. More than a century ago Burns sang of the quality of men, and in that song there are all the stars and stripes that are in the American flag:

> A man's a man for a' that * * *
> An honest man, though e'er so poor,
> Is king of men for a' that.[32]

We believe in the philosophy of Burns. We believe that a man can only help himself by helping his fellow men; that we are dependent upon one another; that we should have a thought, a care for our fellows, and especially for those who are less fortunate than ourselves. Suppose that I am born with superior mental endowments, keen foresight, good judgment, and business capacity, and I am enabled to take advantage of my surroundings because of my superiority over my fellow men. Suppose I have a half-witted brother who has the brand of inferiority upon him, who is unable to provide himself with the common necessities of life. He is as little responsible for his condition as I am for mine, as little to blame as I am entitled to credit. What kind of a man would I be if I were to surround myself with wealth and riot and revel in luxury and let my brother starve to death?

We look upon the human race as constituting one family. Every man who is in the right, regardless of his color or conditions, or who is trying to be in the right, is my brother. *[Applause.]* I believe in the brotherhood of man. I believe in looking beyond the family boundary alone; looking out into the world, knowing something of all the unfortunate conditions that prevail, and giving ourselves the duty of doing what little we can to correct them.

A man cannot afford to be mean and selfish and contemptible; life is too short. We are only here a little while—a few ticks of the pendulum of time and we pass from the scene of action. The world is not just, and is a long way from being generous, but it is getting to be a little better, and I believe that a labor day is coming when the workingmen shall stand as free and independent as any in the land, and shall be rewarded for this toil of brain and hand. For the right is marching on.

I thank you from the depths of my heart for the patience and the kindness with which you have listened to me.

The American University and the Labor Problem†
February 4, 1896

———————————————————————————————

Terre Haute, Ind., February 4, 1896

Strictly speaking, the American university is doing little, if anything, toward solving the "great labor problem," and the reason why, if sought, is found in the fact that neither the American nor the European universities were founded for any purpose directly or remotely connected with the solution of any labor problem, great or small. Such is the history of European universities, and in the founding of American universities history may be said to have repeated itself.

In replying to the interrogatories addressed to me by the editor-in-chief of *The Adelbert*,[33] "Is the American university doing its share in solving the great Labor Problem? If not, where is it lacking and what suggestions would you make for its improvement in that direction?" hypercriticism of the American university is not required, and yet facts should be courageously stated regardless of consequences.

As a general proposition, universities are aristocratic institutions. This is preeminently true of European universities, and to make matters still worse they were from the date of inception hedged about with ecclesiastic prerogatives and bigotries which, *nolens volens*,[34] created a class of superior beings as separate and distinct from labor as if the lines defining their limits had been rivers of fire.

That American universities, as in the case of Harvard and Yale, should have inherited the defects of European institutions is of easy and satisfactory explanation. The French, English, and German universities were creations of kings and popes, and within their sacred precincts no labor problem was ever considered except to find the most effective methods of enslaving the masses,

———————————————————————————————

†   Published in *The Adelbert* (Case Western Reserve University, Cleveland), vol. 6, no. 8 (February 1896), 167–169.

and how effectively this work has gone forward in Europe for the past 600 years the merest novice in investigation may find abundant proof; indeed, exclusiveness is the distinguishing characteristic of the ancient and modern university, and no amount of learned sophistication can obscure the fact. It was true of the Lyceum when Aristotle taught, when Grecian philosophy was in its meridian glory, and the academy of Plato was not invaded except by the favored few, and it is as true now as then that a university education is reserved for those who have money to purchase it, and the fact that universities confer degrees is in itself a power employed for constituting a species of nobility which, however well deserved in certain cases, considered from an educational point of view as rewards for merit, always served the purpose of creating an aristocracy of DDs, LLDs, etc.,[35] often as obnoxiously exclusive as a titled nobility created by kings.

The graduates of universities, with their diplomas and degrees, boasting of their *alma maters,* as a rule, regard themselves, as compared with the "common people," of superior mold, and this fact is scarcely less conspicuous in America than in Europe. The rule is stated: There are numerous exceptions, but observation verifies the proposition and that such defects and infirmities are largely the result of inheritance, few will be found to question the averment.

Referring directly to the interrogatory "Is the American university doing its share in solving the great Labor Problem?" after grouping all the facts, the reply must be in the negative; but just what is meant by the "great labor problem" is susceptible of so many and such varied conclusions that the difficulties evoked are well calculated to involve discussion in ceaseless entanglements. Labor in the United States is confronted with numerous problems, and which one should be designated as the "great labor problem" must be of necessity left to the judgment of those who are interested in such questions.

There are those who are constantly championing the hypothesis that there exists something in the nature of an irrepressible conflict between labor and capital, and that to harmonize the belligerents constitutes the solution of the "great labor problem" and the error, for such it is, so permeates discussion that confusion becomes worse confounded as the debate proceeds and necessarily so, because the premise is a myth—the truth being that capital and labor, instead of occupying a hostile attitude toward each other, enjoy the most peaceful relationship. This must of necessity be the condition, since the truth is axiomatic that labor, and only labor, creates capital. But when it is stated that a conflict exists between laborers and capitalists, a problem is presented worthy of the attention of the American university. It so happens, however, that the university, to use a figure of speech, is itself a capitalist and has never had anything in common with labor, and therefore is not doing its "share," whatever that may be, in solving any labor problem.

In this there is nothing peculiar to the American university, the facts standing out as prominently in the history of all universities.

What, in this connection, could be more interesting than to know what labor problem has been solved by any of the great universities of Europe? To be more particular and pertinent, because of language inheritance, what labor problems have the great historical and wealthy universities of England solved? For more than 600 years the Cambridge and Oxford universities have flourished, and if either of them has solved any great labor problem for the benefit of the toilers of England, the facts should be stated. A correspondent for a Chicago paper, writing recently from London, after recapitulating numerous and aggravating afflictions of labor in England says, "The result is that England has upon her hands an enormous pauperized population, and the government is seriously embarrassed by continuing demands for relief."

What is true of England is equally true of the United States, for notwithstanding we have Harvard and Yale and perhaps a hundred more American universities. We also have "an enormous pauperized population," and if these universities have solved any labor problem, the present is happily opportune to herald the fact.

If the American university has failed in doing its share in solving the "great labor problem," no laborious research is required to find a plausible reason for its shortcomings, and recent humiliating incidents transpiring in the operation of the University of Chicago become sufficiently explanatory to satisfy the most exacting. The dismissal of Professor Bemis proclaims the fact that the American university is not equipped to solve labor problems, but is arrogantly hostile to labor and further proof of its opposition to labor, if demanded, is found in President Harper's explanation of the dismissal of Professor Bemis, in which he is reported to have said substantially that to "express friendship for workingmen is well enough, *but we get our money from the other side.*"[36]

The American university is not seeking to solve labor problems because the performance of such work would require the arraignment of the capitalistic class from which it "gets its money," and the capitalistic class solves all labor problems by creating environments which pauperize labor and reduce it to vassalage.

Suggestions for the improvement of the "American university" made by anyone identified with labor, though responding to a request to offer hints in that direction, would be regarded by university presidents, professors, and graduates as impertinences, plebeian rudeness, born of ignorance and audacity, and yet it so happens that every advance step taken to solve labor problems, bearing the stamp of common sense and justice, has been made by men within the ranks of labor and not by men wearing university titles and equipped with the advantages their *alma maters* could confer.

But such statements are not put forth to indicate intentional culpability on the part of the American university. It was not founded nor endowed for solving labor problems, and its curriculum never includes studies specially designed to aid in the performance of such tasks, and any improvement in that direction would involve such radical changes as would disturb their foundations.

The American university, if it would do any share in solving the "great labor problem," would be required to attack the corrupting power of money wielded by corporations, trusts, and syndicates, as also the American aristocracy, whether built upon coal oil or codfish, watered stocks, banks, bullion, or boodles. This, as in the case of the Chicago institution, it would not do because it is from such sources that it gets its money. It would be required to employ professors to lecture upon the degrading influences of starvation wages, which darken ten thousand American homes. It would be confronted with the exiling power of labor-saving machinery, which is filling the land with armies of enforced idlers which thoughtful men regard as dangerous and threatening to the perpetuity of our republican institutions. It would have to array itself against a corrupt judiciary and hold it up as a target for the maledictions of liberty-loving Americans.

If it is held that the "American university" is solving labor problems by diffusing throughout the land the blessings of a "higher education," including football and other athletic tournaments, as also displays of pyrotechnic oratory, it may be said that ancient Greece and Rome indulged in such classic pastimes and after a few hundred years reached a condition of desuetude without solving any labor problem whatever.

Gladstone, the "grand old man," the justly renowned English statesman and scholar and graduate of Oxford, whose knowledge of Greek is so profound that he could, if required, rival Demosthenes as a Grecian orator, may have during his brilliant career solved some labor problem for which his name will be held in grateful remembrance by English workingmen, but if such is the case the fact is yet to be chronicled. And Daniel Webster, a graduate of Dartmouth University, the great expounder of the Constitution, found out by university processes of reasoning that "government is founded on property"—a heresy advocated by the American university.

If the American university would have any "share" in solving labor problems, a change in its policy will be required. It will have to renounce all allegiances which separate it from the great body of the people and permit its colleges, if need be, to become the tombs of its errors, whether inherited or adopted, that it may in its teachings represent the American democracy rather than the American aristocracy.

Competitive System Pressing Labor Down: Interview with the *Atlanta Constitution*[†]

February 12, 1896

"The day for strikes on a large scale to settle labor troubles has about passed."
The speaker was Eugene V. Debs.

* * *

The labor leader is smooth-shaven and smooth-talking, tall, erect, keen-eyed, and has character written all over his face. He might be mistaken for a relative of Bill Nye's.[37] He said that he had been on an extended trip through the East prior to starting south. Before going east, he was out in the Northwest. Before that he was in jail—for abetting the great strike of 1894. Imprisonment does not appear to have gone hard with him. He says that he read and wrote during his term. He studied then too, and thought more than he had ever done before in the same length of time. It is an individual opinion that Mr. Debs experienced a change of views during his retirement from society.

Four Million Are Idle

He fell to chatting at once about the condition of labor throughout the world and the methods of improving that condition.

There are 4 million idle men in this country. Perhaps they are not idle all the time, but that number are without regular employment. In some places the idle are so numerous that they are a menace to the rest of society. Work is the

---

†   Published as "Debs Talks of Labor" in the *Atlanta Constitution*, vol. 28 (February 13, 1896), 3.

natural lot of mankind, but when he cannot get work, what is he to do? A man who would be a good citizen if he could get employment may become vicious when out of work and starving. The transition is a natural one.

What is the cause of so many being without employment? They want to work, but they cannot get it. We cannot blame them for not having something to do. They are simply victims of circumstances, and if they were all at work there would be another 4 million without any, and you and I might be among them. The different parts of society are not properly adjusted. Improved machinery throws thousands of men out of work all the time. As the machinery is improved, and as it is constantly being improved, the number of idle is increased. The tendency always is to decrease the cost of production.

The competitive system of business is a weight constantly pressing labor down. Then labor competes with itself. So you see, it has to fight itself, improved machinery, and the cunning shrewdness and avarice of corporations and trusts. It is human nature to want great wealth and power. Legislation is unable to check the injustice of corporations to labor and even to their own small investors.

"What is your remedy for the existing conditions?" Mr. Debs was asked.
That is a great problem. The situation is getting worse. Business failures grow more numerous. Some say the tariff is the cause, others say that it is due to the financial policy of the country, and others have still different explanations. I do not think that legislation on the tariff or finances can bring about a permanent improvement. It is my opinion that justice and morality must be at the bottom of the new condition of things. Nothing that disregards justice can stand permanently. I am not a socialist, but I do not see lasting improvement until there is a radical change somewhere. I am reading a book here which says that the world must be regenerated. I have just finished that Italian work there, which is much on the same line. The heart of mankind must be reached and touched. Man must begin by being just to his fellow. I do not see much hope in legislation. That does not go on to the seat of the trouble, though it can aid.

Shorter hours of employment would give work to more men. Complete organization will better enable the laboring men to protect themselves against the encroachments of employers. The stronger the labor organizations are, the less prospect of a strike. It is the history of labor organizations that as they grow in strength and years, they become more conservative. Large aggregations of men are more conservative than small groups. There is less impulse proportionally in the larger number than in the few. A wrong idea has gone out about our organization, the American Railway Union. We are not anarchists. We want to secure and retain the sympathy of the masses, and we are confident that when they hear our views and policies they will give us an even chance with the other fellow.

Haven't the corporations consolidated? Haven't the railroads a General Managers' Association? Then why not all the employees of the railroad organize? There has never been much serious trouble in the South between labor and its employers. That is good and makes me think that it is a fine field for organization. There is that much less danger of strikes, and these conflicts are dreadful. The employee stands a chance of losing what little he has, for as I said a while ago, there are millions of men right now clamoring for work, and the corporations are in close touch with each other.

No, I do not look for anything more in the way of strikes except some spasmodic outbreak. My dream is to get the workingmen of all classes on the railroads banded together into a harmonious whole, each class, so to speak, preserving its identity and autonomy for all purposes pertaining to its own affairs. The mere existence of a great organization will be a weighty factor in the settlement of grievances. The plan is perfectly feasible, and the order is growing. There is an opposition to be lived down. I recognize that. Whenever a strike occurs, some of the public are inconvenienced. A shipper or a traveler finds himself inconvenienced. He at once blames the striker, not going back to the first cause and seeing that the railroad company was at fault. In that way we get the worst of it. But that situation will change too.

This should be a country of happy, prosperous, contented people. There is room enough for hundreds of millions. Everybody ought to have work at remunerative wages. The great problem is how to reach the highest possible state of prosperity for all people, eliminating the vast fortunes and the terrible poverty and starvation which we see everywhere.

Mr. Debs will see something of Atlanta tonight, and tonight will have in his audience many prominent citizens. He is a fluent speaker, is intense in the work in which he is engaged, and impresses one very strongly with his energy and force.

What Can the Church Do to Benefit
the Condition of the Laboring Man?
Speech at First Baptist Church, Terre Haute[†]

March 22, 1896

Ladies, gentlemen, and friends:—

First of all, I desire to thank the reverend gentleman[38] and the congregation of this church for the kindness which made it possible for me to stand here tonight. In discussing the question of the relation of the church to the laboring man, it is my purpose to speak in kindness and in the spirit that prompted the invitation. The labor question is the supreme question of the day, the great question into which all other questions are merged, the question which embraces the interests of society. There are many Christian people, I regret to say, who are prejudiced against the laboring classes, or rather against organized labor. Organized labor, as I see it, is for the uplifting of humanity; it is to save those poor creatures who are the victims of circumstance they did not create, but which they are powerless to overcome. We have passed the point referred to by Goldsmith, when he wrote

> Ill fares the land, to hastening ills a prey,
> Where wealth accumulates and men decay.[39]

We have passed this point, I say, and today thousands of human beings are the victims of man's inhumanity and rapacity. In speaking of our beautiful Christian civilization, I desire to call your attention to something I saw in Kalamazoo, Michigan, not a great while ago. Kalamazoo is a great furniture manufacturing point of the country. I went to that city and to one of the factories and there found men working for the pitiful sum of 50 cents a day—$3 per week. I saw more than this—something that should bring the blush of shame to the face of a Christian man or woman. I saw little girls in that factory working at the machines, maidens on whose faces the pangs of hunger were to be seen in every feature and on whose hands there were missing from one to four fingers. We can but exclaim what a commentary on Christian civilization.

---

† Published in *Terre Haute Express,* March 23, 1896. Reprinted as "Eugene V. Debs in the Pulpit" by the *American Nonconformist,* April 2, 1896.

But this brings me to the tramp question, one of the most melancholy phases of life, and a question I have given much attention. I venture the assertion that not one tramp in ten thousand is a tramp from choice. Most of you can remember a time when the sight of a tramp was an uncommon thing. Then people rushed to the windows and exclaimed in horror: "There goes a tramp!" You know what the condition is today.

The tramp question is easily explained. In the march of human ingenuity has come the introduction of the machine. It is to be found everywhere. The introduction of the machine takes men out of positions. He kisses his wife and little children goodbye and starts in search of employment. He has not gone far before he finds he is one of the army of thousands which is being recruited daily. He is an unfortunate as yet, not a tramp. His clothes become ragged as the weeks pass, society frowns on him, all doors are barred against him. He passes the fine church, which is fast filling up with fashionably dressed people. He looks at his own clothes, once more at the church, and then passes on a tramp and social exile.

It has been said by a man, I regret to say a being who is a pillar in one of the Christian churches in Chicago, that the cheapest commodity on the market today is human flesh and blood. Thomas Wickes, of the Pullman Company, says that man is a commodity. I can conceive of no more horrible thing, think of no more terrible condition than the soul of a man being a commodity.

Going back to the subject of tramps, we will picture the man I referred to looking back, as it were, at the little cottage he left with the introduction of the machine. He sees his wife and babe, but oh, how different from what he left them. He has tried to find work, but there is none to be found. It is a fact, friends, that every position has 100 people waiting to fill it. This tramp—we will now call him—becomes embittered against society. I would not be a tramp for $10,000 a day and be compelled to undergo their hardships and experiences.

I know from personal experience that it takes courage to face idleness. I was out of a job, far from home and without money. I know how to sympathize with them, and my heart goes out to him—he is my brother. But society does not permit of his redemption, the doors are closed, and he is an exile. It seems to me the church has done little or nothing to help these unfortunates. I mean the church as an institution, for these pastors are ever doing all in their power to lift up the poor. It cannot be denied the powerful and rich churches have been arrayed against the poor and unfortunate.

Mr. Debs here read from The Arena an article by Carlos Martyn, DD, on "Churchianity vs. Christianity." It is in part as follows:

> [The church] contents itself with alleviation, and does not study to cure. It gives pity, not justice. It provides charity, instead of insisting on a rearrangement of the situation. * * * It builds cathedrals, not men. It meets on Sunday for worship in splendid exclusion and seclusion, and shuts the building through the week, while the congregation is occupied at the theatre, in the ballroom, or on Wall Street. The pulpit, warned off from the treatment of living issues, drones through a parrotlike repetition of the creed, and puts the emphasis on belief when it should put it on conduct.[40]

The man who said this is not a wild-eyed anarchist but is one of the most prominent Christian ministers.

Two years ago, the great Pullman strike was on, and 14,000 men, women, and children were starving because they had the courage to resist conditions that were making them the victims of the greed and rapacity of a great corporation; the churches of Chicago were against them. There were, I am glad to be able to say, a few exceptions. At that time the big ministers, without ever considering the justness of the cause that prompted these men to act as they did, welcomed with loud voice the arrival of the United States troops, which were to send to the souls of some men to the bar of God. These men had done nothing except demand living wages. From their pulpits these ministers denounced the Pullman sufferers. Thus the modern church has departed from the doctrine of Jesus Christ. The Savior preached universal love and equality. The bending sky was the roof of his church, and the walls were measured by the extent of the universe. It occurred to me then that the minister who preached the doctrine of Christ is soon going to find himself minus a congregation, or, rather, without a job. During this dark period there was one minister, the Reverend Dr. [William H.] Carwardine, who took the trouble to investigate before he condemned. He had the courage to tell the whole truth, but he was dismissed for doing it.

The labor question is up now as it never has been before, and is appealing to the hearts of all the people. You can hear it discussed in the banking houses and elsewhere. People are beginning to see. They are able to discern that crime springs from this social disorder, from this present system of production and distribution. Ministers can, in my opinion, discuss these questions in the pulpit and still be in the correct work.

Mr. Debs read from the work of George D. Herron, a professor in an Iowa college, in part as follows:

In fact, we are and have been in a state of industrial anarchy; of social lawlessness. *Selfishness is always social disintegration. Competition is not law,
but anarchy.* That competition is the life of industry is the most profane
and foolish of social falsehoods. Cain was the author of the competitive
theory. The cross of Jesus stands as its eternal denial. It is social imbecility.
It is economic waste. It is the destruction of life.[41]

The whole social question is fast resolving itself into a question of whether
or not capital can be brought into submission to law. Again, if I had made these
statements I should have been called an anarchist. Following Professor Herron's
theory, he says of the social problem, it is explained in the words "survival of
the fittest," which really means the "survival of the strongest." Fitting illustration is given by reference to the large department stores. According to *Dun and
Bradstreet* there are 65 business failures daily. These large department stores are
slowly crowding the smaller concerns out of the business. You may pass up the
streets of Chicago and there see the places where once there was a thriving little
business for rent. They have simply been driven out, and in a little while will
be recruits to the army of the unemployed. We hear people say there are better
times ahead. My friends, I am of the firm belief there will be no better times
under the present system. There can be no improvement in the times so long as
it is possible for one man to achieve success on the failure of another. Phillips
Brooks said that competition running riot would ultimately destroy itself. This
I also believe. We hear of overproduction. It is nothing of the kind. It is under-
consumption. You and I know that if the mills and factories were kept running
the year round there would not be an overproduction.

Wealth is concentrating and that very rapidly. We can number our millionaires by the thousands and the mendicants by the million. But you ask,
what can the church do to remedy this evil? One thing it can do, and it seems
to me with the utmost propriety: Give attention to the social question. This
is a question that will not soon wear out. Ministers sometimes attend labor
meetings, and I have noticed them urge the laboring men to be law-abiding.
Now, this advice may also be given to the rich. There are rich lawbreakers, and
many who feast on spoils are pillars of the churches. Ministers can talk about
these things. It wouldn't do well to do it in Trinity Church. It would be unwise
to condemn a system of which it is a beneficiary.

I do not fail to see the great power of the church for good. If Christ was
here on earth, I am sure he would be on the side of the wronged and suffering.
He would not tolerate the present wrong social system. I believe he would give
some of our courts attention. In some courts, justice has been purchasable.

Like human flesh and blood, it has been a commodity. Judge Dundy of Denver sentenced a tramp to prison for life for stealing one cent. Another man stole $200,000 and got two years. The railroads of this country annually spend $40 million to debauch legislation. This subject can be discussed by the ministers.

Some people believe the strike to be unlawful and I might agree with them. At the same time, it does not occur to the average businessman that the men are driven to it. None of you are in ignorance of the fact that railroad corporations combine. They do this often to reduce wages. Then why has not the employee the right to do the same thing? It is a matter of self-preservation with him. He strikes, and the people are too ready to condemn him. The responsibility should be divided. Labor has made mistakes, serious mistakes. Capital has done the same thing. There is only one right way to settle them. Laboring men do not want charity, they want wages. I can conceive of no more humiliating thing than for an able-bodied man receiving charity. Employers do not willfully wrong their employees. They are simply victims themselves of this wrong system, and, like the laborer, require emancipation.

We see the coal miner come out of that great hole in the ground after having worked for hours. He goes to his hovel—he has no home. He hasn't even a cottage. It's a hovel, a hut or a cave. Talk of home seems a mockery when we think of the home of a section hand on the Louisville & Nashville Railroad, the home of a man getting 65 cents a day for his work. Ruskin said the American nation was one of cottages. It is nothing of the kind.

Let us all believe in the brotherhood of man. The world is not just, not even generous, but I believe it is getting a little better. I have attempted to give a brief outline of the social conditions as they exist. There is a great work before us all and we must be up and doing. From the cradle, where the mother pours her heart in lullaby to her dimpled babe—from there it is but a few short steps to where youth bends above old age and kisses for the last time the clay cold lips of death.

Thanking you, my friends, from the bottom of my heart for your attention and attendance and my good brother whose invitation brought me here, I bid you all good night.

ARU Ready for Another Fight:
Interview with the Associated Press[†]

April 10, 1896

We do not want another big strike and will try to avoid it. All labor troubles should be adjusted through arbitration, and that is our aim. However, while hoping for the best, we will be prepared for the worst. We can make a much longer and harder fight than two years ago. We are well organized in both the East and the West, and the membership is as large as ever and increasing rapidly.

I have just returned from a trip through Georgia, Alabama, and South Carolina.[42] We organized four thousand men in two weeks, and I never witnessed such enthusiasm. We were also very successful in Buffalo and other eastern cities. Our organization is stronger than ever in the West and Northwest. The only places we are weak is in Chicago, Milwaukee, Detroit, and the other cities where the effects of the big strike were felt most. We will begin the work of reorganization in Chicago within 90 days and will have a larger membership here than ever before.

[†]   Associated Press wire copy, datelined Chicago and published as "Another Fight" in *Los Angeles Daily Times,* vol. 15 (April 11, 1896), 3.

"I Will Not Serve for Public Office":
Statement to the Press, Birmingham, Alabama[†]

May 24, 1896

I will state for the public print that I will not serve for public office. I have a fixed conception of a public office, and I do not care to hold one. Politics and labor are two different institutions, and I will not give up labor for politics. The two don't go well together, and I believe I am of more use to labor. No, I will not go into politics, and will not accept the nomination for president.[43]

Open Letter to Alfred S. Edwards,
Editor of the *Coming Nation*[‡44]

June 8, 1896

Terre Haute, Ind., June 8, 1896

Editor, *The Coming Nation*

Dear Brother:—

Your note of the 30th ult. [May 30] with enclosure herewith returned was handed to me at Nashville. I should have answered more promptly but was kept so busy that I was prevented from so doing. Referring to the Birmingham interview, I am not correctly quoted.[45] I used no language such as is credited to me in the line marked by your correspondent. The American Railway Union stands committed to the People's Party by a unanimous vote of its delegates in convention assembled. This being the case, you will perceive how absurd and mendacious I would be to make such a statement as is contained in the enclosed interview. I

---

†   Wire service report. As published in "Not a Politician" in *St. Mary's Star* (Kansas), May 28, 1896, 8.

‡   Published in *The Coming Nation*, whole no. 161 (June 20, 1896), 1.

am not only in favor of organized labor going actively into politics, but I have urged such action in all my addresses during the past two years. Indeed, the action of our convention in this matter was taken upon my recommendation.

What I did say was that I was an official of a labor organization and as such I could not be a candidate for public office. I have always been opposed to self-seekers, and in order to keep myself free from even a suspicion of being one myself, I have resolutely set my face against holding public office. There are special reasons in my own case why this should be so. I am willing to serve the cause of labor in any way in my power, but I cannot see what good would come either to the cause or to myself by accepting a nomination for public office. I prefer to do what little I can in my own way untrammeled by what would be certain to be construed as personal political aspiration.

You are at liberty to use this communication in any way you may see fit. I should say in this connection that I am often placed at a disadvantage by being incorrectly quoted in press interviews and alleged interviews. I am not infrequently made to say what I never said or thought of saying. The Birmingham interview has appeared in various forms and has undergone various changes to suit the purposes of those who have an object in having me appear in a false and self-contradictory light before the public.

I regret very much not having been able to visit you while in Tennessee. When next I visit your state, I hope to have the pleasure of a few hours at Ruskin.[46] I met a number of your members at Nashville and was greatly pleased with them. They impressed me as being men of the right stamp, and if the colony is made up in great part of such as they I have no doubt as to its ultimate success.

With best wishes, believe me always,

Yours fraternally,
Eugene V. Debs

Telegram to Henry Demarest Lloyd, Delegate to the People's Party Convention, Saint Louis[†]

July 25, 1896

Terre Haute, Ind., July 25 [1896]

Hon. Henry D. Lloyd,[47] Delegate,

People's Party Convention, St. Louis:—

Please do not permit use of my name for nomination.

—E. V. Debs

Without the Populists, the Democrats Cannot Win: From a Letter to George P. Garrison[‡]

August 6, 1896

Without the support of the Populists, the Democratic Party could not win. The Populists, animated by patriotism, accorded first honors to the Democratic nominee, and the Democrats, if they are animated by similar motives, will now accord the Populists second place by placing Mr. Watson[48] on the ticket with Mr. Bryan.

Mr. Sewall[49] can well afford to step aside to effect this union of the two great forces and insure the election of the people's candidates. Such action on the part of Mr. Sewall would make him a far greater man than vice president. Failing to accord the People's Party such recognition by giving them a place on

---

[†]   From contemporary wire service reports, multiple published sources.

[‡]   First published in the *Omaha Daily Bee,* date and page unspecified. Republished as part of an Associated Press wire report, datelined Omaha, August 16, 1896, and attributing this correspondence with George P. Garrison of Chadron, Nebraska.

the national ticket, there will be dissatisfaction which may culminate in open revolt, especially in the Southern states, where Populists have suffered all sorts of indignities at the hands of the Bourbon Democracy. And this may cost Mr. Bryan his election and put McKinley and goldbugism in power.

For the mere offices, we care nothing, for we scorn spoils in any form. But for the principle involved we care and have a right to care much. There is a vast difference between Mr. Bryan and the Democratic Party. If the latter's only ambition is to swallow the People's Party so as to place them in power and get possession of the offices, their design will and should be thwarted. I would rather see McKinley elected than have another Democratic administration.

"Give Me Liberty or Give Me Death": A Labor Day Message[†]
September 7, 1896

Patrick Henry of Virginia, at a time when King George of England was engaged in massing the resources of his kingdom to subjugate his American colonies and reduce the American people to slavery, immortalized his name by exclaiming, "Give me liberty or give me death."

Patrick Henry was not, by birth or education, one of Virginia's aristocracy. He had no landed estate. He was eminently a poor man. He was one of the "plain people." He was not, in a university sense, an educated man. Unsuccessful in various business ventures, he was a reader of books and a student of affairs, and finally became an advocate, a lawyer, and in that profession found his rightful place in the list of patriots of his time, and with the stride of a giant became the peer of Washington, Hancock, Adams, Quincy, and Lee,[50] and by his fearless courage and unequaled eloquence, called the American nation to arms in the defense of liberty and independence.

On one occasion, when the perils of his country were being discussed, when the shadows of coming events spread out dark and appalling from

---

†   Published in *Cleveland Press*, Labor Day edition, September 7, 1896. Reprinted in the *Railway Times*, vol. 3, no. 18 (September 15, 1896), 3.

Massachusetts to Georgia, when the choice was between fight or flight, liberty or slavery, British subjugation or American independence, Patrick Henry grasped with prescient genius, cause and effect, the perils and the sacrifices involved, and accepting them all with a courage as dauntless as ever inspired a patriot, and with hope and faith aflame, uttered the imperishable words, "Give me liberty or give me death."

What did he mean, and what do men now mean, who so often quote the words of the illustrious patriot?

Around him, far and near, from the North to the South, there was African chattel slavery. Is it to be supposed that the great Virginian meant give me death rather than chattel slavery? No one imagines such to have been Patrick Henry's idea, but rather than submit to a foreign potentate, aided and abetted by American Tories and traitors, rather than be the vassal of an English king and an English nobility and aristocracy, his choice was death.

History is repeating itself. True, England is not sending over her armies under her Burgoynes and Cornwallises.[51] Her fleets of warships are not hovering upon our coasts. She is not taking armed possession of our cities, but nevertheless she is plotting to overthrow the liberties of American citizens.

In the days of the Revolution, days that "tried men's souls,"[52] England bought 30,000 Hessians, "dumb driven cattle," armed and equipped to subjugate the American colonies. She does not now use her gold to buy Hessians; but she does use it to transform Americans into Hessians, and where there was one Benedict Arnold to betray his country in the dark days of the Revolution, there are now a thousand in alliance with England's moneylenders ready, for gold, to betray their country and establish in the United States English domination in financial affairs.

Whom are these Benedict Arnolds, these Tories, these Hessian cattle? The answer is on every American patriot's tongue. It is borne on every breeze. It glows in every patriot's eye. It is voiced from the Atlantic to the Pacific, from the lakes to the gulf. It is, that they are the ones who manage trusts and syndicates, banks and factories, railroads and mortgages; those who employ workingmen and workingwomen, and ceaselessly strive to reduce wages, that they may grow rich and still richer by their piracies, the millionaires, the men who constitute the money power, who speculate in bonds and gamble in stocks, who contract the currency and create panics at their will, who persuade Grover Cleveland to issue gold bonds for gold barons, and pocket millions by their cunning and their knavery, who grasp the president and his cabinet and transform them into mere automata, and compel them to dance to the jingle of gold in Lombard and Wall Streets.[53]

I unhesitatingly affirm that the subject is eminently and preeminently appropriate for Labor Day discussion.

Those whom I have referred to as being in alliance to secure English domination in American finances have been in alliance also with English capitalists to take possession of vast areas of American land, and to control numerous American industries, especially American railroads, many of which are operated in the interest of English, Holland, and German capitalists, so that now multiplied thousands of American toilers are the vassals of European capitalists and aristocrats, and are being plundered in their interests.

What more do these English lords and Tories want? What further humiliation and degradation of workingmen do they contemplate? The answer is easy. They expect to rob them of their ballots, or what is the same thing, by bulldozing, intimidating, and blacklisting methods, compel them to make their ballots not only record a lie, but that under the lash of their masters, their ballots shall record the fact that American workingmen are like Benedict Arnold and his associate Tory apostates, traitors to truth, to manhood, to liberty and independence, and traitors to their families, their fellow men, and country.

The issue is squarely made. It is up for debate. British emissaries are here.

The alliance between American Tories and English enemies of America is to be perpetuated, and workingmen are to be enslaved.

In view of such things, what will Labor Day orators say? I do not know, but this I do know, if they are true to themselves and to their country, true to liberty and independence, true to their fellow workingmen and to free institutions, free speech, and undebauched judiciary, and to the great body of the people, they will rise and expand with their theme and exclaim as did Patrick Henry, a hundred years ago, "Give me liberty or give me death."

Endorsement of William J. Bryan for President of the United States†

September 1896

To members of the American Railway Union
and all railway employees in the United States:

Greeting:—

The undersigned, constituting the Board of Directors of the American Railway Union, desire to address you upon a matter of momentous import in connection with the great political campaign now in progress. You have no doubt been struck with the unprecedented activity and astounding tactics of railway owners and managers in this campaign. High officials are going up and down the lines addressing employees and warning them against the frightful consequences of free silver coinage. Roundhouses, depots, and shops have been temporarily changed into political wigwams. "Sound money" clubs have been organized and employees intimidated to join them. Circulars and campaign documents are being delivered to employees with their wages, and in many instances employees are given plainly to understand that their continuance in service depends upon their supporting the gold standard candidates. In this proceeding, the money question only is permitted to be discussed, *and only one side of that.*

Now, what of all this? The railroad managers are overwhelming employees with predictions of frightful disaster which will follow in the wake of free coinage. Wages will be cut in two, they say, thousands will be thrown out of employment, and the country ruined. This one issue is forced upon employees to the exclusion of all others. Their minds are not to be diverted from the free silver calamity a single instant. It is to command their united, ceaseless, and terrified gaze to the very election booth, so that by no possibility may the discovery be made that "sound money" is only a pretext for deceiving and hoodwinking employees, and that railroad managers have a totally different motive for transforming the corporations they represent into huge Republican machines in this campaign.

The money question has been in American politics in all its various forms since the foundation of the government. When have railroad corporations

---

† Published as "Address to Railway Employees" in the *Railway Times,* vol. 3, no. 18 (September 15, 1896), 1.

organized, drilled, and openly commanded their employees to vote the company's ticket? Never before to an extent that would even remotely compare with their brazen activity in this campaign. Employees have yielded up everything, and now they are to be stripped of their votes and deprived of their last means of protection against oppression and injustice.

And now, we ask, why this unheard-of activity on the part of railroad managers for Bryan's defeat and McKinley's election? How is it to be accounted for? We appeal to railroad employees to *pause and think.* The like of the present situation has never been witnessed. The country stands amazed in the presence of such bold, bald, and shameless intimidation. Again, we ask, what does it mean? What can be its significance? Why such ceaseless, stupendous, and desperate efforts to control an election? Is it on account of free coinage? No! The absurdity of the proposition is evident upon the very face of it. That railroad companies have some interest in the money question is conceded, but that they would turn earth, heaven, and hell on that account, to prevent an injury to their "poor employees," is not only ridiculous, but an insult to every employee of common intelligence who is not wholly the property of the company.

They have been cutting the wages of their employees by all the means ingenuity could suggest, and if they believed free silver would "cut in two" the wages they are now receiving, we know of nothing in their past record that would warrant the assumption that they would oppose free coinage.

Oh, no; it is not free silver that has unloosened and enraged this railroad Moloch. Then, what is it? Here is the answer: *The attack in the Democratic platform on government by injunction.* Here is the milk in the coconut. We know whereof we speak. The authority upon which we make this avowal is from a source which cannot be questioned. But such authority is scarcely required. Upon second thought, the proposition overwhelmingly confirms itself and becomes clear as the noonday sun. For years, railway managers have been wrestling with the problem of cutting wages and controlling their employees generally. But the employees were more or less organized. The managers found the opposition of these organizations extremely annoying. Committees greatly distressed them. Mr. Ingalls,[54] president of the Big Four system, in his annual report to the board of directors dilated upon the great and growing difficulties of handling employees and treated the question as one of paramount importance. The managers could not treat their employees as they pleased. There was more or less friction, and sometimes strikes occurred, and these were embarrassing and expensive. The dread of a strike restrained the managers and kept them within uncomfortable bounds. Something must be done to overcome these organizations and reduce employees to submission.

Experimenting began in various directions. Finally the right lead was struck. The federal court would solve the problem. The strike of the engineers and firemen on the Toledo, Ann Arbor & North Michigan was paralyzed by a federal court injunction. Other disturbances followed and were settled in like fashion, until Judge Jenkins actually restrained the employees of the Northern Pacific from quitting the service of the company, because of a reduction of wages, under penalty of being adjudged guilty of contempt of court and committed to jail.[55] The railway companies exclaimed in one voice, *"Eureka!"* The problem of problems was solved. Hereafter they might reduce wages, treat employees as they saw fit, and they would have to submit. *Government by injunction* was now established, and the managers were supreme, while the employees were helpless.

How perfectly the scheme worked, the great Pullman strike bore haggard testimony. The federal courts, the federal soldiers, the deputy marshals, in fact, all the tremendous powers of the government, were promptly brought into requisition to crush the employees, and it was all done by the application of government by injunction. There have been sweeping reductions of wages since, amounting to millions, but there has been no protest. There is not likely to be any protest while government by injunction continues. Unconditional submission is the order of the day. Even arbitration is denied, and, in fact, has been made impossible. Railroad managers have things absolutely their own way. Should employees quit work in a body, injunctions would probably be issued and they would be sent to jail without trial. This is what has happened and what will happen again. Employees know this, and however galling the yoke, they submit. They can do nothing else.

Managers are no longer annoyed with committees. Agreements have been arbitrarily abrogated and men reduced to slavish conditions. No doubt some of these employees will deny these statements. Their jobs will depend on their doing so. Corporation hirelings will do likewise, but the facts are of Pike's Peak proportions and defy successful contradiction. Not long since the employees of the Plant System, at Savannah, Georgia, repudiated and denounced the American Railway Union. The company prepared the statement and compelled the employees to sign it under pain of dismissal. We have the documents to prove the assertion. Can corporate despotism go farther, or the abasement of employees be sunk lower?

The election of McKinley means the perpetuation of government by injunction, the supremacy of corporations, and the helpless, hopeless subjection of employees. It will not be confined to railroad corporations in its enslaving operations. All other corporations, trusts, and combines will claim its beneficial protection, and therefore all workingmen, especially those who are organized, are profoundly concerned in this issue. Ex-President Harrison and Bourke Cockran,[56] both corporation attorneys, strenuously defended government by injunction in their New York speeches. It is worth millions of dollars to railroad companies, and all comes out of the pockets of employees.

American railroads consist largely of British gold and American labor. Government by injunction crowns the former king and makes the latter subject. The platform upon which William J. Bryan stands is pledged to abolish this despotic usurpation of judicial power and restore to railway employees their lawful right to resist reduction and injustice by the lawful means provided by their organizations. The railway corporations are united and have massed all their tremendous powers to crush him. This in itself is indisputable proof that he is the friend of workingmen. In saying this, the genuine keynote of the railroad campaign has been struck. It startles like alarm bells at night. There is no mistaking the issue. Its gravity cannot be overestimated. It involves the very existence of organized labor, the bulwark and defense of workingmen against corporate tyranny, which, if swept away, leaves them shorn of every vestige of power and totally at the mercy of corporate capital.

The one federal judge who has proven himself to be immeasurably above the corrupting influences of corporations, who has earned the confidence and gratitude of all railway employees for his unyielding defense of their rights, upon whose fair name there is no scar or blemish, Henry C. Caldwell, has declared that the nomination of William J. Bryan is the greatest since Lincoln. We heartily concur in the declaration of this honest, fearless, and distinguished jurist.

In view of all these facts—facts of tremendous import which cannot be successfully controverted—we pledge our united and unwavering support to William J. Bryan for president, and appeal to railway employees and all workingmen to join with us in rebuking corporate tyranny which attempts to wrest the sacred right of suffrage from employees, in abolishing government by injunction, and in securing and maintaining every right of citizenship vouchsafed by the constitution of our country.

Eugene V. Debs,
James Hogan,
Sylvester Keliher,
R. M. Goodwin,
M. J. Elliott,
William E. Burns,
Board of Directors, American Railway Union

"I Have No Prejudice Against the Rich":
Speech at Houston, Texas†
[excerpt]

September 25, 1896

*   *   *

I have no prejudice against the rich, not in the least. I am simply discussing conditions. The extremely rich of this country are as much the abnormal product of an abnormal system as are the extremely poor. I sometimes think they are as much to be pitied. The life of many of them is a hollow mockery. The man who seeks to accumulate more money than he can use is making a mistake, and sometimes the penalty of that mistake is his life.

Jay Gould died 20 years in advance of his time simply because he had too much money. In this country of ours, the most favored beneath the skies, there is no trouble about wealth or about resources. We have them in fabulous abundance. The trouble is about the distribution. No man in this world ever made a million dollars honestly. No man in this world can show a good title for that amount of money. It may have been wrung from those who produced it, by legal methods, but it is piracy nonetheless.

There is no wrong in the system under which we live, but it so happens that they who produce all the wealth of the world have little or nothing to show for it, and they who produce little or nothing have it all. More than a century ago we achieved our political independence. The divine right of kings and the crown and scepter were relegated to oblivion. The servants became the masters. We have our political independence, but we are in the grasp of industrial servitude. American workingmen under the present system to a very large extent are compelled to work for such wages as the corporations see fit to impose. If I am obliged to work for a man under conditions fixed by that man, that man is my owner, I am that man's slave. I may boast of being a sovereign citizen, but I am a slave nonetheless. As a matter of course, corporations say, "If you are not satisfied, you can quit." And what does that mean? The right to quit nowadays means the right to starve. The corporations well know that there are millions of

---

†   Published as "Speech of Eugene V. Debs: He Gives the Laboring Man Some Good Advice" in *Houston Daily Post,* vol. 12, no. 175 (September 26, 1896), 8.

workingmen in the market. They know that they can reduce wages.

*　　*　　*

This country is dominated by combined syndicates and trusts.

Just a little while ago, in the city of Indianapolis, a few glass manufacturers held their meeting. They concluded to restrict the production of window glass. What for? To increase the price. In order to do this, they concluded to close their factories for a period of four months. This resulted in the dismissal of 15,000 operatives. For the sake of increasing their profits they threw out of employment 15,000 workingmen, which, allowing three to each family, we have 60,000 people thrown upon the world without resources to satisfy the insatiate private greed. Upon the one hand, this little combine of glass manufacturers fix the price of glass absolutely, and the American people are compelled to pay that price; upon the other hand, they fix the price of wages, and the workingmen are compelled to accept that wage. They are masters of the situation, and from their decisions there is no appeal.

What are the workingmen going to do in such a situation as that? This is not only true of the glass manufacturers; it is true of the operatives in every department of labor in this country. It is true very largely of the railroad employees of this country.

*　　*　　*

Labor has organized simply in the interest of self-protection. The railroads are organized; then why not their employees? They organize to fix rates and salaries, and why not the employees organize in their own interests?

*　　*　　*

As a matter of course, I do not declare that all courts are corrupt, because that is not true. There are very many honest, upright judges who administer the law impartially. In the presence of such a judge, I doff my hat; I pay to him the tribute of my admiration and respect. But there are courts in this country where justice is a purchasable quantity and you can commit any crime you choose and escape the consequences if you have money enough. There is something radically wrong in such a state of affairs under which such injustice is possible, but I would not have you believe that I take a gloomy view of the situation.

The courts were the best managers of railroads. When a railroad became wrecked and bankrupted through bad management, it was put in the hands of a receiver and thus turned over to the government. Hence the government was a sort of railroad repair shop, and they managed wrecked roads so well as to create the suspicion in the minds of many people that the management of all the roads should be turned over to the government.

*   *   *

There is very little sympathy for the tramp, but my heart always goes out to them. Some of them become tramps, and when they are reduced to that level, society closes its doors against them. Through his rags I can still see the outline of the man. I happen to know how some of these tramps are made. He loses his position through no fault of his own; he looks about for work and cannot find it. After a while he gets three or four hundred miles from home; his last dollar is gone; he is a stranger among strangers, and his clothes begin to get seedy. Those who pass him on the street look upon him with suspicion. The realization comes that in this world there is no place for him. His sensibilities become blunted. His self-respect deserts him. At long range he can see the little cottage he left behind, and in his fancy, he sees his wife in anguish over his non-appearance and his little children crying for food. He is a tramp on the face of the earth. It is only a few short steps from that condition to crime. Such a man is entitled to all the sympathy and pity we can bestow upon him.

*   *   *

Not long ago in the city of London, all those who were out of employment met at Trafalgar Square. The police were ordered to disperse them, and when they charged upon them, those unemployed men gave three cheers for Jesus Christ.

Some people declared that they were irreverent and profane. I deny it. In this world they had no sympathy, but they remembered that Christ was the friend of the friendless, that Christ was the divine tramp of the universe. If Christ ever had a dollar, history gives no authentic account of it. Christ did not despise the poor and unfortunate, and He did not only preach to them, but He fed them. He pitied the unfortunate and his sympathy went out to the erring. You remember that the rabble pursued the woman who had been guilty of the unpardonable sin, just as Christians are pursuing her today, and you remember that Christ cried out, "Let him who is without sin cast the first stone," and although century after century has been rolled up in the scroll of the ages, that stone has never yet been cast. That stone never will be cast.

*   *   *

[The labor question] will not down in the presence of superior force or before the bayonet. It will never be settled till it is settled right, till every man has the right to work and the right to get what he earns. The workingman is not entirely blameless for existing conditions. They should make better use of their time by expanding their knowledge. Knowledge will eventually free you from industrial bondage. Stay at home and read. The labor problem will never be settled in the saloon. Better buy books than beer.

*   *   *

We are now in the grasp of industrial servitude. I have faith that in time, however, this great question will be settled and settled right. No man who has faith in himself and in his undertaking can ever fail. In the mad pursuit of money, the very heart is being eaten out of our civilization. Man are not now measured by their character, but by what they are worth. We can help ourselves simply in proportion as we help ourselves.

*   *   *

Some people say you should always respect public opinion. I wish to say tonight that I have little respect for what they call public opinion. It is very unreliable as a counselor or guide. Public opinion has sanctioned every outrage that has been perpetrated in this world, public opinion has justified every crime committed against humanity. I admit that public opinion in the course of time gets right, but it sometimes takes two or three thousand years, and that is too long for the average mortal to wait.

The speaker closed his remarks by reciting a poem called "Labor Day is Coming."[37] *In fact, his speech was interspersed with snatches of poetry, all of them used appropriately and well emphasized. His remarks were frequently interrupted with applause, and when he concluded his speech, which consumed about an hour and a half in its delivery, he was the subject of general congratulation . . .*

An Uprising of the People:
Campaign Speech for William Jennings Bryan
at Duluth, Minnesota†

October 21, 1896

Ladies and Gentlemen:—

I regard the campaign fast drawing to a close as the most important political contest in the history of the country.[58] I have faith in the intelligence, independence, and patriotism of the American people, and I believe that on November 3 American manhood will triumph over British gold. This is a campaign of the people. This meeting is significant, and it demonstrates to my satisfaction that the principles of liberty are not nearly extinct in the hearts of American freemen. This is more than a political movement. It is an uprising of the people. It is time for a change, and that is coming as certainly as the rivers find their way to the sea. Let us get together and forget parties for a while, simply remembering that we are American citizens, the proudest title ever borne by any man on this earth. *[Applause.]* You and I and all of us love the Republic, and we are interested in the perpetuation of freedom.

We have been branded as anarchists. Let us trace the compliment to its source. It comes from Wall Street, whence our oppression comes. Some of these days we are going to revise our dictionary and it will have a new definition for anarchy, and under the new definition I will be surprised if it does not embrace the managers of the Republican campaign. *[Laughter and applause.]* The man today who does not do something to draw upon himself the epithet of anarchist is an object of suspicion. *[Laughter.]* Anarchy and patriotism have become synonymous. The real anarchists are trying to press down upon the toiler's brow a crown of thorns.

Just the other day a gentleman of the cloth espoused the cause of gold and with a hammer of gold drove one more nail into the body of a suffering people. Think of this follower of the meek and lowly Nazarene. Christ never deserted the poor. If he ever had a dollar, history has yet to record it, and in this particular at least he does not resemble Archbishop Ireland.[59] *[Laughter and applause.]*

---

†   Published as part of the article "Our Gene" in *Duluth Labor World*, vol. 1, no. 16 (October 24, 1896), 2–3.

The American people are no longer doing their thinking by proxy. The average citizen is standing magnificently erect, and by straining one's vision ever so little one can see the first glimmer of the dawn of emancipation. Some people view with alarm the unrest in our politics and prophesy the failure of free government. I believe that the good old ship of state will breast all billows, face all storms, finally reach the port of prosperity. *[Applause.]*

In this campaign two parties are contending, one of which repudiated the Declaration of Independence. It says that America is not able to legislate for itself. Over 100 years ago American independence was achieved. Today Bryan, Lind,[60] and Towne[61] *[tremendous applause]*, as magnificent men as ever gave glory to American history, are fighting to achieve our financial independence. In the days of Washington were those who hesitated, who said, "Let us have peace." They were willing to sacrifice American independence for the sake of peace. Washington was an anarchist; Franklin was a demagogue. *[Applause.]* All the powers of plutocracy were arraigned against them. The same forces are arraigned today. The fought and passed into history. The fighters of today will pass into history.

Some say that Bryan is going to fail. Bryan cannot fail. *[Cheers.]* His nomination was not of the Democratic Party, it was ordained by the Almighty. *[Applause.]* His nomination was providential, and it is going to be ratified by an overwhelming majority of the American people next month. *[Great applause.]* Bryan was not born to defeat. *[Applause.]* He stands today where Lincoln stood in 1860. *[Applause.]* Lincoln, like [Bryan], was fresh from the loins of the people and was to the end of his life the sole proprietor of himself.[62] His sad and sweet and tragic face has become a permanent benediction. I am just reminded that he said that God must have loved the poor because he made so many of them. *[Laughter.]* I am not prejudiced against the rich, but as between the rich and the poor I am for the poor, because the rich can take care of themselves.

A few men naturally become rich; they can't help it. Many naturally remain poor; they can't help it. If one has a superior brain, he is entitled to no credit. If one gains a fortune, he is entitled to no credit. If a brother is helpless and remains where he started, he can't help it; I have an idea that it is the duty of the man who gets more than he needs to help him. *[Applause.]* Men may say that I am a dreamer, but it sometimes happens that the dreamer of one age is the philosopher of the next. The man who works longest and hardest gets least to show for it. I object to the conditions under which the man who does least gets all. That is something that appeals to all for correction. Wealth has accumulated in the hands of a few, by special legislation and special privilege.

The theory of our government, according to Abraham Lincoln, is: "Life is of more consequence than property. The man before the dollar." We see today the words of the great Lincoln literally interpreted. We see the man before the dollar supplicating on bended knees for the right to live. *[Applause and laughter.]* In the presence of the dollar, the dollar which we have deified, we prostrate ourselves. In the presence of the almighty dollar, we are slaves.

Multiplied thousands complain of man's inhumanity to man. Millions are begging for what the world owes them, an opportunity to work. In the presence of this appalling condition, what does the Republican Party propose? Nothing. The tramp is the spawn of the gold standard. I remember when a tramp was a curiosity, but now there is no need to look in a museum to see one. *[Laughter.]* Let me tell you how the tramp is made. The unfortunate husband comes home at eventide, and there is no work to be found. Then he tells his wife and gathers his children about him and looks sorrowfully about him at the bare table and the fireless stove and the want that has crept into his home, [and declares] that he will go elsewhere and seek for work that he may give them life. He trudges off next morning with the purpose of going to some distant point. He does not take the passenger coach, for he has no money, but he climbs under the coach and rides on the truck. I want all those who think men are tramps from choice to try that. Before he gets to the next station, the brakeman discovers him and he is left along the way. He wearily trudges on in search of work, but his clothes have become seedy and he is soiled and worn and haggard-looking, and the eye of suspicion is directed toward him. The only person he knows is the policeman, but his heart throbs as he wearily trudges on, and he thinks of the little white cottage where his little ones are and where his wife is waiting for him and where there is suffering. As he goes on the suspicion increases. He gets two hundred or three hundred miles away from home and he can obtain no work. People will not have him. All the future is dark, and he begins to realize that on earth there is no room for him. His sensibilities become blunted. His self-respect deserts him, and he is a tramp on the face of the earth.

Let me try the same on you. Let me turn you out into the cold world and have every door locked to you for six months! Let me place you in his position, where the garbage and filth of society is poured upon him, and would you be any better than he? Would you become anything else but a tramp?

The tramp is now to be found in all states and forms a grand army of menace to the Republic. The declaration of the Republican Party on the money question is an insult to every American citizen. They have not the hardihood to declare for the gold standard, but promise to change by the permission of

England. The Democratic Party says we'll change anyway. *[Applause.]* It says that it is time for a change and that we will change without consulting Europe. We should bear in mind that an invitation extended 18 years ago to the nations of Europe to a bimetallic conference has been treated with scorn and contempt. John Bull has no respect for Uncle Sam, and he would not pretend to have any if he did not have his hands in Uncle Sam's pockets up to his elbows. The nations of Europe did not demonetize silver in their own countries to remonetize it in this country. We will never get bimetallism by agreement, and no one knows that better than the gentlemen who wrote the financial plank of the Republican platform. They intended to deceive, but, thank God, the American people are not to be the victims of duplicity this time. *[Great applause.]*

I wish to discuss McKinley for a while. *[Laughter and applause.]* Mark Hanna[63] *[general hisses and groans]* saw that McKinley was in financial difficulty. With great discernment, he saw in McKinley promising presidential timber. He and H. H. Kohlsaat[64] helped the major out of his money troubles. They took up his paper, and Hanna has it in his strongbox today. They have a mortgage on the Republican candidate, and if he is elected, which I think God forbids, they will foreclose it. Mark Hanna is the commander of McKinley's forces. Mr. Kohlsaat wrote the financial plank of the Republican platform. [With] Mark Hanna—I do not want to do him an injustice. I could not if I would. I cannot even do him justice. *[Laughter and applause.]* This is a condition which appeals to the patriotism of every American citizen. I have nothing to say against McKinley, but as the creature of the money power I oppose him.

When I speak of the money power, do you comprehend the tremendous import of the words? We are in its hands. Seventy million people are helpless. It has invaded the Supreme Court and debauched it. The income tax was a law that taxed the wealth of the country. But the highest judicial authority in the land declared it unconstitutional. In declaring the law unconstitutional, the Supreme Court usurped the legislative functions of the government. If, instead of taxing the wealth, the Congress of the country had enacted that the poor be taxed, the Supreme Court would never have declared the law unconstitutional. I have read the opinions of three judges of that court, not demagogues, nor cranks nor anarchists, who say that this decision of their fellows on the bench is in the nature of a revolution.

The decision was a complete surrender to the money power. This is not the declaration of a wild-eyed anarchist, but the calm, deliberative judgment of some of the men who constitute that high judicial tribunal. I cannot but recall the appearance and the language of that grand man, Lyman Trumbull, who was engaged in the defense of myself and colleagues, when after trying to accomplish something for his clients, said: "Mr. Debs, we are hopelessly, helplessly at the mercy of the money power, as represented by the courts."

The American people were never so much aroused as now. They have never been thinking so of great questions, especially the laboring men. The laboring man is asking why he builds palaces but lives in a hovel. They are beginning to think and will soon act. If they cannot get their rights, they will take them. They will not demand that they be given theirs by force, but with the ballot that falls as lightly as the winter snow, yet does the work of lightning from the heavens, will they fight in the future and insure to themselves their right—their equal right with the corporations and the trusts and the elements that seek to crush them down and make them slaves. *[Applause.]*

It is labor that draws out the shining rails from the molten ore and transforms them into the wagon roads of commerce. It is labor that takes the fleeces from animals of the field and manufactures them into articles of commerce. It is labor that fells the green-plumed forest monarch and transforms it into lumber with the gang saw. It is labor that controls the black cavalry of commerce and shapes the destinies of the commercial world. It is labor that goes into the golden harvest field and garners the grain and makes it into bread. And shall not labor come to his own? Let labor everywhere take heart of hope, for the midnight is passing, and joy cometh with the morning. *[Continued applause.]*

The world is not just; it is a long way from being generous, but it is getting better every day. There should be no multimillionaires. When a man schemes to get more than he needs he makes a mistake, and his punishment is sometimes on earth. I love to think of the democracy of death. It enters the home of a Vanderbilt without a card and reduces the occupant to the level of the veriest pauper. Men should remember that shrouds have no pockets. We are here just a little while, and humanity is as far above gold as stars are above earthly mold. Character is better than cash. Men are not equal, but they are entitled to equal opportunities. We have no trouble about wealth; it is about distribution.

After paying his respects to Mark Hanna, Chauncey M. Depew,[65] H. C. Payne,[66] H. C. Frick, and others, Mr. Debs concluded by drawing a beautiful picture of a workingman's home under prosperity . . .

Patriotism Versus Plutocracy:
Speech for William Jennings Bryan in Cleveland[†]
[excerpt]

October 27, 1896

Mr. Chairman, Gentlemen, and Fellow Workingmen:—

My heart is with you. *[Applause.]* The campaign now drawing to an end is by far the most important ever fought in this country. This is a conflict between American manhood and British gold, between man and the dollar. The dollar has ruled long enough. Under the gold standard, born in 1873, 2 million American workingmen have been reduced to the condition of beggars. Lincoln said man was born before the dollar. Now the man is on his bended knees asking for the privilege of living.

The gold standard was born in 1873, the same year the American tramp was born. The gold standard has made him a permanent institution on American soil. There are 3 million of him. He has grown into a grand army. His march, tramp, tramp, has grown into a funeral march to the grave. Many despise the tramp. Through his rags, through his squalor, I can see the [outlines] of a man. *[Applause.]*

*   *   *

I plead for no human sympathy. I ask office from no one. Labor can give me no office. I prefer to remain free and speak the truth. The palpitating, the quivering heart of humanity demands consideration from all true men.

*   *   *

Gold has ruled for three thousand years. Twenty-five years ago, employer and employee worked together and their differences were easily settled. The ear of each was open to the other. Gold has no conscience, no heart. So long as these conditions prevailed, there was heart in employers. Then came the corporation. Ten men each with $100,000 form a corporation. They had ten hearts. The corporation has none. Ten hearts, any one of which would not be responsible for the suffering that has been caused by that corporation.

This conflict is between the heartless aggregation of wealth on the one hand and humanity on the other. It is not a struggle between Republicans, Democrats,

---

[†]   Published as "Fought to Get In" in *Cleveland Plain Dealer*, vol. 55, no. 302 (October 28, 1896), 1–2. The speech was delivered at Cleveland Music Hall.

or Populists, but between plutocracy and democracy, between the Pullmans *[hisses]*, the Carnegies, the Fricks, and the Hannas *[hisses]*—somebody says do not do him an injustice. I can't do him an injustice. Had I the colors of a Michelangelo, the language of a [John] Milton and a [Victor] Hugo combined, I could not do him justice. Between this element and human liberty is the contest.

*   *   *

Wealth is not the test of a man. That magnificent democrat, Death, entered the home of a Vanderbilt. He didn't send up his card. The doctors were there. He pushed them aside and told that palpitating heart to stop. In half a second, that multimillionaire was no better than the lowest mendicant in the land. Remember that shrouds have no pockets. *[Applause.]* But that is what they propose to make the test of American citizenship.

*   *   *

It is the corporation that is everything and nothing. They are the ones who think they are interested in the maintenance of the existing gold standard. It is that element which is endeavoring to coerce you. Major McKinley says it is cooperation. Yes, it is the cooperation of the lamb and the wolf. *[Laughter.]* He says they are cooperating. Perhaps he doesn't know the kind of cooperation it is. Perhaps he doesn't know that the cooperation is to increase millionaires and increase pauperism.

McKinley does not represent himself, and the Republican Party doesn't trust the American people. Let us do no injustice to the major. When Mark Hanna bought that $118,000 worth of McKinley's notes, he was not actuated by philanthropic motives. Oh, no. Mr. Hanna and those associated with him saw the promising presidential timber; they knew well enough that if popular favor continued, it would land him in the president's chair. A man in that chair is useful to plutocracy, but before he will serve plutocracy, he must be under obligations to it. McKinley is under obligations.

What is it that Hanna's mortgaged major promises? A higher tariff tax and confidence. *[Laughter.]* They say we are suffering from a lack of confidence. That lack of confidence, they say, has come from the free silver agitation. Oh, God! I say, Oh, God, reverently, and I wish all the people of this land could hear me. A monetary system that cannot stand the effect of agitation! What a thing to say to an intelligent people, that because they chose to talk about their money system, they are plunged into misery, into degradation, into oppression. Oh, God, what will they not say in this campaign?

By higher taxation they are to restore confidence. For 23 years we have been following their leadership. That is what we are promised.

Every glistening tear upon the face, every suffering child pleads to us for the election of William Jennings Bryan. *[(Long, continued applause.]* They call Bryan an anarchist. *[Applause.]* Who calls him an anarchist and who calls us anarchists? Trace it back to its source and you will find it comes from every stock jobber, every grain speculator, every foreign and domestic shylock, every oppressor of the poor—all yelling "Anarchist!" at Bryan and every man on the side of humanity. McKinley stands for British gold; Bryan stands for humanity. *[Applause.]* McKinley stands for a despotism; Bryan for constitutional liberty. *[Applause.]*

* * *

They say free coinage is wholly in favor of the silver mine operator. I believe the *Cleveland Leader* asked me some questions. *[Hisses.]* No, don't hiss. When I was here a year ago, the *Leader* treated me very fairly and I want to be equally fair. The *Leader* wants to know what good 53-cent dollars will do the workingman. If you working men get 53-cent dollars, you can pay them out again, can't you? You owe your wages before you get them, don't you? If they are 53-cent dollars, where is the benefit to the silver mine owners? *[Applause.]* Then that paper wants to know about benefit to railroad men. I simply want to refer that paper to Henry Clay Caldwell, a federal judge, the only federal judge who ever opened his courtroom to the workingman. He says that if the Union Pacific affairs had been managed properly, that road could have paid decent wages and would not have been compelled to cut their wages.

Railroads still charge three cents a mile when you ride. *[A voice: "Except when you go to Canton." Laughter.]* I think there are some railroad men here *[A chorus of "Yes, yes!" and several hundred men rose up]* and you will hear me out in saying that railroads have doubled the capacity of their engines and cars. They do twice as much work with half as many crews, and yet they claim they are unable to pay decent wages. They can't pay decent wages and interest upon mountains of bonds issued on watered stock. *[Applause.]* Interest must be paid first, wages last. When Bryan is president, you railroad men will not be afraid to attend meetings. He will keep them so busy obeying the laws that they will overlook you. *[Applause.]* Every man who fears the laws will be enforced is crying "Anarchy!" and chief among these are the manipulators of wrecked railroads. *[Applause.]*

It is becoming so now that a man who does nothing to earn the title "anarchist" is a just subject of suspicion. *[Laughter.]* I repeat, this campaign is a conflict between the dollar and humanity, between patriotism and plutocracy, over which stands the sad and tragic face of Abraham Lincoln as a constant benediction. He came from the people; he sympathized with them. The New

York press hailed him as a freak from the morasses of Illinois, and the Boston press said a kangaroo had escaped from his keepers in the West. They are saying practically the same thing with regard to Bryan.

*   *   *

There were Tories during the Revolutionary War. There are Tories now. *[Applause.]* They said we couldn't achieve independence and liberty in 1776. Greene's soldiers tramping barefoot through the Carolinas to help Washington was their answer.[67] Their rifles wore through their clothing. They put bunches of grass on their shoulders. Their arms wore through that, and their blood marked their path to answer the objection that the 13 weak and disorganized colonies were not strong enough to achieve their independence.

The Republican Party says we are not strong enough to achieve our monetary independence without the permission of Europe. Let me tell you, the European sovereigns never demonetized silver for the benefit of the moneyed class, for the purpose of entering into an international agreement to permit America to restore silver to its position as a standard money. *[Applause.]* Since 1878, we have had a law on our statute books inviting an international agreement. The invitation has been treated with contempt. Still, that is the hope Hanna's mortgaged major holds out to you, knowing full well, as he does, that an international agreement is not among the probabilities, scarcely a possibility. *[Applause.]*

In the march of this money power, it has usurped all the functions of government. It comes from its den and robs the American citizen. Nowadays a man lives by permission of the money power. It was my turn to live in jail a while ago, and it may be your turn next.

If Hanna were tried for one of his innumerable crimes, I would insist upon his receiving a trial by jury. People are losing confidence in courts because courts are no longer courts of justice. Men no longer stand upon the basis of equality. Rags are dominated by robes. The millionaire makes the judge, the judge makes the law, and the law crushes the rags. Only the poor go to jail.

It is a question of humanity. The heart of every man and every woman must be touched in the presence of corrosive, corrupting influence of centralized wealth. Yes, do anything you like. Strike down your fellow man, destroy the virtue of your sister, pollute the fountain of all the streams of human happiness, be a monster, be a criminal, do as you like—have money and go free. But woe unto you if you are a moneyless man. Have no money and steal a garment with which to protect the shivering form of your wife, and go to jail. It is that which is involved in the campaign, a campaign of humanity, of the heart, of the intellect, against the aggressive march of human greed.

If you are enormously rich, you may trample underfoot the laws of man and debauch the Supreme Court. They have invaded Congress. They have entered the Christian pulpit, they have touched the robed minister at the altar; they freeze his heart and blotch his soul and send him forth a traitor to his consecrated vows, with the price of his treason in his pocket. The pulpit no longer dares to preach the gospel of Jesus Christ. There are magnificent exceptions, but like Christ they have found themselves like the Divine Tramp. In the early days of the slavery agitation, Wendell Phillips said: "They have prostituted the pulpit."

Christ, in all his beautiful, self-denying life, never had one dollar. In this respect, he differs materially from Archbishop Ireland. This priest of Christ, who has time enough to accumulate $1 million, has no real sympathy with the suffering poor. He is one of those who have, by reason of his priestly robe, authority to press down upon the brow of labor a crown of thorns. Some people may think this irrelevant, but I do not think so. Christ was a poor man. In all his life he never turned his back upon the poor. He met the poor, suffered and sympathized with them. You remember how he received the poor, sinful woman and stayed the mob that wished to stone her. "Let him who is without guilt cast the first stone," He said to them.[68] That first stone was not cast, and it never will be.

In conclusion, Debs spoke for his friend, George H. Gordon,[69] and referred to the Brown strike in general terms, saying that the strikers fought for the right of petition, and asked his hearers to put themselves in their places.[70] He marveled that soldiers were called out only to quiet workingmen and wondered if they are always wrong, that they should always be the destination of the bullet. He closed with an appeal to each man to take stock of his patriotism and voted as his heart dictated on November 3.

Bryan, he said, is a man above the ability of money to corrupt, fresh from the hearts of the people, diligent to their service, and fully fitted to be the highest officer in the land.

Notes

1. Opening couplet from *The Deserted Village* (1770), by Oliver Goldsmith (1728–1774).

2. A frequently repeated, usually misquoted maxim of the Revolutionary War, commonly misattributed today to Thomas Jefferson or Susan B. Anthony. The original motto, proposed for use by Benjamin Franklin as part of a three-member congressional committee named in July 1776 to design a Great Seal of the United States, was "Rebellion to Tyrants is Obedience to God." Jefferson, a fellow member of the committee with Franklin, liked the slogan so much that he made it part of his personal seal, thereby erroneously gaining credit of authorship. Patrick Henry was not involved.

3. George Graham Vest (1830–1904), a former member of both the House of Representatives and Senate of the Confederate States of America, was a Democrat elected to the US Senate in 1878, serving there until 1903.

4. The income tax was ruled by the Supreme Court to be an unconstitutional direct tax in the 1895 case of *Pollock v. Farmers' Loan & Trust Co.* It was only with the adoption of the 16th Amendment to the Constitution in February 1913 that the income tax was legalized in the United States.

5. Stanza from "A Word from a Petitioner" (1843), by John Pierpont (1785–1866).

6. In January 1894, Judge Elmer S. Dundy imposed a mandatory sentence of life in prison upon Louis de France for the armed robbery of a mail carrier at Chadron, Nebraska—a crime that netted the thief one cent. The judge indicated at the time of sentencing that the penalty was excessively harsh, but that his hands were tied by the law.

7. C. W. Mosher was president of the Capital National Bank of Lincoln, a firm that went bankrupt. Mosher was indicted for embezzlement, implicated by a series of false entries in the firm's books. Following a guilty plea, on July 8, 1893, Dundy sentenced Mosher to five years imprisonment in the federal penitentiary at Sioux Falls for his theft, which was estimated to have been in excess of $200,000.

8. This tale of the duality of justice in Judge Dundy's court was repeated by others in the press from 1894, with the facts of the two cases becoming muddled in the telling. Debs probably just repeated a story he had heard, for which he wrote a new punch line.

9. Debs's imaginative excuse for checking in to jail a day late the previous June owing to having eaten "bad cucumbers," while appearing to observers to be badly hungover from overindulgence in alcohol, remained a running joke among his detractors for many years. Playing upon this, this anecdote seems to have been first delivered in his speech in beer-loving Milwaukee one week earlier. The quip's repetition in Buffalo made the news wires.

10. The published transcript reads "Justice Wood"—apparently Debs misspoke.

11. The transcript renders this quotation incorrectly; text corrected here.

12. If Justice Harland ever used this language, he did not use it in his dissent to the decision. What he did write was that "a decision now that a tax on income from real

property can be laid and collected only by apportioning the same among the states, on the basis of numbers, may, not improperly, be regarded as a judicial revolution, that may sow the seeds of hate and distrust among the people of different sections of our common country . . . Any attempt on the part of Congress to apportion among the states, upon the basis simply of their population, taxation of personal property, or of incomes would tend to arouse such indignation among the freemen of America that it would never be repeated." *(158 US 1135, 1137.)*

13. Johann "John" Most (1846–1906) was a German-born anarchist publicist who published a German-language radical weekly, the *Freiheit*, in New York City after his immigration to America in 1882. Most is best remembered for his popularization of the concept of "propaganda by the deed."

14. From Psalms 30:5.

15. Couplet from *The Traveler* (1764) by Oliver Goldsmith (1728–1774).

16. From "Man Was Made to Mourn: A Dirge" (1784), by Robert Burns (1759–1796).

17. Frances Willard (1839–1898) was the founder of the powerful Woman's Christian Temperance Union (WCTU) and an outspoken advocate of voting rights for women.

18. From Willard's address written for the Third Biennial Convention of the World's Woman's Christian Temperance Union, London, June 1895, a text which was to be read to local unions of the WCTU across the United States.

19. John Bright (1811–1889) was a British Liberal Party politician and popular orator.

20. The Sherman Antitrust Act of 1890 was ultimately an effective tool in moderating the anticompetitive behavior of monopolies.

21. Lincoln's exact words were "The Democracy [Democratic Party] of today hold the *liberty* of one man to be absolutely nothing, when in conflict with another man's right of *property*. Republicans, on the contrary, are for both *the man* and the *dollar;* but in case of conflict, the man *before* the dollar." (Letter to Boston Republicans, April 6, 1859.)

22. Cornelius H. Hanford (1849–1926) was the US district court judge for the state of Washington.

23. Henry Clay Payne (1843–1904), former president of the Milwaukee & Northern Railroad, would be named postmaster general by President Theodore Roosevelt in 1902.

24. Couplet from "Three Graves" (1886), by John Boyle O'Reilly (1844–1890).

25. "Every man has his price" is an aphorism sometimes attributed to a 1734 speech by British prime minister Robert Walpole (1676–1745), who allegedly remarked of politicians offering flowery patriotic oratory, "All those men have their price." First published in a biography decades after the alleged utterance, the attributed line should be regarded as apocryphal.

26. Brayton Ives (1840–1914) was president of the Northern Pacific Railroad from 1893 to 1896.

27. Abraham Lincoln (1809–1865) did not utter these words in his frequently cited Chicago speech of July 10, 1858.

28. The connection of this witticism to Lincoln is apocryphal. Origins of the "Lincoln

said" connection dates at least to the 1880s, when the attribution was made at two different Prohibition Party conventions.

29. Thomas Jefferson's exact words were, "Let us found a government where there shall be no extremely rich men and no abjectly poor ones. Let us found a government upon the intelligence of the people and the equitable distribution of property. Let us make laws where there shall be no government partnership with favored classes."

30. From "Stanzas on Freedom" (1849) by James Russell Lowell (1819–1891).

31. Line from the poem "On the Capture of Fugitive Slaves Near Washington" (July 1845).

32. Excerpt from Burns's "For A' That and A' That."

33. *The Adelbert* was a student periodical at Case Western Reserve University in Cleveland. The editor of the magazine was Charles W. Naumann.

34. Like it or not.

35. Doctors of Divinity and Doctors of Law—that is, preachers and lawyers.

36. Edward Webster Bemis (1860–1930) was an associate professor of political economy at the University of Chicago that was forced out of his position for his progressive political and economic views in 1895 by the administration of President William Rainey Harper (1856–1906).

37. Edgar Wilson "Bill" Nye (1850–1896) was a popular humorist, author, and public speaker. Nye would die of meningitis less than two weeks after the publication of this interview.

38. The First Baptist Church of Terre Haute was led by Rev. J. S. Holmes. The building was packed to capacity for Debs's Sunday night speech.

39. Couplet from the poem *The Deserted Village* (1770) by Oliver Goldsmith (1728–1774).

40. From Carlos Martyn, "Churchianity vs. Christianity," *The Arena,* vol. 2, whole no. 8 (July 1890), 155.

41. From George D. Herron, *The New Redempton: A Call to the Church to Reconstruct Society According to the Gospel of Christ* (New York: Thomas Y. Crowell & Co., 1893), 16–17.

42. Debs's tour, which ran from the middle of February through the first week of March, took him as far south as Tallahassee, Florida.

43. An attempt was made by left-wing elements in the People's Party to boom the candidacy of Debs for president. According to the *Chicago Tribune,* a Central E. V. Debs Club was formed in Chicago on May 20, 1896, with Debs's future 1920 Socialist Party running mate Seymour Stedman elected as president of the new organization.

44. Alfred Shenstone Edwards (1848–19XX) was born in Birmingham, England, and immigrated to the United States in 1867. He was active in the Knights of Labor in Minneapolis, where he gained stature as a public speaker and writer. In August 1895, Edwards was tapped as editor of the socialist weekly *The Coming Nation* (official organ of the Ruskin Colony established by J. A. Wayland, and therefore forerunner of the *Appeal to Reason.)* Edwards would also edit the *Social Democratic Herald* from

1898 to 1902, and the *Industrial Worker* from 1906 to 1908.

45. Debs was in Birmingham, Alabama, on May 18 and 19, 1896, where he spoke at a public meeting held at Lakeview Park. The source of the contentious interview is unknown.

46. Ruskin Commonwealth Association was a utopian socialist cooperative community established in rural Dickson County, Tennessee, near Tennessee City. Real estate developer and newspaper publisher J. A. Wayland was the financial angel of the project, and his weekly newspaper, *The Coming Nation,* was the profitable official organ of the enterprise. Wayland left the colony in the summer of 1895 amid acrimony, abandoning his paper to the editorship of Alfred S. Edwards and moving to Kansas City to launch a new publication, the *Appeal to Reason.* The Ruskin colony was dissolved in the fall of 1901.

47. Henry Demarest Lloyd (1847–1903) was a muckraking journalist and prominent booster of Gene Debs to head the presidential ticket of the People's Party. Four days prior to this cable Debs had wired People's Party delegate Victor L. Berger, another member of the left-wing "Middle of the Road" faction, expressing Debs's hopes to join him at the St. Louis convention shortly—a communication provided to the press as evidence that Debs was potentially softening in his opposition to any effort to draft him for the presidential nomination. This telegram quashed that effort.

48. Thomas E. Watson (1856–1922) was first elected to Congress from Georgia in 1890 on the Democratic ticket. A supporter of the Farmers' Alliance, Watson soon abandoned the Democratic Party to join the People's Party, which sought his inclusion on the fusion Democratic-Populist ticket in 1896. Watson later ran as the People's Party's nominee for president in 1904 and 1908, the final two national campaigns. An opinionated newspaper publisher, Watson espoused the ideology of white supremacy in his later years.

49. Arthur Sewall (1835–1900) was a wealthy shipbuilder and industrialist from Maine who was tapped by William Jennings Bryan as his running mate in 1896.

50. Charles Lee (1731–1782) was a top general in the Continental Army.

51. John Burgoyne (1722–1792) and Charles Cornwallis (1738–1805) were leading British generals who fought against the revolutionaries in the American revolutionary war.

52. "These are the times that try men's souls" is the opening line from "The Crisis" (December 1776) by Thomas Paine (1737–1809).

53. Lombard Street in London was the center of British finance capital, akin to its American cousin, Wall Street.

54. Melville Ezra Ingalls (1842–1914) was head of the Cleveland, Cincinnati, Chicago & St. Louis Railroad, the so-called "Big Four."

55. James Graham Jenkins (1834–1921) was a judge of the US District Court for the Eastern District of Wisconsin from 1888 to 1893.

56. William Bourke Cockran (1854–1923) was a Democratic member of the House of Representatives from New York who broke with his party over their nomination of free silver advocate William Jennings Bryan, supporting Republican William

McKinley instead.

57. "A Labor Day is Coming" (1889) by Col. J. B. Maynard.

58. This 1896 speech on behalf of the Democratic Party–People's Party fusion candidacy of William Jennings Bryan was attended by an estimated five thousand people at a venue called the "car barn." When Debs made his appearance, he was greeted by three minutes of continuous applause, according to this news account.

59. John Ireland (1838–1918) was the archbishop of St. Paul, Minnesota, from 1888 until his death.

60. John Lind (1854–1930) was the fusion Democratic and People's Party candidate for governor of Minnesota. He lost to his Republican opponent by fewer than 3,600 votes out of more than 337,000 cast.

61. Charles Arnette Towne (1858–1928) first won election to Congress from Minnesota in November 1894 as a Republican. A progressive and an advocate of free silver, Towne was dumped by his party but chose to run for reelection in 1896 as an Independent, losing the race. He would later decline nomination for vice president of the United States at the 1900 convention of the People's Party.

62. The line "No party has a mortgage on me—I am the sole proprietor of myself" was uttered by Robert Ingersoll in an 1880 campaign speech on behalf of the Republican Party.

63. Millionaire businessman Mark Hanna (1837–1904), soon to be elected to the US Senate from Ohio, was the manager of William McKinley's campaign and was regarded as one of the most influential conservative political figures of his era.

64. Herman Henry Kohlsaat (1853–1924), a staunch Republican partisan and outspoken supporter of the gold standard, was a newspaper publisher who in 1896 was the owner of the *Chicago Times Herald* and the *Chicago Evening Post*.

65. Chauncey M. Depew (1834–1928) was the president of the New York Central Railroad, a line engaged in continual combat with its workers. He would be elected a Republican US senator from New York in November 1898.

66. Henry Clay Payne (1843–1904) was president of the Milwaukee & Northern Railroad. He would be appointed postmaster general in 1904 by Republican president Theodore Roosevelt.

67. General Nathanael Greene (1742–1786) was commander of the Southern Department of the Continental Army during the American revolutionary war.

68. From John 8:7.

69. George H. Gordon was a Cleveland labor activist and Democratic candidate for Cuyahoga County clerk who was one of four who were arrested speaking for free silver on the Cleveland public square to a crowd of 300 on September 15, 1896. The serial arrest of the four speakers from the soapbox, ostensibly for violating park regulations, foreshadowed the later "free speech fights" of the Industrial Workers of the World.

70. On Monday, May 25, 1896, all 800 employees of the Brown Hoisting and Conveying Works of Cleveland were sent home at noon and locked out over a stalemate between the machinists union and the company over an effort to reduce

the company's ten-hour day by one hour. The company announced that it would no longer bargain collectively with its workers and that any hired back would have to apply individually. An extremely bitter strike ensued, with violence being used against strikebreakers, scores of strikers beaten by police guards, and the gunfire of state militia and armed strikers causing the death of several strikers in the conflict, which lasted through the summer.

Appendix

Declaration of Principles of the
American Railway Union,
Embracing All Classes of Railway Employees[†]
April 16, 1893[1]

In the creation of a new organization of railway employees, certain reasons prompting the movement are demanded and should be set forth with becoming candor.

The number of employees now in the service of the railroads in America has been variously estimated from 800,000 to 1 million. It is safe to assume that this vast army of employees is, at the present time, not less than 1 million.

Accepting the highest claims of the various railway organizations as a basis of calculation, less than 150,000 of these employees are members of such organizations, leaving more than 850,000 who are not enrolled in the ranks of organized labor.

To state the proposition concisely, organization is union. It is a self-evident truth that "in union there is strength," and conversely, without union weakness prevails. Therefore, the central benefit to be derived from organization is strength—power to accomplish that which defies individual effort.

Defects in Organization

Experience, the great teacher, whose lessons sooner or later must be heeded, points out with unerring certainty the defects and demonstrates the inefficiency of the organizations as they now exist.

1. They do not provide for all classes of employees, it being shown that 850,000 of them, or 85 percent of the whole number, remain unorganized. These may be divided into three general classes: (1) those who are eligible but decline to join, (2) those who have been expelled because of their inability or refusal to bear the financial burdens which membership imposes, and (3) the multiplied thousands in various departments of the service who are totally ineligible, there being no provision for their admission.

These facts, in the light of 30 years of organization, establish beyond all

---

†   As published in Sylvester Keliher, "Dawn of a New Era," *Railway Carmen's Journal,*
      vol. 3, whole no. 26 (May 1893), 259. Also published in pamphlet form in May
      1893 under the title appearing here.

controversy the truth of the declarations herein set forth and emphasize the demand for an order in which there shall be room and protection for all whose hearts throb responsive to union sentiments, and whose desire it is to march under union banners in the great struggle for the triumph of union principles.

2. The existing organizations, designed to promote and preserve harmonious relations between employer and employee, have met with only limited success, if indeed it can be shown that any progress in that direction has been made. Never has there existed that mutual confidence, without which it were misleading to assume that peace, amity, and goodwill will prevail. At best, therefore, this relation between employer and employee has been little better than an enforced compliance with conditions rarely satisfactory to either party.

3. What must be said of organizations which have failed to establish friendship and goodwill even among themselves? From the first there have existed antagonisms and jealousies, culminating in warring factions, instead of a harmonious whole. Organization has been pitted against organization, bringing upon themselves not only disaster but lasting reproach.

4. Protection is the cardinal principle of the present organizations, but they do not protect. Since "an injury to one is the concern of all," a failure to protect all is an exhibition of a purpose without the power to enforce it, and this fact emphasizes the necessity of the federation of organizations, but which under existing conditions is impracticable, if not impossible.

5. It is universally conceded that one of the most serious objections to the existing organizations is their excessive cost to the membership, the sum totals of which, were the facts known, would amaze the labor world. So enormous have they become that tens of thousands, unable to bear the burden, have been forced back into the ranks of the unorganized.

6. Another defect in existing organizations is their secrecy, as for instance, the secret ballot, by virtue of which thousands of worthy applicants have been excluded. The air of mystery surrounding their proceedings is not calculated to inspire confidence. On the contrary, in the relations between employer and employee, in carrying forward great enterprises in which the people at large are profoundly interested, mystery is not required and is productive of suspicion and distrust. Open, fearless, and above-board work is far more in consonance with the spirit of independence and free institutions.

7. The tremendous power conferred upon chief officers has been a source of widespread dissatisfaction. The mere dictum of an individual determines whether a strike involving thousands of employees and millions of dollars shall or shall not occur. He is, in this sense, an absolute monarch. From his decision

there is no appeal. The unanimous vote of the organization cannot prevail against it. Such autocratic power vested in a single person is not only dangerous to a degree that defies exaggeration, but is at war with the American idea of government, in which one-man rule has no place. The responsibility often involved in a final decision is too great and too grave to rest upon any one man, however sturdy his integrity or unerring his judgment.

8. The subject of grievances and grievance committees has itself become a grievance that cries aloud for correction. The petty complaints that ceaselessly arise among employees and keep them in a state of agitation and unrest have brought odium upon organizations and weakened their power for good in directions where real grievances demand adjustment. The very term "grievance committee" has become a reproach and a byword. This brood of evils is in a large measure due to the personal jealousies and enmities flowing out of the inharmonious relations existing between organizations, each of which seeks supremacy without regard to the welfare of the other.

The complex grievance machinery entailing prolonged delays, the vast number of local, general, and joint committees, an army in themselves, are well calculated to increase rather than diminish grievances. For every complaint that is remedied another takes its place, and thus they multiply until railway officials lose patience and seek refuge in refusal to make further concessions.

Such petty grievances as are herein indicated ought not to exist at all, and once correct methods of organization are inaugurated will entirely disappear. Righteous complaints and just demands are always in order, and should receive prompt attention and be pressed to a speedy and satisfactory adjustment.

9. Organizations have become so numerous, and their annual and biennial conventions occur so frequently, that the question of furnishing free transportation for delegates, their families, and friends, is being seriously considered by railway officials as an abuse of privileges without a redeeming feature. This incessant demand for special trains, special cars, the recognition of credentials and passes without limit is compromising the character and dignity of organizations and placing their officers and members under obligations which must sooner or later, in view of the constant agitation for increased pay and other concessions, prove a source of embarrassment and humiliation.

10. The extraordinary fact cannot be overlooked that while present organizations are provided with expensive striking and boycotting machinery, and while millions of dollars, wrung from their members, have been expended in support of strikes, they have with scarcely an exception been overwhelmed with defeat. The history of railroad strikes, as conducted by railroad organizations,

is a recital of brave but hopeless struggle, of strikers defeated, impoverished, blacklisted, pursued, and driven to the extremity of scabbing or starvation. Under present conditions this result is inevitable, and a century of organization on present lines will not change it. Railway employees have contributed from their earnings untold millions in support of organizations and are therefore entitled to protection instead of promises that can never be fulfilled.

It cannot be denied that the policy of present organizations has filled the land with scabs, who swarm in the highways and byways awaiting anxiously, eagerly, the opportunity to gratify their revenge by taking positions vacated by strikers. Thoughtful men have no difficulty in accounting for the failure of railroad strikes. Neither are they at a loss to suggest a remedy. Organized upon correct principles, governed by just laws, and animated by unselfish purposes, the necessity for strikes and boycotts among railway employees will disappear.

Experience teaches that defective organization leads to strikes and defeat as certainly as perfect organization will insure peace and success.

11. The ever-increasing body of idle engineers, conductors, etc., seeking in vain for employment is the legitimate fruit of promotion on the seniority basis. The pernicious effects of this system can scarcely be overestimated. A lifetime of faithful service counts for nothing. When dismissal comes, ofttimes for trivial offense, the victim finds the doors of his calling everywhere barred against him. He is compelled to go to the very bottom and serve again his entire apprenticeship. The natural tendency is to weaken organized labor by creating a surplus of experienced men whose necessities make them available to corporations in recruiting their service in times of trouble. It is not strange that the victims of the seniority iniquity renounce organization and take their places with the unorganized.

What is required is a system of promotion that recognizes and rewards merit rather than seniority. Other things being equal, seniority should of course have the preference. In filling vacancies, selection should be made from the line of promotion and from the unemployed in a ratio evincing due regard to the rights of both.

The New Order

The American Railway Union will include all classes of railway employees separately organized, yet all in harmonious alliance within one great brotherhood.

There will be one supreme law for the order with provisions for all classes, one roof to shelter all, each separate and yet all united when unity of action is required. In this is seen the federation of classes which is feasible, instead of the federation of organizations, which has proved to be utterly impracticable. The reforms sought to be inaugurated and the benefits to be derived therefrom briefly stated are as follows:

1. The protection of members in all matters relating to wages and their rights as employees is the principal purpose of the organization. Railway employees are entitled to a voice in fixing wages and determining conditions of employment.

Fair wages and proper treatment must be the return for efficient service faithfully performed.

Such a policy insures harmonious relations and satisfactory results. The new order, while pledged to conservative methods, will protect the humblest of its members in every right he can justly claim. But while the rights of members will be sacredly guarded, no intemperate demand or unreasonable proposition will be entertained.

Corporations will not be permitted to treat the organization better than the organization will treat them. A high sense of honor must be the animating spirit, and even-handed justice the end sought to be attained.

Thoroughly organized in every department, with a due regard for the right wherever found, it is confidently believed that all differences may be satisfactorily adjusted, that harmonious relations may be established and maintained, that the service may be incalculably improved, and that the necessity for strike and lockout, boycott and blacklist, alike disastrous to employer and employee, and a perpetual menace to the welfare of the public, will forever disappear.

2. In every department of labor, the question of economy is forced to the front by the logic of necessity. The importance of organization is conceded, but if it costs more than a workingman is able to pay, the benefits to accrue, however great, are barred. Therefore, to bring the expenses of organization within the reach of all is the one thing required, a primary question which must be settled before those who stand most in need can participate in the benefits to be derived.

The expenditures required to maintain subordinate and grand lodges, every dollar of which is a tax upon labor, operate disastrously in two ways: first by repelling men who believe in organization, and second by expelling members because of inability to meet the exactions, and in both of which the much vaunted fraternity feature, it is seen, is based entirely upon the ability to pay dues. In this it is noted that the organizations as now conducted are for men, as a general proposition, who have steady work at fair pay, while others less fortunate in these regards are forced to remain outside to be the victims of uncharitable criticism.

Hence to reduce the cost to the lowest practicable point is a demand strictly in accord with the fundamental principles of economy, and any movement which makes it possible for all to participate in the benefits ought to meet with popular favor.

This reduction of cost the new organization proposes to accomplish in a way that, while preserving every feature of efficiency that can be claimed by existing organizations, will so minimize expenses that members will not be forced to seek relief, as is now the case, in the abandonment of organization. To accomplish this reduction a number of burdens such as grand and subordinate lodges, annual and biennial conventions, innumerable grievance committees, etc., will be eliminated. As these unnecessary features will not exist, the entire brood of taxes necessary to maintain them will be unknown.

3. The new organization will have a number of departments, each of which will be designed to promote the welfare of the membership in a practical way and by practical methods. The best thought of workingmen has long sought to solve the problem of making labor organizations protective, not only against sickness, disability, and death, but against the ills consequent upon idleness, and those which follow in its train. Hence there will be established an employment department in which it is proposed to register the name of every member out of employment. The department will also be fully informed where work may be obtained. It is doubtful if a more important feature could be suggested. It evidences fraternal regard without a fee, benevolence without alloy.

4. In the establishment of a department of education, a number of important features are contemplated, as for instance, lectures upon subjects relating to economics, such as wages, expenses, the relations of employer and employee, strikes, their moral and financial aspects, etc. In this connection a daily paper will be established whose mission it will be to advocate measures and policies in which labor had vital interests, and also the publication of a standard monthly magazine which will occupy a still broader field in the discussion of questions which engage the attention of the best writers and thinkers of the times.[2]

5. There will be a department designed to promote legislation in the interest of labor—that is to say, the enactment of laws by legislatures and by Congress having in view well-defined obligations of employer and employees, such as safety appliances for trains, hours of labor, the payment of wages, the rights of employees to be heard in courts where they have claims to be adjudicated, and numerous others in which partisan politics will play no part, the common good being the animating purpose.

6. In the department of insurance, sound business principles will be

introduced, something that has not hitherto engaged the serious attention its importance merits. At present, insurance entails grievous burdens without corresponding benefits. To lessen the cost while maintaining every security and every benefit will be the problem the department will solve. It is the purpose to have a life as well as an accident department, both to be optional with the membership.

With this declaration of its purposes and with boundless faith in its conquering mission, the American Railway Union consecrates itself to the great cause of industrial emancipation.

It comes with a message of greeting and good cheer to all organizations and all men who stand pledged to the sacred work of lightening the burden and lifting up the bowed form of labor.

It hails with a glow of satisfaction the signs of the times indicating with unerring certainty the coming of the new and better era when heart, brain, and conscience in holy alliance shall be the controlling power in human affairs.

In this spirit it enters upon its chosen field and will labor with all the zeal, devotion, and ability at its command to attain the cherished objects of its high ambition.

Eugene V. Debs,
G. W. Howard,
W. S. Missemer,
S. Keliher,
L. W. Rogers,
W. H. Sebring,
J. A. Clarke

Interview with Eugene V. Debs at Woodstock Jail, by Nellie Bly[†]

January 19, 1895

Chicago, Ill. January 19 [1895]—Eugene Victor Debs says he makes only one sacrifice by being in jail.[3] That is the absence from his family circle in their Sunday evening reunions.

It has been the invariable custom of the Debs family to spend their Sunday evenings together. As children it was the unbroken rule and as sons and daughters grew up and got homes of their own, they still came back on Sunday evenings with husbands or wives and children to their parents' fireside.

"All days are alike to one in jail," Mr. Debs said to me. "I forget whether it's Monday or Wednesday, but intuitively and without effort I know when it's Sunday. I suppose one would say it was due to some occult influence, for then the family are together and my chair is vacant."

While I attended the strikes at Pullman last summer I did not meet Mr. Debs, who, as the leader of the ARU, became so widely known through them. So I was rather glad to take the tiresome trip to Woodstock, Illinois, to see Mr. Debs.

Woodstock is a small country town. The jail is a very small affair in the rear of the sheriff's house and adjoining the courthouse.

The reason Mr. Debs and his seven fellow sufferers are in Woodstock is because the jail in Chicago is overflowing with prisoners, guilty and innocent, and, unlike the streetcars, it cannot squeeze in another one. They have at present four men in every small cell, and the entire place is crawling with vermin and deep in filth. So Mr. Debs and his companions have good reasons for congratulating themselves that there was no room for more.

There are no signs of a jail about the front of the Sheriff's house. It is a plain brick, with unbarred windows. I rang the bell and was admitted by a young girl, who stared at me wonderingly.

"I would like to see Mr. Debs. Can I do so?" I asked.

"I guess so," she said, and then added, hesitatingly, "The sheriff's in court and won't be out till 12:00, so I guess I'd better ask Mother."

[†]   Published as "Nellie Bly in Jail: Chat with Eugene Victor Debs, the Imprisoned Labor Leader" in *New York World,* January 20, 1895.

She disappeared after telling me to be seated, and presently a woman came in and I made known to her my wishes.

"Are you his wife?" she asked, curiously.

"No," I replied, "merely a friend."

"I guess you can see him. Come this way," she said.

I followed her through the dining room to a hall in the rear and along this hall to where iron bars, newly painted white, shut off the jail from the house.

Glancing through the bars I could see a number of men sitting in a sunlit corridor. They all sat in perfect silence, deeply interested in the books they were reading.

"Here's a friend of yours, Mr. Debs," the woman called, and Mr. Debs came close to the gate.

I did not want everybody to know who I was, so I whispered through the bars.

"I am Nellie Bly,[4] Mr. Debs, and I would like to have a talk with you."

"I am glad to see you, Miss Bly," was the quiet reply, and then he addressed the woman.

"Can you let me come out for a little while, Mrs. Eckert?" he said.

"I'll let you out alone," she replied, and taking a huge key from her pocket endeavored to unlock the door.

The lock stuck.

"Push on the door, Mr. Debs," she ordered, and Mr. Debs lent his aid to undo the stubborn bolt.

His Own Jailer

"The other night I had to lock myself in," Mr. Debs observed dryly.

In another moment the bolt shot back, the door swung open, and Eugene Victor Debs stood in the corridor before me.

For an instant we looked at each other, his tall figure looming up before me, and then simultaneously we stretched out our arms.

"I am glad to meet you," said Mr. Debs.

"And I am glad to meet you," I replied.

Side by side we walked through the corridor, through the dining room, and to the sitting room which I had first entered.

There we sat down facing each other.

"They don't seem much afraid of your getting away," I observed.

"They know we are on our honor here, and they can trust us," Mr. Debs replied. "The day we were brought here I was to appear in court at 10:00, so I ran all the way to court and arrived there just one minute to 10. I was on my honor, and I would not have been a minute late for anything in the world. Several persons said to me that I was the first man they ever saw run to get into jail."

"Do you find your imprisonment very hard to bear?" I asked.

"No; the only sacrifice I make is the separation from my family. It has always been the custom of our family to have a reunion Sunday nights, and to miss them is the only cross I have to bear. My father and mother are old, my father being 75, and it is hard to miss even one night that I could be with them."

The Debs family is a very happy and lucky one. There are four daughters and two sons, and there has never been a death.[5] The daughters married and the sons married, and it only increased the family circle. Even the very slightest of family quarrels or strife has never come among the Debses.[6]

Eugene Victor Debs says the most perfect harmony and affection have always existed in the home, even with those who have married into his family.

He has been married ten years, and he has never had even one cross word with his wife. She is a daughter, fond and loving, to his parents, and she is in the family circle these Sunday evenings that he spends in jail.

Until within a short time the family all lived in Terre Haute, Indiana, but now one married sister lives in New York and another is on a visit to Paris, while Mr. Debs is in jail, making a break in the home that the parents feel deeply.

"Don't you think it is rather hard to be in jail on the silly charge of contempt of court, when Carnegie is at liberty?" I asked.

Mr. Debs smiled.

"Everybody understands what makes the difference," he answered. "You know," he added, "they declared me guilty under the bill known as the Interstate Commerce law. This bill was supposedly enacted for the protection of small farmers and producers. Before the law was passed, the small farmers were crushed to the wall by combines and large companies, who could get low rates because of the quantity they shipped, and consequently were always able to undersell the small farmer.

Since the Santa Fe Railroad has been in the hands of receivers, Expert Little, who made an examination of the company's books, finds that J. W. Reinhart, president of the company, paid out, within a year, $8 million in rebates to favored shippers, the very thing the Interstate Commerce law was designed to put a stop to. No one was ever prosecuted. Mr. Reinhart was permitted to resign his position, and the matter ended there. Notwithstanding the Santa Fe Company was in the hands of a receiver, therefore in the custody of the court. The court took no judicial knowledge of the crime, and nothing has been said of it from that day to this. Had it been a labor leader guilty of this crime, the press would have insisted on his being prosecuted and punished by fine and imprisonment, and there would have been no end until this was done.

Compared with Millionaires

I looked at Mr. Debs as he sat before me and compared him with two millionaires—Pullman and Carnegie.

Mr. Debs is unusually tall—an inch or two over six feet, I should judge. He is well built, slender, but not thin. His shoulders are broad and there is a look of strength about him.

His face is rather long, beardless and smooth cut. He has the strong, large nose of a successful man. His mouth is small and pleasantly shaped, and he smiles frequently, a fleeting but pretty smile that shows two rows of strong white teeth.

His eyes are blue and at present have slightly reddish rings about them, as though from too much reading. Gold-rimmed glasses that run behind the ears he wears constantly.

Mr. Debs's forehead was originally high and broad, and much thought has placed four lines across it, with a short one above the right eye. There are evidences that in a short time Mr. Debs's forehead will be still higher. His hair is very thin on top.

There was no sign of the prisoner about Mr. Debs's clothes. He wore a well-made suit of gray tweed, the coat being a cutaway, and a white starched shirt with a standing collar and a small black-and-white scarf tied in a bowknot.

There was a plain gold button in his shirt front, a gold chain crossing from buttonhole to vest pocket, and an agate ring upon the third finger of his left hand.

"You don't seem very fond of jewelry," I observed.

"No; I've had a great deal given to me, but I do not like it. I only wear this ring, and I've worn it for 15 years, for one reason. You can see why."

He took off the ring and handed it to me, and I saw inscribed on the inside: "Mother to Eugene."

Eugene Victor Debs's parents were born in France, but all their children were born in America. Mr. Debs, Sr., was a grocer in Terre Haute. His son

Eugene was born November 5, 1855, and attended the public schools until he was 14 years old, when he went to work in the Vandalia Railroad paint shops.

For a year and a half he earned 50 cents a day, until ill health forced him to stop. Afterward he "fired" on a locomotive for the same company for three years and a half. He was passionately fond of railroading, and might have been working at it yet had not a wreck occurred in which two of his comrades, the engineer and the fireman, were killed. This affected his mother so strongly that she insisted upon his leaving the business.[7]

So Eugene Debs left railroading for the grocery business. There is a wholesale grocery house in Terre Haute that is considered the most complete in America. In this the young man worked for five years and held one of the most responsible positions in the house, when he became ambitious politically. He was successful in his first campaign, and in 1880 became city clerk. Five years later he was elected to the legislature.

This, he says, settled all his political aspirations. He saw that if he expected to accomplish anything he must adapt himself to the existing methods, and this he could not do and retain his self-respect.

Since 1876 Mr. Debs had been a member of the Brotherhood of Locomotive Firemen, and when, some four years later, the secretary was found to be a defaulter, the order being bankrupted and demoralized in consequence, Mr. Debs was called upon to fill the unexpired term.

Refused a Tip

This he did with great success, and in a short time he had succeeded in paying off the debt of $8,000. After that he was appointed editor of the *Locomotive Firemen's Magazine* and held that position until 1893.[8] He resigned then, though unanimously reelected, with the privilege of fixing his own salary. The order also voted him $3,000 and a six-month vacation, but Mr. Debs refused to take the money, and it still remains in the treasury of the Brotherhood.

Mr. Debs's reason for quitting the paper was that he might lend his aid to the order in other ways. He thought he had a mission to perform, and he set out to do it. He had recognized the fact that all the railroads were secretly coming together, and that they meant to reduce wages, not everywhere at once, but quietly, first one place and then another, until a wholesale reduction would result.

This is what Eugene Victor Debs wanted to work against. And if past records are anything, I don't know of any man who would make a better leader for any class of people. Eugene Debs has been in labor organizations for 20 years.

While success invariably creates enemies, and the most malicious of all enemies, failure also produces enemies, but Eugene Debs has never had a vote cast against him in all these 20 years.

That says a great deal for the man.

In addition to this, it was plain to everybody that his motive must be an honest one, since he never tried to make money from his position, but on the contrary at every convention has always asked to have his salary reduced from one to two thousand dollars.

He gave up a yearly salary of $3,000 to work for the [American Railway Union] at $75 per month, and when the trouble broke out the convention voted to raise his salary to $3,000, but he decided the order needed the money, and he has stopped his salary and has not received any since.

"How have you managed to live?" I asked, impertinently perhaps, but curiously.

"Through my family," he replied. "Whatever one has is for all. There is not a discord in our entire connection, and whatever the others have is at the command of any who may need it."

"Are you worth any money?" I asked.

"The extent of my worldly possessions is a house and lot," he answered. "I owe no man a dollar and no man owes me. You might say that I am square with the world."

"Have you no ambition to get rich?"

"Not the least. If I had to take my choice between being extremely rich or extremely poor, I would choose the latter. I think the very rich deserve pity instead of censure, just as Oscar Wilde says in his latest essay; we ought not to be severe with the very rich, they as well as the poor are entitled to our commiseration. Money-getting is a disease as much as paresis, and as much to be pitied."

"What is your highest ambition?"

"All my life, from my earliest recollection, my highest ambition has been to be an orator," he answered, his earnest blue eyes looking steadily at me. "I have always thought the personality or power to move people was the greatest on earth. If I had my choice of the gifts that come to men, I would choose that. If a woman, I would want to be the most beautiful singer."

When Mr. Debs was "firing," he worked all night, slept in the forenoon, and attended school in the afternoon. He has heard all the orators with any pretensions to greatness and power.

Fond of Music

Mr. Debs is passionately fond of music. His wife and her sisters and his own are all musical. The piano, mandolin, and guitar are all played in his house.

Mr. Debs understands French and speaks German. He doesn't care much for novels, except for those of Hugo, Sue, and Dumas. Lately he reads only economic works.

He smokes, is temperate, but enjoys a good dinner and is fond of pets. He has two—Fay, an Irish setter, and a canary named Sweetie.

He is passionately fond of children, and one can readily believe him when he says all the children at home know him.

He told me a little incident that happened just before he left his home this last time, and which warmed his heart to endure the trial before him.

On the morning of the day he left, there came a timid knock upon his door and, opening it, he saw two little tots, a boy and a girl, on the step. Each carried a little red savings bank.

The little boy was spokesman.

"I got $13," he said, "and sister's got $2 in her bank, and we're going to give it to you to pay those men so they won't take you off to jail."

They had evidently heard their parents discussing Mr. Debs's fate and had made up their baby minds to save their favorite.

Mr. Debs has no children of his own.

There is much of a poetic nature in Eugene Debs. He has a soft, pleasing voice that is soothing and caressing. His manner is most mild and gentle. For some reason which I cannot explain, he reminds me of James Whitcomb Riley. He and Riley are warm personal friends.

"Riley says every man lives his life in a circle," he said to me during our conversation. "A man starts here (drawing an imaginary circle upon his knee), a farm lad. He drifts out to a city to make wealth but suffers after a while; he tires of this money and the hurry and bustle of the world, and he buys a farm, and after a while his friends go out to see him and find him happy at work among his cattle, just where he began as a boy. So he completes his circle."

"I know how my life is to be," he continued in a dreamy fashion, his blue eyes gazing out through the window, where everything glistened with snow. "I am going to die in perfect quiet on a farm. I know just what that farm is like, though I have never seen it. A winding creek cuts through it and there is an immense orchard."

He stopped suddenly as if he thought he was too confidential, and he smiled. "You see," he explained, "I want a little poetry in it. I always considered a farmer's life should be the freest and best in the world. If any man knows liberty, it should be the farmer. If any man is wise, it should be the farmer. It is a perfect life. I never pass a farmhouse that I do not envy the inmates. In the country one does as one likes; in the city one does as others like. The country is the only place a man can be true to himself."

In the lapel of his coat, Mr. Debs wore a very brilliant pink flower. He evidently thought I noticed it.

"I suppose people might think this seems out of place—a carnation on a convict!" he observed with a merry smile, "and that I should wear weeping willow or something like that. It was among a box of flowers which the wife of one of my comrades sent all the way from Ogden, Utah.[9] They came in a beautiful condition; just as fresh as if newly cut."

Mr. Debs is a close student of Shakespeare, and always carries a volume with him. He can repeat *Romeo and Juliet* and *Julius Caesar* almost entire.

He is getting pretty well used to the newspapers now, but once found untruthful stories hard to bear. Now he tries to be philosophical and believes truth will live and lies die. He says everybody in Terre Haute knows him, infirmities and all, and he is sure old and young, black and white, rich and poor, can say nothing against him.

"A man hasn't anything, after all, but his reputation," he observed, "and if he won't defend that, it's because it isn't worth defending."

"Don't you think you could do labor some good by lecturing through the country?" I asked.

"There are two things I won't do," he replied promptly. "I won't write a book or lecture for money. I think it would be disreputable to thus take advantage of the notoriety I gained through workingmen's trouble. If I can survive all the talk, then I think I can do some good. If it's temporary notoriety then I shall, as a New York paper suggested, go into that obscurity from which I emerged.

"If I ever get time," Mr. Debs said, earnestly, "I want to devote some study to prisoners. During the heat of excitement over the last strike, I was arrested and spent eight days in the Chicago jail. I would not give up that experience for any consideration. There were 50 women and 500 men in that jail, and it was marvelous to see the bond of comradeship that existed among them. All the time I was there I was deluged with food and flowers. I distributed them among the other prisoners, and if I gave a man a cigar he would cut it in two or three and divide with friends. There was more fellowship among them than I have ever seen elsewhere in my life. Poor fellows!

They are confined four to a small cell, and they are in that cell 22 of the 24 hours. It is horrible.

"I became very friendly with all the men," he continued, "and I am willing to believe that if I had put them on their honor and let them out for so many hours, every one of them would have returned at the appointed time.

"I had a funny letter from one of the prisoners after my conviction," Mr. Debs said, smiling. "He began it 'Dear Brother—I am glad to hear you got six months,' he wrote, 'and that you'll be coming back to us. You'll be welcomed with open arms.'"

Woman's Rights

In a little while I changed the subject by asking the convicted labor leader what he thought of woman's rights.

"Woman's suffrage is one of my hobbies," he said enthusiastically. "I believe in women having all the rights men have. Until they do, I do not think we are civilized. I firmly believe every social condition will be improved if women have the right to vote. Women have more integrity, more honor than men. A woman's vote couldn't be bought with a drink of whiskey. If I have done any good, I owe it entirely to the influence of my mother, my wife, and my sisters.

"Marriage is another hobby of mine," he added, earnestly. "I think it is brutal for a woman to take a husband merely for the sake of getting married or being supported. I think this alleged reproach for woman staying single, or being an old maid, is wrong. All honor to a woman, I say, who stays single because she does not find a congenial mate and is courageous enough to refuse anything else. I call it brave and deserving credit instead of reproach.

"My brother and I always declared our sisters should never marry unless they loved. Without any prompting from anyone, we secretly vowed that one of us would never marry while our sisters were single and by so doing possibly force them to consider marrying for the sake of a home. And we didn't. My three sisters were married and the fourth engaged when I became engaged."

"Are you religious?" I asked. "I think I have heard you called an infidel."

"I don't subscribe to any creed," he replied gravely, "nor do I profess any religion. I am not an unbeliever. I accept the Christ standard as the highest standard of morality. I believe in the religion of the golden rule.[10] I wouldn't if I could disturb the religion of any human creature. Whatever a man's creed may be, if he sincerely believes it, it is the right creed. As for another world, I haven't time to think about it. I am interested in doing all the good I can in this."

"But don't you think it comforting to believe we'll meet those we love in another life?" I asked.

"It would be horrible not to think so," he answered, quickly. "I hate death. I never allow myself to think about it. It is enough to set one crazy. We've never had a death in our family. If I believed as Christians profess, I would look on death as a benediction. I go to the extent of hoping, if I cannot believe in an afterlife."

One of Mr. Debs's unbroken rules is not to receive presents or banquets. He says he does not think it right to let men give him what they can't afford to have for themselves, and that when he reads of managers and presidents of corporations receiving gifts as testimonials of esteem, he knows it is more a testimonial of slavery.

His Greatest Compliment

"The greatest compliment I ever had in my life was after we won a strike on the Great Northern for the section men. We got their wages raised from 80 cents a day to $1.25. The men wanted afterward to give me a banquet, but I didn't think it right to look as if rejoicing over our victory. I would have no public demonstration. As my train drew out of the station the conductor asked me to come out on the platform, and there, lining either side of the railroad, were the section men, bent and worn from exposure, each man leaning on his shovel with his hat in his hand. It touched me deeply."

"Do you ever get blue?"

"Sometimes; but I was never discouraged an instant in my life."

"How do you feel about the future for labor?" I asked.

"Very cheerful," he answered. "Government ownership of railroads is looming up in the distance. That will mean mutualism. I don't think we will ever have another great railroad strike, though there will be other strikes in other departments of industry.

"It would be foolish," he added, seriously, "to strike again. We know inevitably what the results will be. Courts will enjoin, authorities reprove them. With all the organized forces of society against them, as well as the powers of government, failure is inevitable."

I asked Mr. Debs if I might stay and share the prison dinner, and he said he would be delighted to have me and wanted to have extra fare provided for me. I could scarcely make him understand that it was his fare I wanted to share.

Sheriff Eckert came in about 12:30, and Mr. Debs introduced me and explained my mission. The sheriff is a pleasant man and seems to think his prisoners are a well-behaved lot. We told him I wanted a photographer, and he kindly offered to send for one.

It is a country jail and town, and things are not conducted just as they might be in cities. Three prisoners at a time are an event in Woodstock, so it is easy to understand the commotion raised by eight.

The only other thing that has ever happened in Woodstock was a hanging. A man killed an alderman in Chicago some years ago, and the man was taken to Woodstock and hanged. A pump now stands where the gallows stood, about 15 feet from the jail window.

There are two prisoners in jail besides the labor leaders. One is a simple fellow who could not get the wages due him from a niggardly old farmer, and so threatened to burn down his barn. The other is a German boy who stole silverware from his uncle.

At 1:00 Mrs. Eckert told us dinner was served, and Mr. Debs and I went into the dining room, where I was introduced to his seven comrades—William Burns, Sylvester Keliher, G. W. Howard, L. W. Rogers, R. M Goodwin, James Hogan, and M. J. Elliott.

The table was neatly spread, and a bowl of soup stood at every plate. After the soup we had roast beef and boiled potatoes, Mr. Debs carving, and after that lemon pie for dessert. Everybody had a large cup of coffee.

The hour spent at dinner was most enjoyable. Everybody was in a good humor and everybody had a healthy appetite.

Then we went out into the sunlit corridor of the jail, where these men, if not admitted to bail, will spend the most of their six months.[11]

The corridor is long and narrow, with huge bars on one side and three large barred windows on the other. There were two tables strewn with books and papers, a shelf around the windows, also covered with books, and eight chairs, one of which was a barber's chair. On the table was a small bunch of flowers, to which the men proudly called my attention. Above the table was the picture of a bunch of violets.

The Prison Rules

Upon the wall were pinned the rules these men made and live up to. They arise at 6:30 and have breakfast at 7:30. Breakfast consists of meat, potatoes, bread, and coffee.

From 8:00 until 12:00 the men sit in the corridor in absolute silence, reading and studying. They have been active men, and stillness was a trial, so they impose a fine of ten cents on every man who forgets and speaks aloud. This fine is given to the good, for, as Mr. Debs says, if wrongdoing be punished, it follows that goodness shall be rewarded.

So far four men have been fined, and Mr. Goodwin had the best record for goodness, so he won the reward—40 cents.

But that spoiled him, and amid much laughter they told me that Mr. Goodwin had since then been fined twice!

Mr. Goodwin, by the way, is a relative of Nat Goodwin,[12] the comedian, and the resemblance, except that Mr. Goodwin is more youthful, is very strong.

From 12:00 to 1:00 the men have what they call indifferently a "cake walk" and a "dress parade." At 1:00 they have dinner. At 2:00 they go into session again, and for the rest of the afternoon a pin could be heard drop.

From 6:30 until 7:00 they have supper, and afterward they devote an hour to discussion, or, as Mr. Debs says, "to good fellowship."

Someone proposes a subject, and they discuss it or what they have read during the day.

"We did tell stories at first," Mr. Debs said with his quick smile, "but we find after we've been in jail a week or so that we begin to repeat the same story four or five times. Then it isn't so funny."

At 9:30 sharp the solitary lamp, a hanging one, is put out, and everybody goes into his cell, and the good sheriff locks his prisoners up for the night.

The cells are small, with two cots to a cell, and two men are in each cell. There are only two tiers, comprising ten cells in all.

Each man makes his own bed. It is an iron cot fastened to the wall, and has a mattress, sheet, blanket, and pillow.

Sometimes the men forget to make their beds, and then they are fined. One man had forgotten the day I was there, and he rushed into his cell hoping to escape notice until his work was done. But someone saw him, and amid great laughing he was pulled forth and made to pay his fine, which he did, blushing like a schoolboy.

The men have basins to wash in; three towels are provided the ten prisoners, and they have to last for two days.

Four men smoke and four do not. They may smoke when they wish.

I took a glance at their books. There was not a light work of fiction among them. The books were brought by the men from their homes.

Intellectual Development of Europe, by Draper; *Social Problems,* by Henry George; Harvey's *Coin's Financial School; Civilization Civilized,* by Stephen Maybell; *Holy Bible; Text Book of Rhetoric; Our Destiny,* by Gronlund; *Better*

Days, by Fitch;[13] *The Cooperative Commonwealth,* by Gronlund, and volumes of Hawthorne and Shakespeare.

That is only a small list, but it gives some idea of the style of reading enjoyed by these men who are fighting for workingmen's rights.

Debs's Busy Life in Jail:
Interview with the *Chicago Chronicle*[†]
June 18, 1895

> I intend to use all my influence, and it is very little, toward the Cooperative Commonwealth and against monopolistic ownership. I have given my liberty for my convictions and I am ready to give my life for them.

As he spoke these words yesterday [June 18, 1895] Eugene V. Debs glanced quietly at the little group seated around him in the McHenry County Jail at Woodstock.[14] Seated beside the famous labor leader, with his dark eyes fixed on the tier of cells in front of him, was L. W. Rogers. On a rude barber chair William E. Burns stretched his length, puffing at a pipe and giving serious attention to the words of his chief. Sylvester Keliher, James Hogan, M. J. Elliott, and R. M Goodwin, the other directors of the American Railway Union undergoing sentence for contempt of court, lounged about the cell room in lazy attitudes and listened.

"There will be no more prosperity in this country until the money power, that great force which is combining and centralizing capital in every branch of industry, is supplanted by a commonwealth where every man will receive the full product of his brain and hands," went on Mr. Debs in his firm, convincing way.

Mr. Debs is a trifle thinner than he was a few weeks ago, but indoor life has not yet begun to tell on his ruddy cheek. He was comfortably attired in negligee costume, as were all the other prisoners. Rogers alone seems to show the effects of confinement, as his face is overspread by a sickly pallor which is heightened by a stubble growth of beard.

---

†   Published in *Chicago Chronicle,* June 19, 1895.

Comforts for Prisoners

The room in which the seven prisoners sat talking is about 30 feet long and 10 feet wide. A flood of light and air is admitted by three large windows, and here the world-famous officers of the American Railway Union study, write, and talk. At the west end of the room, close under a barred window, is a pine table, piled high with books and writing materials. The north wall is composed of a latticework of steel, and beyond that are the ten cells of the McHenry County Jail.

Life in the prison is not irksome to Debs and his companions, for every moment is occupied. All are deeply interested in the study of economic questions, and the books are constantly in use. On the south wall is pinned a code of rules, drawn by a committee of the prisoners. Here they are:

> Rise, 6 a.m.
> Study hours, 8:30 to 10:30 a.m.
> Recess, 10:45 to 12:15 p.m.
> **DINNER**
> Study hours, 2 to 3:30 p.m.
> Recess, 3:45 to 5 p.m.
> Drill, 5 sharp.
> **SUPPER**
> Debate, 7:30 to 9 p.m.
> Retire at 10 p.m.
>
>
> Positively no talking or leaving bed after the lights go out.
> Entire silence must be preserved during study hours.
> All interruptions by reading aloud or talking aloud or asking questions of any kind are strictly prohibited.
> Visitors—During visits rules are suspended, but are instantly in force when visitor departs.
> Each man shall be turnkey one day at a time, and if he neglects his duty he shall serve an additional day.
> Cells must be inspected and kept clean; all beds to be made during morning session.

Live Up to Rules

"There are our rules," said Mr. Debs, with a sweep of his arm toward them, "and we live up to them. Inspector Elliott, there, will allow no trifling. At five minutes to ten he gives the signal for bed, and every man is allowed five minutes to get into his cell, undress, and become quiet. At 10:00, off goes the light, and not a loud breath is allowed after that."

Mr. Elliott grinned good-naturedly at this recital of his capabilities as a martinet, and Burns, lazily rolling over in the barber chair, observed that a variation of five minutes in some of the watches the night before almost caused a riot.

"Have you seen our gymnasium?" asked Mr. Debs. "You must not miss the punching bag. Stay for the big show," and he led the way into the cell room where a punching bag is rigged up. "There is where we get our magnificent proportions," said Mr. Debs, giving the bag a lusty jab, "and here is our military branch," he said as he produced an old army musket from a corner. "Colonel Hogan, there, puts us through the manual with this to limber us up, and all the boys are well drilled except me. Then we march up and down here and do the arm movements, so you see we can keep down the weight."

Time Profitably Occupied

As he ceased his banter and again seated himself with his chair tilted back against the steel bars, Mr. Debs took a graver tone, and said:

"Every minute here is profitably occupied. During study hour you could hear a pin drop. Here are some of our books," and he lifted a copy of Kidd's *Social Evolution*. [Other books included] Richard Ely's *Political Economy; Freeland—A Social Anticipation*, by Professor Hertzka; Lawrence Gronlund's *Cooperative Commonwealth; Live Questions*, by Altgeld; and all the new books on the silver question. "So, you see, we keep ourselves busy. Every night we have a debate or speeches. Here is the program for this evening," and the studious-looking prisoner picked up a sheet of paper on which was written:

> Tuesday evening, 7:30 to 9:00.
> Resolved, That a sincere belief in any religion helps, rather than retards, the reform movement.
> Affirmative, Burns; negative, Hogan.
> Time rule—Affirmative, 15 minutes; negative, 15 minutes; audience, 7 minutes each; negative concludes in 10 minutes; affirmative concludes in 10 minutes; statement next subject and remarks, 5 minutes; adjourn.

"Tomorrow evening will be given up to speeches," went on Mr. Debs, "and Brother Rogers has arranged this little program:"

Ten-minute speeches on special subjects:
Goodwin: "Abuse of Natural Law and Its Consequences."
Debs: "What Monopolies Should First Be Destroyed, and Why."
Keliher: "Gymnastic Development and Its Benefits."
Elliott: "The Effects of Importing Foreign Labor."
Rogers: "Outline Lessons in Science We Should Understand."
Hogan: "Use and Abuse of Military Power."
Burns: "Power of Corporation Lobbies in 'Reform Legislatures.'"
Two-minute speeches on the subject just discussed permitted between the
   ten-minute speeches.

Official Letter Writing

"As for myself, in addition to taking part in these little interchanges of
thought, I am keeping up all my necessary correspondence on behalf of the
American Railway Union, and I am writing for a number of labor papers. I
expect before long to get into the magazines. I have been invited to contribute to the *North American Review* and to *The Arena*. A book might be written
on this experience of ours, but the trouble would be to know where to stop.
The case stands without precedent in this country and is worth of being preserved in book form.

"As for the future, I am not worrying. I think when this sentence is served
there will not be another one to follow. Judge Woods agreed to make the records show that the sentences were concurrent, and I think he will do it. When
I get out of here I will take up the threads where they were laid down and do
my best to help the dawn of day we are all hoping for, when the poor man will
have a show. As it is, he has none. The trend of the times is toward capitalization, toward centralization of everything, and when each branch of industry is
controlled by a trust that monopoly doles out such wages as it pleases. All this
is wrong, and only a Cooperative Commonwealth can right it.

"In this country we have no longer a republic, no longer a Congress. If the
Congress places upon the statute books a law inimical to the interests of the
allied money power, of capital, it is wiped out by the Supreme Court. What is
the Supreme Court? Nine gentlemen who owe their appointments to corporation influence, seven of whom are corporation lawyers, men whose lives have
been spent in service of corporations, whose affiliations and sympathies are all
with the corporations. Is there the slightest chance that they would decide any
question in favor of the workingman, in favor of a class from which they turn
with disgust, and which might as well be on another planet for all they know

of its struggles and ambitions? Events have proven that such hope is futile and that the money power, capital, which is daily and hourly growing more centralized, already supersedes every department of the government and has the country by the throat.

Is Not an Anarchist

"All this may be termed buncombe and anarchistic, but we are American citizens, we are not anarchists. Had we been, we would be free today, for we would be on the other side of the question. The time will never again come in this country when there will be enough work to go around. Every day more men are forced out of work by machinery. The machinery produces what they formerly did, but the men remain to be provided for, and every year it is growing worse. Just so long as all that machinery and everything it produces is controlled by monopoly, the workingman will stand begging for employment at the door of the trust. The country has outgrown the wage system. That is the sum and substance of it. The system which was in vogue 25 and 30 years ago is still in force, but conditions are entirely revolutionized. When I was a boy, every man who worked for another hoped someday to be his own employer, to set up his own business. The blacksmith's apprentice worked a few years and then started his own shop. Nowadays all the horseshoe nails and nearly all the horseshoes are made by trusts. The printer learned his trade, and what use is it to him? Ten years from now a hand compositor will be a rarity. They have been driven out by machines. But the men are still here, clamoring for the work which machinery deprives them of, and capital, controlling the machinery and its product, holds the upper hand. The way out is a question too large for me to handle. But toward the Cooperative Commonwealth, the solution of this problem of the day, all my energies shall be directed."

Treatment by the Sheriff

Sheriff Eckert, who rules the prisoners with so light a hand, is a genial, hearty gentleman who has a deep respect for Mr. Debs and his fellow prisoners. The men eat every meal in the dining room of the sheriff's residence, and the fare is the same as that of Mr. Eckert's family.

"I make no distinction in the matter of feeding the boys," said Sheriff Eckert. "They eat the same food my family does, and I buy the best I can afford. To prepare their meals and serve them in the cells would be too much work for my family, so I just gave orders that the boys should eat in my dining room. I guess they are satisfied."

The cells of the labor leaders are scrupulously clean. Mr. Debs sleeps alone in a 6 x 4 cell, but the others bunk two in a cell. A narrow iron bunk is hung from the wall by chains and on this is a mattress, pillow, and bedclothing. When the men are in their cells, three heavy barred doors are between them and the outer world.

There are five other prisoners in the jail at present, and they seem to enjoy almost as many privileges as the Debs party. Sheriff Eckert does not see the wisdom or necessity of locking prisoners in a narrow cell all day. The five men are free in the corridor to smoke, punch the bag, or sleep, as fancy may dictate. All of the prisoners declared they were well and as happy as could be expected of seven strong men with locks on every side and a glimpse of the world obtained only by gazing through steel bars.

How I Became a Socialist[†15]

April 1902

As I have some doubt about the readers of *The Comrade* having any curiosity as to "how I became a socialist," it may be in order to say that the subject is the editor's, not my own; and that what is here offered is at his bidding—my only concern being that he shall not have cause to wish that I had remained what I was instead of becoming a socialist.

On the evening of February 27, 1875, the local lodge of the Brotherhood of Locomotive Firemen was organized at Terre Haute, Indiana, by Joshua A. Leach, then grand master, and I was admitted as a charter member and at once chosen secretary. "Old Josh Leach," as he was affectionately called, a typical locomotive fireman of his day, was the founder of the brotherhood, and I was instantly attracted by his rugged honesty, simple manner, and homely speech. How well I remember feeling his large, rough hand on my shoulder, the kindly eye of an elder brother searching my own as he gently said, "My boy, you're a little young, but I believe you're in earnest and will make your mark in the brotherhood." Of course, I assured him that I would do my best. What he

†   Published in *The Comrade* (New York), vol. 1, no. 7 (April 1902), 146–148.

really thought at the time flattered my boyish vanity not a little when I heard of it. He was attending a meeting at St. Louis some months later, and in the course of his remarks said: "I put a towheaded boy in the brotherhood at Terre Haute not long ago, and some day he will be at the head of it."[16]

Twenty-seven years, to a day, have played their pranks with "Old Josh" and the rest of us. When last we met, not long ago, and I pressed his good, right hand, I observed that he was crowned with the frost that never melts; and as I think of him now:

> Remembrance wakes, with all her busy train,
> Swells at my breast and turns the past to pain.[17]

My first step was thus taken in organized labor, and a new influence fired my ambition and changed the whole current of my career. I was filled with enthusiasm and my blood fairly leaped in my veins. Day and night I worked for the brotherhood. To see its watchfires glow and observe the increase of its sturdy members were the sunshine and shower of my life. To attend the "meeting" was my supreme joy, and for ten years I was not once absent when the faithful assembled.

At the convention held in Buffalo in 1878, I was chosen associate editor of the magazine, and in 1880 I became grand secretary and treasurer. With all the fire of youth I entered upon the crusade which seemed to fairly glitter with possibilities. For 18 hours at a stretch I was glued to my desk, reeling off the answers to my many correspondents. Day and night were one. Sleep was time wasted, and often, when all oblivious of her presence in the still small hours, my mother's hand turned off the light, I went to bed under protest. Oh, what days! And what quenchless zeal and consuming vanity! All the firemen every-where—and they were all the world—were straining:

> To catch the beat
> On my tramping feet.[18]

My grip was always packed; and I was darting in all directions. To tramp through a railroad yard in the rain, snow, or sleet half the night, or till day-break, to be ordered out of the roundhouse for being an "agitator," or put off a train, sometimes passenger, more often freight, while attempting to deadhead over the division, were all in the program, and served to whet the appetite to conquer. One night in midwinter at Elmira, New York, a conductor on the Erie kindly dropped me off in a snowbank, and as I clambered to the top I ran into the arms of a policeman who heard my story and on the spot became my friend.

I rode on the engines over mountain and plain, slept in the cabooses and bunks, and was fed from their pails by the swarthy stokers who still nestle close to my heart, and will until it is cold and still.

Through all these years I was nourished at Fountain Proletaire. I drank deeply of its waters, and every particle of my tissue became saturated with the spirit of the working class. I had fired an engine and been stung by the exposure and hardship of the rail. I was with the boys in their weary watches, at the broken engine's side, and often helped to bear their bruised and bleeding bodies back to wife and child again. How could I but feel the burden of their wrongs? How the seed of agitation fail to take deep root in my heart?

And so I was spurred on in the work of organizing, not the firemen merely, but the brakemen, switchmen, telegraphers, shopmen, track-hands, all of them in fact, and as I had now become known as an organizer, the calls came from all sides, and there are but few trades I have not helped to organize and less still in whose strikes I have not at some time had a hand.

In 1894 the American Railway Union was organized, and a braver body of men never fought the battle of the working class.[19]

Up to this time I had heard but little of socialism, knew practically nothing about the movement, and what little I did know was not calculated to impress me in its favor. I was bent on thorough and complete organization of the railroad men, and ultimately the whole working class, and all my time and energy were given to that end. My supreme conviction was that if they were only organized in every branch of the service and all acted together in concert, they could redress their wrongs and regulate the conditions of their employment. The stockholders of the corporation acted as one, why not the men? It was such a plain proposition—simply to follow the example set before their eyes by their masters—surely they could not fail to see it, act as one, and solve the problem.

It is useless to say that I had yet to learn the workings of the capitalist system, the resources of its masters, and the weakness of its slaves. Indeed, no shadow of a "system" fell athwart my pathway; no thought of ending wage-misery marred my plans. I was too deeply absorbed in perfecting wage-servitude and making it a "thing of beauty and a joy forever."[20]

It all seems very strange to me now, taking a backward look, that my vision was so focalized on a single objective point that I utterly failed to see what now appears as clear as the noonday sun—so clear that I marvel that any working-man, however dull, uncomprehending, can resist it.

But perhaps it was better so. I was to be baptized in socialism in the roar of conflict, and I thank the gods for reserving to this fitful occasion the fiat, "Let there be light!"—the light that streams in steady radiance upon the broad way to the socialist republic.

The skirmish lines of the ARU were well advanced. A series of small battles were fought and won without the loss of a man. A number of concessions were made by the corporations rather than risk an encounter. Then came the fight on the Great Northern, short, sharp, and decisive. The victory was complete— the only railroad strike of magnitude ever won by an organization in America.

Next followed the final shock—the Pullman strike—and the American Railway Union again won, clear and complete. The combined corporations were paralyzed and helpless. At this juncture there were delivered, from wholly unexpected quarters, a swift succession of blows that blinded me for an instant and then opened wide my eyes—and in the gleam of every bayonet and the flash of every rifle *the class struggle was revealed.* This was my first practical lesson in socialism, though wholly unaware that it was called by that name.

An army of detectives, thugs, and murderers were equipped with badge and beer and bludgeon and turned loose; old hulks of cars were fired; the alarm bells tolled; the people were terrified; the most startling rumors were set afloat; the press volleyed and thundered, and over all the wires sped the news that Chicago's white throat was in the clutch of a red mob; injunctions flew thick and fast, arrests followed, and our office and headquarters, the heart of the strike, was sacked, torn out, and nailed up by the "lawful" authorities of the federal government; and when in company with my loyal comrades I found myself in Cook County Jail at Chicago with the whole press screaming conspiracy, treason, and murder, and by some fateful coincidence I was given the cell occupied just previous to his execution by the assassin of Mayor Carter Harrison, Sr., overlooking the spot, a few feet distant, where the anarchists were hanged a few years before, why then I had another exceedingly practical and impressive lesson in socialism.

Acting upon the advice of friends, we sought to employ John Harlan,[21] son of the Supreme Justice, to assist in our defense—a defense memorable to me chiefly because of the skill and fidelity of our lawyers, among whom were the brilliant Clarence Darrow and the venerable Judge Lyman Trumbull, author of the 13th Amendment to the Constitution, abolishing slavery in the United States.

Mr. Harlan wanted to think of the matter overnight; and the next morning gravely informed us that he could not afford to be identified with the case, "for," said he, "you will be tried upon the same theory as were the anarchists, with probably the same result." That day, I remember, the jailer, by way of consolation, I suppose, showed us the bloodstained rope used at the last execution and explained in minutest detail, as he exhibited the gruesome relic, just how the monstrous crime of lawful murder is committed.

But the tempest gradually subsided, and with it the bloodthirstiness of the press and "public sentiment." We were not sentenced to the gallows, nor even to the penitentiary—though put on trial for conspiracy—for reasons that will make another story.

The Chicago jail sentences were followed by six months at Woodstock, and it was here that socialism gradually laid hold of me in its own irresistible fashion. Books and pamphlets and letters from socialists came by every mail, and I began to read and think and dissect the anatomy of the system in which workingmen, however organized, could be shattered and battered and splintered at a single stroke. The writings of Bellamy and Blatchford[22] early appealed to me. *The Cooperative Commonwealth* of Gronlund also impressed me, but the writings of Kautsky were so clear and conclusive that I readily grasped not merely his argument, but also caught the spirit of his socialist utterance— and I thank him and all who helped me out of darkness into light. It was at this time, when the first glimmerings of socialism were beginning to penetrate, that Victor L. Berger—and I have loved him ever since—came to Woodstock, as if a providential instrument, and delivered the first impassioned message of socialism I had ever heard—the very first to set the "wires humming in my system." As a souvenir of that visit there is in my library a volume of *Capital,* by Karl Marx, inscribed with the compliments of Victor L. Berger, which I cherish as a token of priceless value.[23]

The American Railway Union was defeated but not conquered—overwhelmed but not destroyed. It lives and pulsates in the socialist movement, and its defeat but blazed the way to economic freedom and hastened the sunrise of human brotherhood.

The Federal Government and the Chicago Strike: A Reply to Grover Cleveland[†]

July 1904

In the July issue of *McClure's Magazine,* ex-president Grover Cleveland has an article on "The Government in the Chicago Strike of 1894."[24] That there may be no mistake about the meaning of "government" in this connection, it should be understood that Mr. Cleveland has reference to the federal government, of which he was the executive head at the time of the strike in question, and not to the state government of Illinois, or the municipal government of Chicago, both of which were overridden and set at defiance by the executive authority, enforced by the military power of the federal government, under the administration of Mr. Cleveland.

Cleveland Vindicates Himself

The ex-president's article not only triumphantly vindicates his administration, but congratulates its author upon the eminent service he rendered the Republic in a critical hour when a labor strike jarred its foundations and threatened its overthrow.

It may be sheer coincidence that Mr. Cleveland's eulogy upon his patriotic administration, and upon himself as its central and commanding figure, appeared on the eve of a national convention composed largely of his disciples who were urging his fourth nomination for the presidency for the very reasons set forth in the article on the Chicago strike.

His Knowledge Secondhand

However this may be, it is certain that of his own knowledge, ex-President Cleveland knows nothing of the strike he discusses; that the evidence upon which he acted officially and upon which he now bases his conclusions was *ex parte,* obtained wholly from the railroad interests and those who represented or were controlled by these interests, and it is not strange, therefore, that he falls

---

[†]   Written circa July 7, 1904. Published in *Appeal to Reason* (Girard, KS), whole no. 456 (August 27, 1904), 1–2. Reprinted as a pamphlet by Debs's Standard Publishing Co., Terre Haute, IN, 1904. Revised edition published by Charles H. Kerr & Co., Chicago, February 15, 1910.

into a series of efforts beginning with the cause of the disturbance and running all through his account of it, as may be proved beyond doubt by reference to the *Report on the Chicago Strike* by the United States Strike Commission, of his own appointment.[25]

What Was the Chicago Strike?

Simply one of the many battles that have been fought and are yet to be fought in the economic war between capital and labor. Pittsburgh, Homestead, Buffalo, Lattimer, Pana, Coeur d'Alene, Cripple Creek, and Telluride recall a few of the battles fought in this country in the worldwide struggle for industrial emancipation.

When the strike at Chicago occurred, did President Cleveland make a personal investigation? No.

Did he grant both sides a hearing? He did not.

In his 14-page magazine article, what workingman, or what representative of labor, does he cite in support of his statements or his official acts? Not one.

I aver that he received every particle of his information from the capitalist side, that he was prompted to act by the capitalist side, that his official course was determined wholly, absolutely by and in the interest of the capitalist side, and that no more thought or consideration was given to the other side, the hundreds of thousands of workingmen whose lives and whose wives and babes were at stake, than if they had been so many swine or sheep that had balked on their way to the shambles.

The Object of Federal Interference

From the federal judge who sat on the bench as the protégé of the late George M. Pullman, to whose influence he was indebted for his appointment—as he was to the railroad companies for the annual passes he had in his pocket—down to the last thug sworn in by the railroads and paid by the railroads to serve the railroads as United States deputy marshals, the one object of the federal court and its officers was not the enforcement of law and the preservation of order, but the breaking up of the strike in the interest of the railroad corporations, and it was because of this fact that John P. Altgeld, governor of Illinois, and John P. Hopkins, mayor of Chicago, were not in harmony with President Cleveland's administration and protested against the federal troops being used in their state and city for such a malign purpose.

This is the fact, and I shall prove it beyond doubt before this article is concluded.

Cleveland Omits Reference to Judge Woods

The late Judge William A. Woods figured as one of the principal judges in the Chicago affair, issuing the injunctions, citing the strikers to appear before him, and sentencing them to jail without trial; but President Cleveland discretely omits all reference to him; and although he introduces copies of many documents, his article does not include copies of the telegrams that passed between Judge Woods, from his home in Indianapolis, and the railroad managers at Chicago before he left home to hold court in the latter city.

Judge Woods had the distinction of convicting the writer and his colleagues without a trial and of releasing William W. Dudley, of "Blocks of Five" memory, in spite of a trial.

Judge Woods is dead, and I do not attack the dead. I have to mention his name, and this of itself is sufficient.

Pullman's Contempt of Court

During the strike the late George M. Pullman was summoned to appear before the federal court to give testimony. He at once had his private car attached to an eastbound train and left the city, treating the court with sovereign contempt. On his return, accompanied by Robert Todd Lincoln,[26] his attorney, he had a *tête-à-tête* with the court "in chambers," and that ended the matter. He was not required to testify nor to appear in open court. The striker upon whom there fell even the suspicion of a shadow of contempt was sentenced and jailed with alacrity. Not one was spared, not one invited to a "heart-to-heart" with his honor "in chambers."

A Challenge to Cleveland

In reviewing the article of ex-President Cleveland I wish to adduce the proof of my exceptions and denials, as well as the evidence to support my affirmations, but I realize that in the limited space of a single issue it is impossible to do this in complete and satisfactory manner; and as the case is important enough to be revived after a lapse of ten years by Mr. Cleveland, and as the side of labor has never yet reached the people, I am prompted to suggest a fair and full hearing of both sides on the public rostrum or in a series of articles, and I shall be happy to meet Mr. Cleveland, or anyone he may designate, in such oral or written discussion, and if I fail to relieve the great body of railroad men who composed the American Railway Union of the criminal stigma which Mr. Cleveland has sought to fasten upon them, or if I cannot produce satisfactory evidence that the crimes charged were instigated by the other side—the side in whose interest President Cleveland brought to bear all the powers of the federal government—I will agree to publicly beg forgiveness of the railroads, apologize to the ex-president, and cease my agitation forever.

The Cause of the Pullman Strike[27]

That Mr. Cleveland knows nothing about the Chicago strike except what has been told him by the railroads and their emissaries, that he has not even read the report of his own strike commission, is apparent from the very beginning of his article. He says, "The strike was provoked by a reduction of wages." This is not true. The fact is that although wages had been repeatedly reduced, the employees did not strike. They appointed a committee to meet the officials and ask why, if their wages had to be reduced, the high rents they were obliged to pay the Pullman company were not correspondingly lowered. Failing to secure redress, they called upon Mr. Pullman himself. He promised to investigate. They returned happy. The following day the committee was discharged, and thereupon all the employees laid down their tools and walked out of the shops. That is what provoked the strike and the report of the strike commission proves it.

The Court's Partiality to the Railroads

It is easy for Mr. Cleveland and others who were on the side of the railroads to introduce copies of documents, reports, etc., for the simple reason that the federal court at Chicago compelled the telegraph companies to deliver up copies of all our telegrams and copies of the proceedings of our convention and other meetings of the American Railway Union, including secret sessions, but the federal court did not call upon the railroads to produce the telegrams that passed among themselves, nor between their counsel and the federal authorities, nor the printed proceedings of the General Managers' Association, for public inspection and as a basis for criminal prosecution.

Had the Strike Won

Nevertheless, there is available proof sufficient to make it clear to the unprejudiced mind, to the honest man who seeks the truth, that the United States government, under the administration of President Grover Cleveland, was at the beck and call of the railroad corporations, acting as one through the General Managers' Association, and that these corporations, with the federal courts and troops to back them up, had swarms of mercenaries sworn in as deputy marshals to incite violence as a pretext for taking possession of the headquarters of the American Railway Union by armed force, throwing its leaders into prison without trial, and breaking up a strike that was fairly won without a blow being struck, and breaking down the union that was victorious—maligning, brow-beating, and persecuting its peaceable and law-abiding members and putting the railroad corporations in supreme control of the situation.

That was the part of President Cleveland in the Chicago strike, and for this achievement the railroad combine and the trusts in general remember him with profound gratitude and are not only willing but anxious that he shall be president of the United States forever more.

A Precedent for Future Action

In the closing paragraph of his article Mr. Cleveland compliments his admin-istration upon having cleared the way "which shall hereafter guide our nation safely and surely in the exercise of its functions which represent the people's trust." The word, "people's" is not only superfluous but mischievous and fatal to truth. Omit that and the ex-president's statement will not be challenged.

Cleveland's First Move

How did President Cleveland begin operations in the Chicago strike? Among the first things he did, as he himself tells us, was to appoint Edwin Walker as special counsel for the government.

Who was Edwin Walker?

"An able and prominent attorney," says Mr. Cleveland.

Is that all?

Not quite. At the time President Cleveland and his attorney general, Rich-ard Olney, designated Edwin Walker, upon recommendation of the railroads, as special counsel to the government, for which alleged service he was paid a fee that amounted to a fortune, *the said Edwin Walker was already the regular counsel of the Chicago, Milwaukee & St. Paul Railway.*

Turning for a moment to *Who's Who in America,* we find:

> Walker, Edwin.—Lawyer, * * * removed to Chicago in 1865; has repre-sented several railroads as general solicitor since 1860. Illinois counsel for C. M. & St. P. RR since 1870; also partner in firm of W. P. Rend & Co., coal miners and shippers. Was counsel for the railway companies and special counsel for the United States in the lawsuits growing out of the great railroad strike of 1894.

The Significance of Walker's Appointment[28]

What is the significance of such an appointment under such circumstances? Can it be in doubt a single moment? Does it not indicate clearly that the railroads controlled the government, that President Cleveland did the bidding of the General Managers' Association by appointing as special counsel of the government their own attorney to prosecute the striking employees and use the powers of the government to crush them into submission? Can there be any shadow of doubt about it in the mind of any candid man?

Why the Mails were Obstructed

Here is the situation: There is a conflict between the General Managers' Association, representing the railroads, and the American Railway Union, representing the employees. Perfect quiet and order prevail, as I shall show, but the railroads are beaten to a standstill, utterly helpless, cannot even move a mail car, simply because their employees have quit their service and left the premises in a body. Note also that the employees were willing to haul the mail trains, and all other trains, refusing only to handle Pullman cars until the Pullman Company should consent to arbitrate its disagreement with its striking and starving employees. But the railroad officials determined that if the Pullman cars were not handled, the mail cars should not move.

This is how and why the mails were obstructed and this was the pretext for federal interference. In a word, President Cleveland, obedient to the railroads, took sides with them and supported them in their conflict with their employees with all the powers of the federal government.

Commission's Report vs. Cleveland

To bear out these facts it is not necessary to go outside of the official report of the strike commission, which anyone may verify at his pleasure. The only reason I do not incorporate the voluminous evidence is that the space at my command must be economized for other purposes.

It is thus made clear that President Cleveland and his cabinet placed the government at the service of the railroads.

Edwin Walker, their own attorney, made the agent of the government and put in supreme command of the railroad and government forces! What an unholy alliance! And what a spectacle and object lesson!

Upon Walker's representations, Cleveland acted; upon Walker's demand, the federal soldiers marched into Chicago; upon Walker's command, the great government of the United States obeyed with all the subserviency of a trained lackey.

Suppose Cleveland Had Appointed Darrow?

Suppose that President Cleveland had appointed Clarence S. Darrow, attorney for the American Railway Union, instead of Edwin Walker, attorney of the General Managers' Association, as special counsel to the government!

And suppose that Darrow had ordered the offices of the General Managers' Association sacked, the books, papers, and correspondence, including the unopened private letters of the absent officers, packed up and carted away and the offices put under the guard of federal ruffians, in flagrant violation of the constitution of the United States, as was done by order of Walker with the offices of the American Railway Union!

And suppose, moreover, that the American Railway Union, backed up by Darrow, agent of the United States government, had sworn in an army of "thugs, thieves, and ex-convicts" (see official report of Michael Brennan, superintendent of Chicago police to the Council of Chicago) to serve the American Railway Union as deputy United States marshals and "conservators of peace and order"!

And suppose, finally, that the expected trouble had followed, would anyone in possession of his senses believe that these things had been done to protect life and property and preserve law and order?

That is substantially the case that President Cleveland is trying to make for himself and his administration out of their participation in the Chicago strike.

Railroads the Real Lawbreakers

The implication that runs through Mr. Cleveland's entire article is that the railway corporations were paragons of peace and patriotism, law and order, while the railway employees were a criminal, desperate, and bloodthirsty mob, which had to be suppressed by the strong arm of government.

No wonder the ex-president is so dear to the iron heart of the railroad trust, and every other trust that uses the government and its officers and soldiers to further its own sordid ends.

Let us consider for a moment these simple questions:

Who are the more law-abiding, the predatory railroad corporations or the hard-worked railroad employees?

What railroad corporation in the United States lives up to the law of the land? Not one.

What body of railroad employees violates it? Not one.

Brazen Defiance of the Law by Railroads

The railroad corporations are notorious for their brazen defiance of every law that is designed to curb their powers or restrain their rapacity.

The railroad corporations have their lobby at Washington and at every state capital; they bribe legislators, corrupt courts, debauch politics, and commit countless other legal and moral crimes against the commonwealth.

The railway employees are a body of honest, useful, self-sacrificing, peace-loving men, who never have and never will be guilty of the crimes committed by their corporate masters.

And yet President Cleveland serves the corporate masters and exalts and glorifies the act while he attempts to absolve the criminals and fasten the insufferable stigma upon honest men.

Nothing further is required to demonstrate beyond all cavil the capitalist class character of our present government.

The Strike Commission's Report

Now for a few facts about the strike. It began May 11, 1894, and was perfectly peaceable and orderly until the army of "thugs, thieves, and ex-convicts," as Superintendent of Police Brennan called them in his official report to the Council of Chicago, were sworn in as deputies by the United States marshal at the command of Edwin Walker, attorney of the General Mangers' Association and special counsel to the government. Let us quote the report of the strike commission, consisting of Carroll D. Wright, commissioner of labor, who served ex officio; John D. Kernan, of New York; and N. E. Worthington, of Illinois, two lawyers appointed by President Cleveland.

Let it be noted that the railway employees, that is to say labor, the working class, had no representative on this commission.

From the report they issued, we quote as follows:

ARU Leaders Advise Against Strike

> It is undoubtedly true that the officers and directors of the American Railway Union did not want a strike at Pullman and advised against it . . .

Yet the people were told over and over and still believe that Debs ordered the strike.

Railroads Set the Example

It should be noted that until the railroads set the example, a general union of railroad employees was never attempted. . . .

The refusal of the General Managers' Association to recognize and deal with such a combination of labor as the American Railway Union seemed arrogant and absurd, when we consider its standing before the law, its assumptions, and its past and obviously contemplated future action. . . .

. . . the rents (at Pullman) are from 20 to 25 percent higher than rents in Chicago or surrounding towns for similar accommodations.

Strike Commission Contradicts Cleveland

The strike occurred on May 11, and from that time until the soldiers went to Pullman, about July 4, 300 strikers were placed about the company's property, professedly to guard it from destruction or interference. This guarding of property in strikes is, as a rule, a mere pretense. Too often the real object of guards is to prevent newcomers from taking the strikers' places, by persuasion, often to be followed, if ineffectual, by intimidation and violence. The Pullman Company claims this was the real object of these guards. *These strikers at Pullman are entitled to be believed to the contrary in this matter, because of their conduct and forbearance after May 11. It is in evidence and uncontradicted that no violence or destruction of property by strikers or sympathizers took place at Pullman, and that until July 3* (when the federal troops came upon the scene) *no extraordinary protection was had from the police or military against even anticipated disorder.*

This paragraph from the report of Mr. Cleveland's own commission is sufficient answer to Mr. Cleveland's article. It is conclusive, crushing, overwhelming.

Deputies Started the Trouble

There was no trouble at Pullman, nor at Chicago, nor elsewhere, until the railroad United States deputy marshals were sworn in, followed by the federal troops.

Governor Altgeld, patriot and statesman, knew it and protested against the troops.

Mayor John P. Hopkins knew it and declared that he was fully competent to preserve the peace of the city.

Superintendent of Police Called Them "Thugs"

Michael Brennan, superintendent of the Chicago police, knew it and denounced the deputy marshals, Edwin Walker's hirelings, the General Managers' Association's incendiaries and sluggers, as "thugs, thieves, and ex-convicts."

These were the "gentlemen" President Cleveland's government pressed into service upon requisition of the railroads, to preserve order and protect life and property, and this is what the ex-president calls "the power of the national government to protect itself in the exercise of its functions."

As to just what these "functions" are, when Grover Cleveland is president, the railroad corporations understand to a nicety and agree to by acclamation.

Peace Reigned Supreme

The only trouble there was when the "deputies" were sworn in, followed by the soldiers, was that there was no trouble. That is the secret of subsequent proceedings. The railroads were paralyzed. Profound peace reigned. The people demanded of the railroads that they operate their trains. They could not do it. Not a man would serve them. They were completely defeated, and the banners of organized labor floated triumphant in the breeze.

Beaten at every point, their schemes all frustrated, outgeneraled in tactics and strategy, the corporations played their trump card by an appeal to the federal judiciary and the federal administration. To this appeal the response came quick as lightning from a storm cloud.

Peace Fatal to Managers' Association

Peace and order were fatal to the railroad corporations. Violence was necessary to them as peace was to the employees. They realized that victory could only be snatched from labor by an appeal to violence in the name of peace.

First, deputy marshals. The very day they were appointed, the trouble began. The files of every Chicago paper prove it. The report of the strike commission does the same.

That was what they were hired for, and their character is sufficient evidence of their guilt.

Second, fires (but no Pullman palace cars were lighted), and riots (but no strikers were implicated).

Third, the capitalist-owned newspapers and Associated Press flashed the news all over the wires that the people were at the mercy of a mob and that the strikers were burning and sacking the city.

Fourth, the people (especially those at a distance, who knew nothing except what they saw in the papers) united with the frenzied cry, "Down with anarchy! Down with the ARU! Death to the strikers!"

Disturbances Started by Deputy Marshals

The first trouble instigated by the deputy marshals was the signal for the federal court injunctions, and they came like a succession of lightning flashes.

Next, the general offices of the American Railway Union were sacked and put under guard and communication destroyed. (Later Judge Grosscup rebuked the federal satraps who committed their outrageous crime, but he did not pretend to bring them to justice.)

Next, the leaders of the strike were arrested, not for crime, but for alleged violation of an injunction.

Next, they were brought into court, denied trial by jury, pronounced guilty by the same judge who had issued the injunction, and sent to jail from 3 to 6 months.

The Concluding Words Not Yet Written

The Supreme Court of the United States, consisting wholly of trained and successful corporation lawyers, affirmed the proceedings, and President Cleveland says that they have "written the concluding words of this history."

Did the Supreme Court of the United States write the "concluding words" in the history of chattel slavery when it handed down Chief Justice Taney's decision that black man had "no rights that the white man was bound to respect"?

These "concluding words" will but hasten the overthrow of wage-slavery as the "concluding words" of the same Supreme Court in 1857 hastened the overthrow of chattel slavery.

The railroad corporations would rather have destroyed their property and seen Chicago perish than see the American Railway Union triumphant in as noble a cause as ever prompted sympathetic, manly men to action in this world.

Peace Overtures Turned Down

The late Mayor Pingree, of Detroit, came to Chicago with telegrams from mayors of over 50 of the largest cities urging that there should be arbitration. He was turned down without ceremony and afterward declared that the railroads were the only criminals and that they were responsible for the consequences.

On June 22, four days before the strike against the railroads, or rather the boycott of Pullman cars, took effect, there was a joint meeting of the railroad and Pullman officials. At this meeting it was resolved to defeat the strikers, wipe out the American Railway Union, and, to use their exact words, "That we act unitedly to that end."

This was the only joint meeting of the kind that had ever been held between the officials of the railroad companies and the Pullman Company. They mutually determined to stand together to defeat the strike and destroy the union.

Now, to show what regard these gentlemen have for courts and law and morals, this incident will suffice:

Railroad Officers Perjure Themselves

When the officers of the American Railway Union were indicted by a special and packed grand jury and placed on trial for conspiracy, the general managers of the railroads were put on the witness stand to testify as to what action had been taken at the joint railroad and Pullman meeting above described, and each and every one of them perjured himself by swearing that he had no recollection of what had taken place at that meeting. Sitting within a few feet of them, I saw their faces turn scarlet under the cross-examination, knowing that they were testifying falsely, that the court knew it, and that everyone present knew it, but they stuck to their agreement and uniformly failed to remember that they had resolved to stand together, the railroads agreeing to back the Pullman Company in defeating their famishing employees, and the Pullman Company pledging itself to stand by the railroads in destroying the American Railway Union.

That is what their own record shows they resolved to do, and a little later they concluded to forget all about it, and to this they swore in a federal court of law.

I have copies of the court records, including the testimony, to prove this, and the files of all the Chicago dailies of that time contain the same testimony.

These are the gentlemen who have so much to say about law and order; the vaunted guardians of morals and good citizenship.

When A. B. Stickney, president of the Chicago & Great Western, who had been victimized by them, told them to their faces that there was not an honest official among them and that he would not trust one of them out of his sight, they did not attempt any defense, for they knew that their accuser was on the inside and in a position to make good his assertions.

The Deputies as Viewed by the Commission

I must now introduce a little evidence from the report of the strike commission bearing upon the United States deputy marshals, who were sworn in by the railroads "to protect life and property and preserve the peace!"

Superintendent Brennan, of the Chicago police, testifies before the commission that he has a number of deputy marshals in the county jail *arrested while serving the railroads as United States deputy marshals for highway robbery.*

Newspaper Reporters' Evidence

Ray Stannard Baker, then a reporter for the *Chicago Record,* now on the staff of *McClure's Magazine,* testified as follows, in answer to the question as to what he knew of the character of the deputy marshals: "From my experience with them it was very bad. I saw more cases of drunkenness, I believe, among the United States deputy marshals than I did among the strikers."

Malcomb McDowell, reporter for the *Chicago Record,* testified:

> The United States deputy marshals and the special deputy sheriffs were sworn in by the hundreds about the 3rd and 4th of July [1894], and prior to that, too, and everybody who saw them knew they were not the class of men who ought to be made deputy marshals or deputy sheriffs. * * * In regard to most of the deputy marshals, they seemed to be hunting trouble all the time. * * * At one time a serious row nearly resulted because some of the deputy marshals standing on the railroad track jeered at the women that passed and insulted them. * * * I saw more deputy marshals drunk than I saw strikers drunk.

These were Edwin Walker's justly celebrated guardians of the peace. Herold I. Cleveland, reporter for the *Chicago Herald,* testified:

> I was on the tracks of the Western Indiana 14 days. * * * I saw in that time a couple of hundred deputy marshals. I think they were a very low, contemptible set of men.

Deputies Hired and Paid by the Railroads

Now follows what the strike commissioners themselves have to say about the deputy marshals, and their words are specially commended to the thoughtful consideration of their chief, President Cleveland:

> United States deputy marshals, to the number of 3,600, were selected by

and appointed at request of the General Managers' Association, and of its railroads. They were armed and paid by the railroads and acted in the double capacity of railroad employees and United States officers. While operating the railroads they assumed and exercised unrestricted United States authority when so ordered by their employers, or whenever they regarded it as necessary. They were not under the direct control of any government official while exercising authority. This is placing officers of the government under control of a combination of the railroads. It is a bad precedent that might well lead to serious consequences.

The Government Serves the Corporations

Here we have it, upon the authority of President Cleveland's own commission, that the United States government under his administration furnished the railroad corporations with government officers, in the form of deputy marshals, to take the places of striking employees, operate the trains, and serve in that dual capacity in any way that might be required to crush out the strike. This is perhaps more credit than the ex-president expected to receive. His own commission charges him, in effect, with serving the railroads as strikebreaker by furnishing government employees to take the places of striking railroad men and arming them with pistols and clubs and with all the authority of government officials.

Page after page bears testimony of the disreputable character of the deputy marshals sworn in to the number of several thousand and turned loose like armed bullies to "preserve the peace."

The report of the strike commission contains 681 pages. I have a mass of other testimony, but for the purpose of this article have confined myself to the report of Mr. Cleveland's own commission.

How the Strikers Were Defeated

Hundreds of pages of evidence are given by impartial witnesses to establish the guilt of the railroad corporations, to prove that the leaders of the strike counseled peace and order, that the strikers themselves were law-abiding and used their influence to prevent disorder; that there was no trouble until the murderous deputy marshals were sprung upon the community, and that these instigated trouble to pave the way for injunctions and soldiers and change of public sentiment, thereby defeating the strike.

Confirmed by Cleveland

President Cleveland unwittingly, perhaps, confirms this fact. On page 232 of his article, he quotes approvingly the letter written to Edwin Walker, special counsel of the government and regular counsel of the railroads, by Attorney General Richard Olney as follows: "It has seemed to me that if the rights of the United States (railroads?) were vigorously asserted in Chicago, the origin and center of the demonstration, the result would be to make it a failure everywhere else, and to prevent its spread over the entire country."

That is the point, precisely the point, and Mr. Cleveland admits it. It is not the "obstruction of the mails," nor disorder, nor the violation of law that arouses Mr. Cleveland's government and prompts it to "vigorous" assertion of its powers, but the "demonstration," that is the strike against the railroads, and to put this down, not to move the mails or restore order, a mere pretext, which was fully exposed by Governor Altgeld, was the prime cause of federal interference, and to "make it a failure everywhere" all constitutional restraints were battered down, and as a strikebreaker President Cleveland won imperishable renown.

Strike Leaders Exonerated by Commission

Particular attention is invited to the following, which appears upon page XLV:

> There is no evidence before the commission that the officers of the American Railway Union at any time participated in or advised intimidation, violence, or the destruction of property. *They knew and fully appreciated that as soon as mobs ruled, the organized forces would crush the mobs and all responsible for them in the remotest degree, and that this means defeat.*

And yet they all served prison sentences. Will President Cleveland please explain why? And why they were refused a trial?

In Whose Interest Were These Crimes Committed?

Read the above paragraph from the report of the strike commission and then answer these questions:

To whose interest was it to have riots and fires, lawlessness and crime?

To whose advantage was it to have disreputable "deputies" do these things?

Why were only freight cars, largely hospital wrecks, set on fire?

Why have the railroads not yet recovered damages from Cook County, Illinois, for failing to protect their property? Why are they so modest and patient with their suits?

The riots and incendiarism turned defeat into victory for the railroads. They could have won in no other way. They had everything to gain and the strikers everything to lose.

The violence was instigated in spite of the strikers, and the report of the commission proves that they made every effort in their power to preserve the peace.

When a crime is committed in the dark, the person who is supposed to have benefited by it is sought out as the probable culprit, but we are not required to rely on presumption in this case, for the testimony against the railroads is too clear and complete and convincing to admit of doubt.

Imprisoned Without Trial

If the crimes committed during the Chicago strike were chargeable to the strikers, why were they not prosecuted? If not, why were they sentenced to prison?

The fact that they were flung into prison without evidence and without trial and the fact that the Supreme Court affirmed the outrage seemed to afford Mr. Cleveland special satisfaction and he accepts what he calls the "concluding words" of the court as his own final vindication.

Judge Trumbull's Opinion

The late senator and judge Lyman Trumbull, for many years United States senator, chairman of the Senate Committee on Judiciary, supreme judge of Illinois, author of the 13th Amendment to the Constitution of the United States, personal friend of Abraham Lincoln, and, above all, an honest man, wrote: "The doctrine announced by the Supreme Court in the Debs case places every citizen at the mercy of any prejudiced or malicious federal judge who may think proper to imprison him."

President Cleveland doubtless understands the import of these ominous words. Let the people—the working people—whom the ex-president regards merely as a mob to be suppressed when they peaceably protest against injustice—let them contemplate these words at their leisure.

When the strike was at its height and the railroads were defeated at every turn, the federal court hastily empaneled a special grand jury to indict the strikers. The foreman of this jury was chosen because he was a violent union-hater, and he afterward betrayed his own capitalistic colleagues in a matter they had entrusted to his integrity.

The jury was empaneled not to investigate, but to indict.

A *Tribune* reporter, who refused to verify a false interview before the jury, and thereby perjure himself, to incriminate the writer, was discharged. The *Chicago Times* published the particulars.

An indictment was speedily returned. "To the penitentiary," was the cry of the railroads and their henchmen. A trial jury was empaneled. Not a juror was accepted who was of the same political party as the defendants. Every possible effort was made to rush the strike leaders to the state prison.

The Failure of the Prosecution

After all the evidence of the prosecution had been presented, they realized that they had miserably failed. Not one particle of incriminating testimony could the railroads produce with all the sleuth hounds they had at their command.

Next came our turn. The general managers were dumbfounded when they were, one after the other, put on the stand. Eighty-six witnesses were in court to testify as to the riots and fires. Assistant Chief Palmer and other members of the fire department were on hand to testify that when they were trying to extinguish the flames in the railroad yards they caught men in the act of cutting the hose, and that these men wore the badges of deputy marshals. Other witnesses were policemen who were ready to testify that they had caught these same deputies instigating violence and acts of incendiarism.

The Jury Dumbfounded

The jury had been packed to convict. When our evidence began to come in, their eyes fairly bulged with astonishment. There was a perfect transformation scene. The jurors realized that they had been steeped in prejudice and grossly deceived.

The general managers testified that they did not remember what had taken place at the joint general managers' and Pullman meeting. Their printed proceedings were called for. They looked appealingly to Edwin Walker. The terror that overspread their features can never be forgotten by those who witnessed it. Their proceedings would expose their mendacity and convict them of conspiracy and crime. Something must be done and done quickly. Court adjourned for lunch. When it reconvened, Judge Grosscup gravely announced that a juror had been suddenly taken ill and that the trial could not proceed.

The Suspicious "Illness" of a Juror

The next day and the next, the same announcement was repeated. We offered to proceed in any of the several ways provided in such exigencies. The prosecution objected. The cry "To the penitentiary" had subsided. To "let go" was now the order of the railroads. Not another session of court must be held, for their printed proceedings, the private property in the strong box of each manager, and full of matter that would convict them, would have to be produced. All the proceedings of the American Railway Union had been produced in evidence by order of the court, and the court could not refuse to command the railroad officials to produce the proceedings of their association. These proceedings were brought in at the closing session of the trial, but by order of the court the defendants were forbidden to look into them, and Edwin Walker, the government counsel, watched them with the faithful eye of a trusted guardian.

We were not allowed to examine the proceedings of the General Managers' Association, notwithstanding our proceedings, telegrams, letters, and other private communications had been brought into court by order of the judge, inspected by Edwin Walker and others, and printed in the court records for public inspection.

It was at just this point that the court adjourned and the juror was taken ill.

Ten years have elapsed. He is still ill, and we are still waiting for the court to reconvene and the trial to proceed.

Government Refused to Go on with Case

Every proposition to continue the case was fiercely resisted by Edwin Walker, special counsel of the government and general counsel of the railroads.

Clarence S. Darrow objected to Mr. Walker's appearing in that dual capacity, representing at the same time the government and the railroads, the supposed justice of the one and the vengeful spirit of the other, but Judge Grosscup overruled the objection.

The trial was postponed again and again, the interest in it gradually subsiding, and many months afterward, when it was almost forgotten, it was quietly stricken from the docket.

Jurors Grasped Debs's Hand

When the remaining 11 jurors were discharged by the court, Edwin Walker extended his hand to them, but they rushed by him and surrounded the writer and his codefendants, grasping their hands and assuring them, each and every one of them, that they were convinced of their innocence and only regretted that they had been prevented from returning their verdict accordingly. The details appear in the Chicago papers of the time.

At the very time we were being tried for conspiracy, we were serving a sentence in prison for contempt, the program being that six months in jail should be followed by as many years in penitentiary.

For a jury to pronounce us innocent in substantially the same case for which we were already serving a sentence would mean not only our complete vindication but the exposure of the federal court that had, at the behest of the railroads, sentenced us to prison without a trial.

And so the trial was abruptly terminated on account of the alleged illness of a juror, and they could find no other to take his place.

These are the facts, and I have all the documentary evidence in detail, and only lack of space prevents me from making the exhibits in this article.

If President Cleveland or the railroad managers doubt it, I stand ready to meet them face-to-face in discussion of the issue upon any platform in America.

The Greatest Industrial Battle in History

The Chicago strike was in many respects the grandest industrial battle in history, and I am prouder of my small share in it than of any other act of my life.

Men, women, and children were on the verge of starvation at the "model city" of Pullman. They had produced the fabulous wealth of the Pullman Corporation, but they, poor souls, were compelled to suffer the torment of hunger pangs in the very midst of the abundance their labor had created.

A hundred and fifty thousand railroad employees, their fellow members in the American Railway Union, sympathized with them, shared their earnings with them, and, after vainly trying in every peaceable way they could conceive to touch the flint heart of the Pullman Company, every overture being resented, every suggestion denied, every proposition spurned with contempt, they determined not to pollute their hands and dishonor their manhood by handling Pullman cars and contributing to the suffering and sorrow of their brethren and their wives and babes. And rather than do this, they laid down their tools in a body, sacrificed their situations, and submitted to persecution, exile, and the blacklist; to idleness and poverty, crusts and rags, and I shall love and honor these moral heroes to my latest breath.

There was more of human sympathy, of the essence of brotherhood, of the spirit of real Christianity, in this act than in all the hollow pretenses and heartless prayers of those disciples of mammon who cried out against it, and this act will shine forth in increasing splendor long after the dollar-worshippers have mingled with the dust of oblivion.

Had the Carpenter of Nazareth been in Chicago at the time he would have been on the side of the poor, the heavy-laden and sore at heart, and he would have denounced their oppressors and been sent to prison for contempt of court under President Cleveland's administration.

President Cleveland says that we were put down because we had acted in violation of the Sherman Antitrust Act of 1890. Will he kindly state what other trusts were proceeded against and what capitalists were sentenced to prison during his administration?

A Tribute to Governor Altgeld

He waited ten years to cast his aspersions upon the honor of John P. Altgeld, and if that patriotic statesman had not fallen in the service of the people, if he were still here to defend his official acts, it is not probable that the ex-president would have ventured to assail him.

Reluctantly indeed do I close without the space to incorporate his burning messages to President Cleveland, and at least some brief extracts from his masterly speech on "Government by Injunction."

His memory requires no defense, but if it did I could speak better for him than for myself. He never truckled to corporate wealth, he did not compromise with his conscience, he was steadfast in his devotion to truth and in his fidelity to right, and he sought with all his strength to serve the people, and the people will gratefully remember him as one of the true men, one of the great souls, of his sordid age.

The Chicago strike is not yet settled, and its "concluding pages" are *yet to be written.*

A Sheriff I Loved†
February 1923

The type of the average human who functions as sheriff is not of a lovable nature. A sheriff is ex officio beyond words the official creature who is willing for a paltry fee to serve as the executioner, the legal assassin of a human being, even though that human being be condemned as the lowest, vilest, and most degraded on earth.

But there are exceptions to the rule and beneath the official vesture of the sheriff there may be the soul of a man.

Such an exception was George Eckert, the sheriff of McHenry County, Illinois, in 1895, when I served a sentence of six months in his custody in the county jail at Woodstock.

The sentence resulted from the railroad strike of the preceding year. The farce of a trial had been pulled off in the federal court at Chicago. A jury had been denied. The sentence had been arbitrarily pronounced in surrender to the clamor of the mob spirit aroused to such a pitch of insane fury by the capitalist press, bravely backed, as usual, by the capitalist clergy. The appeal to the Supreme Court of the United States, on behalf of which Lyman Trumbull, the friend of Lincoln and the author of the 13th Amendment abolishing slavery, made his personal plea, and also his last one, proved fruitless, as expected. The court confirmed the sentence by evading the issue, as it did a quarter of a century later in the infamous espionage cases.

Fortunately for me and my convicted associates, the filthy, rotten, unspeakably vile and notorious Cook County Jail at Chicago, wherein the anarchists had been hanged and we had been temporarily detained and all but devoured by sewer rats and body lice, was so crowded that the court ordered us transferred to the McHenry County Jail at Woodstock, some 50 miles west of Chicago.

The prejudice and hate engendered by the lies and calumnies of the capitalist press and the pious vassals in the capitalist pulpit were more bitter and relentless than can well be imagined. The farmers of McHenry County protested even against my being imprisoned there, and it was reported that

† Published in *Miami Valley Socialist* (Dayton, OH), vol. 10, whole no. 570 (February 9, 1923), 2.

they would meet the train on which I was to arrive and that a lynching might follow. Heavily guarded, I was thus delivered to George Eckert, sheriff of McHenry County, who met the train at the station and took me into custody. The farmers were there with their threats and mutterings, and with some other sheriff than George Eckert in charge might have attempted their cowardly program.

But George Eckert was a man as well as a sheriff, and he told them, in words they did not fail to understand, that I was his prisoner, and that it was his duty to protect as well as to jail me, and that he proposed to do it.

The would-be lynchers knew George Eckert, and slunk away in the darkness. They knew he would protect me—if necessary with his own life. He was a small man, but a whole one. As a boy he had been all through the Civil War, and he did not fear to face an enemy, even though that enemy happened to be his own neighbor and had helped to put him in office.

This was my introduction to George Eckert. He had read and heard all about me that was false and slanderous and had been led to believe that I was a desperate and dangerous criminal and that I should be treated accordingly. But this did not alter his determination to accord to me the treatment due to any other prisoner in his custody.[29]

That night I slept in a clean cell. The following morning the sheriff came to see me, and I had a friendly chat and soon came to a perfect mutual understanding which was never once violated on either side. From that hour George Eckert was my friend and I was his, and though 27 years have passed, not one of them brought its holidays without the exchange of mutual greetings and remembrances.

This morning there came to me the following telegram:

Woodstock, Ill., January 28, 1922

Eugene V. Debs,
Terre Haute, Indiana
Father died this morning.   *—Georgie C. Eckert.*

This sad message came to me from his daughter, the daughter he adored, and I and all of our family feel as if our own household had been stricken by the sorrowful bereavement. Only a few weeks ago while I was in the sanitarium at Elmhurst,[30] Mr. Eckert and his daughter Georgie drove 50 miles on a cold, gusty day to pay me a visit and to comfort me with their sympathy and companionship. The visit was to be the last with my loyal old friend, and I shall never forget how touched at the parting.

George Eckert had been a true friend to me when friendship is possible only in the heart and soul and conscience of a genuine human being. I recalled to him the answer he made to those of his constituents who wanted him to subject me to rough treatment; how kind he and his wife and daughter had been to my wife and family, and how the tears of gladness and regret stood in his eyes as well as mine the day I left his custody and started for home. When last we exchanged farewells we were clasped in each other's arms.

George Eckert has passed on to his next beautiful adventure, leaving to his friends, his neighbors, and to the world the memory of a man.

May he rest in peace and flowers bloom where he sleeps.

Notes

1. In February 1893 an early organizing meeting for the future American Railway Union named a three-member Committee on Constitution and Declaration of Principles consisting of Debs; George W. Howard, former head of the Brotherhood of Railroad Conductors; and Sylvester Keliher, secretary-treasurer and editor for the Brotherhood of Railway Carmen. This document should be considered a collective work of the three. The draft document was reported to the founding conference of the ARU at the Hotel Greene in Chicago on April 12, 1893, and approved at that closed session. This manifesto was first published as "New Railway Union" in the *Chicago Inter Ocean,* vol. 22, no. 23 (April 16, 1893), 6, and perhaps other Chicago newspapers on that same day, and was subsequently reprinted by other newspapers.

2. Neither of these publishing objectives were ultimately fulfilled, with the ARU managing to launch a weekly newspaper, *The Railway Times,* under the editorship of L. W. Rogers, on January 1, 1894. No monthly magazine of the ARU was ever issued. *The Railway Times* was eventually rechristened *The Social Democrat* in 1897.

3. Debs was jailed in conjunction with his six-month contempt of court sentence on January 8, 1895 and released on bail on January 24—less than a week after this interview—for review of his case by the US Supreme Court. Following a unanimous Supreme Court ruling upholding the judgment, Debs was reincarcerated on June 12 of that same year, remaining in jail until the completion of his sentence on November 22.

4. Nellie Bly, pen name of Elizabeth Jane Cochran Seaman (1864–1922), was one of the most famous female journalists of the nineteenth century. For her 1887 work feigning insanity in order to expose the practices of a New York mental hospital, Bly is regarded as a founder of undercover investigative journalism. She further enhanced her fame late in 1889 when she embarked upon a 72-day trip around the world in emulation of Jules Verne's novel *Around the World in Eighty Days.* Bly married an aging industrialist in 1895 and subsequently retired from journalism.

5. There were actually ten Debs children, six of whom survived childhood and four who died.

6. One questions this idyllic assertion. Certainly in later years there was great tension between Gene's brother, Theodore, and his wife, Katherine.

7. This account of the early railroading years of Debs is prosaic but not precise.

8. Debs actually retained a connection with the magazine until the issue published October 1, 1894.

9. Hometown of ARU board member and fellow prisoner James Hogan.

10. Allusion to Luke 6:31.

11. Only Debs was sentenced to a term of six months, with the other seven ARU directors drawing three-month sentences.

12. Nathaniel C. "Nat" Goodwin (1857–1919) was a prominent actor and vaudevillian known for his work in burlesques.

13. *Better Days; or, A Millionaire of Tomorrow* (1891), a novel by Thomas Fitch and Anna A. Fitch.

14. This interview was conducted the week after Debs's return to jail on June 12, 1895, following the loss of his appeal for a writ of habeas corpus to the United States Supreme Court. Debs would remain incarcerated until the completion of his six-month sentence on November 22, 1895.

15. This autobiographical piece by Debs was part of a running series of articles sharing this title by prominent socialists of the day in the glossy illustrated magazine *The Comrade*. It was accorded a place of honor at the front of the frequently republished 1908 Debs presidential campaign collection, *Debs: His Life, Writings, and Speeches*.

16. "Old Josh Leach" (1843–1919) was born May 8, 1843, making him 31 years old at the time of his meeting the 19-year-old "towheaded boy" Gene Debs.

17. Couplet from "The Deserted Village" (1770), by Oliver Goldsmith (1728–1774).

18. Source of this couplet is unknown.

19. Debs misstates the 1893 date of origin of the ARU by a year.

20. Allusion to the eponymous poem by John Keats (1795–1821).

21. Chicago attorney John Maynard Harlan (1864–1934) was the son of John Marshall Harlan (1833–1911) and the father of John Marshall Harlan II (1899–1971), both of whom were appointed associate justices of the Supreme Court of the United States.

22. Manchester socialist Robert Blatchford (1851–1943), a member of the Fabian Society, was the founder of the radical weekly *The Clarion*. Blatchford is best rememebered for his *Merrie England* (1894), a frequently reprinted pamphlet popularizing socialist ideas. In 1897, Debs wrote an introduction for an edition of this pamphlet published by Charles H. Kerr & Co. before releasing his own edition through Debs Publishing Co. in 1899.

23. When read in conjunction with journalistic accounts of his time in Woodstock Jail that paid attention to the prisoners' bookshelf, it seems likely that six and a half years after the event Debs grossly exaggerates here the influence on his thinking of books by Karl Kautsky and Karl Marx. Nor does he mention the documented visit to Woodstock on September 4, 1895, by Chicago Socialist Labor Party activist Tommy Morgan and Scottish Labour Party leader Keir Hardie that resulted in the signing of an agreement establishing a stillborn "International Bureau of Correspondence and Agitation." Instead, he heaps all praise upon his close Socialist Party associate Victor L. Berger and intimates that it was a direct appeal by Berger, rather than the organic development of his own thinking, that brought Debs to socialism.

24. This version of the article is based upon the original text published in the pages of the *Appeal to Reason*. Cleveland's original article appeared in the July 1904 issue of *McClure's Magazine*. Publisher S. S. McClure rejected Debs's article with a letter dated July 15, 1904, which Debs responded to with a letter of his own dated July 22, 1904. Both of these documents were published in facsimile on page 1 of the *Appeal* of July 30, 1904. The text was checked against the two subsequent pamphlet editions overseen by Debs himself.

25. Reference is to *Report on the Chicago Strike of June–July, 1894, by the United States Strike Commission, Appointed by the President July 26, 1894, under the Provisions of*

Section 6 of Chapter 1063 of the Laws of the United States Passed October 1, 1888, with Appendices Containing Testimony, Proceedings, and Recommendations. (Washington, DC: Government Printing Office, 1895). For an extensive excerpt of Debs's testimony, see this volume, 317–54.

26. Robert Todd Lincoln (1843–1926) was the eldest son of Abraham Lincoln. Lincoln was general counsel of Pullman's Palace Car Company during the Pulllman strike and was named president of the corporation upon Pullman's death in 1897.

27. This paragraph was omitted from all subsequent reprints of this document dating back to the 1904 pamphlet edition, which was republished as part of the 1908 volume *Debs: His Life, Writings, and Speeches.*

28. This paragraph was omitted from all subsequent reprints of this document dating back to the 1904 pamphlet edition, which was republished as part of the 1908 volume *Debs: His Life, Writings, and Speeches.*

29. It should go without saying that this account, written more than a quarter century after the fact, is highly melodramatic, and that if a handful of Illinois farmers did indeed conduct a mass lynching of eight white trade-union leaders on January 8, 1895, it would have been an event without parallel in the annals of American history.

30. In frail health during his final years, Debs spent time recuperating at the Lindlahr Sanitarium in Elmhurst, Illinois, a facility that emphasized the purportedly curative properties of fresh air, sunbathing, and hydrotherapy.

Index

Hertzka, Theodor, 637
Hill, James J., 8, 227, 238–39, 321, 361,
　509–10
　bust, 43
Hinman, Marshall Littlefield, 233, 382n
Hippocrene, 521, 538n
Hirzel's Hall (Terre Haute), 381n
*History of the Intellectual Development of
　Europe* (Draper), 634
Hogan, James, 17, 30n, 460, 463, 468,
　535n, 593, 633, 635–38 passim, 668n
　portrait, 42
Hogan, William, 388n
Holland, 176, 589
Homelessness. *See* Tramps
Homestead Strike of 1892. *See* Strikes,
　Homestead Strike of 1892
Homestead Works. *See* Carnegie Steel
　Company
Homestead, Illinois, 47, 48, 51
Hood, Thomas, 538n
Hopkins, John Patrick, 332–35, 387n, 393,
　646, 653
Hotel Greene (Chicago) 179n, 387n, 668n
Hottentot people, 111, 255
Howard, George W., 4–6, 12, 15, 178n,
　179n, 240, 293, 298, 317–18, 320,
　322, 328, 331, 333, 341, 381n, 384n,
　386n, 473–74, 622, 633, 668n
　breaks with ARU, 17–18
　establishes American Industrial Union, 17
　founder Brotherhood of Railway
　　Conductors, 26n
　indicted and arrested, 15, 385n
　originator of ARU idea, 4–5, 27n
　portrait, 35, 42
　sentenced, 15
Hugo, Victor, 604, 629
Hun (ethnic slur), 104
Hunt, James Henry Leigh, 178n

Idaho, 7, 107, 156
Illinois Central Railroad, 30n, 31n, 270,

　271, 327, 354, 385n
Illinois, 13, 17, 25n, 141, 179n, 239–40,
　295, 298, 369–70, 372–73, 383n,
　384n, 385n, 386n, 387n, 388n, 391,
　439, 505, 526, 532n, 535n, 536n,
　560, 606, 645–46, 649, 652, 659–60,
　665, 670
Immigration, 175–76, 350–51, 381n
Income Tax Act of 1894, 535n, 544, 608n
Independent Labour Party (ILP), 31n
India, 56, 174, 370, 519
Indian wars, 106, 428
Indianapolis, Indiana, 344, 534n, 595, 647
Indians. *See* Native Americans
Industrial Worker, The, 611n
The Inferno (Dante), 104
Ingalls, Melville Ezra, 591, 611n
Ingersoll, Robert, 149, 239, 558, 612n
Injunctions, 7, 13, 15, 17, 192, 216,
　221–22, 255, 285, 327–29, 346, 357,
　372, 388n, 397, 399, 402–3, 415,
　418–20, 432, 436, 438, 440, 442, 463,
　471, 479, 481, 484, 512, 515, 544–45,
　558, 559–60, 591–93, 632, 643, 647,
　655, 658, 664
Inquisition, the 426, 441
International Association of Machinists
　(IAM), 31n, 613n
International Bureau of Correspondence and
　Agitation, 18, 669n
Interstate Commerce Commission (ICC),
　193, 197, 385, 540
Interstate Commerce law of 1887, 248, 530,
　565–66
Iowa College, 536n
Iowa, 26n, 201, 381n, 580
Iran. *See* Persia
Ireland, 250
Ireland, John, 598, 607, 612n
Irons, Martin,
　caricatured, 41
Italy, 176
Ives, Brayton, 566, 609n

About the Editors

Tim Davenport is involved with several online radical history projects, including his Early American Marxism website, Marxists Internet Archive, and Wikipedia. He is a member of the Historians of American Communism, the Organization of American Historians, the Society for Historians of the Gilded Age and Progressive Era, and the Labor and Working-Class History Association. He is coeditor with Paul LeBlanc of *The "American Exceptionalism" of Jay Lovestone and His Comrades, 1929–1940* (Haymarket Books, 2018).

David Walters is a lifelong socialist and trade unionist. He was one of the founders of the Marxists Internet Archive and remains with the MIA as a volunteer. He is currently director of the Holt Labor Library in San Francisco.

About Haymarket Books

Haymarket Books is a radical, independent, nonprofit book publisher based in Chicago. Our mission is to publish books that contribute to struggles for social and economic justice. We strive to make our books a vibrant and organic part of social movements and the education and development of a critical, engaged, international left.

We take inspiration and courage from our namesakes, the Haymarket martyrs, who gave their lives fighting for a better world. Their 1886 struggle for the eight-hour day—which gave us May Day, the international workers' holiday— reminds workers around the world that ordinary people can organize and struggle for their own liberation. These struggles continue today across the globe— struggles against oppression, exploitation, poverty, and war.

Since our founding in 2001, Haymarket Books has published more than five hundred titles. Radically independent, we seek to drive a wedge into the risk-averse world of corporate book publishing. Our authors include Noam Chomsky, Arundhati Roy, Rebecca Solnit, Angela Y. Davis, Howard Zinn, Amy Goodman, Wallace Shawn, Mike Davis, Winona LaDuke, Ilan Pappé, Richard Wolff, Dave Zirin, Keeanga-Yamahtta Taylor, Nick Turse, Dahr Jamail, David Barsamian, Elizabeth Laird, Amira Hass, Mark Steel, Avi Lewis, Naomi Klein, and Neil Davidson. We are also the trade publishers of the acclaimed Historical Materialism Book Series and of Dispatch Books.

Also available from Haymarket Books

The American Socialist Movement, 1897–1912
Ira Kipnis

The Bending Cross: A Biography of Eugene Victor Debs
Ray Ginger, introduction by Mike Davis

Lucy Parsons: An American Revolutionary
Carolyn Ashbaugh

The Labor Wars: From the Molly Maguires to the Sit Downs
Sidney Lens

A Short History of the U.S. Working Class: From Colonial Times to the Twenty-First Century (Revolutionary Studies)
Paul Le Blanc